T0202911

Lecture Notes in Computer Science   14814

Founding Editors

Gerhard Goos
Juris Hartmanis

Editorial Board Members

Elisa Bertino, *Purdue University, West Lafayette, IN, USA*
Wen Gao, *Peking University, Beijing, China*
Bernhard Steffen ⓘ, *TU Dortmund University, Dortmund, Germany*
Moti Yung ⓘ, *Columbia University, New York, NY, USA*

The series Lecture Notes in Computer Science (LNCS), including its subseries Lecture Notes in Artificial Intelligence (LNAI) and Lecture Notes in Bioinformatics (LNBI), has established itself as a medium for the publication of new developments in computer science and information technology research, teaching, and education.

LNCS enjoys close cooperation with the computer science R & D community, the series counts many renowned academics among its volume editors and paper authors, and collaborates with prestigious societies. Its mission is to serve this international community by providing an invaluable service, mainly focused on the publication of conference and workshop proceedings and postproceedings. LNCS commenced publication in 1973.

Osvaldo Gervasi · Beniamino Murgante ·
Chiara Garau · David Taniar ·
Ana Maria A. C. Rocha ·
Maria Noelia Faginas Lago
Editors

Computational Science and Its Applications – ICCSA 2024

24th International Conference
Hanoi, Vietnam, July 1–4, 2024
Proceedings, Part II

 Springer

Editors
Osvaldo Gervasi ⓘ
University of Perugia
Perugia, Italy

Beniamino Murgante ⓘ
School of Engineering
University of Basilicata
Potenza, Italy

Chiara Garau ⓘ
Department of Civil and Environmental
Engineering and Architecture
University of Cagliari
Cagliari, Italy

David Taniar ⓘ
Faculty of Information Technology
Monash University
Clayton, VIC, Australia

Ana Maria A. C. Rocha ⓘ
Algoritmi Research Centre
University of Minho
Braga, Portugal

Maria Noelia Faginas Lago ⓘ
Department of Chemistry, Biology
and Biotechnology
University of Perugia
Perugia, Italy

ISSN 0302-9743   ISSN 1611-3349 (electronic)
Lecture Notes in Computer Science
ISBN 978-3-031-64607-2   ISBN 978-3-031-64608-9 (eBook)
https://doi.org/10.1007/978-3-031-64608-9

This Springer imprint is published by the registered company Springer Nature Switzerland AG
The registered company address is: Gewerbestrasse 11, 6330 Cham, Switzerland

If disposing of this product, please recycle the paper.

Preface

These two volumes (LNCS volumes 14813–14814) consist of the peer-reviewed papers from the 2024 International Conference on Computational Science and Its Applications (ICCSA 2024) which took place during July 1–4, 2024. In addition, the peer-reviewed papers of the 55 Workshops, the Workshops proceedings, are published in a separate set consisting of 11 volumes (LNCS 14815–14825).

The conference was held in a hybrid form, with some participants present in person, hosted in Hanoi, Vietnam, by the Thuy Loi University. We enabled virtual participation for those who were unable to attend the event, due to logistical, political and economic problems, by adopting a technological infrastructure based on open source software (jitsi + riot), and a commercial Cloud infrastructure.

ICCSA 2024 was another successful event in the International Conference on Computational Science and Its Applications (ICCSA) conference series, previously held in Athens, Greece (2023), Malaga, Spain (2022), Cagliari, Italy (hybrid with few participants in presence in 2021 and completely online in 2020), whilst earlier editions took place in Saint Petersburg, Russia (2019), Melbourne, Australia (2018), Trieste, Italy (2017), Beijing, China (2016), Banff, Canada (2015), Guimaraes, Portugal (2014), Ho Chi Minh City, Vietnam (2013), Salvador, Brazil (2012), Santander, Spain (2011), Fukuoka, Japan (2010), Suwon, South Korea (2009), Perugia, Italy (2008), Kuala Lumpur, Malaysia (2007), Glasgow, UK (2006), Singapore (2005), Assisi, Italy (2004), Montreal, Canada (2003), and (as ICCS) Amsterdam, The Netherlands (2002) and San Francisco, USA (2001).

Computational Science is the main pillar of most of the present research, industrial and commercial applications, and plays a unique role in exploiting ICT innovative technologies, and the ICCSA conference series have been providing a venue to researchers and industry practitioners to discuss new ideas, to share complex problems and their solutions, and to shape new trends in Computational Science. As the conference mirrors society from a scientific point of view, this year's undoubtedly dominant theme was the machine learning and artificial intelligence and their applications in the most diverse economic and industrial fields.

The ICCSA 2024 conference is structured in 6 general tracks covering the fields of computational science and its applications: Computational Methods, Algorithms and Scientific Applications – High Performance Computing and Networks – Geometric Modeling, Graphics and Visualization – Advanced and Emerging Applications – Information Systems and Technologies – Urban and Regional Planning. In addition, the conference consisted of 55 workshops, focusing on very topical issues of importance to science, technology and society: from new mathematical approaches for solving complex computational systems, to information and knowledge in the Internet of Things, new statistical and optimization methods, several Artificial Intelligence approaches, sustainability issues, smart cities and related technologies.

We accepted 53 full papers, 6 short papers and 3 PhD Showcase papers from 207 submissions to the General Tracks of the conference (acceptance rate 30%). For the 55 workshops we accepted 281 full papers, 17 short papers and 2 PhD Showcase papers. We would like to express our appreciation to the workshops chairs and co-chairs for their hard work and dedication.

The success of the ICCSA conference series in general, and of ICCSA 2024 in particular, vitally depends on the support of many people: authors, presenters, participants, keynote speakers, workshop chairs, session chairs, organizing committee members, student volunteers, Program Committee members, Advisory Committee members, International Liaison chairs, reviewers and others in various roles. We take this opportunity to wholeheartedly thank them all.

We also wish to thank our publisher, Springer, for their acceptance to publish the proceedings, for sponsoring part of the best papers awards and for their kind assistance and cooperation during the editing process.

We cordially invite you to visit the ICCSA website https://iccsa.org where you can find all the relevant information about this interesting and exciting event.

July 2024

Osvaldo Gervasi
David Taniar
Beniamino Murgante
Chiara Garau

Welcome Message from Organizers

After the very hard times of COVID, ICCSA continues its successful scientific endeavors in 2024, hosted in Hanoi, Vietnam. This time, ICCSA moved from the Mediterranean Region to Southeast Asia and was held in the metropolitan city of Hanoi, the capital of Vietnam. Hanoi is a vibrant urban environment known for the hospitality of its citizens, its rich history, vibrant culture, and dynamic urban life. Located in the northern part of the country, Hanoi is a bustling metropolis that combines the old with the new, offering a unique blend of ancient traditions and modern development.

ICCSA 2024 took place in a secure environment, allowing for safe and vibrant in-person participation. Combined with the active engagement of the ICCSA 2024 scientific community, this set the stage for highly motivating discussions and interactions regarding the latest developments in computer science and its applications in the real world for improving communities' quality of life.

Thuyloi University, also known as the Water Resources University, is a prominent institution in Hanoi, Vietnam, with a strong reputation in engineering and technical education, particularly in water resources and environmental engineering. In recent years, the University has expanded its academic offerings to include computer science, reflecting the growing importance of technology and digital skills in all sectors. This year, Thuyloi University had the honor of hosting ICCSA 2024. The Local Organizing Committee felt the burden and responsibility of such a demanding task and put all necessary energy into meeting participants' expectations and establishing a friendly, creative, and inspiring scientific and social/cultural environment that allowed for new ideas and perspectives to flourish.

Since all ICCSA participants, whether informatics-oriented or application-driven, realize the tremendous advancements in computer science over the last few decades and the huge potential these advancements offer in coping with the enormous challenges of humanity in a globalized, 'wired,' and highly competitive world, the expectations for ICCSA 2024 were high. The goal was to successfully match computer science progress with communities' aspirations, achieving progress that serves real, place- and people-based needs and paves the way towards a visionary, smart, sustainable, resilient, and inclusive future for both current and future generations.

On behalf of the Local Organizing Committee, I would like to sincerely thank all of you who contributed to ICCSA 2024.

Nguyen Canh Thai

Organization

ICCSA 2024 was organized by Thuyloi University (Vietnam), the University of Perugia (Italy), the University of Basilicata (Italy), Monash University (Australia), Kyushu Sangyo University (Japan), the University of Minho (Portugal), and the University of Cagliari (Italy).

Honorary General Chairs

Norio Shiratori	Chuo University, Japan
Kenneth C. J. Tan	Sardina Systems, UK

General Chairs

Nguyen Canh Thai	Thuyloi University, Vietnam
Osvaldo Gervasi	University of Perugia, Italy
David Taniar	Monash University, Australia

Program Committee Chairs

Beniamino Murgante	University of Basilicata, Italy
Chiara Garau	University of Cagliari, Italy
Ana Maria A.C. Rocha	University of Minho, Portugal
Bernady O. Apduhan	Kyushu Sangyo University, Japan

International Advisory Committee

Jemal Abawajy	Deakin University, Australia
Dharma P. Agarwal	University of Cincinnati, USA
Rajkumar Buyya	Melbourne University, Australia
Claudia Bauzer Medeiros	University of Campinas, Brazil
Manfred M. Fisher	Vienna University of Economics and Business, Austria
Pierre Frankhauser	University of Franche-Comté/CNRS, France
Marina L. Gavrilova	University of Calgary, Canada

Sumi Helal   University of Florida, USA & University of
                                    Lancaster, UK
Bin Jiang   University of Gävle, Sweden
Yee Leung   Chinese University of Hong Kong, China

International Liaison Chairs

Ivan Blečić   University of Cagliari, Italy
Giuseppe Borruso   University of Trieste, Italy
Elise De Donker   Western Michigan University, USA
Maria Noelia Faginas Lago   University of Perugia, Italy
Maria Irene Falcão   University of Minho, Portugal
Robert C. H. Hsu   Chung Hua University, Taiwan
Yeliz Karaca   University of Massachusetts Medical School,
                                    Worcester, USA
Tae-Hoon Kim   Zhejiang University of Science and Technology,
                                    China
Vladimir Korkhov   Saint Petersburg University, Russia
Takashi Naka   Kyushu Sangyo University, Japan
Rafael D. C. Santos   National Institute for Space Research, Brazil
Maribel Yasmina Santos   University of Minho, Portugal
Anastasia Stratigea   National Technical University of Athens, Greece

Workshop and Session Organizing Chairs

Beniamino Murgante   University of Basilicata, Italy
Chiara Garau   University of Cagliari, Italy

Award Chair

Wenny Rahayu   La Trobe University, Australia

Publicity Committee Chair

Elmer Dadios   De La Salle University, Philippines
Nataliia Kulabukhova   Saint Petersburg University, Russia
Daisuke Takahashi   Tsukuba University, Japan

Shangwang Wang	Beijing University of Posts and Telecommunications, China

Local Organizing Committee Chairs

Doan Quang Tu	Academy of Military Science and Technology, Hanoi, Vietnam
Ho Sy Tam	Thuyloi University, Vietnam
Le Quang Tuan	Thuyloi University, Vietnam
Nguyen Huu Quynh	Thuyloi University, Vietnam
Ta Quang Chieu	Thuyloi University, Vietnam

Technology Chair

Damiano Perri	University of Perugia, Italy

Program Committee

Vera Afreixo	University of Aveiro, Portugal
Vladimir Alarcon	Northern Gulf Institute, USA
Filipe Alvelos	University of Minho, Portugal
Debora Anelli	Polytechnic University of Bari, Italy
Hartmut Asche	Hasso-Plattner-Institut für Digital Engineering, Germany
Ginevra Balletto	University of Cagliari, Italy
Socrates Basbas	Aristotle University of Thessaloniki, Greece
David Berti	ART SpA, Italy
Michela Bertolotto	University College Dublin, Ireland
Debnath Bhattacharyya	Koneru Lakshmaiah University, India
Sandro Bimonte	CEMAGREF, TSCF, France
Ana Cristina Braga	University of Minho, Portugal
Tiziana Campisi	Kore University of Enna, Italy
Yves Caniou	Lyon University, France
José A. Cardoso e Cunha	Universidade Nova de Lisboa, Portugal
Rui Cardoso	University of Beira Interior, Portugal
Leocadio G. Casado	University of Almeria, Spain
Mete Celik	Erciyes University, Turkey
Maria Cerreta	University of Naples Federico II, Italy
Mauro Coni	University of Cagliari, Italy

Eric Pardede	La Trobe University, Australia
Ana Isabel Pereira	Polytechnic Institute of Bragança, Portugal
Damiano Perri	University of Perugia, Italy
Massimiliano Petri	University of Pisa, Italy
Telmo Pinto	University of Coimbra, Portugal
Maurizio Pollino	ENEA, Italy
Alenka Poplin	Iowa State University, USA
Marcos Quiles	Federal University of São Paulo, Brazil
Humberto Rocha	University of Coimbra, Portugal
Marzio Rosi	University of Perugia, Italy
Manna Sheela Rani Chetty	Koneru Lakshmaiah University, India
Lucia Saganeiti	University of L'Aquila, Italy
Tamie Salter	Citizen Alerts Inc., Canada
Francesco Scorza	University of Basilicata, Italy
Marco Paulo Seabra dos Reis	University of Coimbra, Portugal
Jie Shen	University of Michigan, USA
Chien Sing Lee	Sunway University, Malaysia
Francesco Tajani	Sapienza University of Rome, Italy
Rodrigo Tapia-McClung	Centro de Investigación en Ciencias de Información Geoespacial, Mexico
Eufemia Tarantino	Polytechnic of Bari, Italy
Sergio Tasso	University of Perugia, Italy
Ana Paula Teixeira	Universidade do Minho, Portugal
Maria Filomena Teodoro	IST ID, Instituto Superior Técnico, Portugal
Yiota Theodora	National Technical University of Athens, Greece
Carmelo Torre	Polytechnic of Bari, Italy
Giuseppe A. Trunfio	University of Sassari, Italy
Toshihiro Uchibayashi	Kyushu University, Japan
Marco Vizzari	University of Perugia, Italy
Frank Westad	Norwegian University of Science and Technology, Norway
Fukuko Yuasa	High Energy Accelerator Research Organization, Japan
Ljiljana Zivkovic	Republic Geodetic Authority, Serbia

Additional Reviewers

Michal Abrahamowicz	McGill University, Montreal, Canada
Lidia Aceto	Università del Piemonte Orientale, Italy
Marco Baioletti	University of Perugia, Italy
Birol Ciloglugil	Ege University, Turkey

Maria Danese	National Research Council, Italy
Alexander Degtyarev	Saint Petersburg State University, Russia
Alexander Derendyaev	Institute for Information Transmission Problems, Russia
Joana Dias	University of Coimbra, Portugal
Ivan Gerace	University of Perugia, Italy
Alessandra Marra	University of Salerno, Italy
Giovanni Mauro	University of Campania Luigi Vanvitelli, Italy
Paolo Mengoni	Hong Kong Baptist University, China
Marco Reis	University of Coimbra, Portugal
Cristiano Russo	University of Napoli Federico II, Italy
Valentino Santucci	University for Foreigners of Perugia, Italy

Workshops

1. *Advances in Artificial Intelligence Learning Technologies: Blended Learning, STEM, Computational Thinking and Coding (AAILT 2024)*
2. *Advanced and Innovative Web Apps 2024 (AIWA 2024)*
3. *Advanced Processes of Mathematics and Computing Models in Complex Computational Systems (ACMC 2024)*
4. *Advances in Information Systems and Technologies for Emergency Management, Risk Assessment and Mitigation Based on the Resilience Concepts (ASTER 2024)*
5. *Advances in Web-Based Learning 2024 (AWBL 2024)*
6. *Blockchain and Distributed Ledgers: Technologies and Applications (BDLTA 2024)*
7. *Computational and Applied Mathematics (CAM 2024)*
8. *Computational and Applied Statistics (CAS 2024)*
9. *Cyber Intelligence and Applications (CIA 2024)*
10. *Computational Methods, Statistics and Industrial Mathematics (CMSIM 2024)*
11. *Computational Optimization and Applications (COA 2024)*
12. *Computational Astrochemistry (CompAstro 2024)*
13. *Computational Methods for Porous Geomaterials (CompPor 2024)*
14. *Workshop on Computational Science and HPC (CSHPC 2024)*
15. *Cities, Technologies and Planning (CTP 2024)*
16. *Sustainable Digital Circular Economy (DiCE 2024)*
17. *Evaluating Inner Areas Potentials (EIAP 2024)*
18. *Econometrics and Multidimensional Evaluation of Urban Environment (EMEUE 2024)*
19. *Environmental, Social, Governance of Energy Planning (ESGEP 2024)*
20. *Ecosystem Services in Spatial Planning for Resilient Urban and Rural Areas (ESSP 2024)*
21. *Ethical AI Applications for a Human-Centered Cyber Society (EthicAI 2024)*
22. *14th International Workshop on Future Computing System Technologies and Applications (FiSTA 2024)*

Sponsoring Organizations

ICCSA 2024 would not have been possible without the tremendous support of many organizations and institutions, for which all organizers and participants of ICCSA 2024 express their sincere gratitude:

Springer Nature Switzerland AG, Switzerland (https://www.springer.com)

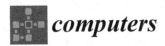

Computers Open Access Journal (https://www.mdpi.com/journal/computers)

Thuyloi University, Hanoi, Vietnam (https://en.tlu.edu.vn/)

University of Perugia, Italy (https://www.unipg.it)

University of Basilicata, Italy (http://www.unibas.it)

Monash University, Australia (https://www.monash.edu/)

Kyushu Sangyo University, Japan (https://www.kyusan-u.ac.jp/)

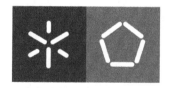

University of Minho, Portugal (https://www.uminho.pt/)

University of Cagliari, Italy (https://en.unica.it/en)

Venue

ICCSA 2024 took place on the main campus of Thuyloi University in Hanoi, Vietnam.

Plenary Lectures

Harnessing Artificial Intelligence for Enhanced Spatial Analysis of Natural Hazard Assessments

Prof. Dr. Biswajeet Pradhan

Director - Centre for Advanced Modelling and Geospatial Information Systems (CAMGIS), School of Civil and Environmental Engineering, Faculty of Engineering and IT, University of Technology Sydney, Australia

Abstract. In the realm of natural hazard assessments within spatial domains, the advent of Artificial Intelligence (AI) represents a paradigm shift, revolutionizing the way we conceptualize, model, and interpret environmental risks. This keynote address illuminates the profound impact of AI technologies, particularly machine learning algorithms and data-driven approaches, in reshaping our understanding and prediction capabilities concerning natural disasters.

By assimilating and scrutinizing vast spatial datasets, AI-driven models offer unparalleled accuracy and efficiency, facilitating timely and precise hazard assessments. Real-time processing of geospatial information not only enables rapid predictions but also forms the cornerstone of proactive disaster management strategies. Furthermore, AI's capacity lies in its adeptness at deciphering intricate spatial patterns inherent to natural hazards, unraveling subtle cues and previously unnoticed correlations within the data fabric.

This keynote delves into how AI's nuanced interpretation, coupled with advanced algorithms, elevates hazard modeling, providing deeper insights into the spatial dynamics of environmental risks. By augmenting traditional methodologies and revealing hidden patterns, AI fosters comprehensive risk assessments, fostering informed decision-making processes. The fusion of AI and natural hazard assessments in spatial domains heralds a more resilient approach to disaster preparedness and response.

Join us in embracing this transformative era, where AI's sophisticated modeling techniques and precise spatial interpretations converge, heralding proactive and effective mitigation strategies amidst the ever-evolving landscape of environmental challenges.

Short Bio. Distinguished Professor Dr. Biswajeet Pradhan is an internationally established scientist in the field of Geospatial Information Systems (GIS), remote sensing and image processing, complex modelling/geo-computing, machine learning and soft-computing applications, natural hazards and environmental modelling. He is the Director of the Centre for Advanced Modelling and Geospatial Information Systems (CAMGIS) at the Faculty of Engineering and IT at the University of Technology, Sydney (Australia). He was listed as the World's Most Highly Cited Researcher by the Clarivate Analytics Report for five consecutive years, 2016–2020 as one of the world's most influential minds.

He ranked number one (1) in the field of "Geological & Geomatics Engineering" during the calendar year 2021–2023, according to the list published by Stanford University Researchers, USA. This list ranks the world's top 2% most highly cited researchers based on Scopus data. In 2018–2020, he was awarded as World Class Professor by the Ministry of Research, Technology and Higher Education, Indonesia. He is a recipient of the Alexander von Humboldt Research Fellowship from Germany. Between 2015–2021, he served as "Ambassador Scientist" for the Alexander Humboldt Foundation, Germany.

Professor Pradhan has received 58 awards since 2006 in recognition of his excellence in teaching, service and research. Out of his more than 850 articles (Google Scholar citation: 70,000, H-index: 129), more than 750 have been published in science citation index (SCI/SCIE) technical journals. He has authored/co-authored ten books and thirteen book chapters.

Software Engineering Research in a New Situation

Prof. Carl K. Chang

Professor Emeritus, State University of Iowa, USA

Abstract. With the rise of Generative Artificial Intelligence (GAI), epitomized by Large Language Models (LLMs), a profound shift has unfolded in software engineering research. In this presentation, I will traverse my four-decade journey in software engineering research, focusing on situational awareness in the era of the Internet of Things (IoT). I have witnessed the turbulence brought forth by the AI community that demands changes in our approaches. Meanwhile, owing to the pervasiveness of services computing, services became the first-class citizen in modern-day software engineering methodologies.

I argue that situational awareness must permeate the entire lifecycle to consistently deliver software services that align with the dynamic needs of users and the ever-evolving environments. I will elucidate this argument by reviewing the Situ framework, offering a comprehensive illustration of my perspective. Furthermore, I will outline my vision regarding the formidable research challenges considering the rapidly shifting landscape dominated by an irresistible and profoundly disruptive generative AI tsunami.

Short Bio. Carl K. Chang is a former department chair and Professor Emeritus of Computer Science at Iowa State University. His research interests include requirements engineering, net-centric computing, situational software engineering and digital health. Chang was the 2004 President of the IEEE Computer Society. Previously he served as the Editor-in-Chief for IEEE Software (1991–1994), and as the Editor-in-Chief of IEEE

Computer (2007–2010). He was the 2012 recipient of the Richard E. Merwin Medal from the IEEE Computer Society. Chang is a Life Fellow of IEEE, a Fellow of AAAS, and a Life Member of the European Academy of Sciences (EurASc).

Interpretability and Privacy Preservation in Large Language Models (LLMs)

Prof. My Thai

University of Florida (UF) Research Foundation Professor
Associate Director of UF Nelms Institute for the Connected World

Abstract. Large Language Models (LLMs) have transformed the AI landscape, captivating researchers and practitioners with their remarkable ability to generate human-like text and perform complex tasks. However, this transformative power comes with a set of critical challenges, particularly in the realms of interpretability and privacy preservation. In this keynote, we embark on an exploration of these pressing issues, shedding light on how LLMs operate, their limitations, and the strategies we can employ to mitigate risks. We begin by examining the interpretability in LLMs, which often function as enigmatic "black boxes." Their complex neural architectures make it challenging to understand how they arrive at specific outputs. This lack of transparency raises questions of trust and accountability. When deploying LLMs in real-world applications—whether for chatbots, content generation, or decision-making—it becomes crucial to demystify their decision paths.

We will use explainable AI (XAI) to offer faithful explanations, from the black-box to white-box models, and from feature-based [1, 2] to neuron circuits-based [3, 4] explanations. By visualizing attention mechanisms, feature importance, and saliency maps, we empower users to comprehend LLM predictions. XAI not only fosters trust but also encourages responsible utilization of LLMs.

We next turn our attention to one of the utmost concerns and challenges: data privacy. LLMs process vast amounts of data, raising risks of data leakage, model inversion, the right to be forgotten, and inadvertent exposure of sensitive information. Furthermore, the integration of LLMs into diverse applications also significantly brings these challenges to the next level [5].

This talk explores strategies to protect privacy, including differential privacy, federated learning, and data encryption.

Short Bio. My T. Thai is a University of Florida (UF) Research Foundation Professor, Associate Director of UF Nelms Institute for the Connected World, and a Fellow of IEEE and AAIA. Dr. Thai is a leading authority who has done transformative research in Trustworthy AI and Optimization, especially for complex systems with applications to healthcare, social media, critical networking infrastructure, and cybersecurity. The results of her work have led to 7 books and 350+ publications in highly ranked international journals and conferences, including several best paper awards from the IEEE, ACM, and AAAI.

In responding to a world-wide call for responsible and safe AI, Dr. Thai is a pioneer in designing deep explanations for black-box ML models, while defending against explanation-guided attacks, evident by her Distinguished Papers Award at the Association for the Advancement of Artificial Intelligence (AAAI) conference in 2023. At the same year, she was also awarded an ACM Web Science Trust Test-of-Time award, for her landmark work on combating misinformation in social media. In 2022, she received an IEEE Big Data Security Women of Achievement Award. In 2009, she was awarded the Young Investigator (YIP) from the Defense Threat Reduction Agency (DTRA), and in 2010 she won the NSF CAREER Award. She is presently the Editor-in-Chief of the Springer Journal of Combinatorial Optimization and the IET Blockchain Journal, and editor of the Springer book series Optimization and Its Applications.

References

1. Vu, M., Thai, M.T.: PGM-explainer: probabilistic graphical model explanations for graph neural networks. In: Advances in Neural Information Processing Systems (NeurIPS) (2020)
2. Nguyen, T., Lai, P., Phan, H., Thai, M.T.: XRand: differentially private defense against explanation-guided attacks. In: AAAI Conference on Artificial Intelligence (AAAI) (2023)
3. Vu, N., Nguyen, T., Thai, M.T.: NeuCEPT: learn neural networks' mechanism via critical neurons with precision guarantee. In: IEEE International Conference on Data Mining (ICDM) (2022)
4. Conmy, A., Mavor-Parker, A., Heimersheim, S., Garriga-Alonso, A.: Towards automated circuit discovery for mechanistic interpretability. In: Advances in Neural Information Processing Systems (NeurIPS) (2023)
5. Vu, M., Nguyen, T., Jeter, T., Thai, M.T.: Analysis of privacy leakages in federated large language models. In: International Conference on Artificial Intelligence and Statistics (AISTATS) (2023)

Contents – Part II

PHD Showcase Papers

Short Papers

Contents – Part I

Geometric Modeling, Graphics and Visualization

Advanced and Emerging Applications

Urban and Regional Planning

High Performance Computing
and Networks

e-CLAS: Effective GPUDirect I/O Classification Scheme

Jungmyoung Kim and Jaechun No[✉]

Department of Computer Science and Engineering, Sejong University,
209 Neungdong-ro, Gwangjin-gu, Seoul, Korea
jano@sejong.ac.kr

Abstract. GPUs are widely used in various computational areas, due to their massive multithreading platform capable of high-level parallelism. Especially, to speedup I/O processing, GPUDirect I/O has been developed to enable direct data access between GPU memory and either NVMe or NVMe-oF. However, GPUDirect I/O does not always enhance the I/O performance of applications, because of reducing the benefit of page cache. In this paper, we present an effective I/O scheme, called *e*-CLAS, that can categorize I/Os through machine learning algorithms, to maximize the benefit of GPUDirect I/O while managing NVMe device storage at cost-effective way. The performance evaluation shows that our scheme effectively works to increase I/O performance, by appropriately classifying I/Os generated from applications.

Keywords: GPUDirect · I/O classification · NVMe · Direct I/O · machine-learning

1 Introduction

As GPU technology has been rapidly developed, several areas requiring high computation power, such as deep learning or HPC applications, increasingly facilitate GPUs due to their potential of high processing capability through massive multithreading and parallel executions [1–5, 8]. In order to leverage GPUs in user applications, users should link with API provided at GPU runtime library (e.g. CUDA).

In such an environment, to execute I/O processing, the necessary data should be transferred from storage to host memory and then moved to GPU memory by using the runtime library such as CUDA. Such a data transmission can restrict I/O processing throughput by going through multiple layers or external device (e.g. PCI-e), incurring the significant I/O performance degradation. GPU Direct I/O [6, 7] has been developed to overcome such a drawback in I/O path, by providing the direct data access between GPU memory and either NVMe (Non-Volatile Memory access) or NVMe-oF.

However, providing the direct I/O path in GPUDirect would not always enhance I/O performance [5] because of host kernel bypass capabilities, reducing the benefit of page cache such as data prefetching. There is a need to differentiate the I/O path

O. Gervasi et al. (Eds.): ICCSA 2024, LNCS 14814, pp. 3–16, 2024.
https://doi.org/10.1007/978-3-031-64608-9_1

required in applications between GPUDirect Scheme (GDS interchangeably) and CPU-GPU Scheme (GPU or GPU I/O interchangeably), according to I/O characteristics such as data size or access pattern.

In this paper, we propose a machine-learning based I/O classification scheme, called *e*-CLAS(*e*ffective GPUDirect I/O **CLAS**sification Scheme), capable of categorizing I/Os through machine learning algorithms, to maximize the benefit of GPUDirect I/O while managing NVMe device storage at cost-effective way.

In this paper, we first compare the I/O performance of GDS and GPU (typical GPU I/O) by various benchmark tools and leverage the comparison results to organize ML-based classes, together with application I/O parameters and system status information including file size, I/O access pattern, and memory usages of CPU, GPU and memory.

To choose the appropriate data for GDS, *e*-CLAS extracts features affecting I/O performance of applications facilitating GPUs for computations and I/Os, and then classifies the proper data for GDS to separately store them to NVMe.

As a result, I/O operations on those selected data would utilize GDS capability by allowing the direct access between NVMe where the desired data are stored and GPU memory, using cuCIM library. In *e*-CLAS, the ML-based models built for categorizing I/Os have been implemented by using multiple ML algorithms including Support vector machine, Random Forest and Logistic regression. Among those models, the one enabling the best performance can automatically be selected, to exploit I/O speedup.

The rest of paper is organized as follows: In Sect. 2, we present the performance comparison between GDS and GPU to describe our motivations. In Sect. 3, we represent the overall structure of *e*-CLAS, and demonstrate its performance evaluation in Sect. 4. We conclude our paper in Sect. 5.

2　Motivation

In Figs. 1 and 2, we analyzed the I/O bandwidth of GDS on the local environments, while comparing it with GPU (CPU-GPU Scheme). In these figures, GDS creates the direct I/O path between the local NVMe device and the GPU memory. Such an I/O path is activated by going through either the network adaptor or the storage-based DMA engine to transfer data to GPU memory, while avoiding CPU bounce buffer.

The experimental platform used for the evaluation includes a 3.10 GHz 6-core Intel Xeon CPU i5-10500, NVIDIA RTX A4000 GPU, four 8 GB of Samsung DDR4 (total 32 GB), a 1 TB of Western Digital WD5000AZLX, and a 1 TB of KLEVV CRAS c710 NVMe. We used Ubuntu 20.04 with kernel 5.4.0 for our evaluation.

The evaluation results of Figs. 1 and 2 were obtained by using gdsio and fio, respectively. The file sizes are varied from 1 GB to 16 GB, while changing I/O sizes between 4 KB and 16 KB. As the I/O sizes increase, the performance gap between GDS and GPU becomes significant due to multiple data paths to reach GPU memory for computations, except for results with 16 GB of file size.

In Fig. 1, with 4 KB of file size, the I/O throughput of GPU shows about 15% of I/O degradation compared to that of GDS because of multiple I/O paths until the necessary data reaches GPU memory. However, such a difference is smaller than that with the large I/O size because the effect of bypassing cache do not help enhance GDS performance.

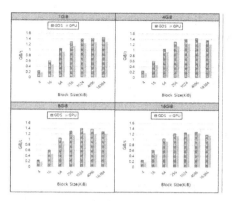

Fig. 1. gdsio read performance comparison

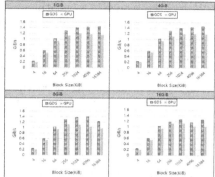

Fig. 2. fio read performance

With large I/O sizes, the beneficial of GDS becomes apparent, except for results with 16 GB of file size where I/O access latency to storage is large compared to that of other file sizes. We can observe the similar I/O execution behavior in Fig. 2, measured with *fio* benchmark.

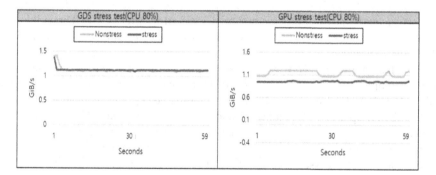

Fig. 3. Performance comparison using stress tool

Figure 3 illustrates how the existing I/O stress impacts I/O performance of GDS and GPU. In this comparison, we used Linux stress tool. In the figure, we can notice that the existing I/O stress would cause more performance variation with the typical GPU I/O than with GDS, since GPU I/O going through more I/O layers can be significantly influenced by the I/O stress. In GDS, fewer I/O layers are involved in I/O operations, resulting in more consistent performance compared to GPU I/O.

To collect appropriate performance results for implementing *e*-CLAS, we performed a lot of performance comparisons, although not all of them can be presented in this paper due to page limitations. Based on the evaluation, we attempt to achieve the following main objectives:

1) We try to categorize I/Os based on various application execution parameters, such as file and I/O sizes, access pattern, and current resource statuses including CPU, GPU and memory.
2) To choose the appropriate I/O scheme for applications, we utilize various machine learning (ML) algorithms. The ML algorithms being used for e-CLAS can be easily integrated with the system, for both training and evaluating the associated I/O models.
3) e-CLAS can effectively manage the NVMe storage capacity, by transferring only the data needed for GDS into it. Also, it stores the I/O categorization result for applications in the repository, to avoid redundant model evaluation or data transmission for further processing.

As the potential of GPUs has become evident in massive computational areas, extensive research has been conducted in various ways. For instance, Silberstein et al. [2] attempted to integrate GPU code to host's filesystem through POSIX-like API, while extending the host buffer cache to GPU memory, to retain GPU advantages such as massive parallelism. In the scheme, the GPUfs library caching filedata in both CPU and GPU memory is linked with user GPU code, to enable data accesses to the host filesystem.

Zhang [9] tried to provide a way of directly connecting GPU memory to SSD devices by mapping physically shared system memory blocks. By doing this way, their scheme can mitigate the overhead of data movement while reducing user/kernel switching.

Vesely et al. [10] tried to support standard POSIX semantics for GPU, instead of using special system calls. SPIN [5] proposed a way of integrating GPUDirect into file I/O layer, to leverage the benefit of page cache, such as prefetching, while maintaining POSIX file consistency.

Also, there are several GPU works for optimizing irregular memory accesses [11–14]. For example, Segura et al. [11] proposed IRU that can reorder irregular data accessed by threads, to improve memory coalescing in graph-based GPGPU applications. Li et al. [12] worked on optimizing irregular memory accesses by providing both fine-grained and coarse-grained L1 cache line management, without requiring additional memory structure for tag storage. Guo et al. [13] also tried to resolve the problem of mismatching between the size of accessed data and the wide GPU cache line, by utilizing run-time memory access profiling.

Chen et al. [14] argued that the current GPU cache might not enhance application performances retaining a lot of multiple irregular access patterns, due to its aim for the speedup architecture through multithread-based structure. They proposed GPGPU's cache policy that can control the number of active warps at run-time, to avoid cache contention.

ActivePointers [15] was proposed to eliminate CPU interference with active pointer in handling both page fault and GPU address translation occurring mmap system calls. It provides a pointer-based interface to directly access to storages from GPU. Also, GaiaGPU [16] was developed to combine CPU and GPU memories to extend OS page cache, while integrating it with OS file I/O layer. It employs mmap system calls to extend page cache space into GPU memory while addressing false sharing overhead through a lazy release consistency model.

3 Implementation Details

3.1 System Architecture

The main objective of *e*-CLAS is to categorize applications that can accelerate I/O performance through GPUDirect I/O. To achieve this, we classify the appropriate datasets generated by those applications using machine learning and store the data in advance on NVMe device storage, allowing for direct access when possible.

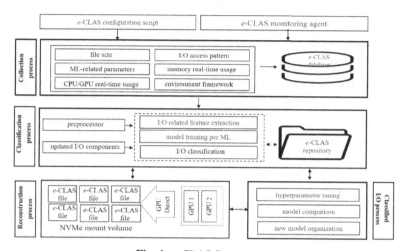

Fig. 4. *e*-CLAS Structure

Figure 4 illustrates *e*-CLAS structure. The *e*-CLAS is composed of four processes: collection process, classification process, reconstruction process, and classified I/O process. The collection process obtains the necessary information to categorize the I/O scheme enhancing application performance, such as the dataset for evaluating model training, the system environment parameters including the real-time states of host memory, CPU, and GPUs. The dataset for evaluating models would be continuously updated as new applications are executed on the *e*-CLAS.

The classification process extracts I/O characteristics (features) needed for categorizing the proper I/O scheme through machine learning (ML). *E*-CLAS can organize diverse I/O models to search for the proper applications whose dataset is appropriate for performing GPUDirect I/O. The ML algorithm necessary for organizing I/O models is either specified in the collection process as a part of *e*-CLAS configuration, or automatically selected by comparing the performance comparison ratio during the model training in the classification process. The organized models are stored in *e*-CLAS repository to be used for further processes.

In the reconstruction process, *e*-CLAS updates the existing models by optimizing steps, such as hyperparameter tuning. During this process, newly recognized, effective I/O characteristics are used to update and reorganize *e*-CLAS models, which are then stored for further use.

Based on the output of the reconstruction process, data sets not residing in NVMe device storage are copied to NVMe storage during the classified I/O process, enabling the utilization of GPUDirect in I/O steps available in the corresponding applications. As a result, if the applications running on the host generate the appropriate datasets for GPUDirect, the datasets would be directly accessed between NVMe storage and GPU memory.

To avoid redundant steps in organizing and analyzing the required I/O models for applications, the previously obtained performance comparison ratio for each application is stored in the *e*-CLAS repository for reuse in subsequent executions.

3.2 *e*-CLAS Collection Process

Table 1 shows an example of datasets used for training *e*-CLAS I/O models. Currently, we collect the dataset by executing *gdsio* and *fio* benchmarks. Because the system environment can significantly impact I/O performance, we generate datasets by introducing various system statuses, while changing the system environment in the collection process.

Table 1. An example of dataset for training *e*-CLAS I/O model

	file size	I/O access pattern	GPU usage	memory usage	CPU usage	framework	I/O class
1	0.2	1	0	16	0	0	0
3	4.0	1	32	42	85	0	0
4	2.9	1	39	17	1	1	0
2214	3.7	1	42	38	84	0	1

```
file_size    = os.path.getsize(name)
steam1       = os.popen("free| grep ^Mem | awk '{printf $3*100/$2}'")
stream2      = os.popen("nvidia-smi | grep % | awk '{print $13}' | cut -d '%' -f1")
dockerframe  = "docker"
randpat      = "randomread"
if pattern == randpat:
     A_new = np.array([[file_size3, 0, 1, inout1, inout, inout2]])
```

Fig. 5. An example of *e*-CLAS configuration

Figure 5 shows the *e*-CLAS configuration script used for categorizing the proper I/Os. The initial I/O parameters for determining resource statuses at the time of collection would be specified in the configuration file. After identifying the I/O parameters used for analyzing associated I/O performance, the monitoring agent updates the real-time statuses of the selected system component, to provide a more accurate performance comparison ratio for the classification.

The I/O parameters can be easily added to the configuration file, without involving the model reorganization. The current parameters for choosing the appropriate I/O scheme include file size, machine learning algorithm for model training, I/O access pattern, and usages of GPU, CPU and memory.

3.3 I/O Categorization

The classification process selects the appropriate features for performing *e*-CLAS and organizes the necessary models for producing the accurate performance comparison ratio. Once the classification module obtains the datasets from the collection module, it preprocesses the dataset in such a way that it takes the abnormal values away to prevent I/O errors. The preprocessed I/O dataset is used for categorizing I/O schemes through model training.

We use Random Forest (RF), Support Vector Machine (SVM) and Logistic Regression (LR) to organize *e*-CLAS models. However, user can specify more ML algorithms to provide the higher performance ratio, by specifying them in the configuration file. Since different algorithms can lead to different performance ratios when applied to the same dataset, the choice of ML algorithm depends on various factors such as the nature of the dataset, computational resources where applications execute, or performance requirements. *E*-CLAS attempts to consider those factors by flexibly providing them to the system and to compare their performance ratios, to select the most suitable one for application executions. The trained models and the performance comparison ratios are stored in the *e*-CLAS repository for further uses.

Table 2 shows an example of the performance comparison ratio obtained from the *e*-CLAS classification process. In this example, the evaluation values including precision, recall, and F1-score are used, and also SVM shows the highest ratio.

Table 2. An example of performance comparison ratio

		precision	recall	F1-score	support
RF	I/O	0.99	0.94	0.97	533
	accuracy			0.94	555
	weighted avg.	0.97	0.94	0.95	555
SVM	I/O	0.99	0.99	0.99	533
	accuracy			0.98	555
	weighted avg.	0.98	0.98	0.98	555
LR	I/O	0.99	0.92	0.96	533
	accuracy			0.92	555
	weighted avg.	0.97	0.92	0.94	555

3.4 I/O Reconstruction Process

The reconstruction process is to update *e*-CLAS models by applying either a new ML algorithm, or accepting additional I/O parameters from the configuration script. In this case, *e*-CLAS extracts new features affecting the I/O performance through hyperparameter tuning and organizes new models to update the performance. Figure 6 shows an example of *e*-CLAS reconstruction process to update the models.

At the initial step, *e*-CLAS mounts its volume to store the selected datasets through the classified scheme. If the dataset is already available outside *e*-CLAS storage, the associated dataset is duplicated into *e*-CLAS directory in advance, to make them available for *e*-CLAS process.

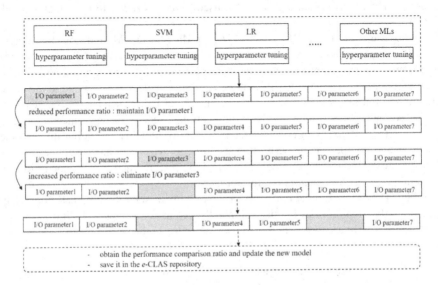

Fig. 6. *e*-CLAS reconstruction process

In order not to repeatedly execute the classification process of *e*-CLAS, the previously measured performance comparison ratio of the application is stored in the repository, and reused for the next execution, unless user triggers to update the new result. The procedures for categorizing I/O schemes are as follows:

1. Preprocess the datasets by eliminating parameter errors. If multiple ML candidates are determined in the *e*-CLAS configuration, select the better candidate by comparing their registered performance ratio stored in the repository.
2. Execute the optimization steps including hyperparameter tuning by updating I/O parameters and then choose the effective features significantly influencing the performance ratio enhancement. Perform steps repeatedly until effective I/O parameters are chosen.
3. Train and evaluate the *e*-CLAS models by leveraging the selected features, and store the trained models per ML in the repository.

4. Mount *e*-CLAS volume to perform the classified I/O process, by leveraging the models residing in the repository and the real-time system environment provided by the system agent. When applications begin, access the repository to check the proper I/O scheme and perform the selected I/O scheme. The real-time application and environment data are updated in the database to be used for the further model training and analysis.

Table 3 shows an example of I/O parameters used for hyperparameter tuning and model training in the *e*-CLAS classification process.

Table 3. I/O parameters used in *e*-CLAS

Attributes	Parameters
Hyperparameter tuning	GridSearchCV
ML algorithm	Support vector machine(SVM) Random forest(RF) Logistic regression(LR)
RF parameter	n_estimators, max_features, max_depths
SVM parameter	C, gamma
LR parameter	max_iter, C

4 Performance Evaluation

Figures 7 and 8 are the performance comparisons of *e*-CLAS and GPU I/O (CPU-GPU I/O), while reading 1 GB of data to GPU local memory. We measured the performance on the local environment in Fig. 4 and on the docker environment in Fig. 8.

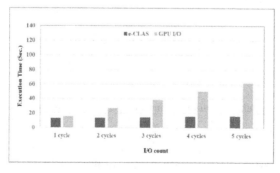

Fig. 7. Time comparison of seq. read operation on the local environment

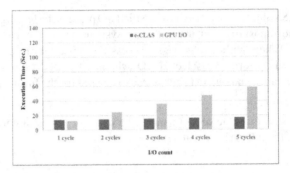

Fig. 8. Time comparison of seq. read operation on the docker environment

On the local environment, reading the file using *e*-CLAS takes about 13 s. and the time for reading using GPU I/O takes about 16 s. After the first step of reading data, *e*-CLAS approximately adds 0.75 s. for each read operation, while GPU I/O adding about 11 s. The reason for generating more I/O overhead in the existing GPU I/O is that every I/O step of GPU I/O needs to retrieve files from the host storage to CPU and to transfer those files to GPU memory for further computation.

Whereas in *e*-CLAS, although the necessary files should be copied to NVMe device storage at the first step, those files can be accessed from NVMe to GPU memory directly in the next I/O steps. Therefore, *e*-CLAS produces less I/O overhead in accessing the desirable files from NVMe to GPU, to utilize those files in the GPU computation.

Also, in GPU I/O, while I/O cycles increase the performance gap between 1 cycle and 5 cycles becomes large, nearly tripling in magnitude. On the other hand, the gap of *e*-CLAS within the same cycle is only about 22%. This suggests that GPU I/O is more affected by the system status during the performance measurement.

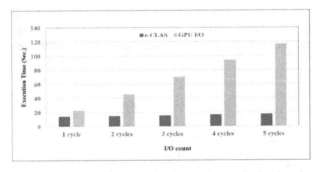

Fig. 9. Time comparison for random read operation on the local environment

Figures 9 and 10 show the random read performance comparison of *e*-CLAS and GPU I/O, by measuring *gdsio* benchmark on the local (Fig. 9) and the docker (Fig. 10) environments, respectively. Like in the previous experiments in Figs. 7 and 8, the performance of *e*-CLAS shows the better throughput compared to that of GPU I/O. Furthermore, the

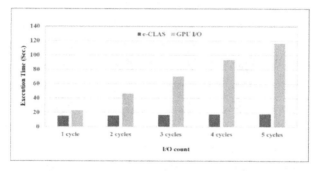

Fig. 10. Time comparison for random read operation on the docker environment

performance difference between the two schemes is more significant than that in the previous experiment, primarily due to the random read access pattern.

Even in the random access pattern, *e*-CLAS shows minimal differences as the number of I/O cycles increases, whether the performance was measured on the local environment or on the docker environment. However, with GPU I/O, the performance gap between 1 cycle and 5 cycles is nearly four times larger, even exceeding the gap shown in Fig. 7, due to the increased influence of system statuses.

In Fig. 11, we measured the throughput of cuCIM read operation, because we used cuCIM library for the performance comparison. In this evaluation, we vary the size of files from 1GiB to 4GiB. As can be seen, the read bandwidth in *e*-CLAS is higher than that of GPU I/O, although the performance gap is smaller than in the previous experiment.

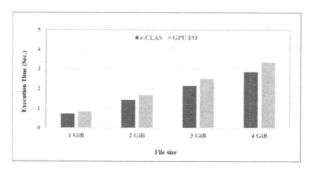

Fig. 11. cuCIM read performance

In Fig. 12, we compared the F1-score of ML algorithms used in *e*-CLAS, including RF, SVM, and LR. As can be seen, the SVM shows the best accuracy in organizing *e*-CLAS models. Even though, we set SVM models as default in the current implementation, users can easily switch to the other algorithm producing the better performance. Also, the *e*-CLAS can automatically detect the better models once their performance is registered in the repository.

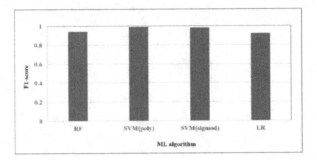

Fig. 12. F1-score of ML algorithms used in *e*-CLAS

Figures 13 and 14 are the comparison where two I/O schemes are installed on the remote server where clients access the desired data through NFS server. In the figures, Figs. 13 and 14 are the throughput of sequential read operations and random read operations, respectively. In this experiment, we can notice that even with the network overhead produced by NFS protocol, two I/O schemes generate the similar behavior, leading to the larger performance gap in GPI I/O as I/O counts increase.

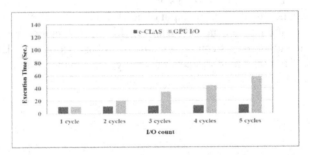

Fig. 13. Time comparison for seq. read operation where two I/O schemes are installed on the NFS server.

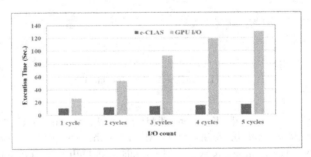

Fig. 14. Time comparison for random read operation where two I/O schemes are installed on the NFS server.

5   Conclusion

In this paper, we presented a machine-learning based I/O classification scheme, called *e*-CLAS, that categorizes I/Os using machine learning algorithms, to optimize GPUDirect I/O scheme (GDS) while efficiently managing NVMe device storage. To select the suitable data for each I/O scheme, *e*-CLAS extracts performance-affecting features from applications that facilitate GPUs for computations and I/Os. It then classifies the relevant data for GDS to separately store them to NVMe. We compared our scheme to the typical GPU I/O and demonstrated that *e*-CLAS can improve the I/O throughput on a large scale. As a future work, we would verify our scheme with more benchmarks in various ways to prove its effectiveness.

Acknowledgements. This work was supported by the National Research Foundation of Korea (NRF) grant funded by the Korea Government (MSIT) (No. 2022R1A2C1004156).

References

1. Ravikumar, K., Appelhans, D., Yeung, P.K.: GPU acceleration of extreme scale pseudo-spectral simulations of turbulence using asynchronism. In: Proceedings of the International Conference for High Performance Computing Networking, Storage and Analysis (SC 2019), Denver (2019)
2. Silberstein, M., Ford, B., Keidar, I., Witchel, E.: GPUfs: integrating a file system with GPUs. ACM Trans. Comput. Syst. **1**(1) (2013)
3. Hong, C., Spence, I., Nikolopoulos, D.: FairGV: fair and fast GPU virtualization. IEEE Trans. Parallel Distrib. Syst. **28**(12) (2017)
4. Suzuki, Y., Kato, S., Yamada, H., Kono, K.: GPUvm: GPU virtualization at the hypervisor. IEEE Trans. Comput. **65**(9) (2016)
5. Bergman, S., Brokhman, T., Cohen, T., Silberstein M.: SPIN: seamless operating system integration of peer-to-peer DMA between SSDs and GPUs. In: USENIX Annual Technical Conference (ATC 2017), Santa Clara (2017)
6. https://doc.nvidia.com/gpudirect-storage/overview-guide/index.html
7. Bayati, M., Leeser, M., Mi, N.: Exploiting GPU direct access to non-volatile memory to accelerate big data processing. In: IEEE Conference on High Performance Extreme Computing (HPEC) (2020)
8. Eduardo, V., Bona, L., Zola, W.: Speculative encryption on GPU applied to cryptographic file systems. In: 17th USENIX Conference on File and Storage Technologies (FAST 2019), Boston (2019)
9. Zhang, J., Donofrio, D., Shalf, J., Kandemir, M., Jung, M.: NVMMU: a non-volatile memory management unit for heterogeneous GPU-SSD architecture. In: PACT, pp. 13–24 (2015)
10. Vesely, J., Basu, A., Bhattacharjee, A., Loh, G., Oskin, M., Reinhardt, S.: Generic system calls for GPUs. In: ACM/IEEE 45th Annual International Symposium on Computer Architecture (2018)
11. Segura, A., Arnau, J., Gonzalez, A.: Irregular accesses reorder unit: improving GPGPU memory coalescing for graph-based workloads. J. Supercomput. **79**, 762–787 (2022)
12. Li, B., Wei, J., Sun, J., Annavaram, M., Kim, N.: An efficient GPU cache architecture for applications with irregular memory access patterns. ACM Trans. Architect. Code Optimiz. **16**(3) (2019)

13. Guo, H., Huang, L., Lu, Y., Ma, S., Wang, Z.: DyCache: dynamic multi-grain cache management for irregular memory accesses on GPU. IEEE Access **6**, 38881–38891 (2018)
14. Chen, X., Chang, L.-W., Rodrigues, C., Lv, J., Wang, Z., Hwu, W.: Adaptive cache management for energy-efficient GPU computing. In: IEEE/ACM International Symposium on Microarchitecture (MICRO) (2014)
15. Shahar, S., Bergman, S., Siberstein, M.: ActivePointers: a case for software address translation on GPUs. In: ACM/IEEE 43rd Annual International Symposium on Computer Architecture (ISCA) (2016)
16. Gu, J., Song, S., Li, Y., Luo, H.: Gaia GPU: sharing GPUs in container clouds. In: IEEE International Conference on Big Data and Cloud Computing (2018)

A Real-Time Visualization Tool of Hardware Resources for Flutter Applications

Felipe Bedinotto Fava and Claudio Schepke[✉]

Laboratory of Advanced Studies in Computation, Federal University of Pampa
(UNIPAMPA), Alegrete, RS, Brazil
{felipefava.aluno,claudioschepke}@unipampa.edu.br

Abstract. Mobile development is a constantly evolving field. Several options are available for developing cross-platform applications, such as Flutter, React Native, Ionic, and Xamarin. These options have the potential to achieve excellent performance compared to native applications, and they can also facilitate the development process by reducing the need for separate projects for each platform. One of the main challenges in developing mobile applications is finding potential changes that could affect the application's performance. To address this topic, we develop a Flutter plugin. It helps identify performance issues for developers in their applications while developing and testing them. The plugin increases the speed of detecting bugs and keeps the application running smoothly. We develop the performance tool in Dart. It features three main aspects to be visualized by the developer: frames rendered per second, number of bytes sent and received through the network, and RAM's information of total available, occupied, and free memory. We validated the tool on three Dart applications running on a physical smartphone, displaying the performance results in real time. The results show variations in FPS, RAM, and network collected values during the execution of the applications.

Keywords: Flutter · Plugin · Network Monitor · FPS · Memory

1 Introduction

Mobile application development is a field that is constantly evolving [3,4]. Several options are available to developers, each with its advantages and disadvantages. Choosing the best option for a project will depend on its specific needs. One popular option is native development, which involves platform-specific languages and tools like Swift and Objective-C for iOS [2], and Java and Kotlin for Android [9]. That often results in high-performing applications but can also be more laborious and expensive due to the need to create and maintain two different source codes. Alternatively, there are development tools such as Flutter, React Native, Ionic, and Xamarin, which allow the development of multiplatform applications with the potential to achieve excellent performance compared to native applications [5,6,12]. These tools also facilitate process development by reducing the need for different teams and projects for each platform.

To be accepted by users, a system must work efficiently and meet their needs [1]. It can be frustrating when users open an application and notice that it drains their device battery faster than usual. Poor system performance can also be a crucial turnoff for new users. An application that performs poorly can cause issues such as slowness, crashes, and errors, which lead to user lack of satisfaction, application uninstallation, and even financial loss. Therefore, the system design needs optimal performance to ensure a positive user experience.

Flutter [8] provides developers with a helpful set of tools called DevTools [11] for debugging code and analyzing performance. It is powerful and allows developers to understand how their application is performing. However, this process is still complex and, in some ways, costly, as it requires external application monitoring. To access the DevTools interface, the developer needs to use a link provided by the Flutter SDK when launching the application through the SDK or access using a new tab of Visual Studio Code if all dependencies were already correctly configured. Moreover, the tool's interface has a steep learning curve, making it difficult for many developers to use.

After considering all the aspects presented, we propose a Flutter plugin to help developers identify possible performance issues and detect bugs more efficiently in real-time. Thus, it can used during the development of Flutter applications. The specific objectives pursued during the plugin's development are as follows:

- Be easy for the developers to use;
- Make the interface as less invasive as possible;
- Display an indication of the number of frames generated per second;
- Show values of memory usage;
- View indicators of network traffic.

The contributions of the work are:

(i) the description of a simple, non-invasive plugin alternative to help Flutter developers identify performance problems in their applications while developing them;
(ii) an extension of Flutter's bibliography, given that it is still a topic that is not yet very present in academic works.

The organization of this paper is in four sections. Section 2 points the related work. Section 3 shows aspects of methodology like implementation and parameters for the modules. Section 4 details the results obtained through the plugin execution. Section 5 presents the conclusion of the paper and future works.

2 Related Work

We discuss in this section the packages and plugins found in the official Dart and Flutter repository [10]. We consider these packages to be related work due to their relevance to our work. Our research criteria include the terms Flutter, Android, or iOS that address CPU, memory, or network traffic monitoring. We used the base application created by executing the `flutter create {name_for_flutter_project}` command to test these packages and plugins. We have listed the packages that are most suitable for our work below.

1. **show_fps**[1] - The package provides a simple FPS viewer as shown in Fig. 1a. We encounter some issues while using the code example on the official page. The frame counter didn't appear in the application despite following the instructions. It only displays a text reading *FPS* in the top right corner of the page. However, changing the *showChart* parameter from *false* to *true* resolved the issue, and the counter started working alongside the chart. It's worth noting that the chart updates very quickly, which makes it challenging to follow events.

2. **performance_fps**[2] - This package displays the FPS rate of an application. However, the package did not include interface elements and was only accessible to the developer. The developer can call a function that will return two values: the FPS rate and the number of dropped frames, referred to as *dropCount*. It is worth noting that this plugin uses specific mechanisms of the target platforms to obtain data. But it stood discontinued.

3. **lemberfpsmonitor**[3] - It provides the developer a chart as shown in Fig. 1b. At the upper right corner of its interface to the left, it displays the frame rate per second, the lowest and the highest frame rates recorded within the sample window. The visualization of these two last data is inside a parenthesis, split by a hyphen. By default, it has a *maxFPS* variable set to 60. It locks the maximum displayed value of FPS in the chart, The package's *widget* provides an option to change the maximum displayed value of FPS.

4. **statsfl**[4] - The previous *lemberfpsmonitor* package and its official documentation inspired this package. It has the same interface as its predecessor. However, this one does not display any graphs. Instead, it only shows the achieved frame rate values and a small line indicating which frames reached the target of 60 FPS.

5. **memory_info**[5] - This package does not have a pre-built data presentation interface for developers. However, it provides some methods to retrieve information about the device's RAM and internal storage. The available information includes the total RAM of the device, the amount of free RAM, the total size of internal storage, and the amount of free space on it.

6. **performance**[6] - This particular package served as an inspiration for the development of our project. It generates three charts on the primary application that display, from left to right, the frames produced by the UI isolate,

---

[1] https://github.com/mantreshkhurana/show_fps.
[2] https://github.com/allenymt/flutter_fps.
[3] https://github.com/lember-ecu/fpsmonitoring.
[4] https://github.com/gskinnerTeam/flutter-stats-fl.
[5] https://github.com/MrOlolo/memory_info/tree/master/memory_info.
[6] https://github.com/creativecreatorormaybenot/performance.

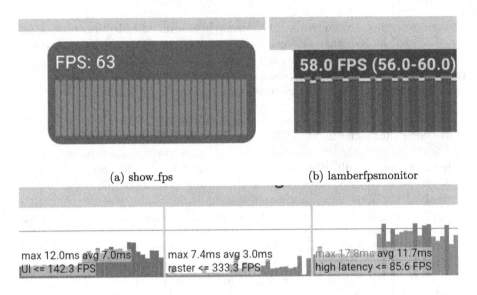

(a) show_fps (b) lamberfpsmonitor

(c) performance

Fig. 1. Related work interfaces

raster, and the total time interval between the beginning of sync and the completion of rasterization, as shown in Fig. 1c and Fig. 2. This package has an important feature that updates the graphics only when there is an update on the screen. Nothing appears in the graphics if there is no need for screen refreshment. However, when there is interaction, the graphics get updated.

The **performance** package uses Flutter's resources to gather data to generate charts to achieve this behavior. It motivates us to find ways to capture other data types for monitoring the device while developing an application. The evolution of the tool became the focus of our work. Table 1 presents FPS rate/info, RAM, and Network as monitoring aspects and compares the evaluated packages and our proposal over these aspects.

Table 1. Related Plugins and Packages

Packages	FPS rate	Other FPS info	RAM	Network
show_fps	x			
performance_fps	x	x		
lemberfpsmonitor	x	x		
statsfl	x	x		
memory_info			x	
performance	x	x		
Our Work	x		x	x

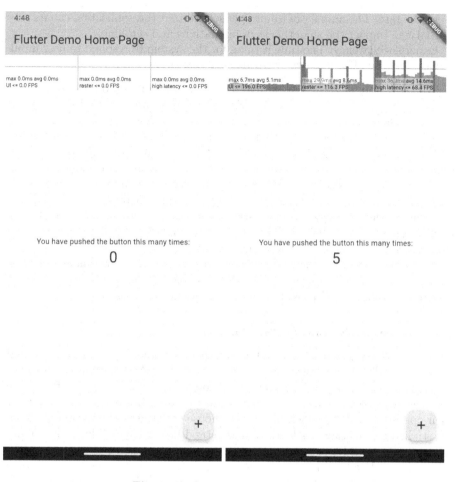

Fig. 2. **performance** package test

3 Methodology

This section describes the creation process of a performance tool application. The objectives of the tool were defined based on the following factors considered:

- CPU usage: The amount of processing power the application requires and the impact on device performance.
- Memory usage: The amount of memory the application uses while running.
- Battery usage: The influence of the app has on the device's battery life.
- Network usage: The amount of data the system transfers over the network and the effect on network performance.
- Startup time: The time it takes for the application to start and be ready for use.

- Frame rate: The number of frames per second that the application can display that can impact the smoothness of animations and scrolling.
- Experience latency: The time it takes for the system to respond to user input.
- Crashes rate: The number of crashes per user or session.

All these points are significant and analyzed during the development and life of an application. However, to identify one or more problems all of the time, several of these factors are observed and analyzed to find ways to fix them.

It's important to remember that most factors will depend on the application and its intended use. It is also worth evaluating application performance on different devices and under conditions to understand its performance. Among all these factors, we chose three for the first implementation of the tool: memory usage, network usage, and frame rate. Using these three factors together, it is now possible for the developer to understand what is the regular behavior of their application while developing. We can see the impacts in real time, analyzing these three factors with each new code change.

The developed tool allows developers to evaluate the performance of their applications quickly and easily. It provides valuable information to improve application performance and provide a better experience for users.

3.1   Frame per Second (FPS) Counter

During the development of the tool, we reached a stage where we needed to find references and implementation examples. In Sect. 2, we had previously presented the requirement of displaying frames per second. After researching, we found five packages that could provide the desired functionality. However, after analyzing their operation and implementations, we choose only the **performance** package. We studied this package in-depth to understand how it is possible to obtain and manage data until its presentation on the screen.

As shown detailedly in [7], there is a `mixin` available in the `scheduler` library, the `SchedulerBinding` that is a crucial mechanism in Flutter's **performance** package and which is native to Flutter. Therefore, there's no need to install any external modules.

Using `SchedulerBinding`, we can acquire a list of `FrameTiming`, which is a class available in `dart:ui`. This library provides low-level services for the Flutter framework when initializing applications. The `FrameTiming` class stores metrics related to the timing of a frame, such as `vsyncStart`, `buildStart`, `buildFinish`, `rasterStart`, and `rasterFinish`. By combining reactivity, `SchedulerBinding`, and callbacks, we can readily and effectively collect the necessary data to present in the frame counter. Figure 3a shows how the frames per second counter interface looks.

3.2   Memory Usage

While Flutter excels at managing frame rates entirely within Dart code, accessing memory hardware details necessitates a platform-level approach due to limitations in Dart itself. Due to the inclusion of code specific to the Android platform,

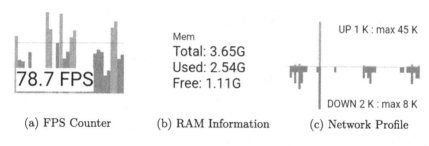

(a) FPS Counter   (b) RAM Information   (c) Network Profile

Fig. 3. Performance Aspects

the functionality presented in this paper is called a plugin rather than a package, which solely relies on Dart code. Using Kotlin as a programming language for specific development for Android, the MemoryInfo class was used to return the information to the Dart code through MethodChannel and thus present the memory data on the screen. The *plugin* shows three memory data information, as presented in Fig. 3b, which are total, used, and free device memory in *gigabytes*.

The executed routine does not use Flutter's internal reactivities. It fetches information from the platform. It is invoked every second within a function in Dart code. Because of this behavior, when the frame monitor is run alone in a newly created application, it behaves the same as the **performance** package, for example. There are updates to the graph only when there are changes to the interface. However, when the memory or network traffic monitoring module runs together with the frame monitor, there is an interface update every second.

3.3   Network Traffic

In today's world, where many mobile applications act as mere interfaces to APIs, constantly sending and receiving data, traffic monitors play a crucial role. These tools allow developers to measure the exact amount of data flowing in and out of their applications via the Internet during each request-response cycle. This granular insight is invaluable for identifying anomalies. Imagine an API request programmed to receive a specific amount of data (X) but instead returns a significantly different amount (Y). A traffic monitor can flag such discrepancies, helping developers diagnose and fix issues before they impact user experience.

Flutter does not have direct access to the network layer of devices. This layer is only available through system APIs. We sought a solution for the Android operating system since it is not possible to acquire data through Flutter or Dart The TrafficStats class provides the capture of values through its methods. We use the getTotalTxBytes and getTotalRxBytes methods to get the number of bytes sent and received throughout the system, respectively. Figure 3c shows the results of this invocation. As this class collects data at the network layer, it does not differentiate between TCP and UDP packets.

3.4   Customization Parameters

There are several parameters to customize plugins, making it easier for developers to manipulate the modules on the screen. Here are the parameters and their default values that each one indicates:

- **bool disable**: Whether the plugin will be disabled or not, preventing it from being initialized. Its default value is *false*.
- **bool activateFPS**: Whether the frame generation module will be or not activated. Its default value is *true*.
- **double scaleFPS**: The rendered scale of the frame generation module. Its default value is *1*.
- **Alignment alignmentFPS**: The frame generation module alignment within the device screen. Its default value is *Alignment.topRight*.
- **int sampleSizeFPS**: The extrapolated number of 'frame time' samples to the frame generation module. Its default value is *32*.
- **Duration targetFrameTimeFPS**: The maximum time to build a frame. All frames that take longer than this parameter will appear in red. Otherwise, they will draw in the *chartBarsColor* parameter color. This parameter also tells the plugin where to draw the horizontal black line present in the frame generation module. Its default value is *16.7 milliseconds*. This value is equivalent to 60 frames per second.
- **Color backgroundFPS**: The background color of the frame generation module. Its default value is *Color(0x00ffffff)*. ☐
- **Color textColorFPS**: The text color of the frame generation module. Its default value is *Color(0xff000000)*. ■
- **Color textBackgroundColorFPS**: The background color of the text of the frame generation module. Its default value is *Color(0xffffffff)*. ☐
- **Color chartBarsColor**: The rectangles color representing the frames superior to the *targetFrameTimeFPS* of the frame generation module. Its default value is *Color(0xff4caf50)*. ■
- **bool activateMemory**: Whether the memory module will be or not activated. Its default value is *true*.
- **Alignment alignmentMemory**: The memory module alignment within the device screen. Its default value is *Alignment.topRight*.
- **double scaleMemory**: The rendered scale of the memory module. Its default value is *1*.
- **Color backgroundMemory**: The background color of the memory module. Its default value is *Color(0x00ffffff)*. ☐
- **Color textColorMemory**: The text color of the memory module. Its default value is *Color(0xff000000)*. ■
- **Color textBackgroundColorMemory**: The background color of the memory module text. Its default value is *Color(0xffffffff)*. ☐
- **bool activateNetwork**: Whether the network module will be or not activated. Its default value is *true*.

- **Alignment alignmentNetwork**: The network module alignment within the device screen. Its default value is *Alignment.topLeft*.
- **double scaleNetwork**: The rendered scale of the network module. Its default value is *1*.
- **Color backgroundNetwork**: The background color of the network module. Its default value is *Color(0x00ffffff)*. ☐
- **Color textColorNetwork**: The color of the network module text. Its default value is *Color(0xff000000)*. ■
- **Color textBackgroundNetwork**: The background color of the network module text. Its default value is *Color(0xffffffff)*. ☐
- **int timeBox**: The seconds shown in the network chart. Its default value is *60*.

4   Experimental Results

This section provides an overview of the interface of the developed plugin, tested on two real applications named *Wonderous* and *OpenLeaf*, both of which are available for download on the *Play Store*. Additionally, both of these applications have public repositories on GitHub[7],[8]. During the development of this plugin, we also created a test application.

We obtain the results presented in this section by running the applications on a physical smartphone, a Motorola Z3 Play. It has a Qualcomm SDM636 Snapdragon 636 processor and 4GB of RAM. By doing so, we can evaluate the impact of applications on hardware that is somehow outdated and considered with characteristics of a low-level device.

Although the plugin is available in debug mode, we recommend analyzing the application's behavior in profile or even release mode to obtain results consistent with the actual performance of the application. Debug mode includes functions that can impact and harm the values found during the execution of the application.

We publish the first version of the plugin in the official package repository for Dart and Flutter applications[9]. An open repository is available to track the plugin's entire development[10].

4.1   Sample Test Application

We developed a sample test application, a plugin that performs simple actions such as sending HTTP requests to an online API, incrementing variables through button interaction, and generating a list of 1000000 objects displayed on a different application page. Figure 4 illustrates the difference in the application's behavior before (left screen) and after (right screen) an HTTP request.

---

[7] https://github.com/JideGuru/FlutterEbookApp.
[8] https://github.com/gskinnerTeam/flutter-wonderous-app.
[9] https://pub.dev/packages/perf_view.
[10] https://github.com/bedinotto/perf_view.

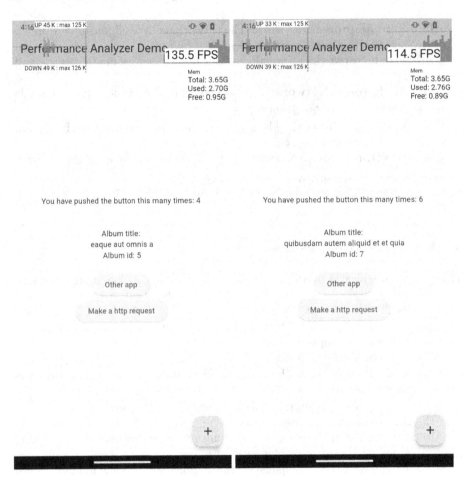

Fig. 4. Comparison of application behavior when making a request to the Internet

4.2   Wonderous

This application is a resource for information on some of the most famous structures in the world, including the Great Wall of China, Christ the Redeemer, and the Pyramids of Giza. The application uses various layout features in Flutter, showcasing the platform's impressive styling and animation capabilities.

In Fig. 5, we can see the Wonderous application page, which provides information, specifically on Christ the Redeemer. At the top of each screen, we can see the value in real-time of network traffic (UP and DOWN), the Frame Per Second Counter, and the memory usage (Total, Used, and Free). Unfortunately, the page experiences a significant drop in performance in one section (right screen). There are many animations and visual effects. Specifically, the frame rate drops to one quarter (87.6 to 19.6 FPS) of what is present on the rest of the page (as the left screen).

Fig. 5. Two pages about Christ the Redeemer with active plugin on the top of the screen

We notice that the application's other pages, which have the *layout* component filled with animations, exhibited the same behavior. We observe this behavior in Fig. 6, which also shows customized alignment settings for the plugin components.

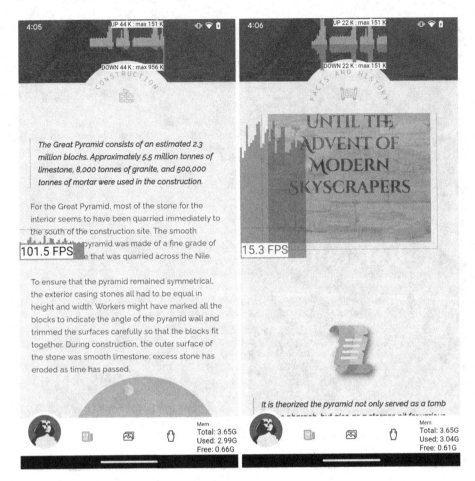

Fig. 6. Page about The Great Pyramid with active plugin

4.3   OpenLeaf

This application functions as a virtual library and offers a range of public domain books that are readily accessible. It also doubles up as a PDF file reader. Figure 7 illustrates the difference between the application's regular performance (left screen) while the interface is loading (right screen). An exceptional frame generation of the test device results when a new page is loaded. We also see more DOWN network traffic and usage of memory resulting from the requested information on the second screen.

Fig. 7. Comparison between loaded and loading page of the OpenLeaf application

5   Conclusion and Future Works

In this article, we discuss the development of a plugin that measures the performance of applications built using Flutter. We explain the steps taken during the software development, including how the tool provides the visualization for frames generated per second, memory total, free and occupied, and network data transmission. We evaluate the plugin over a sample test application and two applications: Wonderous and OpenLeaf.

With the tool developed, we created a new option for Flutter developers to use while working on their Flutter application, not completely chained to DevTools. The plugin is free and available in the official repository of Dart and Flutter packages and plugins. Additionally, we host the source code in the platform's versioning Github repository. It is also available for free. By making this work available to the Flutter community, we hope to encourage other developers to use and disseminate it.

In future work, we plan to evaluate the feasibility of using the features introduced in Flutter version 3.16. It recently made the DevTools feature extension available to package authors. We also intend to assess the plugin's computational impact on application performance and explore the possibility of creating similar projects for other application development tools to help developers who use those tools. It includes the application communication in a distributed environment.

Acknowledgment. The authors would like to thank the National Council for Scientific and Technological Development - CNPq (Process Number 407827/2023-4) and Fundação de Amparo à Pesquisa do Estado do Rio Grande do Sul - FAPERGS (07/2021 PqG project N° 21/2551-0002055-5).

References

1. Amaravadi, C., Lessard, Z.L.: The characteristics of good systems. Lond. J. Res. Comput. Sci. Technol. **17** (2017). https://journalspress.com/the-characteristics-of-good-systems/
2. Apple Inc: Objective-C and C++ interoperability with Swift (2024). https://developer.apple.com/swift/#objective-c
3. Caminade, J., von Wartburg, M.: The Success of Third-Party Apps on the App Store (2022). https://www.apple.com/newsroom/pdfs/the-success-of-third-party-apps-on-the-app-store.pdf
4. Ceci, L.: How many apps are there in the play store? (2024). https://www.statista.com/statistics/266210/number-of-available-applications-in-the-google-play-store/
5. Demedyuk, I., Tsybulskyi, N.: Flutter vs native vs react-native: examining performance (2020). https://inveritasoft.com/blog/flutter-vs-native-vs-react-native-examining-performance
6. Ebone, A., Tan, Y., Jia, X.: A performance evaluation of cross-platform mobile application development approaches. In: 2018 IEEE/ACM 5th International Conference on Mobile Software Engineering and Systems (MOBILESoft), pp. 92–93 (2018)
7. Flutter. Schedulerbinding (2024). https://github.com/flutter/flutter/blob/master/packages/flutter/lib/src/scheduler/binding.dart
8. Google. Flutter documentation (2024). https://docs.flutter.dev
9. Google. Learn Kotlin for Java developers (2024). https://developer.android.com/kotlin/learn-kotlin-java-pathway
10. Google. The official package repository for Dart and Flutter apps (2024). https://pub.dev
11. Google. What is DevTools? (2024). https://docs.flutter.dev/tools/devtools/overview#what-is-devtools
12. Zahra, H.A., Zein, S.: A systematic comparison between flutter and react native from automation testing perspective. In: 2022 International Symposium on Multidisciplinary Studies and Innovative Technologies (ISMSIT), pp. 6–12 (2022). https://doi.org/10.1109/ISMSIT56059.2022.9932749

Optimizing Cloud-Fog Workloads: A Budget Aware Dynamic Scheduling Solution

Phuoc Hung Pham[1(✉)], Nguyen Thanh Binh[2], Md. Golam Rabiul Alam[3], and Md. Motaharul Islam[4]

[1] Providence College, Rhode Island, USA
hung205a2@gmail.com
[2] University of Finance – Marketing, Hochiminh, Vietnam
ntbinh@ufm.edu.vn
[3] BRAC University, Dhaka, Bangladesh
rabiul.alam@bracu.ac.bd
[4] United International University, Dhaka, Bangladesh
motaharul@cse.uiu.ac.bd

Abstract. With the rise of demanding computational applications, individuals and businesses reap significant benefits. However, processing power limitations on local devices hinder further progress. These local resources also require substantial financial and human investment. Fortunately, the adoption of cloud computing (CC) platforms alleviates these concerns. CC enables offloading computationally intensive tasks to the cloud, reserving local resources for simpler jobs. However, as CC operates on a pay-as-you-go model, finding an approach that minimizes both execution time and cost is crucial. While research efforts have attempted to address this challenge, solutions remain limited. This paper proposes a novel architecture leveraging cloud provider resources and local computing power on fog computing devices. The core of this framework is a dynamic task scheduling solution that minimizes completion time within the cloud service while considering network conditions and customer costs for service usage. Simulations and comparisons with existing scheduling approaches demonstrate that our proposed method delivers robust performance with significant cost savings for cloud users.

Keywords: Cloud Computing · Fog Computing · Task Scheduling · Distributed System · High Performance Computing

1 Introduction

The advent of the Internet of Things (IoTs) generates a huge demand for big data management. It is estimated that by the year 2025, there will be nearly 40 billion IoT devices in the world, most of which consist of sensors and low-power end devices that are not powerful for data processing [15]. Even with advanced devices, their processing power still falls short for complex business workflows with large data volumes, high frequencies, and intricate structures. Cloud computing (CC) [17] emerges as a solution, shifting heavy data processing and storage to powerful centralized servers in data centers. This leaves local devices with minimal tasks, maximizing cloud resource utilization for high performance. However, the challenge of extensive data transmission arises when confronted with bandwidth limitations. Moreover, the inherent system delays hinder the cloud's ability to deliver effective services for real-time applications. This is where the fog computing paradigm becomes pivotal. The benefits of fog computing go beyond just reducing latency for real-time applications. It also holds the key to unlocking intelligent location-based mobility support. With the ever-growing use of smart devices and wearables, maintaining user proximity during resource allocation becomes crucial. This is where the highly distributed and low-latency nature of fog computing shines. Combined with diverse network connections between cloud, fog, and mobile networks, fog seamlessly integrates with 5G technology, a boon for IoT [1] thanks to its high-speed data rates.

But fog computing's impact extends beyond simple data transfer. Vehicular networks can leverage their capabilities for task offloading and execution. These computationally intensive and latency-sensitive operations highlight the importance of bringing computing resources closer to the network edge. By doing so, fog computing tackles latency constraints and reduces the traffic burden on the cloud, paving the way for a more responsive and efficient mobile future.

While fog computing boasts numerous benefits, it's not without limitations. Resource-constrained fog devices, significantly less powerful than cloud servers, necessitate effective resource allocation and service placement methods to ensure end-to-end service based on user preferences like latency, bandwidth usage, and cloud cost. Thus, balancing these trade-offs for cloud-fog collaboration is where task scheduling strategies come in for Cloud Service Customers (CSCs). These strategies aim to distribute workload efficiently, and minimize completion time, as well as cloud cost for resource usage.

However, task scheduling is still a challenge [23]. Large-scale workflows involve diverse workloads, requiring efficient scheduling to map tasks onto processing systems while respecting task dependencies and minimizing completion time. This is a complex problem due to the NP-completeness of scheduling in heterogeneous environments like CC. Previous approaches mainly focused on minimizing execution time (makespan) without considering cost, which is a significant concern for CSCs paying for rented resources. For example, Amazon EC2 [12] charges CSCs according to the number of virtual machines initialized by CSCs and how long they have been used.

In heterogeneous environments like CC, exhaustive searches are impractical. Existing scheduling methods often trade performance for cost-effectiveness. Some prioritize execution time but incur high monetary costs, hindering CSCs from fulfilling demands while processing complex applications. Efficient task scheduling balancing completion time and cloud cost is vital for improved performance, Quality of Service (QoS), and user satisfaction, especially in active environments.

Therefore, in this paper we propose a novel algorithm to optimize task scheduling for dynamic processing systems, allowing continuous task arrival. It considers network contention and cloud service costs, crucial factors for user satisfaction in a collaboration between the cloud network and fog computing resources to elevate QoS. Traditionally, fog computing clients handled user interface functionalities and offline mobile processing. In our architecture, they leverage their processing power to execute dispatched tasks and store user data when needed. Fog devices comprise heterogeneous resources with storage and processing capacities less powerful than the cloud, e.g., such as routers, access points, and micro data centers. Additionally, there is a broker functioning as a centralized management node between fog devices and cloud resources. Moreover, extensive simulations demonstrate the efficiency and effectiveness of our approach compared to existing methods. The results highlight improved performance and a valuable trade-off between workflow performance and cost-effectiveness.

Subsequent sections of this paper are organized as follows: Sect. 2 equips you with knowledge of existing solutions, while Sect. 3 lays the groundwork by exploring the system description itself. Section 4 confronts the challenge head-on, introducing our unique method for tackling it. Then, Sect. 5 presents the rigorous testing process and its illuminating results. Finally, Sect. 6 delivers the concluding remarks and charts the course for future exploration.

2 Related Studies

This section covers the foundational elements of the proposed method, including the fog computing environment.

The explosion of data from countless IoT devices has exposed limitations in traditional cloud computing, namely slow communication and high monetary cost. To address these challenges, a new paradigm called fog computing has emerged. Imagine it as a bridge between the network edge – sensors, smartphones, etc. – and the distant cloud data centers, forming a three-tier architecture.

Think of the fog layer as a distributed network of mini data centers located near the devices. Instead of sending all data straight to the cloud, fog nodes handle local processing, storage, and tasks like data management and networking. These nodes, although less powerful than their cloud counterparts, offer several advantages.

- Firstly, by processing data locally, fog computing drastically reduces transmission time and bandwidth usage. This is crucial for real-time applications like healthcare, traffic management, and connected vehicles, where even slight delays can be detrimental.
- Secondly, fog computing improves the overall Quality of Service (QoS) by bringing application services closer to users. Consider an air quality monitoring system. Filtering and processing sensor data at the fog layer before sending it to the cloud significantly reduces data volume and network load, leading to faster analysis and actionable insights.

However, it's not all sunshine and rainbows. Bringing services closer to users can also lead to increased network congestion and energy consumption due to more data hops and communication within the network. In conclusion, fog computing offers a promising solution to the challenges of managing massive IoT data. By placing processing power closer to the devices, fog computing reduces latency, improves QoS, and optimizes network resources. Although there are potential drawbacks, task scheduling can mitigate these concerns, paving the way for a smoother and more efficient IoT ecosystem.

Several research proposals have been anticipated for efficient task scheduling in heterogeneous as well as homogeneous systems. Despite numerous research proposals, task scheduling still remains a challenging open problem in heterogeneous CC environments [8, 20]. Several graph template-based task scheduling methods are presented in [9, 11, 13, 18]. The obliviousness of network contention is the major shortcoming of those proposals. Although a network contention-based method of task scheduling is presented in [21], it ignores the monetary cost of cloud customers (CCs) in utilizing cloud resources. Authors in [24] introduce a cost-efficient approach to select the most proper system (private or public cloud) to execute the workflow according to a deadline constraint as well as cost savings. Lingfang et al. in [16] propose budget-conscious scheduling algorithms to satisfy strictly the budget constraint. Juan et al. proposed an algorithm of scheduling in [14], to schedule applications of massive graph processing. The schedule length and cost are considered in that proposal. Sen et al. in [25] and Chandrashekhar et al. in [22] present methods to minimize the schedule length or cost in dynamic cloud computing but do not study trade-off optimality.

Liu et al. [4] present an approach that can reduce service delay in heterogeneous fog networks but the most important cost-latency trade-off problem in heterogeneous fog networks is not considered. In [5], a dynamic tasking scheduling algorithm is proposed to reduce average service delay but the performance of the system is less in a more complex homogenous fog network. Raafat et al. [1] model the scheduling of IoT service requests as an optimization problem using integer programming in hybrid fog-cloud computing to minimize the overall service request latency, however, it does not include the cost usage.

Therefore, the envisioned proposal should take into account all three efficiency factors: i) completion time ii) network contention iii) cost of cloud resources with the intervention of fog computing in a dynamic cloud environment. This motivates us to provide a system that can solve a task scheduling approach for optimality in a dynamic cloud environment while taking into account those factors and navigating these trade-offs in the realm of scheduling strategies.

3 System Architecture

The following section gives an insight into our system architecture to address the issues discussed above:

The system to which the proposed algorithm is applied follows a distributed data flow model. Each application is modeled as a series of application modules or tasks that can communicate with each other. The output of one application module can serve as the input of the other. This data dependency between application modules is modeled as a directed acyclic graph (DAG), in which the vertices denote modules and the edges represent the dependencies among them. The tuple type (TT) of the data stream is represented on these edges. Tuples are data emitted from sensors or other application modules. These data streams contain raw data if emitted from sensors. In the case of the emission from other modules, each of them is labeled with a specific type which determines to what application module the tuple needs to be transmitted. Resources such as fog devices also tend to produce data streams in the form of usage details processed by the information collector to provide information on the state of the devices.

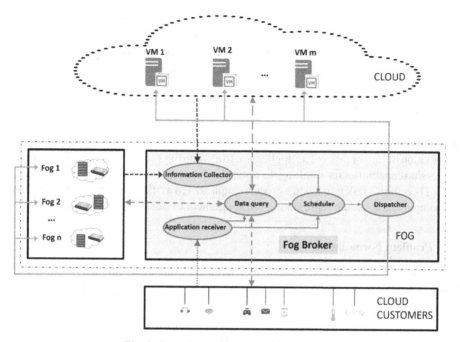

Fig. 1. Layering architecture of the proposal

The proposed architecture as depicted in Fig. 1, consists of three layers i) cloud provider (CP) layer: composed of a pool of VMs, ii) fog layer consisting of fog devices, for example, routers, access points, and micro data centers,…, and iii) customer (CC) layer including IoT devices such as sensors, smartphones, actuators, etc.… The fog layer is structured in a geographically distributed fashion, by placing its resources chiefly within the close vicinity of IoT devices, and consequently of the users. The workload is then divided into smaller chunks, and each chunk is sent from the associated CC to a suitable fog broker or node for processing and is temporarily stored in fog micro data centers as they cannot hold the data permanently due to storage limitations [7]. The main advantage of this approach is the reduction in the transmission time of a data packet as fewer hops need to be crossed, which happens to be crucial in latency-sensitive IoT applications e.g., healthcare, traffic, and connected vehicles. For instance, in an ambient air monitoring system, huge amounts of data gathered from air quality sensors need to be transferred through network layers to get filtered, aggregated, analyzed, and stored. Should these pieces of information get filtered at primary network levels, their volume would decrease, and the less voluminous the data becomes, the lower the network usage will be.

The fog broker acts as a centralized node for management. The functions of the broker in our proposal are as follows: i) It accepts users' requests from IoT devices ii) It manages processing resources (e.g., capacity, cost, and bandwidth) from both fog and cloud, and returns query data. Iii) It prepares an efficient, effective, and optimal schedule concerning input workflow, query data, and resource information. The broker uploads the data to the CP layer through a single connection but VMs of the CP layer send data to the CC layer through the broker, then the broker divides those data into non-uniform chunks. Afterward, the broker delivers those chunks to corresponding CCs [3, 10].

In the next section, we formulate the problem and describe our proposed approach.

4   Problem Domain

Task scheduling of complex systems having hierarchical topology is analogous to the distribution of jobs or tasks of an application to a group of processors with heterogeneous processing capabilities for fulfilling the optimization goal of minimization of completion time. Therefore, a task graph and a process graph are fed as the inputs of task scheduling. The output is a schedule representing the assignment of tasks to processors.

4.1   Problem Formulation

Before problem formulation, we state here the used terms in the problem formulation. Then a dynamic cost-time aware task scheduling method is presented elaborately.

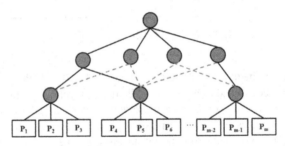

Fig. 2. A processor graph

Definition 1. A processor graph $PG = (N,D)$ demonstrated in Fig. 2 is a graph that represents the network topology between vertices (heterogeneous processors) that are virtual machines (VMs) on cloud servers or fog devices. In this graph, N is the finite set of vertices, and a directed edge $d_{kl} \in D$ means a directed link from vertex P_k to vertex P_l with $P_k, P_l \in N$. Each processor P_k controls the processing rate μ_k and bandwidth on the link connecting it to other processors. Due to the high stability of Local Area Network (LAN) compared with the Internet, the data transfer rate of internal communication among fog devices is always better than that of external communications between cloud VMs.

Definition 2. A task graph, as shown in Fig. 3, is denoted by a Directed Acyclic Graph (DAG) $G = (V, E, W, C)$ where the vertices set $V = \{v_1, v_2, ..., v_k\}$ presents the parallel application modules or tasks. The edge $e_{ij} = (v_i, v_j) \in E$ of the DAG symbolized as a communication link between the task v_i and task v_j. The communication time from task

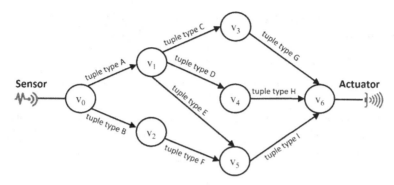

Fig. 3. A sample DAG

v_i to task v_j is denoted by $c(e_{ij})$, whereas $d(e_{ij})$ represents the transferred data. The weight $w(v_i, P_k)$ of task v_i is its computation time on processor P_k. It is supposed that a task v_i contains a set of preceding subtasks $prec(v_i)$ and a set of successive subtasks $succ(v_i)$. A task without any predecessors, $prec(v_i) = 0$, is a start-up task v_{entry}, and a task that does not have any successors, $succ(v_i) = 0$, is an end task v_{end}. The workload belonging to task v_i is represented as $l(v_i, P_l)$, which delimits amount of work (e.g. the number of instructions) processed with certain computing resource P_l. Let $t_s(v_i, P_l)$ denote Start Time of task v_i on processor P_l. Hence, the finish time of that task is given by $t_f(v_i, P_l) = t_s(v_i, P_l) + w(v_i, P_l)$.

A sample representation of an IoT application, consisting of 7 modules ranging from v_0 to v_6 and tuple types A to I, is depicted in Fig. 3. In a sense-process-actuate scenario, all the information emitted from IoT sensors is transferred to module v_0 as raw data, and then the generated output tuples are delivered to modules v_1, v_2, and from v_1 to other modules v_3, v_4, v_5, and from v_2 to v_5 respectively. After that, output tuples from v_3, v_4, v_5 are delivered to their destination v_6. After an application loop has been completed, the actuator is activated if necessary. For example, a bell might begin to play sounds.

Assume that the conditions mentioned below are satisfied:

Condition 1. Application made up of task v_1, task v_2 ...task v_n, the broker knows the sequencing of tasks, e.g. task v_1 first, task v_2 second.

Condition 2. When there are several different tasks running, if new tasks need to be started at anytime, the broker will check available processors and allocate the most appropriate processors to the tasks to result in the shortest completion time.

Condition 3. Some tasks of the task graph are already scheduled, we may reschedule them upon the arrival new task.

Condition 4. A task can start its execution after all of its parent tasks have already been executed. Each task appears only once in the schedule.

Condition 5. The ready time $t_{ready}(v_i, P_l)$ is the time that processor P_l completes its last running assigned task and be ready to execute task v_i. Therefore,

$$t_{ready}(v_i, P_l) =$$
$$\max\{t_f(v_y, P_l), \max_{e_{zi} \in E, v_z \in prec(v_i), k \in N} (t_f(v_z, P_k) + c(e_i^{kl}))\} \tag{1}$$

where v_y is a task being executed at processor P_l and $prec(v_i)$ is a set of preceding tasks of v_i, and $c(e_i^{kl})$ is the communication time of connection between processors P_k and P_l. It can be defined as:

$$c(e_i^{kl}) = \begin{cases} (do_{zi})\frac{1}{bw_{kl}} & \text{if } k \neq j \\ 0 & \text{otherwise.} \end{cases} \tag{2}$$

Here do_{zi} is volume of outgoing data transferred from P_k to P_l.

Condition 6. Let $[t_A, t_B] \in [0, \infty]$ be an idle time interval on processor P_l in which no task is executed. A free task $v_i \in V$ can be scheduled on processor P_l within $[t_A, t_B]$ if

$$\max\{t_A, t_{ready}(v_i, P_l)\} + w(v_i, P_l) \leq t_B. \tag{3}$$

4.2   Task Scheduling Solution

Given a task graph $G = (V, E, W, C)$ and a processor graph $PG = (N, D)$, our approach is to produce the most appropriate scheduled list of tasks. Because our method tries to minimize the completion time while considering the network contention and cloud cost, the following section exemplifies the formation of Earliest Finish Time (*EFT*) and the cost of task v_i on a processor from its Earliest Start Time (*EST*) as well as the element costs.

EST of a task v_i executed on a processor P_l can be calculated as follows:

$$EST(v_i, P_l) = \begin{cases} t_{ready}(v_i, P_l), & \text{if } v_i \neq v_{entry} \\ 0, & \text{otherwise} \end{cases}, \tag{4}$$

Suppose that p_{il} is the probability of task v_i processed at processor P_l, then the overall task arrival rate for each arrival rate λ_{il} at processor P_l can be calculated as:

$$\sum p_{il} \lambda_{il}$$

Thus, given service rate Ω_l at processor P_l, the computation time to execute task v_i on processor P_l is defined as:

$$w(v_i, P_l) = |\frac{l(v_i)}{\Omega_l - \sum p_{il} \lambda_{il}}| \tag{5}$$

Consequently, *EFT* of the task v_i is designed as:

$$EFT(v_i, P_l) = w(v_i, P_l) + EST(v_i, P_l), \tag{6}$$

Additionally, the algorithm also takes into account the cost for using cloud resources or fog resources to finish tasks. Given $x_{v_i}^{f_i} \in \{0, 1\}$, the cost $C(v_i, P_l)$ to execute task v_i at VM P_l or local fog device P_l is defined by:

$$C(v_i, P_l) = (C_{comm}^{(v_i, P_l)} + C_{disc}^{(v_i, P_l)}) * x_{v_i}^{f_i} + C_{proc}^{(v_i, P_l)} + C_{queue}^{(v_i, P_l)} + C_{str}^{(v_i, P_l)} + C_{mem}^{(v_i, P_l)}, \quad (7)$$

In Eq. (7), each cost is calculated as follows:
Processing cost is expressed as:

$$C_{proc}^{(v_i, P_l)} = c_1 * w(v_i, P_l), \quad (8)$$

where c_1 is the processing cost per time unit of workflow execution on processor P_l.

Let t_{assign} be the time point when task v_i is assigned to processor P_l. c_2 be the queuing cost per time unit of the task v_i until it can be executed. Then the queuing cost is as:

$$C_{queue}^{(v_i, P_l)} = c_2 * (EST(v_i, P_l) - t_{assign}(v_i, P_l)) \quad (9)$$

Assume that the amount of money per time unit for transferring outgoing data from processor P_k to P_l is c_3, then the communication cost is defined as follows:

$$C_{comm}^{(v_i, P_l)} = c_3 * (\sum_{v_z \in (prec(v_i) \cap exec(k))} do_{zi}) \frac{1}{bw_{kl}} \quad (10)$$

We presume that the distribution of disconnection events between a cloud or a fog device and clients is a Poisson distribution with the parameter μ_T, which represents the stability of the network. The expected number of arrivals over an interval of length τ is $E[N_T] = \mu_T * \tau$. Let L be a random variable for the length of an offline event, μ_L be the mean length and c_4 be the disconnection cost per unit time. Therefore, the expected duration of a disconnection event, which can affect the completion time of task v_i, is $\mu_T * \tau * \mu_L$. Hence, the cost of disconnection can be derived as:

$$C_{disc}^{(v_i, P_l)} = c_4 * (\mu_T * \tau * \mu_L), \quad (11)$$

Let c_5 be the storage cost per data unit and st_i be the storage size of task v_i on processor P_l. Then we can present the storage cost of task v_i on processor P_l as:

$$C_{str}^{(v_i, P_l)} = c_5 * st_i, \quad (12)$$

In addition, the memory cost of processor P_l for task v_i is computed as follows:

$$C_{mem}^{(v_i, P_l)} = c_6 * s_{mem}, \quad (13)$$

where s_{mem} is the size of the memory used and c_6 is the memory cost per data unit.

Lastly, an optimal function that calculates the tradeoff U can be formulated as a convex combination of EFT and monetary cost for each processor $P_l \in N$ in fog or cloud where task $v_i \in E$ running as follows:

$$U = Min \sum_{v_i, v_j \in V, P_k \in N} (\partial \frac{EFT(v_i, P_l) - Min[EFT(v_j, P_k)]}{Max[EFT(v_j, P_k)] - Min[EFT(v_j, P_k)]} + (1 - \partial) \frac{C(v_i, P_l) - Min[C(v_j, P_k)]}{Max[C(v_j, P_k)] - Min[C(v_j, P_k)]}), \quad (14)$$

where $\partial \in [0, 1]$ is a cost-conscious factor that represents a user's preference for the completion time and the monetary cost.

By considering the above function that combines $cost(v_i, P_l)$ and $EFT(v_i, P_l)$, we can determine the most appropriate schedule. This indicates that its combination of $cost(v_i, P_l)$ and $EFT(v_i, P_l)$ should demonstrate the minimum value of the tradeoff U.

Due to evaluate the performance of the proposal, we have compared our approach with state-of-the-art task scheduling algorithms. These minimize the total completion time of the workflow or reduce the cloud's task processing cost. Algorithm 1 is Greedy approach to cost reduction, which allocates tasks to processors following greedy principle that minimizes cloud cost. In algorithm 2, network contention-aware task scheduling [21] is presented. In the meantime, algorithm 3 shows that our approach, a dynamic Cost-Time aware method, stands on both network contention and cloud cost. Therefore, it can justify the tradeoff of cloud cost and completion time.

Algorithm 1. Greedy approach for cost reduction

Input   : Task graph G, processor graph PG
Output   : Scheduled list of tasks
Function greedyForCostScheduling(G, PG)
1. Sort task v_n in the descending order by its priority;

2. **for each** $v_n \in V$ **do**

3.   Find the most appropriate processor P_l that minimizes the cost of accomplishing the task v_n;

4. Assign v_n to P_l;

5. **end**

6. **return** scheduled list of tasks;

Algorithm 2. Contention aware task scheduling

Input   : Task graph G, processor graph PG
Output   : Scheduled list of tasks
Function networkCostScheduling (G, PG)
1. Sort task v_n in the descending order by its priority;

2. **for each** $v_n \in V$ **do**

3.   Find the most appropriate processor P_l that allows EFT of v_n, considering network bandwidth usage;

4. Assign v_n to P_l;

5. **end**

6. **return** scheduled list of tasks;

Algorithm 3. Dynamic Cost-Time aware method

Input   : Task graph G, processor graph PG
Output   : Scheduled list of tasks
Function DCTScheduling (G, PG)
1. Sort task v_n in the descending order by its priority;

2. **for each** $v_n \in V$ **do**

3.   Find the most appropriate processor P_l that allows *EFT* of v_n, considering network bandwidth usage and monetary cost;
4.   Assign v_n to P_l;
5. **end**
6. **return** scheduled list of tasks;

---

5   Implementation and Analysis

5.1   Experimental Settings

Several different experiments have been performed to evaluate the efficiency of our approach with varying conditions such as communication costs and upcoming tasks, network usage as well as a varying number of application modules. To check the performance, we compare the results obtained from the proposed dynamic Cost-Time aware Scheduling (DCTS) and the existing ones: Contention aware Task Scheduling (CaTS) [19] just taking account of network contention, Greedy approach for Cost Reduction (RCR) concerning the monetary cost. The experimental setup configurations are provided in Tables 1, 2, 3 and 4.

Task graphs are created with number of tasks in the graph ranging from 10 to 120. The task graphs are scheduled on a multiprocessor system a combination of 22 heterogeneous VMs and 8 fog devices located at the local system of CCs for the above algorithms. The metrics used for comparison are the completion time and monetary cost. We assume the communication network is fully connected. Each communication link has its own randomly generated cost. And simulation settings are developed in Java with JDK-7u7-i586 and Netbeans-7.2. The proposed algorithm is evaluated using the iFogSim simulator. This JAVA-based simulator is an extension of CloudSim [6] designed to simulate fog computing environments [2]. CloudSim is a framework for modeling and simulation of cloud computing infrastructures and services. In our simulation, we use MI (Millions of Instructions) and MIPS (Million Instructions per Second) to represent the processing capacity of processors.

5.2   Experimental Results

In the following figures, we present the experimental results to demonstrate that our method, DCTS, can be more efficient in terms of schedule length and cloud cost. Figures 4 and 5 show that although GCR obtains the worst result regarding the completion time, it provides the highest cost saving for CCs. In contrast, CaTS delivers the best performance but maximum cost. In the meantime, our solution conduces to the benefits

Table 1. Features of the simulated system

Parameter	Value
Topology model	LAN, fully connected
Operating system	Windows 10 Professional
Number of processors	30
Number of tasks	[10, 110]
Processing rate	[15, 800]
Bandwidth	[20, 100, 512, 1024] Mbps
Cost per time unit executed on processor P_1	[0.2, 0.6]
Cost per outgoing data unit from processor P_1	[0.1, 0.5]
Cost of waiting time	[0.2, 0.5]
Cost of a disconnection time	[0,03, 0.3]

Table 2. Latency between devices.

Source	Destination	Latency (ms)
Sensor	End device	0.6
Actuator	End device	0.1
End device	Fog device	2.0
Fog device	Proxy-server	4.0
Proxy-server	Cloud datacenter	100.0

Table 3. Configuration of devices.

Device type	CPU (MIPS)	RAM (MB)	Uplink bandwidth (Mbps)	Downlink bandwidth (Mbps)
Cloud Data Center	44,800	40,000	100	10,000
Proxy-server	2800	4000	10,000	10,000
Fog device	2800	4000	10,000	10,000
End device	1000	1000	10,000	270
Cloud Data Center	44,800	40,000	100	10,000

of balance between acceptable completion time for workflow and the corresponding cost for utilizing cloud resources. In particular, compared with CaTS, our method can save nearly 19% cost for CCs and it is 21% faster than GCR.

The evaluation of the effect of varying numbers of processors on the cloud cost and the schedule length only in DCTS with a stable number of tasks is also made and given in

Table 4. Description of application tuples.

Tuple type	CPU length	Network length
TT_A	44,800	40,000
TT_B	2800	4000
TT_C	2800	4000
TT_D	1000	1000
TT_E	1400	5000
TT_F	1000	1000
TT_G	1000	500
TT_H	1000	500
TT_I	1000	4000

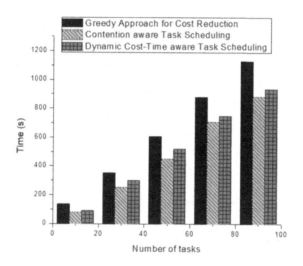

Fig. 4. Schedule length comparison

Figs. 6 and 7, respectively. It is clear to see that there is a great improvement in the speed obtained through DCTS. This improvement rises as the number of processors increases. However, the cost is higher.

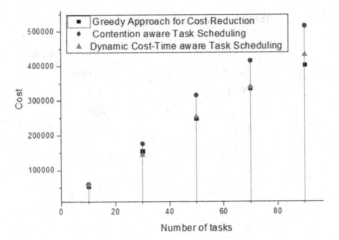

Fig. 5. Cost comparison

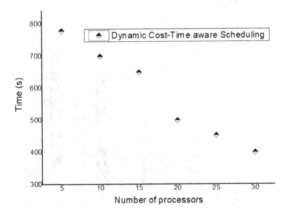

Fig. 6. Schedule length with numbers of processors

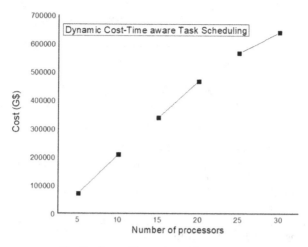

Fig. 7. Cost with numbers of processors

6 Conclusion

This paper proposes a collaboration between fog and cloud resources within a cloud platform to leverage the combined computing power of both internal and external infrastructure. Additionally, we introduce a novel method to extend dynamic task scheduling, aiming to achieve desired completion times while balancing system performance and cloud service costs. Furthermore, we conduct simulations to assess our approach and compare it with alternative methods. The experimental findings demonstrate that the proposed scheduling approach yields improved performance while requiring less monetary expenditure. In future work, we plan to refine our scheduling method across various scenarios, including considerations of energy consumption, to enhance trustworthiness and effectiveness with optimal efficiency.

References

1. Raafat, O., Mazin, A., Taha, L., Khaled, E.: Scheduling Internet of Things requests to minimize latency in hybrid Fog–Cloud computing. Future Gen. Comput. Syst. (2020)
2. Gupta, H., Dastjerdi, A.V., Ghosh, S., Buyya, R.: iFogSim: a toolkit for modeling and simulation of resource management techniques in the internet of things, edge and fog computing environments. Softw. Pract. Exp. **47**(9), 1275–1296 (2017)
3. Entezari-Maleki, R., Sarrafzade, N., Sousa, L.: A genetic-based approach for service placement in fog computing. J. Supercomput. (2022)
4. Liu, Z., Yang, X., Yang, Y., Wang, K., Mao, G.: DATS: dispersive stable task scheduling in heterogeneous fog networks. IEEE Internet Things J. **6**(2), 3423–3436 (2018)
5. Yang, Y., Zhao, S., Zhang, W., Chen, Y., Luo, X., Wang, J.: DEBTS: delay energy balanced task scheduling in homogeneous fog networks. IEEE Internet Things J. **5**(3), 2094–2106 (2018)
6. Cloudsim. https://code.google.com/p/cloudsim/downloads/list (2014)
7. Ehsan, M., Saima, I.: Novel approaches for scheduling task graphs in heterogeneous distributed computing environment. Int. Arab J. e-Technol. **12**(3) (2014)

8. Fatma, A.O., Mona, M.A.: Genetic algorithms for task scheduling problem. J. Parallel Distrib. Comput. **70**(1), 13–22 (2010)

9. Gopalakrishnan, A.K.: A subjective job scheduler based on a backpropagation neural network. HCIS **3**(1), 1–15 (2013). https://doi.org/10.1186/2192-1962-3-17

10. Hung, P.P., Bui, T.A., Eui-Nam, H.: Optimal collaboration of thin–thick clients and resource allocation in cloud computing. Pers. Ubiquit. Comput. **18**(3), 563–572 (2014)

11. Huynh, T.T.B.: Multi-objective genetic algorithm for solving the multilayer survivable optical network design problem. J. Converg. **5**(1), 20–25 (2014)

12. Amazon Web Services. http://aws.amazon.com/ec2/

13. Joel, W., et al.: SODA: an optimizing scheduler for large-scale stream-based distributed computer systems. In: International Conference on Middleware, pp. 306–325 (2008)

14. Juan, L., Sen, S., Xiang, C., Zhongbao, Z.: Cost-conscious scheduling for large graph processing in the cloud. In: IEEE International Conference on High Performance Computing and Communications, pp. 808–813 (2011)

15. Pham, H., Eui-Nam, H.: An adaptive procedure for task scheduling optimization in mobile cloud computing. Math. Prob. Eng. **2015**, 1–13 (2015)

16. Lingfang, Z., Veeravalli, B., Xiaorong, L.: ScaleStar: budget conscious scheduling precedence-constrained many-task workflow applications in cloud. In: Advanced Information Networking and Applications (AINA), pp. 534–541 (2012)

17. Hung, P.P., Bui, T.-A., Morales, M.A.G., Van Nguyen, M., Huh, E.-N.: Optimal collaboration of thin–thick clients and resource allocation in cloud computing. Pers. Ubiquit. Comput. **18**(3), 563–572 (2013)

18. Byungsang, K., Chan-Hyun, Y., Yong-Sung, P., Yonggyu, L., Wan, C.: An adaptive workflow scheduling scheme based on an estimated data processing rate for next generation sequencing in cloud computing. J. Inf. Process. Syst. **8**(4), 555–566 (2012)

19. Mohammad, A., Salama, H., Sulieman, B.: On static scheduling of tasks in real time multiprocessor systems: an improved GA-based approach. Int. Arab J. e-Technol. **11**(6) (2013)

20. Nguyen, D.M., Eui-Nam, H.: Cost and efficiency-based scheduling on a general framework combining between cloud computing and local thick clients. In: Computing, Management and Telecommunications, pp. 258–263 (2013)

21. Oliver, S.: Communication contention in task scheduling. IEEE Trans. Parallel Distrib. Syst. **16**(6), 503–515 (2005)

22. Chandrashekhar, S., Rajnikant, B.: Priority based dynamic resource allocation in cloud computing. In: International Symposium on Cloud and Services Computing, Mangalore (2012)

23. Siva, T.M., Srikant, R.: Stochastic models of load balancing and scheduling in cloud computing clusters. In: IEEE Infocom, pp. 702–710 (2012)

24. Ruben, V., Vanmechelen, K., Broeckhove, J.: Cost-efficient scheduling heuristics for deadline constrained workloads on hybrid clouds. In: Cloud Computing Technology and Science (CloudCom), pp. 320–327 (2011)

25. Sen, S., Jian, L., Qingjia, H.: Cost-efficient task scheduling for executing large programs in the cloud. Parallel Comput. J. (2013)

Information Systems and Technologies

A Process to Identify Players' Motivational Profiles for Designing a Gamification Project

Cristiane Soares Ramos[1] ⓘ, Mylena Angélica Silva Farias[1] ⓘ,
Sergio Antônio Andrade de Freitas[1](✉) ⓘ, Marcus Vinícius Paiva Martins[1] ⓘ,
Juan Mangueira Alves[1] ⓘ, and Leda Cardoso Sampson Pinto[2] ⓘ

[1] Faculdade UnB Gama – Universidade de Brasília (UnB), Area Especial Industria Proj. A,
Gama, DF, Brasil
{cristianesramos, sergiofreitas}@unb.br,
paiva.marcus@aluno.unb.br
[2] Instituto Brasileiro de Informação em Ciência e Tecnologia (IBICT), Setor de Autarquias Sul,
Quadra 5, Lote 6, Bloco H, Brasília, DF, Brasil
ledapinto@ibict.br

Abstract. This article presents an innovative process for identifying the motivational profiles of a specific target audience using three distinct strategies: assessment by judges, application of game dynamics, and the Intrinsic Motivation Inventory (IMI) questionnaire. Each strategy aims to align with the Octalysis framework, emphasizing the importance of personalization and adaptability in gamification. The process is tested on a gamification project within a Brazilian government portal for scientific dissemination, focusing on engaging Brazilian students in science. The analysis reveals differences in strategy outcomes, highlighting the requirement of a multifaceted approach to accurately capture the target audience's motivational profiles and improve gamification effectiveness.

Keywords: Gamification · Motivational Profile · Design Project · Octalysis

1 Introduction

Gamification, defined as the application of game design elements in non-game contexts, has emerged as an innovative approach at the intersections of technology, human behavior, and engineering. This concept, extensively explored by Deterding et al. [1], aims to engage individuals and motivate them to achieve specific goals, enhancing interactivity across a variety of activities. Its implementation has been notable in sectors such as education and corporate, as highlighted by Hamari et al. [2] and Robson et al. [3]. Gamification has improved motivation and learning in complex areas like computer science and engineering, as well as played a vital role in enhancing productivity and fostering collaboration in the corporate environment [4].

Research shows that gamification in educational and corporate environments enhances engagement and learning outcomes. Luarn et al. [5] analyzed the influence of gamification in educational contexts, emphasizing its impact on student engagement

O. Gervasi et al. (Eds.): ICCSA 2024, LNCS 14814, pp. 49–67, 2024.
https://doi.org/10.1007/978-3-031-64608-9_4

and learning effectiveness. In the corporate realm, the studies by Fábregas Grau et al. [6] discussed the role of gamification in corporate communication, suggesting its potential to improve employee training and internal communication strategies. This research collectively illustrates the versatile benefits of gamification across different sectors.

The relevance and growth of gamification are further emphasized by the study of Schöbel et al. [7], which explores the need for adaptive and personalized gamification designs. This work emphasizes the need to account for users' diverse motivations and needs for the success of gamification, drawing support from Ryan and Deci's Self-Determination Theory [8]. They discuss the future of gamification and the need for adaptive and personalized strategies to improve the relevance outcomes of gamification.

The aim of this paper is to present an innovative process for identifying the motivational profile of a specific target audience, using three distinct strategies: assessment by judges familiar with the target audience's profile, application of dynamics, and use of the Intrinsic Motivation Inventory (IMI) questionnaire. Each strategy is designed to identify a motivational profile aligned with the Octalysis framework [9], in line with the trend of personalization and adaptability in gamification highlighted by Schöbel et al. [7]. The identified profiles are then harmonized into a single detailed Octalysis motivational profile, providing specific insights into suitable gaming techniques.

In this study, we emphasize the importance of personalization and adaptability in gamification, an aspect still underexplored in previous research. While studies such as those by Deterding et al. [1] and Hamari et al. [2] have laid the foundations of gamification, our research advances by developing an innovative process for the identification of motivational profiles. This process not only aligns with the growing trend of personalization, as highlighted by Schöbel et al. [7], but also fills an important gap: the practical application of adaptive gamification strategies based on an in-depth understanding of the target audience's needs and motivations. Thus, our work significantly contributes to the field of gamification, offering a practical and theoretically grounded model for the implementation of personalized and effective solutions in various contexts.

This paper is structured to provide a comprehensive overview of the proposed process. Section 2 reviews the related literature in gamification, contextualizing the study within the existing field and expanding the discussion based on the findings of Schöbel et al. [7]. Section 3 details the three strategies used for the identification of motivational profiles. Section 4 illustrates the practical application of the process and its validation. Section 5 discusses the obtained results, and Sect. 6 concludes the article, summarizing the main findings and proposing directions for future research in the area.

2   Literature Review

In this review, we explore the evolution of gamification, underscoring its growing relevance across various sectors, including education and corporate environments. We begin with an overview of gamification applications, highlighting their impact on learning, student engagement, and corporate communication. The analysis focuses on gamification's influence on motivation and educational effectiveness, as well as its role in the workplace, particularly under the conditions of increased remote work prompted by the pandemic.

The study by Luarn et al. [5] is relevant to this discussion. This research investigates the influence of specific gamification elements in the educational environment and their impact on students' intrinsic motivation to learn. The authors consider factors such as perceived collaboration, perceived competition, positive feedback, self-expression, and sense of control, analyzing how each contributes to intrinsic learning motivation. The study adopts a quantitative approach, employing a survey with a 26-item questionnaire measuring seven constructs related to gamification and intrinsic motivation.

The findings from this study aid in understanding how to structure gamification in educational contexts [10]. They suggest that certain gamification elements, like collaboration and positive feedback, are particularly effective at enhancing students' intrinsic motivation. These insights offer valuable guidance on how educators can incorporate gamification elements into their teaching practices to improve knowledge retention and student motivation. This study's contribution provides a foundation for future research and educational practices aiming to integrate gamification effectively.

Luarn et al. [5] research, by highlighting the efficacy of specific gamification elements in education, draws a parallel to the proposition of this article. Our work focuses on expanding this understanding, proposing a process that not only incorporates key gamification elements but also personalizes them according to users' motivational profiles. This focus on customization is inspired by evidence that certain aspects of gamification, such as collaboration and positive feedback, can significantly increase motivation and engagement. Thus, our study aims to develop a method for identifying and harmonizing these motivational profiles within the context of gamification, aiming to maximize its effectiveness in various settings, including education. By aligning the customization of gamification elements with the individual needs and preferences of users, we seek to provide a more effective and adaptable gamification model, applicable in teaching and other areas, such as corporate training.

In this context, Yu-kai Chou's Octalysis framework [9] emerges as a tool, deepening our understanding of gamification's practical application. This framework is distinguished by its holistic and multidimensional approach, examining human motivations and the behavioral drivers underlying gamification's effectiveness. Structured around eight core drives, Octalysis provides valuable insights for creating more engaging and gamification experiences. The core drives of Octalysis include: Epic Meaning & Calling (CD1); Inspiring users to be part of something greater; Development & Accomplishment (CD2): Focusing on progress and achievement; Empowerment of Creativity & Feedback (CD3): Allowing for experimentation and continuous interaction; Ownership & Possession (CD4): Strengthening users' sense of ownership; Social Influence & Relatedness (CD5): Exploring aspects such as mentorship and camaraderie; Scarcity & Impatience (CD6): Creating a desire for items or experiences not immediately accessible; Unpredictability & Curiosity (CD7): Keeping users engaged with the unknown; and Loss & Avoidance (CD8): Motivating users to avoid negative consequences.

Octalysis framework enables the possibility of creating personalized and adapted approaches to users' motivations, a central aspect in our study. For example, consider a motivational profile based on the Octalysis framework, which might identify an individual primarily motivated by CD2 and CD3. Such a profile suggests that this user is highly driven by personal growth, achievement, and the ability to experiment and receive feedback on their actions.

The study conducted by Fábregas Grau et al. [6], focused on the application of gamification in remote job contexts during the pandemic, reveals critical aspects of business communication in small and medium enterprises. The research investigates how remote job, intensified using digital technologies, impacts interpersonal relationships and the understanding of strategic goals and values of the company. The study points to the potential of gamification as a tool to improve internal communication but also highlights a lack of effective implementation and knowledge about gamification in the studied companies. The qualitative methodology, based on semi-structured interviews with managers, provides insights into perceptions and attitudes towards gamification, suggesting a need for greater practical exploration of this tool.

In the context of the findings by Fábregas Grau et al., the process of identifying target audience motivational profiles proposed in our study gains relevance. By understanding the motivations, preferences, and needs of employees in a remote job environment, gamification can be more personalized and adapted.

Implementing a gamification approach based on detailed motivational profiles can address various challenges identified in the study by Fábregas Grau et al. In a remote job scenario, where face-to-face interaction is limited, personalized gamification can offer a means to keep employees engaged, motivated, and aligned with corporate objectives [11, 12]. Furthermore, gamification adapted to the individual characteristics of employees can facilitate the understanding of the company's values and strategic goals, improving internal communication and strengthening organizational culture. Therefore, our study proposes a model that not only fills a gap in gamification research but also offers a practical solution to emerging challenges in the modern workplace.

In the study by Tatarinova et al. [13], the application of gamification technologies in employee training in Russian and international companies is examined. The central goal is to assess the efficacy of gamification in the educational context and its capacity to address practical challenges in various public life sectors. The research tests the influence of gamification on training efficiency and the learning process.

The relevance of this study is anchored in the digital transformation impacting businesses and societies, especially in corporations as reported by Assis and Freitas [4]. The work of Tatarinova et al. was conducted with a specific focus on enhancing educational systems in Russia through the integration of new technologies and educational methodologies. The adopted methodology includes a meta-analysis of international scientific literature and practical cases, complemented using neuroimaging techniques to analyze participants' brain activity during gamification activities.

The results indicate that gamification contributes to improved productivity and attention, although its effect on player engagement is more limited, a result reinforced by Ishaq et al. [14]. The authors conclude that gamification offers significant benefits for training but also caution against the need for careful design to avoid potential distractions or divisions among participants.

Integrating these findings into our work, we propose a gamification model that personalizes the training experience based on detailed motivational profiles of players. This model aims to align gamification with organizational strategic objectives, maximizing its impact on learning and employee engagement. This approach responds to the needs identified in the study by Tatarinova et al., offering a practical strategy to overcome the challenges of implementing and evaluating gamification.

Aligned with the scenario outlined by Schöbel et al. [7], this article proposes a new process for customization in gamification. This process is divided into three distinct strategies, each aiming to identify and harmonize users' motivational profiles in gamification contexts.

The first strategy involves assessment by judges who have in-depth knowledge about the target audience's profile [12, 15]. In the second strategy, interactive dynamics are applied to elicit behavioral responses and preferences from users in a controlled environment. The third and final strategy of the process uses the IMI questionnaire [8]. This instrument is employed to capture quantitative data on users' motivations and preferences, offering a detailed view of their motivational profiles. Combining these three strategies allows for the creation of an Octalysis motivational profile [9], reflecting a personalized and adaptive approach in gamification.

This proposed process not only aligns with the trend of personalization and adaptability in gamification, as highlighted by Schöbel et al. [7], but also fills a significant gap in the field. We offer a practical and theoretically grounded model for the implementation of personalized and effective gamification solutions, suitable for various contexts and user needs.

Our work also establishes a connection between the gamification customization process we propose and some psychological theories. By highlighting the importance of meeting the diverse motivations and needs of users to make gamification experiences effective, we rely on Ryan and Deci's Self-Determination Theory [8].

Applying the Self-Determination Theory in our process involves analyzing users' basic psychological needs - autonomy, competence, and relatedness. In the motivational profile evaluation phase, the goal is to identify and integrate users' intrinsic motivations. The goal is to design gamification experiences that resonate with these fundamental needs, thereby increasing user motivation and engagement.

Upon concluding the literature review on gamification, we identified specific gaps in current research, especially regarding personalization and adaptability. These gaps indicate promising areas for future research, where deeper exploration could bring significant benefits to both the theoretical development and practice of gamification.

1. **Personalization in Gamification**: A critical gap in gamification is the lack of personalized experiences. Despite trends toward greater customization, substantial research is needed to integrate users' unique preferences into gamification frameworks effectively. Future studies should aim to develop and implement methods for efficiently and ethically gathering and analyzing user data to enhance engagement and tailor experiences.

2. **Adaptability of Gamification Systems**: Another significant gap is the adaptability of gamification systems. Future research should explore how these systems can dynamically respond to user behavior changes. This involves studying algorithms and AI strategies for ongoing adaptation of gamification elements to maintain relevance and motivation over time.

3. **Long-Term Impact of Personalized Gamification**: There is a need for research on the long-term impact of personalized gamification. Important questions include how

personalized gamification experiences affect user engagement over time and whether these experiences can lead to lasting changes in behavior or learning.

Furthermore, our process proposes an adaptive approach, where gamification can be adjusted based on user responses. Through the application of the IMI questionnaire [8] and the Octalysis framework [9], we aim to create a gamification system that responds and adapts to changes in user behavior and preferences over time. This addresses the gap related to the adaptability of gamification systems.

By examining the long-term impact of personalized gamification through this process, our study also aims to investigate how personalized gamification experiences influence user engagement and behavior over time. This contributes to understanding the lasting impact of personalized gamification, an area that requires further investigation.

Finally, by integrating fundamental psychological theories such as Self-Determination Theory into the design of our gamification process, we seek to create experiences that not only motivate but also respect users' autonomy and well-being.

3   The Process

To gain a deeper understanding of players' motivational profiles using the Octalysis framework, a process incorporating three strategies from various perspectives was developed and implemented. These strategies are used in a complementary manner. Figure 1 illustrates the main process through which these strategies are applied.

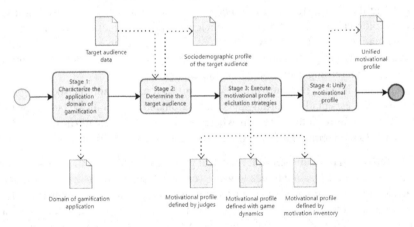

Fig. 1. Process to Identify Players' Motivational Profiles in Gamification Design.

The importance of employing these three strategies is rooted in the fundamental need to address the complexity and multifaceted nature of human motivation. Each strategy offers a unique and complementary perspective, enabling a more holistic and comprehensive analysis. The first strategy (S1), which utilizes judges specialized in the domain of gamification application, leverages the knowledge of these professionals on the specific behaviors of the target audience, ensuring a grounded and contextualized evaluation. The second strategy (S2), based on game dynamics, provides a practical and interactive understanding of motivations, revealing preferences and tendencies in a realistic and engaging context. Finally, the third strategy (S3), employing a motivation inventory, offers a more quantitative and structured approach, allowing for the collection of direct data from the target audience.

The combination of these three methodologies results in a robust and detailed motivational profile, essential for the development of effective gamification solutions that are aligned with the specific needs and preferences of the audience.

The process begins with *"Stage 1: Characterize the Application Domain of Gamification"* whose goal is a detailed analysis of the context in which gamification will be applied. This includes understanding the specific characteristics of the context and identifying key elements that can be enhanced through gamification techniques.

The next step is *"Stage 2: Determine the Target Audience"*, which focuses on identifying and understanding the group of individuals who will interact with the gamified system. Aspects such as age, preferences, needs, challenges, and objectives of the target audience are analyzed to ensure that the gamification approach is relevant and effective.

Based on the identified target audience and application domain, a survey of the target audience's motivational profile is conducted with *"Stage 3: Execute Motivational Profile Elicitation Strategies"*. This stage encompasses three distinct sub-processes, each corresponding to a specific strategy used to achieve this goal.

After applying the three strategies for eliciting the motivational profile, the final stage *"Stage 4: Unify Motivational Profile"* is executed involving the compilation and analysis of the motivational profiles obtained from each strategy to form a unified motivational profile. It is expected that this profile will be comprehensive enough for the development of a gamification approach that ensures the use of techniques aligned with the motivations and preferences of the target audience.

When unifying the different motivational profiles generated by the sub-processes of Stage 3, some guidelines should be considered:

- Identify the core drives that most significantly affect the target audience's motivation, focusing on those with the highest scores – (D1).
- For the initial planning of gamification, strategies S2 (game dynamics) and S3 (motivation inventory) are highly recommended due to their direct contact with the target audience in the data collection phase, as S1 provides a superficial view of the motivational profile since it does not involve the direct engagement of the target audience – (D2).
- The strategy S3, which involves the use of a motivation inventory, is particularly suitable for planning improvements in an existing gamification, offering detailed insights into underlying motivations – (D3).
- For evaluating an ongoing gamification, strategies S3 and S2 are the most indicated, providing an in-depth analysis of user engagement – (D4).
- The strategy S2 stands out in the precise identification of the real motivational profile of users, being a valuable tool both in the planning phase and in the evaluation of gamifications – (D5).

• In selecting game techniques, prioritize those that received the highest scores from judges on each core drive. Given the judges' expertise in the gamification application domain and knowledge of core drives, their evaluations are fundamental for identifying the most effective techniques in motivating the target audience – (D6).

The subprocess "Execution of Motivational Profile Elicitation Strategies" encompasses three distinct sub-processes, each corresponding to a specific strategy used to achieve this goal. The detailed description of these sub-processes is presented in the subsequent sections.

3.1 Subprocess: Eliciting Motivational Profile Through Judges (S1)

This strategy is based on the selection and use of judges' opinions (Fig. 2). Judges are professionals with expertise in the specific area where the gamification will be implemented. Its execution begins with the activity *"Leveling judges' knowledge in gamification"* which is focused on training the judges in essential gamification concepts, with an emphasis on the Octalysis framework [9]. The goal is to equip the judges with a comprehensive understanding of motivational strategies. The subsequent activity, *"Elicit the target audience's motivational profile"* involves the judges filling out a form in which they evaluate various gamification techniques across each core drive of the Octalysis framework, assigning scores that reflect the suitability and effectiveness of these techniques for the target audience. The final activity, *"Determine the Target Audience's Motivational Profile"* consists of analyzing the average scores assigned to the techniques in each core drive, thus establishing the target audience's profile.

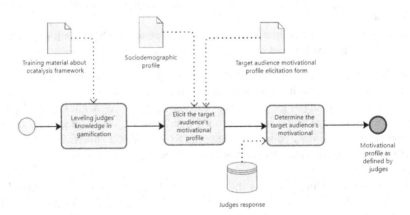

Fig. 2. Subprocess: Eliciting Motivational Profile through Judges (strategy 1).

3.2 Subprocess: Eliciting Motivational Profile with Game Dynamics (S2)

This strategy identifies motivational profiles through the implementation of game dynamics (Fig. 3), directly involving the target audience. In this subprocess, the initial activity,

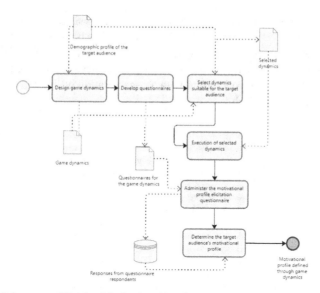

Fig. 3. Subprocess: Eliciting Motivational Profile with Game Dynamics (strategy 2).

"*Design game dynamics*", focuses on developing dynamics that highlight the core drives of the Octalysis framework.

Validating these dynamics with experts is advisable to ensure their effectiveness. Then, "*Develop questionnaires*" involves creating questionnaires to collect data on the target audience's motivational profile, using questions based on the Octalysis core drives, which are answered on a 5-point Likert scale.

Next, "*Select dynamics suitable for the target audience*" involves choosing dynamics that optimize the Octalysis core drives, considering the sociodemographic profile of the target audience. "*Execution of selected dynamics*" occurs with the active participation of the target audience, aiming to foster immersion and interactivity in a playful context. "*Administer the motivational profile elicitation questionnaire*" involves the target audience members responding to the questionnaires. Finally, "*Determine the target audience's motivational profile*" consists of analyzing the collected data, and assessing which Octalysis core drives are most impactful for the target audience.

3.3 Subprocess: Eliciting Motivational Profile Through a Motivation Inventory (S3)

This strategy (Fig. 4) focuses on directly collecting data from the target audience using immersive questionnaires, which are developed based on the analysis of correlations between the IMI [8] and the Octalysis framework [9]. The first activity, "*Map octalysis with IMI*" involved a comparative analysis between the Octalysis framework [9], outlining eight Core Drives, and the Intrinsic Motivation Inventory (IMI) [8], presenting seven distinct scales. This step aimed to identify correlations and emerging patterns between these theoretical structures. Initially, a matching analysis between the Core Drives and the IMI scales was conducted. Subsequently, the analysis was broken down into three sub-activities: (1) targeted comparison of IMI against Octalysis, aiming to identify similarities and differences between the motivations proposed by both theories; (2) reciprocal comparison of Octalysis against IMI, to see if and how Octalysis Core Drives could be interpreted or represented by IMI sub-scales; and (3) synthesis of the results obtained in both comparisons (Table 1), concluding with a consolidation of findings and providing possibilities for future research.

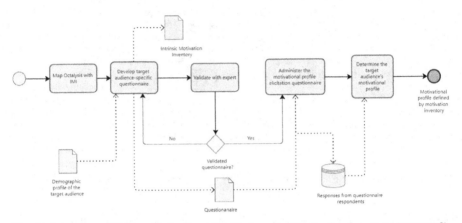

Fig. 4. Subprocess: Eliciting Motivational Profile through a Motivation Inventory (strategy 3).

The "Interest/Enjoyment" subscale (I) measures the pleasure and interest in an activity. It mainly relates to the core drives "Empowerment of Creativity & Feedback" (CD3) and "Unpredictability & Curiosity" (CD7). This emphasizes the link between pleasure, creativity, and the excitement of discovery. The "Perceived Competence" subscale (P), focusing on the sense of skill and mastery, aligns with "Development & Accomplishment" (CD2) and "Ownership & Possession" (CD4), reflecting the significance of personal growth and customization.

Table 1. Mapping of IMI Subscales with the Octalysis Framework Core Drives.

IMI Subscale	I	P	E	T	C	V	R
Octalysis Core	CD 3	CD 2	CD 2	CD 6	CD 2	CD 1	CD3
Drives	CD 7	CD 4	CD 8	CD 8	CD 4	CD 7	CD 5

The "Effort/Importance" subscale (E), assessing the effort and importance assigned to an activity, is related to CD2 and CD8. It highlights the importance of effort in personal growth and minimizing negative outcomes. "Pressure/Tension" (T), measuring internal anxiety or pressure, aligns with CD6 and CD8, indicating the influence of urgency and loss aversion. "Perceived Choice" (C), related to autonomy and choice, finds parallels in CD2 and CD4, showcasing control and customization as motivational factors. "Value/Usefulness" (V), evaluating perceived value and usefulness, is mirrored in CD1 and CD7, underlining the importance of meaningful contributions and exploration. Lastly, "Relatedness" (R), focusing on social connection and belonging, correlates with CD5 and CD3, highlighting the significance of feedback and social interactions in relationship building and the creative process.

The second activity is "*Develop target audience-specific questionnaires*" where questionnaires are tailored from the IMI [8], considering the socio-economic criteria of the audience. This is followed by "*Validate with Expert*" involving the review and evaluation of the questionnaires by professionals experienced in using the IMI and the Octalysis framework. This aims to ensure the accuracy, relevance, and quality of the questions and the suitability of the instrument for the target audience. Then, in the activity "*Administer the motivational profile elicitation questionnaire*" the questionnaires are filled out by the target audience members, for directly gathering information on the participants' motivations. Finally, "*Determine the target audience's motivational profile*" involves analyzing the collected data to identify the motivational profile of the target audience as outlined by the Octalysis framework, offering relevant insights for customizing the gamification experience.

4 Testing the Process in a Complex Domain

This section outlines the execution of the four stages of the process used to identify the target audience's motivational profile in a gamification project within a Brazilian government portal dedicated to scientific dissemination. The phases of this process are presented in the subsections below:

4.1 Stage 1: Characterize the Application Domain of Gamification

The process is applied to the gamification of the Canal Ciência (CC) by Brazilian Institute of Information in Science and Technology (IBICT - https://canalciencia.ibict.br/). CC is a Brazilian government initiative aimed at scientific dissemination, and IBICT is an institution linked to the Ministry of Science, Technology, and Innovation (MCTI). Its mission is to promote competence, resource development, and information infrastructure in science and technology for the production, socialization, and integration of scientific and technological knowledge. CC aims to organize and disseminate scientific information. It contributes to advancing scientific literacy in Brazil, fostering a more informed and engaged population on scientific and technological issues. The purpose of gamifying CC is to increase user motivation and engagement, aiming to boost interest in using the Portal.

4.2 Stage 2: Define the Target Audience

The primary target audience selected for this study is represented by Brazilian students, mainly from elementary to high school, interested in science. This group includes young people seeking knowledge and understanding in these areas, whether through school projects, personal curiosity, or extracurricular activities focused on science. Additionally, it's vital to consider Brazil's cultural and socioeconomic diversity, integrating students from various regions and backgrounds to ensure the gamification of the portal is accessible, relevant, and engaging for a broad spectrum of young learners.

4.3 Stage 3: Execute Motivational Profile Elicitation Strategies

This stage addresses the execution of three sub-processes, each corresponding to a specific strategy. The description of each sub-process provides an understanding of its contribution to the overall process.

S1: Elicit Motivational Profile Through Judges
The study involved the participation of 16 active judges on CC, all acting as researchers or teachers in Brazilian educational institutions. Their scope of work ranges from elementary level 2 to higher education, demonstrating a broad spectrum of educational engagement and contribution to the development and maintenance of the portal. The age range of the participants varies from 27 to 64 years, with an average of about 4 years of involvement with the CC. Notably, at least two of these participants have collaborated with the Channel for over a decade, demonstrating a long-term commitment. In terms of educational experience, the average among the judges is 10 years.

Geographically, the judges represent 80% of Brazilian regions, including the Midwest, North, Northeast, South, and Southeast, reflecting a national scope in their work. The most frequent area of knowledge among them is Social Sciences. Despite their significant contribution to education, most are not linked to a specific type of educational institution and do not work directly in the educational field.

The following activities were performed in this strategy:

Leveling Judges' Knowledge in Gamification: The training of judges was centered on the basic principles of the Octalysis framework [9], with an emphasis on core drive techniques. After the initial class, the judges were organized into 4 teams with 4 participants each. Teams continued with asynchronous study.

Table 2. Average scoring of the Octalysis core drives by team.

Octalysis Core Drives	Team 1	Team 2	Team 3	Team 4	Mean
Epic Meaning & Calling (CD1)	2,63	1,63	1,13	1,75	1.79
Development & Accomplishment (CD2)	1,56	1,31	2,25	1,94	1.77
Empowerment of Creativity & Feedback (CD3)	2,00	1,45	1,36	0,73	1.39
Ownership & Possession (CD4)	1,27	0,91	1,55	2,27	1.50
Social Influence & Relatedness (CD5)	0,77	0,77	1,77	1,31	1.56
Scarcity & Impatience (CD6)	0,83	0,42	1,67	0,75	0.92
Unpredictability & Curiosity (CD7)	1,82	1,18	2,18	2,45	1.91
Loss & Avoidance (CD8)	0,30	0,20	0,50	0,70	0.43

Elicit the Target Audience's Motivational Profile: Considering the sociodemographic profile of the target audience, in this activity, teams were asked to fill out the "target audience motivational profile elicitation form" where they scored, on each core drive of the Octalysis framework, the suitability and impact of each technique on sustaining the motivation of the target audience they were focused on.

Determine the Target Audience's Motivational Profile: The resulting Octalysis of each team was established through the average scoring of individual techniques within each core drive of the Octalysis framework (Table 2).

We observe that the core drives CD7, CD1 and CD2 have the highest scores. These results indicate a trend towards valuing elements associated with surprise, discovery, broader purpose, and personal or professional development. The high score in CD7 highlights the importance attributed to elements that generate surprise and stimulate curiosity. CD1 emphasizes the value of purpose and the pursuit of greater goals. CD2 in turn, reflects the significance of growth and achieving goals.

On the other hand, the core drives CD8 and CD6 score the lowest, suggesting that for the target audience, there is less relevance of factors related to loss, rejection, urgency, scarcity, time, and resource limitations. This indicates a lesser predominance of negative or pressure-based factors compared to those that promote discovery, purpose, and growth. To obtain the final Octalysis of the judges, the average of each core drive was calculated from the team averages.

S2: Elicit Motivational Profile with Game Dynamics

Develop Game Dynamics: The creation of game dynamics and questionnaires was guided to stimulate the most prevalent core drives in the target audience [16]. In total, five dynamics were developed, named: "My Other Half is With You" - focusing on the CD5 core drive; "Characteristics and Quirks" - also related to the CD5 core drive; "The Problem with My City/School" - centered on the CD1 core drive; "Living with Masks" - related to the CD3; and "Two for All" - emphasizing the CD6 core drive. Each dynamic was carefully planned and adapted according to the target audience.

In tailoring the 'The Problem with My City/School' dynamic for ES students, the focus was on everyday challenges within the school environment, such as bullying, social integration, and academic pressures. For MS and HS participants, the adaptation addressed broader societal issues relevant to their urban surroundings, including environmental sustainability, community welfare, educational infrastructure, and civic engagement. These nuanced adjustments ensured that the game dynamics resonated with and were applicable to the developmental stages and thematic interests of each target demographic.

Develop Questionnaires: Regarding the questionnaires, two types were created: one for children and another for teenagers. In the children's questionnaire, a question for each core drive was formulated, and the Likert scale (with 5 points) was adapted using pictures related to each question.

Select Dynamics Suitable for Target Audience: The game dynamics were sent to teachers for them to select those deemed most suitable for their students.

Execution of Selected Dynamics: The selected dynamics were carried out in classrooms under the guidance of teachers, who also acted as judges in the study. They received adequate support materials and assistance to facilitate the implementation of these activities, ensuring an execution aligned with the study's objectives.

Administer the Motivational Profile Elicitation Questionnaire: Participants involved in the dynamics and in filling out the questionnaires are students from public schools in the Brazilian states of Rio de Janeiro and the Federal District. To ensure broad representativeness, the dynamics were conducted with students from elementary school, middle school, and high school. The total number of students who participated in the questionnaire was 593, as indicated in Table 3.

Table 3. Demographic Data of Students Participating in S2.

Target Audience	Group	Age Range	Number of Respondents
Children	Elementary	5–10	44
Youth	Middle school	11–16	97
Youth	High School	16–19	452

In total, 581 complete questionnaires and 12 incomplete questionnaires, where some target audience identification was missing, were received. Analyzing the students' responses provided essential quantitative data on the target audience in different contexts, enabling a careful and diverse evaluation of which game elements could be more effective in sustaining players' motivation.

Determine the Target Audience's Motivational Profile: The data analysis was conducted through the average of responses in each core drive and by assembling the Octalysis chart. Figure 5 represents the motivational profile outlined for the target audience according to the 3 categories: Elementary school (ES), Middle school (MS), and High School (HS).

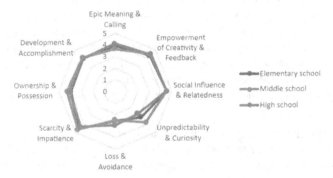

Fig. 5. Octalysis result from S2 for the 3 groups.

It's observed that there is agreement and disagreement regarding which core drives were most prevalent in each group. For all 3 groups, the top-scoring core drives were CD3, CD5 and CD6. However, the ranking of each core drive varied among the groups. For the HS and MS groups, the 1st was CD6 the 2nd was CD5 and the 3rd was CD3. For the HS group, the 1st was CD5, the 2nd was CD3 and the 3rd was CD6.

S3: Eliciting Motivational Profile Through a Motivation Inventory

The process of defining a motivational profile through the IMI followed these activities:

Map Octalysis with IMI: The resulting mapping was described in Sect. 3.

Develop Target Audience-Specific Questionnaires: The questionnaires were developed with adaptations from the IMI questions [8], considering the socio-economic criteria of the target audience. This ensured the questions were relevant and appropriate to the participants' characteristics and contexts. For this reason, two questionnaires were created: one for elementary school children with seven adapted questions, following the mapping from the previous step, and another with 14 questions for middle and high school students, also using the mapping.

Validate with Expert: This step involves the review and evaluation of the developed questionnaires by professionals experienced in using the IMI and the Octalysis framework [9]. The aim is to ensure the accuracy, relevance, and quality of the questions, ensuring the instrument is effective and suitable for the target audience. This becomes an optional but highly recommended step.

Administer the Motivational Profile Elicitation Questionnaire: The questionnaires are filled out by individuals from the target audience. This step is essential for directly collecting data on the participants' motivations, offering valuable information for subsequent analysis.

Determine the Target Audience's Motivational Profile: This activity has not yet been executed. Once it is carried out, an analysis will be conducted to identify correlations between the Octalysis framework core drives and the intrinsic motivation factors from the IMI. This procedure contributes to a deeper understanding of the underlying motivations of participants' behavior in the context of game dynamics.

4.4   Stage 4: Unify the Motivational Profile

The S1 and S2 strategies resulted in 4 Octalysis charts representing the motivational profile of the target audience for the Canal Ciência portal. These are depicted in Fig. 5, and Table 4 summarizes the scores obtained for each core drive.

A significant difference is observed in the core drive CD6 between the judges' averages (S1) and the student participants' averages (S2). This variation can be attributed to the age differences. Judges evaluate gamification strategies from a long-term strategic perspective, whereas students react based on immediate experiences. Integrating both groups' assessments could offer a fuller understanding of gamification strategies' impacts, enhancing their application and effectiveness.

Implementing the first guideline (D1), it's found that, according to the judges' evaluation (S1), the three core drives with the greatest impact on the target audience are CD7, CD1 and CD2. From the target audience's perspective, in Strategy S2, the three most valued core drives across the three groups were CD3, CD5 and CD6 only differing in their order of ranking. Based on these findings, the initial gamification planning followed the target audience's preference, as directed by guideline D2.

Table 4. Scores of the Octalysis framework core drives from strategies S1 and S2.

Octalysis Core drives	S1	S2		
		ES	MS	HS
Epic Meaning & Calling (CD1)	1,79	3,913	3,645	4,075
Development & Accomplishment (CD2)	1,77	3,982	4,082	4,020
Empowerment of Creativity & Feedback (CD3)	1,39	4,309	4,495	4,451
Ownership & Possession (CD4)	1,50	3,939	4,268	4,029
Social Influence & Relatedness (CD5)	1,56	4,597	4,608	4,606
Scarcity & Impatience (CD6)	0,92	4,620	4,713	4,385
Unpredictability & Curiosity (CD7)	1,91	3,208	3,874	2,790
Loss & Avoidance (CD8)	0,43	2,583	2,505	2,958

In selecting game techniques, as per guideline D6, those that received the highest scores from the judges (S1) in each selected core drive were prioritized. The number of techniques to be implemented in each core drive was based on the proportion of scores received.

Thus, core drives with higher scores were allocated a larger number of techniques, aiming to emphasize the elements most valued by the target audience in the gamification. The result, shown in Table 5, follows these guidelines for a balanced approach, focusing on components most effective for engaging the target audience.

Table 5. Scores of the Octalysis Core Drivers from strategies S1 and S2

Selected Core Drives	Selected Game Techniques
1st. Social Influence & Relatedness (CD5)	Mentorship; Trophy Shelves; Group Quest; Friending; Touting; Bragging
2nd. Scarcity & Impatience (CD6)	Patient Feedback; Countdown; Throttles; Torture Break
3rd. Empowerment of Creativity & Feedback (CD3)	Evergreen Mechanics; Voluntary Autonomy; Plant Picker/Meaningful Choices

For the core drive with the highest score, the four techniques with the best scores in S1 were selected. For the second core drive, three techniques were chosen, and for the third, two techniques. In situations where there was a tie in the scores of techniques for the second and third core drives, the tiebreaker will be conducted in consultation with IBICT, considering criteria such as technical feasibility, timeframe, and cost.

Game techniques such as Patient Feedback and Countdown can be implemented together to optimize user engagement, helping to keep them motivated by balancing reflection and immediate action. On the other hand, Throttles and Torture Break regulate interaction with content in a way that prevents overload and enhances anticipation. It is expected that this combination will keep users continuously engaged and interested in the next steps.

5 Discussion

The analysis of the three motivational profile elicitation strategies reveals important differences in their outcomes. The judges' strategy (S1) provided a view based on specialized knowledge, indicating the most suitable game techniques for the target audience, yet it is at a more superficial level. In contrast, the game dynamics strategy (S2) and the motivation inventory strategy (S3) generate more practical results as they involve the target audience's participation, with S3 specifically mapping intrinsic motivation to deepen understanding of the motivational profile. The strategies are complementary, and their concurrent use results in a multifaceted motivational profile. Further studies are needed to determine how to assign appropriate weights to each strategy, according to the context in which they are applied.

Implementing strategy S2 in Canal Ciência faced challenges due to the audience's diversity, with variations in age, educational background, and socio-cultural contexts. This strategy, which includes interactive dynamics, requires adaptations to ensure its relevance and effectiveness across different groups. On the other hand, strategy S3, focused on the motivation inventory, has not yet moved to the application phase on the target audience but is anticipated to face challenges related to user diversity. Implementing S3 requires adjustments in questionnaire development to ensure comprehension and relevance for a broad spectrum of users. This heterogeneity, while enhancing data collection, introduces complexities in analysis and interpretation of the results, posing a challenge in accurately identifying motivational profiles and improving gamification.

6 Conclusion

This research delineates a novel, multifaceted process to identify motivational profiles within gamification contexts, directly aligning with goals of enhancing engagement and learning outcomes in various sectors. Through the integration of expert assessments, dynamic gaming strategies, and the application of the IMI, we have developed a comprehensive methodology that not only adheres to but also advances the personalization and adaptability aspects of gamification strategies. This approach has proven effective in capturing the nuanced motivations of diverse target audiences, thereby offering a granular insight into developing tailored gamification interventions that significantly enhance user engagement and learning outcomes.

Our findings reveal the critical importance of adopting a multifaceted lens to understand and cater to the intrinsic motivations of individuals. By leveraging the Octalysis framework, we were able to systematically dissect and reconstruct the motivational drives of our target audience, demonstrating the impact of personalized gamification on fostering meaningful engagement. Moreover, the study underscores the dynamic nature of motivation, advocating for the continuous adaptation of gamification strategies to accommodate evolving user preferences and technological advancements.

Future studies will explore the enduring impact of customized gamification across different groups and settings. Additionally, integrating cutting-edge technologies and psychological insights could sharpen gamification's effectiveness. This research significantly enriches the gamification field, offering a novel perspective for creating more captivating, efficient, and user-focused gamification strategies.

References

1. Deterding, S., Dixon, D., Khaled, R., Nacke, L.: From game design elements to gamefulness: defining "gamification." In: Proceedings of the 15th International Academic MindTrek Conference: Envisioning Future Media Environments, MindTrek 2011, pp. 9–15 (2011)
2. Hamari, J., Koivisto, J., Sarsa, H.: Does gamification work? - a literature review of empirical studies on gamification. In: Proceedings of the Annual Hawaii International Conference on System Sciences, pp. 3025–3034 (2014). https://doi.org/10.1109/HICSS.2014.377
3. Robson, K., Plangger, K., Kietzmann, J.H., McCarthy, I., Pitt, L.: Is it all a game? Understanding the principles of gamification. Bus. Horiz. **58**, 411–420 (2015). https://doi.org/10.1016/j.bushor.2015.03.006
4. Assis, L.S., Freitas, S.A.A.: Gamification in organizational contexts: a systematic literature review. In: Nah, F., Siau, K. (eds.) HCI in Business, Government and Organizations, pp. 331–352. Springer, Cham (2023). https://doi.org/10.1007/978-3-031-35969-9_23
5. Luarn, P., Chen, C.-C., Chiu, Y.-P.: The influence of gamification elements in educational environments. Int. J. Game-Based Learn. **13**, 1–12 (2023)
6. Fábregas Grau, J., Tejedor, S., Salla García, J.: La gamificación como recurso telemático en la comunicación empresarial en tiempos de pandemia. Comunicación 57–75 (2021). https://doi.org/10.18566/comunica.n44.a04
7. Schöbel, S., Schmidt-Kraepelin, M., Janson, A., Sunyaev, A.: Adaptive and personalized gamification designs: call for action and future research. AIS Trans. Hum.-Comput. Interact. **13**, 479–494 (2021). https://doi.org/10.17705/1thci.00158
8. Ryan, R.M., Deci, E.L.: Self-Determination Theory: Basic Psychological Needs in Motivation, Development, and Wellness. The Guilford Press, New York (2018)
9. Chou, Y.-K.: Actionable gamification: beyond points, badges, and leaderboards. Leanpub (2016)
10. Chugh, R., Turnbull, D.: Gamification in education: a citation network analysis using CitNetExplorer. Contemp. Educ. Technol. **15**, ep405 (2023)
11. Knutas, A., van Roy, R., Hynninen, T., Granato, M., Kasurinen, J., Ikonen, J.: A process for designing algorithm-based personalized gamification. Multimed. Tools Appl. **78**, 13593–13612 (2019). https://doi.org/10.1007/s11042-018-6913-5
12. Borotic, G., Jagust, T.: Enhancing student engagement with personalized gamification and adaptive learning strategies. In: 2022 IEEE Frontiers in Education Conference (FIE), pp. 1–5. IEEE, Uppsala (2022). https://doi.org/10.1109/FIE56618.2022.9962647
13. Tatarinova, E.A., Sycheva, S.M., Mezina, T.V., Khalimon, E.A., Ciric Lalić, D.: Gamification technologies in staff training of Russian and foreign companies. In: Sustainable and Innovative Development in the Global Digital Age. Dela Press Publishing House (2022)
14. Ishaq, A., Asghar, M., Mubashir, S.: Application of gamification in human resource management– an empirical research to increase employees' motivation and productivity. Int. J. Comput. Appl. **177**, 11–13 (2019). https://doi.org/10.5120/ijca2019919728

15. Sant' Ana Van Erven, R.C.G., De Almeida Jubé, D., Santos, H.R., Andrade De Freitas, S.A., Canedo, E.D.: Gamification project to receive continuous feedback in the context of the evolution of public service for lawyers. In: 2023 IEEE Frontiers in Education Conference (FIE), pp. 1–8. IEEE, College Station (2023)
16. Freitas, S.A.A., Lacerda, A.R.T., Calado, P.M.R.O., Lima, T.S., Dias Canedo, E.: Gamification in education: a methodology to identify student's profile. In: 2017 IEEE Frontiers in Education Conference (FIE), pp. 1–8. IEEE, Indianapolis (2017). https://doi.org/10.1109/FIE.2017.8190499

The Effectiveness of Using AutoML in Electricity Theft Detection: The Impact of Data Preprocessing and Balancing Techniques

Suhad A. Yousif[1] and Venus W. Samawi[2]([envelope])

[1] Computer Science Department, Al-Nahrain University, Baghdad, Iraq
[2] Department of MIS/Smart Business, Isra University, Amman, Jordan
venus.samawi@iu.edu.jo

Abstract. Electricity theft is a significant threat to the economy and society's security. Machine learning models are applied to consumption data obtained from smart meters to detect and prevent it. The consumption data must undergo preprocessing and feature selection techniques to enhance detection accuracy. Moreover, the data is imbalanced, where it contains rare malicious samples. This study uses AutoML to detect electricity theft by utilizing its useful services, such as data preprocessing, feature engineering, algorithm selection, and model hyperparameter optimization. We will showcase and evaluate two prominent platforms, TPOT and H2O, and analyze the effectiveness and accuracy of each. The study will examine whether applying additional preprocessing for outlier detection and handling impacts TPOT's and H2O's performance. Additionally, we will examine the performance of each platform on the unbalanced datasets related to electricity theft and compare it with their performance after balancing the dataset using three different techniques - Random Oversampling, Synthetic Minority Oversampling Technique (SMOTE), and adaptive synthetic (ADASYN). After analyzing the results, the Random Oversampling Accuracy technique was the best among the three techniques for balancing the dataset. The TPOT achieved the highest accuracy of 99% on the balanced dataset with Random Oversampling, while H2O reached an accuracy of 96.8%. However, H2O outperforms TPOT when applied to the unbalanced dataset. The results demonstrate that inappropriate handling of outliers reduces accuracy, particularly with imbalanced datasets. However, accuracy is improved after balancing it.

Keywords: Electricity theft detection · Data Balancing Techniques · AutoML · TPOT · H2O · Outlier Detection and Handling

1 Introduction

The smart grid (SG) is crucial in managing electricity production, distribution, and control. However, power losses often occur during the production, distribution, and transmission of electrical energy due to technical (TLs) and non-technical factors (NTLs). Electricity theft is a significant cause of (NTLs) [1, 2]. It occurs when users fraudulently

O. Gervasi et al. (Eds.): ICCSA 2024, LNCS 14814, pp. 68–82, 2024.
https://doi.org/10.1007/978-3-031-64608-9_5

consume energy by stealing electric energy from power grids, resulting in non-technical losses in the power sector. Three main strategies could be used to detect power theft: *network-oriented methodology*, *data-oriented technique*, and a *hybrid approach* that combines the two methods. Implementing network- and hybrid-oriented solutions is often not feasible due to security risks and high installation costs, as it requires regular modification of the network architecture [3]. Consequently, data-driven techniques have been implemented for Electricity Theft Detection (ETD). This approach uses data obtained from smart meters to forecast electricity theft. Research has demonstrated that using data-driven techniques enhances the precision of ETD, as stated by [2, 4]. Deep learning (DL) and machine learning (ML) techniques are commonly employed to predict instances of electricity theft by identifying abnormal electricity consumption patterns [5–8]. Furthermore, a combination of DL and ML techniques can be used to detect electricity theft by analyzing data collected from smart meters [1, 9]. ML algorithms analyze vast amounts of data to detect anomalous patterns. Since the data collected may contain noise, inaccuracies, and missing values, it needs to be cleaned and preprocessed first. After that, engineers apply feature engineering techniques to the data to enhance the effectiveness of ML algorithms. On the other hand, deep learning algorithms are capable of generating features from raw data; however, the data still needs to be cleaned, and data noise should be handled. Moreover, the data available for identifying electricity fraud is complex and imbalanced, making it difficult to identify fraudulent patterns through traditional machine learning and neural network techniques [10]. However, AutoML platforms can be a useful solution, as they offer valuable services such as data preprocessing, feature engineering, algorithm selection, and model hyperparameter optimization. The advantage of using Auto ML platforms is that researchers do not need to be experts in machine learning and deep learning techniques. These platforms also help to select the most appropriate technique for solving the problem [11]. Imbalanced data is biased towards the majority class, and data balancing techniques can address this issue.

Using data-oriented techniques for electricity theft detection (ETD) faces challenges in handling large electricity consumption datasets due to missing values, data variance, and nonlinear data relationship issues [4, 12]. Therefore, an effective preprocessing phase is needed to address this problem and prepare the dataset for the classification (or clustering) phase to get more accurate results [1]. Primary data preprocessing involves imputing missing values, handling outliers, and normalizing data [10, 12, 13]. Another crucial step in ML is feature engineering, including transforming raw data into new features and creating new variables by extracting them from the raw data (feature extraction). This helps train new ML models to tackle new tasks effectively, leading to more accurate predictions and insights [14]. AutoML platforms can automatically perform feature engineering to improve the handling of certain data types [15]. Finally, imbalanced data is a common issue in data science that requires data balancing techniques to overcome bias towards the majority class [16]. Resampling techniques are employed to address the imbalanced data problem. These techniques include oversampling methods such as Random oversampling, SMOTE, and ADASYN, as well as under-sampling methods like Random under-sampling, NearMiss, and Tomek-links. Choosing between under-sampling and oversampling techniques depends on the dataset characteristics and the problem to be solved. Some studies have utilized both methods (under-sampling and oversampling) to balance the dataset [12]. According to the literature, oversampling is generally considered more effective for data balancing [17]. Based on this, we decided to investigate three oversampling techniques (Random, SMOTE, ADASYN) to balance the electricity consumption datasets and study their effect on the behaviour of the theft detection model used.

This study aims to use AutoML to tackle the problem of electricity theft prediction. We will test and assess the effectiveness and precision of two platforms, TPOT and H2O. These platforms provide multiple tools and services for data preprocessing and feature engineering, algorithm selection, and hyperparameter tuning for model building. Our study addresses challenges concerning handling outliers and unbalanced classes included in the used ETD dataset. Furthermore, the best AutoML platform (between TPOT and H2O) will be specified based on the results achieved by each of them. The best classifier in each of TPOT and H2O is specified based on the algorithm selection and model hyperparameter optimization provided by each platform. Additionally, our study intends to answer the following questions: 1) Which AutoML platform is better for identifying electricity fraud - TPOT or H2O? 2) To what extent do outlier detection and handling as a preprocessing step improve the performance of TPOT and H2O? 3) Do TPOT and H2O have similar outcomes to an imbalanced dataset? 4) Finally, we will investigate which data balancing technique (Random, SMOTE, and ADASYN) is more effective in enhancing the performance of TPOT and H2O on the used dataset.

Henceforth, this paper is organized in the following manner. Section 2 reviews AutoML platforms. Section 3 summarizes data preprocessing and feature engineering. Section 4 illustrates data balancing using resampling techniques. The system model is explained in Sect. 5. Section 6 summarizes the scenarios of experimental results of both TPOT and H2O and assesses the outcomes of the experiments. Ultimately, we stated the main findings in Sect. 6 and provided an outline for future work.

2   AutoML

AutoML (Automated Machine Learning) is an ML platform used to develop an ML model by automating the training and learning process. These platforms enable experts and non-experts to apply machine learning models to solve various problems such as regression, classification, and clustering [11, 13]. Many AutoML platforms, including Auto-Keras [21], Azure, TPOT, and H2O, are available. Each offers different features and capabilities. Some of them provide data preprocessing and feature engineering (H2O, MLBox, and TPOT), in addition to selecting the appropriate algorithms and optimizing the model's hyperparameters (H2O, MLBox, Auto-SKLearn, TPOT) [18, 19]. AutoML platforms provide a variety of tools and services for machine learning. *Azure* AutoML is particularly useful for supervised learning and time series forecasting. In contrast, *Google Cloud* AutoML uses reinforcement learning to interact with its environment and receive feedback. *Run:ai* is designed to automate resource management and workload orchestration for machine learning infrastructure [18, 20]. *Auto-Keras* uses a DL library and provides building blocks for performing architecture searches. It searches for the most suitable neural network architecture based on the dataset and task [21]. *H2O* utilizes ML and artificial intelligence technologies to accomplish various tasks. The tool offers model interpretation to assist users in comprehending the model's decision-making process. This is crucial for specific applications [22, 23]. Finally, *TPOT* is a tree-based optimization tool. It optimizes machine learning pipelines using genetic programming [24]. In this work, we are interested in studying the performance of two AutoML platforms, TPOT and H2O. TPOT and H2O use different approaches. Several research papers outline TPOT [25, 26]; however, limited information is available on H2O. Therefore, H2O will be explained in more detail.

In this work, we aim to utilize AutoML to address the problem of detecting electricity theft. The performance and accuracy of the two platforms, TPOT and H2O, will be tested and evaluated. Each platform provides its version of tools and services concerning data preprocessing and feature engineering, selecting the appropriate algorithms, and optimizing the model's hyperparameters.

2.1 H2O AutoML Platform

H2O is an AutoML platform used to handle complex models and datasets while maintaining scalability. When using H2O AutoML, users can customize the training model by specifying the runtime or choosing which models to combine. H2O AutoML provides automated tasks, including feature engineering, model selection, and hyperparameter tuning based on Bayesian optimization and Random search algorithms and others, simplifying machine learning workflows. It also selects the performance model based on validation techniques. It is worth mentioning that H2O can combine predictions from various models using stacked methods to improve accuracy, which involves a mental learner. Therefore, for data predictions, either the performing model or an ensemble of models is produced. H2O also provides interpretability tools to explain the decision-making process [22, 27, 28]. The ML stages in H2O include (see Fig. 1):

1. Data preparation: In this stage, the dataset passes through cleaning and transformation processes, where data imputation, encoding variables, and normalizing data are performed.
2. Features Engineering: H2O AutoML improves model performance by generating new features from input data and applying feature selection algorithms to reduce dimensionality and increase efficiency.
3. Exploring Models: In this stage, H2O tests different machine learning algorithms, namely linear models, tree-based methods such as Random Forests and Gradient Boosting Machines (GBMs), DL models, and ensemble methods. Each algorithm performs hyperparameter tuning to find optimal model parameters by using grid search, random search, or Bayesian optimization.
4. Models Evaluation: Cross-validation is applied to data to ensure model reliability and prevent overfitting to a subset of data. Furthermore, a leaderboard is maintained to rank models based on performance metrics such as accuracy, RMSE, AUC, and F1_mesure. The best classifier is selected from the model that tops the leaderboard.
5. Deploying in Real World Scenario: The chosen model can be easily deployed for making predictions in a production environment.

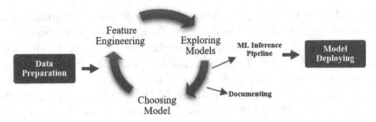

Fig. 1. The ML stages in H2O

H2O is an open-source ML platform with customized versions of algorithms for enhanced performance. AutoML automates tasks like feature engineering, model tuning, and deployment. H2O is available in multiple languages and integrates well with big data platforms. However, it is difficult to use with other frameworks like scikit learn. H2O architecture has multiple layers. The topmost layer, API, provides REST API clients for various platforms (such as Python, R, Excel, Tableau, and Flow Web UI using socket connections). The bottom layer is a big data platform that runs on a JVM process. An H2O cluster has nodes, each with a JVM process split into three layers: language, algorithms, and core infrastructure, as shown in Fig. 2 [22].

API Layer: Provides REST API Clients for Various Platforms			
Python	F	Excel/ Tableau	Flow Web
Network			
Language Layer			
R-expression evaluation engines	Scale		Client Algorithm
The Algorithm Layer			
Parse	ML Algorithms XGBoost, GBM, Random Forest, K-Means, etc.	Prediction Engine	Client Algorithm
Core Infrastructure Layer			
Manages resources such as memory and CPU			
Big Data Platform			
Spark	Hadoop		Standalone H2O

Fig. 2. H2O Architecture

2.2 TPOT AutoML Platform

TPOT is open-source software (written in Python) that automates building ML pipelines by combining expression tree representation with stochastic search algorithms. It uses the Python-based scikit-learn library as its ML menu [25, 26]. TPOT intelligently explores thousands of possible pipelines to find the best one for the data. This package uses genetic programming to help recognize the best pipeline for a specific task. Unlike H2O, TPOT discovers the best models and pipelines with preprocessors, feature selectors, and ML/DL. It provides services concerning feature engineering, model selection, and hyperparameter tuning [25, 26]. The ML Pipeline automated by TPOT is shown in Fig. 3.

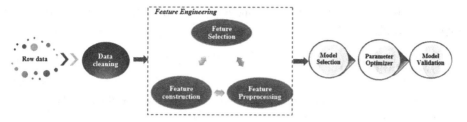

Fig. 3. ML Pipeline Automated By TPOT

3 Data Preprocessing and Feature Engineering

Machine learning often involves feature engineering and data preprocessing, which includes selecting, manipulating, and transforming raw data into features easily understood by learning algorithms. It involves handling inappropriate data, missing values, errors caused by human intervention, insufficient data sources, and other issues. Popular data preprocessing and feature engineering techniques include cleaning up datasets by fixing or removing incorrect, corrupted, duplicate, or incomplete data. The imputation technique handles irregularity in the dataset instead of removing rows or columns with missing data. It is used to fill in missing values with estimates to retain data in datasets (default values or means/medians can impute missing numerical data; for categorical data, the most frequent value in a column can replace the missing values). Datasets may contain outliers (extreme values). These outliers can significantly affect the classification accuracy. Therefore, outliers must be identified and handled before the classification phase to improve accuracy. Feature scaling (data normalization) is used to enhance model training performance and stability by adjusting the range of data. Some popular data normalization techniques include scaling to a range, clipping, log scaling, and z-score. Finally, Logarithm transformation, or log transform, is a mathematical technique used in ML to normalize skewed data and reduce the effect of outliers on the data, which makes the model more robust.

Data preprocessing and feature engineering are crucial for improving ML models and achieving more accurate predictions for real-world data. Both TPOT and H2O provide a set of services for data preprocessing and feature engineering. However, although Both H2O and TPOT integrate robust models and preprocessing techniques that can reduce the influence of the outliers, they do not explicitly detect or handle outliers as a separate step. Therefore, it is better to handle outliers manually before applying the AutoML tools. Consequently, we propose an algorithm based on Z-scores to detect and handle outliers in the original dataset.

Algorithm One: Preprocessing to filter out rows with Outliers.

1. Iterate over columns.
   a. Find Mean μ, and standard deviation δ.
   b. Let x_i be a value current column, $dx_i = |x_i - \mu|$ // deviation of each value from the mean of the column
   c. If $dx_i >$ threshold, then drop the corresponding row from the dataset # threshold is set $3 \times \delta$, which represents the cutoff for outlier

The study examines the impact of removing rows with outliers as a preprocessing step before applying TPOT and H2O and evaluates its effect on their performance.

4 Data Balancing

The dataset for detecting electricity theft is unbalanced, with a majority normal class and a minority theft class. This can cause skewness and bias issues, which can be addressed with resampling techniques. Resampling is a technique that transforms the training dataset by creating a new version with a different class distribution. The change in class distribution is only applied to the training dataset, not the test dataset. The purpose of resampling is to influence model fit, so selecting an appropriate technique for the specific problem is essential. To address the rarity of malicious samples in the used electricity consumption dataset, three oversampling data balancing techniques, namely, Random Oversampling, SMOTE, and ADASYN are experimented with to find the best method to balance the dataset, which improves the ML performance. Random oversampling is based on duplicating examples from the minority class. Although it is simple to implement and fast for large datasets, it sometimes can lead to overfitting. Random oversampling is suitable for binary and multi-class classification problems. On the other hand, SMOTE involves generating synthetic samples of the minority class by interpolating between existing minority class examples [12, 29]. Unlike random oversampling, SMOTE does not increase overfitting as it does not use copies of minority class data [17]. SMOTE and ADASYN are similar in that both of them oversample the minority class in unbalanced datasets by generating synthetic data. However, ADASYN generates synthetic samples for a given instance x_i, which are proportional to the number of neighboring samples that do not belong to the same class as x_i. This means that ADASYN focuses more on generating new examples for the minority class outliers rather than just oversampling the existing instances [16]. In this study, each AutoML platform (TPOT and H2O) is applied to both the unbalanced and balanced datasets. Their behavior will be studied by comparing their performance before and after balancing the dataset. Moreover, we will investigate which data balancing technique (Random, SMOTE, and ADASYN) is more effective in enhancing the performance of TPOT and H2O on the used Dataset.

5 Electricity Theft Predictions: The Proposed System Model

Machine learning generally comprises five phases: data preprocessing, feature engineering, Dataset balancing, learning phase, and evaluation phase. Most AutoML platforms include data preprocessing, feature engineering, algorithm selection, and model hyperparameter optimization as part of their built-in functionalities. As mentioned, this study utilizes AutoML to detect electricity theft. Two prominent platforms, TPOT and H2O, will be investigated to assess the effectiveness and accuracy of each. The study will investigate the effect of two preprocessing and feature selection algorithms, described in Sect. 3, on TPOT and H2O beyond their built-in capabilities. Furthermore, we will investigate whether TPOT and H2O have similar performance when used with imbalanced datasets related to electricity theft. Three techniques are used to understand the impact of balancing methods on TPOT and H2O's performance: Random Oversampling,

SMOTE, and ADASYN. We propose a four-phase system model to achieve the main research goals (as shown in Fig. 4).

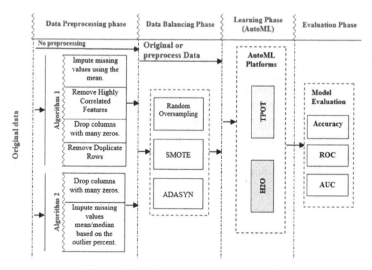

Fig. 4. ETD: The proposed system model.

The four phases are data preprocessing and feature selection, data balancing, learning, and model evaluation. Initially, the dataset is directly passed to the learning or balancing phases or undergoes two preprocessing and feature selection algorithms. These algorithms remove highly correlated features, duplicate rows, drop columns with many zeros, and impute missing values to improve the learning process of TPOT and H2O. To investigate the performance of TPOT and H2O on an imbalanced dataset and to explore whether balancing methods affect their behavior, TPOT and H2O were trained on the original data and data balanced with three methods. After completing the learning phase, the selected models from TPOT and H2O are evaluated using the testing dataset and compared based on accuracy, AUC, and ROC. The TPOT and H2O stages are illustrated in Figs. 1 and 3, respectively.

6   Experimental Results: Assessment

This research uses a real dataset containing 9956 rows and 367 columns. The first column contains alphanumeric consumer IDs, while the 2nd to 366 columns contain daily electricity consumption data. The last column, "flag," contains binary values (0 for normal and 1 indicating theft). The dataset is an unbalanced dataset that contains (8562 normal vs. 1394 theft). It also includes missing values and requires slight cleaning. The dataset can be utilized to classify electrical theft as positive or negative. Additionally, it is valuable for exploring class balancing techniques since it is an unbalanced dataset. Moreover, it can be used for time series forecasting of electrical consumption. Three scenarios were used to evaluate the developed model's performance and answer the research questions.

Scenario One (exploring whether balancing methods affect the behavior of TPOT and H2O): This investigation aims to study the impact of data balancing on the performance of H2O and TPOT. Specifically, we want to identify which method of balancing (Random, SMOTE, or ADASYN) is more effective in improving the performance of TPOT and H2O. To achieve this, we will apply TPOT and H2O to both the original and balanced datasets using the three methods.

Scenario Two (Investigating the effect of data preprocessing): This investigation aims to determine whether additional preprocessing concerning outlier handling can improve the performance of TPOT and H2O beyond their built-in capabilities. To achieve this, we will apply TPOT and H2O to the preprocessed data (using Algorithm One) before and after data balancing (using Random, SMOTE, or ADASYN).

For performance evaluation, cross-validation with 10-fold is used in both AutoML platforms (TPOT and H2O), with 30% of the dataset hold-out for testing. The best platform for detecting electricity theft will be identified based on three performance measures:

1. *Accuracy*: is one of the metrics used in ML to measure the performance of a model (see Eq. (1)).

$$\text{Accuracy} = \text{Number of correct predictions/Total number of predictions} \dots \quad (1)$$

2. *Roc Curve*: The ROC curve plots a true positive (TP) rate against a false positive (FP) rate at different thresholds, showing a classification model's performance.
3. *Area Under the Curve (AUC):* is a metric that measures the effectiveness of a binary classifier in distinguishing between classes. The higher the AUC, the better the model's performance in distinguishing between the two classes.

The results of the two scenarios are shown in Tables 1 and 2, while Figs. 5, 6, 7, and 8 depict the ROC and AUC results.

Tables 1 and 2 illustrate that when working with an unbalanced dataset, regardless of the scenarios, TPOT and H2O perform well with or without preprocessing. However, H2O outperforms TPOT (0.89606 and 0.7728. compared to 0.8898 and 0.7487, respectively). On the other hand, after data balancing (regarding the balancing technique), TPOT outperforms H2O in most cases. The best theft detection accuracy (0.99182 and 0.9846) is reached when applying TPOT to the original dataset balanced with Random-sampling. At the same time, the TPOT performance is comparable when applied to data balanced with SMOT and ADASYN in both scenarios. On the other hand, When Algorithm One is used to handle outliers in unbalanced data, it negatively affects the performance of H2O and TPOT, reducing accuracy to 0.7728 and 0.7487, respectively. After balancing the data, their performance returned to its average. TPOT achieves the best accuracy when applied to data balanced with random sampling (0.9846), whereas H2O performs best on data balanced with ADASYN (0.8819).

Based on the experimental results, it was discovered that the most effective pipeline is usually achieved by using ensemble machine learning. Combining multiple machine learning models using bagging, boosting, or stacking techniques. Tables 3 and 4 display the best pipeline for Scenario 1 and 2, respectively, as determined by TPOT and H2O.

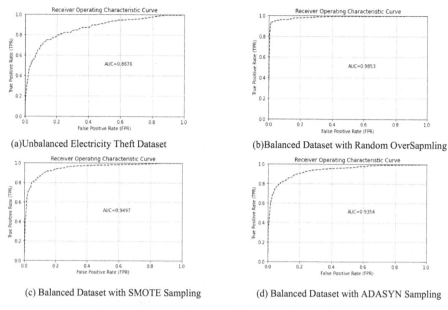

(a)Unbalanced Electricity Theft Dataset   (b)Balanced Dataset with Random OverSapmling

(c) Balanced Dataset with SMOTE Sampling   (d) Balanced Dataset with ADASYN Sampling

Fig. 5. ROC Curve: Apply H2O on the original dataset

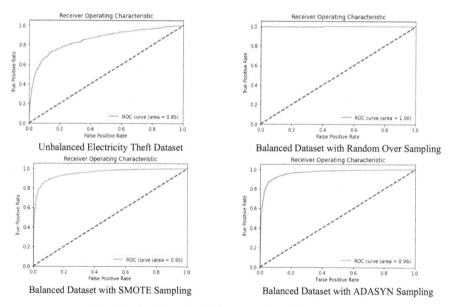

Unbalanced Electricity Theft Dataset   Balanced Dataset with Random Over Sampling

Balanced Dataset with SMOTE Sampling   Balanced Dataset with ADASYN Sampling

Fig. 6. ROC Curve: Apply TPOT on the original dataset.

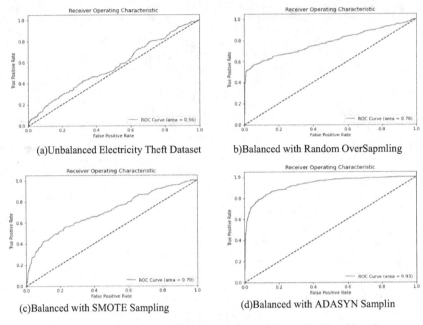

Fig. 7. ROC Curve: Apply H2O on preprocessed data with Algorithm One

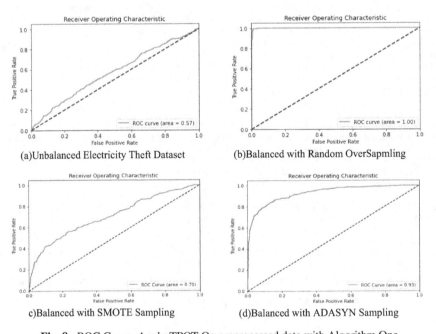

Fig. 8. ROC Curve: Apply TPOT On preprocessed data with Algorithm One

Table 1. The accuracy of applying AutoML on the original dataset

		Balanced Sampling Methods		
AutoML	Unbalanced Data	Random Oversampling	SMOTE	ADASYN
H2O	0.8960	0.9683	0.9034	0.8918
TPOT	0.8898	0.9918	0.8923	0.90618

Table 2. The accuracy of applying AutoML to the dataset after handling the outliers with algorithm one

		Balanced Sampling Methods		
AutoML	Unbalanced Data	Random Oversampling	SMOTE	ADASYN
H2O	0.7728	0.8237	0.7433	0.8819
TPOT	0.7487	0.9846	0.9250	0.9250

Table 3. The Best pipeline For Scenario One considering the four cases

Cases	TPOT: Best pipeline	H2O
Unbalanced Dataset	GradientBoostingClassifier with GaussianNB	Stacked Ensembles All produce the best results for all cases
Random Oversampling	RandomForestClassifier with RBFSampler	
SMOTE	RandomForestClassifier with CombineDFs	
ADYSAN	GradientBoostingClassifie with PCA	

Table 4. The Best pipeline For Scenario One considering the four cases.

Cases	TPOT: Best pipeline	H2O
Unbalanced Dataset	ExtraTreesClassifier	Stacked Ensembles All produce the best results for all cases
Random Oversampling	RandomForestClassifier With PCA	
SMOTE	MLPClassifier with RobustScaler	
ADYSAN	MLPClassifier with RobustScaler	

7 Discussion and Conclusion

The objective of this study is to use two AutoML platforms, specifically H2O and TPOT, to detect electricity theft based on data collected by smart meters. The study addresses the challenges of handling outliers and unbalanced classes in the ETD dataset. The experimental results indicate that TPOT outperforms H2O in terms of accuracy for electricity theft detection on the balanced dataset, while H2O performs better on the unbalanced dataset. This is because H2O can handle complex models and datasets, while TPOT performs better in combining and selecting the best model as optimizes ML pipelines using genetic programming. Sampling methods can address the class imbalance problem, but their effectiveness depends on the dataset's nature and method. Random sampling outperforms SMOTE and ADASYN, which have shown comparable accuracy as they both create synthetic samples. However, the generated samples may not accurately represent the classes if the original data includes noise or outliers, negatively affecting classification accuracy. The variation in model performance highlights the importance of thorough data preparation in predictive modeling, especially in complex tasks like fraud or theft detection. Lastly, handling outliers by removing the data row containing at least one outlier will reduce the dataset size. Therefore, the training process will be negatively affected, leading to a reduction in classification accuracy. However, after balancing the resulting dataset, the performance of TPOT and H2O significantly improved. It's worth noting that leveraging AutoML platforms enables experts to concentrate on data analysis instead of the classification phase. As part of our upcoming work, we intend to explore different techniques to handle outliers explicitly before feeding the data to the AutoML platform.

Disclosure of Interests. The authors have no relevant competing interests to declare regarding the content of this article.

References

1. Munawar, S., et al.: Electricity theft detection in smart grids using a hybrid BiGRU–BiLSTM model with feature engineering-based preprocessing. Sensors **22**, 7818 (2022). https://doi.org/10.3390/s22207818
2. Ul Haq, E., Pei, C., Zhang, R., Jianjun, H., Ahmad, F.: Electricity-theft detection for smart grid security using smart meter data: a deep-CNN based approach. Energy Reports **9**(Supplement 1), 634–643 (2023). https://doi.org/10.1016/j.egyr.2022.11.072
3. Messinis, G.M., Hatziargyriou, N.D.: Review of non-technical loss detection methods. Electr. Power Syst. Res. **158**, 250–266 (2018)
4. Glauner, P., et al.: Identifying irregular power usage by turning predictions into holographic spatial visualizations. In: Proceedings of the 2017 IEEE International Conference on Data Mining Workshops, pp. 258–265 (2017)
5. Zhu, L., Wen, W., Li, J., Zhang, C., Zhou, B., Shuai, Z.: Deep active learning-enabled cost-effective electricity theft detection in smart grids. IEEE Trans. Indust. Inf. **20**(1), 256–268 (2024). https://doi.org/10.1109/TII.2023.3249212
6. Johncy, G., Anisha Felise, A.: An efficient power theft detection using mean-shift clustering and deep learning in smart grid. IOP Conf. Ser.: Mater. Sci. Eng. **983**, 012003 (2020). https://doi.org/10.1088/1757-899X/983/1/012003

7. Lepolesa, L.J., Achari, S., Cheng, L.: Electricity theft detection in smart grids based on deep neural network. IEEE Access **10**, 39638–39655 (2022). https://doi.org/10.1109/ACCESS.2022.3166146

8. Xia, X., Xiao, Y., Liang, W., Cui, J.: Detection methods in smart meters for electricity thefts: a survey. Proc. IEEE **110**(2), 273–319 (2022). https://doi.org/10.1109/JPROC.2021.3139754

9. Ul Haq, E., Huang, J., Xu, H., Li, K., Ahmad, F.: A hybrid approach based on deep learning and support vector machine for the detection of electricity theft in power grids. Energy Rep. **7**(6), 349–356 (2021). https://doi.org/10.1016/j.egyr.2021.08.038

10. Badr, M.M., Ibrahem, M.I., Kholidy, H.A., Fouda, M.M., Ismail, M.: Review of the data-driven methods for electricity fraud detection in smart metering systems. Energies **16**, 2852 (2023). https://doi.org/10.3390/en16062852

11. Samawi, V.W., Yousif, S.A., Al-Saidi, N.M.G.: Intrusion detection system: an automatic machine learning algorithms using auto-WEKA. In: 2022 IEEE 13th Control and System Graduate Research Colloquium (ICSGRC), Shah Alam, Malaysia, pp. 42–46 (2022). https://doi.org/10.1109/ICSGRC55096.2022.9845166

12. Khan, I.U., Javeid, N., Taylor, C.J., Gamage, K.A.A., Ma, X.: A stacked machine and deep learning-based approach for analysing electricity theft in smart grids. IEEE Trans. Smart Grid **13**(2), 1633–1644 (2022). https://doi.org/10.1109/TSG.2021.3134018

13. Yousif, S.A., Samawi, V.W., Al-Saidi, N.M.G.: Automatic machine learning classification algorithms for stability detection of smart grid. In: 2022 IEEE 5th International Conference on Big Data and Artificial Intelligence (BDAI), Fuzhou, pp. 34–39 (2022). https://doi.org/10.1109/BDAI56143.2022.9862710

14. Punmiya, R., Choe, S.: Energy theft detection using gradient boosting theft detector with eature engineering-based preprocessing. IEEE Trans. Smart Grid **10**(2), 2326–2329 (2019). https://doi.org/10.1109/TSG.2019.2892595

15. Mumuni, A., Mumuni, F.: Automated data processing and feature engineering for deep learning and big data applications: a survey. J. Inf. Intell. (2024). https://doi.org/10.1016/j.jiixd.2024.01.002

16. Ali, A., Khan, L., Javaid, N., Aslam, M., Aldegheishem, A., Alrajeh, N.: Exploiting machine learning to tackle peculiar consumption of electricity in power grids: a step towards building green smart cities. IET Gen. Transmis. Distrib. **18**(3), 413–445 (2024)

17. García, V., Sánchez, J.S., Marqués, A.I., Florencia, R., Rivera, G.: Understanding the apparent superiority of over-sampling through an analysis of local information for class-imbalanced data. Exp. Syst. Appl. **158**, 113026 (2020). https://doi.org/10.1016/j.eswa.2019.113026

18. Moatz, N., Yousif, S.A.: COVID-19 detection via blood tests using an automated machine learning tool (auto-sklearn). Iraqi J. Sci. 6013–6024 (2023)

19. Feurer, M., Klein, A., Eggensperger, K., Springenberg, J.T., Blum, M., Hutter, F.: Auto-sklearn: efficient and robust automated machine learning. In: Hutter, F., Kotthoff, L., Vanschoren, J. (eds.) Automated Machine Learning. The Springer Series on Challenges in Machine Learning. Springer, Cham (2019). https://doi.org/10.1007/978-3-030-05318-5_6

20. What Is Automated Machine Learning (AutoML)? Run.ai (2023). https://www.run.ai/guides/automl

21. Matti, R., Yousif, S.A.: AutoKeras for fake news identification in Arabic: leveraging deep learning with an extensive dataset. Al-Nahrain J. Sci. **26**(3), 60–66 (2023)

22. H2O AutoML. Automatic Machine Learning, H2O.ai (2023). https://docs.h2o.ai/h2o/latest-stable/h2o-docs/welcome.html

23. Schmitt, M.: Automated machine learning: AI-driven decision making in business analytics. Intell. Syst. Appl. **18**, 200188 (2023). https://doi.org/10.1016/j.iswa.2023.200188

24. Sohn, A., Olson, R.S., Moore, J.H.: Toward the automated analysis of complex diseases in genome-wide association studies using genetic programming. In: Proceedings of the Genetic and Evolutionary Computation Conference (GECCO 2017), pp: 489–496. ACM Digital Library, Berlin (2017). https://doi.org/10.1145/3071178.3071212
25. Moatz, N., Yousif, S.A.: An automated machine learning model for diagnosing coronavirus disease 2019 (COVID-19) infection. IAES Int. J. Artif. Intell. **12**(3), 1360 (2023)
26. Le, T.T., Weixuan, F., Moore, J.H.: Scaling tree-based automated machine learning to biomedical big data with a feature set selector. Bioinformatics **36**(1), 250–256 (2020)
27. LeDell, E., Poirier, S.: H2O AutoML: scalable automatic machine learning. In: 7th ICML Workshop on Automated Machine Learning (AutoML) (2020). https://www.automl.org/wp-content/uploads/2020/07/AutoML_2020_paper_61.pdf
28. Gooday, A.: Automated Machine Learning: An Introduction to AutoML. Google, Amazon & H2O.ai AutoML (2020). https://medium.com/analytics-vidhya/an-introduction-to-automl-8356b6ceb091
29. Qu, Z., Li, H., Wang, Y., Zhang, J., Abu-Siada, A., Yao, Y.: Detection of electricity theft behavior based on improved synthetic minority oversampling technique and random forest classifier. Energies **13**, 2039 (2020). https://doi.org/10.3390/en13082039

On the Use of Predictive Deep Learning Approaches in the Frequency and Uniqueness-Based Representation of Sequential Browsing Events

Hakan Hakvar[1], Cansu Cavuldak[1], Oğulcan Söyler[1], Yusuf Subaşı[1],
Yıldız Karadayı[1], Ilgın Şafak[1(✉)], Nail Taşgetiren[2],
and Mehmet S. Aktaş[3]

[1] Fibabanka R&D Center, Istanbul, Türkiye
{hakan.hakvar,cansu.cavuldak,ogulcan.soyler,yusuf.subasi,
yildiz.karadayi,ilgin.safak}@fibabanka.com.tr
[2] Hepsiburada R&D Center, Istanbul, Türkiye
nail.tasgetiren@hepsiburada.com
[3] Yıldız Technical University, Computer Engineering Department, Istanbul, Türkiye
aktas@yildiz.edu.tr

Abstract. To gain a more comprehensive understanding of how users navigate, this study investigates the potential of predictive deep learning techniques. To properly describe user's browsing events such page visits, this paper first provides an overview of two embedding methodologies based on natural language processing and graphical representations. Secondly, this study presents two aggregation methods, one based on frequency and the other on uniqueness, that can be used to depict the possible sequence of events that may occur during a user's surfing session. With an emphasis on online banking, this research summarizes data representation approaches to model customers' digital footprints and learn about their banking product purchase intents. When we analyze a customer's digital footprint in the digital banking domain during the early stages of the application's lifecycle, we find that there are insufficient digital user footprints to model and comprehend users' behavior. Consequently, new approaches are needed to increase the quantity of session recordings kept by customers' digital footprints. We consider the possibility of increasing the quantity of digital footprints of bank customers by employing predictive deep learning techniques. To enhance the quantity of user navigational behaviors, we present a predictive technique based on long short-term memories. According to the findings, the newly generated customer sequences facilitate testing the suggested method, and accurately represent the initial client session data.

Keywords: Customer Embedding · Customer Behavior · Digital Banking · Graph Based Embedding · Representation Learning · Word Embedding

1 Introduction

In the ever-changing realm of digital banking, the analysis and thorough comprehension of users' digital footprints become crucial undertakings with significant consequences. A user's digital footprint is comprised of a wide range of interactions, including the complex series of events that occur when he or she uses banking software. These footprints, consisting of patterns of movement, records of transactions, and changes over time, are extremely significant sources of information. Accurate modeling and interpreting these digital footprints enable us to get valuable insights into user habits, preferences, and intentions. We can then create strong predictive models and customize tailored services to enhance overall efficiency, security, and user experience, as well as to determine future directions in digital banking, and to promote a mutually beneficial relationship between financial institutions and their customers.

As part of the complex network of online traces, we examine specifically the surfing behavior of consumers on digital banking websites. These patterns, which represent how users interact with the online banking interface, contain a significant amount of important information that is crucial for understanding user habits and preferences. Modeling and comprehending these navigational sequences are of utmost importance, since they directly mirror the intentions of users, the paths they take to complete transactions, and their levels of involvement. Valuable information can be extracted by analyzing browsing behaviors to improve user experience, optimize service offerings, and strengthen security measures. This helps determining the future of personalized, efficient, and secure digital financial transactions.

The depiction of users' browsing behaviors, especially in the context of consecutive occurrences, is a complex and diverse problem. A major challenge stems from the intrinsic intricacy and variety of users each with distinct and changing navigational preferences. The ever-changing characteristics of digital interactions exacerbate the difficulty, as users connect with financial services on various devices and in different settings. Furthermore, large amounts of consecutive occurrences produced during user sessions present difficulties in terms of scalability, computational requirements and efficient representation. The complexities arising from temporal dependencies and contextual nuances in event sequences introduce an additional level of intricacy, requiring novel approaches to capture and simulate the dynamic nature of user interactions. Developing strong representation approaches is crucial in order to accurately capture the varied and ever-changing sequential browsing behaviors of users in digital banking settings.

Various methodologies, including natural language processing (NLP)-based, and graph-based techniques, show potential in accurately capturing the complexities of user behaviors in digital banking. Even so, there is a significant lack of research that examines the effectiveness of various methods for recognizing and describing user behaviors in the literature. While each strategy has its own advantages, little research has been conducted to explore how well they perform in accurately interpreting the intricate details of successive user interactions. Hence it is difficult to gain a comprehensive understanding of their strengths and limitations, which hinders progress in optimizing and improving event modeling techniques.

Different methodologies may be used for combining representations of event sequences, especially in the context of user browsing sessions. This study uses frequency and uniqueness-based aggregation approaches to create embedding vectors that accurately capture the complex dynamics of user interactions. This enables the creation of a standardized and efficient embedding methodology specifically designed for event sequences that occur during user browsing sessions. We present strategies that combine different ways of representing events, creating a coherent and informative framework that can capture the complex patterns observed in the behaviors of digital banking users.

Most digital banking apps lack the user data necessary to model and understand customer behavior based on the examination of their digital footprints. This study provides a comprehensive analysis of how data representation is utilized to model users' digital behaviors and determine their level of interest in banking products. To this end, we update and extend our previous work [6], which is a machine learning (ML) pipeline that we implemented for predicting customer purchase behavior for a particular banking product, i.e., FX. We evaluate the prediction performance of the updated ML pipeline.

We also enhance frequency and inverse frequency-based weighting methodologies. In the frequency based weighting approach in [6], a frequency weight is calculated based on the weights of the pages visited by each customer. However, in this study, the optimized frequency-based weighting is achieved by normalizing the number of times a page appears in a session by the total number of pages in the session. Inverse frequency weighting reduces the importance given to the most visited pages by taking the inverse of the frequency of visits to the page for each customer. In contrast with the approach followed in [6], the inverse frequency-based weighting in this study involves taking the logarithm of the term for inverse frequency-based weighting in [6]. This logarithmic scaling is used to ensure that highly frequent web pages do not dominate the inverse page frequency score.

Furthermore, this study extends [6] by introducing a predictive deep-learning based methodology in enhancing banks' ability to gather more data on customer's digital footprints. We use a Long Short-Term Memory (LSTM) based predictive model to gain deeper insights into user behavior on the website. To facilitate testing of this method, we introduce an evaluation methodology that can measure how newly generated session sequences successfully represent the original user's browsing behavior. The ultimate goal is to create an optimized ML business process that can learn from the temporal sequences, recorded during user's browsing sessions, and that can predict user's next actions, such as purchasing actions. By conducting a methodical analysis, we aim to uncover the potential of these cutting-edge methodologies for collecting and analyzing the patterns of user interactions in the digital banking domain. This will ultimately enhance our understanding of user browsing behaviors.

Therefore, we address the following issues in this study:

1. How can we design a methodology that can synthetically generate customer session data using predictive deep learning techniques?

2. How can we understand whether the generated session sequences successfully represent the original user's browsing behavior?
3. How can we evaluate the effectiveness of the optimized version of the ML pipeline capability for predicting customers' financial behavior? This includes their likelihood of purchasing specific financial products or engaging in certain transactions.

The remainder of this article is organized as follows: Sect. 2 reviews the literature. Section 3 presents the methodology used in our research. Section 4 discusses the implementation of our framework and data set used in experimental work. Section 5 discusses the experimental work conducted. Conclusions and future work are presented in Sect. 6.

2   Fundamental Concepts and Literature Survey

To better predict customers' time-based activities in digital banking applications, compact and dynamic representations of customers are required. The use of embedding techniques provides a solution to this problem by digitizing customer transactions in banking applications and transforming their behavior into numerical representations that can be used to accurately predict their future behavior [2]. This section discusses the fundamental concepts of embedding mechanisms and reviews previous studies analyzing embedding approaches to representing user navigational behavior.

2.1   Embedding Approaches

Digital analytics and user behavior modeling require accurate representation of events in user browsing activity. One thus needs techniques to accurately represent customers' navigational footprints both over time and on a frequency basis. To this end, one may follow three separate embedding approaches, each based on core notions that support their effectiveness. Embeddings based on NLP utilize linguistic patterns to encode textual information, offering a nuanced comprehension of user interactions. Graph-based embeddings utilize network topologies to capture links and dependencies in browsing activity, providing a comprehensive understanding of user interaction. Autoencoder-based embeddings, in contrast, utilize neural network structures to acquire condensed representations of data, enabling effective storage and retrieval of significant insights. These three embedding approaches are crucial to investigate the core concepts necessary for the analysis and interpretation of user interactions in the digital environment. Embedding techniques have evolved over time into sub-fields such as word embedding and graph embedding.

NLP based Embedding Approaches: NLP-based embedding provides a vector representation of words in a corpus, which captures both semantic and syntactic information [33]. This technique enables similarity analysis, speech labeling, clustering, and syntactic parsing in NLP applications [4]. Word embedding has facilitated numerous analyses and predictions in supervised, semi-supervised, and unsupervised ML algorithms by converting words to vectors [33]. The Word2Vec model consists of two approaches: Continuous Bag of Words (CBoW) and Skip-gram [34]. CBoW predicts a specific word by analyzing its neighboring words. Words are converted into one-hot encoded vectors and fed into a neural network, with the predicted word being output as the result. Skip-gram, on the other hand, predicts neighboring words around a specific word, which is then converted into a one-hot encoded vector and used as input to a neural network, with the neighboring words predicted as output [34]-[10].

Graph-Based Embedding Approaches: As opposed to word embedding, graph embedding uses graphs to represent nodes as vectors in a low-dimensional space. The graph-based embedding is a powerful technique to solve problems related to social networks, community detection, node classification [35] and clustering [30]. This embedding approach uses computationally intensive eigenvalue decomposition techniques [27]. The graph embedding approach is a powerful technique that solves problems related to social networks and community detection. This approach helps to create vectorized features for graph attributes, such as nodes, edges, and subgraphs [14]. Some common graph embedding methods are Node2vec [5], DeepWalk [20], Struc2vec [26], Graph Convolutional Networks (GCNs) [11], GraphSAGE [7], LINE [29], and TransE [1]. The Node2vec algorithm generates random walks on a graph and uses a skip-gram model to learn node embeddings. In the same way, DeepWalk generates random walks on a graph, but instead of a skip-gram model, it uses a neural network for learning node embeddings. Struc2Vec is a powerful method for graph embedding that is particularly effective at capturing the structural information of a graph. GNCs use convolutional neural networks (CNNs) to learn node embeddings by aggregating the features of neighboring nodes. GraphSAGE extends the GCN idea by using a differentiable aggregator function to combine neighboring nodes' features. LINE preserves local and global network structures by optimizing nodes' first- and second-order proximity, while TransE is a method for embedding directed graphs that utilizes a translation-based scoring function to learn embeddings.

Among these graph embedding methods, we are particularly interested in DeepWalk, a popular and effective graph embedding technique. This technique maintains higher-order proximity by maximizing the likelihood of monitoring the last node and subsequent nodes in each random walk [28]. It works in two stages: In the first stage, random walks are generated in the graph to optimize embedded representations of nodes by randomly wandering near neighbors [13]. In the second stage, the Word2Vec Skip-gram algorithm is applied to every created walk to vectorize the nodes. When DeepWalk is applied to successful word embedding, the nodes are set so that the occurrence frequencies of pairs in short random walks are preserved [27]. There are different implementations of DeepWalk graph representations, such as Hierarchical Softmax, which uses the Huffman binary tree as an alternative representation of the vocabulary [9].

DeepWalk has been used successfully in many applications, such as community detection, link prediction, and recommendation systems [27,31].

Autoencoder-Based Embedding Approaches: Autoencoder-based embeddings are notable in the field of analysis, data representation and feature learning since they can effectively capture nuanced patterns and inherent structures in large datasets. Autoencoders are unsupervised learning methods that utilize neural network architecture to encode input data into a compact representation known as an embedding. The encoder network facilitates the encoding process, which prioritizes the extraction of important elements while eliminating unnecessary information. The decoder network can reconstruct the input data from its compressed representation. Autoencoders intrinsically acquire the ability to accurately reproduce the original input, enabling them to effectively capture the fundamental characteristics of the data. This makes autoencoders a versatile tool that may be used for various tasks such as reducing dimensionality, detecting anomalies, and extracting features.

2.2 Other Embedding Methods

Other embedding methodologies have been proposed and surveyed in the literature [31]. Pattern-based embedding approaches [16,17] have been widely used to analyze customers' navigational behavior. A number of studies have employed word-based embedding techniques [3,15,18,32] to understand customer behavior and generate graphical customer interface testing scripts. There are, however, few comparative analyses of embedding methods in digital footprint studies. The embedding methods that take time-based datasets into account are insufficient.

3 Methodology

In this section, we discuss the contributions of this study in two fold. Firstly, we give an overview of a ML process that can analyze and model customer's browsing behavior data. Secondly, we introduce a methodology that synthetically generates customer user sequences in order to improve the prediction capability of the ML process.

3.1 An Overview of the ML Business Process

The customer embedding framework proposed in this study involves six stages, including data pre-processing, embedding, post-processing, training and prediction.

1. **Pre-processing stage:** Raw data, that refers to customers' digital footprints obtained from mobile application platforms, is cleaned, and irrelevant features are removed. Features selected are Customer Number, Page Sequence, Page Durations, Session Start Date, FX Event Flag (see Table 1 for a description of the features). Pages that customers visit by default, such as login and logout, and pages that are rarely visited, are eliminated. The time duration spent by a customer on each page is calculated.

Table 1. Browsing data on mobile banking application pages of bank customers

Feature	Explanation
Customer Number	Unique customer number
Page Sequence	Chronologically ordered page numbers the customer browsed in the mobile app during the session
Page Durations	How long has the customer been on a specific page (in seconds)
Session Start Date	The date and time the customer created the session via logging into the mobile app
FX Event Flag	Whether the customer executes the FX transaction during the session (1 = True, 0 = False)

2. **Embedding stage:** A suitable embedding technique is applied to the preprocessed data to represent customer behavior in a high-dimensional vector
   space. The word embedding method employed in this study is Word2Vec
   (CBoW). An extension to the DeepWalk algorithm is used as a graph embedding method to capture mobile banking customers' tendencies towards specific
   financial products. The proposed extension incorporates a new metric, namely
   the frequency with which customers visit the pages of a mobile banking application. To achieve this, we introduce frequency-based weighting approach at
   the post-processing stage.

3. **Post-processing stage:** The embeddings are further processed to eliminate noise and enhance embedding quality. This involves generating customer
   embedding vectors using visit frequency-based weighting techniques. Event
   frequency-based weighting: This approach, that involves calculating an event
   frequency value for each page based on the frequency of customer C visits,
   aims to represent customers' digital footprints. The event frequency weighted
   vector for a customer is obtained using the following equation:
   Event frequency-based weighting: Involves calculating an event frequency value for each page based on the frequency of customer visits. The
   event frequency weighted vector for a customer is obtained using the following
   equation:

$$NF_C = \frac{VF_C}{\sum_{i=1}^{K} f_C(i)}. \tag{1}$$

Here, NF_C is the matrix consisting of customer C's normalized event frequency values of all sessions, VF_C is customer C's event frequency matrix of
all sessions, K is the total number of sessions, and $f_C(i)$ is the total frequency
of all pages visited by customer C in session i. The embedded session vectors
are multiplied by this matrix to obtain the normalized event frequency based
weighted session vectors. In this approach, the most frequently visited pages
are given greater importance.

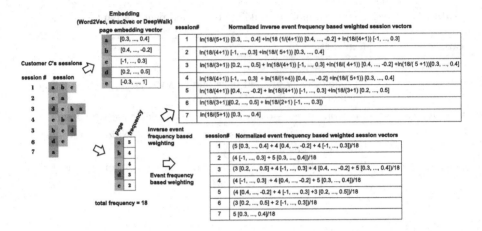

Fig. 1. An example of frequency and inverse frequency-based weighting mechanism

Let us consider the example with seven sessions as illustrated in Fig. 1. According to the session data, the customer visits five pages, namely a, b, c, d and e. The first session includes pages a, b and c, the second session includes pages c and a, and so on. The frequency of visits to each page is calculated, and the normalized event frequency-based weighting matrix is obtained using Eq. 1. Each page is represented with an embedding vector by using one of the embedding methods, Word2Vec or Deepwalk. Lastly, the embedding vectors are multiplied by the normalized frequency based weighting vector to obtain the normalized event frequency based weighted session matrix. In this example, the total page visit frequency count of all sessions is 18, which is used as the normalization value. Note that the same customer session data and embedding vectors are used in frequency, inverse frequency and event time duration based weighting methods.

Inverse event frequency-based weighting: In this weighting approach, more frequently visited pages are given less weight. This is obtained by taking the inverse and then the natural logarithm of Eq. 1, and adding 1 to the denominator in order to scale and prevent division by zero. The inverse frequency weighted matrix for a customer is thus given by:

$$INF_C = \ln\left(\frac{\sum_{i=1}^{K} f_C(i)}{VF_C + 1}\right). \tag{2}$$

Here, INF_C is the matrix consisting of the inverse of the frequency values of pages visited by customer C in all sessions. The embedded session vectors are multiplied by this matrix to obtain the normalized inverse event frequency based weighted session vectors. Overall, our proposed approach aims to represent customers' digital footprints. It also enables more accurate predictions of their behavior on mobile banking applications. This methodology answers the first research question mentioned in the Introduction section.

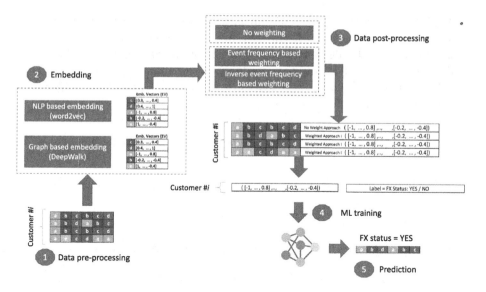

Fig. 2. An example flow using the customer embedding framework

An example flow using the customer embedding framework is illustrated in Fig. 2. In the example shown in Fig. 1, each page's visit frequency is obtained using the session data, and each page is represented with an embedding vector. The embedding vectors are multiplied by the normalized inverse frequency matrix obtained by using Eq. 2 to determine the normalized inverse frequency-based session vectors. After generating session embedding vectors using the DeepWalk algorithm and applying frequency-based weighting techniques, customer-based vectors are calculated to represent each customer with an embedding vector. The customer embedding vectors are generated by taking the arithmetic mean of the session embedding vectors. This represents the customer's overall navigational behavior. The average of all session embedding vectors for each customer results in a n dimensional customer-based vector, where the so-called framework parameter n shows the embedding vector's dimension. The customer-based vectors thus obtained are used as input for clustering algorithms to segment customers based on their navigational behavior.

4. **Training phase:** During this stage, the labeled embedding datasets are partitioned into a training dataset (80%) and a test dataset (20%). ML algorithms are trained on the training dataset to create ML models using customer embedding vectors to predict customer behavior. These models are then validated using the test dataset.

The performance of the framework was evaluated by using the ML algorithm called as Isolation Forest that detects anomalies by assuming that instances that deviate from the central data cluster are abnormal. It uses random sampling to create binary trees and aggregates them to build a model for a given

- dataset. This study utilized an unbalanced dataset due to a small number of customers conducting FX transactions. As a result, Isolation Forest was selected as the ML algorithm for testing the proposed framework [12].

5. **Prediction stage:** Resulting embeddings are utilized to predict customer behavior and preferences. The generated ML model is employed to forecast new users' navigational behavior.

3.2   A Novel Methodology for Generating User Sequences

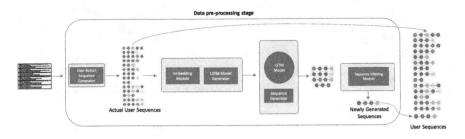

Fig. 3. Predictive Deep Learning Based Methodology for Generating User Sequences

When working with small labeled datasets in supervised ML, one of the techniques used is data augmentation. This involves generating new training samples from existing ones by applying various transformations. A predictive deep learning approach is used in this study to create hidden navigational behaviors of customers. The proposed approach is illustrated in Fig. 3. The details of the proposed data augmentation methodology is given below:

1. **User Action Sequence Generator:** The customer's navigational behaviors are reflected by user sequences. These sequences are then transformed by embedding so that they can be applied as input for an LSTM algorithm. LSTM-based predictive model is used for learning certain patterns from data, so that when presented with some prompt, it can produce an output in the same way as the pattern that was learned. Next, this model is used to generate new sequences. These newly generated sequences are checked against original user sequences. A final output is generated by filtering out only those sequences that differ from the actual user actions and that are feasible considering the user interfaces of digital banking mobile applications. As a result, the original and newly generated user action sequences are obtained.

2. **Embedding Module:** This module is responsible for converting the web page labels to integers. Each unique web page label is converted a distinct integer. With this approach, user sequences are represented as sequence of integers.

3. **Predictive Deep Learning Model Generator:** LSTM [8] is a type of recurrent neural network that is widely used in deep learning. It is particularly effective at capturing long-term dependencies, making it a suitable tool for predicting sequences.
4. **Sequence Generator:** This module is responsible for generating new sequences based on the trained LSTM model.
5. **Sequence Filtering Module:** This module is responsible for eliminating sequences that match to one of the actual sequences. This way, new and distinct sequences are generated.

4 Proposed Framework Implementation

The proposed framework was implemented using Python-3 (version 3.6.13) [24]. To generate the embedding vectors, we utilized the Gensim (version 4.2.0) library, which provides implementations of Word2Vec algorithms such as CBoW and Skip-gram [21]. For converting sessions to graphs, we used the NetworkX (version 2.5.1) library [22]. Pandas (version 1.1.5) and Numpy (version 1.19.5) libraries were utilized for data processing operations [23,25]. We employed the scikit-learn (version 0.24.2) library for implementing the Isolation Forest model and metrics. To evaluate the framework's functionality, we conducted tests using clickstream data from Fibabanka's mobile banking application. The dataset consists of 2,971,999 rows with five attributes and 36,160 distinct customers. The data captures online activities of mobile banking customers, including page views and actions such as FX transactions, loan applications, and account openings.

Figure 4 depicts the histogram of the session lengths per customer in the dataset. It is observed that the majority of customers have sessions with less than 200 events.

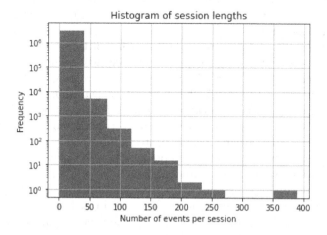

Fig. 4. Histogram of the number of events per session per customer

Table 2. FX rate in dataset

FX Status	Train	Test
FX=1	4.39	1.07
FX=0	24.53	6.15
FX=1 Rate	15.2%	14.9%

Table 2 shows the rate at which customers perform FX transactions in sessions in the dataset. Here, FX=1 means that an FX transaction occurs, and FX=0 implies that no FX transaction occurred in a customer session. 'FX=1 Rate' is the percentage of FX transactions in the test or train dataset.

Each session in the clickstream data includes the unique customer number, pages visited during the session, time spent on each page, date and time of the session, and whether the customer executed the target event, which in this case, is an FX transaction.

The study focused on customers who had 50 or more sessions during 76 d between April 1, 2022, and June 15, 2022. By analyzing the dataset, we predicted customer behavior over an extended period and comprehensively analyzed customer intent and behavior.

The clickstream data captured for each session includes two significant features with equal lengths: "Page Sequence" and "Page Durations". The "Page Sequence" shows the list of pages a customer navigated throughout a session in the order they were visited. For example, if a customer visited the Login page, Main Page, Loan Application, Calculate Loan, Main Page, Money Transfer, and Logout page in that order, the "Page Sequence" feature would be represented as [Login, Main Page, Loan Application, Calculate Loan, Main Page, Money Transfer, Logout]. The customer's overall navigational behavior can be better described by using the "Page Sequence" data to calculate the frequency of each page sequence visited by each customer. Frequency-based weighting enhances the framework's accuracy.

The "Page Durations" feature represents a list of time spent on each page visited by the customer during the session, in seconds. For instance, the time spent on each page of the "Page Sequence" above is represented by the "Page Durations" [0.5, 0.7, 1.1, 1.2, 0.5, 2.4, 0.2]. "Page Durations" data is used to compute customer-based time duration weighting for the embedding vectors in order to improve the framework's accuracy in predicting customers' intent, as the duration spent on a specific page indicates interest.

The proposed framework's data pre-processing stage involves several steps. To begin with, we remove some pages, such as login and logout pages, as well as pages rarely visited by customers, from the clickstream dataset pages. After eliminating these pages, the duration of each page in each session is calculated. If there are any missing page duration values, the average page duration of all sessions for the customer is calculated to replace the null values.

In the embedding stage of the framework, we employed the embedding methodologies, Word2Vec CBoW and DeepWalk, to generate session-based representations in order to capture customer behavior and intent effectively. To further enhance the generated embedding vectors, we utilized novel frequency-based weighting techniques in the post-processing stage.

We analyzed data from previous mobile sessions to predict whether customers would buy or sell FX in their next mobile session. To accomplish this, we used the "FX Event Flag" attribute as the target label for our dataset. We experimented with different empirically-selected embedding vector sizes of 20, 50, and 100. Due to the relatively small size of our training dataset, which contains only 36K distinct entities, we selected smaller vector sizes.

5 Experimental Work

We conducted two different types of experiments in order to determine how practical the study's frameworks were. The first examines how well synthetic user sequences are generated, and the second examines how well optimized ML pipelines are implemented. The second research question posed in the Introduction is addressed by the first experimental study, and the third research question by the second.

First Experimental Study employed an Autoencoder LSTM architecture to generate novel yet plausible synthetic sessions. Aiming to ensure the novelty of the generated sessions, we eliminated those that were exact duplicates of existing sessions and selected only the technically feasible sessions from the remainder. We then measured the similarity between the generated sessions and the existing ones using the Bilingual Evaluation Understudy (BLEU) score metric [19]. A BLEU score is a value between zero and one that determines how similar the machine-translated text is to a collection of high-quality reference translations. A BLEU score close to unity indicates a high degree of similarity between the machine-generated text and the reference translation. The newly generated session set and the eliminated session set were compared with the existing sessions. The sessions with the highest BLEU scores were identified as the most suitable for adding new sessions (see Table 3).

As for the second Experimental Study, we investigated the prediction performance of the optimized/updated ML pipeline and compared the results against our previous study. For our experiments, we utilized two base embedding methodologies, namely Word2Vec and DeepWalk. These methodologies are applied directly to customers' navigational behavior data to create benchmark datasets. These datasets are then used in the training and prediction stages without transformations and weighting methods introduced in our proposed framework. The models are trained on unbalanced datasets in order to predict customers who execute FX transactions. The results of experiments conducted to evaluate the performance of the proposed optimized ML pipeline in predicting customers who execute FX transactions are presented in Table 4 for an embedding vector size of 100 and prediction using the Isolation Forest ML algorithm.

Table 3. BLEU Score of generated sequence and most similar sequence

No.	Generated Hidden Sequence	Most Similar Sequence	BLEU Score
1	PRODUCTS ACCOUNT DETAIL, ALL DOCUMENTS, PRODUCTS ACCOUNT ACTIVITIES, TRANSACTIONS, FIBA FX	PRODUCTS ACCOUNTS, PRODUCTS ACCOUNT DETAIL, PRODUCTS ACCOUNT ACTIVITIES, HOME PAGE, FIBA FX	0,75984
2	LOGIN, HOME PAGE, PPPPSCREENTSX, PPPPSCREENTSX, TRANSFER ORDER DETAIL	LOGIN, HOME PAGE, PRODUCTS ACCOUNTS, TRANSACTIONS, FIBA FX	0,70711
3	HOME PAGE, NOTIFICATIONS, HOME PAGE, TRANSACTIONS, FIBA FX	HOME PAGE, NOTIFICATIONS, PRODUCTS ACCOUNTS, TRANSACTIONS, FIBA FX	0,99871

The results indicate that the optimized ML pipeline (Isolation Forest pipeline) prediction performance is improved as in the followings: a) for frequency based weighting mechanism and word2vec embedding approach, F1 Score is improved approximately by 20%; b) for inverse frequency based weighting mechanism and word2vec embedding approach, F1 score is improved approximately by 31%; c) for frequency based weighting mechanism and deepWalk embedding approach, F1 Score is improved approximately by 15%; d) for inverse frequency based weighting mechanism and word2vec embedding approach, F1 score is improved approximately by 6%;

Table 4 show the F1 score, Precision, Recall and Accuracy for different weighting options of the optimized Isolation Forest ML pipeline. The F1 score provides a balanced view of Precision and Recall, making it an effective means of evaluating the performance of models in imbalanced datasets. This is valid in this case since positive cases are rare. The proposed framework's prediction outputs are compared with base models' plain embeddings, i.e., Word2Vec and DeepWalk embeddings. Hence, NONE stands for no weighting, FREQ shows frequency-based weighting and FREQ-1 denotes inverse frequency-based weighting. Table 4 shows that, for Word2Vec embedding, both the frequency based weighting and inverse frequency based weighting methods outperform the baseline performance where no weighting, NONE. Inverse event frequency-based weighting displays the highest performance. For DeepWalk embedding, the frequency based weighting method is seen to have a higher performance than the baseline model's performance, NONE. This experimental study answers research question 3 listed in the Introduction.

Table 4. Experimental study results for the optimized Isolation Forest ML Pipeline

	Word2Vec				DeepWalk			
	Accuracy	Precision	Recall	F1	Accuracy	Precision	Recall	F1
NONE	74,01%	14,86%	15,16%	15,01%	74,09%	14,90%	15,68%	15,28%
FREQ	74,40%	15,12%	14,98%	15,05%	74,60%	15,66%	16,05%	15,85%
FREQ-1	74,20%	15,43%	15,71%	15,57%	74,17%	13,76%	13,91%	13,84%

As a result, Table 4 shows that the proposed framework improves the performance of base embedding models in predicting customers who execute FX transactions. The best performance is achieved with inverse frequency-based weighting. The proposed framework generally outperforms the base embedding models in terms of F1 score for predicting customers who execute FX transactions. As demonstrated by the experimental results, the proposed framework is more effective at predicting FX transactions than the baseline embedding models. Also note that the F1 scores of the proposed framework outperforms the base models in most cases. This indicates that the weighting techniques used in the framework effectively improve the base models' performance. It is observed that the performance of the models depends on the size of the vector, and larger vector sizes generally result in better results. However, it is worth considering the computational complexity of larger vector sizes and balancing this against potential performance improvements. Overall, these results suggest that the proposed framework can effectively improve the performance of embedding models in predicting customer behavior on online platforms. These results provide an answer to research questions listed in the Introduction section.

Overall, the study provides insights into the application of embedding models for predicting customer behavior in the FX domain. It proposes a novel framework to improve prediction accuracy. Further experimentation may be needed to identify the optimal approach for various types of data. Overall, the results demonstrate the potential of the proposed framework to improve customer behavior prediction tasks. Future research may investigate how the proposed framework performs in other financial domains and the further evaluation of its performance using larger datasets.

6   Conclusions and Future Work

This study introduces a novel customer embedding framework that leverages temporal and repetitive dynamics of navigational footprints generated in mobile banking applications. The framework utilizes cutting-edge embedding algorithms such as Word2Vec and DeepWalk, incorporating the overall customer tendency based on visit frequency to enhance the generated embedding representations. Using embedding vectors to predict customers' preferences for a financial product, the effectiveness of the proposed framework was evaluated. The results indicated that the proposed framework outperformed the baseline models in almost all test scenarios, and demonstrated its ability to capture customers' intent more accurately. It is important to note that the choice of embedding algorithm may vary depending on the dataset and the specific problem at hand. Further experimentation may be necessary to identify the optimal approach for different types of data. This study contributes to the development of a framework for capturing customer intent using digital financial footprints in mobile banking applications. The potential applications of this framework are not limited to the banking industry, but can also be applied in other fields where customer behavior analysis plays a key role, including e-commerce, healthcare, and social media. The framework proposed provides an avenue for organizations to better understand their customers and tailor their services accordingly. Aside from the findings presented in this study, the authors intend to further improve their pro- posed framework by incorporating multi-modal data and improving its ability to predict customer intention towards a wide range of products. In addition, they intend to incorporate RNN-based algorithms into the framework to predict when customers will use specific products in the near future.

Acknowledgements. The authors of this study would like to express their gratitude to Fibabanka for their support in facilitating this research. In addition, one of the authors, Nail Tasgetiren, would like to thank Hepsiburada for providing the flexible working atmosphere to support this study.

References

1. Bordes, A., et al.: Translating Embeddings For Modeling Multi-relational Data. In: Advances in Neural Information Processing Systems. Burges, C.J. et al. (eds.), vol. 26. Curran Associates, Inc. (2013)
2. Chitsazan, N., et al.: Dynamic customer embeddings for financial service applications (2021). arXiv: 2106.11880
3. Erdem, I., et al.: Test script generation based on hidden markov models learning from user browsing behaviors. In: 2021 IEEE International Conference on Big Data (Big Data), pp. 2998–3005 (2021)
4. Ghannay, S., et al.: Word Embedding Evaluation and Combination. In: Proceedings of the Tenth International Conference on Language Resources and Evaluation (LREC 2016). Calzolari, N.: (eds.) et al. Portorož, Slovenia: European Language Resources Association (ELRA), May 2016, pp. 300–305 (2016)
5. Grover, A., Leskovec, J.: Node2vec: scalable feature learning for networks. In: Proceedings of the 22nd ACM SIGKDD International Conference on Knowledge Discovery and Data Mining. KDD 2016. San Francisco, California, USA: Association for Computing Machinery, pp. 855–864 (2016). ISBN: 9781450342322
6. Hakvar, H., et al.: Time-sensitive embedding for understanding customer navigational behavior in mobile banking. In: Computational Intelligence, Data Analytics and Applications. García Márquez, F.P. et al. (eds.), pp. 257–270 Springer International Publishing, Cham (2023). ISBN: 978-3-031-27099-4, https://doi.org/10.1007/978-3-031-27099-4_20
7. Hamilton, W.L., Ying, R., Leskovec, J.: Inductive representation learning on large graphs (2018). arXiv: 1706.02216
8. Hochreiter, S., Schmidhuber, J.: Long Short-Term Memory. In: Neural Computation 9.8, pp. 1735–1780 (Nov. 1997). ISSN: 0899-7667
9. Hou, M., et al.: Network embedding: taxonomies, frameworks and applications. Comput. Sci. Rev. **38**, 100296 (2020). ISSN: 1574-0137
10. Jang, B., Kim, I., Kim, J.W.: Word2vec convolutional neural networks for classification of news articles and tweets. PLOS ONE **14**(8) 1–20 (2019)
11. Thomas N. Kipf and Max Welling. "Semi-Supervised Classification with Graph Convolutional Networks". In: 5th International Conference on Learning Representations, ICLR 2017, Toulon, France, April 24-26, 2017, Conference Track Proceedings. OpenReview.net, 2017

12. Ajay Kulkarni, Deri Chong, and Feras A. Batarseh. "5 - Foundations of data imbalance and solutions for a data democracy". In: Data Democracy. Ed. by Feras A. Batarseh and Ruixin Yang. Academic Press, 2020, pp. 83- 106. ISBN: 978-0-12-818366-3
13. Juzheng Li, Jun Zhu, and Bo Zhang. "Discriminative Deep Random Walk for Network Classification". In: Annual Meeting of the Association for Computational Linguistics. 2016
14. Makarov, I., et al.: Survey on graph embeddings and their applications to machine learning problems on graphs. PeerJ Comput. Sci. **7**, e357 (2021). ISSN: 2376-5992
15. Oguz, R.F., Erdi Oz, M., Olmezogullari, E., Aktas, M.S.: Extracting information from large scale graph data: case study on automated UI testing. In: Chaves, R., et al. Par 2021: Parallel Processing Workshops, vol. 13098. Springer, Cham (2022). https://doi.org/10.1007/978-3-031-06156-1_29
16. Olmezogullari, E., Aktas, M.S.: Pattern2Vec: representation of clickstream data sequences for learning user navigational behavior. Concurrency Comput. Pract. Experience **34**(9), e6546 (2022)
17. Olmezogullari, E., Aktas, M.S.: Representation of click-stream data sequences for learning user navigational behavior by using embeddings. In: 2020 IEEE International Conference on Big Data (Big Data), pp. 3173–3179 (2020)
18. Oz, M., et al.: On the use of generative deep learning approaches for generating hidden test scripts. Int. J. Software Eng. Knowl. Eng. **31**, 1447–1468 (2021)
19. Papineni, K., et al.: BLEU: a method for automatic evaluation of machine translation. In: Proceedings of the 40th Annual Meeting on Association for Computational Linguistics. ACL 2002. Philadelphia, Pennsylvania: Association for Computational Linguistics, pp. 311–318 (2002)
20. Perozzi, B., Al-Rfou, R., Skiena, S.: DeepWalk: online learning of social representations. In: Proceedings of the 20th ACM SIGKDD International Conference on Knowledge Discovery and Data Mining. KDD 2014. Association for Computing Machinery, pp. 701–710 (2014)
21. Python Gensim library offical website. http://pypi.org. Accessed 22 Nov 2023
22. Python Networkx library offical website. http://networkx.org. Accessed 22 Nov 2023
23. Python Numpy library offical website. http://numpy.org. Accessed 22 Nov 2023
24. Python offical website. http://www.python.org. Accessed 22 Nov 2023
25. Python Pandas library offical website. http://pandas.pydata.org. Accessed 22 Nov 2023
26. Ribeiro, L.F.R., Saverese, P.H.P., Figueiredo, D.R.: struc2vec: learning node representations from structural identity. In: Proceedings of the 23rd ACM SIGKDD International Conference on Knowledge Discovery and Data Mining. KDD 2017. Halifax, NS, Canada: Association for Computing Machinery, pp. 385–394 (2017). ISBN: 9781450348874
27. Rossi, R.A., Zhou, R., Ahmed, N.K.: Deep inductive graph representation learning. IEEE Trans. Knowl. Data Eng. **32**(3), 438–452 (2020)
28. Rizi, F.S., Granitzer, M.: Properties of vector embeddings in social networks. Algorithms **10**(4) (2017). ISSN: 1999-4893
29. Tang, J., et al.: LINE: large-scale information network embedding. In: Proceedings of the 24th International Conference on World Wide Web. WWW 2015. Florence, Italy: International World Wide Web Conferences Steering Committee, pp. 1067–1077 (2015). ISBN: 9781450334693

30. Tasgetiren, N., Şafak, I., Aktas.,M.S.: On the use of graph embedding techniques for clustering user browsing navigational behaviours. In: International Journal of Web and Grid Services, Special Issue for ICCSA 2023 (2024)
31. Taşgetiren, N., Aktas, M.S.: Mining web user behavior: a systematic mapping study. In: Computational Science and Its Applications - ICCSA 2022 Workshops. In: Gervasi, O., Murgante, B., Misra, S., Rocha, A.M.A.C., Garau, C. (eds), pp. 667–683. Springer International Publishing, Cham (2022). ISBN: 978-3-031-10536-4, https://doi.org/10.1007/978-3-031-10536-4_44
32. Uygun, Y., et al.: On the large-scale graph data processing for user interface testing in big data science projects. In: 2020 IEEE International Conference on Big Data (Big Data), pp. 2049–2056 (2020)
33. Wang, B., et al.: Evaluating word embedding models: methods and experimental results. APSIPA Trans. Signal Inform. Process. **8**, e19 (2019)
34. Wu, L., et al.: Word mover's embedding: from word2vec to document embedding. In: Proceedings of the 2018 Conference on Empirical Methods in Natural Language Processing. Riloff, E. (ed.) et al. Brussels, Belgium: Association for Computational Linguistics, Oct. 2018, pp. 4524–4534 (2018)
35. Zuckerman, M., Last, M.: Using graphs for word embedding with enhanced semantic relations. In: Proceedings of the Thirteenth Workshop on Graph-Based Methods for Natural Language Processing (Text- Graphs-13). Ustalov, D. (ed.) et al. Hong Kong: Association for Computational Linguistics, Nov. 2019, pp. 32-41 (2019)

MPCD: An Algorithm for Discovering Multilevel Prevalent Co-location Patterns from Heterogeneous Distribution of Spatial Datasets

Vanha Tran$^{(\boxtimes)}$ ⓘ, Thiloan Bui, and Hoangan Le

FPT University, Hanoi 155514, Vietnam
{hatv14,loanbt7}@fe.edu.vn, anlhhe163613@fpt.edu.vn

Abstract. Discovering spatial prevalent co-location patterns (SPCPs) is an important area of research in spatial data analysis, aiming to identify hidden spatial relationships between objects (spatial instances), e.g., their simultaneous occurrences in space. The significance of discovering SPCPs is evident in various fields such as medicine, biology, urban planning, and many others. However, many challenges are currently faced in the process of discovering SPCPs, including dealing with heterogeneous distribution spatial datasets and the computational cost required for multilevel SPCP discovery, which often encounters inefficient time complexity. To address these challenges, in this paper, we propose a new method applied density-wise clustering. After splitting the dataset into clusters based on both density levels and distribution, which we called 'density-wise clusters', we adopt the Bron-Kerbosch algorithm and utilize a MC-hash structure to enhance the SPCP mining process. Our method is examined and compared with other two efficient methods on both simulated and real-world datasets. The results show that our proposed method not only effectively addresses the mentioned difficulties but also yields noteworthy results in discovering SPCPs in spatial data.

Keywords: Multilevel co-location patterns · Heterogeneous distribution · Density-wise clusters · MC-hash structure

1 Introduction

With the relentless advancement of technology, a vast amount of spatial data is collected daily. Among these, spatial prevalent co-location pattern (SPCP) mining is considered a crucial component since it can expose. SPCPs demonstrate sets of objects co-occurring in space with significant frequency [8]. Therefore, exploring and studying SPCPs have the potential to provide insights for the development and application in various fields such as urban planning [18], public health [11], business [20], transportation [21], agricultural science [13], etc.

However, determining SPCPs faces many challenges due to the uneven distribution of real-world data. Figure 1 is an example of data points in space with

O. Gervasi et al. (Eds.): ICCSA 2024, LNCS 14814, pp. 101–119, 2024.
https://doi.org/10.1007/978-3-031-64608-9_7

different distributions and density variations. Traditional SPCP mining methods often rely on a single threshold to measure the association (e.g., neighbor relationship) between objects (spatial instances) in space. This can lead to inaccuracies in output, e.g., if the threshold is too low, sparse events may be easily underestimated, or conversely, if the threshold is set too high, less significant events may be wrongly evaluated. Other existing methods consider the relationships between instances by partitioning data into regions or clusters with different densities [15,19]. While this strategy demonstrates high efficiency with relatively accurate results, computational costs increase significantly, slowing down the mining process due to the need to leverage abundant data volumes at the current time.

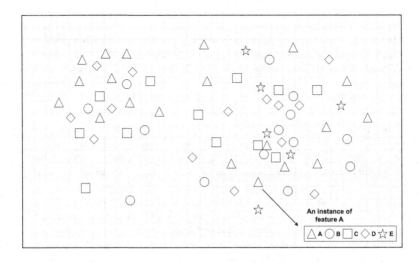

Fig. 1. Example of heterogeneous distribution data.

To address these limitations, we propose a method to improve the accuracy and speed of mining SPCPs in heterogeneous distribution spatial data. Our method consists of three stages, as follows:

1. We partition the input dataset into different subsets based on density levels of data objects. Subsequently, on each subset, the fuzzyDBSCAN [9] algorithm is employed to separate the points into 'density-wise clusters'.
2. Within each density-wise cluster, all maximal cliques are determined using the robust Bron-Kerbosch algorithm [10]. From there, candidate co-location patterns are identified. In this stage, a compressed maximal clique hash (MC-hash for short), which is developed to store the neighbor relationships between instances compactly, is used for reducing computational cost.
3. Finally, across all regions, combining SPCPs in these regions are examined to determine whether they are prevalent enough to become global patterns based on the global index (GI). If not, they are claimed as local patterns.

The remaining portion of the paper is organized as follows. Section 2 reviews relevant studies on this topic. Then, we detail the specific steps of the proposed method in Sect. 3. Section 4 presents experiments and analysis. Finally, the conclusion is led in Sect. 5.

2 Related Work

An important branch of spatial data mining is spatial co-location mining, which focuses on discovering co-occurring patterns of spatial objects within the same geographic area. Shekar et al. [16] laid the foundation for the field of SPCP mining and introduced algorithms for finding SPCPs based on set intersection operations. However, this algorithm has several drawbacks such as low efficiency, insufficient accuracy, and limited scalability. After that, there are many efficient algorithms developed such as joinless [23], overlapping maximal-based [17], instance driver schema [1], and so on.

In SPCP mining, the challenge lies in effectively handling large data and uneven distribution densities. This is because certain patterns may only emerge in specific regions (without clear hierarchical partitioning). However, in the context of mining multiple levels, this significantly impacts the accuracy and efficiency of the task. The existing algorithms for mining multilevel SPCPs currently can roughly divided into three categories, i.e., rule-based [12,15], clustering-based [3,13,19], and network constrained-based [6,14] algorithms. In which, employing clustering across the entire space is proved more efficiently to address the drawback in mining multilevel SPCPs in heterogeneous distribution data [19].

DBSCAN [5] is a clustering algorithm that uses density to determine clusters and noise points in data space. It does not require prior knowledge of the number or shape of clusters. This makes DBSCAN an effective tool in many real-world applications such as image analysis, signal processing, and spatial data mining. Compared to DBSCAN, Fuzzy DBSCAN [9] has several outstanding advantages, e.g., parameter selection is simple, it only requires a single parameter, i.e., the degree of fuzziness, instead of two parameters ϵ and $MinPts$ in DBSCAN. Fuzzy DBSCAN also has better ability to handle clusters with different densities and shapes, enhancing the effectiveness and flexibility of the clustering algorithm.

In paper [2], L-density is used to measure the density of data points in space. L-density, or density level, is a new concept that distinguishes between clusters with different densities and identifies clusters with varying density in data space. The L-density calculation method in k-DBSCAN provides a new approach to improving the performance and results of clustering algorithms, especially when data exhibits density variations.

Eppstein et al. presented the Bron-Kerbosch algorithm [4] as a recursive algorithm to enumerate all maximal cliques in a graph. This algorithm works by narrowing down potential candidate sets and recursively calling to search for maximum cliques. It is quite simple, easy to understand, highly efficient for sparse graphs, and significantly improves performance compared to previous methods, making the analysis of complex networks more feasible.

Multi-level SPCP mining allows the detection of co-locations at different scales, from detailed and specific patterns to general and common patterns, or vice versa. This helps create a comprehensive view of the structure of geographical space and the close relationships between objects or locations. In this work, we design an efficient algorithm that employs the above technique, i.e., Fuzzy DBSCAN, maximal cliques, and SPCP mining to discover multilevel SPCPs.

3   Proposed Method

To efficiently explore multilevel SPCPs, the entire spatial dataset needs to be partitioned into subsets for processing based on their differing appearances. Data points with close relationships, holding the potential for co-location patterns, often exhibit similarity in density and distribution. This is the driving force behind the formation of density-wise clusters.

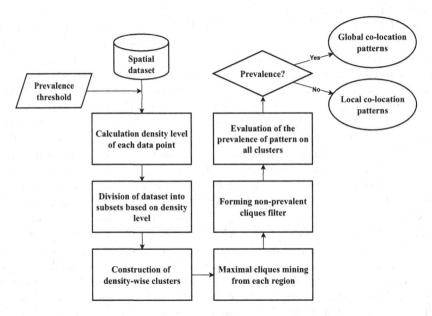

Fig. 2. The proposed framework for discovering multilevel SPCPs form heterogeneous distribution of spatial datasets.

Figure 2 shows the pipeline of the proposed method for discovering multilevel SPCPs from heterogeneous distribution of spatial dataset. Once density-wise clusters are formed across the entire dataset, SPCPS are explored. Starting with the search for maximal cliques, we optimize computation costs and operational time by leveraging the Apriori property and a compressed MC-hash. After SPCPs are found across all density-wise clusters, the global index (GI) is used to classify patterns into global and local categories. The following sections will provide specific instructions for this method.

3.1   Construction of Density-Wise Clusters

Heterogeneous spatial data always exhibit regions with varying densities and distributions. To achieve high efficiency and accuracy, the entire dataset will be partitioned into smaller groups based on the density and distribution of the data points. Partitioning the data based on only one of the two factors, density or distribution, is insufficient, as illustrated in the Fig. 3. Therefore, it is necessary to process the data based on both factors to form sets of data points in space that are more closely linked, which we will refer to as density-wise clusters.

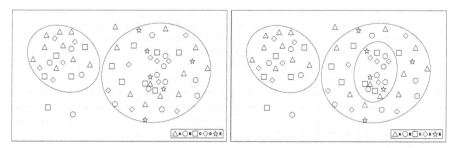

(a) Data clustered based on distribution   **(b)** Data clustered based on density

Fig. 3. Illustration of spatial data clustered by different factors.

Firstly, the dataset is partitioned into subsets based on density value using the k-level partitioning method. We borrow the definition from KDBSCAN [2]:

Definition 1 (l-Density). *The l-density of a point P, denoted as l-density(P), is defined as follows:*

$$l - density(P) = \frac{1}{l} \sum_{i=1}^{l} d_i \qquad (1)$$

Definition 2 (Density Level). *Density level of a point P, denoted by density − level(P) is an integer number, labeled by k-means algorithm. For two points P and Q, if their density levels are the same, then the l − density of P and Q are approximately similar. Note that, density-level is only a categorical parameter.*

After applying the k-level partitioning method, we obtain subsets of data with the same density level, or subsets containing points with the same density. On each subset, we further proceed to partition the data points based on distribution using the Fuzzy DBSCAN [9] algorithm. The result we obtain is density-wise clusters containing points that are similar in density and distribution, demonstrating close coherence with each other. An example of density-wise clusters is shown in Fig. 4.

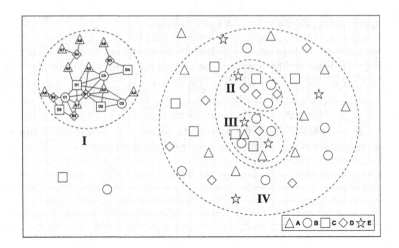

Fig. 4. Density-wise clusters forming based on both density and distribution.

3.2 Multi-level SPCP Mining from Clusters

After obtaining the density-wise clusters, the next step is to conduct mining on each of these clusters. Firstly, we will utilize the robust Bron Kerbosch algorithm [10] to find maximal cliques in each cluster.

Algorithm 1. Bron-Kerbosch-Pivot

P: A data set vertices of a cluster
R: A maximal clique
X: A set of vertices excluded from the clique
1: **if** $P \cup X = \emptyset$ **then**
2:     report R as a maximal clique and store in MC-hash
3: **end if**
4: choose a pivot $u \in P \cup X$ {choose u to maximize $|P \cap \Gamma(u)|$}
5: **for** each vertex $v \in P \setminus \Gamma(u)$ **do**
6:     BronKerboschPivot($P \cap \Gamma(v)$, $R \cup \{v\}$, $X \cap \Gamma(v)$)
7:     $P \leftarrow P \setminus \{v\}$
8:     $X \leftarrow X \cup \{v\}$
9: **end for**

Algorithm 1 operates by traversing through potential vertex subsets and checking if they can be extended into maximal vertex subsets. This process is carried out recursively, with the selection of pivot vertices and removal of visited vertices aiding in improving the algorithm's efficiency. The final result is all maximal vertex subsets in the cluster. When applying algorithm 1 to cluster 5 in Fig. 4, discovered the maximal cliques show in the left side of Fig. 5.

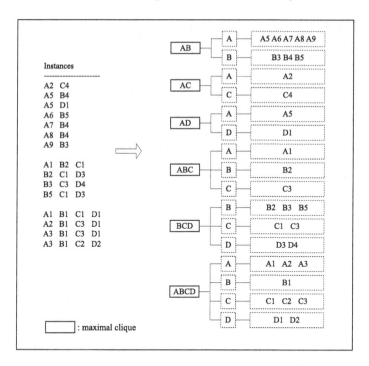

Fig. 5. MC-hash structure with the maximal cliques in cluster 5 of Fig. 4.

Each maximal cliques is saved into the MC-hash structure as shown in the right side of Fig. 5, with the key being the co-location pattern and the corresponding value being the list of neighbor objects. From the maximal cliques, patterns are mined based on one of the fundamental theories of data mining, namely the Apriori property, i.e., all subsets of a frequent item set must be frequent. If an item set is infrequent, all its super sets will be infrequent. Starting with patterns of size = 2, we use the participation index (PI) (that is shown in Eq. 2) as a measure of popularity:

$$PI(C_i) = min_{f_j \in C_i} \{Pr(C_i, f_i)\} \qquad (2)$$

$$Pr(C_i, f_j) = \frac{|I(C_i, f_j)|}{|I(f_j)|} \qquad (3)$$

where $|I(C_i, f_j)|$ is the number of unique instances of feature f_j in instances of Ci, and $|I(f_j)|$ is the number of instances of feature f_j in the entire study area or a sub-region. Given a threshold T, if $PI(C_i) \geq T$; then, C_i will be identified as a prevalent pattern; otherwise, C_i will be classified as a non-prevalent pattern.

Algorithm 2 checks the cliques in the MC-hash, χ. First, the prevalent patterns of size 2 are preserved, while the non-prevalent patterns of size 2 are used as a standard to eliminate non-prevalent patterns of larger sizes, helping to by

---

Algorithm 2. Discovering SPCP algorithm

1: $Sk = \emptyset$, $L1 = \emptyset$, $L2 = \emptyset$
2: **for** each clique zi in χ **do**
3:     **if** size of $zi = k$ **then**
4:         check zi in Sk with conditional and add value χ of zi to Sk
5:     **else if** size of $zi > k$ **then**
6:         $subcliques = generate\_combinations(zi)$
7:         **for** each clique wi in $subcliques$ **do**
8:             check wi in Sk with conditional and add all instances of wi to Sk
9:         **end for**
10:     **end if**
11: **end for**
12: **for** each co-location pattern cp in Sk **do**
13:     **if** cp not in non_prev_2 **then**
14:         $Pi = calculate\_pi(cp)$
15:         **if** $Pi \geq \theta$ **then** $L1$ add cp
16:         **else** $L2$ add cp
17:         **end if**
18:     **end if**
19: **end for**
20: **return** $L1, L2$

---

pass redundant computations. The set S will be used to contain non-prevalent size 2 patterns. Then, patterns of larger sizes, starting from 3, 4, 5, and so forth, will be mined. For each pattern, if the pattern contains any pattern from set S, then that pattern will be non-prevalent. If the pattern does not contain any pattern from set S, we will calculate the PI value of that pattern. If the PI value is greater than the threshold, the pattern will be considered prevalent. This entire process is further accelerated by utilizing a compressed maximal clique hash structure, i.e., MC-hash.

The search for prevalent patterns is carried out sequentially across all clusters. Once all prevalent patterns have been identified across the entire dataset, they are classified into global and local patterns. We propose a Global index (GI) calculated as the ratio of the number of clusters in which the pattern is prevalent to the total number of clusters:

$$GI(P) = \frac{\text{number of density - wise clusters that pattern P is prevalent}}{\text{total number of density - wise clusters}} \quad (4)$$

All patterns with a GI greater than the predefined threshold will be classified as global patterns. Correspondingly, the remaining patterns will be considered as local patterns.

The MPCD algorithm, i.e., Algorithm 3, initially, the algorithm construction of density-wise clusters by KD-tree structure, K-means and fuzzy DBSCAN to cluster data points into groups based on density. Subsequently, the algorithm multi-level pattern mining from clusters by mining maximal cliques and utilizes

---

Algorithm 3. The proposed algorithm, MPCD

    Input: ρ: A data set points, θ: Prevalence threshold, α: Global threshold

    Output: Γ: List of global co-location patterns, Λ: List of local co-location patterns

1: $\Gamma = \emptyset$, $\Lambda = \emptyset$, $S = \emptyset$

2: root = build_kdtree(ρ)

3: $k\_neigh = 100$

4: Find_k_nearest_neighbors for each point in ρ with root

5: η = find_Ldens(ρ, root)

6: Δ = KMeans(η)   ▷ Hash density level of all point

7: $\Theta = \emptyset$

8: **for** each data in Δ **do**

9:     Θ = fuzzyDBSCAN(Δ_i)   ▷ Hash of all cluster after using fuzzy K-DBSCAN
        algorithm

10: **end for**

11: **for** each cluster Θ_i in Θ **do**

12:     $prev\_2 = \emptyset$, $non\_prev\_2 = \emptyset$

13:     χ = BronKerboschWithPivot(Θ_i)   ▷ Using MC-hash structure

14:     $prev\_2, non\_prev\_2 \leftarrow$ mining_cliques_lv2(χ, θ)

15:     $S \leftarrow S \cup prev\_2$

16:     max_len_co-location = max(χ)

17:     **for** $N = 3$ to max_len_co-location **do**

18:         $S \leftarrow S \cup$ mining_cliques_lvk($\chi, N, non\_prev\_2, \theta$)   ▷ List prevalence
        co-location pattern

19:     **end for**

20: **end for**

21: **for** each prevalence co-location pattern ρ_i in S **do**

22:     **if** $\rho_i \geq \alpha$ **then** $\Gamma \leftarrow \Gamma \cup \rho_i$

23:     **else** $\Lambda \leftarrow \Lambda \cup \rho_i$

24:     **end if**

25: **end for**

26: **return** Γ, Λ

---

a data structure called MC-hash to store neighbor object subgroups of previously generated clusters. Finally, the algorithm classifies the discovered patterns into two types: global and local, based on a provided prevalence threshold.

4 Experiments and Analysis

In this section, comprehensive experiments were conducted to evaluate the effectiveness and efficiency of the proposed method. We carefully selected the following algorithms for comparison: For the KNNG method, the distance variation threshold is set at 0.6, as determined from experimental analysis conducted in the original study. For the Joinless method, the distance threshold is also determined using the L-function, as proposed by Yoo and Bow (2012) [22]. For our method, the parameter k-neighbors is set to 100 based on experimental results. All algorithms were coded in C++ and run on a computer with the configuration of Chip Apple M1, Memory 16 GB, MacOS Ventura 13.0. All algorithms were run on both artificial and real datasets for comparison.

4.1   Experiments on Synthetic Datasets

This process generates simulated spatial datasets for evaluating three methods of spatial data handling. A 200×200 research area is divided into four 100×100 subareas and named regions I, II, III, and IV. Random parent points are generated in each subarea, controlled by the parameter $n - parent$. Child points are created around each parent point within a buffer zone defined by $r - parent$. These child points are then replaced by grandchildren points, each associated with a randomly chosen feature type from a set of $n - feature$ types. Noise points are added to increase data diversity, with parameters such as feature point density, interaction range, number of features, and noise level controlled by $r - parent$, $n - feature$, and $n - noise$. This process enables the generation of diverse datasets for evaluating spatial data processing methods.

4.1.1   Parameter Setting and Evaluation Measure

To efficiently explore co-location patterns within a heterogeneous distribution of spatial datasets, experiments have established a PI of 0.2 to avoid discovering insignificant small localities of local co-location patterns. The parameters for the three comparison methods were configured according to recommendations provided in the original studies:

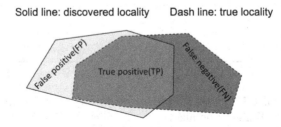

Fig. 6. Illustration of the measures for assessing the quality of discovered localities.

The measure developed by Guo and Wang (2011) [7] was employed to assess the accuracy of the multilevel co-location patterns discovered by the three methods. In Fig. 6, the dashed polygon represents a predefined area of the co-location pattern, while the solid polygon represents the area detected by the co-location pattern mining method. For each dataset, precision and recall can be calculated as follows:

$$Precision = \frac{\sum_{i=1}^{n} TP/(TP_i + FP_i)}{n} \qquad (5)$$

$$Recall = 1 - \frac{\sum_{i=1}^{n} TP/(TP_i + FN_i)}{n} \tag{6}$$

Precision is calculated as the average ratio of true positive (TP) regions (the intersection of patterns generated by the specified instances and features on the ground truth dataset) over the total number of true positive and false positive (FP) regions (the sum of these regions represents what the methods explore, where FP is the complement region of TP). Additionally, the measurement method provides a Recall index with similar TP and false negative (FN) regions. A Precision score approaching 1 indicates that what the methods explore is more accurate. However, we also need to consider the Recall parameter to determine whether the algorithm is truly accurate. In order to make it easier to observe here, we use the recall formula in Eq. (6) that is using 1 to subtract the original recall value. Thus, in Eq. (6), as a higher Recall score indicates that many co-location patterns are still unexplored or misidentified.

4.1.2   Effect of Number Instance of Spatial Features

The data is generated with the following parameters: noise = 50, and the number of instances gradually increases: 5,000, 10,000, 15,000, 20,000, 25,000. Five features are generated as follows: [A, B, C] within region [I, III], [B, C, D, E] within region [II, IV]. Ten features are generated as follows: [C, D, E, F, G] within region [I, III], [A, B, C, D, H, I, J] within region [II, IV]. Fifteen features are generated as follows: [A, B, C, D, E, F, G, H, I, J] within region [I, III], [A, B, C, D, E, K, L, M, O] within region [II, IV]. The generated data set is illustrated in Fig. 7.

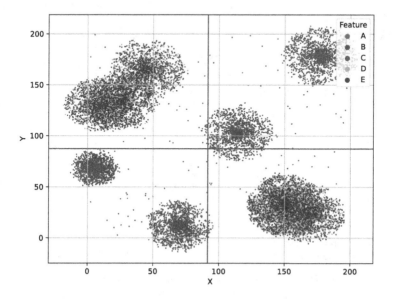

Fig. 7. The generated data set.

When conducting experiments simultaneously increasing the number of features and instances and providing indices regarding precision and neglect in exploring multilevel co-locations in Fig. 8, it can be observed that the proposed method exhibits a higher precision (0.93) compared to the Joinless method (0.76) and the KNNG method (0.65). Combining this with recall, the proposed method (0.12) outperforms the Joinless method (0.35) and the KNNG method (0.42). This demonstrates that the proposed method is more effective than the other two

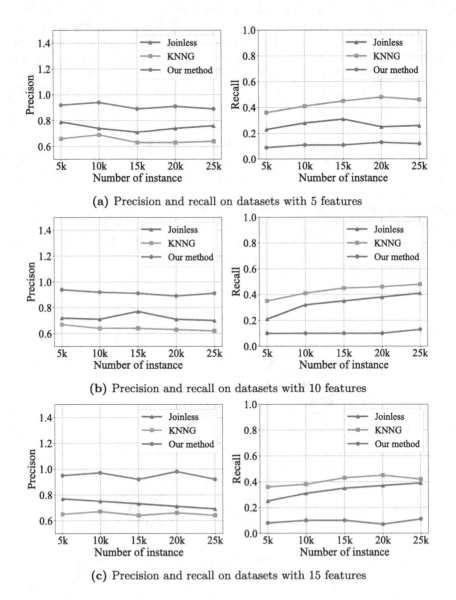

(a) Precision and recall on datasets with 5 features

(b) Precision and recall on datasets with 10 features

(c) Precision and recall on datasets with 15 features

Fig. 8. The effect of the number of instances on mining multilevel SPCPs.

methods. The main reason is that the Joinless method overlooks many sparse data regions that still hold value, while the KNNG method evaluates various candidate locations differently.

4.1.3 Scalability of Density and Instance

In this experiment, we tested the scalability of density and instance on a self-generated dataset with large feature and instance parameters to demonstrate the ability to expand the density of neighboring regions, describing the number of cases with the same location generated within the same neighboring region, controlled by the concentration level. We utilized 20 features, increased the number of instances gradually by 40.000, with clumpy values ranging from 1 to 5.

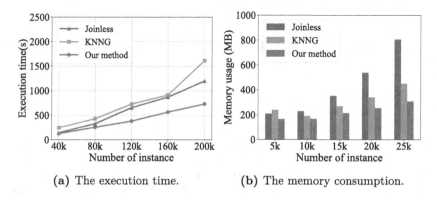

(a) The execution time.   (b) The memory consumption.

Fig. 9. The execution time and memory consumption of three algorithms on different numbers of instances (prevalence threshold is 0.2 for all cases).

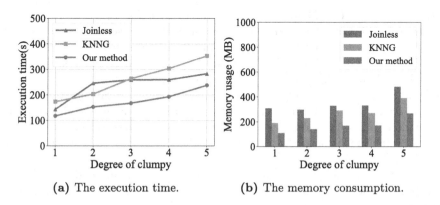

(a) The execution time.   (b) The memory consumption.

Fig. 10. The scalability of the three algorithms on different densities of neighborhood areas.

From Fig. 9, we can observe that the scalability of the KNNG and Joinless methods is relatively low due to the large range and dense density, resulting in a high number of instances within the space around the large distance threshold.

Performance is further compared based on the concentration level of the dataset in Fig. 10. We can see that as the clumpy increases, the runtime and RAM usage of the other two methods are higher compared to the proposed method. This is because the distance threshold parameters of the Joinless and KNNG methods need to be increased to accommodate sparse data regions, significantly affecting their ability to process densely populated areas. On the other hand, the proposed method demonstrates flexibility in handling heterogeneous distributions of spatial datasets.

4.2 Experiments on Real Datasets

This experiment utilizes real-world Point Of Interest (POI) data from various geographical regions to evaluate both the effectiveness and scalability of identified multilevel co-location patterns. Four distinct datasets are employed for this purpose.

The Shenzhen POI dataset consists of 100,000 data points and is used to assess the efficacy of the three methods under investigation. California POI Alpha dataset encompasses 97,000 data points and 26 different feature types, with instances ranging from a maximum of 13,481 for feature A to a minimum of 835 for feature W. Shanghai POI dataset, comprising 120,000 data points and 15 feature types, exhibits varying instance counts across its features, with feature A having the highest instance count at 25,476 and feature O the lowest at 240 instances. The Beijing POI dataset contains 241,000 data points and includes 30 feature types, with feature A registering the highest instance count at 35,453 instances and feature D the lowest at 2,423 instances. These datasets are instrumental in examining the scalability of instance counts.

4.2.1 Effect of the Discovered Multilevel SPCPs

The experiment was conducted on the Shenzhen POI dataset with the following parameter settings: a prevalence threshold of 0.2 to determine co-location pattern levels. In Table 1, the experiment listed important co-location patterns and their levels for each method. For the proposed method, PI is calculated as GI according to the formula mentioned. For the other two methods, PI is calculated using the original formula. To determine the local levels in the Joinless, we also consider co-locations below the prevalence threshold as local patterns. For the KNNG, we determine global patterns by averaging the PI of each co-location pattern across the data regions.

Let's consider co-location pattern {C,D,G}. With our method, we found it with a PI value of 0.43 and identified it as a global pattern. This is correct because the children of {C,D,G}, namely $PI(\{C,D\}) = 0.76$, $PI(\{C,G\}) = 0.74$, and $PI(\{D,G\}) = 0.72$, are all global patterns. However, both Joinless and KNNG methods also found co-location patterns that are children of {C,D,G}

Table 1. The multilevel SPCPs discovered by the KNNG, Joinless, and MPCD

Multi-level co- location patterns	The Proposed Method		Joinless		KNNG	
	Level	PI	Level	PI	Level	PI
{A,C}	Global	0.76	Global	0.69	Global	0.58
{A,D}	Global	0.76	Global	0.64	Global	0.49
{B,K}	Local	0.13	Local	0.17	–	–
{C,D,G}	Global	0.43	Local	0.18	Local	0.18
{C,D}	Global	0.76	Global	0.64	Global	0.26
{C,G}	Global	0.74	Global	0.64	Global	0.23
{D,G}	Global	0.72	Local	0.17	Local	0.14
{D,P}	Local	0.12	Local	0.17	–	–
{F,J}	Local	0.15	–	–	Local	0.06
{F,P}	Local	0.13	–	–	–	–
{G,R}	Local	0.17	–	–	Local	0.06
{H,M}	Local	0.15	Local	0.13	Local	0.03
{N,P}	Local	0.17	–	–	Local	0.03

and identified them as global patterns, whereas {C,D,G} is only at the local
pattern level. This can be explained by the fact that the other two methods
missed many patterns during the exploration process, especially in regions with
heterogeneous spatial data. This is evident in patterns such as {B,K}, {D,P},
{F,J}, {F,G}, {N,P}, {G,R}, and many others not listed in this experiment.

Through Table 1, the multilevel co-location patterns detected by Joinless,
KNNG, and the proposed method are listed. It can be observed that the multilevel co-location patterns detected by the proposed method generally differ from
those detected by the other methods.

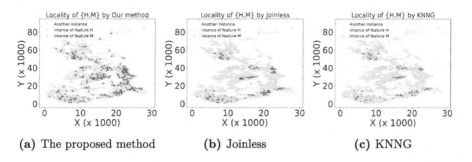

(a) The proposed method   (b) Joinless   (c) KNNG

Fig. 11. Comparison of the locality co-location pattern {H,M} detected by Joinless,
KNNG, and the proposed method.

The proposed method identifies more global and local co-location patterns
compared to the other two methods. We further evaluate all the detected

multilevel co-location patterns based on listing the top co-location patterns with the highest PI at the global and local levels. Subsequently, we compute the PI value for each co-location pattern across the methods.

This experiment has selected two co-location patterns and illustrates the instances of the patterns discovered by the three compared methods. Through visualization, we can better understand the data presented in Table 1.

To further compare the performance of the three methods, some instances of the local co-location patterns detected by all three methods are displayed in Fig. 11. We can observe that the Joinless method, depicted in Fig. 11(b), only identifies locality patterns H,M within densely populated areas with a small exploration range, thus missing out on {H,M} patterns in sparsely populated regions. On the other hand, Fig. 11(c) illustrates that the KNNG method fails to detect {H,M} locality patterns at the outer edges of large regions, and some regions misidentify {H,M} locality patterns.

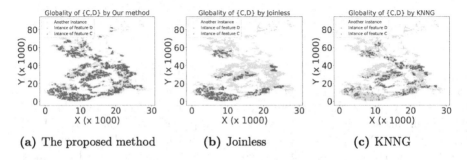

(a) The proposed method   (b) Joinless   (c) KNNG

Fig. 12. A comparison of the locality co-location pattern {C,D} detected by Joinless, KNNG, and the proposed method is presented.

Through Fig. 12(a), it is evident that the proposed method effectively explores global patterns {C,D} across various regions and density levels. However, Fig. 12(b) demonstrates that the Joinless method only searches within densely populated data regions, thus missing global patterns {C,D} in sparsely populated areas due to the inflexible distance threshold parameter. On the other hand, Fig. 12(c) illustrates that the KNNG method predominantly delineates global patterns {C,D} within regions of similar and discrete densities, overlooking many global patterns in sparsely populated areas.

4.2.2 Scalability

To verify the performance and scalability when varying the dataset sizes, this experiment divides three large datasets into smaller datasets with sizes corresponding to 20, 40, 60, and 80 percent of the original data points randomly. The experiment is conducted with PI of 0.2 across all three comparison methods. For the Joinless method, the experiment sets the distance threshold to 200 for the Beijing and Shanghai datasets, and to 800 for the California dataset. For the

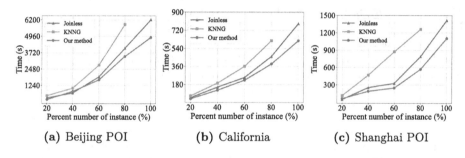

Fig. 13. The execution time of the compared algorithms.

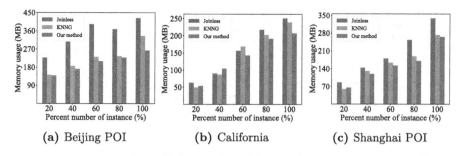

Fig. 14. The memory usage of the compared algorithms.

KNNG method, the experiment sets epsilon to 0.6 and alpha to 0.001. Regarding the method proposed in this paper, the global threshold is set to 0.5.

As the number of data points increases shown in Fig. 13, the runtime of our method is lower compared to the other two methods. This is because our method efficiently partitions the data based on heterogeneous density, resulting in faster and more effective processing. On the other hand, the presence of multiple feature types in the data slows down the other two methods.

All parameters in this experiment are kept constant to record the memory usage during the execution of the three methods. The results are depicted in Fig. 14. The heterogeneous distribution of the data makes it challenging to control the number of neighbors within the distance threshold range, as it can vary significantly. Moreover, the diversity in the number of features results in the other two methods consuming more memory space, while our method partitions the data into smaller regions and employs prevalence co-location pattern exploration.

5 Conclusion

In this study, we propose a novel method for exploring spatial co-location patterns. Initially, the data is clustered based on both density level and distribution, forming density-wise clusters. Subsequently, candidate co-location patterns are generated using the powerful Bron-Kerbosch algorithm and employing the MC-hash structure. Finally, the Global Index is utilized to classify patterns into Global and Local categories. Experiments conducted on both simulated and real-world datasets have demonstrated the effectiveness of this method. We compare the proposed method with two other well-known approaches.

References

1. Bao, X., Wang, L.: A clique-based approach for co-location pattern mining. Inf. Sci. **490**, 244–264 (2019)
2. Debnath, M., Tripathi, P.K., Elmasri, R.: K-dbscan: identifying spatial clusters with differing density levels. In: DMIA, pp. 51–60. IEEE (2015)
3. Deng, M., Cai, J., Liu, Q., He, Z., Tang, J.: Multi-level method for discovery of regional co-location patterns. Int. J. Geogr. Inf. Sci. **31**(9), 1846–1870 (2017)
4. Eppstein, D., Löffler, M., Strash, D.: Listing all maximal cliques in large sparse real-world graphs. J. Exp. Algorithm. **18**, 3 (2013)
5. Ester, M., Kriegel, H.P., Sander, J.: A density-based algorithm for discovering clusters in large spatial databases with noise. In: KDD, vol. 96, pp. 226–231 (1996)
6. Ghosh, S., Gupta, J., Sharma, A., An, S., Shekhar, S.: Towards geographically robust statistically significant regional colocation pattern detection. In: ACM SIGSPATIAL, pp. 11–20 (2022)
7. Guo, D., Wang, H.: Automatic region building for spatial analysis. Trans. GIS **15**, 29–45 (2011)
8. Huang, Y., Shekhar, S., Xiong, H.: Discovering colocation patterns from spatial data sets: a general approach. IEEE Trans. Knowl. Data Eng. **16**(12), 1472–1485 (2004)
9. Ienco, D., Bordogna, G.: Fuzzy extensions of the dbscan clustering algorithm. Soft. Comput. **22**(5), 1719–1730 (2018)
10. Johnston, H.: Cliques of a graph-variations on the Bron-Kerbosch algorithm. Int. J. Comput. Inf. Sci. **5**(3), 209–238 (1976)
11. Li, J., Adilmagambetov, A., Mohomed Jabbar, M.S.: On discovering co-location patterns in datasets: a case study of pollutants and child cancers. GeoInformatica **20**, 651–692 (2016)
12. Li, Y., Shekhar, S.: Local co-location pattern detection: a summary of results. In: 10th International Conference on Geographic Information Science (GIScience 2018). Schloss-Dagstuhl-Leibniz Zentrum für Informatik (2018)
13. Liu, Q., Liu, W., Deng, M.: An adaptive detection of multilevel co-location patterns based on natural neighborhoods. Int. J. Geogr. Inf. Sci. **35**(3), 556–581 (2021)
14. Liu, W., Liu, Q., Deng, M.: Discovery of statistically significant regional co-location patterns on urban road networks. Int. J. Geogr. Inf. Sci. **36**(4), 749–772 (2022)
15. Qian, F., Chiew, K., He, Q., Huang, H.: Mining regional co-location patterns with kNNG. J. Intell. Inf. Syst. **42**, 485–505 (2014)
16. Shekhar, S., Huang, Y.: Discovering spatial co-location patterns: a summary of results. In: Jensen, C.S., Schneider, M., Seeger, B., Tsotras, V.J. (eds.) SSTD 2001. LNCS, vol. 2121, pp. 236–256. Springer, Heidelberg (2001). https://doi.org/10.1007/3-540-47724-1_13
17. Tran, V., Wang, L., Zhou, L.: Mining spatial co-location patterns based on overlap maximal clique partitioning. In: MDM, pp. 467–472 (2019)

18. Tran, V., Wang, L., Zhou, L.: A spatial co-location pattern mining framework insensitive to prevalence thresholds based on overlapping cliques. Distrib. Parall. Datab. **41**(4), 511–548 (2023)
19. Wang, D., Wang, L., Wang, X., Tran, V.: An approach based on maximal cliques and multi-density clustering for regional co-location pattern mining. Exp. Syst. Appl. **248**, 123414 (2024)
20. Wang, L., Tran, V., Do, T.: A clique-querying mining framework for discovering high utility co-location patterns without generating candidates. ACM Trans. Knowl. Discov. Data **18**(1), 1–42 (2023)
21. Yao, X., Jiang, X., Wang, D., Yang, L., Peng, L., Chi, T.: Efficiently mining maximal co-locations in a spatial continuous field under directed road networks. Inf. Sci. **542**, 357–379 (2021)
22. Yoo, J.S., Bow, M.: Mining spatial colocation patterns: a different framework. Data Min. Knowl. Disc. **24**, 159–194 (2012)
23. Yoo, J.S., Shekhar, S.: A joinless approach for mining spatial colocation patterns. IEEE Trans. Knowl. Data Eng. **18**(10), 1323–1337 (2006)

Leveraging Wav2Vec2.0 for Kazakh Speech Recognition: An Experimental Study

Zhanibek Kozhirbayev$^{(\boxtimes)}$ (iD)

National Laboratory Astana, Nazarbayev University, Astana 01000, Kazakhstan
zhanibek.kozhirbayev@nu.edu.kz

Abstract. In the fast-growing world of neural networks, models trained on extensive multilingual text and speech data have shown great promise for improving the state of low-resource languages. This study focuses on the application of state-of-the-art speech recognition models, specifically Facebook's Wav2Vec2.0 and Wav2Vec2-XLSR, to the Kazakh language. The primary objective is to evaluate the performance of these models in transcribing spoken Kazakh content. Additionally, the research explores the possibility of using data from other languages for initial training and examines whether fine-tuning the model with target language data can improve its performance. More so, this work gives insights into how effective pre-trained multilingual models are when used on low-resource languages. The fine-tuned wav2vec2.0-XLSR model demonstrated impressive results, achieving a character error rate (CER) of 1.9 and a word error rate (WER) of 8.9 when tested against the test set of the Kazcorpus dataset. These findings may help create robustness in Automatic Speech Recognition (ASR) systems for Kazakh which could be used for various applications such as voice-activated assistants; speech-to-text translators among others.

Keywords: Automatic speech recognition · Kazakh language · Wav2Vec 2.0 · Wav2Vec2-XLSR · Pre-trained transformer models · Speech representation models

1 Introduction

Recently, sequence-based models have demonstrated remarkable advances in speech recognition compared to traditional automatic speech recognition systems. These sequence-based models use neural networks to convert speech into text, which simplifies the modeling process. Among them, Transformer [1] stands out as widely used and has demonstrated noteworthy achievements in the creation of end-to-end speech recognition systems [2–4]. Despite the substantial headway in the advancement of ASR models, the development of reliable models for languages other than English remains a challenge. This problem is mainly related to the fact that in order to obtain satisfactory results using advanced models, it usually takes many hours of work with annotated speech data for training. This is especially true of Kazakh, the Turkic language spoken by the global community of more than 13 million people.

O. Gervasi et al. (Eds.): ICCSA 2024, LNCS 14814, pp. 120–132, 2024.
https://doi.org/10.1007/978-3-031-64608-9_8

Recent advances in the development of self-learning methodologies have demonstrated the potential to address the limited availability of language data in the absence of sufficient resources. Self-supervised is a unique approach to improving speech recognition systems, allowing to use a huge amount of unlabeled speech data to obtain a valuable representation of speech signals. Unlike traditional supervised learning, in which labeled data is required to train the model, self-supervised learning algorithms extract knowledge from raw data without the need for explicit annotations. As part of self-learning, models are honed to perform tasks that are closely related to the main task of speech recognition, but do not require labeled input. An example involves training a model to predict the next frame of a speech signal based on previous frames—a concept called contrastive predictive coding (CPC) [5]. Another strategy involves training the model to distinguish between two different speech segments, for example, to distinguish a pair of speech frames that are close in time from those that are significantly separated from each other. The potential of self-supervised training to recognize Kazakh speech lies in its ability to benefit from significant amounts of unlabeled data, which is an important advantage for languages where annotated data is still scarce. Using self-supervised techniques to train a speech recognition model based on unlabeled data, the model can skillfully decode key aspects of the speech signal, including phonemes and acoustic nuances necessary for accurate transcription. In addition to the ability to improve the accuracy of speech recognition systems, self-supervised method promises to reduce the amount of labeled data needed for learning. This reduction can significantly reduce the costs and time spent on creating a reliable Kazakh speech recognition system, which will make it more accessible to researchers and developers. Recent advances in self-supervised audio encoders, such as Wav2Vec2.0 [6], have made it possible to effectively assimilate high-quality audio representations. However, their unsupervised approach to pre-learning makes it difficult to effectively translate these ideas into practical results. Therefore, a fine-tuning step is required to effectively apply these models to tasks such as automatic speech recognition (ASR). The motivation of my work can be outlined as follows:

- Bridging the language gap: This experimental study is motivated by the need to bridge this gap and improve ASR capabilities for languages with limited resources.
- Use of unlabeled data: This study builds on the potential of self-learning techniques to use valuable information about unlabeled speech data. Moreover, the key motivation for this study is to study the effectiveness of self-supervised learning in reducing dependence on labeled data for training ASR models.

Two iterations of Wav2Vec2.0 pre-trained models exist: the first is solely pre-trained for a single language, and the second, is a multilingual pre-trained (XLSR-53) model. This study was undertaken to contrast these two approaches to ascertain their efficacy in facilitating robust ASR for the Kazakh language. The primary contributions of this study encompass:

1. Supplementary to the available Kazakh language speech corpora, we procured audio recordings along with their corresponding texts from publicly accessible sources. The aggregate data amassed equated to around 1000 h. Each audio file corresponds to an individual text file containing audiobook content. Notably, it is imperative to

acknowledge that synchronization was absent between the audio and text, implying a lack of alignment at the sentence or word level. To address this challenge of misalignment, we employed a segmentation technique grounded in the connectionist temporal classification (CTC) [7] algorithm. This approach facilitated the precise extraction of audio-text alignments.

2. A series of experiments were conducted utilizing the Wav2Vec2.0 base and XLSR-53 architectures, encompassing various pre-training and fine-tuning scenarios.

3. An extensive comparative analysis was performed between two methodologies: Wav2Vec2.0 and Wav2Vec2.0-XLSR.

This paper is structured as follows: Sect. 2 delves into a comprehensive examination of the technical nuances underlying the Wav2Vec2.0 and XLSR-53 architectures within the context of ASR. Additionally, this section provides insights into recent advancements in the domain of Kazakh speech recognition. The particulars concerning the dataset employed in our experimentation are detailed in Sect. 3. The strategies involving Wav2Vec2.0 and XLSR-53 architectures are expounded upon in the same section. Section 4 outlines the outcomes derived from the conducted experiments. Finally, Sect. 5 encapsulates our discoveries and conclusions from the undertaken experiments, shedding light on potential avenues for future exploration.

2 Background and Related Work

This section furnishes a concise outline of the pertinent literature related to this article, classified into two subsections: Wav2Vec2.0 and XLSR-53, and Kazakh ASR.

2.1 Wav2Vec 2.0 and XLSR-53

Wav2Vec 2.0. is meticulously crafted for transcribing speech embedded within audio signals, leveraging a self-supervised pre-training methodology that imbibes insights from vast volumes of unlabeled audio data. It amalgamates principles from several precursor models, namely, Contrastive Predictive Coding (CPC) [5], Model Predictive Control (MPC) [8], wav2vec [9], and vqwav2vec [10]. The architecture of Wav2Vec2 harmonizes convolutional neural networks (CNNs) and transformers, enabling it to apprehend both local nuances and overarching patterns within audio data. The model utilizes a multi-layer convolutional feature encoder, denoted as $f : X \rightarrow Z$, to encode raw audio waveforms, X, into latent speech representations, $z_1, \ldots, z_T$, which are then fed into a transformer-masked network, denoted as $g : Z \rightarrow C$, that maps the representations from the latent space to a discrete set of outputs, $q_1, \ldots, q_T$, that represent targets in the self-supervised learning objective [6, 12]. The transformer module contextualizes the quantized representations using attention blocks, resulting in a set of discrete contextual representations, $c_1, \ldots, c_T$. The feature encoder is composed of seven convolutional blocks, each with 512 channels, kernel widths of $\{10, 3, 3, 3, 3, 2, 2\}$, and strides of $\{5, 2, 2, 2, 2, 2, 2\}$. On the other hand, the transformer network is made up of 24 blocks, with 1024 dimensions and inner dimensions numbering 4096. It also has 16 attention heads.

Demonstrating its prowess, this model has achieved remarkable feats across various benchmark datasets, substantially propelling the boundaries of speech recognition technology.

XLSR-53, a product of Facebook AI Research [11], is a multilingual language model with a foundation in cross-lingual language model XLM-R, tailored to cater to multilingual and cross-lingual natural language processing (NLP) tasks. Building upon the Wav2Vec 2.0 model, XLSR-53 possesses the capacity to acquire latent quantization spanning various languages. This is accomplished through the utilization of product quantization to cherry-pick quantized representations from codebooks. The selection process employs the Gumbel-Softmax technique, ensuring complete distinction. The architecture of XLSR-53 bears resemblance to that of Bidirectional Encoder Representations from Transformers (BERT) [12], with a notable deviation: it encompasses 53 language-specific embeddings, catering to each of the supported languages. This intricate design empowers the model to process diverse languages, capturing their subtleties even in cases of similar spellings or pronunciations. Furthermore, XLSR-53 boasts an expansive parameter count of 500 million, positioning it among the largest multilingual language models available. This model is trained on an extensive and diverse corpus comprising speech text data extracted from over 53 languages. The inherent ability of XLSR-53 to comprehend multiple languages renders it exceptionally advantageous for cross-lingual transfer learning. This entails adapting a model trained in one language to perform well in another language, requiring only minimal supplementary training.

2.2 Kazakh ASR

Recent advances in ASR have led to the emergence of new end-to-end architectures that provide impressive accuracy when sufficient data sets are available.. The basic principle underlying these end-to-end models is the direct conversion of input speech signals into sequences of characters. This streamlined approach simplifies learning, fine-tuning, and logical inference procedures. In the field of ASR research, experts predominantly gravitate towards two distinct methodologies for training ASR systems: fully supervised and self-supervised models.

In the context of the first category, Yessenbayev et al. [13] undertook an extensive study aimed at surmounting the challenge of automatic, speaker-independent recognition of continuous Kazakh speech, focusing on a specific vocabulary foundation, while contending with noisy environments. The authors' proposed system exhibited commendable outcomes in diverse tasks, encompassing phonetic recognition of English speech as well as the recognition of continuous Kazakh speech. Notably, the system displayed a relative enhancement in recognition quality of up to 20%. Noteworthy is the achievement of a recognition quality of 94.5% for Kazakh speech. In essence, this research stands as a foundational step, laying the groundwork for the subsequent development of more advanced frameworks catering to the domain of continuous Kazakh speech recognition.

Kozhirbayev [14] focuses on experimenting with three state-of-the-art speech recognition models, namely Facebook's Wav2Vec2.0 and Wav2Vec2-XLS-R, OpenAI's Whisper, on the Kazakh language. This work can provide insights into the effectiveness of using pretrained multilingual models in under esourced language settings. The wav2vec2.0 model achieved a Character Error Rate (CER) of 2.8 and a Word Error Rate

(WER) of 8.7 on the test set, which closely matches the best result achieved by the end-to-end Transformer model. The large whisper model achieves a CER of approximately 4 on the test set. Kozhirbayev and Islamgozhayev [15] first created a dedicated speech translation dataset ST-kk-ru based on the ISSAI Corpus to develop the cascade speech translation system. The ST-kk-ru dataset comprises a large collection of Kazakh speech recordings along with their corresponding Russian translations. The automatic speech recognition (ASR) module of the system utilizes deep learning techniques to convert spoken Kazakh input into text. The machine translation (MT) module employs state-of-the-art neural machine translation methods, leveraging the parallel Kazakh-Russian translations available in the dataset to generate accurate translations.

In their research, Mamyrbayev et al. [16] delve into stream speech recognition through the implementation of the RNN-T model. This architecture is structured with neural networks like LSTM and BLSTM, leveraging a training dataset of over 300 h comprising both prepared (reading) and spontaneous speech recordings. The outcomes of the study underscore the RNN-T model's capability to attain a CER of 10.6.

In a distinct study by the same authors, Mamyrbayev et al. [17] introduce a hybrid Transformer + CTC (Connectionist Temporal Classification) model. It was honed using a speech dataset spanning 400 h. Notably, the study's findings spotlight the model's performance, registering a CER of 3.7 and a WER of 8.3.

Certainly, it's noteworthy to highlight the collaborative efforts of researchers from the Center for Speech Technologies at St. Petersburg National Research University of Information Technologies, Mechanics, and Optics, along with Kostanay State University named after A. Baitursynov [18]. These researchers embarked on a project centered around the recognition and synthesis of the bilingual (Kazakh-Russian) language. Their endeavors focused on advancing the field of bilingual speech processing, thereby contributing to the broader spectrum of language technology research.

Khassanov et al. [19] have introduced a significant contribution to Kazakh speech recognition research in the form of the KSC 1 database. This comprehensive database serves as an open benchmark, constituting around 332 h of transcribed audio. The database encompasses over 153,000 utterances spoken by individuals from diverse age groups, regions, and genders. The authors employed a Transformer-based end-to-end (E2E) model, achieving a Character Error Rate (CER) of 2.8% and a Word Error Rate (WER) of 8.7% on this dataset. In a related development, Mussakhojayeva et al. [20] extended the KSC database to a staggering 1128 h. This augmentation involved the incorporation of additional data from diverse sources, including television news, television and radio programs, parliamentary speeches, and podcasts. The authors meticulously defined the corpus specifications and substantiated its utility by employing a Transformer-based ASR model. This model yielded promising outcomes, with an overall Word Error Rate (WER) of 15.1% on the validation set and 15.6% on the test set. These efforts significantly bolster the resources available for advancing Kazakh speech recognition technology.

Although the ongoing development of models has demonstrated remarkable performance, a significant portion of them rely heavily on supervised learning techniques, which requires significant amounts of annotated data. Unfortunately, the process of collecting and annotating data is resource-intensive, expensive and time-consuming, often requiring manual intervention. Moreover, there may be circumstances in which obtaining such data becomes impractical due to limitations or unavailability. Unlike fully controlled models, recent research has focused on the use of powerful acoustic models prepared using self-supervised methods and extensive amount of unlabeled data. An example is the work of Meng and Yolvas [21], who implemented unsupervised pretraining using Wav2Vec2.0. They integrated the factorized TDNN level to maintain the connection between voice and time steps, thereby increasing the effectiveness of speech recognition in the Kazakh language. In addition, they used multilingual pre-training and speech synthesis techniques to further enhance productivity. The results of their experiments highlighted the benefits of assimilating unlabeled data from languages other than the target language and using data enhancement techniques using speech synthesis. These approaches, in particular, have led to a significant reduction in the frequency of errors in words in test suites. This study indicates significant progress in optimizing speech recognition systems while reducing dependence on extensive labeled datasets.

3 Materials and Method

This section is dedicated to data sets specially designed for speech recognition in the Kazakh language. It also examines the methodologies used to develop accurate speech recognition modules designed for a given linguistic context.

3.1 Dataset

In these experiments, several sets of data on the Kazakh language were used. Some of them were used for pre-training phase, while others were used for fine tuning phase. ISSAI KSC [19] and Kazcorpus [22] were selected for fine-tuning and evaluation due to their comprehensive coverage, diverse linguistic content and suitability for solving specific tasks. They offer a rich variety of linguistic data, which makes them ideal for fine-tuning models to effectively solve target tasks. On the other hand, KazLibriSpeech was chosen for pre-training because of its large-scale audio data, which can facilitate the study of high-level acoustic characteristics and improve the performance of the model in speech-related tasks.

ISSAI KSC. The ISSAI KSC database is the most extensive open resource created to support Kazakh speech and language data processing applications. This substantial dataset contains over 332 h of content collected using a web-based platform designed for speech recording. this platform invited volunteers to formulate suggestions taken from various sources, including books, laws, Wikipedia, news portals and blogs. The KSC dataset is diverse and includes speakers and audio recordings from various regions of Kazakhstan, which use a variety of devices such as smartphones, tablets and laptops. The speaker group consists of representatives from five different regions, with 51.7% of female speakers and 48.3% of male speakers in the screening and testing kits.

Kazcorpus. The kazcorpus acoustic corpus includes two separate subcorpuses: kazspeechdb and kazmedia. The foundation for the creation of the broadcast news corpus was laid using the kazspeechdb corpus. This subcorpus consists of fragments of speech, namely 12,675 sentences spoken in Kazakh, recorded in controlled studio conditions. The speakers represent different genders, ages and regions of Kazakhstan. In total, the performance of the subgroup lasted 22 h, 169 speakers took part in it, including 73 male and 96 female voices. Each speaker delivered 75 sentences.

On the other hand, the KazMedia subcorporation combines audio and text data collected from the official websites of television news agencies, in particular Khabar, Astana TV and Channel 31. Text data represents the entire set of news materials in the Kazakh language published on the official websites of these channels. Audio data consists of WAV format files, which are audio tracks extracted from various news videos broadcast on these channels in the Kazakh language. Collectively, this subcorpus includes 21 h of speech.

KazLibriSpeech. We have collected audio recordings in combination with relevant texts from open sources, accumulating a total of about 1,000 h of data. Each audio file corresponds to the corresponding text contained in the audiobook, although there is no alignment at the sentence or word level. Therefore, the subsequent attempt is to segment these audio files into smaller intervals, whether they are words, phrases, or sentences. Then each such segment must be compared with the corresponding voiced text that was created during the same interval. Although the alignment and segmentation process can be complex, this method allows to create extensive datasets covering various sources and areas with minimal cost.

Given that the quality of the collected audiobooks varies, the cleaning and normalization process has been launched. This included removing noise, working with homoglyphs, transliteration, extracting non-reproducible fragments, replacing abbreviations and abbreviations with their full forms, normalizing numerical composition, replacing characters with their phonetic counterparts, initial chapter-level segmentation and dividing the source text into compressed sentences using punctuation marks. In addition, all the musical elements accompanying the audiobook at the beginning and at the end were removed. Our segmentation approach involved the use of the CTC algorithm, which ensures accurate alignment of the audio text, even if the audio recording contains incomprehensible fragments of speech at the beginning or end. Our method is to train an end-to-end network based on pre-aligned data using a CTC/attention based ASR system. CTC, as a mechanism for neural network inference and scoring, plays an important role in training recurrent neural networks to solve sequence-based tasks, taking into account variable time. This mechanism does not depend on the basic structure of the neural network. In our context, this model identifies speech segments in audio files at the sentence level. The ASR model requisite for segmentation was honed using the ISSAI KSC dataset and the Espnet tool [23].

For a comprehensive overview of the corpora designed for speech recognition in the Kazakh language, please consult Table 1. This table presents the dataset structures, the division of the dataset into training, testing, and development sets, and the methodologies employed for dataset acquisition, the number of WAV files, the aggregate duration of WAV files in hours.

Table 1. The structure of the corpora for the Kazakh language.

Structure	Name of the corpus/ sets	Data type	Amount of wav-files	Overall duration of wav-files in hour
1	**ISSAI KSC**	Crowdsourced recordings	**153853**	**332.6**
1.1	Train		147236	318.4
1.2	Dev		3283	7.1
1.3	Test		3334	7.1
2	**Kazcorpus**	Mixed type: studio recordings, prepared speech + spontaneous speech in different acoustic conditions	**13425**	**44.16**
2.1	kazspeechdb		12675	22.61
2.1.1	Train		11175	19.92
2.1.2	Dev		750	1.36
2.1.3	Test		750	1.34
2.2	KazMedia		740	21.55
2.2.1	Train		561	18.04
2.2.2	Dev		49	1.00
2.2.3	Test		130	2.51
3	**KazLibriSpeech**	Audio books	**575243**	**992**

3.2 Methods

In the context of this research, an evaluation was conducted on two variants of wav2vec: (1) Wav2Vec 2.0, pre-trained and fine-tuned exclusively for the Kazakh language, and (2) XLSR-53, initially pre-trained across 53 languages, followed by continuous pre-training and fine-tuning for the Kazakh language.

Wav2Vec 2.0. The experimentation was carried out utilizing the Fairseq platform [24]. The Wav2Vec 2.0 base model underwent pre-training using varied configurations, encompassing an encoder layerdrop set to 0.05, dropout_input, dropout_features, feature_grad_mult set to 0.1, and an encoder_embed_dim established at 768. Training hyperparameters encompassed a learning rate of 5×10^{-4}, with a warm-up phase in the initial 10% of the training duration. The number of updates was specified as 800,000, while the maximum token count was set at 1,200,000. Consistently, the Adam optimizer was applied, in line with the original approach.

For fine-tuning, conventional procedures were followed, with parameters set as follows: the number of updates reached 160,000, while the maximum token count stood at 2,800,000. Similar to pre-training, the Adam optimizer was engaged, utilizing a learning rate of 3×10^{-5} and a gradient accumulation of 12 steps. The training batch size was dynamically determined by the framework, factoring in the predefined token maximum. Throughout training, the optimal model was chosen based on the lowest WER achieved on the validation set.

XLSR-53. The XLSR model underwent pre-training with identical configurations as those employed for the Wav2Vec large model. The encoder block encompassed 24 layers, each with a dimension of 1024, and a set of 16 attention blocks was utilized, without incorporating dropout. Fine-tuning parameters were determined in line with the configurations applied in the original XLSR experiment with Wav2Vec 2.0.

Language Model. Subsequent to the fine-tuning process, the model undergoes decoding, facilitated by a 3-g language model [25]. The language model was trained using the transcriptions from all the accessible datasets outlined in Table 1, utilizing the Kenlm toolkit [26]. For decoding purposes, a beam search decoder is employed, with the beam size configured to 1500.

4 Result and Discussion

The evaluation of Wav2Vec2.0 models utilized the datasets described in Sect. 3.1. The ASR systems' performance, as indicated by WER and CER scores, is presented in Table 2. Various training scenarios were employed for each architecture with different parameters. The experiments took place on the NVIDIA DGX-1 server, equipped with 8 V100 GPUs.

Table 2 displays the character error rate and word error rate scores of the fine-tuned Wav2Vec 2.0-base and XLSR-53 models. During the pre-training phase, the KazLibriSpeech corpus was exclusively employed, while the ISSAI KSC1 and Kazcorpus were used for fine-tuning. Results highlight the exceptional performance of the pre-trained XLSR-53 model. After undergoing pre-training with the KazLibriSpeech corpus and fine-tuning with the Kazcorpus (train + dev) data, it achieves a CER of 1.9 and a WER of 8.9 on the test set. These figures are notably higher by 28.2% and 26.9% compared to the Wav2Vec 2.0-base model in terms of WER and CER, respectively. These findings underscore the significant enhancement in model performance due to pre-training, where the dataset size used for pre-training plays a pivotal role. Conversely, the Wav2Vec 2.0-base model, having undergone pre-training with the KazLibriSpeech corpus and fine-tuning with the ISSAI KSC1 (train + dev) data, exhibits superior results compared to the XLSR-53 model. This occurrence might have been triggered due to the fact that the initial model underwent pre-training using a dataset containing audiobook content.

Table 2. Wav2Vec 2.0 models performance.

ID	Initial model	Pretrain dataset	Finetune dataset	Evaluation set	LM dataset	Test	
						WER	CER
1	Wav2Vec 2.0 Base	KazLibriSpeech	Kazcorpus (train + dev)	Kazcorpus (test)	3-g KenLM	12.4	2.6
2	Wav2Vec 2.0 Base	KazLibriSpeech	ISSAI KSC1 (train + dev)	ISSAI KSC1 (test)	3-g KenLM	10.1	2.8
3	XLSR-53	KazLibriSpeech	Kazcorpus (train + dev)	Kazcorpus (test)	3-g KenLM	8.9	1.9
4	XLSR-53	KazLibriSpeech	ISSAI KSC1 (train + dev)	ISSAI KSC1 (test)	3-g KenLM	15.1	4.8

The training progression during the pre-training and fine-tuning phases is illustrated in Figs. 1 and 2. These visuals depict the changes in loss values throughout training, offering insights into the optimization process of the models.

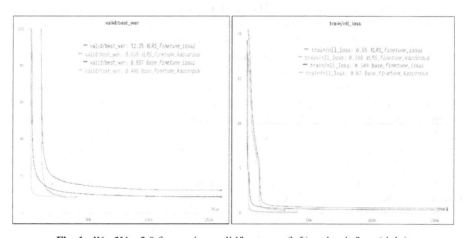

Fig. 1. Wav2Vec 2.0 fine-tuning: valid/best_wer (left) and train/loss (right).

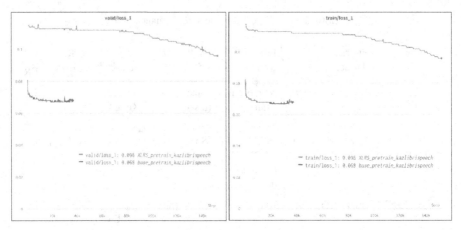

Fig. 2. Wav2Vec 2.0 pre-training: valid/loss (left) and train/loss (right).

5   Conclusion

The main purpose of this study is to evaluate the effectiveness of advanced speech recognition models in transcribing the Kazakh language, which belongs to the category of languages with a low level of resources. Our analysis includes a comprehensive comparison of these models, taking into account the nature and volume of data used during the pre-training and fine-tuning stages. In addition, the study aims to uncover the potential benefits of pre-training using data from other languages, followed by fine-tuning using data from the target language. The study includes a series of experiments using the Wav2Vec2.0 and Wav2Vec2-XLS-R architectures, during which various scenarios of pre-training and fine-tuning are studied. Thanks to these experiments, we not only get an idea of how these models work specifically for the Kazakh language, but also identify the consequences applicable to other languages and settings.

In fact, this study highlights the prospects for using advanced multilingual models and comparing self-supervised and fully supervised methods for reliable ASR in conditions of limited language resources. The findings and methodologies presented in this study have broader implications, including reducing the limitations of language resources and advancing the development of an ASR system for a wide range of languages.

Acknowledgments. This research has been funded by the Science Committee of the Ministry of Education and Science of the Republic of Kazakhstan (Grant No. AP13068635).

References

1. Vaswani, A., et al.: Attention is all you need. In: Advances in neural information processing systems, vol. 30 (2017)
2. Karita, S., et al.: A comparative study on transformer vs rnn in speech applications. In: 2019 IEEE Automatic Speech Recognition and Understanding Workshop (ASRU), pp. 449–456 (2019). https://doi.org/10.1109/ASRU46091.2019.9003750

3. Nakatani, T.: Improving transformer-based end-to-end speech recognition with connectionist temporal classification and language model integration. In: Proceedings of Interspeech (2019). https://doi.org/10.21437/Interspeech.2019-1938

4. Dong, L., Xu, S., Xu, B.: Speech-transformer: a no-recurrence sequence-to-sequence model for speech recognition. In: 2018 IEEE International Conference on Acoustics, Speech and Signal Processing (ICASSP), pp. 5884–5888 (2018). https://doi.org/ https://doi.org/10.1109/ ICASSP.2018.8462506

5. Oord, A. V. D., Li, Y., Vinyals, O.: Representation learning with contrastive predictive coding. arXiv preprint arXiv:1807.03748 (2018)

6. Baevski, A., Zhou, Y., Mohamed, A., Auli, M.: wav2vec 2.0: A framework for self-supervised learning of speech representations. In: Advances in Neural Information Processing Systems, vol. 33, pp. 12449–12460 (2020)

7. Kürzinger, L., Winkelbauer, D., Li, L., Watzel, T., Rigoll, G.: CTC-segmentation of large corpora for german end-to-end speech recognition. In: Proceedings of Speech and Computer: 22nd International Conference, SPECOM 2020, pp. 267–278 (2020). https://doi.org/10.1007/ 978-3-030-60276-5_27

8. Jiang, D., et al.: Improving transformer-based speech recognition using unsupervised pre-training, arXiv preprint arXiv:1910.09932 (2019)

9. Schneider, S., Baevski, A., Collobert, R., Auli, M: wav2vec: unsupervised pre-training for speech recognition. In: Proceedings of Interspeech, pp. 3465–3469 (2019). https://doi.org/ 10.21437/Interspeech.2019-1873

10. Baevski, A., Schneider, S., Auli, M.: vq-wav2vec: Self-supervised learning of discrete speech representations. arXiv preprint arXiv:1910.05453 (2019)

11. Conneau, A., Baevski, A., Collobert, R., Mohamed, A., Auli, M.: Unsupervised cross-lingual representation learning for speech recognition. In: Proceedings of Interspeech, pp. 2426–2430 (2021). https://doi.org/10.21437/Interspeech.2021-329

12. Devlin, J., Chang, M., Lee, K., Toutanova, K.: Bert: Pre-training of deep bidirectional transformers for language understanding. In: Proceedings of the 2019 Conference of the North American Chapter of the Association for Computational Linguistics: Human Language Technologies, pp. 4171–4186 (2019). https://doi.org/10.21437/10.18653/v1/N19-1423

13. Yessenbayev, Z., Karabalayeva, M., Shamayeva, F.: Large vocabulary continuous speech recognition for Kazakh. In: Proceedings of the I International Conference on Computer processing of Turkic Languages, Astana, pp. 217–221 (2013)

14. Kozhirbayev, Z.: Kazakh speech recognition: Wav2vec 2.0 vs. Whisper. J. Adv. Inform. Technol. **14**(6), 1382–1389 (2023). https://doi.org/10.21437/10.12720/jait.14.6.1382-1389

15. Kozhirbayev, Z., Islamgozhayev, T.: Cascade speech translation for the kazakh language. Appl. Sci. **13**(15), 8900 (2023). https://doi.org/10.3390/app13158900

16. Mamyrbayev, O., Oralbekova, D., Kydyrbekova, A., Turdalykyzy, T., Bekarystankyzy, A.: End-to-end model based on RNN-T for Kazakh speech recognition. In: 2021 3rd International Conference on Computer Communication and the Internet (ICCCI), pp. 163–167 (2021). https://doi.org/10.1109/ICCCI51764.2021.9486811

17. Mamyrbayev, O., Oralbekova, D., Alimhan, K., Nuranbayeva, B.: Hybrid end-to-end model for Kazakh speech recognition. Inter. J. Speech Technol., 1–10 (2022). https://doi.org/10. 1007/s10772-022-09983-8

18. Khomitsevich, O., Mendelev, V., Tomashenko, N., Rybin, S., Medennikov, I., Kudubayeva, S.: A bilingual Kazakh-Russian system for automatic speech recognition and synthesis. In: Proceedings of Speech and Computer: 17th International Conference, SPECOM 2015, Athens, Greece, 20–24 September, pp. 25–33 (2015). https://doi.org/10.1007/978-3-319-23132-7_3

19. Khassanov, Y., Mussakhojayeva, S., Mirzakhmetov, A., Adiyev, A., Nurpeiissov, M., Varol, H.: A crowdsourced open-source Kazakh speech corpus and initial speech recognition baseline. In: Proceedings of the 16th Conference of the European Chapter of the Association for Computational Linguistics: Main Volume, pp. 697–706 (2021). https://doi.org/10.18653/v1/2021.eacl-main.58

20. Mussakhojayeva, S., Khassanov, Y., Varol, H.: KSC2: an industrial-scale open-source Kazakh speech corpus. In: Proceedings of the INTERSPEECH, Incheon, Republic of Korea, pp. 18–22 (2015). https://doi.org/10.21437/Interspeech.2022-421

21. Meng, W., Yolwas, N.: A study of speech recognition for kazakh based on unsupervised pre-training. Sensors **23**(2), 870 (2023). https://doi.org/10.3390/s23020870

22. Makhambetov, O., Makazhanov, A., Yessenbayev, Z., Matkarimov, B., Sabyrgaliyev, I., Sharafudinov, A.: Assembling the kazakh language corpus. In: Proceedings of the 2013 Conference on Empirical Methods in Natural Language Processing, pp. 1022–1031 (2013)

23. Watanabe, S., et al.: Espnet: End-to-end speech processing toolkit. arXiv preprint arXiv:1804.00015 (2018)

24. Ott, M., et al.: fairseq: a fast, extensible toolkit for sequence modeling. In: Proceedings of the 2019 Conference of the North American Chapter of the Association for Computational Linguistics (Demonstrations), pp. 48–53 (2019)

25. Myrzakhmetov, B., Kozhirbayev, Z.: Extended language modeling experiments for Kazakh. In: Proceedings of 2018 International Workshop on Computational Models in Language and Speech, p. 42 (2018)

26. Heafield, K.: KenLM: Faster and smaller language model queries. In: Proceedings of the Sixth Workshop on Statistical Machine Translation, pp. 187–197 (2011)

The 2018 Brazilian Presidential Run-Off: A Complex Network Analysis Approach Using Twitter Data

Juliano E. C. Cruz[1]($\boxtimes$) and Marcos G. Quiles[2]

[1] Applied Computing Postgraduate Program, National Institute for Space Research (INPE), São José dos Campos, Brazil
`juliano.cruz@inpe.br`
[2] Institute of Science and Technology, Federal University of São Paulo (UNIFESP), São José dos Campos, SP, Brazil
`quiles@unifesp.br`

Abstract. The political role of social networks has increased significantly in recent years. It has shifted from simple data analytics, employed to understand characteristics and desires of social groups, to a crucial digital platform for political campaigns and social influence. Here, we present an exploratory study of social data gathered from Twitter during the second round of the 2018 Brazilian Presidential Election. The study used complex network analysis to identify hidden communication patterns, important features, and key actors within Twitter data. The results were used to better understand how political polarization is embedded into Twitter during presidential campaigns. Moreover, the model also provided a straightforward manner to scrutinize the data and infer hypotheses from the obtained patterns. In summary, the number of communities of the network revealed an unbalanced division between the candidates and a lack of moderate behaviors.

Keywords: complex network · elections · social network analysis

1 Introduction

Social media has an important role in political discourse worldwide [4]. A considerable part of the global population uses Internet to read about general and political news. Many people who intend to have a more active role in politics, use social networks, blogs, or other online communities [9,10]. A smaller group ends up organizing themselves in private communities, in which most members have homogeneous think alike and usually are aligned to the same party, political view, or ideological currents [10,18]. Nowadays, one of the most popular social media for politicians is Twitter, which allows both direct and public communication with their supporters or ordinary citizens.

Supplementary Information The online version contains supplementary material available at https://doi.org/10.1007/978-3-031-64608-9_9.

Brazil had become increasingly polarized starting with the 2014 presidential elections, oscillating during four years that followed and reaching a peak during the 2018 campaign. For the first time since the end of the military dictatorship, the far-right candidate won the 2018 election. After many years of centrist and left-wing tenures, the far-right coalition won by putting political "outsiders" on the ticket with a political agenda that appealed to the electorate.

Thus, this paper discusses Twitter data collected during the second round of the 2018 elections to verify the structure and patterns of communication and the shape and features of clusters and communities.

In this first section, background information on political polarization, the Brazilian political scenario up to the 2018 elections is presented. . Related studies are analyzed in Sect. 2, followed by methodology. Next, centrality metrics and community detection algorithms employed in this paper are presented. The final section presents the resultant network topology, main nodes, clusters, and communities along with concluding remarks.

1.1 Political Polarization

Lee [16] defines polarization as the growth of extremists and the decline of moderates within an ideological spectrum. DiMaggio *et al.* [12] describe it as both a state and a process, indicating the opposition of opinions and its intensification over time. Polarization can be categorized into elite, mass, or pernicious types. Elite polarization occurs among political actors and institutions [8], while mass polarization involves the electorate's divided opinions and behaviors [1,2]. Pernicious polarization combines elite and mass polarization into large opposing blocks, often around a binary division, and tends to last beyond the event that caused the polarization [8,17].

The evolution of polarization is often fueled by the echo chamber effect, where beliefs are amplified within a closed system, leading to ideological segregation and political polarization [3,22]. This effect is driven by selective exposure and confirmation bias, as individuals engage with information that aligns with their pre-existing beliefs, ignoring contrary viewpoints [3].

1.2 The Brazilian Political Scenario

The second round of the 2018 Brazilian presidential election had candidates from totally opposite political positions.

Jair Bolsonaro, a 63-year-old retired army officer and a seven-term federal congressman, represented the Social Liberal Party (PSL), advocating for a liberal economy and social conservatism. Known for his pro-gun stance and alignment with the United States and Israel, Bolsonaro's far-right views and "outsider" image underscored by his distance from national corruption scandals, made his campaign victorious.

Contrastingly, the Workers' Party (PT) nominated Fernando Haddad, a 55-year-old former São Paulo mayor and Minister of Education under PT administrations, after Luis Inácio Lula da Silva was barred from running due to legal convictions. Haddad's platform focused on expanding social welfare, opposing privatization, and enhancing Latin American and African ties.

Bolsonaro won with over 55% of the valid votes, securing victory in sixteen of the wealthiest states, while Haddad prevailed in eleven of the poorest. The election saw high rates of abstention (21.30%), blank (2.14%), and null (7.43%) votes, reflecting moderate voters' disillusionment with the polarized choice [13].

This polarization traced back to the 2014 elections and was exacerbated by corruption scandals involving PT, leading to widespread protests in 2013 and 2014. The impeachment of President Dilma Rousseff in 2016 and the subsequent presidency of Michel Temer marked a temporary dip in polarization. However, the announcement of the 2018 presidential candidates reignited polarization, reaching its zenith during the run-off.

2 Related Work

Twitter was founded in 2006 and since then, it has been used for many purposes, like product advertisement, news, propaganda, and social networking for ordinary people. There are research articles that discuss the Twitter usage patterns.

Retweet is the main information dissemination mechanism on Twitter, but it was not known why certain information spread faster than others. Thus, Suh et al. [23] evaluated several features that may affect the propagation of tweets through retweets. The results showed that links and hashtags are strongly correlated to the retweet rate, as well as, followed user numbers, follower numbers, and account age.

There are also studies regarding exclusively political analysis on Twitter that can be cited. They analyze situations in Austria [15], Canada [14], Egypt [7], Germany [19], the United Kingdom [11], and the United States [10,24].

Cram et al. [11] analyzes the data from one month before the 2017 British general election. It used over 34 million posts, where 9.6 million are original tweets and 25 million are retweets. The study employed time series analysis regarding relevant news, most cited topics, and most active and popular users. It detected the overwhelming dominance of pro-Labour posts and a disproportionate presence of the Scottish National Party, even though only Scottish voters could elect this party. The study found that, in this case, social media was just an extension of traditional media. It also claimed that, even though Twitter cannot be used to predict elections due to lack of representativeness, it was a useful tool to access the mood of a particular population niche.

As for the 2017 German federal elections, Morstatter et al. [19] measured the election dynamics using Twitter data, from a dataset of more than 39 million tweets, with a little more than 130 thousand users. The study analyzed how the party Alternative for Germany (AfD), was able to take control of a large number of parliament seats. Initially, the study performed community detection to then identify how each cluster interacted with others and also to determine the most relevant themes for each cluster.

Yaqub et al. [24] reports on the 2016 American presidential election, where the main candidates were Hillary Clinton and Donald Trump. The dataset had almost 2.9 million tweets, which were acquired during the elections. One of the objectives was to evaluate how accurately tweets represented the public opinion. It found that sentiment and topics expressed on Twitter could be a good proxy for public opinion. Another finding was that little original content was created by users. They normally retweeted opinions and the user-to-user communication rate was quite low. Finally, the last relevant finding was that sentiments generated by Donald Trump discourses were more optimistic and positive than those generated Hillary's, directly reflecting the comment sentiments of Twitter users at the time.

3   Methodology

3.1   The Abstraction Model

The proposed abstraction model is able to keep all the information extracted from tweets by merging different nodes and relationship types into a unique network. In addition, it also allows node and relationship types to be filtered out in particular queries. The node types are: users, hashtags, retweets and words, called stems. The relationships are: copresence and authorship. Thus, in a scenario in which it is necessary to filter out only the users with a copresence relationship, it can be easily done with this approach. Figure 1 shows what a tweet looks like initially (a) and, in (b), the colored particles are the ones which are selected to become nodes in the preprocessing phase, as detailed in Sect. 3.2. Some words are not tagged due to stop word removal procedure.

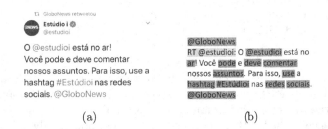

(a)   (b)

Fig. 1. (a) Original tweet and (b) extracted text with color tag representing the node types, where pink highlights users, yellow-retweets, red-words, and blue-hashtags (Color figure online)

The example shown in Fig. 1(a) is a retweet of a TV news account. It was chosen for having all of the node types in just one tweet. The translation is: "@estudioi is on air! You can and should comment our stories. Therefore, use the hashtag #Estúdioi on social networks. @GloboNews"

Networks would not exist with only nodes. Therefore, connections are also a really important feature. The copresence relationship in Fig. 2(a) refers to the relationship created when the terms appear in the same tweet body. It is not directional because the terms are together and there is no action between them. The authorship relationship in Fig. 2(b) refers to the act of a user writing a tweet. In this case, the relationship is directional and goes from the user to tweet body terms. Both edge types are weighted, where it means the number of times that particular relationship happened.

(a) Copresence relationships   (b) Authorship relationships

Fig. 2. Node relationship types: (a) represents terms that appear in the same tweet and (b) represents a user that wrote a tweet with certain terms. This example refers to the Fig. 1(b)

3.2   Dataset and Preprocessing

The data used in this study was acquired during the second round of the 2018 Brazilian presidential election, from October 8th to 27th. It has 1 million public tweets with user name and tweet body. For a faster and more dynamic analysis, an abstraction model, described in Sect. 3.1, was employed. Several processing approaches were employed to design the model some of which are related to Natural Language Processing (NLP).

The following steps were performed in the preprocessing phase: (A) Relational database read; (B) language detection; (C) translation to Portuguese when applicable; (D) tweet segmentation in hashtags, user mentions, author users, retweets and words (regular text); (E) stop word removal (colloquial writing was not considered) and word stemming; (F) insertion in document-oriented database and data transformation; and (G) insertion in graph database.

There was a considerable amount of tweets in other languages. So, language detection was needed for each tweet, which was done in step B. About 91.7% (917,311) of the tweets were in Portuguese, 5.5% (55,169) in English, 1.7% (17,293) in Spanish and 0.4% (4,015) in French. In step C, non-Portuguese tweets were automatically translate to Portuguese to avoid language clusters and create a network that focused on meaning.

Step D performed the tweet segmentation, where tweet body words were separated into five classes or, what we call, tweet particles: hashtag, author user, user mention, retweet, and text. This segmentation procedure is very important for Step G, which needs to know what type of tweet particle it is handling, so it can than create the right type of node and relationship. Due to the fact that each term type has a well-defined pattern, simple regular expressions were used to perform such segmentation. Step E seeks to avoid words that do not have intrinsic meaning and to avoid meaning duplicity by performing stop word removal and stemming, respectively. In step F, the tweets were stored in the document-oriented database, where the document properties are the five tweet particles obtained in segmentation performed by step D. The objective of this task was to transform how data were organized. In step G, all nodes and relationships among them were inserted in graph-oriented database.

4   Methods

The methods employed for further network analysis are explained in this section.

4.1   Centrality Metrics

Centrality metrics measure how important a node is to the network. There are several approaches, but the ones used in this paper are approaches that consider the influence beyond the first connection layer. The methods are eigenvector centrality and PageRank.

Eigenvector Centrality. Eigenvector centrality was proposed in 1986 [6]. It is the first centrality metric to consider the transitive importance of a node in a graph rather than just its direct connections. Thus, relationships with high scoring nodes can be said to contribute more to the scoring of a particular node than connections to low scoring nodes.

PageRank. PageRank was initially created to rank websites in Google search [20]. The score is based on the inbound link quantity and quality. It also relies on the assumption that an Internet user can get bored after several clicks, going then to a random page. It can be understood as a Markov chain, where states are pages and transitions are links, all of which have equally transition likelihood. Thus, if the method reaches a page with no outbound link, it will randomly choose a page to continue the process. PageRank pragmatically considers that pages without outbound links are connected to all pages in the network. Therefore, scores found for this particular page are divided equally among all other pages. This residual transition probability is typically set to 0.85. The value is estimated by averaging how often users use their bookmark list to go to a new page.

4.2   Community Detection

The objective of community detection methods is to find clusters in the network. Contrary to clustering methods that group samples in terms of their features, community detection only uses nodes and theirs relationships. This study employs label propagation and Louvain methods.

Label Propagation. The Label Propagation algorithm is a fast algorithm for finding communities in graphs, which was proposed by Raghavan *et al.* [21]. It can detect communities using only the network structure but it has a feature allows to use initial labels to narrow down the final solution.

The algorithm assumes that a single label can easily become dominant in a densely connected group of nodes, which is unlikely to happen in a poorly connected region. At the end, nodes with the same label belong to the same community. The algorithm's name comes from the fact that some labels propagate through the network during the iterative process of label updating. Densely connected groups of nodes quickly reach consensus on a single label during the iterations. So, only a few labels will remain at the end.

The Louvain Algorithm. Proposed by Blondel *et al.* [5] the Louvain algorithm performs hierarchical community detection. It is based on modularity and is one of the fastest algorithms, also performing well on very large graphs [5]. The basic idea consists in optimizing the communities' modularity and then, aggregating the community nodes. The modularity score quantifies the assignment quality of a community to a node by comparing how densely connected that community has become compared to a scenario in which it is a random network.

Louvain is a hierarchical method. Thus, it tries to go a level further every iteration, merging communities whenever possible. The overall stop criterion is met when an iteration does not result in any reassignments.

5   Results

5.1   Network Basic Features

The network under study comprises 468,643 nodes and 3,854,159 edges, featuring four distinct node types: 338,899 unique users, 66,831 unique stems, 40,790 unique retweets, and 22,123 unique hashtags. The edges are divided into 2,178,039 copresence relationships and 1,676,120 authorship relationships. Notably, 52% (176,079) of user nodes were active in writing tweets, while 48% (162,820) were mentioned without actively participating. A significant portion of nodes (32%, 149,095) lacked connections, often due to tweets containing only links or images without text.

Table 1 compares network segments by average degree, connection weight, and clustering coefficient. The network's average degree stood at 2842.0, with an edge weight of 3.65 per node, indicating the diversity of tweet particles and the frequency of node usage in tweets. The clustering coefficient, averaging over 0.16, reflects the degree of neighbor connectivity, with 1 indicating full connection and 0 none. The authorship-only network segment exhibited a markedly lower clustering coefficient (0.0007), suggesting less interconnectedness compared to the broader network. In contrast, retweets had a slightly higher average clustering coefficient (0.2269), hinting at more dense connections among these nodes. This structural analysis reveals the network's complexity and the varying interaction patterns among different node types.

Table 1. Average degree, average weight per node, and average clustering coefficient for the entire network and for different node types.

Node Type	Population	Avg. Degree	Avg. Weight	Avg. Clustering Coef
all	468,643	2842.0	3.65	0.1618
all (authorship)	236,563	2345.3	1.00	0.0007
all (copresence)	139,055	1746.9	6.09	0.0455
hashtags	22,123	6145.0	8.59	0.1303
stems	66,831	1823.4	3.94	0.1682
retweets	40,790	789.0	8.10	0.2269
users	338,899	259.1	1.55	0.1548

In analyzing the network by node type, hashtags lead with an average degree of 6145.0, followed by stems (1823.4), retweets (789.0), and users (259.1) due to their frequency and repetition in tweets. Hashtags, indexing keywords or topics, appear more repetitively (8.59 times on average) and are crucial for topic identification. Stems, representing morphological roots, are often neutral and used across political discussions, explaining their high repetition but lower average weight compared to hashtags and retweets. Retweets, reflecting endorsements of views, show high repetition due to the verbatim sharing of messages, enhancing their relationship weight.

User nodes exhibit the least diversity (259.1) and repetition (1.55), impacted by the predominance of single-use authorship relationships, with over 72% of user nodes not repeating tweet particles. This uniqueness of user nodes stems from their mandatory role in authorship relationships, directly affecting their average weight and degree distribution.

Degree distribution, illustrated in Fig. 3, reveals distinct patterns for each node type. Users and stems start with higher magnitudes (10000), while hashtags and retweets start at 1000. Notably, user nodes display a significant plateau, ending at degree 17, whereas retweets show a smaller plateau, concluding at degree 7, indicating varied engagement levels across node types.

Figure 4 segments the network's degree distribution by connection type, revealing distinct patterns. The authorship relationship, depicted in Fig. 4(a), mirrors the user node distribution from Fig. 3(b), highlighting the significant role of user nodes in authorship connections. Conversely, the copresence relationship, shown in Fig. 4(b), aligns more closely with the distribution patterns of hashtags, retweets, and stems, indicating their prevalent use in tweets. The combined network view in Fig. 4(c) predominantly reflects the copresence relationship's distribution but also features a secondary peak from degrees 12 to 17, attributable to authorship connections.

The network's average weight per node is 3.65, with 87% (296,354) of nodes having an average weight between 1 and 2, as shown in Fig. 5. This metric indicates the frequency of interactions between nodes, underscoring the network's dynamic nature.

The highest degree nodes are predominantly hashtags, with five stems and one user also making the list. Degrees range from approximately 17,000 to over 42,000, with most nodes having an average weight below 10, highlighting the significant role of hashtags in the network. Notably, three candidate-related

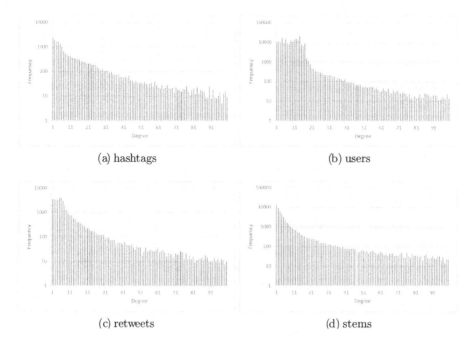

(a) hashtags

(b) users

(c) retweets

(d) stems

Fig. 3. Degree distribution for different node types.

hashtags (#haddad13, #bolsonaropresidente, and #bolsonarosim) and one candidate account (@jairbolsonaro) have higher average weights, reflecting their central role in the network's discourse.

Focusing on hashtags, all of which are associated with the two main candidates, indicating a lack of neutral hashtags among the top ranks. The distribution of average weights suggests varying degrees of engagement and repetition among these hashtags, with no direct correlation between degree and average weight. This pattern underscores the hashtags' importance in organizing and amplifying political discourse on Twitter.

Stems, ranking second in average degree, exhibit lower average weights compared to hashtags. Their neutrality and widespread use across political discussions contribute to their high degree but lower repetition rate.

Retweets and user nodes, despite their lower ranking in degree, show significant engagement levels, with retweets particularly standing out for their higher average weights, indicative of their role in disseminating messages verbatim across the network.

The cumulative distribution function (CDF) of the network and its subnetworks, presented in Fig. 6, contrasts with example power-law and Poisson distributions. The overall network and authorship subnetwork distributions deviate from these models, suggesting a unique network structure not fully captured by traditional distribution models. However, the copresence subnetwork's alignment with a power-law distribution hints at the scale-free nature of these interactions.

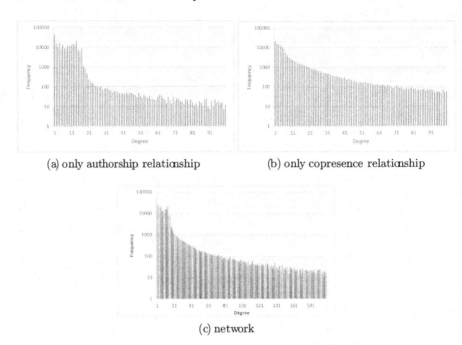

(a) only authorship relationship   (b) only copresence relationship

(c) network

Fig. 4. Degree distribution for each relationships and for the entire network.

This analysis elucidates the complex interplay of node types within the network, highlighting the pivotal role of hashtags in structuring political discourse and the distinct patterns of engagement across different types of connections. Detailed information about each node type or other analyses done can be found in Supplementary Material.

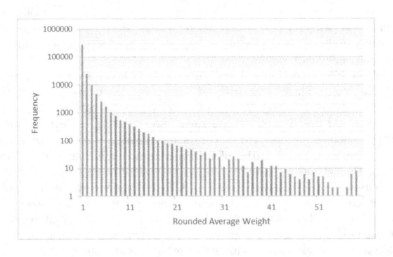

Fig. 5. The distribution of average connection weight per node.

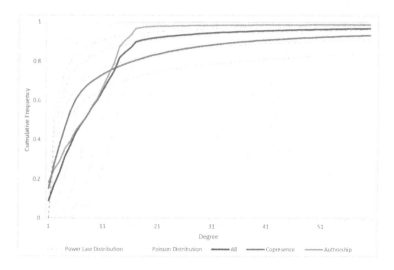

Fig. 6. Cumulative distribution functions of the network and its subnetworks (solid lines), example of power law distributions (dash-dot lines), and example of Poisson distributions (dashed lines).

5.2 Authorship Relations

Analyzing authorship relationships between users and retweets reveals the network's main influencers. Popularity is gauged not just by the number of retweets or mentions but by the diversity of users engaging. This approach values breadth over depth of interaction, focusing on user-user and user-retweet dynamics.

Figure 7 identifies the twenty most cited users, with @jairbolsonaro and @haddad_fernando emerging as principal hubs within their respective clusters. Other notable mentions include @manueladavila, @rogerwaters, and @lulaoficial supporting Haddad, and @lobaoeletrico, @carlosbolsonaro supporting Bolsonaro, alongside neutral entities like @youtube and @tsejusbr. The peculiar case of @jairbolsonarohttps highlights issues in data parsing.

Distinct clusters around these hubs suggest a polarized network structure, with a central cluster engaging with both sides. The comparison between the top 15 users regarding degree and top 20 most mentioned users shows a shift in ranking when focusing solely on inbound authorship connections, underscoring the different interaction patterns in authorship versus copresence relationships.

Retweet analysis regarding the authors with higher degree further illustrates the network's segmentation, with no cross-cluster retweeting among the top 20 retweets. This isolation reflects echo chamber dynamics, as discussed by Conover *et al.* [10]. The majority of retweets support Haddad, with a smaller fraction backing Bolsonaro or remaining neutral. Detailed information about the analyses done can be found in Supplementary Material.

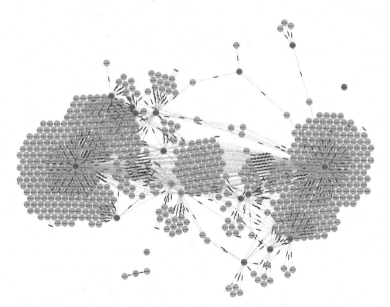

Fig. 7. The twenty most mentioned users and the main users who mentioned them (light blue). The color of mentioned users represent which side they were related to. Blue is for nodes supporting Bolsonaro, red Haddad and gray neutral. (Color figure online)

5.3 Top 50

Centrality analysis using eigenvector and PageRank metrics reveals the network's key nodes. The eigenvector centrality, shown in Fig. 8, highlights a network with 771 connections, including fifteen users, twelve hashtags, and twenty-three stems, but no retweet nodes. This mix of nodes indicates diverse political affiliations and topics of discussion, from election-related hashtags to neutral stems and media outlets.

PageRank centrality, detailed in Fig. 9, presents a slightly different composition with nineteen hashtags, nineteen stems, nine retweets, and three users. This variation underscores the different focuses of the two centrality measures, with PageRank incorporating a broader array of retweets and hashtags into the top ranks.

Both centrality measures capture the network's critical nodes but from different perspectives. Eigenvector centrality emphasizes users and stems, while PageRank gives more weight to retweets and hashtags, reflecting their role in disseminating and amplifying content.

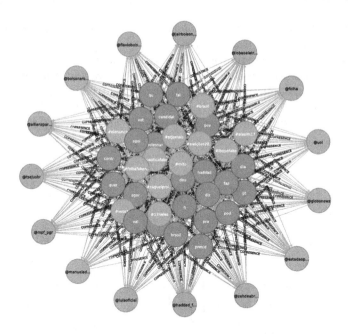

Fig. 8. Top 50 using eigenvector centrality.

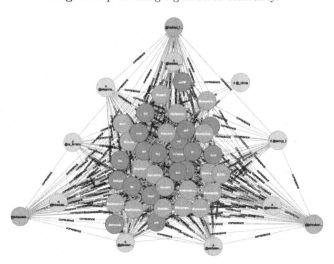

Fig. 9. Top 50 using PageRank.

5.4 Communities

Community detection using the Louvain algorithm identified 150,574 communities, with the 23 largest encompassing 67.7% of all nodes. These communities range from large, politically aligned clusters to smaller, topic-specific groups. The largest community had 43,415 nodes, while the smallest in the top 23 had

84 nodes. Communities with only one node accounted for over 32% of the total, highlighting the network's fragmentation.

Figure 10 shows the distribution of these communities by size and political affiliation, with Bolsonaro-related communities numbering nine and Haddad-related six. Neutral communities, often hosting debates between political sides, make up eight of the total. Notably, some communities focus less on political debate and more on specific themes or events, such as concerts or personal discussions.

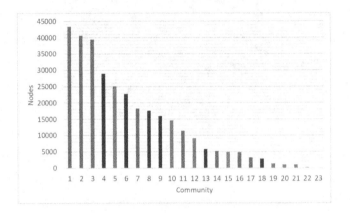

Fig. 10. Largest communities obtained with Louvain algorithm. Blue are Bolsonaro-related, red-Haddad-related, and gray-neutrals. (Color figure online)

The internal organization of these communities, as depicted in Fig. 11, reveals a predominance of user nodes, with significant variation in the presence of other node types like retweets, stems, and hashtags. This diversity indicates the range of discussion and interaction patterns within each community.

PageRank scores within communities, shown in Fig. 12 and Fig. 13, suggest a wide disparity in influence, with most nodes holding low scores. This distribution points to a few highly influential nodes within communities, surrounded by a large number of less influential ones.

PageRank was chosen because it generated a top 50 composed of all node types, which did not happen with eigenvector centrality, see Sect. 5.3. Having a more diverse node population, theoretically, helps in order to have a better inference about community theme. Thus, from visually analyzing the top 30 of every community it is possible to note that only two communities (19 and 11) do not have all node types present. Also, most of the top 30 have stems as the majority nodes, except for Community 1. Stems do not have the highest PageRank scores on average (Fig. 14), but at the top 30 they are the majority in most communities. Another notable trend is that, the smaller the community is with the top 30, the more likely it is to be less connected.

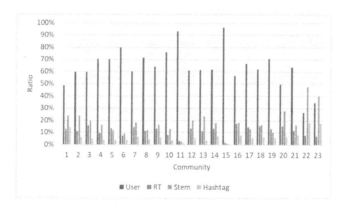

Fig. 11. Node-type ratio for each community.

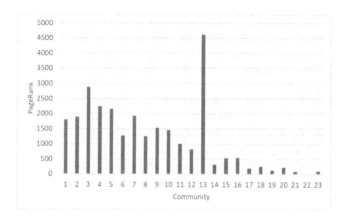

Fig. 12. Highest PageRank scores for each community.

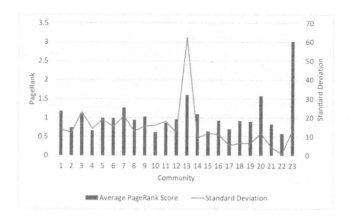

Fig. 13. PageRank score average and standard deviation for each community.

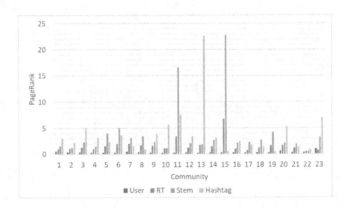

Fig. 14. PageRank average per node type in each community.

The analysis of community themes, based on the top 30 nodes by PageRank, reveals a rich tapestry of political affiliations, key issues, and public figures dominating the discourse. While political nodes are prevalent, the presence of neutral and thematic nodes underscores the network's complexity and the multifaceted nature of online political discourse.

In summary, the network's structure, from its influencers to its communities, paints a detailed picture of the online political landscape during the election period. The interplay of user interactions, centrality measures, and community dynamics offers insights into the digital public square's polarized yet interconnected nature. Detailed information about all the analyses done can be found in Supplementary Material.

6   Conclusions

The objective of this paper was to discuss Twitter data from the Brazilian 2018 presidential run-off election. The study employed tools and methods to facilitate storage, processing, and analysis of unstructured data.

The employed tweet abstraction model made the network analysis easier and much more dynamic. Just one network was necessary. Analysis was performed by queries that allowed selecting multiple types of nodes and connections. The copresence subnetwork seems to follow a power-law distribution, while the entire network and authorship subnetwork do not seem to follow either power-law or Poisson distribution. When the most mentioned users were filtered, the resultant hubs coincide with the most prominent personalities and organizations during the period of the political campaign. The main users are both presidential candidates and secondarily there are users orbiting them. The fact that there is just a medium-size group of users connected to both candidates may suggest that the majority of users might get focused exclusively on attacking or supporting one of the sides, with regard to user mention.

The claim that users who support opposite parties or politicians hardly interact through retweets [10] was confirmed by the analysis done. In addition, no user retweeted more than one node from the top 20.

The results from Label Propagation algorithm were not satisfactory. However, the Louvain algorithm produced good results. The community sizes have logarithmic-alike distribution, then only the main ones where analyzed, the 23 largest communities. Most of the top 30 nodes of the communities had stems as majority. Their main node was hashtag (9 communities), followed by stems (6 communities).

Frequently research creates more questions than answers. Further studies should examine the communities in greater depth, to study main user roles and influences, hashtag and stem themes. They also should probe the relationship among communities in order to understand the relationship structure and to examine whether neutral communities orbit polarized groups or form an independent major group.

Finally, polarization normally means expanding extremists and diminishing moderates. Moderate numbers diminish, but do not disappear completely. Therefore, except for Community 15, one could not find explicitly moderate users or moderate behavior in the data analyzed. It is impossible to say if moderates ignored the second round election completely or supported one of the sides; there is no data to establish by what ratio either happened. Nor can it be ascertained what role moderates had in communities, or even if they were present in the major ones.

References

1. Abramowitz, A.: The disappearing center: engaged citizens, polarization, and American democracy. Yale University Press (2011)
2. Abramowitz, A.A., Saunders, K.L.: Is polarization a myth? J. Politics **70**(2), 542–555 (2018)
3. Barberá, P., Jost, J., Nagler, J., Tucker, J., Bonneau, R.: Tweeting from left to right: is online political communication more than an echo chamber? Psychol. Sci. **26**(10), 1531–1542 (2015)
4. Barberá, P., Gohdes, A.R., Iakhnis, E., Zeitzoff, T.: Distract and divert: how world leaders use social media during contentious politics. Inter. J. Press/Politics **29**(1), 47–73 (2024)
5. Blondel, V.D., Guillaume, J., Lambiotte, R., Lefebvre, E.: Fast unfolding of communities in large networks. J. Stat. Mech: Theory Exp. **2008**(10), P10008 (2008)
6. Bonacich, P.: Power and centrality: a family of measures. Am. J. Sociol. **92**(5), 1170–1182 (1987)
7. Borge-Holthoefer, J., Magdy, W., Darwish, K., Weber, I.: Content and network dynamics behind egyptian political polarization on twitter. In: Proceedings of ACM Conference on Computer Supported Cooperative Work & Social Computing, pp. 700–711 (2015)
8. Carothers, T., O'Donohue, A.: Democracies Divided: The Global Challenge of Political Polarization. Brookings Institution Press (2019)

9. Chan, M., Yi, J.: Social media use and political engagement in polarized times. examining the contextual roles of issue and affective polarization in developed democracies. Political Commun., 1–20 (2024)
10. Conover, M.D., Ratkiewicz, J., Francisco, M., Gonçalves, B., Menczer, F., Flammini, A.: Political polarization on twitter. In: AAAI Conference on Weblogs and Social Media (2011)
11. Cram, L., Llewellyn, C., Hill, R., Magdy, W.: Uk general election 2017: a twitter analysis. arXiv:1706.02271 (2017)
12. DiMaggio, P., Evans, J., Bryson, B.: Have American's social attitudes become more polarized? Am. J. Sociol. **102**(3), 690–755 (1996)
13. Federal, S.T.: Brazilian electoral data repository. http://www.tse.jus.br/hotsites/pesquisas-eleitorais/index.html, (Accessed Jan 10 2020)
14. Gruzd, A., Roy, J.: Investigating political polarization on twitter: a canadian perspective. Policy & Internet **6**(1), 28–45 (2014)
15. Kušen, E., Strembeck, M.: Politics, sentiments, and misinformation: an analysis of the twitter discussion on the 2016 austrian presidential elections. Online Soc. Netw. Media **5**, 37–50 (2018)
16. Lee, J.M.: The political consequences of elite and mass polarization. Ph.D. thesis, University of Iowa (2012)
17. McCoy, J., Somer, M.: Toward a theory of pernicious polarization and how it harms democracies: Comparative evidence and possible remedies. Annals Am. Acad. Political Soc. Sci. **681**
18. Moe, H., Lindtner, S., Ytre-Arne, B.: Polarisation and echo chambers? making sense of the climate issue with social media in everyday life. Nordicom Rev. **44**(1), 23–43 (2023)
19. Morstatter, F., Shao, Y., Galstyan, A., Karunasekera, S.: From alt-right to alt-rechts: twitter analysis of the 2017 german federal election. In: Proceedings of the The Web Conference, pp. 621–628 (2018)
20. Page, L., Brin, S., Motwani, R., Winograd, T.: The pagerank citation ranking: bringing order to the web. Stanford InfoLab (1999)
21. Raghavan, U.N., Albert, R., Kumara, S.: Near linear time algorithm to detect community structures in large-scale networks. Phys. Rev. E **76**(3), 036106 (2007)
22. Rum, S.N.M., Mohamed, R., Asfarian, A.: Identifying political polarization in social media: a literature review. J. Adv. Res. Appli. Sci. Eng. Technol. **34**(1), 80–89 (2023)
23. Suh, B., Hong, L., Pirolli, P., Chi, E.H.: Want to be retweeted? large scale analytics on factors impacting retweet in twitter network. In: IEEE International Conference on Social Computing, pp. 177–184 (2010)
24. Yaqub, U., Chun, S.A., Atluri, V., Vaidya, J.: Analysis of political discourse on twitter in the context of the 2016 us presidential elections. Gov. Inf. Q. **34**(4), 613–626 (2017)

A Descriptive and Predictive Analysis Tool for Criminal Data: A Case Study from Brazil

Yan Andrade[1(✉)], Matheus Pimenta[3], Gabriel Amarante[3],
Antônio Hot Faria[2,3], Marcelo Vilas-Boas[2], João Paulo da Silva[2],
Felipe Rocha[2], Jamicel da Silva[2], Wagner Meira Jr.[3], George Teodoro[3],
Leonardo Rocha[1], and Renato Ferreira[3]

[1] Universidade Federal de São João del-Rei, São João del Rei, Brazil
`yrandrade123@aluno.ufsj.edu.br, lcrocha@ufsj.edu.br`
[2] Polícia Militar de Minas Gerais, Belo Horizonte, Brazil
`{1265677,1357516,1369016,jamicel.silva}@pm.mg.gov.br`
[3] Universidade Federal de Minas Gerais, Belo Horizonte, Brazil
`{matheuspimenta,gabriel.amarante,antonio.hot,`
`meira,george,renato}@dcc.ufmg.br`

Abstract. Addressing the challenge of crime is crucial for governing bodies, requiring informed strategies. This article examines the underutilization of detailed criminal data, collaborating with the Military Police of Minas Gerais, Brazil. We propose a new methodology, materialized in a tool, that is able to transform raw data into strategic information for public security decision-making. The tool evaluation unfolds in three phases: characterizing the data, a descriptive analysis of a real case study, and a predictive analysis. This work highlights the untapped potential in detailed criminal data, emphasizing the pivotal role of precise analysis in deciphering complex dynamics. Collaborating with law enforcement aims to bridge the gap between data abundance and actionable insights for effective public security strategies.

1 Introduction

Security impacts all dimensions of everyday life, from personal development to the business landscape [3]. The effects of the feeling of insecurity influence the quality of life, restrict mobility, and impact the economy, undermining investor confidence and market stability. The persistent fight against crime poses a significant challenge for governments, requiring well-founded and effective strategies. The inherent complexity of this challenge, connected to a network of social, demographic, and educational factors, highlights the need for a precise understanding for an effective approach [10]. In this context, understanding and characterizing crime and how all the factors inherent to it are related becomes a crucial task for proposals of effective and comprehensive solutions.

Considering this, the capacity of public security organizations to collect and store detailed data on criminal events has experienced significant growth, resulting in the daily generation of large volumes of information. These data, enriched

O. Gervasi et al. (Eds.): ICCSA 2024, LNCS 14814, pp. 151–169, 2024.
https://doi.org/10.1007/978-3-031-64608-9_10

with spatial and temporal details, offer a comprehensive overview of criminal dynamics. However, within this scenario, with excess information, a problem emerges: the underutilization of these data [12]. The lack of appropriate analysis compromises the extraction of valuable insights and constitutes an obstacle to informed decision-making and the development of effective public policies in the fight against crime.

In the face of this challenging context, in this paper, we present a methodology for characterizing previously stored criminal data that allows it to be transformed into information that helps develop assertive crime-fighting and prevention tactics. Our methodology aims to understand the dynamics of crime occurrence from two different perspectives: temporal and spatial. Based on this understanding, in this work, we also evaluate the application of regression models that can correlate information from the two perspectives considered, helping predict where and when crimes will occur in the future. The entire methodology is materialized in a tool focused on a simple and intuitive interface to be used by public agents responsible for security.

The tool comprises six distinct modules: Scenario Filtering, Trend Analysis, Distribution Analysis, Temporal Heat Map, Layered Event Map, and Regression Models. In the first module, we provide a series of filters that allow us to select the data set for the scenario we want to analyze, for example, theft crimes on weekdays during the afternoon in the downtown neighborhood. Several scenarios can be selected and contrasted. The second module (Trend Analysis) provides visual metaphors that allow us to assess the temporal evolution of a particular type of criminal occurrence. In the scenario previously presented, we can assess the trend of theft occurrences in the city center. The third module (Distribution Analysis) provides intuitive visualizations that allow us to analyze how the distribution of criminal occurrences occurs in different regions and periods (dawn, morning, afternoon, and evening). The tool is flexible enough and allows the inclusion of new distributions for analysis. The fourth module (Temporal Heat Map) provides an intuitive visualization of the distribution of criminal occurrences in a given period by combining a heat map with a calendar. In the fifth module (Layered Event Map), we implemented a georeferenced visualization from a map in multiple layers. In the first layer, the neighborhoods of a given city are delimited according to official city data. Over this first layer, a heat map allows us to identify the neighborhoods with the highest incidence of a specific crime regionally. In the third layer, we provide a map with the distribution of points that represent the incidents, and in the fourth layer, through the integration with a clustering algorithm that groups occurrences according to geographical proximity, identifying and highlighting the critical points according to the concentration of crime incidents. Finally, our last module comprises a series of implemented geospatial regression algorithms that allow us to create predictive models on crime incidence, helping to identify when and where there is the highest probability of incidence of a particular crime. All these modules working together are essential to help the competent authorities decide about optimized public policies to combat and prevent crime.

We instantiated our methodology using data from Brazil, one of the 20 countries with the highest crime rates in the world, according to the Global Organized Crime Index[1]. More specifically, we used the criminal records stored by the Military Police of the State of Minas Gerais (PMMG), Brazil, which is subordinate to the Public Security Secretariat of Minas Gerais, one of the most violent states in Brazil. Since 2005, the PMMG has had a system for recording criminal occurrences and currently has over 40 million cases related to the 853 municipalities in Minas Gerais. These occurrences range from violent crimes, such as theft, robbery, and homicide, to less impactful occurrences from a public security standpoint, such as arguments and verbal aggression. The occurrences are defined employing 224 attributes that provide a wide range of information, from aspects such as temporal data, including the date and time of the occurrence, spatial aspects such as latitude, longitude, municipality, and address, to bureaucratic details associated with each registered incident.

Among the various results we obtained from the instantiation of our tool in this database, we highlight some that demonstrate the potential of our tool. In a more specific analysis, we compared the crime map before, during, and after Carnival, the world's most famous Brazilian popular festival. We focused our analysis on Belo Horizonte, the capital of the State of Minas Gerais. We observed a significant change in criminal behavior during Carnival, with a substantial increase in crimes, concentrated in places where specific events occur (carnival blocks), with a large concentration of tourists. Identifying and characterizing this atypical behavior is essential for developing specific combat and prevention strategies, helping to allocate public security agents more efficiently. In addition to this descriptive analysis, we detail a predictive data analysis in our results. Also, considering the city of Belo Horizonte during January, we trained and evaluated two crime prediction models. Both models demonstrated satisfactory performance, presenting predicted values close to the actual data. These prediction models allow public security to develop preventive actions more assertively. Integrating all modules of the proposed tool offers an approach with complete descriptive and predictive analyses, contributing more effectively to improving public safety.

2   Related Work

Crime data analysis is the subject of several works investigating different data mining techniques for identifying patterns and relationships between criminal events. In [11], the authors propose using association rule algorithms to find correlations between descriptive attributes and crime types. Using Apriori [8], recognized for its effectiveness in several domains, the authors identified rules that correlated attributes such as day of the week, weather conditions, holiday, time of day, and crime type with the location of the occurrence. Notably, most crimes tended to occur on days without rain and in residential areas. Another relevant observation of the authors was the absence of frequent pairs for sexual

---

[1] https://ocindex.net/rankings?f=rankings&view=List.

crimes, suggesting the possibility of occurring randomly at different times and places. The rules found were contrasted with a heatmap of occurrences showing great correspondence. Based on this last observation, we opted for our tool to use heatmaps.

Another set of techniques widely used in criminal characterizations is clustering [19] and outlier detection [17]. In [16], the authors present a study that analyzes spatio-temporal patterns of crimes in micro-locations (streets) in six major US cities using clustering algorithms. The authors identify the micro-locations with the highest crime incidence at different times and perform a comparative temporal evaluation between them. In their conclusions, the authors identify a pattern, and many regions with the highest crime rates are persistent over time. Our tool also uses clustering algorithms. More specifically, we perform a georeferenced grouping of criminal occurrences, identifying and highlighting the points of highest incidence, which we call critical points, on the map. This analysis is also integrated with a calendar, allowing us to expand the scale of the spatial analysis and provide a more comprehensive view of crime patterns over time.

In another research line, we identified works that analyze the importance of applying pre-processing techniques before conducting analyses on criminal data. In [14], the authors present a taxonomy composed of two types of errors: systematic (underreporting and undercounting of crimes) and random (inconsistencies in the reporting and recording processes of crimes between victims, areas, and police forces). In the evaluations, the authors show that measurement errors can lead to biased estimates in all prediction models. Our work takes a similar stance to the article [14]. Both recognize the importance of processing the data before analyzing it. In our case, we implemented specific processing methods, such as logarithmic transformation, as proposed in this study, for discrepancies in criminal data records.

As mentioned in the previous paragraph, in addition to works on characterization in understanding criminal data, we observe a growing line of works that aim to build spatio-temporal predictive models [2], with emphasis on time series. These are notable for the chronological indexing of their observations [20] and, consequently, crucial in analyzing trends and patterns over time. This approach is divided into three main components: Trend, which reflects the long-term structural direction of the data; Seasonality, related to repetitive patterns at fixed intervals, capturing regular fluctuations; and Noise, representing residuals after removing seasonality and trend, expressing non-systematic and random variation in the data. A relevant study [5] employed the ARIMA model [21] to perform temporal regression, exploring different parameters and their impacts. Focusing on the Chicago region, the goal was to identify critical areas of the state. Using hotspot and clustering techniques, the study outlined these regions and applied regression algorithms to identify specific trends in each one. They demonstrated the need to adjust the model's hyperparameters for each region. This integrated approach offered a deeper understanding of the temporal behavior in specific regions. Similar work is presented in [9] using ARIMA with criminal data from India. In [15], the authors present a temporal analysis technique for criminal

data called Heartbeat, which overlays spatial, temporal, and intensity information, separated by crime type, into a predictive model. The authors observed
that the Heartbeat was able to indicate specific moments of higher occurrence
for different types of crime. Going a little further, [18] analyzes the impact of
well-made criminal predictions on the proper allocation of patrolling and, consequently, on crime reduction.

As we will see in the next section, our tool also allows training models capable of performing spatio-temporal predictions. We provide a series of filters that
allow the creation of various scenarios for training predictive models, from more
specific scenarios (i.e., theft crimes during the night in central neighborhoods)
to more general scenarios (i.e., crimes in general throughout the city). This
allows the development of crime-fighting tactics customized according to region,
time, and type of crime, the development of articulated strategies between different public security agents from different regions, and even the development of
medium- and long-term public safety policies. We will detail our proposal below.

3   Criminal Analysis Tool

The objective of the proposed tool is to transform criminal records into valuable information that can assist public security officials in the development of
(1) assertive crime-fighting strategies, as well as (2) the construction of crime
prevention public policies. Our tool uses both descriptive models, which aim to
continuously map occurrences (crime-fighting strategies), and predictive models, which aim to anticipate where and when crimes will occur (crime prevention
public policies). Thinking about these objectives, we created a complete tool
that, in addition to geographic visualization, provides in-depth data visualization, scenario simulation, identification of trends in the number of occurrences,
data distribution analysis, visual representation through temporal heat maps,
and methodology to highlight points that require special attention. The tool was
implemented using the Python programming language and the Streamlit library
due to their ability to create dashboards that comprehensively and intuitively
present data. An overview of the tool is presented in Fig. 1, and in this section,
we present a detailed description of each component of the tool, highlighting how
they complement each other to provide a comprehensive and effective decision-
making tool. Our focus is on the ability of the tool to transform complex data
into actionable insights and increase a deep understanding of the crime landscape
to optimize public security strategies.

3.1   Scenario Filtering

Typically, criminal records are composed of several attributes that detail the
occurrences. These attributes can be related to temporal perspectives (date
and time of the occurrence), geographic (city, neighborhood, street, etc.), and
descriptive (type of crime, total victims, etc.). Performing a global analysis of all
data can be computationally infeasible and also uninformative from the point

of view of the conclusions that can be generated. In addition, public security actions and responsibilities are segmented in most countries. That is, specific organizations are responsible for combating and preventing crime according to the locality. For this reason, the first component of our tool is filters (item 1 in Fig. 1) that allow users to analyze different scenarios by segmenting the data representation according to specific criteria. The filters provided by our tool are:

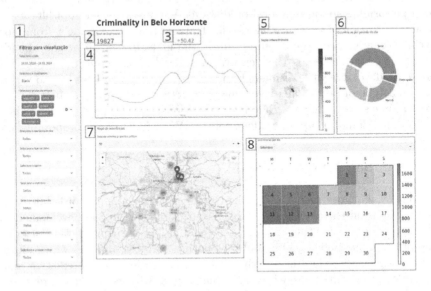

Fig. 1. Main page of the tool

- **Time interval**: Provides a custom time visualization by selecting a specific date range to perform the analysis;
- **Granularity**: Offers the ability to visualize data at different temporal granularities, such as daily, monthly, or annual, allowing for a more detailed or more generalized view of the data;
- **Day of the week**: Allows users to select specific days of the week for analysis, helping to identify patterns of events in different periods, for example, only weekends, only weekdays, or only a specific day of the week.;
- **Time of day**: By dividing the day into four periods (early morning, morning, afternoon, and evening), it is possible to analyze more accurately the difference in crime rates at different times of the day;
- **Neighborhoods**: We standardized the data based on latitude and longitude, allowing users to select specific neighborhoods within each municipality and providing more localized analyses. For an adequate neighborhood analysis, it is necessary to integrate this filter with the official map of the cities, where the boundaries between the neighborhoods are highlighted;
- **Address**: Facilitates the more detailed selection of the location, including street information for a more fine-grained analysis;

- **Crime types**: Covers all types of incidents found in the data, allowing for a detailed analysis of the different types of crimes registered;
- **Department**: Allows the choice of the responsible department, such as police stations or police posts, contributing to an analysis by area of responsibility. For an adequate department analysis, it is necessary to integrate this filter with the official distribution of police stations/departments of each city;
- **Unit**: Allows the selection of the responsible unit, following the pre-established hierarchy by the public security agency. For an adequate unit analysis, it is necessary to integrate this filter with the pre-established hierarchy of a given country or state;

Based on these filters, various scenarios can be constructed for analysis. For example, one could investigate the distribution of robberies in neighborhood "X" in the early morning hours on weekends from January to April, contrasting it with a similar scenario but evaluating weekdays. Alternatively, one could perform an analysis with the same configuration evaluating different neighborhoods. Another interesting example would be to analyze entire and nearby neighborhoods, contrasting the information found with and without a specific event, such as a soccer game or a concert. In short, through these filters, we have infinite scenarios that can be created and contrasted in various analyses.

3.2 Trend Analysis

The first analysis module of the tool focuses on three key elements to provide a comprehensive understanding of the temporal trends of events. The first field (item 2 in Fig. 1) displays the total number of incidents based on the filters used, allowing you to see the number immediately. The second graphical component (item 4 in Fig. 1) visually highlights the behavior of the event, allowing cumulative analyses over time-based on the defined granularity, including day, month, or year.

This section highlights the fusion of trend lines obtained by applying a regression algorithm to the graph points. We decided to use linear regression as our model for its simplicity and efficiency in simple cases and online systems. This technique provides functions that model the relationships between points in a graph, allowing us to obtain a mathematical expression for the defined time flow. We use the derivative of the regression function at the last point of the graph to determine if the trend is increasing or decreasing (item 3 in Fig. 1). The arrows next to the numerical value indicate the rate of change in the number of cases, highlighting the derived values. It is important to note that this value does not directly correspond to the rate of change but provides a relative measure of the slope of the trend. This approach combines visual interpretation with powerful mathematical analysis to provide valuable insights into the temporal patterns of events.

3.3 Distributions Analysis

The distribution analysis module is designed to provide a detailed and comprehensive view of criminal events' spatial and temporal aspects, including updated distribution by neighborhood and time of day. Each of these distributions represents critically important aspects of the data, allowing for a deeper analysis of the spatial and temporal nuances of the events.

In our neighborhood analysis (item 5 in Fig. 1), we highlight the neighborhoods with the highest incident rates, providing a clear visual view of the most impacted geographic areas, where the redder the neighborhood, the higher its crime rate. This spatial analysis is important for identifying concentration patterns in certain areas and guiding specific public safety strategies.

The assignment by the time of day (item 6 in Fig. 1) completes this analysis by examining the variation in occurrences during the different times of day. Dividing the day into specific periods, such as early morning, morning, afternoon, and evening, this distribution allows for the identification of temporal patterns that can influence the allocation of resources and the effectiveness of preventive measures.

It is important to note that the flexibility of this module allows for the inclusion of multiple distributions for different attributes present in the data. This adaptability adjusts the tool to meet specific cases, ensuring a personalized and in-depth approach to criminal data analysis. This adaptability reinforces the tool's versatility, making it a valuable ally in various public safety scenarios.

3.4 Temporal Heat Map

The Temporal Heatmap module was developed to provide an efficient and intuitive visualization of the distribution of occurrences over a given period. This approach combines two important and complementary concepts: a heat map (item 7 in Fig. 1) that identifies and highlights areas of high concentration and a calendar (item 8 in Fig. 1) that displays the days of the month. Combining these factors provides a dynamic visual representation of the concentration of incidents on each day of the month, allowing for a comprehensive and detailed analysis. The integration provides visibility of all months within the selected interval, allowing for comparative analysis and the identification of recurring patterns over the months. This broader temporal perspective contributes to a comprehensive understanding of the distribution of incidents over time.

3.5 Layered Event Map

One of the fundamental pillars of our tool is the ability to analyze data based on its georeferenced properties. We adopt a cartographic presentation through maps (item 7 in Fig. 1) to do this. We implemented four distinct layers to provide information about the geography of crime, aiming to provide a rich and complete experience in spatial event analysis.

The first layer demarcates the city's neighborhoods, Fig. 2 a), providing a clear geographic context and facilitating the identification of areas with higher incident rates. The second layer is a heatmap (Fig. 2 b) that highlights areas with the highest density of incidents. It varies color hue and uses the distance between points to provide a clear view of areas with large concentrations of incidents.

The third layer marks the points on the map, Fig. 2 c). Initially, these points are grouped based on distance, but with user interaction, as they are zoomed in, they move apart, allowing for more detailed access to each occurrence. Each point aggregates three essential pieces of information: date, time, and type of event, enriching the analysis with details about the time and classification of the event.

The fourth and final layer highlights critical points, Fig. 2 d), identified through a clustering process based on a maximum distance limit between points. In a simplified way, we define a radius in meters, for which we want to perform the neighborhood grouping, and a minimum value of grouped occurrences to be considered a critical point. From these parameters, a clustering algorithm is applied; in our case, we consider the k-means [7], which will do the grouping and define the critical points highlighted on the map. We add details such as date, time, neighborhood, and complements for these points.

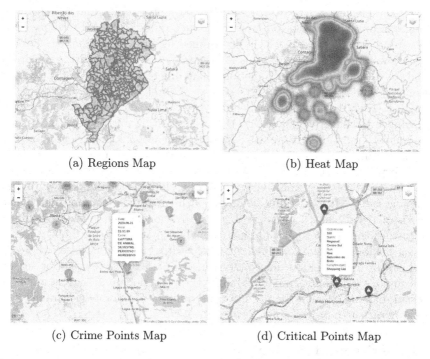

(a) Regions Map   (b) Heat Map

(c) Crime Points Map   (d) Critical Points Map

Fig. 2. Description of Event Map Layers. In (b), concentrations increase on a scale from blue to red. (Color figure online)

It is important to note that all these layers are integrated into a single map, allowing them to be modified and combined as needed. This approach provides a comprehensive view of the geography of crime, allowing users to customize their analysis and explore different aspects of crime in an efficient and organized way. This flexibility also extends to the ability to add new layers, maintain the organizational structure of the panel, and expand the analytical capabilities of the tool.

3.6   Regression Models

The application of regression models for forecasting has proven to be a promising tool. ARIMA (AutoRegressive Integrated Moving Average) and Facebook (FB) Prophet models are relevant in various areas. Their versatility lies in capturing trends, seasonality, and temporal patterns in various domains, significantly contributing to predictive analytics in different contexts. In our case, it has proven to be a promising tool in helping police forces to assist strategic planning and efficient resource allocation [4]. In order to facilitate the analysis and understanding of the data, as well as to make predictions that generate relevant insights for the user, we created two sections in our tool, one for each model mentioned below.

The ARIMA model is a powerful tool for forecasting time series, composed of three key elements: AR (AutoRegressive), I (Integrated), and MA (Moving Average), represented by the parameters 'p', 'd', and 'q'. The AR term uses past values to predict the next, with 'p' determined by the PACF (Partial Autocorrelation Function). The MA term uses past prediction errors, with 'q' identified by the ACF (Autocorrelation Function). The differentiation order, 'd', ensures stationarity and is defined by tests such as ADF (Augmented Dickey-Fuller) and KPSS (Kwiatkowski-Phillips-Schmidt-Shin). These components are crucial to maximize the effectiveness of ARIMA in forecasting a variety of time series.

On the other hand, FBProphet, developed by Facebook and released in 2017, is a robust and effective tool for analyzing and forecasting time series. It is straightforward and robust, and it handles time series that exhibit seasonal patterns and holidays very well, being especially suitable for datasets with gaps or missing values. It is an additive model with three main components: Trend, which is modeled using a piecewise linear regression model, allowing flexibility in adjusting the trend to the data; Seasonality, modeled using Fourier series, allowing flexible modeling of different seasonal patterns; and Noise, where the model captures the random fluctuations in the data that the trend or seasonality components cannot explain. Finally, the posterior prediction is made via Bayesian inference, where the posterior distribution of the model parameters is estimated rather than just point estimates.

4   Experimental Evaluation

To evaluate the applicability of the crime analysis tool proposed in this article, we instantiated it using criminal data from Brazil, one of the countries with the highest crime rates in the world, according to the Global Organized Crime Index (See Footnote 1). More specifically, we used the criminal records stored by the Military Police of the State of Minas Gerais (PMMG), one of the most violent states in Brazil. The PMMG is subordinate to the Public Security Secretariat of Minas Gerais (SSPMG), which currently maintains a Research, Development, and Innovation Project with the universities of the authors of this article.

Our evaluation is divided into three complementary parts: the characterization of the data, aimed at the treatment and understanding of the same; the practical application of the tool, allowing a dynamic interaction of different scenarios; and the application and testing of predictive models. The objective is to iterate over all the modules of the tool, previously described in the previous section.

4.1   Data Characterization

The Military Police of Minas Gerais (PMMG) has had a system for recording criminal occurrences and police actions since 2005. The system has over 40 million cases related to the 853 municipalities. Each instance in the database represents a police report and is characterized by 224 attributes that provide a wide range of information. These attributes cover several aspects, such as temporal data, including the date and time of the recording; spatial aspects, such as latitude, longitude, and municipality; and descriptive attributes, such as the specific nature of the incident, the responsible battalion, and the police units involved.

To ensure the effectiveness of subsequent analyses, we treated the data by manually inspecting each attribute. In this inspection, we identified a significant challenge related to the large volume of null values, which would affect the usefulness of the attributes in data analysis algorithms. Another fundamental criterion for attribute selection was identifying a high correlation between them. Eliminating redundant attributes was based on the premise that highly correlated attributes can offer similar information. The exclusion of attributes unique to each instance, such as the unique identifier, was also performed to simplify the dataset's structure. In total, 164 attributes were discarded, providing efficient data cleaning. The set of attributes that we will consider in our analysis are already consolidated in the literature, as observed in the systematic review [6]. These attributes cover spatial, temporal, and categorical factors and are considered essential for defining scenarios through the tool proposed in this work. After data treatment and selection, we analyzed its behavior in different aspects.

Our first analysis, presented in Fig. 3, shows the evolution of the number of records over the years. There is an initial adaptation period in the early years, marked by relatively low numbers of records. This phenomenon can be attributed to implementation and adjustment processes in data collection, reflecting a period of database construction and consolidation. In the last ten years, there has been stability in the volume of annual occurrences, with modest variations and no sharp trends of increase or decrease. Even during the pandemic, we can

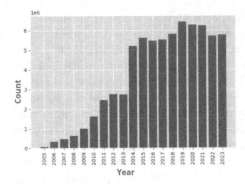

Fig. 3. Occurrence frequency per year in MG

observe that the total number of criminal occurrences in Minas Gerais in Brazil did not decrease.

The importance of analyzing data at different spatial levels is highlighted in the study [1], in which the analyses conducted in Vancouver are divided into three perspectives: census tracts, dissemination areas, and street segments (blocks). These perspectives provide different levels of detail and scope. Census tracts are the most comprehensive perspective, providing information about large geographic areas. Dissemination areas provide an intermediate level of detail, providing information about smaller areas. Street segments provide the most detailed information about tiny areas. Considering the importance of analyzing data at different spatial levels, for our study, we will consider three regions: the most comprehensive, the state of Minas Gerais; the intermediate, the most incident municipality; and the most detailed, the most incident neighborhood.

(a) Mesoregion of MG   (b) Municipality of MG   (c) Neighborhood of BH

Fig. 4. Temporal distributions of occurrences in MG and BH by color intensity, ranging from light to dark.

To identify the regions to be analyzed, we performed the spatial distribution of occurrences, as illustrated in Fig. 4. In Fig. 4 (a), we can see a large concentration of crimes in the Metropolitan Region of Belo Horizonte (RMBH), which houses the state capital, Belo Horizonte (BH). This city has the highest number of occurrences, as shown in Fig. 4 (b). When we analyze the city of BH, we can see a concentration of occurrences in the Seção Urbana Primeira (SUP), as shown in Fig. 4 (c), a densely populated region characterized by large commercial centers. In addition, the SUP has the most significant number of tourist attractions compared to other neighborhoods.

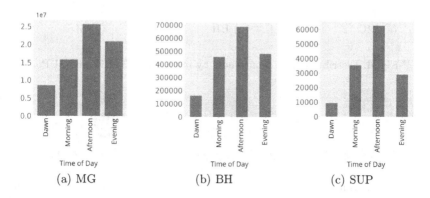

(a) MG   (b) BH   (c) SUP

Fig. 5. Distributions of occurrences by time of day in MG, BH, and the SUP

In our second analysis, we evaluated the distribution of occurrences throughout the day, considering the same levels of vision established previously. As shown in Fig. 5, the behaviors are similar in the data. We can see a higher crime rate in the afternoon shift and a lower rate in the early morning, regardless of the spatial level analyzed.

In our third analysis, we present the total number of occurrences each month for each spatial level established, which reveals distinct behaviors, as shown in Fig. 6. Figures 6(a) and (b) show that considering the state and the city as a whole, there is a balance of occurrences during the months. However, when considering smaller areas, such as neighborhoods, Fig. 6(c), there is a higher rate in February, March, July, and December. This trend may be related to the events related to each month. In the first two months, we have the occurrence of Carnival, a popular festival in Brazil, which will be analyzed separately in the case study. In July and December, we have the school vacation period. Both periods are marked by the concentration of many people celebrating or walking around the major commercial centers. Thus, we observe that smaller and more populous regions tend to be more sensitive to such events.

In our fourth analysis, we compare the percentage of violent crimes to other occurrences, Fig. 7. We observe a difference in behavior with a growing increase in the representation of violent crimes as we move from the most comprehensive region to the most specific, representing a higher concentration of crimes in smaller areas.

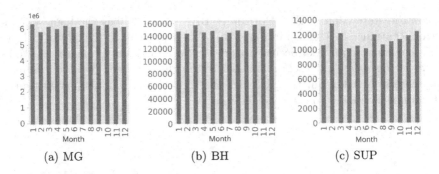

Fig. 6. Distributions of occurrences by month in MG, BH, and SUP.

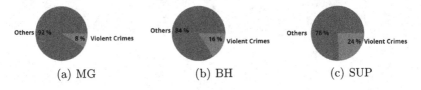

(a) MG   (b) BH   (c) SUP

Fig. 7. Violent crimes (blue) and other crimes (red) in MG, BH, and SUP. (Color figure online)

4.2   Case Study

After the characterization of the data, in this section, we aim to present case studies that demonstrate the tool's applicability. In our first case study, we chose to analyze the Brazilian Carnival. Carnival is one of the largest popular festivals in Brazil, attracting millions of people to the streets annually in February and/or March. The event moves billions of reais and is recognized for its joy, cultural diversity, and grandeur. However, this grandeur is also a factor that contributes to the increase in crime rates. Criminals take advantage of the crowds to commit crimes, such as theft, robbery, and even murder. This reality worries the authorities, who seek strategies to combat crime during the event.

To assist in decision-making in this context, we will demonstrate the application of our tool that can be used to understand the behavior of the data during this period. The tool allows us to identify patterns and trends, which can be used to define priority points for allocating security resources, such as patrol schedules and route definition. In this study, we will analyze the data for theft related to the 2023 Carnival, specifically in the district *Seção Urbana Primeira*, in Belo Horizonte, Minas Gerais. This region was shown to be a region of high crime concentration, as illustrated in Fig. 4(c). The official Carnival period in the region lasted from February 4 to 26. All filtering, such as date range, crime type, and location, are defined interactively and simplified through the filters in the tool, as discussed in Sect. 3.1.

First, to highlight the impact of theft rates on this festive event, we can observe Fig. 8, which presents the trend module of the tool encompassing the first quarter of 2023. In this graph, it is evident that there was a significant increase in crime in February. Another point to note is the similarity of the occurrences in January and March, periods that precede and follow Carnival, highlighting that in February when Carnival took place, the behavior is quite atypical and requires a differentiated strategy by the public security agents.

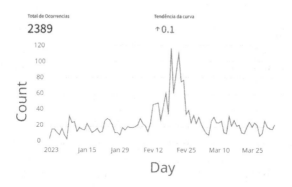

Fig. 8. Tool trend analysis module for the first quarter of 2023

By analyzing the map using the layers of neighborhoods, occurrence points, and critical points, it is possible to contrast these data with the location of carnival blocks, which indicate large concentrations of people and are generally spread throughout the city. Figure 9 illustrates the location of the blocks through markers, and Fig. 10 represents three distinct moments: before, during, and after Carnival.

Fig. 9. Locations of the 2023 Carnival blocks, SUP neighborhood demarcated

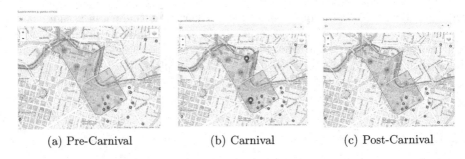

(a) Pre-Carnival   (b) Carnival   (c) Post-Carnival

Fig. 10. Comparison of the spatial distribution of occurrences in the SUP neighborhood, before, during, and after the 2023 Carnival

A significant increase in crime is noted in the downtown region during Carnival, Fig. 10 (b), highlighting the presence of critical points during this period. These critical points are highly correlated with the location of the blocks, thus highlighting areas of greater danger that should receive greater attention, along with police reinforcement. Another point to note is that, as with the number of occurrences, crime points before and after Carnival, Fig. 10(a and c), tend to maintain a pattern. This reinforces the importance of using the tool not only during special events but also in general and daily use to discover insights about crime incidence. The tool allows resources to be distributed and patrols to be scaled more efficiently in places that demand attention, all based on filters that can define multiple scenarios for analysis.

As discussed in Sect. 3.6, in addition to descriptive analyses, which allow the identification of patterns and trends, the tool also has predictive modules that provide valuable information for public safety. Based on the study of [13], these modules do not generate predictions of where and when the next crime will be committed, but rather the relative risk level that a crime will be committed at a given time and location. The tool allows users to define the "where" and "when" questions through filters. The crime level is provided through regression models. This functionality allows public safety to identify with greater precision the areas and periods of greatest risk, which can assist in the planning of preventive actions and the allocation of resources more efficiently.

To illustrate the functioning of this module, we tested and evaluated the two algorithms implemented by the tool (ARIMA and Prophet), considering two distinct granularities for prediction: day and week. First, we selected the data from 01/01/2022 to 01/29/2023, i.e., one year and 29 days, related to theft to perform the training. From the generated model, we predicted crimes for the next two days (01/30/2023 to 01/31/2023), contrasting with the actual occurrences in this period. At the second granularity, we performed the training with data from 01/01/2022 to 01/24/2023. However, the model was evaluated with predictions for the entire following week (01/25/2023 to 01/31/2023). In Figs. 11 and 12, we present the results of this analysis for two days and a week, respectively, considering the two algorithms implemented in the tool.

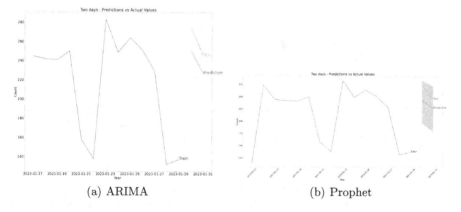

(a) ARIMA   (b) Prophet

Fig. 11. Two-day prediction. In blue, is the last training interval, in green is the prediction (in light green, the confidence interval), and in orange/red, is the actual value (Color figure online)

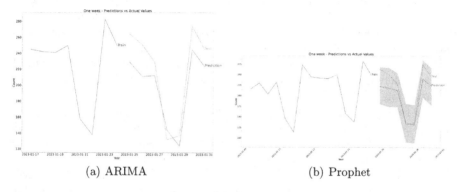

(a) ARIMA   (b) Prophet

Fig. 12. A week-long prediction. The last training interval is in blue, the prediction is in green (the confidence interval is in light green), and the actual value is in orange/red. (Color figure online)

We can see that both models performed well in the prediction task, with values close to the real ones for both granularities. When evaluating the performance of the two models, we observed promising results. Both models performed satisfactorily, presenting predicted values close to the actual data. These studies provide valuable insights into how to quickly apply these models in similar contexts, highlighting both their advantages and specific limitations when predicting crimes. The integration of these models provides a comprehensive approach to predictive analytics, contributing more effectively to the improvement of public safety.

5   Conclusions

In this work, we present a tool for criminal data analysis that is able to characterize the data and transform it into information that helps develop assertive crime-fighting and prevention tactics. Our tool understands the dynamics of crime occurrence from two different perspectives: temporal and spatial, considering two types of analysis: descriptive and predictive, presenting a simple and intuitive interface to be used by public agents responsible for security. To assess the applicability of the criminal analysis tool proposed in this article, we instantiated it using criminal data from Brazil, one of the countries with the highest crime rates in the world, using the criminal records stored by the Military Police of the State of Minas Gerais (PMMG). We perform two descriptive and predictive analyses, considering data from Belo Horizonte, the capital of Minas Gerais. In the descriptive analysis, we compared the crime map before, during, and after Carnival, the world's most famous Brazilian festival, demonstrating a significant change in criminal behavior during the festival, with an increase of crimes concentrated in specific tourist points, which can help to allocate public security agents more efficiently. In predictive analysis, we trained and evaluated two crime prediction models that present predicted values close to the actual data, consequently allowing public security to develop preventive actions more assertively. In sum, we demonstrate that the proposed tool offers an approach with complete descriptive and predictive analyses, contributing more effectively to improving public safety.

Our tool is not limited to static analysis. Its adaptability to future models and the ability to integrate new layers of information emphasizes the dynamic and evolutionary nature of the system. This flexibility ensures the tool can evolve in response to changing criminal dynamics, maintaining its relevance over time. In summary, this work highlights the achievements made in crime data analysis and points to untapped potential and ongoing possibilities for improvement. The strategic partnership between research and security institutions is essential to drive innovation and face complex challenges related to public security. In this scenario, the developed tool emerges as a valuable contribution, offering valuable insights and a model for future approaches to crime management.

References

1. Andresen, M.A., Malleson, N.: Testing the stability of crime patterns: implications for theory and policy. J. Res. Crime Delinquency **48**(1), 58–82 (2011)
2. Bappee, F.K., Soares Júnior, A., Matwin, S.: Predicting crime using spatial features. In: Bagheri, E., Cheung, J.C.K. (eds.) Canadian AI 2018. LNCS (LNAI), vol. 10832, pp. 367–373. Springer, Cham (2018). https://doi.org/10.1007/978-3-319-89656-4_42
3. Bogomolov, A., Lepri, B., Staiano, J., Oliver, N., Pianesi, F., Pentland, A.: Once upon a crime: towards crime prediction from demographics and mobile data. In: Proceedings of 16th International Conference on Multimodal Interaction (2014)
4. Borowik, G., Wawrzyniak, Z.M., Cichosz, P.: Time series analysis for crime forecasting. In: 26th International Conference on Systems Engineering (2018)

5. Catlett, C., Cesario, E., Talia, D., Vinci, A.: A data-driven approach for spatio-temporal crime predictions in smart cities. In: 2018 IEEE International Conference on Smart Computing (2018)
6. Du, Y., Ding, N.: A systematic review of multi-scale spatio-temporal crime prediction methods. ISPRS Int. J. Geo-Inf. 12, 209 (2023)
7. Hamerly, G., Elkan, C.: Learning the k in k-means. In: Advances in Neural Information Processing Systems, vol. 16 (2003)
8. Han, J., Pei, J., Tong, H.: Data Mining: Concepts and Techniques. Morgan Kaufmann (2022)
9. Kumar, M., et al.: Forecasting of annual crime rate in India: a case study. In: International Conference on Advances in Computing, Communications and Informatics (2018)
10. Mandalapu, V., Elluri, L., Vyas, P., Roy, N.: Crime prediction using machine learning and deep learning: a systematic review. IEEE Access 11, 60153–60170 (2023)
11. Marzan, C.S., Baculo, M.J.C., de Dios Bulos, R., Ruiz Jr., C.: Time series analysis and crime pattern forecasting of city crime data. In: Proceedings of the 1st International Conference on Algorithms, Computing and Systems, pp. 113–118 (2017)
12. McCue, C.: Data Mining and Predictive Analysis: Intelligence Gathering and Crime Analysis. Butterworth-Heinemann, Boston (2014)
13. Perry, W.L.: Predictive Policing: The Role of Crime Forecasting in Law Enforcement Operations. Rand Corporation, Washington, DC (2013)
14. Pina-Sánchez, J., Buil-Gil, D., Brunton-Smith, I., Cernat, A.: The impact of measurement error in regression models using police recorded crime rates. J. Quant. Criminol. 39(4), 975–1002 (2023)
15. Prieto Curiel, R.: Weekly crime concentration. J. Quant. Criminol. 39(1), 97–124 (2023)
16. Walter, R.J., Tillyer, M.S., Acolin, A.: Spatiotemporal crime patterns across six us cities: analyzing stability and change in clusters and outliers. J. Quant. Criminol. 39(4), 951–974 (2023)
17. Wang, H., Bah, M.J., Hammad, M.: Progress in outlier detection techniques: a survey. IEEE Access 7, 107964–108000 (2019)
18. Wooditch, A.: The benefits of patrol officers using unallocated time for everyday crime prevention. J. Quant. Criminol. 39, 161–185 (2021)
19. Xu, R., Wunsch, D.: Survey of clustering algorithms. IEEE Trans. Neural Networks 16(3), 645–678 (2005)
20. Yan, W.: Toward automatic time-series forecasting using neural networks. IEEE Trans. Neural Networks Learn. Syst. 23(7), 1028–1039 (2012)
21. Zhang, G.P.: Time series forecasting using a hybrid ARIMA and neural network model. Neurocomputing 50, 159–175 (2003)

Approach to the Formation and Visualization of the Competency Profile of the Staff of Organizations Using the UGVA Method

Viktor Uglev[1]($\boxtimes$) iD, Michail Kuznetsov[1,2] iD, and Sergey Meshkov[1,3] iD

[1] Siberian Federal University, Zheleznogorsk, Russia
vauglev@sfu-kras.ru
[2] JSC Information Satellite Systems, Zheleznogorsk, Russia
[3] Mining and Chemical Combine, Zheleznogorsk, Russia

Abstract. Decision support as part of the task of managing the human capital of organizations largely depends on the extent to which the decision-maker possesses the relevant information about summarized characteristics of the employees and departments. Formation of competency profiles of employees and their visualization by Data Mining methods allows to obtain justification for decisions, even if the profession does not have clear standards and evaluation criteria. The paper considers formation of the competency profile model on the example of the research and teaching staff of organizations and visualization of profiles in the form of anthropomorphic images using the method of the Unified Graphic Visualization of Activity (UGVA). The step-by-step formation of images in UGVA notation and the approach to their analysis for decision-making are described. The competency profiles of the staff members of the Applied Physics and Space Technologies department in Siberian Federal University are shown using their activity database. The results of the analysis of the profiles and the identified patterns are presented. The conclusion provides recommendations on the use of UVGA method for visualization of competency profiles in organizations, its prospects and limitations on its use.

Keywords: Decision Support Systems · competency profile · Data Mining · cognitive visualization · UGVA Method

1 Introduction

The effective functioning of any organization primarily depends on its employees. Therefore, management of human and intellectual capital is directly related to the methods of improving the performance of individual employees, departments and organizations as a whole [15]. But in order to set a management task, it is necessary to record the data on employees' performance, generalize these data taking into account their dynamics and present them in such a way that it is possible to make a well-reasoned management decision. For this purpose, special models and visualization tools are used to form a profile of an employee and the whole staff.

Recording of performance indicators and competencies of employees largely depends on the profile of the organization's activity. The indicators are especially sensitive for humanitarian professions, as there are no clear and generally recognized output rates and methods of performance evaluation [17]. As a rule, staff assessment begins with the formation of individual competency profiles (CP), which are then generalized. As an object of study, let us consider the research and teaching staff of a higher educational institution as bright representatives of a "weakly standardized" profession (i.e., teacher and research worker).

The competency profile of employees of an educational organization has its own specifics: working with people, different abilities to pedagogy and research activity, delayed effect on the evaluation of results, specific types of expertise, non-obvious indicators of commercial return, etc. In Russia Federation the specifics of centralized financing, difficulties of cooperative work (especially of international nature), specifics of mentality are added to this. For this reason, it was decided to consider the use of artificial intelligence methods and cognitive visualization tools (data Visualization from Data Mining [8]) to form CPs.

Analysis of CPs in educational institutions allows to reveal hidden patterns and justify many management decisions. For example, [6] describes how ontological modeling allows assessing the state of a department and identifying its hidden potential. But it is possible only when the data are collected promptly, comprehensively and they have been verified. Further it is necessary to generalize these heterogeneous data and use some complex method of visualization, i.e. "see" the hidden patterns. Let us consider one of the approaches to the formation of the CP and its visualization, which allows to increase the level of reasoning of staffing decisions.

2   Existing Solutions

Methods of assessing CPs and similar indicators result in the formation of a set of generalized quantitative/qualitative characteristics of employees [2,20], departments [6] and organization [1] as a whole. As a result, a profile is formed, in the structure of which it is necessary to combine all the indicators: this allows to perceive the data entirely, to form an image for comparison with similar profiles.

Since Miller's constraints [10] are true for most people (including analysts), the use of data concentration mechanisms is required. In this case, arrays of numbers (time series) and tables significantly lose out to visualization tools [14]. Based on the specifics of physiology, visual concentration is most naturally perceived by humans. Figure 1-a-c shows examples of several profiles summarizing characteristics within organizational structures.

Works in the field of data visualization highlight a number of approaches to concentrating data in the form of graphical images. Let us consider the following: star charts, Chernoff faces, clustering, mapping, dashboards, semantic networks

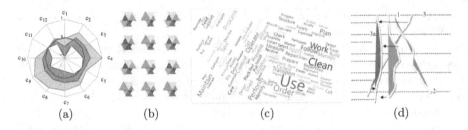

Fig. 1. Profiles of characteristics of one employee (a, [20]), group (b, [11]), profession (c, [16]) and organization (d, [1])

and ontologies, conceptual and mental maps, cognitive maps of knowledge diagnosis and the Unified Graphic Visualization of Activity (UGVA) method. To compare these methods, we use the following characteristics:

1. Convergence to a flat image
2. Integrity of the image
3. Possibility to compare multiple images at the same time
4. Scalability (e.g., employee-department-organization)
5. Ease of interpretation
6. Possibility to reflect the dynamics of indicators
7. Combining an integral assessment and a variety of individual characteristics
8. Ease of implementation

The performance assessment results and research examples are shown in Table 1). It shows that a more or less comprehensive approach for the selected characteristics can be implemented using UGVA notation (including the indicators of the research and teaching employees). The purpose of this study is to show the essence and principles of applying the UGVA notation for assessing the CPs of employees of research and educational departments of organizations. For this purpose, we will briefly describe the approach to the formalization of data on the research and teaching employees, the UGVA method and its adaptation to the display of CP data (Sect. 3); we will consider an example of using the proposed approach in the educational and training department of the university (Sect. 4); analyze the results of the study and formulate recommendations for the use of CP visual representation (Sect. 5). We conclude with the prospects of the method development and our plans for its further application.

3 Method

3.1 Conceptualization of the Subject Area

The applied value of the CP in knowledge management of the organization depends on how systematic the approach to the formation of the factor space of fixed indicators is. Formalization of information for formation of employees' CPs can be conditionally divided into the following categories:

Table 1. Characterization of different graphic notations for CP visualization

Visualization method	Example	1	2	3	4	5	6	7	8
Star charts	[20]	V	V	V	–	V	–	–	V
Chernoff faces	[3]	V	V	V	–	V	–	–	~V
Clustering	[8]	V	-	-	-	~V	–	–	~V
Mapping in the low-dimensional space	[7]	V	V	V	~V	~V	–	–	–
Dashboards	[4]	V	-	-	~V	V	V	~V	V
Semantic networks, knowledge graphs and ontologies	[6]	~V	–	–	–	~V	–	~V	~V
Conceptual and mental maps	[12]	V	~V	–	–	V	–	–	~V
Cognitive maps of knowledge diagnosis	[19]	V	V	–	V	V	~V	–	–
UGVA method	[21]	V	V	V	~V	V	V	V	~V

1. requirements of the professional plan (typical competencies, work functions, areas of labor activity) and data on compliance of a particular employee with them (including violation of work discipline, safety, etc.);
2. specifics of work organization at a particular employer's facility (secrecy regimes, industry experience, admission regimes for certain types of work, forms of issuing and reporting on work assignments, business trips, etc.) and data on compliance of a particular employee with them;
3. personal work experience (by place of employment and profession) and the results of employee assessment for compliance with it (including career progression);
4. educational experience (diplomas of education, professional development courses) and the practice of its application in the performance of labor duties;
5. declared personal goals and expectations and facts confirming the compliance of the employee's behavior with them;
6. professional initiatives (participation in unplanned activities, mentoring) and their results;
7. self-assessment of the employee as a staff member (integration into the corporate culture) and feedback from colleagues/management;
8. social contacts of the employee within the work or educational team (their role, significance, sustainability) and the reflection of these contacts on the activity results;
9. other data about the person (family status, gender, age, psychological characteristics, etc.).

In essence, the CP should correlate expectations (through the introduction of a metric factor space and scaling in it) and reality (manifestation of the person's indicators in this space). It is important to remember, however, that the interpretation of the data should depend on to whom the CP is intended to be demonstrated (the "point of view" of the various persons of interest on the profile). Obviously, it is difficult to collect the entire list of data presented about each employee. Therefore, a preliminary analysis is made to form the CP and it forms a basis for decision made about the particular configuration of the collected data and methods of their interpretation, generalization and visualization.

Having made a system analysis of the research and teaching staff activity, we have revealed the structure of activity of departmental staff, the central categories of which are teaching and educational activity, research and project activity, expert activity. Figure 2 shows the conceptual map of the factor space of the activity data of the research and teaching staff (conceptualization is given in SysML notation according to ISO/IEC/IEEE 42010:2011). Since it was important to find out how the department looks from the point of view of the head (head of the department), the whole organization and the partner enterprise (the organization that forms the request for specialists on the regional labor market), only a part of the possible categories of data was included in the CP.

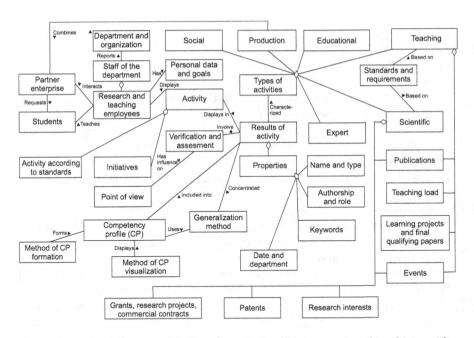

Fig. 2. Conceptual diagram of data on the activity of the research and teaching employees for concentration within the CP

The CP for a department implies the formation of a profile model, collection of primary data, compilation of the profile and its analysis, and making management decisions. In the framework of this study, we are most interested in the stages of profile model formation and its analysis on the basis of cognitive visualization tools. In this case, the dynamics of indicators (activity), reflecting the specifics of the employee's activity, is put into the structure of the image.

Since one of the central characteristics of a CP is competency, it is important to determine the method to be used for its quantitative assessment. We are going to rely mainly on the method presented in [20]. Therefore, the more data on the employee's activity we manage to record, the more confidence we will have in the result of testing each hypothesis about the development of this or that competency.

3.2 The Model of the Profile of Research and Teaching Staff of the Department

Having chosen the research and teaching employees as an object for CP formation, let us distinguish the main groups of activity indicators that we will be interested in within the framework of this study:

- personal qualification (S_1) – activity, which will include indicators related to the profession (education, professional development courses, length of employment, authority in the team, etc.);
- teaching activity (S_2) – activity that will include indicators related to work experience in the educational institution (teaching, work with students, educational initiatives, preparation of teaching materials and e-courses);
- research activity (S_3) – activity related to the research interests of the employee or students supervised by her/him (participation in research projects, results of intellectual activity, research initiatives, research collaborations);
- expert activity (S_4) – (participation in commercial projects, board memberships, expertise, consulting employers, integration into the real production process, training postgraduate students).

In order to identify the activity facts themselves, a questionnaire is formed, including indicators of the research and teaching employees for the reporting period (usually a year or half a year). The following data are recorded for each activity (event):

- employees and their affiliation with departments/organization;
- name of the activity, its type and time of the event (date or just year);
- keywords (entered by the employee or automatically extracted from the name);
- additional vector of characteristics specific to each activity type.

An illustrative example of primary data of different types is given in Table 2. Such data form a database of events, which should be further generalized and visualized as part of the CP.

In the initial phase of analysis, generalization can be done for each indicator separately. Let's consider, for example, keywords, which we will turn into

Table 2. Example of primary data to be collected to form the CP

Employee's Name	Activity's Name	Type	Affiliation	Year	Keywords	Specification
John	IT course	My education	Univ.	2023	computer, programming, C++	Sertificat #=21
Marry and Peter	Article #284	Science	Univ.	2024	satellite, ballistic trajectory	DOI=10.1/5, Journal=LNCS
Tom	Patent #45	IP	Factory	2022	solar battery, reliability	Number= 123, Type= industrial design
Marry	Stud. dissertation	Education	Univ.	2023	automatization, regulation, correction engine	Title= Development of a method for automatic regulation of the navigation satellite correction engine, Regime= Secret, Date=June 28 2023

concepts (by analogy with HumaNeTrust [13]). Let employee i has j indicators, each of which is characterized by k keywords. Then the undirected graph G_{ij} will be given by a set of concepts N_k and a set of links R_{ijk}. The set of graphs of one research and teaching staff $G_i = <G_{ij}, R_{ijk}>$ forms an individual concept graph, where at each intersection of nodes of subgraphs, 1 is added to the weight of a node, and at intersection (overlapping) of edges, 1 is added to the thickness of an edge. The result is a graph abstracted from specific achievements, characterizing the specificity of research and teaching interests. The coloring of the graph substructures can be done based on the selected keyword, year, type of achievement, employee affiliation or some combination of them. Taking this approach a step further, it is possible to color a subgraph formed by any combination of the above conditions, including addition and intersection operations. If the graph $G = <G_{ij}, R_{ijk}>$ denotes the set of subgraphs G_i of a department/organization, then individual employees can become the basis for coloring. In this case, it becomes possible to track the contribution of an individual, group, or their joint types of indicators relative to the entire disposition in the department/organization (to the general graph). Figure 3 shows an example of such a graph for a university department.

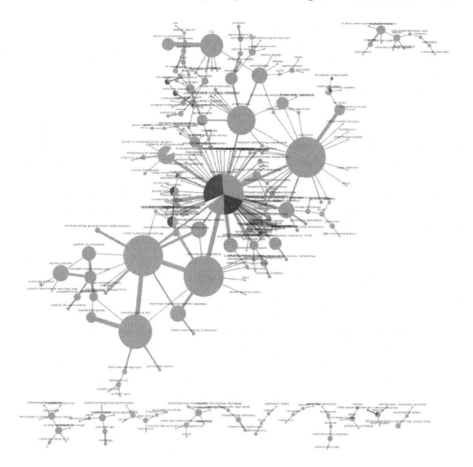

Fig. 3. General graph of the department by employee activity keywords (patents are highlighted)

The use of the mechanism of indicator-based construction of the graph allows to obtain interesting results within the framework of the CP of the employee team, but they do not give a comprehensive picture. Since the set of indicators is not homogeneous and there are many of them (it is practically Big Data), the search for patterns should be complex. This leads to the need to use a more efficient way of data convolution.

Concentration of heterogeneous attribute data can be described in general terms in the form of the following sequence of operations:

1. representation of the flow of activity precedents in the form of vectors having a group specification (each vector a priori belongs to one or more competency groups S_m);
2. estimation of each vector for its influence on the manifestation of an attribute from the groups S_m;

3. summarizing and scaling of estimates of the contribution of the influence of each vector to the total estimate for each attribute;
4. normalization of the obtained estimates and their grouping in accordance with the distinguished S_m;
5. calculation of indicators of balance between the elements S_m.

This process was described in more detail in [21] (see the diagram in Fig. 5) and analyzed by an example. In that paper the estimation was performed by an expert (manual input of coefficient values). Here it is reasonable to implement the operation #2 in automatic mode, operating with collections of production rules (knowledge base). The estimations obtained in this case for a set of compared objects should be presented to the person who makes the decisions. As the analysis of graphic Data Mining methods of data generalization and concentration has shown (see Table 1), the UGVA method has a potential to be applied to visualization of CPs with generalized heterogeneous attributes.

3.3   Methodological Approach to Visualization

The Unified Graphic Visualization of Activity (UGVA) method is an approach to visual representation of a profile of a complex multi-parametric object expressed as an anthropomorphic image in order to show the features of its functional (activity) and structural parameters dependent on them, as well as to compare such profiles [18]. The sets of compared objects in UGVA notation are shown in Fig. 4: the competency profiles of a group of master's students are located on the left, the competency profiles of six enterprise employees are located on the right. When forming such images in this graphic notation, the following sequence of steps should be implemented:

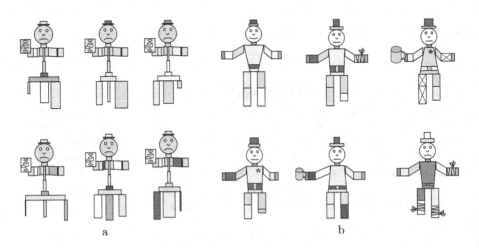

a   b

Fig. 4. Examples of comparable objects in UGVA notation: university students and enterprise employees

1. to prepare a framework diagram of the profession by specifying axis types and symmetry types (sketch or framework);
2. to describe the structural scheme of the activity (profession) in the form of an anthropomorphic image reflecting the activity of parameters (structural image);
3. to adapt the image for a particular department/organization (basic image);
4. to form an image for each employee (image of a particular object);
5. to overlay data on current generalized indicators and their dynamics on the image of an employee (image with overlaid data);
6. to contrast a set of images within the employee team to search for patterns, features, to compare and make subsequent decisions (depends on the research task).

An example of applying the UGVA method to support the educational process when implementing ITS-based e-learning was described in detail in [21]. Therefore, here we will focus on the formation of an anthropomorphic image of the research and teaching employees based on a set of activity indicators S_m.

We will correspond a part of the anthropomorphic image (see structural image in Fig. 5-a to each group of indicators S_m. The upper horizontal (evaluative) stratum includes the parameters of the balance between the four main activity groups (encoded in the "emotion" of the image, the parameter μ) and position (radius of the head circumference, the parameter σ). The middle horizontal stratum reflects data on educational activities (on the left), on professional requirements (in the middle), on the employee's research activities but without individual work with students (on the right). Similarly, the lower horizontal stratum reflects educational and research activity, but realized in interaction with individual students or small project groups. Vertically, the strata related to educational and research activities are highlighted with red and green boundaries. Each block of the image has two segments: the segment located closer to the body reflects data for the past reporting period, the segment located further from the body reflects the current period (in Fig. 5-a they are colored green and blue, respectively). Dotted boxes mark the areas of additional parameters (artifacts). According to the classification from [18] the image will have the configuration $\lambda 6Bit$. Turning a basic image into an image of a particular object is a task associated with the consideration of the actual data set on the activity of the research and teaching employees within a particular department/organization.

Interpretation of an employee's CP image, as well as in the Chernoff faces method [3], involves perception of proportions and color, which convey the specificity of each person's activity for the reporting period. But in UGVA notation, facial expression is an integral estimate of the balance μ of the main groups of CP indicators (the algorithm of calculating the balance value is given in [21]). Let's consider the work with CP images in UGVA notation on the example.

4   Case Study

The Department of Applied Physics and Space Technologies in Siberian Federal University as of the beginning of 2024 is chosen as an object for forming the CP

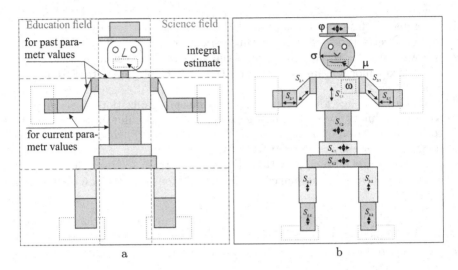

Fig. 5. Structural image of the CP for the research and teaching employees (as a profession) and basic image for the staff of the Department of Applied Physics and Space Technologies (Color figure online)

of employees and the department. It prepares master's students in three technical specialties corresponding to the regional request of the rocket and space industry enterprise JSC Information Satellite Systems (the base enterprise engaged in satellite production). There are 21 research and teaching employees working at the department, 78% of which are also employees of the basic enterprise engaged in high-tech production. In this connection, the visualization model should provide the possibility to evaluate the image from three points of view: in relation to the department (view from the inside), in relation to the whole university (view on the subordinate department) and in relation to the partner enterprise (view from the industry customer on the training of highly qualified specialists). Figure 3 shows the graph of key words of activities of the research and teaching staff of the department (more than 2000 nodes) highlighting the direction of patents for the last 5 years. But we are interested in CP in the form of an anthropomorphic image in UGVA notation.

The transition from the basic image to the image of a particular object (i.e., from Fig. 5-a to Fig. 5-b) was facilitated by the following data specification:

- the degree of interaction between the employee and the base partner enterprise is reflected through the headdress in the evaluation stratum (the parameter φ);
- the presence and effectiveness of educational work is indicated through the artifact badge (the parameter ω);
- availability of active grants with the partner enterprise through the department is shown through the limb artifact on the right side of the image;

– the presence of graduate students is shown through the limb artifact on the left side of the image.

Color coding on the images is used in a scale from green to red with a transition through white in the center: red color indicates low quality of activities in the current group of indicators, green color indicates high quality, white color reflects neutral value, and transitions from white to red or green show the degree of deviation of attribute assessments from neutral.

To accumulate data on the activities of the research and teaching employees, an information system was developed. It was filled with data for the last period of the department's work (from 2018 to the beginning of 2024). The total number of activities of different types in the database amounted to more than 2000. A special analytical module was created for automatic formation of graphs and anthropomorphic images in UGVA notation.

Here is an example for four employees of the department, whose CP data are displayed in the form of anthropomorphic images in UGVA notation (see Fig. 6).

Fig. 6. Example of CP images in UGVA notation for four employees of the department

The image of the first employee (Doctor of Engineering Sciences, professor, holding a managerial position at the partner enterprise) characterizes his activity as follows: educational activity is minimal and stable (he supervises some master's and postgraduate students), there is little research activity, scientific works with students are of low quality. Personal professional growth is minimal, the expert activity is little if any. The balance of activity groups S_m is 0.43, which confirms the unbalanced proportions of the anthropomorphic image in the UGVA notation.

By analogy, we can characterize the activity of other employees. To compare the images of CPs, it is necessary to display them in a single space (as in Fig. 6) and, knowing the principles of image interpretation, to identify the necessary attributes. For example, the images of four employees show that their research work with master's students is rather weak, and the presence of a scientific laboratory (the second image reflects the activity of its head) does not contribute to this.

5 Data Analysis and Results

The proposed approach to CP visualization made it possible not only to take a snapshot of the current state of the activity of the research and training staff of the Department of Applied Physics and Space Technologies, but also to obtain a rationale for decisions related to personnel management. The most significant of them are the following:

- to motivate the most active employees with bonuses based on the dynamics of objective indicators;
- to identify the main and secondary directions in scientific research of employees and correlate them with the development plans of the department (including the justification of "scientific schools");
- to identify social ties within the staff team;
- to identify hidden patterns (strategies) in the approaches to publishing research articles by different employees;
- to evaluate the effectiveness of the work of scientific advisers with students in the implementation of master's theses in the context of each of the three domains of study;
- to analyze the degree of "usefulness" of the employees in relation to the goals of the department, the whole university and the partner enterprise.

The last item implied the presence in the image of a detailed mode of data output to the image, reflecting the affiliation of the employee when declaring certain types of activities (e.g., scientific publications and patents): for example, Fig. 7 shows the images of the employee with indicators that have different contribution to the goals and plans of the department (left), the whole university (center) and the partner enterprise (right). The analysis of these and other results in graphical form obtained by the decision-maker allowed the new head of the department (a new employee who just took office at the beginning of the 2023/2024 academic year) to orient more quickly in the peculiarities of the research and teaching staff and to obtain arguments for decision-making.

Despite the high degree of automation and the availability of interactive tools for working with graphs and anthropomorphic images in UGVA notation, we encountered the following significant difficulties in implementing the project:

- not all research and teaching employees conscientiously entered data on their activities (omissions were discovered during the verification process);
- verification of special methods for assessing precedents in terms of contribution to groups S_m for certain indicators resulted in contradictory feedback from the research and teaching employees (there was a systematic tendency to overestimate the significance of the results of their own activity);
- a number of indicators important for management were never recorded (e.g., assessment of satisfaction with working conditions by Q12-Human Sigma [5] or [9], and use data on participation in projects outside the department);

Fig. 7. Display of one employee's CP with details regarding different points of view

- the lack of competency profiles of master's students integrated into the information system (following the example of [21]) and the lack of elaboration of the CPs of entire domains of study reduced the analytical potential of the proposed approach.

The experience gained allows us to formulate the following recommendations for working with anthropomorphic images reflecting CPs of employees of organizations:

- while emphasizing strata and lines of symmetry in the image try to balance them relative to the center of symmetry (they should be visually comparable, and the balance between them is achievable and desirable);
- allow the employee to see the image of his/her CP, as well as its place in the summary map of anthropomorphic images of the department, using it as a motivation tool;
- document in detail the description of the image structure and the methodology of calculating indicators, making them available in an interactive interaction with the user;
- do not apply the same basic images for different professions, even in the same department;
- when highlighting different points of view on the image, use those indicators that show contradictions in their interpretation (this will make the result illustrative and practically useful);
- do not limit yourself to one method of visualization, if there is a reason to apply several of them (the combination of approaches can give the best result).

The beneficial effect of using UGVA notation to analyze CPs at the Department of Applied Physics and Space Technologies in Siberian Federal University can be improved and we will continue to work in this direction.

6   Conclusion

The use of cognitive visualization tools to represent and analyze competency profiles reflects the general trend in applying the Data Mining approach to big data. Employee teams of research and educational organizations are not an exception. Our proposed approach to formalize the CP of an employee and visualize it in the Unified Graphic Visualization of Activity (UGVA) notation has shown its usefulness for decision makers. We plan to continue this research in the following directions: expansion of the list of factors to be taken into account in the CP; integration of the department profile with the CPs of students; expansion of the points of application of the approach to other departments (in particular, those departments that function purposefully to provide personnel with higher qualification to our common partner enterprise).

The visualization of profiles in UGVA notation allows to work with profiles of various objects and structures outside of research and education organizations. Similarly, it can be applied to form CPs of employees and subdivisions of industry enterprises. We are also actively working in this direction.

References

1. Alekhin, A., Alekseev, O.: Organizational balance as a key to enterprise reorganization. Vestnik Plekhanov Russian Univ. Econ. **19**(5), 190–205 (2022). https://doi.org/10.21686/2413-28292022-5-190-205, in Russian
2. Blömeke, S., Kaiser, G., König, J., Jentsch, A.: Profiles of mathematics teachers' competence and their relation to instructional quality. ZDM **52**, 329–342 (2020)
3. Chernoff, H.: The use of faces to represent points in k-dimensional space graphically. J. Am. Stat. Assoc. **68**(342), 361–368 (1973). https://doi.org/10.1080/01621459.1973.10482434
4. Few, S.: Information dashboard design: The effective visual communication of data. O'Reilly Media, Inc. (2006)
5. Fleming, J.H., Asplund, J.: Human sigma: managing the employee-customer encounter. Gallup Press (2007)
6. Gavrilova, T., Kuznetsova, A., Lesheva, I.: On the issue of the development of ontologies of scientific and academic work. In: XXI National Conference of Artificial Intelligence, vol. 1, pp. 60–67. Print-Express, Smolensk, Russia (2023) (In Russian)
7. Gorban, A.N., Zinovyev, A.: Fast and user-friendly non-linear principal manifold learning by method of elastic maps. In: 2015 IEEE International Conference on Data Science and Advanced Analytics (DSAA), pp. 1–9. IEEE (2015). https://doi.org/10.1109/DSAA.2015.7344818
8. Han, J., Kamber, M., Pei, J.: Data mining concepts and techniques third edition. Morgan Kaufmann Ser. Data Manag. Syst. **5**(4), 83–124 (2011)
9. Hogan, R.: Hogan development survey manual. Hogan Assessment Systems Tulsa, OK (2009)
10. Miller, G.: The magical number seven, plus or minus two: Some limits on our capacity for processing information. Psychol. Rev. **63**(2), 81–97 (1956)
11. Pareto, L., Snis, U.L.: An interactive visualization model for competence management: an integrative approach. In: Proceedings of I-KNOW, vol. 7, pp. 440–447. Citeseer (2007)

12. Peer, M., Brunec, I.K., Newcombe, N.S., Epstein, R.A.: Structuring knowledge with cognitive maps and cognitive graphs. Trends Cogn. Sci. **25**(1), 37–54 (2021)
13. Pouydebat, O., Courtin, C., Bemmami, K.E., Gardet, E., Habchi, G.: Automation of competences extraction-humanetrust: an experimental computer system used in an academic laboratory. In: CIGI-Qualita21: Conférence Internationale Génie Industriel QUALITA-Grenoble (2021). https://hal.science/hal-03203592/document
14. Qin, X., Luo, Y., Tang, N., Li, G.: Making data visualization more efficient and effective: a survey. VLDB J. **29**, 93–117 (2020)
15. Rezaei, F., Khalilzadeh, M., Soleimani, P.: Factors affecting knowledge management and its effect on organizational performance: Mediating the role of human capital. Adv. Hum.-Comput. Interact., 16 (2021). https://doi.org/10.1155/2021/8857572, article ID 8857572
16. Różewski, P., Prys, M.: How to visualize the competence: the issue of occupational information network visualization. Proc. Comput. Sci. **192**, 4845–4852 (2021). https://doi.org/10.1016/j.procs.2021.09.263
17. Simpson, B., Revsbæk, L.: Doing Process Research in Organizations: Noticing Differently. Oxford University Press (2022)
18. Uglev, V.: Unified graphic visualization of activity (UGVA) method. In: Novel and Intelligent Digital Systems 2022. LNNS. pp. 255—265. Springer (2022). https://doi.org/10.1007/978-3-031-17601-2_25
19. Uglev, V., Gavrilova, T.: Cross-cutting visual support of decision making for forming personalized learning spaces. In: Novel and Intelligent Digital Systems 2022. LNNS. pp. 3–12. Springer (2022). https://doi.org/10.1007/978-3-031-17601-2_1
20. Uglev, V., Shangina, E.: Assessment and visualization of course-level and curriculum-level competency profiles. In: International Conference on Computational Science and Its Applications. LNCS, pp. 478–493. Springer (2023). https://doi.org/10.1007/978-3-031-37105-9_32
21. Uglev, V., Sychev, O.: Evaluation, comparison and monitoring of multiparameter systems by unified graphic visualization of activity method on the example of learning process. Algorithms **15**(21) (2022). https://doi.org/10.3390/a15120468

Elevating Wearable Sensor Authentication with Hybrid Deep Learning and Squeeze-and-Excitation

Sakorn Mekruksavanich[1]([✉])[iD] and Anuchit Jitpattanakul[2][iD]

[1] Department of Computer Engineering, School of Information and Communication Technology, University of Phayao, Phayao, Thailand
sakorn.me@up.ac.th
[2] Intelligent and Nonlinear Dynamic Innovations Research Center, Department of Mathematics, Faculty of Applied Science, King Mongkut's University of Technology North Bangkok, Bangkok, Thailand
anuchit.j@sci.kmutnb.ac.th

Abstract. Smartphones often contain users' private and sensitive information. Thus, continuous verification of identity is crucial to prevent unauthorized access. While sensor-based solutions have been explored before, recent advancements in machine learning have provided alternative deep-learning approaches for constantly checking if the smartphone's user is genuine. We put forward a hybrid deep convolutional neural network model named SE-DeepConvNet, which includes squeeze-and-excitation elements to improve representation learning from streams of smartphone sensor information. Using a benchmark human movement dataset, our experiments show state-of-the-art performance boosts with SE-DeepConvNet, realizing 99.78% accuracy and 0.38% equal error rate for user verification – surpassing other evaluated deep learning models. Our distinctive combination of the squeeze-and-excitation system and deep convolutional neural network framework enables optimized feature extraction from sequence information for accurate constant verification.

Keywords: Continuous authentication · Smartphone sensors · Squeeze-and-excitation module · Deep learning · Accurate continuous authentication

1 Introduction

Wearable devices like smartphones aim to bolster security through recurrent user identity verification using continuous authentication techniques. These methods can be broadly classified into two categories: those grounded in analyzing physiological biometrics and those centered around behavioral biometrics. Physiological techniques confirm static bodily attributes, encompassing facial patterns [8], fingerprints [28], Iris patterns [27], voice [3], and pulse [18]. In contrast, behavioral methods concentrate on identifying distinctive patterns in user interactions with

O. Gervasi et al. (Eds.): ICCSA 2024, LNCS 14814, pp. 186–197, 2024.
https://doi.org/10.1007/978-3-031-64608-9_12

the device over time [19]. Specifically, the former relies on unchanging physical traits, necessitating the user's direct involvement in the authentication process. On the other hand, behavioral biometric approaches leverage patterns like touch gestures [37], gait [24], and GPS movements [4]. Extracting unique features from a user's natural interactions with the smartphone, these approaches gather data from various built-in components such as accelerometers, gyroscopes, magnetometers, and touch screens [20]. These methods implicitly model invariant user-specific traits by analyzing these multi-modal signals, eliminating the need for the user's active participation in the authentication process.

Continuous authentication has seen a surge in the adoption of gait recognition, primarily because of the unique walking patterns distinctive to each individual [2]. Techniques based on gait strive to automatically discern whether the current user of a wearable device is the rightful owner or an impersonator. This is accomplished by scrutinizing their motion signatures, extracted from the device's onboard motion sensors, and matching them against the owner's established profile. The fundamental concept here is to verify identity seamlessly by exploiting the individuality of one's walking gait compared to that of an imposter. If, during authentication checks, the deviations in the current user's gait surpass a predefined threshold, the system raises a flag indicating potential unauthorized access.

Gait analysis has recently been investigated for continuous authentication using wearable sensors [22]. Despite their convenience, current methods based on gait face limitations in accuracy, with many needing help to achieve authentication rates surpassing 95% and equal error rates between 5–10% [6]. To ensure reliable adoption, further research is essential to enhance accuracy. Recent advancements in deep learning for behavioral modeling provide promising alternatives to traditional manual feature engineering [26,29]. Deep neural networks can automatically learn representative features from sensor data, freeing us from the complexities of labor-intensive hand-crafted approaches. This enables the deployment of user authentication based on pervasive behaviors like gait captured through onboard sensors.

While deep learning has proven successful in classifying images and speech, its application to non-image/speech data, such as recognizing human behavior through raw sensor data, poses unique challenges. The presence of abundant noise in raw data introduces the risk of errors in behavior recognition during deep learning-based authentication. In addressing this issue, our work introduces a new deep learning model called SE-DeepConvNet, designed explicitly for continuous authentication based on sensor data. This model incorporates fully interactive layers by utilizing squeeze-and-excitation modules to tackle the challenges associated with continuous authentication. Experiments were conducted using the publicly available HMOG dataset to validate its effectiveness. The results of these experiments demonstrate that the proposed SE-DeepConvNet surpasses other baseline deep learning models, achieving higher accuracy and a lower equal error rate (EER).

The remainder of this article follows a structured outline. Recent related works are introduced in Sect. 2. Details about the SE-DeepConvNet model are outlined in Sect. 3. Our experimental results are presented in Sect. 4. Finally, Sect. 5 concludes this work and highlights challenging areas for future exploration.

2   Related Works

2.1   Continuous Authentication

Continuous authentication seeks to comprehend human behaviors, allowing computing systems to assist users proactively based on their needs. Human activities, like walking, sitting, working, and running, can be described as actions the user performs within a specific timeframe and protocol. Over the past decade, extensive research has been conducted on continuous authentication.

The growing number of sensors in standard mobile phones has directed attention towards gait features for authentication. Gait features are stable, distinguishable, and easy to collect but are also gaining significance due to people having their phones with them for longer durations. Additionally, there is a wealth of available gait features. An implicit authentication method based on gait identifies users by their walking style. Gait signal data from built-in sensors like accelerometers and gyroscopes can be easily accessed through mobile phones. By collecting these continuous data streams, discriminative gait features can be extracted and trained by a classifier for authentication. Various methods have been proposed for gait-based implicit authentication on mobile devices, differing primarily in how features are extracted from raw data or the authentication algorithm employed.

The study by Mantyjarvi et al. [17] employed methods utilizing correlation, frequency domain analysis, and data distribution statistics. Thang et al. [32] and Muaaz et al. [21] utilized the dynamic time warping method. Rather than relying on gait cycles for feature extraction, Nickel et al. [23] employed hidden Markov models for gait recognition. The mentioned methods require feature selection and extraction before user authentication, making these procedures intricate and laborious.

Zhong et al. [36] introduced a sensor direction-invariant gait representation called gait dynamic images. This method captures three-dimensional time series using a triaxial accelerometer, expressing GDI as the cosine similarity of the motion measurement at time t with the lag time signal. Damaševicius et al. [7] utilized random projections to reduce feature dimensionality to two, then computed the Jaccard distance between two probability-distributed functions of the derived features for identification. Kašys et al. [15] conducted user identity verification through a linear support vector machine (SVM) classifier on walking activity data captured by a mobile phone.

Xu et al. [34] introduced Gait-watch, a context-aware authentication system based on gait feature recognition and extraction during various walking activities. Abo El-Soud et al. [1] employed filter and wrapper approaches for feature selection of gait data, utilizing a random forest classifier for authentication. Papavasileiou et al. [25] proposed GaitCode, a continuous authentication mechanism based on multi-modal gait-based sensor data. They used a network of auto-encoders with fusion for feature extraction and SVM for classification.

2.2   Deep Learning in Continuous Authentication

The realm of advanced learning [11] has showcased its effectiveness in domains connected to recognizing walking styles. This spans discerning actions [13], categorizing videos [14], and identifying faces [31]. Nevertheless, the training of advanced learning models demands copious data, posing a challenge due to the constraints in collecting abundant walking data, given the limitations in battery life and processing power of mobile devices. In comparison to conventional machine learning approaches, applications of advanced learning in problems related to implicit authentication through walking styles are relatively scarce.

Gadaleta et al. [9] introduced an authentication framework for users based on motion signals gathered from smartphones, labeled as IDNet. IDNet leverages convolutional neural networks (CNN) as versatile feature extractors, utilizing one-class SVM as a classifier. They directly input the original walking signal into the CNN, a method that is not ideal for CNNs as they are less adept at processing one-dimensional signals. Giorgi et al. [10] outlined an authentication framework for users, utilizing inertial sensors and incorporating recurrent neural networks (RNN) for deep learning-based classification. However, notable disparities were observed in results between known and unknown identities.

To enhance the effectiveness of deep learning approaches, cross-channel interaction presents evident advantages compared to recently suggested literature. Hu et al. [12] introduced a squeeze-and-excitation (SE) network to fine-tune channel feature responses. Chen et al. [5] employed channel-wise attention for tasks like semantic segmentation and image captioning. Wu and He [33] utilized group normalization, representing a specialized model with channel-wise communication.

However, the interactions across different channels in their models are overly simplistic, involving only the computation of mean and standard deviation of feature maps. In computer vision, Yang et al. [35] proposed cross-channel interaction at the same layer. This encourages communication among channels within the same layer, improving performance.

3   The Sensor-Based Continuous Authentication Framework

The continuous authentication system based on sensors utilized in our study encompasses four main phases:

1. Gathering raw data streams from sensors,
2. Pre-processing the signals to address missing values and eliminate noise,
3. Converting the refined signals into representative data instances,

4. Conducting supervised training and evaluation of machine learning models using the generated datasets.

This sequential processing pipeline facilitates the robust learning and assessment of authentication systems from sensor streams, illustrated in Fig. 1.

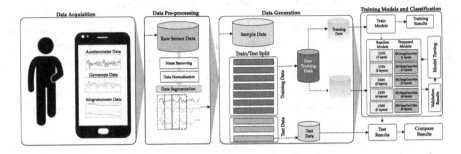

Fig. 1. The proposed framework of gait-based continuous authentication using wearable sensors.

3.1 HMOG Dataset

Experiments utilize the available HMOG smartphone sensor dataset to assess our proposed advanced learning approach, specifically designed for continuous authentication [30]. The HMOG dataset comprises readings from accelerometers and gyroscopes, gathered from 100 participants (53 male, 47 female) using 10 Samsung Galaxy S4 devices at a 100 Hz sampling rate. The participants engaged in sessions lasting 2-6 h, involving activities like reading documents, typing, and navigating maps. However, HMOG encounters challenges such as data gaps and aberrant readings for certain participants [16]. Consequently, we excluded 10 participants from the HMOG dataset for this study.

3.2 Data Pre-processing

Initially, the untreated sensor data streams underwent preliminary adjustments to purify signals and standardize distributions. In particular, filtering methods were applied to eliminate noise from the readings. Subsequently, the refined signals from accelerometers and gyroscopes were standardized to reduce variations across different sensor scales. Ultimately, the processed multi-sensor chronological sequences were partitioned into non-overlapping segments lasting 2.56 s each, employing a sliding window approach. This resulted in fixed-width instances, capturing user behavior patterns over time for the learning algorithms to analyze.

3.3   Training Deep Learning Models

We present SE-DeepConvNet, a concise CNN designed for continuous authentication based on sensor data. The model autonomously derives spatial representations through convolutional layers directly from the unprocessed input sequences. SE blocks are subsequently introduced to recalibrate feature responses channelwise, amplifying informative features. Further optimization during training is achieved through additional batch normalization and ReLU activation layers, which normalize activations and address the vanishing gradient issue. Illustrated in Fig. 2, this cohesive structure facilitates effective learning of distinctive behavioral characteristics from sensor data noise, ensuring dependable user authentication.

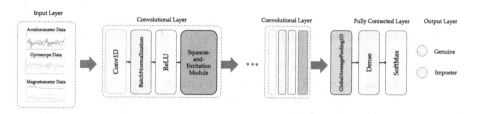

Fig. 2. The proposed SE-DeepConvNet model.

The recalibration of filter responses to accentuate significant features is achieved through SE blocks, initially introduced in [34]. These blocks function in two primary stages — squeeze and excitation. During the squeeze phase, spatial information is consolidated across channels through global average pooling to create channel-wise statistics. The subsequent excitation phase captures inter-channel dependencies using this aggregated information. More precisely, a straightforward gating mechanism employing two fully connected layers activated by ReLU and sigmoid functions, respectively, learns scalar weights for each channel. As demonstrated in Fig. 3, this re-weighting process selectively amplifies influential channels while suppressing less valuable ones, leading to enhanced representation learning.

3.4   Performance Measurement Criteria

The primary measures for evaluating authentication performance are three standard metrics. True Acceptance (TA) corresponds to accurately classifying patterns attributed to the legitimate user as Genuine. True Reject (TR) signifies the correct classification of patterns unrelated to the genuine user as an Imposter. Conversely, False Acceptance (FA) refers to misclassifying patterns not associated with the genuine user as Genuine. Finally, False Reject (FR) denotes the misclassification of patterns belonging to the genuine user as Imposter.

We assess the performance of authentication through three essential metrics:

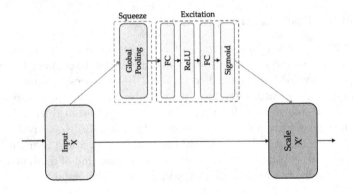

Fig. 3. The Squeeze-and-Excitation module.

1. False Acceptance Rate (FAR) quantifies the ratio of imposter access attempts wrongly identified as genuine users. Reduced values signify heightened security.
2. False Rejection Rate (FRR) measures the ratio of legitimate user attempts to erroneously denied access. Lower values prioritize user convenience.
3. Equal Error Rate (EER) denotes the error rate when FAR equals FRR. As FAR and FRR trade-off, EER balances security and convenience.

The mathematical formulas for these three metrics are presented as follows:

$$FAR = \frac{FA}{FA + TR} \tag{1}$$

$$FRR = \frac{FR}{FR + TA} \tag{2}$$

$$EER = \frac{FAR + FRR}{2} \tag{3}$$

where $|FAR + FRR|$ is minimum.

4   Experiments and Research Findings

In this section, we describe the experiments carried out to assess the proposed SE-DeepConvNet model for continuous authentication. We assess the model's performance on a publicly available dataset by employing data from accelerometer, gyroscope, and magnetometer sensors. We provide information on evaluation metrics, comparisons with baseline models, parameter configurations, and accuracy analyses across various sensing modalities. The presented vital findings showcase cutting-edge authentication rates, affirming the success of incorporating SE blocks into deep convolutional neural networks for reliable user verification from motion sequences captured by wearable devices.

4.1 Experimental Setting

The experimentation is conducted using Python on Google Colab Pro+ with the aid of a Tesla-V100 GPU to expedite computations. The assessments involve pitting the proposed SE-DeepConvNet model against conventional deep learning structures, such as standard CNNs and long short-term memory (LSTM) networks, specifically for continuous authentication based on sensor data. The comparative outcomes gauge enhancements in recognition achieved by incorporating SE blocks into our deep convolutional network.

4.2 Experimental Results and Discussion

The sensor dataset underwent partitioning through a 10-fold cross-validation protocol, ensuring a rigorous evaluation of the model's performance. The authentication results, showcased in Table 1, affirm the improvements introduced by the SE-DeepConvNet model. These results highlight its cutting-edge accuracy and EER compared to conventional methods.

Table 1. Performance metrics of baseline deep learning models including the proposed SE-DeepConvNet using HMOG dataset.

Gait-based Activity	CNN		LSTM		SE-DeepConvNet	
	EER(%)	Accuracy(%)	EER(%)	Accuracy(%)	EER(%)	Accuracy(%)
Read-Walk	0.75(±2.67)	99.51(±1.73)	0.60(±1.81)	99.60(±1.21)	0.38(±1.13)	99.78(±6.67)
Write-Walk	1.33(±2.86)	99.09(±1.86)	1.55(±2.79)	98.97(±1.82)	1.26(±2.32)	99.13(±1.55)
Map-Walk	1.24(±4.73)	99.08(±4.25)	0.77(±1.44)	99.48(±0.96)	0.83(±1.40)	99.43(±0.98)

Table 1 reveals noteworthy observations from the results, leading to several key findings. In the Read-Walk activity, where participants read while walking, the SE-DeepConvNet model demonstrates superior performance. It achieves the highest accuracy at 99.78% and the lowest EER at 0.379%, showcasing a substantial advancement over the baseline CNN and LSTM models.

In the Write-Walk activity involving writing while walking, the SE-DeepConvNet again outshines other models. It attains a top accuracy of 99.13% and an EER of 1.264%. However, the performance gap compared to baselines is slightly narrower than observed in Read-Walk. A similar trend is noticeable in the Map-Walk activity, where map navigation while walking is involved. Here, the SE-DeepConvNet exhibits a marginally higher accuracy of 99.431% and a lower EER of 0.829% compared to CNN and LSTM models.

The advantage gained from incorporating SE blocks is more pronounced in the Read-Walk activity than in other activities, suggesting that SE recalibration is particularly effective in this context. Notably, all models exhibit a comparatively lower performance in the Write-Walk activity than in other activities. This implies that writing while walking may introduce more variability or noise than reading or map-based interactions.

The findings from these experiments indicate that the SE-DeepConvNet surpasses alternative deep learning networks, achieving the highest accuracy at 99.778% and the lowest EER at 0.379% when applied to sensor data from the activity of reading while walking. In the case of the activity involving writing while walking, the SE-DeepConvNet outperforms the baseline deep learning models (CNN and LSTM). These comparative outcomes have been depicted graphically in Fig. 4.

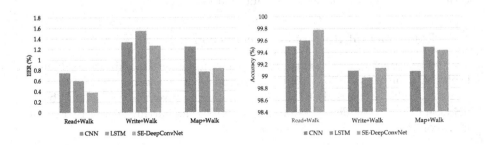

Fig. 4. Comparative results of deep learning models used in this work: (left side) EER, and (right side) accuracy.

5   Conclusion and Future Works

This research introduced SE-DeepConvNet, a CNN incorporating squeeze-and-excitation modules. These modules recalibrate feature responses channel-wise within each convolutional layer to highlight significant representations. The experiments conducted demonstrate cutting-edge authentication accuracy, reaching 99.78% and a low equal error rate of 0.38% on a publicly available gait analysis dataset, surpassing the capabilities of standard deep learning approaches.

Future endeavors in this line of research should focus on verifying our model's adaptability across diverse datasets encompassing various activity modalities. To boost performance, consideration could be given to implementing more sophisticated lightweight architectures and integrating data inputs transformed in time and frequency. In summary, the SE mechanism promises to ensure robust continuous verification using mobile sensor data.

Acknowledgments. This research project was supported by Thailand Science Research and Innovation Fund; University of Phayao under Grant No. FF67-UoE-214; National Science, Research and Innovation Fund (NSRF); and King Mongkut's University of Technology North Bangkok with Contract no. KMUTNB-FF-67-B-10.

Disclosure of Interests. The authors have no competing interests to declare that are relevant to the content of this article.

References

1. Abo El-Soud, M.W., Gaber, T., AlFayez, F., Eltoukhy, M.M.: Implicit authentication method for smartphone users based on rank aggregation and random forest. Alex. Eng. J. **60**(1), 273–283 (2021). https://doi.org/10.1016/j.aej.2020.08.006

2. Baig, A.F., Eskeland, S., Yang, B.: Novel and efficient privacy-preserving continuous authentication. Cryptography **8**(1) (2024). https://doi.org/10.3390/cryptography8010003

3. Bimbot, F., et al.: A tutorial on text-independent speaker verification. EURASIP J. Adv. Signal Process. **2004**, 430-451 (2004). https://doi.org/10.1155/S1110865704310024

4. Buthpitiya, S., Zhang, Y., Dey, A.K., Griss, M.: n-gram geo-trace modeling. In: Lyons, K., Hightower, J., Huang, E.M. (eds.) Pervasive 2011. LNCS, vol. 6696, pp. 97–114. Springer, Heidelberg (2011). https://doi.org/10.1007/978-3-642-21726-5_7

5. Chen, L., Zhang, H., Xiao, J., Nie, L., Shao, J., Liu, W., Chua, T.: Sca-cnn: spatial and channel-wise attention in convolutional networks for image captioning. In: 2017 IEEE Conference on Computer Vision and Pattern Recognition (CVPR), pp. 6298–6306. IEEE Computer Society, Los Alamitos, CA, USA (2017). https://doi.org/10.1109/CVPR.2017.667

6. Choi, J., Choi, S., Kang, T.: Smartphone authentication system using personal gaits and a deep learning model. Sensors **23**(14) (2023). https://doi.org/10.3390/s23146395

7. Damaševičius, R., Vasiljevas, M., Salkevicius, J., Woźniak, M.: Human activity recognition in aal environments using random projections. Comput. Math. Methods Med. **2016**, 1–17 (2016). https://doi.org/10.1155/2016/4073584

8. Fathy, M.E., Patel, V.M., Chellappa, R.: Face-based active authentication on mobile devices. In: 2015 IEEE International Conference on Acoustics, Speech and Signal Processing (ICASSP), pp. 1687–1691 (2015). https://doi.org/10.1109/ICASSP.2015.7178258

9. Gadaleta, M., Rossi, M.: Idnet: smartphone-based gait recognition with convolutional neural networks. Pattern Recogn. **74**, 25–37 (2018). https://doi.org/10.1016/j.patcog.2017.09.005

10. Giorgi, G., Saracino, A., Martinelli, F.: Using recurrent neural networks for continuous authentication through gait analysis. Pattern Recogn. Lett. **147**, 157–163 (2021). https://doi.org/10.1016/j.patrec.2021.03.010

11. Hinton, G.E., Osindero, S., Teh, Y.W.: A fast learning algorithm for deep belief nets. Neural Comput. **18**(7), 1527-1554 (2006). https://doi.org/10.1162/neco.2006.18.7.1527

12. Hu, J., Shen, L., Sun, G.: Squeeze-and-excitation networks. In: 2018 IEEE/CVF Conference on Computer Vision and Pattern Recognition, pp. 7132–7141 (2018). https://doi.org/10.1109/CVPR.2018.00745

13. Ji, S., Xu, W., Yang, M., Yu, K.: 3d convolutional neural networks for human action recognition. IEEE Trans. Pattern Anal. Mach. Intell. **35**(1), 221–231 (2013). https://doi.org/10.1109/TPAMI.2012.59

14. Karpathy, A., Toderici, G., Shetty, S., Leung, T., Sukthankar, R., Fei-Fei, L.: Large-scale video classification with convolutional neural networks. In: 2014 IEEE Conference on Computer Vision and Pattern Recognition, pp. 1725–1732 (2014). https://doi.org/10.1109/CVPR.2014.223

15. Kašys, K., Dundulis, A., Vasiljevas, M., Maskeliūnas, R., Damaševičius, R.: Body-Lock: human identity recogniser app from walking activity data. In: Gervasi, O., et al. (eds.) ICCSA 2020. LNCS, vol. 12250, pp. 307–319. Springer, Cham (2020). https://doi.org/10.1007/978-3-030-58802-1_23

16. Li, Y., Hu, H., Zhou, G., Deng, S.: Sensor-based continuous authentication using cost-effective kernel ridge regression. IEEE Access 6, 32554–32565 (2018). https://doi.org/10.1109/ACCESS.2018.2841347

17. Mantyjarvi, J., Lindholm, M., Vildjiounaite, E., Makela, S.M., Ailisto, H.: Identifying users of portable devices from gait pattern with accelerometers. In: Proceedings. (ICASSP2005). IEEE International Conference on Acoustics, Speech, and Signal Processing, 2005, vol. 2, pp. ii/973–ii/976 (2005). https://doi.org/10.1109/ICASSP.2005.1415569

18. Martinovic, I., Rasmussen, K., Roeschlin, M., Tsudik, G.: Authentication using pulse-response biometrics. Commun. ACM 60(2), 108-115 (2017). https://doi.org/10.1145/3023359

19. Mekruksavanich, S., Jitpattanakul, A.: Deep residual network for smartwatch-based user identification through complex hand movements. Sensors 22(8) (2022). https://doi.org/10.3390/s22083094

20. Mekruksavanich, S., Jitpattanakul, A.: Fallnext: a deep residual model based on multi-branch aggregation for sensor-based fall detection. ECTI Trans. Comput. Inform. Technol. (ECTI-CIT) 16(4), 352-364 (2022). https://doi.org/10.37936/ecti-cit.2022164.248156

21. Muaaz, M., Mayrhofer, R.: An analysis of different approaches to gait recognition using cell phone based accelerometers. In: Proceedings of International Conference on Advances in Mobile Computing & Multimedia,MoMM 2013. pp. 293-300. Association for Computing Machinery, New York (2013). https://doi.org/10.1145/2536853.2536895

22. Muaaz, M., Mayrhofer, R.: Smartphone-based gait recognition: from authentication to imitation. IEEE Trans. Mob. Comput. 16(11), 3209–3221 (2017). https://doi.org/10.1109/TMC.2017.2686855

23. Nickel, C., Busch, C., Rangarajan, S., Möbius, M.: Using hidden markov models for accelerometer-based biometric gait recognition. In: 2011 IEEE 7th International Colloquium on Signal Processing and its Applications, pp. 58–63 (2011). https://doi.org/10.1109/CSPA.2011.5759842

24. Nickel, C., Wirtl, T., Busch, C.: Authentication of smartphone users based on the way they walk using k-nn algorithm. In: 2012 Eighth International Conference on Intelligent Information Hiding and Multimedia Signal Processing, pp. 16–20 (2012). https://doi.org/10.1109/IIH-MSP.2012.11

25. Papavasileiou, I., Qiao, Z., Zhang, C., Zhang, W., Bi, J., Han, S.: Gaitcode: gait-based continuous authentication using multimodal learning and wearable sensors. Smart Health 19, 100162 (2021). https://doi.org/10.1016/j.smhl.2020.100162

26. Peinado-Contreras, A., Munoz-Organero, M.: Gait-based identification using deep recurrent neural networks and acceleration patterns. Sensors 20(23) (2020). https://doi.org/10.3390/s20236900

27. Qi, M., Lu, Y., Li, J., Li, X., Kong, J.: User-specific iris authentication based on feature selection. In: 2008 International Conference on Computer Science and Software Engineering, vol. 1, pp. 1040–1043 (2008). https://doi.org/10.1109/CSSE.2008.1060

28. Shabrina, N., Isshiki, T., Kunieda, H.: Fingerprint authentication on touch sensor using phase-only correlation method. In: 2016 7th International Conference of

Information and Communication Technology for Embedded Systems (IC-ICTES), pp. 85–89 (2016). https://doi.org/10.1109/ICTEmSys.2016.7467127

29. Shiraga, K., Makihara, Y., Muramatsu, D., Echigo, T., Yagi, Y.: Geinet: view-invariant gait recognition using a convolutional neural network. In: 2016 International Conference on Biometrics (ICB), pp. 1–8 (2016). https://doi.org/10.1109/ICB.2016.7550060

30. Sitová, Z., et al.: Hmog: new behavioral biometric features for continuous authentication of smartphone users. IEEE Trans. Inf. Forensics Secur. **11**(5), 877–892 (2016). https://doi.org/10.1109/TIFS.2015.2506542

31. Taigman, Y., Yang, M., Ranzato, M., Wolf, L.: Deepface: closing the gap to human-level performance in face verification. In: 2014 IEEE Conference on Computer Vision and Pattern Recognition, pp. 1701–1708 (2014). https://doi.org/10.1109/CVPR.2014.220

32. Thang, H.M., Viet, V.Q., Dinh Thuc, N., Choi, D.: Gait identification using accelerometer on mobile phone. In: 2012 International Conference on Control, Automation and Information Sciences (ICCAIS), pp. 344–348 (2012). https://doi.org/10.1109/ICCAIS.2012.6466615

33. Wu, Y., He, K.: Group normalization. Int. J. Comput. Vision **128**, 742–755 (2018)

34. Xu, W., Shen, Y., Luo, C., Li, J., Li, W., Zomaya, A.Y.: Gait-watch: a gait-based context-aware authentication system for smart watch via sparse coding. Ad Hoc Netw. **107**, 102218 (2020). https://doi.org/10.1016/j.adhoc.2020.102218

35. Yang, J., Ren, Z., Gan, C., Zhu, H., Parikh, D.: Cross-channel communication networks. In: Wallach, H., Larochelle, H., Beygelzimer, A., d'Alché-Buc, F., Fox, E., Garnett, R. (eds.) Advances in Neural Information Processing Systems, vol. 32, pp. 1–10. Curran Associates, Inc. (2019)

36. Zhong, Y., Deng, Y., Meltzner, G.: Pace independent mobile gait biometrics. In: 2015 IEEE 7th International Conference on Biometrics Theory, Applications and Systems (BTAS), pp. 1–8 (2015). https://doi.org/10.1109/BTAS.2015.7358784

37. Zou, B., Li, Y.: Touch-based smartphone authentication using import vector domain description. In: 2018 IEEE 29th International Conference on Application-specific Systems, Architectures and Processors (ASAP), pp. 1–4 (2018). https://doi.org/10.1109/ASAP.2018.8445125

Applying LSTM Recurrent Neural Networks to Predict Revenue

Luis Eduardo Pelin Cardoso[1,3]($\boxtimes$) (iD), André C. P. de Leon F. de Carvalho[2] (iD), and Marcos G. Quiles[3] (iD)

[1] Research Lab, Neural Technology, Campinas, SP, Brazil
luis.pelin@neuraltec.app
[2] Institute of Mathematics and Computer Sciences, University of São Paulo - USP, São Carlos, SP, Brazil
andre@icmc.usp.br
[3] Institute of Science and Technology, Federal University of São Paulo - UNIFESP, São José dos Campos, SP, Brazil
quiles@unifesp.br

Abstract. Predicting a company's revenue is not a trivial task. Attempting to identify a sales pattern for a store's products, considering all possible variables, both internal and external to the business, is a complex task. For companies that sell products, finding a way to predict next day's revenue helps maintain lean inventory, among numerous other factors. As result, fewer resources are wasted in the form of stagnant products, and there are less expenses in purchasing supplies. The main motivation for this study is to accurately forecast a company's revenue for the days, following the prediction day-only for companies that sell products and disregarding those that offer services. To achieve this goal, here, considering a real scenario, we evaluate the use of the Long Short-Term Memory (LSTM) type of Recurrent Neural Network, known for their superior ability to capture long-term temporal dependencies, outperforming traditional forecasting models in this domain. For our experiments, we employ a single real data model across various LSTM architectures, iteratively refining our approach to approximate an ideal state for future revenue prediction. This study not only validates the effectiveness of LSTM networks in handling the temporal complexity inherent in sales data but also investigates the impact of different architectural configurations on forecasting accuracy. By doing so, we aim to identify a robust model that can serve as a reliable tool for businesses in their inventory and supply chain management strategies.

Keywords: Revenue · Prediction · RNN · LSTM

1 Introduction

Well-managed companies aim to achieve three objectives: increased customer satisfaction, increased revenue, and reduced expenses. For such, entrepreneurs need to address various day-to-day questions related to cash flow, future revenues, the cost of purchasing raw materials and finished products, the volume

O. Gervasi et al. (Eds.): ICCSA 2024, LNCS 14814, pp. 198–212, 2024.
https://doi.org/10.1007/978-3-031-64608-9_13

of stagnant inventory, among others. Furthermore, companies must be flexible to respond rapidly to competitive and market changes. They must benchmark continuously to achieve best practice [8].

In the dynamic landscape of business, anticipating future sales becomes a pivotal challenge for entrepreneurs striving to make informed decisions, which is a crucial part of company strategy. Competitive strategy is about being different [8]. To follow this process, suppose a scenario where a business owner could harness the power of advanced technologies to predict future sales with remarkable accuracy.

The main goal of this work is to assist business owners in partially or fully addressing some of the mentioned questions, as well as others related, since answering these questions will contribute to achieving the above-mentioned objectives. Knowing how to find a value close to future revenue not only brings the direct benefit of more resources to the company but also entails indirect benefits, such as better-managed and leaner inventory. This, in turn, leads to another indirect benefit, which is the reduction of the company's costs, since the lean production philosophy considers inventory a form of waste that should be minimized [16].

There are several ways to assist a business owner in achieving their objectives. A financial consultant could provide this service due to their highly specialized knowledge. However, machine learning models could also be used, provided that those capable of handling complex time series are selected [1].

This article delves into the realm of predictive analytics, specifically focusing on the application of Long Short-Term Memory (LSTM) networks. By exploring the potential of LSTM networks in forecasting future sales, it aims to empower business owners with valuable insights, allowing them to navigate the complexities of their operations with greater foresight and efficiency. The integration of cutting-edge technologies in sales prediction not only aligns with the pursuit of increased revenues but also sets the stage for more streamlined inventory management and cost reduction, ultimately contributing to the holistic success of a business.

The Long Short-Term Memory (LSTM) type of Recurrent Neural Networks (RNNs) is a machine learning model that performs well with complex time series, handling variable sequences and non-linear data [7]. Therefore, it has been chosen for the data analysis in this problem due to its intrinsic nature.

The data for training the model were retrieved from the database of an online system called My Bucks [4], owned by a company affiliated with Neural Tec [13] called Blue Forge. All the data used are real, as it was decided that fictitious data would not be used for the study at any point. Furthermore, the available volume was substantial, which would provide more security for the neural network training process. The data was grouped by day and presented to the Neural Network with nineteen features: the sales date, the company, the total revenue for the day, among others. The granularity of the data that is used as an input for time-series forecasting, is an important factor in the process of prediction [7].

The study's objective is to analyze data from 10 previous days before a specified date and attempt to predict the revenue for the following day. If this process proves successful, it would be extended to more subsequent days. However, if unsuccessful, the model's training data would be enriched with new features for further model training and accuracy analysis.

Various neural network architectures were chosen to train the dataset, aiming to find the one that best adapts-that is, the one that best predicts future revenue. This article will present the best architecture, and its result will be displayed to validate its quality.

This article has four sections: related work, methodology, experimental analysis and conclusion. The related work section will present the literature review and compare other articles to this work. The methodology section will indicate how the data was pre-processed and will briefly explain the algorithms used for prediction. Then, the experimental analysis section will be presented, displaying the chosen data format, the configuration used for algorithm comparison, the analysis criteria used to find the best algorithm, and the obtained results of best architecture. Finally, a conclusion will be presented regarding the most successful algorithm to be used for the sales prediction problem.

2   Related Work

This section aims to provide a comprehensive overview of previous studies and relevant research that underpin and contextualize the present work. It addresses a variety of theoretical approaches, methodologies, and findings that have contributed to the development of the field under study.

Related works are organized according to specific themes and topics, allowing for a clearer understanding of the evolution of knowledge in the area. Each work is succinctly summarized, highlighting its significant contributions and its connections to the objectives and methodology adopted in this article.

By exploring related works, it is possible to identify gaps in existing knowledge, unresolved challenges, and opportunities for additional contributions. This section serves as a solid foundation for the argument and relevance of the present study while acknowledging and valuing the contributions of previous researchers.

In [12], the authors provide a tutorial-like introduction to Long Short-Term Memory Recurrent Neural Networks (LSTM-RNN), originally developed as supplementary material for Artificial Intelligence lectures. It emphasizes understanding LSTM-RNN's evolution since the early nineties, noting changes in notation and representation in today's publications. The article highlights the significance of LSTM-RNN and its potential to improve machine learning algorithms, offering valuable insights into their workings and motivating further development within the machine learning community.

In [1], the research aims to develop a reliable sales trend prediction mechanism using data mining techniques to optimize revenue generation in today's data-driven business environment, particularly in the E-commerce industry. Accurate sales forecasting is crucial for effective enterprise planning and decision-making, impacting resource management and market growth. By employing data mining techniques, vast amounts of data can be transformed into actionable insights, facilitating sound budgeting and strategic planning across functional areas. The study focuses on selecting appropriate approaches for precise sales forecasting, involving extensive data analysis and the evaluation of prediction algorithms. The research findings, methodologies, and future directions are discussed comprehensively, emphasizing the importance of predictive analytics in driving business success. The authors compare machine learning techniques such as Generalized Linear Model (GLM), Decision Tree, and Gradient Boosted Trees (GBT), concluding that the GBT algorithm had the best predictive performance. Despite not employing neural network techniques, the article proved useful in studying data preprocessing techniques for sales prediction.

In [7], the text discusses the application of artificial intelligence, particularly deep neural networks like Long Short-Term Memory (LSTM) with CNN-LSTM (Convolutional Neural Network and Long Short-Term Memory) and Convolutional Long Short-Term Memory (ConvLSTM), in time series analysis and forecasting, addressing challenges such as economic complexity and data granularity. It highlights the importance of sentiment analysis in automated opinion classification, particularly in processing large volumes of textual data. The paper proposes a model for company revenue prediction using deep learning techniques, leveraging quantitative stock data and news sentiments as input features, with a focus on sequence classification for binary forecasting.

In [11], the paper addresses the importance of sales forecasting for business decision-making, particularly in resource allocation, cash flow management, and early risk identification. It discusses the use of machine learning techniques, specifically time series models, such as Auto Regressive Integrated Moving Average (ARIMA) and Long Short Term Memory (LSTM) networks, for sales prediction. ARIMA models are explained in terms of their parameters and their application to stationary time series, while LSTM networks are highlighted for their ability to handle sequence dependence. The paper proposes a comparative study of ARIMA, SARIMA, and LSTM models for profit prediction, emphasizing data collection, model development, and forecasting for the next five years. It is structured to discuss literature review, model building, result analysis, and conclusion in subsequent sections.

In [2], a study was conducted on the insurance industry. The insurance industry serves crucial functions in dispersing risks, compensating losses, financing, and social management, contributing to the stability of people's living standards and social stability. With China emerging as a dominant force in the global insurance market, witnessing significant growth in premium income, now ranking third globally, its importance to the national economic system as a financial pillar and GDP growth driver cannot be overstated. As China's economy transitions to a "new normal" characterized by innovation-driven growth, predicting premium income scale has become a pertinent concern. Long Short-Term Memory (LSTM) neural networks, known for their ability to capture long-term relationships in time series data, offer promising prospects for accurate prediction in the financial domain, notably in stock market forecasting, underscoring their applicability and effectiveness across various fields.

In [3], the authors conduct a comparative study for retail sales prediction using LSTM and ARIMA networks. Environmental concerns, particularly regarding food waste, have become increasingly urgent. The disposal of expired or unsold food by grocery stores not only has significant negative environmental impacts but also poses economic implications. To address this, more accurate sales forecasting methods are crucial. By utilizing historical sales data and patterns, time-series forecasting approaches, such as Autoregressive Integrated Moving Average (ARIMA) and Artificial Neural Networks (ANN), have been employed. Among these, Long Short-Term Memory (LSTM) models have gained attention for their ability to remember long-term information in time-series data. Hence, this study focuses on using LSTM and ARIMA models to predict future sales, aiming to mitigate food waste and promote environmental sustainability while optimizing economic outcomes for grocery stores.

In [9], a comparison was made between two RNN models for predicting sales of medium-sized restaurants. The challenge of forecasting sales in small and medium-sized restaurants, often hindered by limited data and resources for analysis, is crucial for efficient employee scheduling and cost-effectiveness. Traditionally, sales predictions are made intuitively or through economic modeling, focusing on factors like guest counts and sales dollars. Despite the shift towards machine learning methods, including neural networks like LSTM, empirical evidence suggests mixed results compared to traditional statistical models like ARIMA. Recent research emphasizes the importance of accurate forecasting methodologies, particularly in the restaurant industry, highlighting the need for comprehensive studies to compare various machine learning techniques and traditional models. This paper aims to address this gap by conducting a thorough survey of forecasting models using real-world data, aiming to identify optimal methods for predicting sales with an emphasis on accuracy and reproducibility.

In [14], a study is conducted on predicting high and low prices of soybeans futures using an LSTM network. Predicting price movements in financial time series is essential for investors to mitigate risks and maximize returns, constituting a significant challenge in finance. Neural networks, renowned for their nonlinear fitting capabilities, have been extensively employed in this endeavor. Researchers have utilized models like the backpropagation (BP) neural network for price prediction, with recent advancements focusing on deep learning techniques such as the long short-term memory (LSTM) neural network. While LSTM models offer improved accuracy, noise in closing prices poses a challenge, prompting exploration into predicting high and low prices of futures. Despite limited research in this area, this paper employs LSTM networks to forecast high and low prices of soybean futures, yielding promising results that, when combined with a simple trading strategy, demonstrate the potential for substantial profits.

In [6], the authors propose an approach based on Long Short-Term Memory with Particle Swam Optimization (LSTM-PSO) for sale forecasting in E-commerce companies. The advancement of economic development and technology, alongside the evolution of logistics systems, has significantly reshaped the purchasing behavior of Chinese consumers, particularly with the rise of e-commerce technology. During the 2019 Double 11 shopping festival in China, various e-commerce platforms shattered sales records, with Tmall alone generating RMB 10 billion in sales within 1 min and 36 s, leading to a total transaction volume of RMB 268.4 billion and 1.292 billion logistics orders. Sales forecasting, crucial for both traditional businesses and modern e-commerce platforms, aids managers in decision-making processes such as call center preparation, logistics scheduling, and resource allocation. However, e-commerce companies face unique challenges due to the dynamic online environment and the influence of marketing behavior on consumer shopping patterns, necessitating sophisticated analytical models like neural networks for accurate sales forecasting. This paper proposes a novel Long Short-Term Memory (LSTM) based approach for sales forecasting in e-commerce companies, optimizing model parameters using Particle Swam Optimization (PSO) metaheuristic. Experimental results demonstrate the effectiveness of the proposed approach in forecasting accuracy, underscoring the importance of advanced machine learning techniques in addressing the complexities of e-commerce sales forecasting. The study proved to be particularly useful due to the context of e-commerce companies, as they could also utilize the technique presented in this study.

In [15], employing a blend of lightGBM (Light Gradient Boosting Machine) and LSTM, this study proposes an effective model for predicting supply chain sales, emphasizing its accuracy, efficiency, and relevance for strategic decision-making in industrial settings. In recent years, the e-commerce and logistics industries' development has transformed supply chain demand's scope and pace, necessitating enterprises to swiftly respond to customer needs to maintain competitiveness. However, increased uncertainty due to complex social relationships and fluctuating market demands has led to excessive costs within the supply chain. Addressing this challenge has become the focal point for supply chain stakeholders. Leveraging big data analysis and AI technologies for accurate long-term sales forecasting is increasingly crucial, offering vital technical support for crafting supply chain solutions. While various prediction models have been proposed, many linear models lack accuracy and stability. To enhance interpretability without compromising accuracy, this paper combines deep learning with traditional machine learning methods, employing an LSTM model for data mining and integrating it with a lightGBM model for its strong interpretability. Through comparative experiments using three sales datasets, the paper demonstrates the proposed model's effectiveness in forecasting supply chain sales, contributing to enhanced predictive accuracy and interpretability.

Sales forecasting serves as a cornerstone for firms in estimating sales revenue and shaping production, operational, and marketing strategies. Despite the ubiquitous understanding that forecasts are inherently imperfect, accurate predictions are crucial for avoiding losses and optimizing operational efficiency. This necessity is particularly pronounced for products with short lifecycles, where traditional time series forecasting models may falter due to limited historical data availability. Inaccurate sales forecasts can lead to inventory imbalances, customer dissatisfaction, and operational challenges, impacting a company's financial health and capital management. To address these challenges, this study explores effective short-term sales forecasting methods, experimenting with different training timeseries lengths, window sizes, and sentiment analysis techniques. The proposed LSTM model combined with sentiment analysis showcases innovation and underscores the significance of accurate sales forecasting in enabling companies to adapt to market dynamics and achieve cost savings, potentially propelling them to industry leadership. In [10], the study introduces a model for short-term goods demand forecasting in E-commerce, integrating LSTM with sentiment analysis of consumer feedback from 'taobao.com'. Results highlight the efficacy of promptly adjusting sentiment weights to enhance forecast accuracy, enabling precise predictions even with limited historical data. The proposed LSTM approach demonstrates high accuracy in forecasting goods with short-term demands.

3   Methodology

3.1   Dataset

For this study, data was extracted from an online financial system called My Bucks [4]. Sales data from three hundred companies between January 2018 and December 2023 were consulted, and the data was grouped by the day of the sale.

The dataset obtained encompasses nineteen features, including sales date, company name, and daily sales figures for each company. A total of 28,049,723 records were extracted from the database. These records were subsequently aggregated based on sales date and company, resulting in a consolidated total of 4,312,935 entries.

3.2   Model Development

A CSV file was generated with this data for processing by a Python program. All data features were standardized to prevent outliers from interfering with the training process.

After standardization, the dataset was split into training and testing data at a ratio of 70%/30%, respectively. Only after this split were the data presented to the LSTM model. The data was further divided into training and validation sets at an 80%/20% ratio, respectively.

The neural network hyperparameters and experimental details are provided in Sec. 4.2.

3.3   Model Evaluation

Following the training process, the goal was to attempt to predict the revenue for the next day. If successful, the process would be extended to predict revenue for subsequent days. However, if unsuccessful, the data would be enriched with new features, and a new training cycle would commence.

4 Experimental Analysis

A CSV file was constructed from the extracted data to be presented to the model for training. Figure 1 illustrates the revenues of three randomly chosen companies from the three hundred in the dataset during the consulted period.

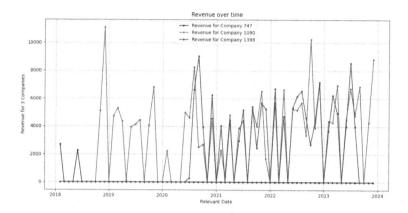

Fig. 1. Revenue of three companies over time

The IQR (Interquartile Range) technique was used to remove outliers and the data was standardized on a scale between 0 and 1, as there are no negative numbers in the dataset, given that it pertains to revenues, i.e., sales of companies. After standardization, the data was split into two sets: training and testing, in a ratio of 70%/30%, respectively. Thus, 3,019,054 records were used for training and 1,293,881 were used for testing.

Due to the nature of LSTM networks, data sequences were prepared with a size according to the chosen configuration to analyze past data. Initially set to analyze the past 10 d, several sequences with subsets of 10 d each were created.

Finally, during the training of all architectures studied, the training data was further split into two sets: training and validation, in a ratio of 80%/20%, respectively.

4.1 Algorithm and Computational Environment Configuration

For model training and subsequent data prediction, a Dell Inspiron 15 5000 notebook, with an Intel Core i7 processor running at 2.7 GHz and 8 gigabytes of memory, operating on Windows 10 64-bit OS build version 19045.3693, was used. In addition to the machine used previously, Google Colab [5] was also utilized with the configuration being CPU hardware accelerator (neither GPU nor TPU were used).

The chosen Python version was 3.7.9. For data manipulation, the Pandas library version 1.3.5 and Numpy version 1.21.6 were utilized. The SKLearn library version 1.0.2 was used for data standardization and splitting into training and testing sets. The Keras library version 2.11.0 was employed for the LSTM neural network.

4.2 Analysis Criteria

The dataset was used to train three different neural network architectures. This study will present the best one, which was considered the winner among them all.

The configuration of the best architecture is presented next:

- LSTM layer with 50 neurons;
- Dense layer with 1 neuron;
- LSTM layer uses the tanh activation function;
- Dense layer use the linear activation function;
- Optimizer: Adaptive Moment Estimation (Adam) with a learning rate of 0.0001;
- Loss function: Mean Squared Error (MSE);
- Number of training epochs: 10;
- Batch size: 100.

Figure 2 illustrates the neural network architecture whose configuration was previously mentioned.

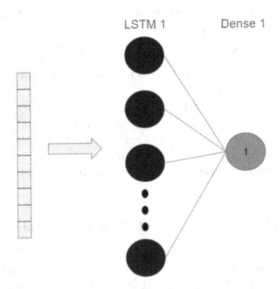

Fig. 2. Best Architecture

Figure 3 shows the training graph with the loss values for training data and this training was done using the batch training method of the Keras package.

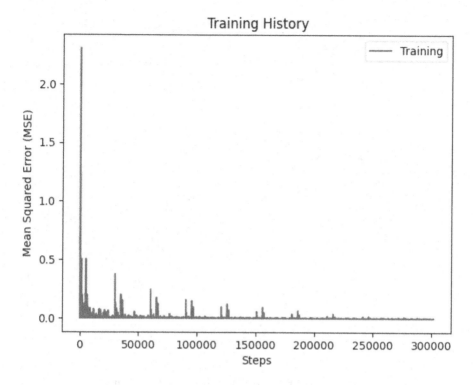

Fig. 3. Training History of Best Architecture

Following the training phase, the prediction algorithm was employed to fore-cast outcomes for both the training and test datasets. This step was under-taken to evaluate the accuracy of the predictions in relation to the original data, thereby assessing the model's performance.

Figure 4 shows the relationship between the original and predicted values in the train dataset. As it can be seen in the comparison between the two sets, the values are very close, indicating that the model can generalize well considering the training set.

Figure 5 shows the relationship between the original and predicted values in the test dataset. As seen in the comparison between the two sets, the values are relatively close, indicating that the model can generalize with the test set, although not as well as with the training set.

Figures 6 and 7 present boxplot graphs comparing the original data with the predicted data in the training and test datasets, respectively. Both graphs demonstrate that the data points are closely aligned, indicating a high degree of similarity between the original and predicted data and suggesting a good level of prediction accuracy, albeit some outliers can be observed in the test data.

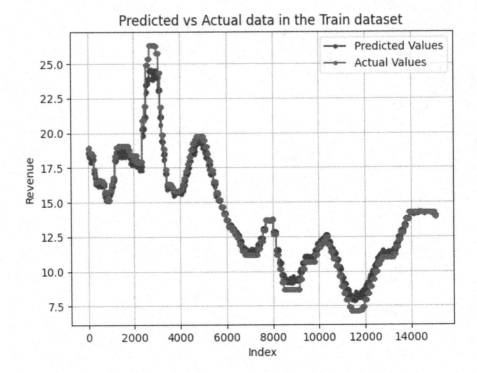

Fig. 4. Predicted vs Original Values in the Train Dataset

4.3   Results

Three distinct architectures were trained, with one emerging as the superior choice based on the outcomes detailed in the preceding section. Table 1 shows the comparison among them. Subsequently, further details regarding the training process of the most effective architecture is provided.

Table 1. Architectures Comparison

Architecture	Train Time (s)	Evaluation Loss	Evaluation MAE	Train Mean Error	Test Mean Error
Arch 1	6032.767805501	0.008931690827012062	0.0705975890159607	0.5106907777806268	1.6352886355469594
Arch 2	7076.006256432	0.105632567421456789	0.0976432567854321	0.6532507004224589	2.3567894783635373
Arch 3	9155.245678363	0.245742467853246487	0.1156894246783666	0.8422225673214567	2.9964245678534680

The selected architecture demonstrated good generalization, evidenced by the relatively modest average error observed on the test set. However, to enhance the model's robustness and predictive accuracy, exploring additional architectures and expanding the dataset to include more features is advisable. This expansion could involve integrating new data directly from the database (internal) as well as incorporating external information, such as consumer sentiment

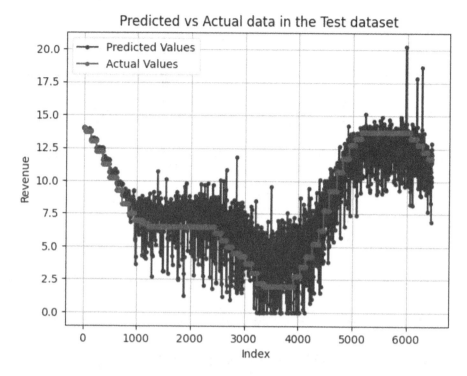

Fig. 5. Predicted vs Original Values in the Test Dataset

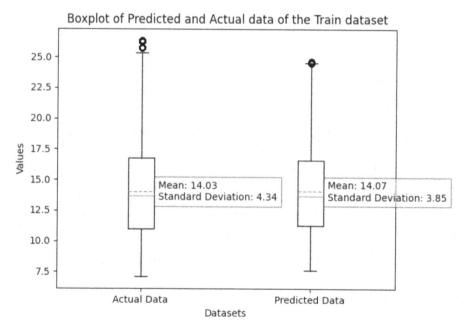

Fig. 6. Boxplot with Actual and Predicted Data in the Train Dataset

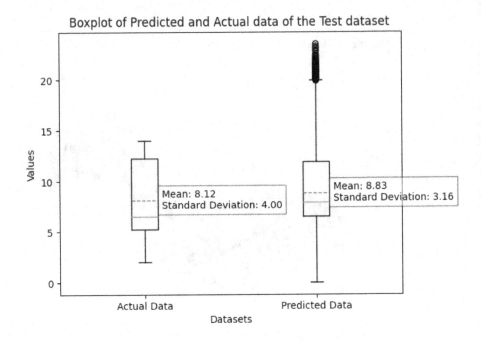

Fig. 7. Boxplot with Actual and Predicted Data in the Test Dataset

analysis related to the companies under study. Moreover, increasing the volume of records for analysis will likely contribute positively to future experiments' depth and reliability.

4.4 Discussion

The outcomes derived from the LSTM model hold significant value for any company that can provide its dataset for future revenue forecasting. Organizations adopting this analytical process benefit from enhanced planning and strategic execution. Moreover, they can minimize inefficiencies in purchasing processes, thereby reducing operational costs.

Ensuring a company's longevity necessitates optimizing its processes through the continuous and systematic application of sophisticated, accurate technologies. These technologies are essential for deciphering complex datasets and converting them into clear, actionable insights for decision-makers. This approach not only streamlines management but also supports the strategic alignment of business operations, contributing to sustainable growth and efficiency.

5   Conclusion

Discovering an automated method to forecast a company's revenue based on its billing history can significantly propel its growth by enabling more effective inventory management and providing estimates of future cash flows. However, selecting the most suitable machine-learning technique for this intricate task is far from straightforward. The neural networks explored in this study shed light on the challenge of generalization within the confines of the available data. It became evident that quantitative and qualitative enhancement of the dataset is essential for neural network models to improve their generalization capabilities. Achieving an optimal equilibrium between the volume and quality of data and the sophistication of algorithms holds the potential to increase the longevity of companies that implement this strategy markedly.

Future work might explore a broader array of machine learning algorithms, including ensemble methods and deep learning variations, to identify models offering superior generalization capabilities. Additionally, incorporating real-time data analytics and exploring the impact of external factors, such as market trends and economic indicators, on revenue predictions could further refine the accuracy of these models.

Acknowledgements. The authors gratefully acknowledge support from FAPESP (São Paulo Research Foundation), projects No. 2020/09835-1 and 2022/09285-7, and the CNPq (National Council for Scientific and Technological Development), project No. 313680/2021-3

References

1. Cheriyan, S., Ibrahim, S., Mohanan, S., Treesa, S.: Intelligent sales prediction using machine learning techniques. In: 2018 International Conference on Computing, Electronics & Communications Engineering (iCCECE), pp. 53–58. IEEE (2018)
2. Diao, L., Wang, N.: Research on premium income prediction based on lstm neural network. Adv. Soc. Sci. Res. J. **6**(11), 256–266 (2019)
3. Elmasdotter, A., Nyströmer, C.: A comparative study between lstm and arima for sales forecasting in retail (2018)
4. Forge, B.: My bucks - financial management (2023). https://www.mybucks.io/ (Accessed 14 December 2023)
5. Google: Google colab (2023). https://colab.research.google.com/ (Accessed 14 December 2023)
6. He, Q.Q., Wu, C., Si, Y.W.: Lstm with particle swam optimization for sales forecasting. Electron. Commer. Res. Appl. **51**, 101118 (2022)
7. Mishev, K., Gjorgjevikj, A., Vodenska, I., Chitkushev, L., Souma, W., Trajanov, D.: Forecasting corporate revenue by using deep-learning methodologies. In: 2019 International Conference on Control, Artificial Intelligence, Robotics & Optimization (ICCAIRO), pp. 115–120. IEEE (2019)
8. Porter, M.E.: What is strategy? Harvard Business Review (reprint 96608), pp. 3–4 (1996)
9. Schmidt, A., Kabir, M.W.U., Hoque, M.T.: Machine learning based restaurant sales forecasting. Mach. Learn. Knowl. Extract. **4**(1), 105–130 (2022)
10. Shih, Y.-S., Lin, M.-H.: A LSTM approach for sales forecasting of goods with short-term demands in E-commerce. In: Nguyen, N.T., Gaol, F.L., Hong, T.-P., Trawiński, B. (eds.) ACIIDS 2019. LNCS (LNAI), vol. 11431, pp. 244–256. Springer, Cham (2019). https://doi.org/10.1007/978-3-030-14799-0_21

11. Sirisha, U.M., Belavagi, M.C., Attigeri, G.: Profit prediction using arima, sarima and lstm models in time series forecasting: a comparison. IEEE Access **10**, 124715–124727 (2022)
12. Staudemeyer, R.C., Morris, E.R.: Understanding lstm–a tutorial into long short-term memory recurrent neural networks. arXiv preprint arXiv:1909.09586 (2019)
13. Tec, N.: Neural tec. https://neuraltec.app/ (2023), (Accessed 14 December 2023)
14. Wang, C., Gao, Q.: High and low prices prediction of soybean futures with lstm neural network. In: 2018 IEEE 9th International Conference on Software Engineering and Service Science (ICSESS), pp. 140–143. IEEE (2018)
15. Weng, T., Liu, W., Xiao, J.: Supply chain sales forecasting based on lightgbm and lstm combination model. Indus. Manag. Data Syst. **120**(2), 265–279 (2020)
16. Womack, J.P., Jones, D.T., Roos, D.: The machine that changed the world. Rawson Associates (1990)

Incentivizing Honesty in Online Decentralized Markets

Tiago Lucas Pereira Clementino$^{(\boxtimes)}$ⓘ and José Antão Beltrão Mouraⓘ

Federal University of Campina Grande, Campina Grande, Paraíba 58425-900, Brazil
tiagolucas@copin.ufcg.edu.br
https://portal.ufcg.edu.br/

Abstract. The Buyers and Sellers Dilemma is an illustration of the risk that every buyer takes when advancing payment for a product or service in a transaction that cannot be verified beforehand. That is the case of transactions involving a buyer who is physically distant from an unknown or anonymous seller as in online, e-commerce scenarios. To increase gains, the seller may be compelled to act dishonestly and not deliver the goods. It is thus of interest to implement solutions that incentivize honesty in said scenarios. For that, this article carried out a literature review in search of decentralized solutions to encourage honesty in non-verifiable transactions. Based on criteria of decentralization, non authentication and non-verifiable transactions tolerance, the solutions found were classified, analyzed and compared based on data from real world operations extracted from the OpenBazaar platform. We ranked the solutions according to effectiveness, although there is still no comprehensive solution that promotes honest behavior under any circumstances.

Keywords: buyers' and sellers' dilemma · decentralization · honesty incentive · decentralized markets · non-verifiable transactions

1 Introduction

A transaction can be seen as a structured protocol composed of a series of operations that facilitate the exchange of values between two parties: an active initiator and a passive responder. In this configuration, the active party (usually, but not necessarily, the buyer) assumes the risk by executing the value transfer (payment) before receiving a response (product or service), leaving room for potential dishonesty on the part of the passive party (seller). Risking transferring values in advance constitutes the Buyers and Sellers Dilemma [3]

Such a dilemma involves a particularly pronounced risk in environments with unverifiable operations, such as in decentralized markets that involve physical currency exchanges. According to Kutera et al [7], the US Federal Trade Commission (FTC, 2021) reported that from October 2020 to March 2021, nearly seven thousand users were victims of digital fraud in the cryptocurrency market due to unfair mediation, causing losses around US$ 80 million.

O. Gervasi et al. (Eds.): ICCSA 2024, LNCS 14814, pp. 213–229, 2024.
https://doi.org/10.1007/978-3-031-64608-9_14

Previous solutions to the Buyers' and Sellers' Dilemma in decentralized markets incorporate costly preconditions that compromise the applicability of the solution. Examples include security deposits [3], arbitration [1,6,9,19], trust assurance in any of the parties involved [3,8], controllable digital content [11,14,20] and payment protocols aimed at products with digitally verifiable authenticity [13]. Such preconditions ensure the verification of all operations throughout the transaction protocol between buyer and seller.

In decentralized markets, two paths can be followed with the aim of reducing such risk: encouraging honesty or validating all operations [3,8,10,11,14,19,20]. A good example of a decentralized market with non-verifiable operations is the e-commerce platform OpenBazaar, which although discontinued its concept remains quite relevant in the literature [4]. This article presents an analysis of the effectiveness of its honesty incentive models in comparing to other honesty incentive models from the literature. Comparison is carried out here on a dataset of OpenBazaar's transactions (purchases) logs from June 15, 2018 to September 3, 2019 collected by Arps and Christina [2].

The research presented here consisted of three phases: 1) Reviewing the literature to collect major decentralized models whose aim is to encourage honesty in transactions with unverifiable operations; 2) Manually tagging transactions as success or failure in OpenBazaar's historical dataset according to annotated reviews and comments on corresponding purchases; and, 3) Comparing such models based on their predictions of success or failure of transactions we were able to infer from the tagged historical dataset. Metrics used to compare these models were inspired by Machine Learning and they are: precision, recall and F1.

For the comparison (phase 3), three main classes of solutions where collected from the literature: decentralized arbitrator, trust network and guarantee deposits. This work extracted from these solution classes the most promising features according to the criteria of decentralization, non-verifiable transactions tolerance and non authentication.

The related Research Question (RQ) for which this paper brings an answer is: *Which of the classes or combinations of their main features present superior performance?*

The results demonstrate that although there are models capable of promoting honesty better than those used in OpenBazaar, the decentralized buying and selling game remains biased towards dishonesty. Further, we find evidence pointing to the solution composed of trust network and decentralized arbiter as the most effective of all. These findings contribute to the research, design, operations and management of smart contracts, e-commerce platforms and decentralized markets in general.

2 Buyers' and Sellers' Dilemma

The Buyers' and Sellers' Dilemma (BSD), a term originally used in the book Prisoners' Dilemma [15], is a racing problem between dishonest players engaged in establishing a trade based in two operations (payment and transference of product, for example), both with advantages in opposite directions. Such transaction is a non equilibrated game, as each party tends to look after its own interests only by betraying the other party, since it offers the most advantageous outcome.

Consider a buyer and a seller, or the active player and the passive player, respectively. The active player is the one who proposes the transaction and assumes the risk of delivering its value first. The passive player is the one who receives the value from the active player and for a moment has in hand its original value (the product or service it is supposed to deliver) and the value of the other. At this point s/he must decide whether to act honestly and deliver her/his consideration or not. This dilemma is based on the assumption that the passive player will always prefer to act dishonestly, and the reason is described below.

One of game theory principles describes the concept of Nash Equilibrium [12], which refers to games in which there is a strategy to be followed by a player in order to always ensure the best possible result no matter the strategies of the other player. This 'safe' strategy is the Nash Equilibrium point.

Definition 1 (Buyers' and Sellers' Dilemma – BSD). *Consider the game* G*, where:*

1. *P consists of the set of exchanged values/products, and $x, y \in P$;*
2. *Q corresponds to the set of players negotiating (generally 2, but it will use $|Q|$ for generalization), and $B, S \in Q$;*
3. *$S^i = \{s_1^i, ..., s_{|S^i|}^i\}$ corresponds to a set of strategies or actions of the player i;*

In the simple game described above and represented in Fig. 1, concluding the negotiation is impossible, as it is advantageous for the buyer (B) never to pay (transfer x) for the item (y), leading the seller (S) to not deliver it. If the buyer does not pay for the product, s/he may retain only the payment value or the payment and the product/service (if the seller delivers the product/service even though s/he has not yet been paid). If the buyers pays for the product/service in advance, s/he may still receive the seller's product, but s/he runs the risk of being left with nothing. The sellers, if s/he does not sent the product (transfer y), can keep just the product/service or the product/service and the received payment; if s/he sends, s/he can still keep the received payment, but runs the risk of being left with nothing. In the just described possibilities, it is always more advantageous to be dishonest.

In despite of the BSD, mutual responsibility and the presence of intermediaries like eBay and Amazon, that for a premium, reimburse the buyer in case of non-delivery of paid for goods, guarantee security in centralized markets. However, legal repercussions or centralized trust intermediaries depend on the verification of all operations and the centralization of authority, conditions that solutions from literature attempt to circumvent.

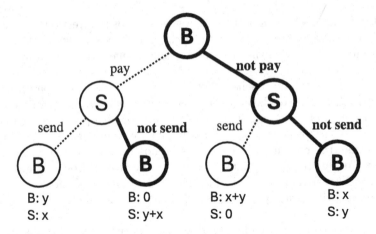

Fig. 1. Representation of the decentralized BSD as an extensive game. The dominant paths are highlighted. It is observed that the dominant strategy always represents better results for the player, buyer (B) or seller (S)

3   Literature Review – Phase 1

This section brings a literature review on solutions solutions applied to BSD. The review was carried out from December, 2023 to January, 2024. The results are divided into three main classes of solutions: trust networks, arbitration and guarantee payments protocols. These three classes are collectively and generally called Honesty Incentive Models (HIMs). Here we also look into combinations of models from more than one class. Our comparative experiment explores the major features of each model class.

Zindros [21] presents the real world OpenBazaar platform, that implements a specific approach of two classes, arbitration and trust network. In OpenBazaar any user can act as a human arbitrator in transactions and this must resolve disputes when a problem occurs in exchange for a monetary reward that is only paid if the referee is called upon. The trust network is based on feedback and the trust in an arbitrator or player depends on such feedback and a text file CV that almost always exposes the arbitrator's identity and the arbitrator is chosen only by the seller.

3.1   Trust Network

The approach introduced by Duong-Trung et al [6], besides automatic conflict resolution, penalizes couriers or carriers who breach contracts based on a reputation system. In the literature there are other works that address decentralized solutions for Cash on Delivery (CoD) and address the BSD in a similar way [1,3,9], although all of them utilize a trust network associated to other models.

3.2   Arbitrator

Son et al [17] employ blockchain and smart contracts to enhance the Cash on Delivery (CoD) protocol for e-commerce. Their approach ensures secure transactions and resolves the BSD by imposing specific rules on players and utilizing smart contracts as intermediaries. Tsabary et al [19] introduced a similar solution called MAD-HTLC, which leverages blockchain miners as contract arbitrators.

Duong-Trung et al [6] introduce a comprehensive CoD model that relies on smart contracts for automatic conflict resolution, eliminating the need for human intermediaries who, according to them, would consume more assets and time for the players involved. However, this approach includes an additional conflict resolution element, penalizing couriers or carriers who breach contracts based on a reputation system. According to the authors, the use of a Smart Contract as an arbiter associated with the reputation system, in addition to the infrastructure provided by decentralized technologies that implement the Smart Contract, is sufficient.

3.3   Payment Guarantee

Le et al [8] introduce a CoD protocol for commercial delivery where drivers are required to mortgage a sum of money for guarantee. More over, an authentication system is used for drivers and a hash code identifies the products.

Tsabary et al [18] introduce the concept of LedgerHedger, a two-party mechanism that ensures timely confirmation of transactions in smart contract protocols. LedgerHedger has the issuing player pay for a transaction in advance, and the other player agrees to pay a required fee, even if it exceeds the value of the transaction. This ensures that the transaction will be confirmed within a defined time frame. Asgaonkar and Krishnamachari [3] also present a solution based on double guarantees. Such double guarantees, although effective, can make transactions unfeasible, especially when they are greater than the negotiated value [18].

Finally, the most complete model of payment guarantee protocols was provided by Schwartzbach [16], where they present two main conclusions: it is not viable to provide a guarantee deposit model without any type of information about player behavior, and it is unlikely that a non-adaptable guarantee deposits protocol based on empirical rules will work. The mathematical approach presented seems the most complete.

3.4   Overall

The difficulty in virtualizing real-world services, cash and products in a decentralized manner is the core problem of non-verifiable transactions and leads most solutions to the BSD to resort to preconditions that limit the application domain or violate the principle of decentralization [3,8,10,11,13,14,19,20]. Table 1 presents all solutions collected from the literature and identifies the preconditions applied by each one to avoid dishonesty. Such preconditions are diverse, but can be classified into four categories, they are:

- Some level of centralization: Models appeal to centralization to verify the transaction in some level, overcoming the difficult of ensure trust without complete information;
- Authentication: Identifies users to intimidate the dishonest ones with legal repercussions;
- Digital verification of delivered products: In a decentralized environment it is applicable only to products that may be completely digitalized;
- Feedback: It is used to build trust, but is more susceptible to fails because may be forged.

Features used for avoiding such preconditions are used to compose the models compared here and described in more details in Sect. 5. As one can see from Table 1, none of the solutions implements exclusively trust network, although without such trust network, some other kind of behavior inference must be provided (as smart contract oracles, for example).

Table 1. Solutions for BSD from the literature

Reference	Model	Centralization	Authentication	Digital Verification	Feedback
[8]	Guarantee deposits	✓	✓	✓	
[18]	Guarantee deposits			✓	
[3]	Guarantee deposits, Trust network			✓	✓
[16]	Guarantee deposits				
[17]	Arbitrator			✓	
[19]	Arbitrator			✓	
[6]	Arbitrator, Trust network	✓	✓	✓	✓
[9]	Arbitrator, Trust network	✓	✓		✓
[1]	Arbitrator, Trust network			✓	

4   Tagging OpenBazaar Historical Data – Phase 2

4.1   OpenBazaar

OpenBazaar, a decentralized e-commerce marketplace, received significant attention from its initial release in 2016 until its closure in 2020. When deciding to use a decentralized platform like OpenBazaar, you should be aware that you are on your own in several aspects. Although the interface sends the same consumer message as centralized markets, in OpenBazaar payment is made by cryptocurrency directly to the seller and there is no refund, nor responsibility on the part of the platform.

It is important to note that OpenBazaar already implements two of the classes of encouraging honesty analyzed here. However, the arbitration model applied is biased, with the seller (BSD's passive player in this case) being solely responsible for choosing a list of possible arbitrators, a contradiction. The reputation model is based on feedback and scoring, without a trust network. Thus, one can compare the effectiveness of the honesty incentive solution applied (arbitration and reputation based on scoring and feedback) with the approaches selected from the literature: decentralized arbitration, trust network without feedback and payments guarantee.

4.2 Dataset

Using multiple daily traces of the OpenBazaar network over approximately 14 months (June 25, 2018 to September 3, 2019), Arps and Christin [2] observed its evolution over time. A total of 6,651 different participants were observed. More than half of all users (3521) were only observed on a single day, and on average only approximately 80 users were active simultaneously on a given day seeking for a total of 4379 listed items. 6292 text messages associated with purchases were also observed.

4.3 Manually Tagging Transactions

From the 6292 text messages, the success or failure of their corresponding transactions was manually inferred and tagged, message by message, yielding a total of 2517 successful transactions and 347 unsuccessful transactions that sums up to a total of 3034 manually tagged transactions; the success or failure of 170 transactions was not possible to infer.

5   Honesty Incentive Models – HIMs

This section describes the strategies behind each honesty incentive model (HIM) we compare. Here it is presented how each model was implemented in order to evaluate its effectiveness in encouraging honesty. Since it is not possible to implement incentive to honesty without any behavior inference strategy [16], decentralized arbitrator and payment guarantee were implemented together with trust network in order to use trust network as a souce of behavior inference.

5.1   Trust Network – T

The reputation network implemented in our comparison describes a more decentralized concept, Web-of-Trust, where there is no feedback (less susceptible to fails) and transactions between users are public, giving each user the freedom to make their own conclusions. Originally, Web-of-Trust deals with a p2p network to establish the authenticity of the connection between a public key and its owner. Over time, users accumulate keys from others they want to designate as trusted introducers, and a trusted network is gradually formed without a centralized certification authority. Users legitimize each other by accumulating and redistributing a collection of third-party certificates. The public key network formed is a flexible, decentralized and fault-tolerant scheme, verified through consensus among users [5].

For transactions with non-verifiable operations, the Web-of-Trust model is capable of providing trust between buyers and sellers who have never had direct interactions based on the experience of those with whom they interacted separately.

Two players $a, b \in A$ evaluate the possibility of carrying out a transaction T. To this end, the network's trust in a given player b is ϕ_b, according to Eq. 1.

$$\phi_b = \frac{\ln\left(\frac{\sum_{a\in A} s_t(b,a)}{P_t}\right)}{\ln\left(\text{MAX}_i\left(\frac{\sum_{a\in A} s_t(i,a)}{P_t}\right)\right)} \tag{1}$$

Where $s_t(b,a)$ refers to the historical balance of transactions between b and a up to the current moment t. Here, balance is understood as the sum of the values in products and currency of the other party in each transaction – thus, dishonest operations by the player contribute negatively to the balance. Finally, P_t represents the total balance of transactions among the entire active population of OpenBazaar up to time t. Here, 'time' means an arbitrary time interval at the end of which trust is recalculated for all players.

Thus, ϕ_a grows as the total balance of a transactions grows in relation to the total balance of the population as a whole. For normalization purposes, it is taken the best reputation among all players $\phi = 1.0$. This best reputation ϕ is represented in Eq. 1 by MAX_i playing the role of normalizer, preserving $\phi \in [0.0, 1.0]$. As the best reputation among all players increases, the others fall in a logarithmic proportion.

Also considering an acceptable trust threshold to carry out a δ transaction, observe Eq. 2.

$$T_{s,b} = \begin{cases} 1 & \text{if } \delta_t < \phi_s \\ 0 & \text{otherwise} \end{cases} \tag{2}$$

Thus, for transaction T to occur, ϕ must be greater than a threshold δ for passive player s (seller). This factor is proportional to the total historical balance of a given player s and inversely proportional to the total balance of the population. Here, trust in the buyer is irrelevant because OpenBazaar's business model leaves no room for dishonesty on the part of buyers as they always transfer their values first.

5.2   Trust Network + Arbitrator – TA

Arbitration is based on the selection of the arbitrator through consensus between the parties and was implemented making the Web-of-Trust proposed in the literature be the source of trust inference. This is because for there to be consensus in the selection of the arbitrator, both parties, even separately, must trust the arbitrator.

Web-of-Trust model works well with the moderation of transactions using reliable decentralized arbitrators, since, given a population Q with a few transactions $S' \ll Q$, it is already possible to estimate the honesty of players involved in a transaction (buyer, seller and arbiter).

Consider Eq. 3. Now three players a, b seeking the transaction, and c candidate for arbitration, where $\gamma_{a,b}(c)$ is the function that defines whether c is trustworthy enough to be the arbiter of transaction $T_{a,b}$.

$$\gamma_{a,b}(c) = \begin{cases} 1 & \text{if } \delta_t < \frac{s_t(c,a)}{\sum_{a \in A} s_t(c,a)} \text{ and } \delta_t < \frac{s_t(c,b)}{\sum_{a \in A} s_t(c,a)} \\ 0 & \text{otherwise} \end{cases} \tag{3}$$

Moreover, to define among the entire population who is the best referee for the operation, see Eq. 4:

$$\gamma_{a,b} = \begin{cases} c & \text{if } \forall_{c \in A} \delta_t < \text{MAX}(\frac{s_t(c,a)}{\sum_{a \in A} s_t(c,a)}) \text{ and} \\ & \delta_t < \text{MAX}(\frac{s_t(c,b)}{\sum_{a \in A} s_t(c,a)}) \\ 0 & \text{otherwise} \end{cases} \tag{4}$$

Which describes an operation of asymptotic complexity $O(n \log n)$, to discover the best arbiter for all operations, with n being the total number of new transactions at each complete time frame t.

5.3   Trust Network + Payment Guarantee – TP

For the collateral deposit protocol, we borrow from the work of Schwartzbach [16], in which the author assumes a decentralized market based on non-verifiable transactions. To this end, Schwartzbach [16] demonstrates the need for some trust inference mechanism between the parties, such as oracles (smart contracts with external access) used in distributed ledgers. Such need was fullfiled by an association to the Trust Network model, as with Decentralized arbitrator Model (see Sect. 5.2

Using the Trust Network to play the role of a source of trust inference as oracles do in Distributed ledgers, consider that two players a, b, buyer and seller, wish to exchange the values x, y, cash and product. According to Schwartzbach [16], the security deposits necessary to guarantee the transaction between a and b are x', y', are given Eqs. 5 and 6.

$$x' = \frac{2\phi_a}{2\phi_a - 1} \, x \tag{5}$$

$$y' = \frac{\phi_b}{2\phi_b - 1} \, y \tag{6}$$

This approach was chosen because it is satisfactorily decentralized and capable of dealing with the uncertainty of an incomplete information environment. Here incomplete information may be considered as the absence of information about the success or failure of transactions (non-verifiable transactions).

6   Experiment Results – Phase 3

Although it achieved some success, OpenBazaar was short-lived when compared to centralized models like Amazon or eBay. Such a fate may have been anticipated due to OpenBazaar's difficulty in encouraging honesty on the system, falling into BSD. In total, of the 3034 transactions observed, approximately 12% were unsuccessful, that is, the seller received payment but did not deliver the products/services, the only form of dishonesty observed. There are still 170 unclassified transactions left, so this proportion could be even more serious. This rate is very high when compared to non-anonymous centralized models, supported by laws and payment intermediary models that make dishonesty within the site very rare.

However, those responsible for OpenBazaar did not ignore the problem and implemented two solutions to verify transactions and encourage honesty: arbitration and score-based reputation. In this section we use the most promising decentralized solutions according to the revised literature, here named T (Trust Network), TA (Trust Network plus Decentralized Arbitrator) and TP (Trust Network plus Payment Guarantee), to predict which transactions would be successful and which would fail, and then checking against the OpenBazaar's manually tagged historical data. With this, we obtained conclusions regarding the evaluated models and the solutions actually implemented in OpenBazaar[1].

6.1   Trust Network only – T

The trust network model based on transaction history without feedback was the one that obtained the best results in avoiding BSD in decentralized environments, according to the literature among the reputation models [1,3,9]. For this experiment, this model also serves as a source for inference to try to estimate the trust of each player, in addition to being compared to the others models.

Notice in Fig. 2a, the total number of unsuccessful transactions (lighter red line) decreases as the δ threshold increases. This is because a bad seller is likely to have a bad reputation, and increasing the threshold predicts the failure of transactions involving sellers with a bad reputation. With the threshold δ very low, most transactions are classified as safe; if this threshold is too high, the model points out almost all transactions as insecure. If the δ threshold is too high, successful transactions may be affected. This is depicted by the rising blue line. For a $\delta \gg 1.0$, most transactions are classified as insecure.

The optimal threshold point δ is shown in Fig. 3a, where the precision and recall metrics cross F1, at approximately $\delta = 0.7$. The green, red and blue lines in Fig. 3a represent the f1, precision and recall metrics, respectively.

---

[1] All results presented here were obtained from the implementation in R language of the proposed models. All source code is openly available at https://github.com/tiago-clementino/honesty_in_openbazaar.

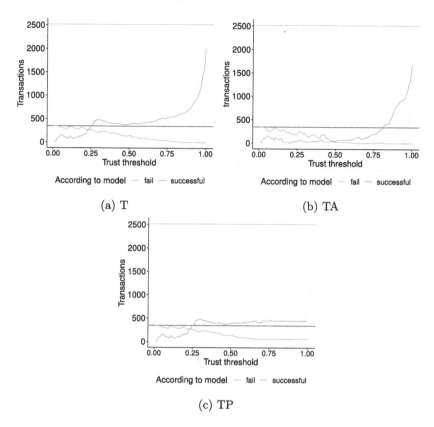

(a) T   (b) TA

(c) TP

Fig. 2. Transactions per trust threshold. Where horizontal dark red line presents the total failed transactions (347 products not delivered), while the horizontal orange line represents the total successful transactions (2517 products delivered) (Color figure online)

6.2   Trust Network + Decentralized Arbitrator − TA

The mechanism behind the decentralized arbiter plus trust network (TA), instead of using buyer-seller mutual trust determines that buyer and seller reach consensus on a third player they both trust. The buyer then transfers payment to the consensual chosen third player who withelds payment to the seller until s/he delivers the product/service. Based on that, this model achieves the best results according to Fig. 3b, where the intersection of f1, recall and precision occurs at 0.965, the best value, and in a trust threshold δ of 0.607, a feasible value.

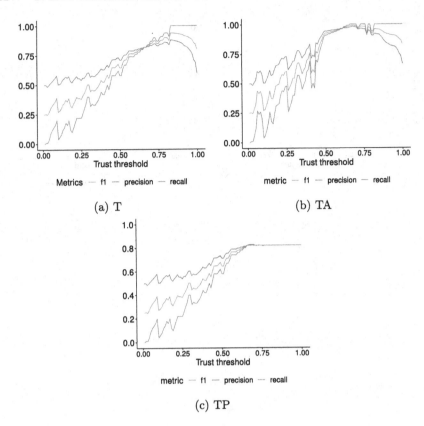

(a) T   (b) TA

(c) TP

Fig. 3. Horizontal axis presents the trust threshold, and vertical axis represents the magnitude of each metric (precision, recall and f1)

The largest results of all model compared are numerically described in Table 2, where the lines represents the metrics and the columns represents the models. The first metric 'Insecurity fail transactions' represents all transactions where the product delivery did not occurs as expected because some dishonest behaviour of the seller. The larger this metric is, the better the model in preventing sellers dishonesty. The second metric is the 'Insecurity successful transactions' which means those successful transactions were wrongly predicted as insecurity by the model. The lower this metric is, the better the model. The third row represents the intersection of the metrics f1, precision and recall, pointing to the best trust threshold of each model. Finally, the last row represents the trust threshold δ where the intersection of metrics f1, recall and precision occurs.

Table 2. Better metrics of each solution compared (T, TA and TB)

Metrics	T	TA	TP
Insecurity fail transactions	287(82.71%)	336(96.83%)	287(82.71%)
Insecurity successful transactions	461(18.31%)	79(3.14%)	445(17.68%)
F1 = recall = precision	0.821	0.965	0.823
Threshold δ	0.666	0.607	0.663

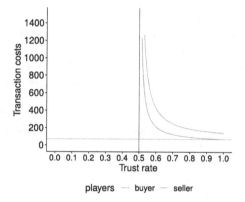

Fig. 4. Cost of payment guarantee (in USD) according to trust rate of seller. The horizontal orange line represents the average transaction amount. The vertical dark blue line represents the trust rate $\phi = 0.5$ (Color figure online)

Looking again at Table 2, you can see numerically that the largest f1, recall and precision intersection is 0.965 for the TA model. For all other metrics, the TA model is significantly better than its competitors.

6.3   Trust Network + Payment Guarantee – TP

Its is important to note that this approach was replicated from the work of Schwartzbach [16]. Schwartzbach concluded that its difficult to provide a viable and effective payment guarantees protocol based on empirical rules, and that design such a protocol without any information about the behavior of players is an intractable problem. This last conclusion motivated us to propose the use of the trust network model as the source of information about the players behavior, as in Arbitration model (TA).

Although such HIM appears to be an effective strategy since the collateral values are always at least equal to the values gained through dishonesty. But there are two drawbacks to consider: 1) First, the protocol is biased towards sellers who can pay as collateral in some situations the same values as the values of their products, but have the chance to end up with their products and the buyer's payment, according to OpenBazaar's business model. 2) As you can see in Fig. 4, which shows the growth of transaction costs (payment guarantee costs in USD) by the trust rate of buyers and sellers, the payments protocol is not even calculable if the trust rate confidence is less than $\phi <= 0.5$ (dark blue vertical line). Otherwise, for higher trust rates, but close to 0.5 (like 0.55), the collateral values are so large that they make such a payment impossible (see red and light blue lines for buyers and sellers respectively).

Therefore, we restrict guarantee payments according to a hybrid model: as long as the trust threshold δ be lower than the reputation/trust rate necessary for the seller to pay more than double its value[2], it is assumed that payment guarantees are not viable and the model falls into the trust network model. This means that if the seller needs to pay more than twice the value of its products as collateral, such collateral will be too expensive to continue the transaction. Since the buyer does not have the opportunity to behave dishonestly, according to the OpenBazaar business model, it is not necessary to demand payment guarantees from him/her.

Going back to Fig. 2c, you can see that the payments guarantee protocol avoids the explosion of fake positives for very large values of δ, where the majority of true transactions are marked as insecurity (light blue line), but it happens after its intersection between f1, precision and recall point (see Fig. 3c). So that, even with serious questions of viability, the payment guarantees protocol plus trust network remains almost as effective as the raw reputation network, as one can see in Fig. 3c and Table 2, where the intersection point of F1, recall and precision are almost the same in both. Because of that, the greatest results (fail transactions marked as insecurity greater and success transactions marked as insecurity lower, according to Table 2) are also almost the same in both models.

Looking again at Fig. 3, we can see that even the least efficient models (T and TP) manage to predict the majority of unsuccessful transactions with sufficient large threshold (light red line below the dark red line). Note also that the HIMs actually applied on the OpenBazaar platform (dark red line in Fig. 1) – i.e., unilateral arbitration and reputation based on feedback, proved to be less effective than all the solutions tested here.

6.4   Answering the RQ and Threats to Validation

From the results in Subsects. 6.1, 6.2 and 6.3, the overall superior performance in terms of honesty incentives and also considering f1, precision and recall is TA. That's the short and simple answer to our Research Question. For a more detailed answer however, one has to take into account situations where T or TP appear superior or even more feasible – e.g., that is the case when honesty is the predominant behavior and any costly mediation strategy is needed – in this case, T appears more applicable; or, on the other hand, when honestly presents "average, typical behavior" and the transactions are critical and must be ensured – in this case, TP is a better choice.

---

[2] seller's + buyer's values assuming, for analysis' tractability, that the values of the buyer and the seller are approximately equal.

Because our results were instrumental to indicate superior HIMs than those applied on the OpenBazaar platform, they should be considered together with an important threat to validity. The analysis presented here is based on historical data and as such, it cannot be used as an impact gauge of the compared solutions for they were not in actual usage.

7 Conclusions and Future Work

7.1 Conclusions

This study compared honesty incentive models (HIMs) elicited from a literature review that was guided by the requirements of decentralization, tolerance for non-verifiable transactions (incomplete information) and non-authentication (anonymity), based on metrics of precision, recall and F1. The elicited HIMs were: trust network without feedback (T), decentralized arbitration (TA, associated to trust network) and payment guarantee (TP, also associated to trust network). The trust network without feedback plays a special role, serving as a source of information regarding the behavior of players. Said role is commonly performed by decentralized oracles in distributed ledger technologies (blockchains, for example).

The comparison was made using the elicited models to predict unsuccessful transactions (products not delivered or delivered with problems) on a manually labeled dataset extracted from the decentralized e-commerce platform Open-Bazaar. Such predictions are based on how much each model is able to classify the security of each transaction, and based on an ideal confidence threshold θ to predict the actual successful and unsuccessful transactions. Such an ideal threshold is one where the precision, recall and F1 metrics intersect. In addition to the comparisons presented here, the advantages and disadvantages of each model are described, as shown in Table 3.

Table 3. Advantages and disadvantages of each model

Models	Advantages	Disadvantages
T	By itself is a good solution, but it may be improved if associated to other solutions	Provide information about behavior of players but not ensures the transaction
TA	The solution that outperformed the others if associated to behavior inference system such as a trust network	It does not work by itself
TP	When viable it is almost infallible	It does not work by itself and most of the time it is not viable because it requires a high trust rating to do so

In conclusion, it was observed that the application of the trust network without feedback associated with decentralized arbitration (TA, see Table 2) showed significantly superior performance than the others based on metrics of recall, precision and F1. The OpenBazaar's original HIMs were found to perform more poorly when compared to the elicited HIMs. TA, the solution that outperformed the others, reached $F1 = 0.965$ (see Table 2), which is quite high.

7.2 Challenges for Future Work

Despite the consistency of the results, there is still no solution in the literature that actually solves the Buyers' and Sellers' Dilemma (BSD) in an anonymous, decentralized environment involving non-verifiable transactions. This finding emphasizes the ongoing nature of the problem and the need for further research and innovative solutions in this domain.

Albeit the above gap in research results, the results reported here contribute to Blockchain and DLTs applications specifically in the field of fraud prevention protocols for online decentralized and anonymous markets dealing with non-verifiable transactions. The main contribution of this study is the provision of a synthesized basis, forming a body of knowledge, for future reference, development and research on the treatment of the BSD in full non-verified, anonymous and decentralized markets.

References

1. AlTawy, R., ElSheikh, M., Youssef, A.M., Gong, G.: Lelantos: a blockchain-based anonymous physical delivery system. In: 2017 15th Annual Conference on Privacy, Security and Trust (PST), pp. 15–1509. IEEE (2017)
2. Arps, J.E., Christin, N.: Open market or ghost town? The curious case of Open-Bazaar. In: Bonneau, J., Heninger, N. (eds.) Financial Cryptography and Data Security: 24th International Conference, FC 2020 , Kota Kinabalu, Malaysia, February 10–14, 2020 Revised Selected Papers, pp. 561–577. Springer International Publishing, Cham (2020). https://doi.org/10.1007/978-3-030-51280-4_30
3. Asgaonkar, A., Krishnamachari, B.: Solving the buyer and seller's dilemma: A dual-deposit escrow smart contract for provably cheat-proof delivery and payment for a digital good without a trusted mediator. In: 2019 IEEE International Conference on Blockchain and Cryptocurrency (ICBC), pp. 262–267. IEEE (2019)
4. Bhawna, Gupta, P., Rai, P., Chauhan, A.: Blockchain application in consumer services: a review and future research agenda. Int. J. Consum. Stud. **47**(6), 2417–2450 (2023)
5. Caronni, G.: Walking the web of trust. In: Proceedings IEEE 9th International Workshops on Enabling Technologies: Infrastructure for Collaborative Enterprises (WET ICE 2000), pp. 153–158. IEEE (2000)
6. Duong-Trung, N., et al.: Multi-sessions mechanism for decentralized cash on delivery system. Int. J. Adv. Comput. Sci. Appl **10**(9) (2019)
7. Kutera, M., et al.: Cryptocurrencies as a subject of financial fraud. J. Entrepreneurship, Manage. Innov. **18**(4), 45–77 (2022)

8. Le, H.T., Le, N.T.T., Phien, N.N., Duong-Trung, N., Son, H.X., Huynh, T.T.: Introducing multi shippers mechanism for decentralized cash on delivery system. Int. J. Adv. Comput. Sci. Appl. **10**(6) (2019)

9. Le, N.N.T., et al.: Assuring non-fraudulent transactions in cash on delivery by introducing double smart contracts. Int. J. Adv. Comput. Sci. Appl. **10**(5), 677–684 (2019)

10. Mamageishvili, A., Schlegel, J.C.: Optimal smart contracts with costly verification. In: 2020 IEEE International Conference on Blockchain and Cryptocurrency (ICBC), pp. 1–8. IEEE (2020)

11. Müller, M., Janczura, J.A., Ruppel, P.: Decoco: blockchain-based decentralized compensation of digital content purchases. In: 2020 2nd Conference on Blockchain Research and Applications for Innovative Networks and Services (BRAINS), pp. 152–159. IEEE (2020)

12. Nash, J.F., Jr.: Equilibrium points in n-person games. Proc. Natl. Acad. Sci. **36**(1), 48–49 (1950)

13. Pande, S.S., Mandolikar, S., Shitole, S.: Bitland-a decentralized commercial real estate platform. In: 2022 IEEE Bombay Section Signature Conference (IBSSC), pp. 1–6. IEEE (2022)

14. Radhakrishnan, R., Ramachandran, G.S., Krishnamachari, B.: Sdpp: Streaming data payment protocol for data economy. In: 2019 IEEE International Conference on Blockchain and Cryptocurrency (ICBC), pp. 17–18. IEEE (2019)

15. Rapoport, A., Chammah, A.M.: Prisoner's dilemma: A study in conflict and cooperation, vol. 165. University of Michigan press (1965)

16. Schwartzbach, N.I.: Payment schemes from limited information with applications in distributed computing. In: Proceedings of the 23rd ACM Conference on Economics and Computation, pp. 129–149 (2022)

17. Son, H.X., et al.: Towards a mechanism for protecting seller's interest of cash on delivery by using smart contract in hyperledger. Int. J. Adv. Comput. Sci. Appl. **10**(4) (2019)

18. Tsabary, I., Manuskin, A., Eyal, I.: Ledgerhedger: Gas reservation for smart-contract security. Cryptology ePrint Archive (2022)

19. Tsabary, I., Yechieli, M., Manuskin, A., Eyal, I.: Mad-htlc: because htlc is crazy-cheap to attack. In: 2021 IEEE Symposium on Security and Privacy (SP), pp. 1230–1248. IEEE (2021)

20. Zhang, P., Wei, J., Liu, Y., Liu, H.: Proxy re-encryption based fair trade protocol for digital goods transactions via smart contracts. arXiv preprint arXiv:2306.01299 (2023)

21. Zindros, D.: Trust in decentralized anonymous marketplaces. National Technical University of Athens (2016)

Boosted HP Filter: Several Properties Derived from Its Spectral Representation

Hiroshi Yamada$^{(\boxtimes)}$ ⓘ

Hiroshima University, Higashi-Hiroshima 739-8525, Japan
yamada@hiroshima-u.ac.jp

Abstract. The Hodrick–Prescott (HP) filter is the most prominent smoothing/trend estimation method for macroeconomic time series such as real gross domestic product. Recently, its modification, the boosted HP (bHP) filter, has been developed, and a number of studies have been conducted on it. This paper contributes to the literature by investigating the properties of the bHP filter. For this purpose, we use the spectral decomposition of the penalty matrix of the HP filter.

Keywords: Hodrick–Prescott filter · boosted HP filter · Whittaker–Henderson graduation

1 Introduction

The Hodrick–Prescott (HP) filter [1] is the most prominent smoothing/trend estimation method for macroeconomic time series such as real gross domestic product. As is well known, it is a kind of Whittaker–Henderson (WH) graduation, which is frequently used in the actuarial literature [2]. Recently, Phillips and Shi [3] developed its modification, the boosted HP (bHP) filter, and a number of studies concerning the filter have emerged [4–10]. In this paper, we contribute to the literature by investigating the properties of the bHP filter. For this purpose, we use the spectral decomposition of the penalty matrix of the HP filter. (The matrix is a symmetric pentadiagonal matrix as shown in the Appendix.) This is because, as we will show later, it allows us to derive the spectral decomposition of the smoother matrix of the bHP filter.

The organization of the paper is as follows. In Sect. 2, we provide some preliminary remarks, which include the spectral decomposition of the penalty matrix of the HP filter. In Sect. 3, we present the spectral representation of the bHP filter. In Sect. 4, we document several properties of the bHP filter. Section 5 concludes the paper. The Appendix contains some proofs.

2 Preliminaries

In this section, we provide some preliminary remarks.

O. Gervasi et al. (Eds.): ICCSA 2024, LNCS 14814, pp. 230–242, 2024.
https://doi.org/10.1007/978-3-031-64608-9_15

Data. Let y_i denote the realization of a variable y at time i for $i = 1, \ldots, n$. In the paper, we assume that y_i cannot be represented as $\phi_1 + \phi_2 i$ for $i = 1, \ldots, n$, where both ϕ_1 and ϕ_2 are real numbers. This is because there is no need for smoothing in the case.

Some of the Notations. Let $\boldsymbol{y} = [y_1, \ldots, y_n]^\top$, $\boldsymbol{x} = [x_1, \ldots, x_n]^\top$, $\boldsymbol{I}_n$ be the $n \times n$ identity matrix, $\boldsymbol{\iota}$ be the n-dimensional column vector of ones, i.e., $\boldsymbol{\iota} = [1, \ldots, 1]^\top$, $\boldsymbol{Q}_\iota = \boldsymbol{I}_n - \boldsymbol{\iota}(\boldsymbol{\iota}^\top\boldsymbol{\iota})^{-1}\boldsymbol{\iota}^\top = \boldsymbol{I}_n - \frac{1}{n}\boldsymbol{\iota}\boldsymbol{\iota}^\top$, $\boldsymbol{\tau} = [1, \ldots, n]^\top$, and

$$\boldsymbol{\Pi} = [\boldsymbol{\iota}, \boldsymbol{\tau}].$$

In addition, let $\boldsymbol{\Delta}_2$ be the $(n-2) \times n$ second differencing matrix such that $\boldsymbol{\Delta}_2\boldsymbol{x} = (x_3 - 2x_2 + x_1, \ldots, x_n - 2x_{n-1} + x_{n-2})^\top$. Explicitly, $\boldsymbol{\Delta}_2$ is the Toeplitz matrix given by

$$\boldsymbol{\Delta}_2 = \begin{bmatrix} 1 & -2 & 1 & 0 & \cdots & 0 \\ 0 & \ddots & \ddots & \ddots & \ddots & \vdots \\ \vdots & \ddots & \ddots & \ddots & \ddots & 0 \\ 0 & \cdots & 0 & 1 & -2 & 1 \end{bmatrix}.$$

For a column vector $\boldsymbol{\eta}$, $\|\boldsymbol{\eta}\|^2 = \boldsymbol{\eta}^\top\boldsymbol{\eta}$. For a full column rank matrix $\boldsymbol{R}$, denote the column space of $\boldsymbol{R}$ by $\mathbb{S}(\boldsymbol{R})$ and let $\boldsymbol{P}_R = \boldsymbol{R}(\boldsymbol{R}^\top\boldsymbol{R})^{-1}\boldsymbol{R}^\top$. Accordingly, $\boldsymbol{P}_R$ is the orthogonal projection matrix onto $\mathbb{S}(\boldsymbol{R})$ and $\boldsymbol{Q}_\iota$ can be represented as $\boldsymbol{I}_n - \boldsymbol{P}_\iota$.

HP Filter. The HP filter is defined by the following minimization problem:

$$\min_{x_1,\ldots,x_n} f(x_1, \ldots, x_n) = \sum_{i=1}^{n}(y_i - x_i)^2 + \lambda \sum_{i=3}^{n}(x_i - 2x_{i-1} + x_{i-2})^2, \quad (1)$$

where $\lambda \in (0, \infty)$ is a smoothing parameter that controls fidelity, $\sum_{i=1}^{n}(y_i - x_i)^2$, and smoothness, $\sum_{i=3}^{n}(x_i - 2x_{i-1} + x_{i-2})^2$. (1) can be represented in matrix form as

$$\min_{x} f(\boldsymbol{x}) = \|\boldsymbol{y} - \boldsymbol{x}\|^2 + \lambda\boldsymbol{x}^\top\boldsymbol{C}\boldsymbol{x}, \quad (2)$$

where

$$\boldsymbol{C} = \boldsymbol{\Delta}_2^\top\boldsymbol{\Delta}_2. \quad (3)$$

Accordingly, $\boldsymbol{C}$ is the penalty matrix of the HP filter. Given that $f(\boldsymbol{x})$ is a quadratic function of $\boldsymbol{x}$ whose Hessian matrix, $2(\boldsymbol{I}_n + \lambda\boldsymbol{C})$, is positive definite, there exists $\widehat{\boldsymbol{x}}^{\mathrm{HP}}$ such that $f(\boldsymbol{x}) > f(\widehat{\boldsymbol{x}}^{\mathrm{HP}})$ for all $\boldsymbol{x} \in \mathbb{R}^n\backslash\{\widehat{\boldsymbol{x}}^{\mathrm{HP}}\}$. Explicitly, it is given by the following linear transformation of $\boldsymbol{y}$,

$$\widehat{\boldsymbol{x}}^{\mathrm{HP}} = \boldsymbol{A}\boldsymbol{y}, \quad (4)$$

where

$$A = (I_n + \lambda C)^{-1}. \tag{5}$$

Note that $(I_n + \lambda C)$ in (5) is nonsingular because it is positive definite [11]. Thus, the HP filter is a linear smoother and A is referred to as the smoother matrix of it. In addition, C in A is referred to as the penalty matrix of the HP filter.

bHP Filter. The trend estimated by the bHP filtering is given by the following linear transformation of y,

$$\widehat{x}^{(m)} = A_m y, \tag{6}$$

where

$$A_m = I_n - (I_n - A)^m. \tag{7}$$

Thus, the bHP filter is also a linear smoother. We refer to A_m as the smoother matrix of the bHP filter. In addition, we refer to m as the degree of boosting. Then, given that

$$A_1 = I_n - (I_n - A)^1 = A, \tag{8}$$

it follows that

$$\widehat{x}^{(1)} = A_1 y = Ay = \widehat{x}^{\mathrm{HP}}. \tag{9}$$

Thus, the bHP filter is a generalization of the HP filter.

Let $A_m = [a_{i,j}^{(m)}]$ and $\widehat{x}_i^{(m)}$ denote the i-th entry of $\widehat{x}^{(m)}$. Then, (6) can be represented as

$$\widehat{x}_i^{(m)} = a_{i,1}^{(m)} y_1 + \cdots + a_{i,n}^{(m)} y_n. \tag{10}$$

Spectral Decomposition of C. Since C in (3) is a real symmetric matrix, it can be spectrally decomposed as

$$C = VDV^\top, \tag{11}$$

where $D = \mathrm{diag}(d_1, \ldots, d_n)$ and $V = [v_1, \ldots, v_n]$ is an orthogonal matrix. Here, $d_1, \ldots, d_n$ are in ascending order. Since C is a positive semidefinite matrix whose rank equals $n - 2$, it follows that $d_1 = d_2 = 0$ and $d_i > 0$ for $i = 3, \ldots, n$. With regard to $d_1 = d_2 = 0$, given $C\iota = 0 \cdot \iota$, $C(Q_\iota \tau) = 0 \cdot (Q_\iota \tau)$, and $\iota^\top(Q_\iota \tau) = 0$, we can let $(d_1, v_1) = (0, \iota/\sqrt{n})$ and $(d_2, v_2) = (0, Q_\iota \tau/\sqrt{\tau^\top Q_\iota \tau})$. With regard to d_n, which denotes the largest eigenvalue of C, it follows that

$$d_n \le 16. \tag{12}$$

For example, when $n = 100$, $d_n = 15.9920$. For proofs of (12), see the Appendix. In summary, the following inequalities apply to the eigenvalues of C, $d_1, \ldots, d_n$:

$$0 = d_1 = d_2 < d_3 \leq \cdots \leq d_n \leq 16, \tag{13}$$

which is used in the next section.

Spectral Decomposition of A. The smoother matrix of the HP filter, A, which is a real symmetric matrix, can be spectrally decomposed as

$$A = VBV^\top, \tag{14}$$

where $B = (I_n + \lambda D)^{-1}$. Let

$$b_i = \frac{1}{1 + \lambda d_i}, \quad i = 1, \ldots, n. \tag{15}$$

Then, $B = \text{diag}(b_1, \ldots, b_n)$.

Spectral Decomposition of A_m. The smoother matrix of the bHP filter, A_m, which is a real symmetric matrix, can be spectrally decomposed as

$$A_m = VB_mV^\top, \tag{16}$$

where $B_m = I_n - (I_n - B)^m$. (16) can be derived from (14) as

$$A_m = I_n - (I_n - A)^m = I_n - (I_n - VBV^\top)^m$$
$$= V\{I_n - (I_n - B)^m\}V^\top = VB_mV^\top.$$

Then, it follows that

$$B_1 = I_n - (I_n - B)^1 = B. \tag{17}$$

This is consistent with (8). It should be noted that (16) is a restatement of the result in [4].

Let

$$b_i^{(m)} = 1 - \left(\frac{\lambda d_i}{1 + \lambda d_i}\right)^m, \quad i = 1, \ldots, n. \tag{18}$$

Then, $B_m = \text{diag}(b_1^{(m)}, \ldots, b_n^{(m)})$. From (15) and (18), it follows that

$$b_i^{(1)} = 1 - \left(\frac{\lambda d_i}{1 + \lambda d_i}\right)^1 = \frac{1 + \lambda d_i - \lambda d_i}{1 + \lambda d_i} = \frac{1}{1 + \lambda d_i} = b_i, \quad i = 1, \ldots, n. \tag{19}$$

3 Spectral Representation of the bHP Filter

From (16), which is a spectral decomposition of A_m, the bHP filter can be represented as

$$\widehat{x}^{(m)} = VB_mV^\top y \tag{20}$$
$$= b_1^{(m)}z_1v_1 + \cdots + b_n^{(m)}z_nv_n, \tag{21}$$

where $z = [z_1, \ldots, z_n]^\top = V^\top y$. We will refer to (20)/(21) as the spectral representation of the bHP filter. It is the linear combination of an orthonormal basis $\{v_1, \ldots, v_n\}$ such that the coefficient of v_i is $b_i^{(m)} z_i$ for $i = 1, \ldots, n$.

We make four points regarding the spectral representation of the bHP filter.

1. Given that

$$\|\boldsymbol{\Delta}_2 v_i\|^2 = v_i^\top C v_i = d_i, \quad i = 1, \ldots, n,$$

from (13), the following inequalities hold.

$$0 = \|\boldsymbol{\Delta}_2 v_1\|^2 = \|\boldsymbol{\Delta}_2 v_2\|^2 < \|\boldsymbol{\Delta}_2 v_3\|^2 \leq \cdots \leq \|\boldsymbol{\Delta}_2 v_n\|^2 \leq 16. \qquad (22)$$

These indicate that with respect to $\boldsymbol{\Delta}_2$,
(a) both v_1 and v_2 are perfectly smooth,
(b) v_i is smoother than v_{i+1} for $i = 2, \ldots, n-1$, and
(c) $\|\boldsymbol{\Delta}_2 v_i\|^2$ is at most 16.
See Fig. 1, which depicts $v_3, \ldots, v_{11}$ when $n = 100$.

2. It follows that

$$1 = b_1^{(m)} = b_2^{(m)} > b_3^{(m)} \geq \cdots \geq b_n^{(m)} > 0. \qquad (23)$$

Therefore, the contribution of eigenvectors corresponding to larger eigenvalues becomes smaller. (In addition, from (23), A_m is positive definite.)

3. It follows that

$$z_i = v_i^\top y = (v_i^\top v_i)^{-1} v_i^\top y = \arg\min_\zeta \|y - \zeta v_i\|^2, \quad i = 1, \ldots, n. \qquad (24)$$

Moreover, denoting the sample correlation coefficient between v_i and y by $\mathrm{cor}(v_i, y)$, it follows that

$$\mathrm{cor}(v_i, y) = \frac{v_i^\top Q_\iota y}{\sqrt{v_i^\top Q_\iota v_i}\sqrt{y^\top Q_\iota y}} = \frac{z_i}{\sqrt{y^\top Q_\iota y}}, \quad i = 2, \ldots, n. \qquad (25)$$

Here, the second equality follows from $v_i^\top v_i = 1$ and $v_i^\top \iota = 0$ for $i = 2, \ldots, n$. (Note that since $y \notin \mathbb{S}(\boldsymbol{\Pi})$ by assumption, $y^\top Q_\iota y$ in (25) is positive.) Therefore, given y, z_i is proportional to $\mathrm{cor}(v_i, y)$.

4. Letting

$$\widehat{\gamma} = \arg\min_\gamma \|y - \boldsymbol{\Pi}\gamma\|^2 = (\boldsymbol{\Pi}^\top \boldsymbol{\Pi})^{-1} \boldsymbol{\Pi}^\top y,$$

it follows that

$$b_1^{(m)} z_1 v_1 + b_2^{(m)} z_2 v_2 = \boldsymbol{\Pi}\widehat{\gamma} = P_{\boldsymbol{\Pi}} y, \qquad (26)$$

which is the orthogonal projection of y onto $\mathbb{S}(\boldsymbol{\Pi})$. For a proof of (26), see the Appendix.

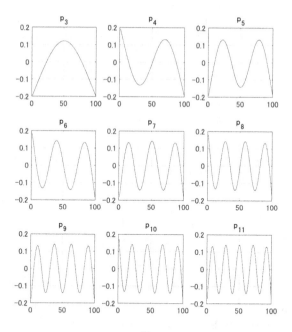

Fig. 1. v_i such that $Cv_i = d_i v_i$ and $v_i^\top v_i = 1$ for $i = 3, \ldots, 11$ when $n = 100$.

4   Several Properties of the bHP Filter

The spectral decomposition of the smoother matrix of the bHP filter given in (16) and the spectral representation of the bHP filter given by (20)/(21) allow us to derive several properties of the bHP filter. In this section, we describe such properties. Those are summarized in Proposition 1.

1. Given that $b_1^{(m)} = 1$ and $z_1 = v_1^\top y$, premultiplying (21) by $v_1^\top$ yields

$$v_1^\top \widehat{x}^{(m)} = b_1^{(m)} z_1 v_1^\top v_1 = v_1^\top y. \tag{27}$$

Since $v_1 = \iota / \sqrt{n}$, multiplying (27) by $\sqrt{n}$ yields

$$\iota^\top \widehat{x}^{(m)} = \iota^\top y. \tag{28}$$

Thus, the mean of the entries of $\widehat{x}^{(m)}$ equals that of y. That is, it follows that

$$\frac{1}{n} \sum_{i=1}^{n} \widehat{x}_i^{(m)} = \frac{1}{n} \sum_{i=1}^{n} y_i. \tag{29}$$

In addition, from (28), it immediately follows that

$$\iota^\top \left(y - \widehat{x}^{(m)} \right) = 0. \tag{30}$$

Thus, the bHP filter trend residuals sum to zero. That is, it follows that

$$\sum_{i=1}^{n}(y_i - \widehat{x}_i^{(m)}) = 0. \tag{31}$$

2. Given that $(b_1^{(m)}, v_1)$ is an eigenpair of A_m and $b_1^{(m)} = 1$, postmultiplying (16) by v_1 yields

$$A_m v_1 = b_1^{(m)} v_1 = v_1. \tag{32}$$

Again, since $v_1 = \iota/\sqrt{n}$, from (32), it follows that

$$A_m \iota = \iota. \tag{33}$$

Thus, each row of the smoother matrix A_m sums to unity. That is, it follows that

$$a_{i,1}^{(m)} + \cdots + a_{i,n}^{(m)} = 1, \quad i = 1, \ldots, n, \tag{34}$$

in (10).

3. Similarly, given that $(b_2^{(m)}, v_2)$ is an eigenpair of A_m and $b_2^{(m)} = 1$, postmultiplying (16) by v_2 yields

$$A_m v_2 = b_2^{(m)} v_2 = v_2. \tag{35}$$

Since $v_2 = Q_\iota \tau / \sqrt{\tau^\top Q_\iota \tau}$, from (35), we obtain

$$A_m(Q_\iota \tau) = (Q_\iota \tau). \tag{36}$$

Then, from (33), it follows that $A_m Q_\iota = A_m - P_\iota$. Thus, (36) becomes $A_m \tau - P_\iota \tau = \tau - P_\iota \tau$, which leads to

$$A_m \tau = \tau. \tag{37}$$

Combining (33) and (37) yields

$$A_m \Pi = \Pi. \tag{38}$$

Let $\xi \in \mathbb{S}(\Pi)$. Then, from (38), it follows that which leads to $A_m \xi = \xi$. Accordingly, since $P_\Pi y \in \mathbb{S}(\Pi)$, we obtain

$$\widehat{x}^{(m)} = P_\Pi y + A_m(y - P_\Pi y). \tag{39}$$

4. Since

$$b_i^{(m)} = 1 - \left(\frac{\lambda d_i}{1 + \lambda d_i}\right)^m \to 0, \quad (n, m : \text{fixed}, \lambda \to \infty)$$

for $i = 3, \ldots, n$, it follows that

$$\begin{aligned} \widehat{x}^{(m)} &= P_\Pi y + b_3^{(m)} z_3 v_3 + \cdots + b_n^{(m)} z_n v_n \\ &\to P_\Pi y, \quad (n, m : \text{fixed}, \lambda \to \infty). \end{aligned} \tag{40}$$

5. Since $b_1^{(m)} = b_2^{(m)} = 1$ and

$$b_i^{(m)} = 1 - \left(\frac{\lambda d_i}{1 + \lambda d_i} \right)^m \to 1, \quad (n, m : \text{fixed}, \ \lambda \to 0)$$

for $i = 3, \ldots, n$, it follows that

$$A_m = V B_m V^\top \to V V^\top = I_n, \quad (n, m : \text{fixed}, \ \lambda \to 0).$$

Therefore, it follows that

$$\widehat{x}^{(m)} = A_m y \to y, \quad (n, m : \text{fixed}, \ \lambda \to 0). \tag{41}$$

6. Since $b_1^{(m)} = b_2^{(m)} = 1$ and

$$b_i^{(m)} = 1 - \left(\frac{\lambda d_i}{1 + \lambda d_i} \right)^m \to 1, \quad (n, \lambda : \text{fixed}, \ m \to \infty) \tag{42}$$

for $i = 3, \ldots, n$, it follows that

$$A_m = V B_m V^\top \to V V^\top = I_n, \quad (n, \lambda : \text{fixed}, \ m \to \infty). \tag{43}$$

See Fig. 2. It illustrates (43) when $n = 100$ and $\lambda = 1600$. (Recall that each row of the smoother matrix A_m sums to unity.) Therefore, it follows that

$$\widehat{x}^{(m)} = A_m y \to y, \quad (n, \lambda : \text{fixed}, \ m \to \infty). \tag{44}$$

7. Given $A_m^k = V B_m^k V^\top$, (23), and (26), it follows that

$$A_m^k y = V B_m^k V^\top y \to V_1 V_1^\top y = P_\Pi y, \quad (n, m, \lambda : \text{fixed}, \ k \to \infty), \tag{45}$$

where $V_1 = [v_1, v_2]$.

8. Since A_m is positive definite and λ is positive, we can let

$$C_m = \lambda^{-1}(A_m^{-1} - I_n). \tag{46}$$

Then, A_m can be represented by C_m as

$$A_m = (I_n + \lambda C_m)^{-1}, \tag{47}$$

which is the Reinsch form representation of A_m. Accordingly, $\widehat{x}^{(m)}$ is the solution of the following penalized least squares problem:

$$\min_x f^{(m)}(x) = \|y - x\|^2 + \lambda x^\top C_m x, \tag{48}$$

and therefore C_m is the penalty matrix of the bHP filter.

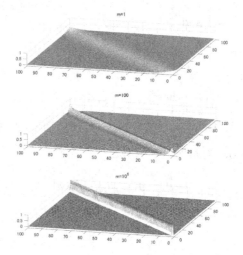

Fig. 2. Smoother matrix $\boldsymbol{A}_m$ in (7) for $m = 1, 100, 10^6$ when $n = 100$ and $\lambda = 1600$.

9. Given $\boldsymbol{A}_m = \boldsymbol{V}\boldsymbol{B}_m\boldsymbol{V}^\top$, it follows that $\boldsymbol{I}_n + \lambda\boldsymbol{C}_m = \boldsymbol{V}\boldsymbol{B}_m^{-1}\boldsymbol{V}^\top$, from which we have $\boldsymbol{C}_m = \boldsymbol{V}\boldsymbol{D}_m\boldsymbol{V}^\top$, where

$$\boldsymbol{D}_m = \lambda^{-1}(\boldsymbol{B}_m^{-1} - \boldsymbol{I}_n). \tag{49}$$

Let

$$d_i^{(m)} = \frac{1}{\lambda}\left(\frac{1}{b_i^{(m)}} - 1\right), \quad i = 1, \dots, n. \tag{50}$$

Then, $\boldsymbol{D}_m = \mathrm{diag}(d_1^{(m)}, \dots, d_n^{(m)})$ and from the inequalities given in (13), it follows that

$$0 = d_1^{(m)} = d_2^{(m)} < d_3^{(m)} \le \cdots \le d_n^{(m)}. \tag{51}$$

10. Since $\boldsymbol{A}_m\boldsymbol{\Pi} = \boldsymbol{\Pi}$, it follows that

$$\boldsymbol{A}_m^{-1}\boldsymbol{\Pi} = \boldsymbol{\Pi},$$

which leads to

$$\boldsymbol{C}_m\boldsymbol{\Pi} = \lambda^{-1}(\boldsymbol{A}_m^{-1} - \boldsymbol{I}_n)\boldsymbol{\Pi} = \lambda^{-1}(\boldsymbol{\Pi} - \boldsymbol{\Pi}) = \boldsymbol{0}. \tag{52}$$

Thus, both $\boldsymbol{\iota}$ and $\boldsymbol{\tau}$ belong to the null space of $\boldsymbol{C}_m$. In addition, given that $0 < b_i^{(m)} < 1$ for $i = 3, \dots, n$, from (49), $\boldsymbol{C}_m$ is a nonnegative definite matrix whose rank is $n - 2$.

11. Let $\boldsymbol{\theta} = \boldsymbol{V}^\top \boldsymbol{x}$. Then, since $\boldsymbol{x} = \boldsymbol{V}\boldsymbol{\theta}$, $f^{(m)}(\boldsymbol{x})$ can be represented by $\boldsymbol{\theta}$ as

$$f^{(m)}(\boldsymbol{x}) = \|\boldsymbol{y} - \boldsymbol{x}\|^2 + \lambda \boldsymbol{x}^\top \boldsymbol{C}_m \boldsymbol{x} = \|\boldsymbol{y} - \boldsymbol{x}\|^2 + \lambda \boldsymbol{x}^\top \boldsymbol{V}\boldsymbol{D}_m \boldsymbol{V}^\top \boldsymbol{x}$$
$$= \|\boldsymbol{y} - \boldsymbol{V}\boldsymbol{\theta}\|^2 + \lambda \boldsymbol{\theta}^\top \boldsymbol{D}_m \boldsymbol{\theta}.$$

12. Let us consider the following generalized ridge regression:

$$\min_{\boldsymbol{\theta}} g^{(m)}(\boldsymbol{\theta}) = \|\boldsymbol{y} - \boldsymbol{V}\boldsymbol{\theta}\|^2 + \lambda \boldsymbol{\theta}^\top \boldsymbol{D}_m \boldsymbol{\theta}. \tag{53}$$

From (51), the first two entries of $\boldsymbol{\theta}$ are not penalized. Let

$$\widehat{\boldsymbol{\theta}}^{(m)} = (\boldsymbol{I}_n + \lambda \boldsymbol{D}_m)^{-1} \boldsymbol{V}^\top \boldsymbol{y}. \tag{54}$$

Then, it follows that $g^{(m)}(\boldsymbol{\theta}) > g^{(m)}(\widehat{\boldsymbol{\theta}}^{(m)})$ for all $\boldsymbol{\theta} \in \mathbb{R}^n \setminus \{\widehat{\boldsymbol{\theta}}^{(m)}\}$. It also follows that

$$\boldsymbol{V}\widehat{\boldsymbol{\theta}}^{(m)} = \boldsymbol{V}(\boldsymbol{I}_n + \lambda \boldsymbol{D}_m)^{-1} \boldsymbol{V}^\top \boldsymbol{y} = (\boldsymbol{I}_n + \lambda \boldsymbol{V}\boldsymbol{D}_m \boldsymbol{V}^\top)^{-1} \boldsymbol{y}$$
$$= (\boldsymbol{I}_n + \lambda \boldsymbol{C}_m)^{-1} \boldsymbol{y} = \boldsymbol{A}_m \boldsymbol{y} = \widehat{\boldsymbol{x}}^{(m)}. \tag{55}$$

Let us summarize the above results.

Proposition 1. *(i) The mean of the entries of $\widehat{\boldsymbol{x}}^{(m)}$ is equal to that of $\boldsymbol{y}$. In addition, the bHP filter trend residuals, $\boldsymbol{y} - \widehat{\boldsymbol{x}}^{(m)}$, sum to zero. (ii) Each row of the smoother matrix $\boldsymbol{A}_m$ sums to unity. (iii) If $\boldsymbol{\xi} \in \mathbb{S}(\boldsymbol{\Pi})$, then $\boldsymbol{A}_m \boldsymbol{\xi} = \boldsymbol{\xi}$. In addition, it follows that $\widehat{\boldsymbol{x}}^{(m)} = \boldsymbol{P}_\Pi \boldsymbol{y} + \boldsymbol{A}_m (\boldsymbol{y} - \boldsymbol{P}_\Pi \boldsymbol{y})$. (iv) When n and m are fixed, as $\lambda \to \infty$, $\widehat{\boldsymbol{x}}^{(m)} \to \boldsymbol{P}_\Pi \boldsymbol{y}$. (v) When n and m are fixed, as $\lambda \to 0$, $\widehat{\boldsymbol{x}}^{(m)} \to \boldsymbol{y}$. (vi) When n and λ are fixed, as $m \to \infty$, $\widehat{\boldsymbol{x}}^{(m)} \to \boldsymbol{y}$. (vii) When n, m, and λ are fixed, as $k \to \infty$, $\boldsymbol{A}_m^k \boldsymbol{y} \to \boldsymbol{P}_\Pi \boldsymbol{y}$. (viii) $\widehat{\boldsymbol{x}}^{(m)}$ is the solution of the penalized least squares problem given by (48). The penalty matrix of the bHP filter can be represented by $\boldsymbol{C}_m$, which is an $n \times n$ nonnegative definite matrix whose null space is identical to $\mathbb{S}(\boldsymbol{\Pi})$. (ix) (53) is a generalized ridge regression representation of the bHP filter.*

Remark 1. Regarding Proposition 1, we make five remarks:

1. Some of the results in Proposition 1 are generalizations of those in [12, Proposition 2.2], which documents several properties of the HP filter. For example, Proposition 1(i) is a generalization of [12, Proposition 2.2(iii)(a)].
2. Given that $\boldsymbol{A}_m$ is symmetric, from Proposition 1(ii), it follows that $\boldsymbol{\iota}^\top \boldsymbol{A}_m = \boldsymbol{\iota}^\top$. Then, Proposition 1(i) can also be derived from it as

$$\boldsymbol{\iota}^\top \widehat{\boldsymbol{x}}^{(m)} = \boldsymbol{\iota}^\top \boldsymbol{A}_m \boldsymbol{y} = \boldsymbol{\iota}^\top \boldsymbol{y}.$$

3. $\widehat{\boldsymbol{x}}^{(m)} = \boldsymbol{P}_\Pi \boldsymbol{y} + \boldsymbol{A}_m (\boldsymbol{y} - \boldsymbol{P}_\Pi \boldsymbol{y})$ in Proposition 1(iii) is a generalization of the result in [13, p. 342] and [14, Eq. (3)]. Given that $\boldsymbol{A}_m$ is a low-pass filter, it indicates that $\widehat{\boldsymbol{x}}^{(m)}$ is the sum of the linear time trend estimated by OLS, $\boldsymbol{P}_\Pi \boldsymbol{y}$, and low-frequency components in the linear trend residuals, $\boldsymbol{y} - \boldsymbol{P}_\Pi \boldsymbol{y}$.

Table 1. List of the relationships between the main matrices

	HP filter	bHP filter
Smoother matrix	A	A_m
Spectral decomposition of smoother matrix	$VBV^\top$	$VB_mV^\top$
Penalty matrix	C	C_m
Spectral decomposition of penalty matrix	$VDV^\top$	$VD_mV^\top$

4. Since $\widehat{x}^{(m)} = A_m y$, for example, $A_m^2 y = A_m \widehat{x}^{(m)}$. Thus, $A_m^k y$ in Proposition 1(vii) represents the result of k times repeated bHP filtering. In addition, from Proposition 1(vii), it follows that

$$\Delta_2(A_m^k y) \to 0, \quad (n, m, \lambda : \text{fixed}, \ k \to \infty), \tag{56}$$

which is a generalization of the result in [2, p. 961].

5. Proposition 1(viii) and (ix) are restatements of the results in [4]. Given that $A_1 = A = (I_n + \lambda C)^{-1}$, by its definition, it follows that

$$C_1 = \lambda^{-1}(A_1^{-1} - I_n) = \lambda^{-1}(I_n + \lambda C - I_n) = C. \tag{57}$$

Therefore, if $m = 1$, then (48) becomes

$$\min_x f^{(1)}(x) = \|y - x\|^2 + \lambda x^\top C x, \tag{58}$$

which is the HP filter. From (15), (19), and (50), it also follows that

$$d_i^{(1)} = \frac{1}{\lambda}\left(\frac{1}{b_i^{(1)}} - 1\right) = \frac{1}{\lambda}\left(\frac{1}{b_i} - 1\right) = d_i, \quad i = 1, \dots, n. \tag{59}$$

from which we obtain

$$D_1 = D. \tag{60}$$

This is consistent with (57).

5 Concluding Remarks

In this paper, we have derived several properties of the bHP filter. For this purpose, we used the spectral decomposition of the penalty matrix of the HP filter. The results of this paper are summarized in Proposition 1. See also Table 1, which lists the relationships between the main matrices such as A_m and B_m.

Finally, we make a remark. The HP filter is a kind of the WH(p) graduation defined by

$$\min_{x_1,\dots,x_n} f_p(x_1,\dots,x_n) = \sum_{i=1}^n (y_i - x_i)^2 + \lambda_p \sum_{i=p+1}^n (\Delta^p x_i)^2, \tag{61}$$

where $\lambda_p \in (0, \infty)$ is a smoothing parameter and $\Delta x_i = x_i - x_{i-1}$. (Note that $\Delta^2 x_i = \Delta(\Delta x_i) = x_i - 2x_{i-1} + x_{i-2}$.) Then, we can consider the boosted version of the WH(p) graduation and establish its properties using the approach adopted in this paper. We are investigating this issue and will report our findings in the future.

Acknowledgments. The author would like to thank three anonymous reviewers for their valuable comments and suggestions. He also thanks Keith Knight for permission to reference his unpublished manuscript. This study was funded by the Japan Society for the Promotion of Science (KAKENHI Grant Number 23K013770A).

Appendix: Some Proofs

Proof of (12)
C in (5) is the following $n \times n$ symmetric pentadiagonal matrix.

$$
C = \begin{bmatrix}
1 & -2 & 1 & 0 & \cdots & \cdots & 0 \\
-2 & 5 & -4 & 1 & \ddots & & \vdots \\
1 & -4 & 6 & \ddots & \ddots & \ddots & \vdots \\
0 & 1 & \ddots & \ddots & \ddots & 1 & 0 \\
\vdots & \ddots & \ddots & \ddots & 6 & -4 & 1 \\
\vdots & & \ddots & 1 & -4 & 5 & -2 \\
0 & \cdots & \cdots & 0 & 1 & -2 & 1
\end{bmatrix}.
$$

From the Gershgorin circle theorem, its eigenvalues, d_i for $i = 1, \ldots, n$, satisfy

$$d_i \in L_1 \cup L_2 \cup L_3, \quad i = 1, \ldots, n,$$

where $L_1 = \{\eta : |\eta - 1| \le 3\}$, $L_2 = \{\eta : |\eta - 5| \le 7\}$, and $L_3 = \{\eta : |\eta - 6| \le 10\}$. Therefore, $d_n \le 16$ follows.

Another Proof of (12)

Kim et al. [13, p. 342] show $\|\Delta_2 x\| \le 4\|x\|$, from which we obtain

$$\frac{\|\Delta_2 x\|^2}{\|x\|^2} \le 16.$$

If $x = v_n$, then the left-hand side is equal to d_n.

Proof of (26)

It follows that

$$b_1^{(m)} z_1 v_1 + b_2^{(m)} z_2 v_2 = V_1 V_1^\top y = V_1 (V_1^\top V_1)^{-1} V_1^\top y = P_{V_1} y,$$

which is the orthogonal projection of y onto $\mathbb{S}(V_1)$. On the other hand, $P_\Pi y$ is the orthogonal projection of y onto $\mathbb{S}(\Pi)$. Since $\mathbb{S}(V_1)$ and $\mathbb{S}(\Pi)$ are identical, (26) holds.

References

1. Hodrick, R.J., Prescott, E.C.: Postwar U.S. business cycles: an empirical investigation. J. Money Credit Banking **29**(1), 1–16 (1997)
2. Weinert, H.L.: Efficient computation for Whittaker-Henderson smoothing. Comput. Stat. Data Anal. **52**(2), 959–974 (2007)
3. Phillips, P.C.B., Shi, Z.: Boosting: why you can use the HP filter. Int. Econ. Rev. **62**(2), 521–570 (2021)
4. Knight, K.: The boosted Hodrick–Prescott filter, penalized least squares, and Bernstein polynomials. Department of Statistical Sciences, University of Toronto (2021). https://www.utstat.utoronto.ca/keith/papers/hp-pls.pdf
5. Biswas, E, Sabzikar, F., Phillips, P.C.B.: Boosting the HP filter for trending time series with long range dependence. Cowles Foundation Discussion Papers No. 2347, Yale University (2022). https://cowles.yale.edu/sites/default/files/2022-12/d2347.pdf
6. Hall, V., Thomson, P.: A boosted HP filter for business cycle analysis: evidence from New Zealand's small open economy. SEF Working Paper 1/2022, Victoria University of Wellington (2022). https://researcharchive.vuw.ac.nz/xmlui/bitstream/handle/10063/9473/Working%20Paper.pdf?sequence=6
7. Mei, Z., Phillips, P.C.B., Shi, Z.: The boosted HP filter is more general than you might think. arXiv:2209.09810 (2022). https://doi.org/10.48550/arXiv.2209.09810
8. Tomal, M.: Testing for overall and cluster convergence of housing rents using robust methodology: evidence from Polish provincial capitals. Empirical Econ. **62**, 2023–2055 (2022)
9. Widiantoro, D.M.: Countercyclical capital buffer: building the resilience or taming the rapid financial cycle? MPRA Paper No. 113507 (2022). https://mpra.ub.uni-muenchen.de/113507/
10. Lu, Y., Pagan, A.: To boost or not to boost? That is the question. CAMA Working Paper 12/2023, Centre for Applied Macroeconomic Analysis, Australian National University (2023). https://crawford.anu.edu.au/sites/default/files/publication/cama_crawford_anu_edu_au/2023-02/12_2023_lu_pagan_0.pdf
11. Danthine, J.-P., Girardin, M.: Business cycles in Switzerland: a comparative study. Eur. Econ. Rev. **33**(1), 31–50 (1989)
12. Yamada, H.: A smoothing method that looks like the Hodrick-Prescott filter. Economet. Theor. **36**(5), 961–981 (2020)
13. Kim, S., Koh, K., Boyd, S., Gorinevsky, D.: ℓ_1 trend filtering. SIAM Rev. **51**(2), 339–360 (2009)
14. Yamada, H.: Why does the trend extracted by the Hodrick-Prescott filtering seem to be more plausible than the linear trend? Appl. Econ. Lett. **25**(2), 102–105 (2018)
15. Abadir, K.M., Magnus, J.R.: Matrix Algebra. Cambridge University Press, Cambridge (2005)

MiSIS: An HL7 FHIR Middleware for Healthcare Information Systems

Ramon Santos Malaquias(✉)®, Itamir de Morais Barroca Filho®,
Jean Mário Moreira de Lima®, André Morais Gurgel®,
and Bruna Alice Oliveira de Brito®

Digital Metropolis Institute, Federal University of Rio Grande do Norte, Natal, Brazil
{malaquias,itamir.filho,jean.lima}@imd.ufrn.br, andre.gurgel@ufrn.br

Abstract. Several e-Health and m-Health technological solutions are increasingly supporting Healthcare services. In this context, Electronic Health Records (EHR) deal with data of different types, which, if integrated, can be of great value for the patient's health care. However, data heterogeneity is a factor that makes this integration difficult, and middleware appears as an option as a solution to this problem. The basic definition of middleware is a software layer that abstracts development details and encourages integration between solutions. This work describes the requirements and implements a middleware for healthcare systems based on HL7 FHIR, an open development standard that enables interoperability between healthcare solutions. As a result, we present a proof of concept that integrates data from 5 different health systems and makes the integrated data available using the HL7 FHIR standard.

Keywords: healthcare · middleware · interoperability · e-Health · m-Health

1 Introduction

With the advancement of technological applications aimed at the healthcare context, there is a need to store, process, and extract information through data used in healthcare to support decisions and optimize processes to improve the service provided. In this sense, Health Information Systems (SIS) emerge, which, according to Fatima et al. [10], can be defined as "a set of interrelated components that collect, process, store and distribute information to support the decision-making process and assist in the control of healthcare organizations."

The use of SIS enables the creation of Electronic Health Records (EHR), defined by Iakovids [15] as digitally stored health information about an individual's life to support continuity of care, education, and research, ensuring confidentiality at all times. In this way, EHR systems allow the clinical team to access patient information [35] easily. Therefore, using EHR-based health systems makes it possible to maintain health data records, integrate services, provide information to different sectors, reduce health treatment costs,

O. Gervasi et al. (Eds.): ICCSA 2024, LNCS 14814, pp. 243–260, 2024.
https://doi.org/10.1007/978-3-031-64608-9_16

avoid loss of information, and contribute to better healthcare provision. Health service [5].

Solutions based on SIS and EHR are examples of *eHealth* solutions. *EHealth* is the field that emerges as an intersection between medical informatics, public health, and business, referring to improved health services through the use of technologies and web technologies [9]. Furthermore, the advancement of mobile communications, which currently support 3G, 4G, and 5G mobile networks for data transport, means that mobile computing promotes countless possibilities for creating solutions for the healthcare sector, bringing to light the concept de *mHealth* [35] [28]. *MHealth* is the area that consists of the use of mobile computing and communication technologies in health [13]. Therefore, systems based on *eHealth* and *mHealth* can support clinical and administrative data management, predictive systems, monitoring vital signs and sending alerts, medication management, and exam and results management.

In this sense, an ecosystem of digital solutions for the health sector can be composed, for example, of solutions aimed at sensing and monitoring patients' vital signs, including solutions for managing exams and results, management data from hospitals and clinics, epidemiological data, personal and sociodemographic data of patients, and etcetera. If integrated, this data could not only promote better support for clinical decision-making and the provision of health services but also help significantly reduce costs in this process. However, the heterogeneity of healthcare data is one of the main challenges in developing integrated solutions for this area [16], along with interoperability, data quality, and security and privacy [17, 21, 34, 41].

Interoperability consists of the ability of a system to transfer data and the ability to interpret the data transferred to other systems [6]. Therefore, nowadays, one of the main requirements for improving the quality of care and services provided in the healthcare domain is to promote interoperability between the applications involved in this context. Therefore, Middleware Platforms aimed at the healthcare context emerge as options to meet the interoperability requirement since they are solutions for distributed applications that make network details transparent and protect functionality implementation details, providing interfaces for customer integration [23].

However, studies indicate that the development of *middleware* platforms for the healthcare area still has limitations, such as the non-use of open standards such as *HL7 FHIR*. In the literature review carried out by Malaquias et al., through a Systematic Mapping [20], 14 *middleware* platforms for the healthcare area were analyzed and none of them presented a solution entirely based on an open communication standard and prepared for data exchange between services *web*, such as *HL7 FHIR*, to promote [27] interoperability.

Based on this context, this paper aims to describe the development and validation process of a Middleware platform called MiSIS based on the *HL7FHIR* Standard for Health Information Systems. The remainder of this work presents the following organization: Sect. 2 deals with related work and middleware solutions aimed at the healthcare area; Sect. 3 details MiSIS from the point of view of its requirements and the software architecture designed to meet the solution's requirements; Sect. 3 deals with the current state of development of MiSIS; Sect. 4 describes the methodology used to validate MiSIS, as well as the results obtained from carrying out proofs of concept and carrying out solution availability tests; and, finally, Sect. 5 presents the conclusions obtained, as well as predictions for future work based on the development of MiSIS.

2   Related Works

To fulfill this work, the authors read and analyzed thirty-four articles to understand how each responds to the questions defined in the research protocol of the review. In this sense, solutions based on the $HL7$ [12] standard are cited as options for the development of *middleware* platforms for [22] healthcare systems. Furthermore, in Zhang et al. [40] some solutions referred to as "standards" by the authors are mentioned, such as: *"Medical Telemonitoring System"* which consists of a method of sending physiological and medical information remotely through the internet for an analysis and diagnostic center; in addition to *middleware* described, *"Mobile Context and Ontology-based Reasoning/Feedback (MCOM)"*, a system that monitors patients' health status using *Smartphone*.

In the work of Alonso et al. [2], authors carried out on several *middleware* platforms, including Kura, a *middleware* proposed and designed by the Eclipse consortium to be part of *gateways*; AllJoyn, proposed by the Linux Foundation, which provides a version for restricted resources and also provides different APIs for developers; Macchina.io, which according to the author, is very modular and extensible, implementing a messaging protocol based on the publish/subscribe model. In the line of applications that use this model, Almadani et al. [1] proposes a *Middleware Real-Time Publish Subscribe (RTPS)*, and Singh et al. [37] that present a *middleware* model for controlling information sharing in a publish/subscribe-based environment.

Madureira et al. [26] describes $My - AHA$, a multiplatform *middleware* designed to perfectly integrate different health and active aging solutions, aiming for well-being. According to the authors, the proposed architecture for $My - AHA$ is a multi-module system architecture, fully scalable and easily implementable, focusing on helping caregivers and seniors improve their current condition, considering changes in cognitive, physical, and physical parameters, social and psychological.

A framework for interoperability between health systems is proposed by Ryan et al. [33]. This framework is *Health Service Bus (HSB)*, a solution based on the *software* architecture of *middleware* Enterprise Service Bus (ESB), which provides a weakly coupled and highly distributed for enterprise systems integration. Another example of *middleware* is $SALSA$, proposed by Rodriguez et al. [32] and which allows developers to create autonomous agents that react to contextual elements of the medical environment and communicate with other agents, users, and services available in the environment.

$POStCODE$ (*POstmarket SurveillanCe Of DEvices*) is a *middleware* proposed by Chaudhry et al. [8] which provides the operational details, taking care to delete private patient data, from devices directly to manufacturers. Thus, it enables manufacturers to monitor and maintain medical devices. In terms of synchronizing medical data, we also have the solution proposed by Lomotey et al. [24], a *middleware* for *mHealth (mobile health)* that facilitates the efficient process of synchronizing medical data, and with minimal latency.

SBUS is *middleware* presented by Singh et al. [36]. *SBUS* is a solution that allows multiple forms of communication that are dynamically reconfigurable. It ensures that the message types of the terminals match and that each transmission (message) conforms to the type scheme. Additionally, *SBUS* supports multiple communication methods, including client-server (request-response and RPC) and *streaming* messages *push/pull*.

Some initiatives to promote interoperability between health systems at the continent or country level have also been identified in the literature. For example, Ferrara [11] proposes *DHE (Distributed Healthcare Environment)*, which is a *middleware* following the proposed European Standard Health Information System Architecture, implementing a distributed repository for all clinical, organizational and managerial information in the healthcare structure, to make it available when and where needed for all applications in the healthcare information system. AlZghoul et al. [3] describes a *middleware* architecture to help healthcare providers in Jordan access electronic health data in a national healthcare database.

Healthcare applications deal with a series of multimedia files, mainly image format exams. In this sense, Kallepalli et al. [19] describes a security *middleware* for *DICOM* images that provide fine-grained access control, policy management, demographic filtering, and log keeping restricted to *Canadian-Manitoban* PHIA and the DICOM standard. Another *middleware* solution proposed for use in health data environments is *CORBA (Common Object Request Broker Architecture)*, applied in the work of Murshed et al. [29], Waluyo et al. [39] and Blobel and Holena [7].

Hsieh et al. [14] uses a series of technologies, systems, and standards to characterize a *middleware* solution, namely: a *Single Sign-On Server* (SSOS) in a Health Information Enterprise Portal (HEIP) and a health information system (HIS). *National Taiwan University Hospital* (NTUH) received this above-cited set of solutions.

Finally, a series of *middleware* platforms are in the analyzed works, including *MiThrilNGN*, *MyHearth* and *X73uHealth* [17], *ANGELAH* (AssistiNG ELders At Home) - proposed in Taleb et al. [38] and *HYDRA*, a solution that allows the integration of different devices into applications through a simple services interface.

The analysis of these works showed us that there are already *middleware* platforms proposed or developed for the healthcare area. However, these solutions are not entirely flexible and applicable in different contexts and, therefore, do not meet all the essential requirements for *middleware* platforms for the healthcare area.

Given this, the opportunity to create *middleware* for health data that uses open standards and facilitates integration between *web* systems, such as *HL7 FHIR*, for integration and interoperability between different solutions health center is still open. Therefore, we propose and develop MiSIS: A Middleware based on the HL7 FHIR Standard for Health Information Systems, described in Sect. 3.

3 MiSIS: A Middleware Based on the HL7 FHIR Standard for Healthcare Information Systems

In this section, MiSIS, a Middleware Platform based on the HL7 FHIR Standard for Health Information Systems, will be described and its implementation and evaluation process. MiSIS aims to promote interoperability between different applications and health information systems, making details of their implementations invisible to developers, focusing only on the communication layer, and enabling integration between heterogeneous solutions.

3.1 Solution Requirements

The main challenges for developing middleware for health information systems consist of the following: Provide solutions that deal with the heterogeneity of data present in the context of health and its applications [11,21,31]; Support devices, systems, and sensors that communicate through different means [17,25], securely provides reliable data, especially considering the degree of sensitivity of health data [4,31].

In this sense, based on these challenges and the state-of-the-art analysis carried out by Malaquias et al. [27] that, below, are described the main requirements that MiSIS must cover:

- **Promote transparent integration of heterogeneous data:** MiSIS should provide a means of treating heterogeneous data with high abstraction, flexibility, and dynamicity in different contexts and environments. Enabling different types of health data to be treated and integrated transparently and with a high level of abstraction makes it possible to centralize health data, facilitating access and cross-referencing between this information.
- **Enable scalability:** MiSIS must provide means by which applications can scale in terms of connected devices and systems, as well as the volume of data transmitted, but without compromising quality requirements, such as reliability, fault tolerance, real-time synchronization, and response;
- **Provide security and privacy:** MiSIS must guarantee the protection and privacy of data used by doctors, patients, and other users using user access control strategies.

Software Architecture strategies were defined and described in the 3.2 subsection to address these requirements and deal with the above challenges.

3.2   Solution Architecture

The *Middleware* proposed in this work supports the integration between different health systems and applications regardless of the type of data managed by each of them. Figure 1 illustrates the role of the proposed solution, where *software* component interconnects different digital solutions aimed at the health area. That software component is responsible for integrating health data from these solutions and making them available to other client applications that use the data, which are, in turn, integrated.

As illustrated, the solutions in Fig. 1 are varied, being systems that deal with patient data, monitoring vital signs, exam management, hospitalization, and bed management. These solutions are examples of health information systems focused on solving specific problems in the health context. However, they initially do not interoperate among them, and there is no integration between their data. Therefore, to enable transparent integration between these systems, an architecture was defined for the proposed solution based mainly on the following items:

- *middleware*, which is responsible for promoting data integration in a transparent, secure, and easy-to-implement manner;
- And the clients, which consist of applications that communicate with the *middleware* component through *HTTP* requests, sending data to be integrated or receiving data already integrated in a structured way.

Figure 2 illustrates the view of MiSIS modules, describing the modules that organize each component of the *solution*, as well as the format and standard (*HL7 FHIR*) that must be followed in the process of integration and communication between health applications.

As a solution based on *WEB* systems, MiSIS must be made available through an application server. Figure 3 illustrates the implementation diagram for MiSIS Fig. 3, and, following this structure, authors carried out two proofs of the concept of the solution.

3.3   Solution Development

MiSIS was developed using the Java Platform *Enterprise Edition* (Java EE), together with the *Spring Framework* [18] tools for developing solutions based on *Web*. Data from client applications integrated by *Middleware* is stored in a *MongoDB*, non-relational and open source database [30]. The open source library *HAPI FHIR* carries out the conversion and interpretation of data to *HL7 FHIR*, and the data is made available through RESTful API services in *JSON* and *XML* formats.

The proposal integrates data from five consolidated but different Health Information Systems used daily by healthcare professionals to carry out the Proofs of Concept and performance tests. These are the considered information systems: the Clinical Data Platform - SigSaúde; the Remote Assistance Platform - PAR; the Beds - Information system based on *web* for managing ICU beds; the SUVEPI System; and the COVID-19 Examination System.

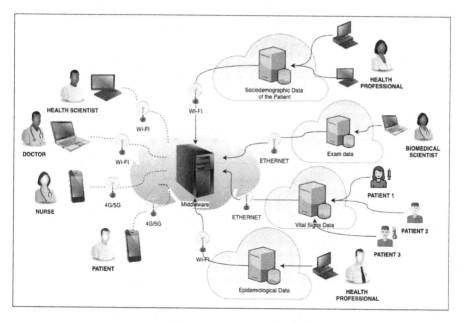

Fig. 1. Conceptual representation of MiSIS: A Middleware Based on the *HL7 FHIR* Standard for Health Information Systems.

4   Studies on the Use and Evaluation of MiSIS

According to the state-of-the-art review carried out in the work of Malaquias et al., [27], *Middleware* Platforms for healthcare systems are evaluated mainly from the point of view of performance, reliability, and direct and indirect costs. The proposal uses two ways to evaluate MiSIS, namely:

- By carrying out two proofs of concept, which consisted of the development of two new applications that consume integrated data and aimed to evaluate cost characteristics of implementing new solutions with the data made available from *middleware*;
- From the execution of stress tests using Apache JMeter, a solution designed to measure the performance of solutions based on the execution of functional behaviors at scale enabled data collection related to the performance and reliability of *middleware*.

Therefore, the details of these evaluations, the methodology used, and the following sections discuss obtained results.

4.1   Analysis of Proofs of Concept

In the context of this work, two new Health Information Systems were developed, one of them being *eHealth* and the other *mHealth*, being *Integrated Health*

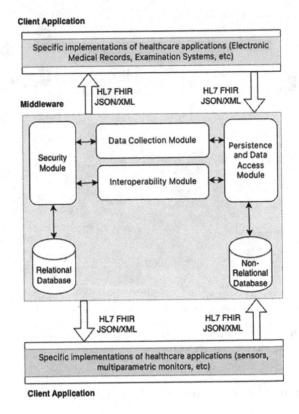

Fig. 2. View of solution modules and the way they communicate.

Application (IHA) and the application "My Medical record", respectively. From the development of these applications, it was possible to analyze whether MiSIS meets the requirements of promoting transparent integration of heterogeneous data and providing security and privacy.

Methodology. Initially, the IHA application was developed, a *eHealth* application based on *web* that aims to present a patient's health data in a unified interface and, for this purpose, performs queries on the RESTful API provided by MiSIS. This application was developed by a single developer, using the Java EE Platform combined with *Spring Framework* solutions. In the experience of developing the application, we noticed the productivity gain when consulting the already integrated data since this application displays four different types of health data (personal data, hospitalization data, exam data, and health data). Completely independent systems collected vital signs, and if they were not connected and integrated from MiSIS, the only way to obtain their data would be if each of them had communication interfaces available, requiring a more significant effort of time and costs for the development of integration.

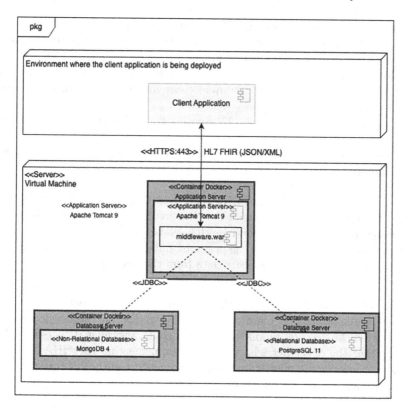

Fig. 3. MiSIS Deployment Diagram.

Secondly, the "My Medical Record" application was developed, a *mHealth* application that aims to facilitate access to a patient's historical health data based on unique identifiers such as CPF and CNS. A team of 3 developers developed this application using the Flutter framework with Dart programming language. To evaluate the experience that developers had in the process of developing a new health application using data integrated from *Middleware* based on the *HL7 FHIR* Standard for Health Information Systems, a *online* questionnaire, built on the *Google Forms* Platform, and can be accessed through the following address: https://forms.gle/rF2BPjUdzynLqXXa6. The questionnaire made available consisted of the following questions:

- **How do you assess your degree of seniority in programming?**
  This question was multiple choice and aimed to identify the degree of programming experience of each developer based on three options: Junior, Full, and Senior;
- **How many hours did you spend developing the application?**
  This question aimed to identify the total number of hours spent developing the application;

– How would you effectively divide the hours allocated to solving technical problems (technology research) and the amount allocated to working on integration activities?
In this question, the objective was to understand the number of hours that each developer needed to work on *middleware* integration and data consumption activities effectively;

– Do you believe using the *JSON* format to exchange data influenced the development process? As?
The objective of this question is to investigate whether the use of an already disseminated standard for exchanging information between *web* systems influenced the development process;

– How do you evaluate, pointing out positive and negative points, the experience in using *Middleware* in developing an application that involves integration between health systems?
This question aims to identify the positives and negatives of the programming experience consuming *middleware* data from the developers' point of view.

Results Obtained. At the end of the application's development, the questionnaire was available so that team members who worked on the development of the "My Medical Record" mobile application could answer it. It is essential to highlight that the developer who worked on implementing the "IHA" application did not answer the questionnaire since he was the author of this work and developer of MiSIS. The responses of each of the developers to the questionnaire, which are also reported in general below:

– How do you assess your degree of seniority in programming?
When answering this question, the three developers classified themselves as "Junior Developers", pointing out their low level of experience and indicating the need for more time required to implement the application;

– How many hours did you spend developing the application?
Table 1 shows that each of the three developers reported having spent 10, 7, and 6 h, respectively, totaling 23 h to develop the application;

Table 1. Number of hours worked by each developer on the development of the 'My Medical Record' app.

Developer	Work hours
A	10
B	7
C	6
Total	23

– How would you effectively divide the hours allocated to solving technical problems (technology research) and the amount allocated to working on integration activities?

Table 2 shows how developers divided their working hours according to demand needs. Each of them stated that they spent only 3 h of work on integration activities and the remaining hours researching technical questions more related to the Flutter programming language, pointing out that the difficulties encountered because they had little experience in programming were the factor that made the development process more complex compared to the difficulties of the health data integration process, as they spent fewer hours working on this process;

Table 2. Number of hours worked by each developer on specific issues of the Flutter programming language and integration

Developer	Hours spent researching inquiries regarding Flutter	Hours spent working on integration
A	7	3
B	4	3
C	3	3
Total	14	9

– Do you believe using the $JSON$ format to exchange data influenced the development process? As?

Unanimously, all developers confirmed that the use of the $JSON$ format had a positive influence on the development process, reporting facilities such as the availability of examples of $FHIR$ online resources in the $JSON$ format and also previous experiences of integrations using this format;

– How do you evaluate, pointing out positive and negative points, the experience in using *Middleware* in developing an application that involves integration between health systems?

As positive points, the developers reported the ease of using data from different databases. They integrated from *middleware* using already known and well-documented standards. In addition, if the integration had not been done with *middleware*, the application would necessarily have to connect several different communication services to obtain the same data. As a negative point, the developers noted the need for a specific mapping for the $FHIR$ resources since the library that handles $HL7\ FHIR$ for the Flutter programming language presented errors during the development process.

In general, the developers who worked on the applications resulting from the Proofs of Concepts attested that *middleware* meets the requirement of promoting transparent integration of heterogeneous data since two solutions that use health data were developed quickly due to the use of *middleware*; it also meets the requirement to provide security and privacy, since to consume health data, applications needed to have a valid access key; and the requirement to provide support for *"plug-and-play"* data collection, considering that to consume the data made available by *middleware*'s RESTful API, applications only had to implement strategies to convert the data received in *HL7 FHIR*. Furthermore, the developers involved in implementing the new applications pointed out the ease brought by the use of *Middleware* based on the *HL7 FHIR* Standard in the process of integration and consumption of health data, showing the possibility of cost reduction development and implementation using *Middleware*.

4.2   Performance Test Analysis

In order to analyze the scalability, availability, and reliability requirements of MiSIS, the proposal carried out stress tests after the development and deployment of the solution on a server available in a private cloud. To carry out the tests, Apache JMeter, a solution that aims to measure the performance of systems based on the execution of functional behaviors at scale, was used to collect data related to the performance and reliability of the tested solution. The test environment configured to carry out the tests, as well as the methodology used to carry out the tests and the results obtained, will be discussed in the Subsects. 4.2, 4.2 and 4.2, respectively.

Test Environment Specification: The environment used to carry out the tests consisted of a virtual machine in a private cloud, which deployed the MiSIS application, and a personal computer with Apache JMeter to simulate client applications that consume integrated data from MiSIS. Below is a description of the configurations of the virtual machine and computer with Apache.

- **Virtual Machine for deploying MiSIS:**
  - **Operating System:** Ubuntu 20.04.1 LTS
  - **RAM memory:** 8Gb
  - **Number of vCPUs:** 8
  - **Disk space:** 20Gb
- **Personal computer to run the client healthcare application simulator:**
  - **Operating System:** macOS Big Sur 11.2.2
  - **RAM memory:** 8Gb
  - **Number of vCPUs:** 8
  - **Disk space:** 512Gb SSD

Figure 4 shows the deployment diagram of the environment used to carry out the performance tests, illustrating the environments with the installed application and the form of communication between the client simulation application and MiSIS that is carried out through *HTTP* requests to the RESTful API, which returns data to clients in the *HL7 FHIR* standard and *JSON* and *XML* formats.

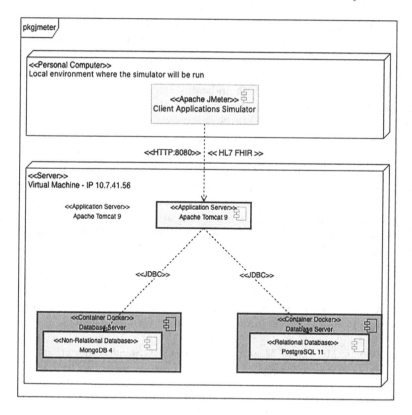

Fig. 4. Diagram of deploy environment performance testing

Methodology: After implementing MiSIS for the virtual machine, the proposal proceeds with data integration from 5 consolidated health systems that are in a productive environment, namely the Clinical Data Platform (SigSaúde), the Remote Assistance Platform (PAR), the COVID-19 Exam Management System, the Bed Management System; and the System for Management of COVID-19 Cases in the State of Rio Grande do Norte (SUVEPI). After processing and integrating data from these systems, the *middleware* database totaled more than 417 thousand health data from 3 different *HL7 FHIR* resources, namely Patients, Observations, and Encounters.

The experiments consisted of 5 sets of tests to evaluate the performance of the integrated data search for each type of *FHIR* resource available. Therefore, tests were carried out based on the number of client applications that simultaneously accessed *middleware* in order to evaluate latency, reliability (error rate), and *throughput* characteristics in data transmission. The number of simulated client applications was 5, 25, 50, 75, and 100 for each of the test batteries and data on request processing time (average, minimum, and maximum latency), standard deviation, error rate, and *throughput* (i.e., the number of requests made every second).

Results Obtained: The results related to the processing time of each request from each of the test batteries are present in Table 3. The minimum latency of requests varies from 196 to 215 milliseconds, showing low variation according to the number of clients that perform queries to the *middleware* API. Authors considered these values low, which indicates that, under ideal infrastructure conditions, request processing can be quite fast. Such an archive is significant as it demonstrates the efficiency of MiSIS.

The average and maximum latency values increased as the number of simulated clients increased. It shows that, quite possibly, the configurations of the environment used for deploying the *middleware* were not ideal for its best functioning, and this is even clearer in the test batteries that simulated more than 50 clients, which showed response from 1745 ms. Furthermore, the high value of the standard deviation in all batteries indicates that there is a difference in the processing time between different requests, and this was due to variations in load on the server during the test batteries (an expected behavior, considering that test batteries queried different types of data).

Table 3. Minimum, mean, maximum, and standard deviation values for the response time (latency) to requests made to the Middleware in each test batch.

Clients	Min (mili)	Mean (mili)	Max (mili)	Standard deviation
5	196	538	1408	213.82
25	202	973	2232	435.94
50	191	1745	3617	881.4
75	215	2654	5395	1267.56
100	215	3487	7014	1870.02

Table 4 shows that in all tests, the percentage of error (that is, requests that did not return *STATUS* 200 of the *HTTP* protocol) was below 2%. The errors presented were server errors caused by concurrency problems, pointing out weaknesses in the *hardware* where *middleware* was installed. Finally, the *throughput* rate was 5.6 requests made per second for the scenario with five clients in the test batteries, but from the moment 25 or more clients were simulated, this rate was between 13.4 and 14.7 requests performed every second. This data is also an indicator that, under ideal computational infrastructure conditions, the *middleware* can process and deliver data quickly, as noticed that as more requests come at the same time, the *middleware* textitmiddleware needed more time to process and return information to clients.

Finally, it is essential to clarify that the results obtained in the simulations and the discussions presented based on them are directly related and influenced by the configurations of the testing environment used to deploy the *middleware* and the simulator. However, the data shows us that the MiSIS presented in this work satisfactorily meets the requirement of providing scalability, as long as it is installed in an environment with better sized *hardware*, being able to process more requests per second and making integrated health data available in an increasingly shorter time.

Table 4. Error rate obtained and the number of requests per second throughput performed in each test batch executed.

Clients	Error Rate	Throughput (req/sec)
5	0%	5.6
25	0.71%	13.4
50	1.03%	14.8
75	2%	14.4
100	1.29%	14.7

5   Conclusions and Future Work

As presented in Sect. 1, there is a strong trend in the development of technological solutions for the healthcare sector. This is primarily aimed at facilitating access to and management of health data by those involved in healthcare service provision (patients, healthcare professionals, managers, or family members), in order to optimize processes, enhance service quality, and reduce costs. Consequently, numerous technological solutions are developed for the healthcare context and often used to address specific problems, resulting in a heterogeneous ecosystem of solutions that are not integrated with each other.

Therefore, Sect. 2 introduced fundamental concepts related to this problem, such as Health Information Systems, *eHealth*, *mHealth*, *Middlewares*, and the $HL7FHIR$ Standards, which were necessary for understanding this work and formed the basis for the creation of MiSIS, a Middleware based on the $HL7FHIR$ Standard for Health Information Systems, detailed in Sect. 3. Section 3 described the requirements of MiSIS, as well as the proposed software architecture to meet these requirements and the current state of the implemented solution.

Furthermore, Sect. 4 outlined the studies conducted to validate MiSIS, which were carried out in two main ways: (i) through Proof of Concepts, involving the implementation of two new Health Systems that consume integrated data from MiSIS, and (ii) through performance tests, aiming to analyze the scalability, availability, and reliability requirements of MiSIS. Overall, the studies indicated that MiSIS effectively meets the requirements related to facilitating integration among heterogeneous healthcare systems, thereby reducing integration implementation costs. On the other hand, performance tests indicated that under ideal conditions for deployment, MiSIS can process and deliver data more quickly.

Finally, future work includes: Conducting further availability tests on infrastructures better than the one where MiSIS was deployed in the context of this work; Deploying MiSIS in a public cloud solution, such as *Amazon Web Services*, to evaluate scalability requirements and real-time data provisioning; Validating MiSIS through case studies in real scenarios involving an ecosystem of healthcare information systems with heterogeneous data, involving healthcare professionals in the validation process (e.g., in a hospital).

Acknowledgement. This study was funded by its authors.

Disclosure of Interests. The authors have no competing interests to declare that they are relevant to the content of this article.

References

1. Almadani, B., Saeed, B., Alroubaiy, A.: Healthcare systems integration using real time publish subscribe (RTPS) middleware. Comput. Electr. Eng. **50**, 67–78 (2016)
2. Alonso, L., Barbarán, J., Chen, J., Díaz, M., Llopis, L., Rubio, B.: Middleware and communication technologies for structural health monitoring of critical infrastructures: a survey. Comput. Stand. Interf. **56**, 83–100 (2018)
3. AlZghoul, M.M., Al-Taee, M.A., Al-Taee, A.M.: Towards nationwide electronic health record system in Jordan. In: 2016 13th International Multi-Conference on Systems, Signals & Devices (SSD). pp. 650–655. IEEE (2016)
4. Arunachalan, B., Light, J.: Middleware architecture for patient care data transmission using wireless networks. In: Proceedings of the 2007 International Conference on Wireless Communications and Mobile Computing, pp. 182–185 (2007)
5. Barroca Filho, I., et al.: Development of a health dashboard for an electronic health record system. In: 2020 20th International Conference on Computational Science and Its Applications (ICCSA), pp. 16–22. IEEE (2020)
6. Bass, L., Clements, P., Kazman, R.: Software architecture in practice (2013)
7. Blobel, B., Holena, M.: Comparing middleware concepts for advanced healthcare system architectures. Int. J. Med. Informatics **46**(2), 69–85 (1997)
8. Chaudhry, J., Valli, C., Crowley, M., Haass, J., Roberts, P.: Postcode middleware for post-market surveillance of medical devices for cyber security in medical and healthcare sector in Australia. In: 2018 12th International Symposium on Medical Information and Communication Technology (ISMICT), pp. 1–10. IEEE (2018)
9. Eysenbach, G.: What is e-health? J. Med. Internet Res. **3**(2), e20 (2001). https://doi.org/10.2196/jmir.3.2.e20, http://www.jmir.org/2001/2/e20/
10. de Fátima Marin, H.: Sistemas de informação em saúde: considerações gerais. J. Health Inform. **2**(1) (2010)
11. Ferrara, F.M.: The standard 'healthcare information systems architecture'and the dhe middleware. Int. J. Med. Informatics **52**(1–3), 39–51 (1998)
12. Foundation, H.F.: Hl7 fhir foundation about page (2021). http://fhir.org/about.html
13. Free, C., Phillips, G., Felix, L., Galli, L., Patel, V., Edwards, P.: The effectiveness of m-health technologies for improving health and health services: a systematic review protocol. BMC. Res. Notes **3**(1), 1–7 (2010)

14. Hsieh, S.L., et al.: An integrated healthcare enterprise information portal and healthcare information system framework. In: 2006 International Conference of the IEEE Engineering in Medicine and Biology Society, pp. 4731–4734. IEEE (2006)
15. Iakovidis, I.: Towards personal health record: current situation, obstacles and trends in implementation of electronic healthcare record in Europe. Int. J. Med. Informatics 52(1–3), 105–115 (1998)
16. Jayaratne, M., Nallaperuma, D., De Silva, D., Alahakoon, D., Devitt, B., Webster, K.E., Chilamkurti, N.: A data integration platform for patient-centered e-healthcare and clinical decision support. Futur. Gener. Comput. Syst. 92, 996–1008 (2019)
17. Ji, Z., Ganchev, I., O'Droma, M., Zhang, X., Zhang, X.: A cloud-based x73 ubiquitous mobile healthcare system: design and implementation. Sci. World J. 2014 (2014)
18. Johnson, R., et al.: Spring framework documentation (2020)
19. Kallepalli, V.N., Ehikioya, S.A., Camorlinga, S., Rueda, J.A.: Security middleware infrastructure for DICOM images in health information systems. J. Digit. Imaging 16(4), 356–364 (2003)
20. Kitchenham, B., Brereton, O.P., Budgen, D., Turner, M., Bailey, J., Linkman, S.: Systematic literature reviews in software engineering-a systematic literature review. Inf. Softw. Technol. 51(1), 7–15 (2009)
21. Kliem, A., Boelke, A., Grohnert, A., Traeder, N.: Self-adaptive middleware for ubiquitous medical device integration. In: 2014 IEEE 16th international conference on e-health networking, applications and services (Healthcom), pp. 298–304. IEEE (2014)
22. Liu, L., Huang, Q.: An extensible hl7 middleware for heterogeneous healthcare information exchange. In: 2012 5th International Conference on BioMedical Engineering and Informatics, pp. 1045–1048. IEEE (2012)
23. Liu, X., Ma, L., Liu, Y.: A middleware-based implementation for data integration of remote devices. In: 2012 13th ACIS International Conference on Software Engineering, Artificial Intelligence, Networking and Parallel/Distributed Computing, pp. 219–224. IEEE (2012)
24. Lomotey, R.K., Nilson, J., Mulder, K., Wittmeier, K., Schachter, C., Deters, R.: Mobile medical data synchronization on cloud-powered middleware platform. IEEE Trans. Serv. Comput. 9(5), 757–770 (2016)
25. Lomotey, R.K., et al.: Using cloud-based middleware to enable mobile medical data management. In: 2016 IEEE International Conference on Mobile Services (MS), pp. 142–149. IEEE (2016)
26. Madureira, P., Cardoso, N., Sousa, F., Moreira, W.: My-aha: middleware platform to sustain active and healthy ageing. In: 2019 International Conference on Wireless and Mobile Computing, Networking and Communications (WiMob), pp. 21–26. IEEE (2019)
27. Malaquias, R.S., Filho, I.M.B.: Middleware for healthcare systems: a systematic mapping. In: Gervasi, O., et al. (eds.) ICCSA 2021. LNCS, vol. 12957, pp. 394–409. Springer, Cham (2021). https://doi.org/10.1007/978-3-030-87013-3_30
28. de Mattos, W.D., Gondim, P.R.: M-health solutions using 5g networks and m2m communications. IT Professional 18(3), 24–29 (2016)
29. Murshed, A.N., Almansoori, W., Xylogiannopoulos, K.F., Elzohbi, M., Alhajj, R., Rokne, J.: Developing an efficient health clinical application: Iiop distributed objects framework. In: 2012 IEEE/ACM International Conference on Advances in Social Networks Analysis and Mining, pp. 759–764. IEEE (2012)

30. Pollack, M., Risberg, T., Gierke, O., Leau, C., Brisbin, J.: Spring data mongodb-reference documentation (2011)

31. Prados-Suarez, B., Molina, C., Peña-Yañez, C.: Providing an integrated access to EHR using electronic health records aggregators. Studies in Health Technol. Informatics **270**, 402–406 (2020)

32. Rodriguez, M.D., Favela, J.: An agent middleware for ubiquitous computing in healthcare. In: Sordo, M., Vaidya, S., Jain, L.C. (eds.) Advanced Computational Intelligence Paradigms in Healthcare-3, pp. 117–149. Springer, Cham (2008). https://doi.org/10.1007/978-3-540-77662-8_6

33. Ryan, A., Eklund, P.W.: The health service bus: an architecture and case study in achieving interoperability in healthcare. Stud Health Technol. Inform. (2010)

34. Shand, B., Rashbass, J.: Security for middleware extensions: event meta-data for enforcing security policy. In: Proceedings of the 2008 Workshop on Middleware Security, pp. 31–33 (2008)

35. Silva, B.M., Rodrigues, J.J., de la Torre Díez, I., López-Coronado, M., Saleem, K.: Mobile-health: a review of current state in 2015. J. Biomed. Inform. **56**, 265–272 (2015)

36. Singh, J., Bacon, J.: Managing health information flows with a reconfigurable component-based middleware. In: 2011 IEEE 12th International Conference on Mobile Data Management, vol. 2, pp. 52–54. IEEE (2011)

37. Singh, J., Vargas, L., Bacon, J., Moody, K.: Policy-based information sharing in publish/subscribe middleware. In: 2008 IEEE Workshop on Policies for Distributed Systems and Networks, pp. 137–144. IEEE (2008)

38. Taleb, T., Bottazzi, D., Guizani, M., Nait-Charif, H.: Angelah: a framework for assisting elders at home. IEEE J. Sel. Areas Commun. **27**(4), 480–494 (2009)

39. Waluyo, A.B., Pek, I., Chen, X., Yeoh, W.S.: Design and evaluation of lightweight middleware for personal wireless body area network. Pers. Ubiquit. Comput. **13**(7), 509–525 (2009)

40. Zhang, W., Thurow, K., Stoll, R.: A knowledge-based telemonitoring platform for application in remote healthcare. Int. J. Comput. Commun. Control **9**(5), 644–654 (2014)

41. Zuehlke, P., Li, J., Talaei-Khoei, A., Ray, P.: A functional specification for mobile ehealth (mhealth) systems. In: 2009 11th International Conference on e-Health Networking, Applications and Services (Healthcom), pp. 74–78. IEEE (2009)

A Novel Leak Localization Method for Water Pipeline Systems Based on Acoustic Emission Monitoring and Event Correlation

Duc-Thuan Nguyen[1] and Jong-Myon Kim[1,2]($\boxtimes$)

[1] Department of Electrical, Electronic and Computer Engineering, University of Ulsan,
Ulsan 44610, South Korea
jmkim07@ulsan.ac.kr
[2] Prognosis and Diagnostics Technologies Co., Ltd., Ulsan 44610, South Korea

Abstract. This paper proposes a novel method for leak localization in water pipeline systems through the monitoring of acoustic emissions and cross-correlation of acoustic emission events. The method is designed to overcome limitations in the calculation of the time difference of arrival by traditional methods such as time-of-arrival detection and cross-correlation. The proposed method combines these two conventional techniques, specifically by examining cross-correlation at positions associated with arrived acoustic emission events. The positions of acoustic emission events are initially identified using the constant false alarm rate signal detection algorithm. Subsequently, the minimum entropy deconvolution is applied at these positions to eliminate noise and reveal signal information. Finally, cross-correlation at the identified positions is computed to determine the time difference of arrival and localize the leak position. Experimental validations on a real-world testbed demonstrate the effectiveness of the proposed method with a high level of accuracy. The proposed method exhibits superior accuracy in comparison to other methods.

Keywords: Leak Localization · Pipeline Systems · Acoustic Emission · Constant False Alarm Rate · Minimum Entropy Deconvolution

1 Introduction

Water pipelines play a vital role in both industrial activities and daily life [1]. Monitoring the condition, detecting, and precisely locating leaks in water pipelines are crucial for minimizing resource losses and ensuring community safety [1, 2]. Current methods for pipeline monitoring include pressure and flow monitoring, acoustic emission monitoring, and image inspection [3]. While pressure and flow monitoring can detect significant leaks, they are less effective for small leaks and challenged in accurately pinpointing the leak location [4, 5]. Image inspection becomes even more challenged when dealing with buried pipes or limited access spaces [6, 7]. Acoustic emission (AE) monitoring is considered suitable for effectively detecting and precisely locating leaks in pipelines due to its high sensitivity and quick response [8]. Recent studies in AE monitoring have

© The Author(s), under exclusive license to Springer Nature Switzerland AG 2024
O. Gervasi et al. (Eds.): ICCSA 2024, LNCS 14814, pp. 261–272, 2024.
https://doi.org/10.1007/978-3-031-64608-9_17

demonstrated its efficiency [9–12], leading to the focus of this research on deploying AE monitoring for leak localization in water pipelines.

The general principle for leak localization involves using two AE sensors placed at the ends of the pipeline to record AE events caused by leaks [12]. The leak position is then determined either based on amplitude differences or the time difference of arrival (TDOA) of the AE events [12, 13]. The first approach requires knowledge of signal attenuation characteristics and consideration of environmental noise effects, presenting challenges due to their inherent instability [14]. Current research often emphasizes the second approach, which involves determining the TDOA [12, 15–17]. Once TDOA is calculated, the difference in distance of the wave travelled can be easily determined based on the wave propagation velocity. It leads to the identification of the source of the AE event i.e., leak location. This approach is simple, highly effective, and easily applicable in practical scenarios, making it a focal point in this study.

In general, there are two main methods for determining TDOA: time of arrival detection and cross-correlation [12]. For the first method, the crucial aspect is accurately determining the arrival time of each acoustic emission event and calculating the time difference between two sensors [18]. This task appears complex and demands precision, as even a slight deviation in arrival time can result in significant errors in predicting the leak location. Moreover, if consecutive AE events occur with overlapping, determining the time of arrival becomes impractical [19]. The second method calculates the cross-correlation of signals between two sensors to find TDOA, identifying the shift time where the correlation is the highest [17, 20]. While this method is simple and highly accurate, it cannot confirm whether there are AE events in the signal or not. Considering the limitations of these two methods, this study aims to propose a hybrid method that leverages the advantages and mitigates the drawbacks of both methods.

The proposed approach involves first detecting AE events in the signal and then using cross-correlation at the positions of the detected events. It eliminates the need for detailed time-of-arrival calculations, taking advantage of the simplicity and effectiveness of cross-correlation. This constitutes the main idea of this research. Specifically, a constant false alarm rate (CFAR) signal detector [21] is initially employed to identify positions with AE events, referred to as AE-active positions. Subsequently, to eliminate noise and reveal signal information, finite impulse response (FIR) filters based on minimum entropy deconvolution (MED) [22] are applied at AE-active positions. The MED is performed after CFAR detection as it is effective only for single AE events identified by CFAR. Finally, cross-correlation is computed at the AE-active positions of two sensors to determine TDOA. Based on the calculated TDOA and known wave propagation velocity, the leak position is determined.

The contributions of this article can be summarized as follows:

- Introducing a novel hybrid method combining time-of-arrival and cross-correlation for leak localization in water pipelines. The proposed method leverages the advantages and addresses the limitations of traditional methods.
- Experimental validations conducted on a real-world testbed to confirm the effectiveness of the proposed method and its superiority over other methods.

2 Background Concepts

2.1 Constant False Alarm Rate Detection

Constant false alarm rate (CFAR) detection is applied in this article to detect AE events caused by leaks. The CFAR detection is a critical aspect of radar signal processing designed to dynamically adjust target detection thresholds in response to varying environmental conditions [23]. In CFAR, cells, or resolution cells, are defined, with a specific cell under test (CUT) selected for target determination. CFAR algorithms calculate the statistical properties of the local environment surrounding the CUT, considering neighboring cells in both range and azimuth. It includes constant false alarm rate-constrained estimation of background noise from the surrounding cells of the CUT, called training cells, but excluding the adjacent cells to the CUT, referred to as guard cells. This comprehensive estimation of background noise allows for the adaptive setting of a detection threshold that maintains a constant probability of false alarms.

Specifically, a configured sliding window includes CUT, guard cells, and training cells as depicted in Fig. 1. The sliding window scans the entire signal with a step equal to the length of CUT for threshold computation detection for each CUT. A CUT is considered to contain a signal if its amplitude exceeds the estimated threshold. The detection threshold for each CUT is determined as follows [23]:

$$T = P_n\left(P_{fa}^{-1/N} - 1\right) \tag{1}$$

where P_n is the sum of samples of training cells, P_{fa} is the constant false alarm rate, and N is the number of training cells. This formula is called cell averaging CFAR (CA-CFAR).

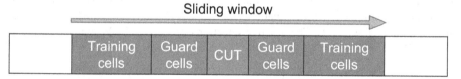

Fig. 1. Components of sliding window in CFAR detection.

2.2 Minimum Entropy Deconvolution

Minimum entropy deconvolution (MED) [22] stands out as a potent signal processing technique meticulously crafted to augment the resolution of signals intricately interwoven with convolutional noise. The core of MED revolves around the design of a finite impulse response (FIR) filter to extract the distinctive features of signals in the form of an impulse. The MED accomplishes this by iteratively fine-tuning the deconvolution process, aiming to maximize the kurtosis of the output signal and, consequently, optimizing its information content.

This concept aligns seamlessly with signals such as the vibrations of rotating machinery or acoustic emissions. However, its true efficacy shines when applied to signals containing only a single impulse, thereby limiting its applicability. To address this limitation, in this research, MED is employed to filter individual AE events detected by CFAR, rather than processing the entire raw signal.

The methodology for implementing the MED-based filter in this context unfolds as follows. We denote $\vec{x} = \begin{bmatrix} x_1\ x_2\ \ldots\ x_N \end{bmatrix}^T$ as the input signal (detected AE event), $\vec{y} = \begin{bmatrix} y_1\ y_2\ \ldots\ y_N \end{bmatrix}^T$ as the output filtered signal, and $\vec{f} = \begin{bmatrix} f_1\ f_2\ \ldots\ f_K \end{bmatrix}^T$ as the impulse response FIR filter. For a causal discrete-time FIR filter, the signal model is represented as in (2), (3):

$$\vec{y} = \vec{f} * \vec{x} = X^T \vec{f} \tag{2}$$

$$X = \begin{bmatrix} x_1\ x_2\ x_3\ \ldots & x_N \\ 0\ x_1\ x_2\ \ldots & x_{N-1} \\ 0\ 0\ x_1\ \ldots & x_{N-2} \\ \vdots\ \vdots\ \vdots\ \ddots & \vdots \\ 0\ 0\ 0\ \ldots\ x_{N-K+1} \end{bmatrix}_{K \times N} \tag{3}$$

The objective of MED is to search for the filter $\vec{f}$ that maximizes the kurtosis of the output signal. This process is formalized in Eq. (4), assuming a zero-mean output $\vec{y}$ [22]:

$$\max_{\vec{f}} \frac{\sum_{n=1}^{N} y_n^4}{\left(\sum_{n=1}^{N} y_n^2 \right)^2} \tag{4}$$

The search process is carried out to find a favorable solution using the Wiggins algorithm [22]. It involves computing the derivative of the kurtosis objective function and then solving the derivative equation with respect to the filter vector $\vec{f}$ iteratively through numerical methods. The iterative selection of $\vec{f}$ derived by Wiggins is outlined in Eq. (5) [22]:

$$\vec{f} = \frac{\sum_{n=1}^{N} y_n^2}{\sum_{n=1}^{N} y_n^4} \left(XX^T \right)^{-1} X \begin{bmatrix} y_1^3\ y_2^3\ \ldots\ y_N^3 \end{bmatrix}^T \tag{5}$$

Accordingly, the initial value of $\vec{f}$ is selected as the centered initial difference filter to compute the initial output $\vec{y}$. Using Eq. (5), the initial $\vec{y}$ is then employed to calculate the updated filter $\vec{f}$, which, in turn, is used to compute a new $\vec{y}$. The termination criteria for this iterative process are commonly defined as a minimum change in filter coefficients between successive iterations [24].

3   Methodology

This section presents the proposed method for addressing the water pipeline leak localization problem. The condition monitoring model utilizes two AE sensors installed at the ends of the pipeline to locate leaks between the two sensors. Figure 2 illustrates the detailed workflow of the implementation steps, which are elaborated as follows:

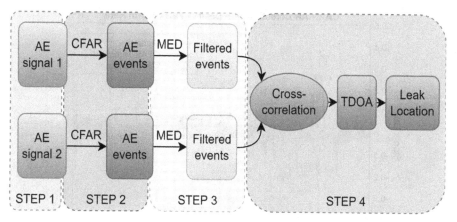

Fig. 2. The workflow of the proposed method.

- Step 1: AE signals are collected from the two AE sensors placed at the ends of the pipeline. It is assumed that the received signals represent the signal at the time the leak occurred.
- Step 2: The CA-CFAR detection algorithm is applied to both received signals to determine the positions of AE events. Specifically, a sliding window is chosen with a CUT size of 1 ms, 4 guard cells (4 ms), and 10 training cells (10 ms). The desired false alarm rate is set to 10^{-6} to ensure the reliability of the detection results. Figure 3 illustrates the use of CA-CFAR for AE event detection, showing an adaptive detection threshold (red line) that accurately identifies AE events, as observed in the grey boxes.
- Step 3: FIR filters based on MED are employed to clean the detected AE events. This is done to reveal the information of the AE signals for accurate cross-correlation calculation. Specifically, filters of length 50 are used for each AE event to find the most suitable filters. Figure 4(a) illustrates the result of using the FIR filter based on MED to clean an AE event, with the optimal filter found in Fig. 4(b). It can be observed that the filtered signal significantly reduces background noise, aiding in minimizing the impact of noise on AE signals and enhancing accuracy for subsequent cross-correlation calculations.
- Step 4: The filtered AE events are input into cross-correlation calculations to determine the TDOA. Specifically, AE events at sensor 1 are cross correlated with neighboring AE events at sensor 2. Neighboring events are defined as those occurring within a time interval not exceeding D/v seconds, where D is the distance between two sensors, and v is the wave propagation velocity ($v = 2600$ m/s in this work). This ensures that the predictions of leak location are positioned between the two sensors. Afterwards, TDOA is determined by the lag time (Δt) where the correlation value is maximum. Finally, the leak location is calculated using the following formula:

$$x = \frac{D - v\Delta t}{2} \tag{6}$$

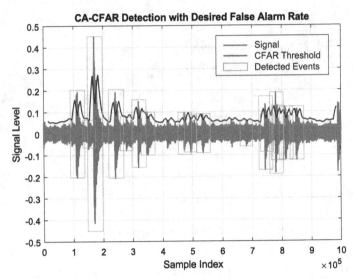

Fig. 3. Illustration of the use of CA-CFAR for AE events detection. (Color figure online)

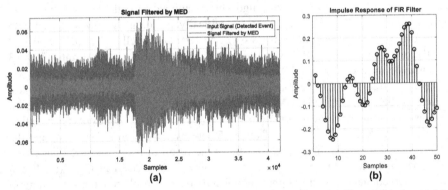

Fig. 4. Illustration of the use of MED for a detected AE event filter: (a) filtered signal, and (b) impulse response of the filter.

4 Experimental Setup

This section details the experimental scenarios conducted to validate the efficacy of the proposed method. Initially, a laboratory-based testbed simulating a water pipeline system was set up, as illustrated in Fig. 5 and Fig. 6. The testbed comprised a pump system and a steel water pipeline. Two R15I-AST AE sensors were strategically placed at the ends of the pipeline, separated by 2.5 m, with specification listed in Table 1. Leakage was simulated by welding perforated screws into the pipeline at a position 1.7 m from sensor 1. A data acquisition (DAQ) module (NI-9223) and a computer were deployed on-site to collect AE signals from the sensors. This experimental setup allows for validation of the proposed leak localization method under realistic conditions. The configuration replicates a simplified yet representative scenario of a water pipeline system, facilitating the performance evaluation of the proposed method.

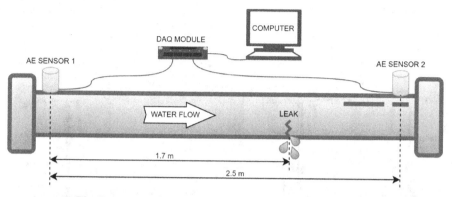

Fig. 5. Experimental testbed for leak simulation in a water pipe.

Table 1. Specification of AE sensors in the testbed.

Parameter	Value	Unit
Peak sensitivity	109	dB
Operating frequency	50 to 400	kHz
Resonant frequency	75	kHz
Directionality	±1.5	dB
Operating temperature	−35 to 75	°C

The data collection scenario unfolded as follows: initially, the pipeline was filled with water to achieve the desired pressure. Subsequently, leaks were activated, and data acquisition commenced for 100 s at a sampling rate of 1 million samples per second (1 MHz). Two leak sizes of 0.3 mm and 0.5 mm, along with two preset pressures of 13 and 18 bar, were considered. Therefore, four datasets were obtained, denoted as follows: 0.3 mm at 13 bar (313), 0.3 mm at 18 bar (318), 0.5 mm at 13 bar (513), and 0.5 mm at 18 bar (518).

Validation experiments were performed on the collected datasets, and evaluation criteria included the estimation of probability density and relative error. To estimate the probability density of predicted leak locations, a kernel smoothing function was employed based on kernel density estimation (KDE) methods [25]. The kernel density estimator can be defined as follows [25]:

$$f(x) = \frac{1}{Nh} \sum_{k=1}^{N} G\left(\frac{x - x_k}{h}\right) \tag{7}$$

where x is the leak location variable, N is the number of observed (predicted) leak locations x_k, G is the Gaussian kernel smoothing function [26], and h is the bandwidth

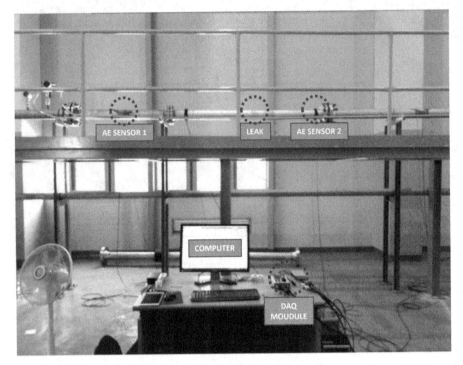

Fig. 6. Actual testbed system in laboratory.

determined based on the Silverman rule of thumb [27]. Subsequently, the final leak location was determined at the point with the highest density from the estimated probability density. This value was then used to compute the relative error according to the following formula:

$$\delta\% = \frac{|x_{leak} - \hat{x}|}{D} \times 100\% \qquad (8)$$

where x_{leak} is the true leak location, $\hat{x}$ is the predicted leak location, and D is the distance between two sensors.

5 Results and Discussion

This section presents the results of experimental verification of the effectiveness of the proposed method, including predictive outcomes and comparisons with other popular methods. Figure 7 illustrates the predicted leak locations through a histogram of leak location predictions across four datasets. In each case, the estimated probability density is depicted to identify the concentration of predictions. Accordingly, the proposed method suggests leak positions extremely close to the actual leaks, with the highest density consistently above 1, near the position of 1.7 m. This observation demonstrates the efficacy of our method in accurately pinpointing leak locations. This achievement is attributed to our approach fully leveraging the strengths of traditional methods. Additionally, all predictions fall within the range of 0 to 2.5 m, as the cross-correlation is constrained to select event pairs within proximity.

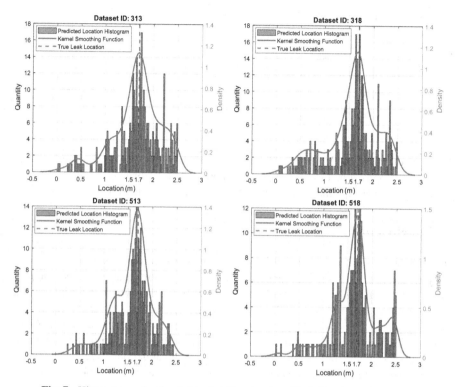

Fig. 7. Histogram and estimated probability density of leak location predictions.

To reinforce the effectiveness of the proposed method, comparative experiments were conducted. The examined methods include: (i) traditional cross-correlation (traditional CC) by calculating cross-correlation on every 10 ms of signal to determine TDOA, and (ii) the proposed method without MED filter named CFAR-CC method. Comparing these methods affirms the superiority of the proposed approach across different aspects.

Table 2 presents a comparative analysis of three leak localization methodologies across four datasets. The traditional CC method displays varying leak position errors ranging from 2.4% to 18.4%, with the highest error occurring in dataset 313. CFAR-CC demonstrates enhanced accuracy, with errors ranging from 1.6% to 5.6%, underscoring the significant improvement resulting from the combination of CFAR and CC due to selective filtering during cross-correlation computation. Notably, the proposed method consistently surpasses the others by providing precise leak positions (1.68 m to 1.70 m) with minimal errors (0.0% to 0.8%). This achievement is attributed to the proposed approach, which integrates both CFAR and CC while leveraging a MED filter to enhance the

Table 2. Comparison between methods for leak localization on pipeline.

Method	Prediction Results	Dataset ID: 313	Dataset ID: 318	Dataset ID: 513	Dataset ID: 518
Traditional CC method	Location (m)	2.16	1.96	1.64	2.08
	Error (%)	18.4%	10.4%	2.4%	15.2%
CFAR-CC method	Location (m)	1.84	1.76	1.66	1.82
	Error (%)	5.6%	2.4%	1.6%	4.8%
Proposed method	Location (m)	1.70	1.68	1.68	1.69
	Error (%)	0.0%	0.8%	0.8%	0.4%

efficiency of cross-correlation calculations. These findings underscore the superior accuracy of the proposed method, highlighting its potential for advancing leak localization precision on water pipelines in comparison to alternative methodologies.

6 Conclusion

This paper introduced a novel and effective method for leak localization in water pipelines using acoustic emissions monitoring and cross-correlation of acoustic events. The proposed method addressed limitations inherent in traditional approaches by integrating and leveraging their respective advantages. Inheriting the merits of both CFAR and CC methods, the suggested approach demonstrated enhanced leak localization. Additionally, FIR filters based on MED were adeptly employed to appropriately enhance the accuracy of computational efficiency. Experimental validations were conducted on a laboratory testbed, and the results substantiated the effectiveness and precision of the proposed method in predicting leak locations. When compared to traditional CC and CFAR-CC, our method exhibited superior accuracy. This positions our proposed method as a promising approach for potential application in the industry.

Acknowledgments. This paper was supported by the Korea Industrial Complex Corporation grant funded by the Korea Government (MOTIE) (SG20220905). This work was also supported by the Korea Institute of Energy Technology Evaluation and Planning (KETEP) grant funded by the Korea government (MOTIE) (RS-2023-00232515, Development of life prediction safety technology and hydrogen embrittlement estimation of LNG pipe mixed hydrogen).

Disclosure of Interests. The authors have no competing interests to declare that are relevant to the content of this article.

References

1. Ahmad, Z., Nguyen, T.K., Rai, A., Kim, J.M.: Industrial fluid pipeline leak detection and localization based on a multiscale Mann-Whitney test and acoustic emission event tracking. Mech. Syst. Signal Process. **189** (2023). https://doi.org/10.1016/j.ymssp.2022.110067

2. Nguyen, D.T., Nguyen, T.K., Ahmad, Z., Kim, J.M.: A reliable pipeline leak detection method using acoustic emission with time difference of arrival and Kolmogorov–Smirnov test. Sensors **23**, 9296 (2023). https://doi.org/10.3390/S23239296

3. Ho, M., El-Borgi, S., Patil, D., Song, G.: Inspection and monitoring systems subsea pipelines: a review paper. Struct. Health Monit. **19**, 606–645 (2020). https://doi.org/10.1177/147592171 9837718

4. Romano, M.: Review of techniques for optimal placement of pressure and flow sensors for leak/burst detection and localisation in water distribution systems. In: Scozzari, A., Mounce, S., Han, D., Soldovieri, F., Solomatine, D. (eds.) ICT for Smart Water Systems: Measurements and Data Science. THEC, vol. 102, pp. 27–63. Springer, Cham (2019). https://doi.org/10.1007/698_2019_405

5. Wan, X., Kuhanestani, P.K., Farmani, R., Keedwell, E.: Literature review of data analytics for leak detection in water distribution networks: a focus on pressure and flow smart sensors. J. Water Resour. Plan. Manag. **148** (2022). https://doi.org/10.1061/(ASCE)WR.1943-5452. 0001597

6. Kazeminasab, S., Sadeghi, N., Janfaza, V., Razavi, M., Ziyadidegan, S., Banks, M.K.: Localization, mapping, navigation, and inspection methods in in-pipe robots: a review. IEEE Access **9**, 162035–162058 (2021). https://doi.org/10.1109/ACCESS.2021.3130233

7. Aitken, J.M., et al.: Simultaneous localization and mapping for inspection robots in water and sewer pipe networks: a review. IEEE Access **9**, 140173–140198 (2021). https://doi.org/10.1109/ACCESS.2021.3115981

8. Siddique, M.F., Ahmad, Z., Kim, J.M.: Pipeline leak diagnosis based on leak-augmented scalograms and deep learning. Eng. Appl. Comput. Fluid Mech. **17**, 2225577 (2023). https://doi.org/10.1080/19942060.2023.2225577

9. Zhang, L., Zhang, T., Chen, E., Ozevin, D., Li, H.: Phased acoustic emission sensor array for localizing radial and axial positions of defects in hollow structures. Measurement **151**, 107223 (2020). https://doi.org/10.1016/j.measurement.2019.107223

10. Fares, A., Tijani, I.A., Rui, Z., Zayed, T.: Leak detection in real water distribution networks based on acoustic emission and machine learning. Environ. Technol. **44**, 3850–3866 (2023). https://doi.org/10.1080/09593330.2022.2074320

11. Banjara, N.K., Sasmal, S., Voggu, S.: Machine learning supported acoustic emission technique for leakage detection in pipelines. Int. J. Pressure Vessels Piping **188**, 104243 (2020). https://doi.org/10.1016/j.ijpvp.2020.104243

12. Hu, Z., Tariq, S., Zayed, T.: A comprehensive review of acoustic based leak localization method in pressurized pipelines. Mech. Syst. Signal Process. **161**, 107994 (2021). https://doi.org/10.1016/j.ymssp.2021.107994

13. Wang, S., et al.: Continuous leak detection and location through the optimal mother wavelet transform to AE signal. J. Pipeline Syst. Eng. Pract. **11** (2020). https://doi.org/10.1061/(ASCE)PS.1949-1204.0000467

14. Negm, A., Ma, X., Aggidis, G.: Review of leakage detection in water distribution networks. IOP Conf. Ser. Earth Environ. Sci. **1136**, 012052 (2023). https://doi.org/10.1088/1755-1315/1136/1/012052

15. Zhang, Z., Zhang, L., Fu, M., Ozevin, D., Yuan, H.: Study on leak localization for buried gas pipelines based on an acoustic method. Tunn. Undergr. Space Technol. **120**, 104247 (2022). https://doi.org/10.1016/j.tust.2021.104247

16. Quy, T.B., Kim, J.-M.: Leak localization in industrial-fluid pipelines based on acoustic emission burst monitoring. Measurement **151**, 107150 (2020). https://doi.org/10.1016/j.measurement.2019.107150

17. Angelopoulos, K., Glentis, G.O.: Cross-correlation assisted and time-difference-of-arrival based leak source localization on fluid-filled pipelines. In: 2022 11th International Conference on Modern Circuits and Systems Technologies (MOCAST), pp. 1–6. IEEE (2022). https://doi.org/10.1109/MOCAST54814.2022.9837640

18. Hassan, Md.M., Khan, Md.T.I., Hasemura, Y., Islam, Md.M.: Performance investigation of two AE source location techniques on a planar multilayer structure. Int. J. Acoust. Vibr. **25**, 226–235 (2020). https://doi.org/10.20855/ijav.2020.25.21635

19. Miller, R.K., Hill, E.K., Moore, P.O.: Nondestructive Testing Handbook: Acoustic Emission Testing (2005)

20. Xiao, Q., Li, J., Sun, J., Feng, H., Jin, S.: Natural-gas pipeline leak location using variational mode decomposition analysis and cross-time–frequency spectrum. Measurement (Lond). **124**, 163–172 (2018). https://doi.org/10.1016/j.measurement.2018.04.030

21. Richards, M.A.: Fundamentals of Radar Signal Processing, 3rd edn. McGraw Hill LLC (2022)

22. Wiggins, R.A.: Minimum entropy deconvolution. Geoexploration **16**, 21–35 (1978). https://doi.org/10.1016/0016-7142(78)90005-4

23. Scharf, L.L., Demeure, C.: Statistical Signal Processing: Detection, Estimation, and Time Series Analysis. Addison-Wesley Publishing Company (1991)

24. McDonald, G.L., Zhao, Q., Zuo, M.J.: Maximum correlated Kurtosis deconvolution and application on gear tooth chip fault detection. Mech. Syst. Signal Process. **33**, 237–255 (2012). https://doi.org/10.1016/J.YMSSP.2012.06.010

25. Botev, Z.I., Grotowski, J.F., Kroese, D.P.: Kernel density estimation via diffusion **38**, 2916–2957 (2010). https://doi.org/10.1214/10-AOS799

26. Hastie, T., Tibshirani, R., Friedman, J.: Kernel Smoothing Methods, pp. 191–218 (2009). https://doi.org/10.1007/978-0-387-84858-7_6

27. Saxena, A., et al.: Metrics for evaluating performance of prognostic techniques. In: 2008 International Conference on Prognostics and Health Management, PHM 2008. (2008). https://doi.org/10.1109/PHM.2008.4711436

Maintaining the Quality of Evolving Ontologies in the Agriculture Domain: Challenges and a Specialised Evaluation Tool

Shyama Wilson[1,2](✉) 🆔, Athula Ginige[1] 🆔, and Jeevani Goonetillake[3] 🆔

[1] Western Sydney University, Parramatta, NSW, Australia
22085197@student.westernsydney.edu.au
[2] Uva Wellassa University, Badulla, Sri Lanka
[3] University of Colombo School of Computing, Colombo 00700, Sri Lanka

Abstract. The development of well-engineered quality ontologies is crucial to ensure capabilities of ontologies such as enhanced communication, knowledge reuse, and knowledge analytical capabilities. Ontology engineers conduct comprehensive evaluations to ensure ontology quality by utilising multiple tools and approaches. However, the ontology evaluators encountered challenges in choosing appropriate evaluation tools and approaches, especially in the context of a decision support system where knowledge accuracy, completeness and relevancy are highly required. This study discusses the challenges encountered when assessing ontology quality, primarily considering the agriculture domain and highlights anomalies in the existing evaluation tools. Consequently, the study developed a tool which addresses the identified limitations in the existing tools. This tool includes measures for assessing crucial quality characteristics related to agriculture ontologies, such as complexity, completeness, consistency, modularity, and comprehensibility. Further, it supports developers in gaining valuable insights to mitigate the issues associated with these key quality characteristics of ontologies.

Keywords: Ontology Evaluation · Agriculture · Quality Characteristics

1 Introduction

Ontologies in computing support represent domain knowledge so that they can be used for multiple purposes. For instance, ontologies support knowledge reuse within a specific domain promoting efficient and consistent knowledge representation [1, 2]. By making domain assumptions explicit, ontologies help clarify underlying concepts and reduce ambiguity. Moreover, ontology can be used as a knowledge base in decision-support systems [1, 2]. Overall, ontology development facilitates comprehensive representation and systematic understanding of domain knowledge, leading to multiple benefits such as enhanced communication, knowledge reuse and inferencing [1].

Developing a well-engineered ontology that guarantees quality is crucial to achieving the aforementioned benefits. Therefore, ontology engineers ensure to conduct comprehensive ontology evaluation as a part of the ontology development process. There are

O. Gervasi et al. (Eds.): ICCSA 2024, LNCS 14814, pp. 273–292, 2024.
https://doi.org/10.1007/978-3-031-64608-9_18

several quality characteristics to be considered when performing ontology evaluation [3, 4]. Some of them are *compliance, complexity, consistency, completeness, modularity, accuracy, relevancy, timeliness, efficiency* and *adaptability* [3, 4]. It is worth noting that all characteristics commonly defined for ontologies are not equally required to be assessed when checking ontology quality [4]. It is sufficient to evaluate the characteristics that are relevant and essential to the considered context of an ontology [5].

Moreover, many tools have been introduced to measure the characteristics that simplify the evaluation process. Notable examples include OOPs! [6], RDF validator [7], OWL validator [8], and OntoMetric [9], which are accessible online for assessing the quality of an ontology. Additionally, OntoQA [10], Domain Ontology Ranking System (DoORS) [11], and OntoKeeper [12] provide a set of measures to evaluate ontology quality characteristics. However, choosing one tool from a list of tools to evaluate a particular ontology is challenging. This is because each tool is limited to a certain set of characteristics. On the other hand, if one tool is considered, it does not comprise all the measurements needed to assess the essential characteristics associated with a given ontology. As a result, multiple tools may need to be used if a single tool does not cover all the required measures for assessing all essential ontology characteristics. Not only that, using multiple tools for the evaluation becomes difficult when doing quality evaluation of evolving ontologies.

We encountered these challenges while assessing ontologies developed for the agriculture domain [4]. To elaborate, we designed a decision support system for agriculture aimed at assisting farmers in making timely and informed decisions. The ontology serves as the primary knowledge source of this system, supplying the necessary information to assist farmers in their decision-making process. Given its critical role, ensuring the quality of the ontology is paramount. This led us to undertake a thorough and comprehensive quality evaluation. Consequently, we started the quality evaluation process using the OOPS! tool that supports the detection of common pitfalls such as *incorrect inverse relationships, isolated classes and properties*, and *incorrect is-a relationships*. When using OOPS!, it was realised that some measures related to complexity (see Table 2) cannot be evaluated [4]. To this end, OntoMetric was used to assess those measures. However, when calculating measures using OntoMetric, it was identified that OntoMetric does not consider the inferred entities (i.e., concepts, relationships, and instances) which can be generated by reasoning the existing ontology axioms. Consequently, some measures such as *concept richness, connected classes*, and *instance richness/ instance usage* were calculated manually. Even though we evaluated ontologies using multiple tools and with manual techniques, as mentioned above, it became difficult to perform iterative quality assessments when multiple versions of an ontology were released. To address this, we developed a tool named OntoQuaL to assess ontology characteristics, primarily taking agricultural ontologies into account. This minimizes the use of multiple tools and addresses certain anomalies found in the existing tools. Not only that any domain that considers the same quality characteristics (see Sect. 3) can utilise OntoQuaL to assess the quality.

The subsequent section reviews the existing tools and approaches (see Sect. 2). Section 3 presents the developed tool and discusses the algorithms implemented in the tool including its experiments (see Sect. 4). Finally, Sect. 5 concludes the findings of this study.

2 Related Work

As presented in the previous surveys [13], a plethora of ontology evaluation tools and approaches have been discussed in the existing work. However, only a few of them are in practice. Thus, this review initially highlights the most common tools and later discusses some approaches specifically developed to evaluate ontologies in the agriculture domain.

OOPS! [6], OntoMetrics [9], OWL Validator [8], RDF Validator [7] and protégé plugins [14] are the readily available tools for ontology evaluation. OOPS! [6] is a comprehensive ontology evaluation tool designed to identify potential pitfalls and issues in ontologies. Primarily, it detects common modelling errors and inconsistencies, providing valuable feedback to ontology developers. Although OOPS! can identify the key problems in an ontology, it does not consider the axioms that can be deduced from explicitly defined axioms. As a result, some issues flagged by OOPS may be nonsensical and unsuitable. For example, OOPS! may highlight missing domains and ranges for specific relationships, but this may not be valid when these domains and ranges can be inferred through their inverse relationships.

OntoMetrics [9] focuses on quantitative measures for ontology evaluation. Mainly, the tool provides numerical assessments that enable developers to make decisions about their ontologies. However, the drawback of this tool is that there is no guidance for evaluators to understand what characteristics the measures are related to. Thus, this tool is good only for ontology developers who have a sound understanding of the provided measures, this may be lacking among new developers. OWL Validator [8] is a web-based tool that specialises in checking ontologies against the OWL (Web Ontology Language) standard. It ensures compliance with OWL specifications, highlighting syntactic errors and offering suggestions for improvement. The tool is particularly useful for ontology developers working with OWL-based ontologies, ensuring adherence to OWL standards. Similarly, the RDF validator [7] is a crucial tool in the realm of Semantic Web technologies. It ensures the compliance and integrity of Resource Description Framework (RDF) data, identifying syntax errors and adherence to RDF specifications. When considering the OWL and RDF validators, these tools have been developed specifically focusing only on the *compliance* quality characteristic [3, 4].

Additionally, there is a quality assurance framework for ontologies named OntoQA [10]. It provides a set of measures related to multiple ontology characteristics, including correctness, coherence, and relevance. However, based on our observation, the tool is not available for the public to use either as an online or standalone tool. Concerning the agriculture domain, the researchers [4, 15] have presented frameworks to evaluate agricultural ontologies. Anat et al. [15] proposed a framework that supports ontology evaluators in selecting appropriate evaluation methods and characteristics to evaluate their agricultural ontologies. On the other hand, Wilson et al. [4] have proposed a streamlined approach to identify ontology quality characteristics and their measures based on the ontology purpose and the considered context. This approach is a general approach that can be applied to any domain. The researchers [4] have demonstrated the application of this approach by using a scenario in the agriculture domain.

To sum up, the discussed tools primarily support assessing ontology characteristics and measures irrespective of the domains in which ontologies are developed. Although they can be considered rich tools, there are some anomalies which can occur when evaluating domain-specific ontologies like agriculture. For instance, the mentioned tools do not support calculating some measures such as *concept richness, connected classes and instance richness/ instance usage* which are essential to consider when evaluating agricultural ontologies [4]. On the other hand, they do not also consider inferred entities (i.e., concepts, relationships, and instances) when calculating measures.

Not only that the existing tools provide a list of values for measures, making it difficult for evaluators to understand what characteristics the measures are related to. To this end, we developed a tool by addressing the mentioned gaps to evaluate the ontologies specifically concerning the essential characteristics and measures relevant to decision support systems, primarily in Agriculture.

3   The OntoQuaL Tool

The tool named OntoQuaL was created to assess the quality of an ontology. Mainly, OntoQuaL supports measuring quality characteristics such as *complexity, modularity, consistency, completeness,* and *comprehensibility.* A set of algorithms was implemented using OWL API [16] to calculate measures related to these characteristics (see Sects. 3.1–3.5). The algorithms primarily consider both explicitly declared and inferred elements while computing the measures. The existing tools, including OOPS!, OntoMetric, and OntoQA, do not have this feature as revealed through the literature review. In this regard, we take a simple example into account. Assume an OWL ontology consists of two concepts: *crop* and *disease*, which are connected with a relationship "*affects*" (i.e., the *disease affects crop*) and the inverse of it is "*isaffectedBy*" (see Fig. 1). Furthermore, assume the below-mentioned definitions have been explicitly defined in the ontology.

- *ObjectPropertyDomain (:affects:disease)*
- *ObjectPropertyRange (:affects:crop)*
- *InverseObjectProperties(:affect:isAffectedBy)*

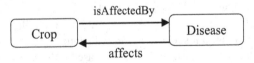

Fig. 1. Relationship between Crop and Disease

Although the domain and range of "*isAffectedby*" relation have not been defined explicitly, it can be inferred through a reasoner that *crop* and *disease* are the domain and range of the relationship "*isAffectedby*" respectively. However, when evaluating such an ontology either through OOPS! or OntoMetrics, the tools detected that *isAffectedBy* is an *isolated object property* without a domain and range. This is because the tools do not consider inferred relationships. This may convey that ontology developers need to explicitly define all the definitions in the ontology. Thus, in turn, ontology can consist of many redundant definitions (i.e., failure of conciseness). Compared to the existing tools, OntoQuaL computes the measures of characteristics by considering such inferred relationships. Additionally, evaluating the necessary and essential quality characteristics which are relevant to a particular domain is a key requirement in quality assessment. Thus, OntoQuaL assesses the most suitable characteristics that are required for ontologies in a decision support system [4, 17]. Furthermore, the tool presents *measures'* results with respect to each quality characteristic, making it simple for users to grasp the state of characteristics separately. Figure 2 presents OntoQuaL with measure values generated for an ontology and Table 1 illustrates the implemented measures and the associated characteristics. The subsequent sections discuss each measure in detail. The implemented tool and the documents have been shared in the GitHub repository and it can be found at https://github.com/shyamaW/OntoQuaL.

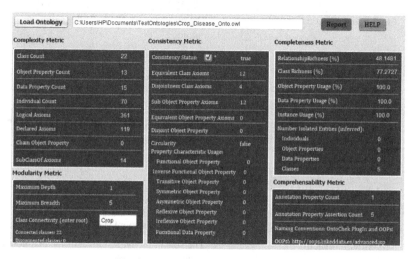

Fig. 2. Prototype of the OntoQuaL tool

3.1 Complexity Measures

Complexity refers to "*the extent of how complicated the ontology is and the measures of it consider the properties of an ontology structure*" [13]. These measures are often useful to observe the dispersion of an ontology [18, 19] and to track the evolution of ontologies easily. Moreover, the measures support the detection of entities (i.e., concepts, relationships, and attributes) which are defined in the requirement document/frame of reference but are not included in an ontology. In addition to that, these measures should be calculated to assess some other measures of *conciseness, completeness* and *consistency* [4]. For instance, *class precision* is a measure of *consistency*. It should be calculated by dividing *the number of correctly covered classes in an ontology* by the *number of classes defined* in an ontology (i.e., class count). Then, the total *class count* is required to perform this *class precision*. Similarly, we recognised the essential complexity measures and automated them with the support of OWL API (see Table 2). Then, they were made available in OntoQuaL for quick calculation.

Table 1. The measures with the corresponding ontology characteristics.

ID	Measure	Description
	Complexity Measures	
M1	Class count	The number of classes defined in an ontology
M2	Object property count	The number of object properties defined in an ontology
M3	Data property count	The number of data properties defined in an ontology
M4	Individual count	The number of individuals defined in an ontology
M5	Logical axioms	The number of logical axioms defined in an ontology
M6	Declared axioms	The number of declared axioms defined in an ontology
M7	Chain object property count	The number of chain object properties defined in an ontology
M8	Subclass axioms	The number of subclass axioms defined in an ontology
	Modularity Measures	
M9	Maximum depth	The size of the longest branch of the taxonomic structure (i.e., is_a) of an ontology
M10	Maximum breadth	The size of the largest level of the taxonomic structure (i.e., is_a) of an ontology
M11	Class connectivity	The number of classes connected with the root class/defined class of an ontology
	Consistency Measures	
M12	Consistency status	Logical consistency and syntax compliance of an ontology
M13	Equivalent class axioms	The number of equivalent class axioms defined in an ontology
M14	Disjoint class axioms	The number of disjoint class axioms defined in an ontology

(continued)

Table 1. (*continued*)

ID	Measure	Description
M15	Subobject property axioms	The number of sub-object properties axioms defined in an ontology
M16	Equivalent object property axioms	The number of equivalent object properties axioms defined in an ontology
M17	Disjoint object property axioms	The number of disjoint object properties axioms defined in an ontology
M18	Circularity status	The number of circles in the taxonomic structure in an ontology
M19	Functional object property	The number of functional object properties axioms defined in an ontology
M20	Inverse functional object property	The number of inverse object properties axioms defined in an ontology
M21	Transitive object property	The number of transitive object properties axioms defined in an ontology
M22	Symmetric object property	The number of symmetric object properties axioms defined in an ontology
M23	Asymmetric object property	The number of Asymmetric object properties axioms defined in an ontology
M24	Reflexive object property	The number of reflexive object properties axioms defined in an ontology
M25	Irreflexive object property	The number of Irreflexive object properties axioms defined in an ontology
M26	Functional data property	The number of functional data properties axioms defined in an ontology
	Completeness Measures	
M27	Relationship richness	The ratio of the number of non-inheritance relationships in an ontology
M28	Class richness	The ratio of the number of populated (explicit/implicit) classes in an ontology
M29	Object property usage	The ratio of the number of object properties (explicit/implicit) with DOMAIN and RANGE in an ontology
M30	Data property usage	The ratio of the number of data properties (explicit/implicit) with DOMAIN and RANGE in an ontology
M31	Instance usage	The ratio of the number of individuals has class type (explicit/implicit) in an ontology

(*continued*)

Table 1. (*continued*)

ID	Measure	Description
M32	Isolated individuals	The number of individuals has no class type (explicit/implicit) in an ontology
M33	Isolated object properties	The number of object properties has no DOMAIN OR RANGE (explicit/implicit) in an ontology
M34	Isolated data properties	The number of data properties has no DOMAIN OR RANGE (explicit/implicit) in an ontology
M35	Isolated classes	The number of classes has no individuals (explicit/implicit) in an ontology
	Comprehensibility Measures	
M36	Annotation property count	The number of annotation properties in an ontology
M37	Annotation property assertion count	The number of annotation assertion properties in an ontology

Table 2. Complexity measures

Measure	OWL Function
Class count	Ontology.getClassesInSignature().size();
Object property count	Ontology.getObjectPropertiesInSignature().size();
Data property count	Ontology.getDataPropertiesInSignature().size();
Individual count	Ontology.getIndividualsInSignature().size();
Logical Axioms	Ontology.getLogicalAxiomCount();
Declared Axioms	Ontology.getAxioms(AxiomType.DECLARATION).size();
Chain object property count	Ontology.getAxioms(AxiomType.SUB_PROPERTY_CHAIN_OF).size();
Subclass axioms	Ontology.getAxiomCount(AxiomType.SUB_CLASSES_OF);

3.2 Modularity Measures

Modularity refers to *the degree to which the ontology is composed of discrete subsets (i.e., modules of a graph, sub-graphs) such that a change to one component has a minimal impact on the other components* [13]. Mainly, the measures of it are associated with the ontology taxonomy (i.e., IS_A graph). On the other hand, these measures are good predictors of ontology reliability [18, 19]. The most discussed two measures are the maximum *depth* and *breadth* of the taxonomic structure of an ontology [20, 21]. These measures were implemented for our evaluation (see Table 3). Notably, OWL API has not provided functions to calculate the depth and breadth of an ontology. Thus, for our study, the algorithms were implemented as illustrated in Fig. 3 and Fig. 4 to determine those two measures by assuming ontology is a graph and taxonomic classes as nodes. In addition to that, *class connectivity* was implemented to observe the connected classes with the given class or root class, either using taxonomic: IS_A or non-taxonomic relationships. For instance, if the ontology presented in Fig. 5 is considered, assuming we want to identify the connected classes with the *crop* class, then, we can observe that *Vegetable, Disease,* and *Control Methods* are the classes connected with the crop class. Additionally, it can be observed that *ApplicationEvent* and *TimeOfApplication* have not been connected with the *crop* class. This connectivity can be identified using the implemented measures (see Fig. 3 and Fig. 4). Mainly, this is more useful in cases where an ontology is large and complex, making it difficult for a developer to understand how cohesively coupled (i.e., well-connected) an ontology's classes are to their root class or specified class. Moreover, it supports identifying the modules that an ontology can be decomposed.

Algorithm 1 Maximum depth of an ontology
```
1:    Data: Root Node: OWL Thing in OWL ontology
2:    Result: Number of classes in the longest path/branch
3:    visited ← NULL
4:    depth ← 0
5:    maxDepth ← 0
6:    circularityClass ← NULL
7:    MAX_DEPTH (root);
8:
9:    function MAX_DEPTH (root)
10:       classList ← get adjacent connected sub-classes of the root
          node
11:       if classList is EMPTY then
12:           Message: Empty Class List
13:       else
14:           for each class of classList do
15:               DFS (class)
16:               if maxDepth ≤ depth then
17:                   maxDepth ← depth
18:               end if
19:           end for
20:       end if
21:       return maxDepth
22:   end function
23:
24:   function DFS (class)
25:       if visited NOT contain the class then
26:           add class to the visited list
27:           depth++
28:           classList ← get adjacent connected sub-classes of the cur-
              rent class
29:           for each class of classList do
30:               DFS(class)
31:           end for
32:       else
33:           Message: No new subclasses in the list and
              CIRCULARITY is dete Algorithm 01 – maximum depth of
              an ontology cted
```

Algorithm 2 Maximum breadth of an ontology
```
1:    Data: Root Node: OWL Thing in OWL ontology
2:    Result: Number of classes in the widest path/branch
3:    visited ← NULL
4:    breadth ← 0
5:    maxBreadth ← 0
6:    subBranchClasses ← NULL
7:    circularityClass ← NULL
8:    MAX_DEPTH (root);
9:
10:   function MAX_BREADTH (class)
11:       if visited NOT contain the class then
12:           classList ← get adjacent connected sub-classes of
              the class
13:           if classList is EMPTY then
14:               Message: Empty Class List
15:           else
16:               breadth ← the number of classes in the classList
17:               if maxBreadth≤ depth then
18:                   maxBreadth ← depth
19:               end if
20:               subBranchClasses.add(classList)
21:               for each class of subbranchClasses do
22:                   MAX_BREADTH(class)
23:               end for
24:           end if
25:       else
26:           No new subclasses in the List and
              CIRCULARITY is detected
27:           circularityClass.add(class);
28:       end if
29:       return maxBreadth
30:   end function
```

Fig. 3. Algorithm 01 – maximum depth of an ontology

Fig. 4. Algorithm 02: maximum breadth of an ontology

Table 3. Modularity measures

Measure	OWL Function/Algorithm[1]
Maximum Depth	Algorithm 01 (see Fig. 3)
Maximum Breadth	Algorithm 02 (see Fig. 4)
Class Connectivity	The same algorithm: Algorithm 01 (see Fig. 3) was implemented by considering both taxonomic and non-taxonomic relationships

[1]Latex file of the algorithms: https://github.com/shyamaW/OntoQuaL/blob/main/Thesis_Algori thms.pdf.

3.3 Consistency Measures

Internal consistency refers to *the extent to which the ontology is free of logical contradictions with respect to particular knowledge representation* [13]. Logical contradictions can be detected easily by using reasoners. However, we recognised that some measures, as listed in Table 4, affect both internal and external consistency. For instance, As highlighted in [4, 13] for agriculture ontologies, defining *functional object property, transitive object property, equivalent object property*, and *disjointness* are required to produce a consistent answer for queries.

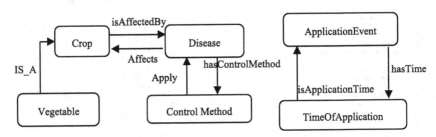

Fig. 5. Snapshot of a crop ontology

Accordingly, the measures in Table 4 were implemented to determine the OWL properties such as *functional, transitive, symmetric, inverse*, and *reflexive*. These provide valuable insights regarding ontology consistency. Moreover, the researchers in [6] have shown that the *circularity* of the ontology taxonomic structure causes inconsistencies and makes results undecidable. Therefore, observing the *circularity* is significant and it also has been included as a measure of consistency (see Table 4).

Table 4. Consistency measures

Measure	OWL Function/Algorithm
Consistency Status	reasoner = hermitreasonerFactory.createReasoner(Ontology); reasoner.isConsistent();
Equivalent class axioms	Ontology.getAxiomCount(AxiomType.EQUIVALENT_CLASSES);
Disjoint class axioms	Ontology.getAxiomCount(AxiomType.DISJOINT_CLASSES);
Sub object property axioms	Ontology.getAxiomCount(AxiomType.SUB_OBJECT_PROPERTY);
Equivalent object property axioms	Ontology.getAxiomCount(AxiomType.EQUIVALENT_OBJECT_PROPERTIES);
Disjoint object property axioms	Ontology.getAxiomCount(AxiomType.DISJOINT_OBJECT_PROPERTIES);
Circularity Status	Algorithm 01 / Algorithm 02 were used to detect the circularity of an ontology (see Fig. 3 & Fig. 4 circularityClass.add (class))
Functional object property	Ontology.getAxiomCount(AxiomType.FUNCTIONAL_OBJECT_PROPERTY);
Inverse functional object property	Ontology.getAxiomCount(AxiomType.INVERSE_FUNCTIONAL_OBJECT_PROPERTY);
Transitive object property	Ontology.getAxiomCount(AxiomType.TRANSITIVE_OBJECT_PROPERTY);
Symmetric object property	Ontology.getAxiomCount(AxiomType.SYMMETRIC_OBJECT_PROPERTY);
Asymmetric object property	Ontology.getAxiomCount(AxiomType.ASYMMETRIC_OBJECT_PROPERTY);
Reflexive object property	Ontology.getAxiomCount(AxiomType.REFLEXIVE_OBJECT_PROPERTY);
Irreflexive object property	Ontology.getAxiomCount(AxiomType.IRREFLEXIVE_OBJECT_PROPERTY);
Functional data property	Ontology.getAxiomCount(AxiomType.FUNCTIONAL_DATA_PROPERTY);

3.4 Completeness Measures

Incomplete definitions of entities such as *concepts (i.e., classes), relationships (object properties), attributes (data properties),* and *instances (individuals)* were considered as a set of indicators for ontology structural incompleteness. This incompleteness is usually caused by errors on the part of ontology developers. The tools OOPS! [6] and OntoMetric [9] consider multiple measures related to this incompleteness. For instance, OOPS! supports identifying the *incomplete domains and ranges* of object properties of an ontology. OntoMetric helps identify measures such as *attribute richness* (i.e., the ratio of the number of attributes defined for a class), *relationship richness* (i.e., the ratio of the number of relationships that are being used by instances of a class in an ontology), and *class richness* (i.e., the ratio of the number classes used). However, some measures (see Table 5), which are important to determine structural completeness, have not been considered in the mentioned tools. On the other hand, as exemplified at the beginning of the section, the existing tools calculate the measures without considering the entities/axioms which can be inferred from the declared entities/axioms in an ontology. Thus, the results of the measures provided through the existing tools are meaningless and insufficient to make a decision about completeness. The measures of completeness that we recognised are listed in Table 5 and the subsequent paragraphs explain the importance of determining those measures.

Relationship Richness (RR) determines the diversity of non-hierarchical and hierarchical relationships. For instance, if *RR* is close to zero, then it implies that an ontology consists of more hierarchical relationships than the other type. In contrast, if RR is close to one, it indicates an ontology consists of more non-hierarchical relationships. Then, this measure supports developers to understand how well the different types of relationships are included in the ontology.

Class Richness determines the ratio of classes that are populated implicitly or explicitly in an ontology. This helps detect the classes which have not been used and isolated. Accordingly, developers can identify the non-populated classes in an ontology. *Object property usage* determines the ratio of the relationships that are connected with classes. For instance, if we consider the *"affect"* relationship between *disease* and *crop* classes (see Fig. 1), then, in an ontology, *disease* and *crop* should be defined as domain and range of *"affect"* respectively in order to connect the two concepts. Otherwise, they (domain/range) should be inferred through the other relationships. If a relationship does not contain a domain or range, it can be considered as an isolated relationship disconnected from the ontology. Thus, this *Object property usage* measure can be used to assess the completeness of relationships within an ontology.

Data property usage considers whether class attributes in an ontology have the domains and ranges (literals). This measure supports identifying the number of attributes defined for classes. *Instance usage* determines the individual completeness of an ontology. For example, if an ontology consists of individuals without a class, then, those individuals would be considered as either non-relevant individuals or incompletely defined individuals. Thus, *Instance usage* supports developers to track isolated individuals without a designated class type.

The measures: *isolated individuals, isolated object properties, isolated data properties* and *isolated classes* are direct measures that support calculating the measures explained in the above paragraph. For instance, *isolated individuals* are the set of individuals without class type, *isolated object properties* are the set of object properties/relationships without domains or ranges, *isolated data properties* are the set of data properties/class attributes without domains or literal and *isolated classes* are the set of classes without any individuals. These measures also support developers in detecting the incompleteness of ontology entities (i.e., classes, object property, data property, and individuals).

3.5 Comprehensibility Measures

Comprehensibility refers to *the degree of annotations (i.e., metadata) of an ontology and how its elements enable users (i.e., ontology developers and consumers) to understand the appropriateness of an ontology* [13]. The OWL API provides some in-built functions to determine the annotation defined in an ontology (see Table 6). In addition to that, OntoCheck [23] and OOPS! [6] provide features to verify the annotation and naming conventions. In this case, the inbuilt functions of OOPS! were called through OntoQuaL to assess the naming conventions and other related annotation measures.

Table 5. Completeness measures

Measure	OWL Function/Algorithm[2]
Relationship richness	$|P| / |P + H|$; where P is the number of non-inheritance relationships and H is the number of inheritance relationships in an ontology. See Algorithm 03 in [22]
Class/Concept richness	$|C'| / |C|$; where C' is the number of used classes or classes with individuals (inferred and explicit) and the number of declared classes in an ontology. See Algorithm 04 in [22]
Object property usage	$|R_{DR}| / |R|$; where R_{DR} is the number of object properties with DOMAIN and RANGE (inferred and explicit) and R is the number of declared object properties in an ontology. See Algorithm 05 in [22]
Data property usage	$|A_{DR}| / |A|$; where A_{DR} is the number of data properties with DOMAIN and RANGE (literal) (inferred and explicit) and A is the number of declared data properties in an ontology. See Algorithm 06 in [22]
Instance/Individual usage	$|I_{type}| / |I|$; where I_{type} is the number of individuals has class type (inferred and explicit) and I is the number of declared individuals in an ontology. See Algorithm 07 in [22]
Isolated individuals	The number of individuals has no class type (inferred and explicit) in an ontology
Isolated object properties	The number of object properties has no DOMAIN OR RANGE (inferred and explicit) in an ontology
Isolated data properties	The number of data properties has no DOMAIN OR RANGE (inferred and explicit) in an ontology
Isolated classes	The number of classes has no individuals (inferred and explicit) in an ontology

[2]Note: Due to the page restriction given by the conference, the algorithms 03–07 are presented in a separate document and can be accessed via https://github.com/shyamaW/OntoEQuaL/blob/main/Thesis_Algorithms.pdf.

Table 6. Annotation measures

Measure	OWL Function
Annotation property count	onto.getAnnotationPropertiesInSignature().size();
Annotation property assertion count	onto.getAxiomCount(AxiomType.ANNOTATION_ASSERTION);

4   Evaluation and Discussion

This section begins by providing a detailed discussion of the evaluation performed to assess the accuracy of the developed measures in the tool. Following this, the experiments which were performed by using an agriculture ontology are presented, emphasizing the utility of the tool.

4.1   Evaluation of the Developed Measures of Characteristics

The implemented algorithms of the measures, which were discussed in the previous section, were tested with seven ontologies (see Table 8). These ontologies were selected from AgroPortal [24], BioPortal [25] and local research data repositories. The considerably small ontologies were selected for testing. The key justification for not choosing the large ontologies is that doing the reasoning and running the algorithms on them would take a long time. On the other hand, the purpose of this testing is to verify the correctness of the implemented algorithms, thus, small-sized ontologies are appropriate. Table 8 illustrates the values produced by OntoQuaL and the evaluation tools: OOPS! and OntoMetric. The detailed results produced from OOPS! and OntoMetrics are stored in the GitHub repository, and can be found at https://github.com/shyamaW/OntoQuaL/tree/main/ExternalEvaluationReports.

In considering the results produced for the *complexity* and *consistency* measures, it was observed that the algorithms of measures developed in this study provide the same results for ontologies as the existing tools. However, some deviations in measure results of the ontologies modelled by importing pre-existing ontologies were investigated. For example, *Home* ontology has been developed by importing *Time* ontology. In this situation, the developed algorithms and OntoMetrics calculate the measures only considering the entities of the *Home* ontology, excluding the imported entities from other ontologies (i.e., time.owl) (see Table 8). Although this is a limitation of OntoQuaL also, the algorithms work correctly for all independent ontologies as illustrated in Table 8. In the future, the study expects to address this limitation and thus to create a complete evaluation tool.

In considering the *modularity* measures, it was examined that the values of the maximum depth and breadth produced through the proposed algorithms agree with the results of OntoMetric and the manual calculations done through protégé. Moreover, the correctness of the results produced for the *class connectivity* was analysed using the OOPS! tool. For example, OOPS! provides the number of unconnected classes in an ontology. If *African wildlife* ontology is considered, OOPS! provides the number of unconnected classes as two out of thirty-one classes. This implies that only twenty-nine (29) classes are connected in the ontology. The algorithm developed in this study also generated the number of connected classes as twenty-nine (29) for the *African wildlife* ontology (see Table 8). Similarly, the correctness of the class connectivity was verified for other ontologies.

When considering the *completeness* and *comprehensibility* measures, it was observed that the existing tools do not provide the facilities to calculate most of the measures (see Table 1: M27 – M32, M35, M36). On the other hand, the results of the supported measures of the existing tool (i.e., M28, M33, M34) are not valid. For instance, in manual analysis, it was examined that the existing tools do not consider the implicit entities as explained in Sect. 3. To further illustrate, if *Time* ontology is considered, it does not contain any isolated object and data properties (M33 and M34) after reasoning the ontology. However, the OOPS! tool calculated M33 and M34 as seven. This value is zero once the reasoning is performed. This issue does not occur in OntoQuaL as the reasoned ontology is considered when calculating completeness measures.

In considering the Relationship Richness (RR), the results produced through the OntoQuaL algorithm agree with the manual calculation performed through protégé. However, it was observed that OntoMetrics and the implemented algorithm in Onto-QuaL produced two different results for RR. The reason is that OntoMetrics counts non-inherited relationships by considering Object Properties, Equivalent Classes and Disjoint Classes. Nonetheless, the algorithm developed in OntoQuaL considers only object property as non-inherited relationships. There is no clear justification in Onto-Metrics why the equivalent and disjoint classes have been regarded as relationships. This may confuse ontology developers when studying the RR in an ontology since in accordance with the original definition [10], the RR compares only the relationships (ISA/NoN-ISA) used for building connections between classes. In brief, the RR measure in the algorithm compares the taxonomy (ISA) and non-taxonomy (object properties) relationship that helps developers to understand the diversity of the ontology structure (i.e., how close or far is the schema structure to a taxonomy) [10].

4.2   Tool Experiments with an Agriculture Ontology

After evaluating the correctness of the developed measures, OntoQuaL was used to evaluate the quality of an ontology developed for agriculture [26]. This experiment demonstrates how the tool effectively supports assessing the quality of an ontology, providing valuable directions for addressing quality issues associated with its relevant characteristics.

The evaluation process involved assessing two versions of an ontology. Initially, the tool was used to evaluate a set of measures of the ontology named *cropDisorderV1*. Following this, the quality issues of the ontology were detected. Consequently, manual quality improvements were made to the ontology at this stage. Subsequently, the tool again was used to assess the improved version of the ontology (i.e., *cropDisorderV2*). Table 7 shows the results of the experiment.

When examining the *complexity* and *modularity* of the ontology, it becomes apparent that there have been minor structural changes, with no alterations to the hierarchical (IS_A) relationships. However, the *class connectivity* measure of the modularity characteristics indicates that the ontology has unconnected classes. This prompts developers to either eliminate the unconnected classes or establish connections with relationships.

Consistency measures indicate that the ontology maintains internal consistency across both versions. Nevertheless, the *completeness* measures, particularly *class richness*, reveal that the ontology contains classes with absent individuals. This directs developers to populate the isolated classes with individuals. Similarly, the tool facilitates the evaluation of a set of characteristics relevant to the agriculture ontologies, providing insights into key areas for enhancing the ontology quality.

Table 7. Tool experiments with the crop disorder ontology

ID	Measure	CropDisorderV1.owl	CropDisorderV2.owl
	Complexity Measures		
M1	Class count	69	73
M2	Object property count	86	96
M3	Data property count	39	40
M4	Individual count	1136	1172
M5	Logical axioms	4619	4723
M6	Declared axioms	1332	1386
M7	Chain object property count	03	03
M8	Subclass axioms	34	34
	Modularity Measures		
M9	Maximum depth	03	03
M10	Maximum breadth	11	11
M11	Class connectivity: Disconnected classes with root node "crop"	04	04
	Consistency Measures		
M12	Consistency status	TRUE	TRUE
M13	Equivalent class axioms	20	20
M14	Disjoint class axioms	339	339
M15	Subobject property axioms	04	04
M16	Equivalent object property axioms	0	0
M17	Disjoint object property axioms	0	0
M18	Circularity status	False	False
M19	Functional object property	16	19
M20	Inverse functional object property	0	01
M21	Transitive object property	02	02
M22	Symmetric object property	0	0
M23	Asymmetric object property	52	52
M24	Reflexive object property	0	0

(*continued*)

Table 7. (*continued*)

ID	Measure	CropDisorderV1.owl	CropDisorderV2.owl
M25	Irreflexive object property	52	52
M26	Functional data property	23	23
	Completeness Measures		
M27	Relationship richness	71.66% (86/120 = 0.7167)	73.8% (96/130 = 0.7384)
M28	Class richness	96% (66/69 = 0.96)	90% (66/73 = 0.90)
M29	Object property usage	94.2% (81/86 = 0.942)	94.8% (91/96 = 0.948)
M30	Data property usage	100%	100%
M31	Instance usage	100%	100%
M32	Isolated individuals	0	0
M33	Isolated object properties	05	05
M34	Isolated data properties	0	0
M35	Isolated classes	03	07
	Comprehensibility Measures		
M36	Annotation property count	05	05
M37	Annotation property assertion count	209	209

Additionally, the authors' previous research demonstrated how the tool can be applied to assess a range of ontologies developed for agricultural purposes, aiding in the selection of suitable ontologies for reuse. This has been explained in [4]. Specifically, the measures provided by the tool assist researchers in gauging the extent of coverage, complexity, and consistency within ontologies, enabling developers to choose the most appropriate ontology for their needs. For example, if a developer seeks to select an ontology from a pool of ontologies with significant domain knowledge coverage, then, they can examine measures related to ontology completeness (M27-M35). Thereafter, the developer can choose the ontologies with high scores for the measures: M27-M30 and low scores for others (M31-M35). Accordingly, the tool can be utilised to analyse the quality of ontologies and choose an appropriate ontology for a specific purpose.

4.3 Future Works

Based on the evaluation and experiments, it can be stated that none of the existing tools supports evaluating all the measures related to ontologies in decision support systems, primarily in agriculture. Moreover, the existing tools only consider explicitly modelled entities when evaluating measurements, ignoring an ontology's implicit nature. The proposed tool in this study, OntoQuaL, has tackled these concerns. Nevertheless, it has a few limitations to be addressed, including its lack of consideration for imported ontologies and its incompatibility with ontologies built using older versions of OWL.

Table 8. Measure comparison

Measure	African Wildlife Ontology			Asthma Ontology			Home Ontology			Stuff Ontology			Time Ontology			Tomato Ontology			Circularity Ontology		
	Our Algorithms	OOPs^/ Protégé	OntoMetric	Our Algorithms	OOPs^/ Protégé	OntoMetric	Our Algorithms	OOPs^/ Protégé	OntoMetric	Our Algorithms	OOPs^/ Protégé	OntoMetric	Our Algorithms	OOPs^/ Protégé	OntoMetric	Our Algorithms	OOPs^/ Protégé	OntoMetric	Our Algorithms	OOPs^/ Protégé	OntoMetric
Complexity																					
M1	31	31	31	289	289	289	48	58	48	65	65	65	13	13	13	29	29	29	24	24	24
M2	5	5	5	0	0	0	10	32	10	32	32	32	24	24	24	53	53	53	0	0	0
M3	0	0	0	0	0	0	29	46	29	2	2	2	17	17	17	42	42	42	0	0	0
M4	0	0	0	0	0	0	0	14	0	0	0	0	14	14	14	72	72	72	0	0	0
M5	56	56	56	283	283	283	110	237	109	187	187	187	128	128	128	539	539	539	21	21	21
M6	37	37		297	297		87	153		96	96		70	70		194	194		24	24	
M7	0			0			0			2			0			0			0		
M8	38	38	38	283	283	283	104	137	104	81	81	81	33	33	33	5	5	5	21	21	21
Modularity																					
M9	3	3	4	3	3	3	4	4	2	8	8	8	4	4	4	2	2	2	6	6	NG
M10	8	8	8	30	30	30	6	6	7	27	27	8	2	2	5	2	2	24	7	7	NG
M11	29			283			47			65			13			29			21		
Consistency																					
M12	T	T	-	T	T	-	T	T	-	T	T	-	T	T	-	T	T	-	T	T	-
M13	3	3	3	0	0	0	0	3	0	17	17	17	3	3	3	0	0	0	0	0	0
M14	7	7	7	0	0	0	0	1	0	14	14	14	1	1	1	0	0	0	0	0	0
M15	1	1	1	0	0	0	3	4	3	23	23	23	1	1	1	10	10	10	0	0	0
M16	0	0	0	0	0	0	0	0	0	0	0	0	0	0	0	0	0	0	0	0	0
M17	0	0	0	0	0	0	0	0	0	0	0	0	0	0	0	0	0	0	0	0	0
M18	F			F			F			F			F			F			T	T*	
M19	0	0	0	0	0	0	0	0	0	0	0	0	0	0	0	18	18	18	0	0	0
M20	0	0	0	0	0	0	0	0	0	0	0	0	0	0	0	2	2	2	0	0	0
M21	2	2	2	0	0	0	0	1	0	1	1	1	1	1	1	0	0	0	0	0	0
M22	0	0	0	0	0	0	0	0	0	0	0	0	0	0	0	0	0	0	0	0	0
M23	0	0	0	0	0	0	0	0	0	0	0	0	0	0	0	20	20	20	0	0	0
M24	1	1	1	0	0	0	0	0	0	0	0	0	0	0	0	0	0	0	0	0	0
M25	1	1	1	0	0	0	0	0	0	0	0	0	0	0	0	20	20	20	0	0	0
M26	0	0	0	0	0	0	0	0	0	0	0	0	0	0	0	3	3	3	0	0	0
Completeness																					
M27	11.6		28	0		0	8.77		8.77	28.32		43.8	42.1		45.9	91.38		91.38	0		0
M28	0	0	0	0		0	2.08		0	10.77			23.08		15.4	96.55		89.7	0		0
M29	20		0	0		0	60		0	90.62		0	100		0	95.23		0	0		0
M30	0		0	0		0	0		0	50		0	100		0	0		0	0		0
M31	0		0	0		0	0		0	0		0	0		0	0		0	0		0
M32	0		0	0		0	0		0	3		0	0		0	0		0	0		0
M33	4	5*	0*	0		0	4	42*		3	23*		0	7*		0	2*		0	0*	
M34	0		0	0		0	28		0	0		0	0		0	2		0	0		0
M35	31			289			47			58			10			1			24		
Comprehensibility																					
M36				10			2			2			2			1			0		
M37	15	15	15	290	292	292	5	5	5	77	77	77	0	0	0	4	4	4	0	0	0

These shortcomings will be resolved in forthcoming updates. Moreover, OntoQuaL has been developed as a desktop application. However, the authors acknowledged the challenges associated with installing and configuring the tool across various operating systems. Therefore, a web-based version of the tool will be launched in the future to address these issues and enhance the ease of use.

5 Conclusion

The research primarily developed OntoQuaL, a quality evaluation tool. It aims to fill gaps in the existing ontology evaluation tools by incorporating measures aligned with key ontology characteristics such as *complexity, modularity, consistency, completeness,* and *comprehensibility*. The developed quality measures were tested for accuracy by comparing their outcomes with those of existing tools. Additionally, the usefulness of the tool was demonstrated by conducting quality evaluations on agriculture ontologies. Unlike previous tools, OntoQuaL evaluates ontologies by considering not only explicit entities but also inferred entities. However, there are limitations such as disregarding external ontologies and lacking compatibility with older OWL versions. Future enhancements aim to address these shortcomings, particularly to improve evaluation efficacy for ontologies in decision support systems.

References

1. Noy, N.F., McGuinness, D.L.: What is an ontology and why we need it. https://pro tege.stanford.edu/publications/ontology_development/ontology101-noy-mcguinness.html. Accessed 26 June 2021

2. Gruninger, M., Fox, M.S.: Methodology for design and evaluation of ontologies. In: Workshop on Basic Ontological Issues in Knowledge Sharing. Proceedings IJCAI 1995 (1995)

3. Wilson, R.S.I., Goonetillake, J.S., Indika, W.A., Ginige, A.: Analysis of ontology quality dimensions, criteria and metrics. In: Gervasi, O. (ed.) Computational Science and Its Applications – ICCSA 2021. LNCS, vol. 12951, pp. 320–337. Springer, Cham (2021). https://doi.org/10.1007/978-3-030-86970-0_23

4. Wilson, S.I., Goonetillake, J.S., Ginige, A., Walisadeera, A.I.: Towards a usable ontology: the identification of quality characteristics for an ontology-driven decision support system. IEEE Access **10**, 12889–12912 (2022). https://doi.org/10.1109/ACCESS.2022.3146331

5. Bevan, N.: Usability is quality of use. In: Advances in Human Factors/Ergonomics, pp. 349–354. Elsevier (1995). https://doi.org/10.1016/S0921-2647(06)80241-8

6. Poveda-Villalón, M., Gómez-Pérez, A., Suárez-Figueroa, M.C.: Oops! (ontology pitfall scanner!): an on-line tool for ontology evaluation. Int. J. Semant. Web Inf. Syst. (IJSWIS) **10**, 7–34 (2014)

7. W3C RDF Validation Service. https://www.w3.org/RDF/Validator/. Accessed 29 Dec 2021

8. Horridge, M.: OWL 2 Validator. http://mowl-power.cs.man.ac.uk:8080/validator/. Accessed 29 Dec 2021

9. Lozano-Tello, A., Gomez-Perez, A.: ONTOMETRIC: a method to choose the appropriate ontology. JDM **15**, 1–18 (2004). https://doi.org/10.4018/jdm.2004040101

10. Tartir, S., Arpinar, I.B., Moore, M., Sheth, A.P., Aleman-Meza, B.: OntoQA: metric-based ontology quality analysis. Presented at the IEEE Workshop on Knowledge Acquisition from Distributed, Autonomous, Semantically Heterogeneous Data and Knowledge Sources (2005)

11. McDaniel, M., Storey, V.C., Sugumaran, V.: Assessing the quality of domain ontologies: metrics and an automated ranking system. Data Knowl. Eng. **115**, 32–47 (2018). https://doi.org/10.1016/j.datak.2018.02.001

12. Amith, M., et al.: OntoKeeper: semiotic-driven ontology evaluation tool for biomedical ontologists. In: 2018 IEEE International Conference on Bioinformatics and Biomedicine (BIBM), pp. 1614–1617 (2018). https://doi.org/10.1109/BIBM.2018.8621458

13. Wilson, R.S.I., Goonetillake, J.S., Indika, W.A., Ginige, A.: A conceptual model for ontology quality assessment. Semant. Web **14**, 1051–1097 (2023). https://doi.org/10.3233/SW-233393

14. protégé. https://protege.stanford.edu/. Accessed 14 Nov 2021

15. Goldstein, A., Fink, L., Ravid, G.: A framework for evaluating agricultural ontologies. Sustainability **13**, 6387 (2021). https://doi.org/10.3390/su13116387

16. OWL API. http://owlapi.sourceforge.net/. Accessed 6 Mar 2020

17. Wilson, R.S.I., Goonetillake, J.S., Ginige, A., Indika, W.A.: Analysis of information quality for a usable information system in agriculture domain: a study in the Sri Lankan context. Procedia Comput. Sci. **184**, 346–355 (2021). https://doi.org/10.1016/j.procs.2021.03.044

18. Sánchez, D.: Semantic variance_An intuitive measure for ontology accuracy evaluation. Eng. Appl. Artif. Intell. **11** (2015)

19. Fernández, M., Overbeeke, C., Sabou, M., Motta, E.: What makes a good ontology? A case-study in fine-grained knowledge reuse. In: Gómez-Pérez, A., Yu, Y., Ding, Y. (eds.) ASWC 2009. LNCS, vol. 5926, pp. 61–75. Springer, Heidelberg (2009). https://doi.org/10.1007/978-3-642-10871-6_5

20. Gangemi, A., Catenacci, C., Ciaramita, M., Lehmann, J.: Modelling ontology evaluation and validation. In: Sure, Y., Domingue, J. (eds.) The Semantic Web: Research and Applications, pp. 140–154. Springer, Heidelberg (2006). https://doi.org/10.1007/11762256_13

21. Ouyang, L., Zou, B., Qu, M., Zhang, C.: A method of ontology evaluation based on coverage, cohesion and coupling. In: 2011 Eighth International Conference on Fuzzy Systems and Knowledge Discovery (FSKD), pp. 2451–2455 (2011). https://doi.org/10.1109/FSKD.2011. 6020046

22. Wilson, R.S.I.: OntoQuaL/Thesis_Algorithms.pdf at main · shyamaW/OntoQuaL, https://git hub.com/shyamaW/OntoQuaL/blob/main/Thesis_Algorithms.pdf. Accessed 16 Apr 2024

23. Schober, D., Tudose, I., Svatek, V., Boeker, M.: OntoCheck: verifying ontology naming conventions and metadata completeness in Protégé 4. J. Biomed. Semanti. 3 (2012). https://doi.org/10.1186/2041-1480-3-S2-S4

24. Jonquet, C., et al.: AgroPortal: a vocabulary and ontology repository for agronomy. Comput. Electron. Agric. 144, 126–143 (2018). https://doi.org/10.1016/j.compag.2017.10.012

25. Salvadores, M., Alexander, P.R., Musen, M.A., Noy, N.F.: BioPortal as a dataset of linked biomedical ontologies and terminologies in RDF. Semant. Web. 4, 277–284 (2013). https://doi.org/10.3233/SW-2012-0086

26. Walisadeera, A.I., Ginige, A., Wikramanayake, G.N.: User centered ontology for Sri Lankan agriculture domain. In: 2014 14th International Conference on Advances in ICT for Emerging Regions (ICTer), pp. 149–155 (2014). https://doi.org/10.1109/ICTER.2014.7083894

Diverse Bagging Effort Estimation Model for Software Development Project

Mohammad Haris⦿, Fang-Fang Chua(✉)⦿, and Amy Hui-Lan Lim⦿

Faculty of Computing and Informatics, Multimedia University, Cyberjaya, Malaysia
1221400087@student.mmu.edu.my, {ffchua,amy.lim}@mmu.edu.my

Abstract. Creating successful projects is challenging and estimation of software development efforts is thus an important activity of the software engineering community. It enables project managers to organize and manage project quality, cost, resources, and timelines. However, standard techniques for estimating development effort struggle due to the increased complexity, dynamic requirements, multifaceted nature, non-linear relationship, and greater interdependencies of modern software. Various machine learning models have been created periodically to tackle the deficiencies of standard estimation techniques. Nevertheless, the deployment is limited due to inefficient model-constructing approaches and inconclusive results. By meticulously optimizing preprocessing and hyperparameter tuning steps, this research presents a Diverse Bagging Effort ESTimation (DBEEST) model for more reliable and accurate software development effort estimation. To accomplish this, six homogeneous ensembles through bagging were applied to the USP05-FT and SEERA datasets. Subsequently, the predictions of each homogeneous ensemble were combined through averaging to generate a more reliable and accurate prediction with improved robustness against inconsistencies and errors. The results demonstrate the DBEEST model outperformed all individual bagging ensembles and produced consistent results by delivering an overall average of low Mean Square Error, Root Mean Square Error, Mean Absolute Error, and Mean Magnitude Relative Error values and an overall average of high Coefficient of determination values across both diverse datasets. Moreover, the proposed model can improve efficiency in handling software development projects, resource optimization, facilitating informed decision-making, and on-time project completion.

Keywords: Software Project Effort Estimation · Ensemble Learning · Ensemble Bagging · Machine Learning Techniques

1 Introduction

As the need for software increases, software development companies must build the software within the agreed budget and timeframe while meeting the client's expectations [1]. This can be achieved by estimating the effort needed to execute a project, as it provides methods to calculate the project's duration and cost for software development. The amount of developer force required to fulfill the requirement for a certain task is known as software effort, and it is typically quantified in units of "person-hours" [1]. Commonly used algorithmic effort estimation techniques such as the Constructive Cost Estimation Model (COCOMO) [2], Putnam's [3], and Function Point Analysis (FPA) [4] which rely on mathematical and statistical work [5], struggle to provide accurate estimations of the effort needed for software project development [6, 7] because they cannot perform early estimations, and the properties utilized could only be calculated after project completion [8, 9]. Furthermore, in the rapidly evolving field of software engineering, these estimation techniques struggle to keep updated particularly with the rise of code reuse and customizable software deployment [10]. For early estimation, expert-based estimation can be a useful non-algorithmic technique for complex or innovative projects, particularly in situations where historical data is restricted [11, 12]. Expert Judgment, Delphi, and planning poker are the most common estimation techniques that rely on Experts [13, 14]. In the Expert judgment, the estimations are done by the Expert, or a group of Experts, based on their own knowledge and expertise [11]. The Delphi technique is a structured interaction technique. It entails privately collecting consensus estimates from a group of experts through iterative rounds of surveys and comments [15], and the Wideband Delphi technique [10] is an extension of the Delphi technique that includes group discussions between rounds. Moreover, Planning Poker is a gamified technique that involves a group determining development effort using a deck of cards, privately assigning values, then disclosing and discussing their choices (especially outliers) until each estimator reaches a consensus [13]. However, overreliance on these expert-based techniques can lead to human bias and subjectivity in the estimation process [2, 14]. Project slippage is a persistent challenge for software project development companies [16]. Therefore, accurate software project effort estimation is essential before developing a project, as it paves the way for successful software development projects, while inaccurate or incorrect estimations can harm companies' sales and reputation, resulting in financial losses [14]. As the procedure of estimating software development effort evolves promptly, it enables ML techniques superior to other standard effort estimation techniques [8, 17]. Hence, the purpose of this research is to propose an ensemble learning-based Diverse Bagging Effort ESTimation (DBEEST) model by utilizing ML algorithms including Linear Regression (LR), Support Vector Regression (SVR), Decision Tree Regressor (DTR), Multi-Layer Perceptron (MLP), Random Forest Regressor (RFR), and K-Nearest Neighbors (KNN). The USP05-FT [6, 17–19], and SEERA [5, 20] datasets were utilized independently for training and testing the proposed model. Therefore, an extensive approach that predicts software project effort more accurately is presented that starts from smart data pre-processing and optimal parameter tuning to the construction and integration of diverse homogeneous ensembles.

2 Literature Review

The standard effort estimation techniques, including algorithmic methods, are designed to provide mathematical equations for estimating the effort required for a software project development [8, 14, 21]. These algorithmic methods are unable to perform early estimates because the variables on which they rely can only be determined after the project is completed [8]. For early estimation, the expert-based non-algorithmic technique is widely used in practice [11, 12]. However, overreliance on expert-based techniques may result in inaccurate and usually overoptimistic estimates due to human bias and subjectivity [2, 10, 14]. Therefore, to overcome the deficiencies of these standard techniques and improve the process of estimating software development effort, a range of ML-based techniques have been periodically proposed over the last two decades [2, 7, 15, 22]. In [23], they proposed a ML-based method to estimate effort for agile-based projects, utilizing an SVM from eight different public-domain project issue appraisals as independent features. The study [24] contributed by developing a new effort estimation dataset that takes into consideration the complexity and dynamic nature of modern software. DT, KNN, and SVM were employed on this dataset to estimate the effort, and the DT performed better than the other two. To assess a project's level of risk, the research [25] has proposed a neural network model with three layers, utilizing the backpropagation method, to accurately predict hazardous software projects. To further enhance the estimation process, an ensemble stacking incorporating RF has been introduced, and the study utilizes seven distinct public datasets for training [15]. The paper [26] used nine regression base estimators within the ensemble model to predict the effort, along with hyperparameter tuning to enhance the model's predictive capability. The authors [10] have presented an ensemble averaging model to estimate the software project duration and effort. In the paper [27], the researchers utilized four distinct public datasets to compare the two ML algorithms (SVM and RF) with two deep learning algorithms (Neuralnet and Deepnet). The results of the experiment showed that RF outperformed all algorithms. The study [1] also plays a part in the building of an ideal ensemble-learning-based model by using DT. Based on predictive accuracy, the proposed DT ensemble model surpasses a single DT algorithm. In [5], MLP, LR, and SVR were contrasted with one another to predict software effort, and a relatively new public dataset (SEERA) was used to train and test the models. Based on the evaluation results, LR performed better by having the highest R-squared value.

In [28], researchers have presented the "COSENS" framework, which integrates Cost-Sensitive learning with an Ensemble technique to predict the risk of outsourcing projects. Moreover, the authors [22] proposed bagging for estimating software effort, employing six base estimators and two variable selection methods, the Genetic Algorithm and BestFit. Paper [29] has developed multiple models. One regression and four ML models are built for comparative evaluation. In the study [17] thirteen ML models are used to identify the best model for effort prediction. RF performs best on the "USP05-FT" dataset, while KStar, Additive Regression, and Reduce Error Pruning Tree excel on the "USP05" dataset. The study [30] used training datasets from public and non-public domains to evaluate and compare individual and ensemble approaches. The results revealed that ensemble methods consistently outperform individual techniques. The paper by [6] has used Naive Bayes (NB) and Artificial Neural Networks (ANN) for estimating effort, and a rough set analysis approach has been considered for selecting independent variables. In [16], the authors used historical data from two substantial governmental ICT projects to train seven base learning classifiers and aggregate their prediction results using the ensemble voting approach to generate more reliable software cost predictions. The paper [31] proposed the AdaBoost ensemble model by utilizing two base learners, SVM and KNN. Based on the findings, the model predicts software effort effectively. In [32], the authors propose a novel approach that integrates ANN with the "Cuckoo Optimization Algorithm (COA)" to improve software project estimation. Further, the researchers in [33] employed K-means clustering throughout the three stages of software development with six classifiers such as DT (J48), RF, DT (C4.5), AdaBoost, NB, and Bagging to examine the efficiency of defect prediction. Another paper [13] proposed an autonomous estimation method for agile methodology story cards, together with supervised learning. As a result of their findings, the researchers exhibited that the DT (J48), Logistic Model Tree (LMT) and Planning Poker, as well as DT (J48) and Planning Poker all outperformed manual Planning Poker.

Upon thoroughly exploring a diverse range of literature related to software project estimation, the ML has the potential to effectively overcome the deficiencies of standard effort estimation techniques, which were observed to be insufficient and outdated [34–36] for estimating today's complex and advanced software project whereas those who do provide early estimates are susceptible to bias and subjective decisions during the estimation process [8, 35–37]. Furthermore, the literature reviews also demonstrated that the ensemble-learning method is notably effective in improving prediction accuracy and robustness [5, 9, 10, 15, 22, 26, 28, 30, 31, 34, 38–40] because it combines the strength of multiple ML algorithms. Ensemble-based models can be constructed as heterogeneous ensembles (train diverse base learners on the same dataset) [41] by utilizing stacking or boosting, or as homogeneous ensembles (train a single base learner on multiple training sets) [10] by utilizing bagging, each with its own distinct strengths and limitations in terms of performance. Therefore, a diverse bagging model that incorporates the strengths of both homogenous and heterogeneous ensembles by integrating six distinctive bagging ensembles is proposed in this study to achieve more accurate and reliable effort estimation for software development projects.

3 Methodology

This section discusses the methodology in stages for constructing a machine learning model by utilizing ensemble bagging for software development effort estimation.

3.1 Stage 1: Data Collection

In this research, two PROMISE [42] repository datasets, namely USP05-FT and SEERA, were used. The USP05-FT [6, 17, 18, 43] is a widely adopted dataset within the field of software project effort estimation. It comprises 76 distinct client/server architecture and web development projects that were completed at the "University of Calgary" in 2005. Each project is described by 15 variables, of which the dependent variable is "Effort," quantified in "person-hours (unit)," and the remaining 14 are independent variables, of which 4 are numerical variables and 10 are categorical variables. Whereas SEERA (Software enginEERing in SudAn) [5, 20] is a relatively new dataset. It aggregates information from 120 diverse software development projects conducted by 42 software development companies in Sudan. This dataset encompasses a total of 76 variables, where "Actual effort," which is quantified in "person-hours (unit)," serves as the dependent variable, and the other 75 are independent variables, of which nearly 80% of these independent variables are categorical, which contain information about different software applications across different domains such as Bespoke applications, Enterprise Resource Planning (ERP), Financial and Managerial applications, Banking system applications, Web applications, and Mobile applications. Both datasets are ideally suited for conducting software engineering experiments, which encompass all the necessary variables for predicting software development effort and will be crucial for the training process of the proposed DBEEST model. Table 1 summarizes the proposed datasets based on source repository information, number of attributes, number of projects, and unit of dependent variables.

Table 1. Summary of the proposed datasets

Dataset	Source	No. of Projects	No. of Variables	Unit of Dependent Variable
USP05-FT	PROMISE	76	15	Person-hours
SEERA	PROMISE	120	76	Person-hours

3.2 Stage 2: Data Preprocessing

Effective data preprocessing stands as a crucial stage in the construction of machine learning models [10, 44]. In this stage, considering insights from the previous related studies, four different data preprocessing techniques were implemented.

Detection and Handling of Missing Values. In the data preprocessing stages, instances with missing values in the proposed datasets were addressed by applying imputation techniques such as mean, median, and k-nearest neighbors (KNN) imputation. These imputation techniques were chosen because missing values in both datasets followed a pattern of Missing Completely at Random (MCAR) [45, 46]. Little's test was conducted to validate this pattern. It is a statistical test that evaluates the Null Hypothesis (HO) that the missing values are missing completely at random. It assists in determining whether the missing values occur completely at random or if there is a systematic pattern to the missingness [45, 47]. This test's result demonstrated that the p-value exceeded the predetermined significance level of 0.05, indicating the null hypothesis was not successfully rejected. This implies that the missingness in the datasets is MCAR. In the USP0F-FT dataset, there were a total of 37 missing values across 8 columns (Number of External Outputs, Unadjusted Function Point, Programming Language, Tools, Tool Experience, Database Management System, Method, and Architecture). For columns containing fewer than 5 missing values, numerical columns were imputed using the mean imputation technique, and categorical columns were imputed using the median imputation technique. This involved substituting the values that are missing with the respective median or mean of the observed values [45, 47, 48]. Additionally, the KNN-Imputation technique was employed for the column (Method) with 14 missing values. KNN-Imputation imputes missing values based on the values of their closest neighboring data points. It considers how similar these nearby data points are to the one with the missing value and uses that information to make an estimate for the missing value [48]. In the second SEERA dataset, 42 columns were identified as containing missing values. The 3 columns (Estimated Size, Outsourcing Impact, Degree of Standards Usage) that have more than 90 missing values were simply dropped. The remaining 39 columns (Object Points, Government Policy Impact, Management Structure Clarity, Developer Hiring Policy, Developer Incentives Policy, Developer Training, Development Team Management, Clarity of Manual System, Project Manager Experience, Consultant Availability, Precedentedness, Software Tool Experience, Programming Language Experience, Programmers Capability, Analysts Capability, Team Selection, Team Contracts, Team Continuity, Team Cohesion, Income Satisfaction, Schedule Quality, Development Environment Adequacy, Tool Availability, Technical Stability, Level of Outsourcing, Degree of Software Reuse, Degree of Risk Management, Use of Standards, Process Reengineering, Requirement Accuracy Level, Technical Documentation, Comments in the Code, User Manual, Required Reusability, Performance Requirements, Product Complexity, Security Requirements, Reliability Requirements, and Specified Hardware) have less than 4 missing values, and the mean imputation was applied to numerical columns, while the median imputation was used for categorical columns to impute the missing values.

Detection and Handling of Outlier Data Points. Handling outliers ensures model robustness, enhances generalization, and prevents biased predictions by addressing data points exhibiting substantial deviations from the remaining values [9, 49]. In this stage, outliers were detected through statistical measures, particularly leveraging the Interquartile Range (IQR). The IQR describes the range of the dataset, and the formula to calculate it is mentioned below.

$$IQR = Q3 - Q1 \tag{1}$$

In the formula, the IQR is the Interquartile Range, Q3 is the value at which 75% of the distribution is obtained, and Q1 is the value at which 25% of the distribution is obtained. In IQR, outliers can usually be detected with a threshold of 1.5 times the IQR [49, 50]. The upper fence is calculated as "Q3 + 1.5 × IQR," while the lower fence is calculated as "Q1 − 1.5 × IQR." Therefore, in the USP05-FT dataset, 2 variables, namely Number of External Inputs and Unadjusted Function Point, were identified that have outliers with the highest values. The calculated upper fence values of these variables are 14 and 25. In order to preserve meaningful information, only those outliers that were close to their calculated upper fence values are converted to their respective upper fence values. In IQR, this process is known as capping. On the other hand, in the SEERA dataset, 7 variables with outliers were identified, namely Estimated Duration, Actual Duration, Object Point, Estimated Effort, Actual Effort, Team Size, Dedicated Team Members. The calculated upper fence values of these variables are 13, 22, 778, 13921, 21912, 10, and 11, respectively. First, the IQR trimming method was applied to those outliers that were extremely high compared to their upper fence values. Then, the IQR capping method was utilized for other outliers that were close to their calculated upper fence values.

Feature Selection. The variables obtained from the proposed datasets were sequentially analyzed to assess their suitability for feature extraction and to uncover the potential relationships or dependencies among them. In this study, Karl Pearson's product-moment correlation coefficient was initially used as a statistical metric to ascertain the association between numerical independent and numerical dependent variables [16]. The coefficient falls within the range of $+1$ to -1. A positive coefficient value denotes a direct correlation. A negative value denotes a negative correlation. A coefficient of zero ("0") denotes that there is no correlation observed between the variables [16, 26]. After employing the correlation coefficient to examine the relationships between numerical dependent and numerical independent variables in both datasets, it was observed that in the USP05-FT dataset, 2 independent numerical variables, Number of External Inputs and Number of Data Files, exhibited very weak negative correlations, approaching zero ("0"), with values of -0.0061 and -0.0512, respectively. Meanwhile, in the SEERA dataset, 2 independent numerical variables, Daily Working Hours and Team Continuity, exhibited weak positive correlations, and 1 independent numerical variable, Multiple Programming Languages, exhibited weak negative correlation, approaching zero ("0") with values of $0.0197, 0.0806$, and -0.0487, respectively. The crucial categorical independent variables across both datasets were identified by employing Analysis of Variance (ANOVA) [51]. It is typically utilized when the independent variables are categorical in nature and the dependent variable is numerical. In ANOVA, variables with high F-statistic values and low p-values (generally less than 0.05) are usually considered more important variables. Conversely, low F-statistic values and high p-values (generally greater than 0.05) denote that the independent categorical variable may not have a significant impact on the dependent numerical variable [51, 52]. The ANOVA test identified a total of 17 insignificant independent categorical variables by analyzing their associated F-values and p-values. Specifically, 2 variables, Project ID and Method, from the USP05-FT dataset, exhibited low F-values of 0.0000 and 0.0006 respectively, and high p-values (>0.05) of 0.9965, and 0.9796, respectively, and 15 variables from the SEERA dataset such as Management Structure Clarity, User Manual, Software Tool Experience, Degree of Software Reuse, Performance Requirements, Requirements Flexibility, Use of Standards, Tool Availability, Reliability Requirements, Economic Instability Impact, Users Stability, Organization ID, Project ID, Technical Stability, and Schedule Quality, exhibited low F-values of 0.0017, 0.0048, 0.0049, 0.0060, 0.0061, 0.0097, 0.0145, 0.0423, 0.0435, 0.0789, 0.0930, 0.1426, 0.1521, 0.1610, and 0.1654, respectively, and high p-values (>0.05) of 0.9671, 0.9446, 0.9442, 0.9380, 0.9375, 0.9216, 0.9040, 0.8374, 0.8352, 0.7793, 0.7609, 0.7063, 0.7432, 0.6890, and 0.6850, respectively. Therefore, irrelevant numerical variables identified through Pearson's correlation and irrelevant categorical variables identified through ANOVA were eliminated from both datasets to enhance the proposed model's performance, interpretability, and computational efficiency [51, 52].

Feature Scaling. The purpose of feature scaling is to modify the range of independent numerical variables, making them more compatible with one another while preventing certain variables from dominating the learning process [26]. In this stage, the standardization method for feature scaling was utilized for both proposed datasets [1]. This was necessary because certain proposed models, such as SVR, KNN, and MLP, are sensitive to variations in the scale of input variables [26]. The standardization centers the data on a mean of "0" and scales it to a standard deviation of "1." The following formula is used to calculate the standard scale for the variable 'p' [43]:

$$S_{standardized} = \frac{p - \mu}{\sigma} \tag{2}$$

where "$S_{standardized}$" is the standardized values of the variables, "p" is the initial variable values, "μ" is the mean of the considered training samples, "σ" is the standard deviation of the variable values.

The data preprocessing entails cleaning, standardizing numerical variables, reducing irrelevant variables, and splitting the datasets into an 80–20 ratio, 80% training sets, and 20% test sets. This sets the stage for effective model training and testing.

3.3 Stage 3: Hyperparameter Tunning

The hyperparameters are the set of parameters that are not explicitly assigned or learned by the estimators or models [26]. These parameters are not predefined as defaults by any estimator. However, hyperparameter tuning is the technique of systematically searching for the optimum setting of these hyperparameters, which govern the performance of ML models [26, 28, 53, 54]. In this stage, the Grid Search Cross-Validation (GridSearchCV) hyperparameter tuning technique [55] is implemented. As it systematically explores all potential parameter combinations, this technique is deemed to be more effective [26, 55]. In the context of GridSearchCV, Cross Validation (CV) is an essential step in the hyperparameter tuning process. The training data serves as the input, and the cross-validation technique handles the dynamic creation of validation sets while examining various hyperparameter settings [55]. It performed K-fold cross-validation at each point on the predefined hyperparameter grid to evaluate performance [26, 53, 54]. Moreover, as GridSearchCV handles cross-validation internally, there is no need to explicitly specify a separate validation set [54]. The optimum parameter settings for the proposed base estimators, as well as their corresponding ensemble bagging models, were determined on both proposed datasets through this GridSearchCV hyperparameter tuning technique. In each dataset, 10-fold cross-validation was applied. This entailed splitting the respective training set into 10 subsets (folds), 9 for training and 1 for validation in each iteration. This process was repeated 10 times to ensure that each subset was utilized as a validation set at least once. Furthermore, these parameter settings were determined based on the set of hyperparameters that produced optimal 10-fold cross-validated results.

3.4 Stage 4: Construction of Proposed Model (DBEEST)

To construct the proposed DBEEST model, six base estimators, MLP, SVR, LR, DTR, RFR, and KNN, are utilized to construct six separate homogenous ensembles through the bagging method. Each homogeneous ensemble is constructed on a distinct estimator that leverages the diverse learning capabilities of these models or estimators to identify a broad spectrum of patterns and relationships within the data. To train each of these six separate homogeneous ensembles, the training sets (80%) acquired from the proposed datasets are utilized independently. Bagging is implemented on all six homogeneous ensembles, yielding six distinct prediction outcomes. The final prediction was derived by combining the predictions from all six homogeneous ensembles using the averaging method. Therefore, the estimate will be more reliable and accurate. The six base estimators and bagging method proposed for constructing the DBEEST model have been successfully employed in multiple prior studies. The estimators and bagging method were chosen for their proven effectiveness in software estimation and their ability to provide adequate predictions. The descriptions of the base estimators and ensemble bagging are presented in the following sections.

Base Estimators. MLP is a supervised algorithm that gains insights from a training dataset using a function $f(a) : S^m \rightarrow S^q$ in which 'm' denotes the quantity of variables with regard to input and 'q' denotes the quantity of variables with regard to output [56]. The MLP is capable of learning a non-linear function for a given set of variables signified as $W = w1, w2, ..., wm$ and a dependent variable d through neural layers that are related to one another [17]. This allows the MLP to address regression or classification problems effectively [26]. SVR is another supervised learning Support Vector Machine (SVM) method for regression problems [26]. It utilizes the use of support vectors to generate a hyperplane that depicts the relationship between independent variables and continuous dependent variables [26, 34]. LR is a parametric model that is utilized in regression scenarios when the dependent variable is assumed to be a combination of other variables in a linear manner [22]. It seeks to identify the best-fitting linear line that minimizes the difference between the actual and predicted values [26]. While DT is a non-parametric method designed to develop a model using decision rules derived from data variables [16]. It is a binary tree, with its root positioned at the top, and the data is arranged into a tree structure to handle different ML-related problems. DT utilizes a collection of predictor variables to demonstrate how a target variable is predicted [2]. In dealing with regression problems with DT, the Decision Tree Regressor (DTR) is used [26]. Furthermore, RF is an ensemble meta-estimator composed of several decision trees [9]. It works by constructing numerous Decision Trees (DTs) and then aggregating their predicted results to make ultimate predictions. Every decision tree is trained on a randomly generated portion of the training data and attributes [17]. To generate a prediction, the RF takes a set of attributes and distributes them under each tree in the forest. Random Forest Regressor (RFR) is implemented when dealing with regression problems [13, 26]. Lastly, KNN is another non-parametric method based on proximity that generates predictions by locating the K nearest observations to a provided input and averaging their dependent values (for regression) or choosing the majority class (for classification) [17]. The fundamental concept of this method is case-based reasoning, which includes processes like detecting cases, collecting related cases, and adopting cases. Regression-based neighboring methods are employed when dealing with continuous data [26].

Ensemble Bagging. Bagging, short for "Bootstrap Aggregation", is an ensemble learning method that assists ML models to increase their stability and accuracy [33]. It is well-effective for managing the balance between underfitting and overfitting, reducing the variance of the predictive model [22]. Bagging generates several bootstrap samples from the training set, each of which is used to train multiple base estimators of same type. To obtain a final prediction, all base estimator predictions are aggregated [28]. Mathematically, this bagging process can be described as follow.

$$\hat{f} = \frac{1}{E} \sum_{a=1}^{E} t_a(d) \tag{3}$$

where $\hat{f}$ is the final prediction, E is the total no of base estimators, t_a denotes the a-th base estimator, and d denotes the individual data points. Each base estimator t_a is trained on a distinct bootstrap sample, and their predictions are aggregated by using averaging method for regression problem or majority voting method for classification problem.

3.5 Stage 5: Proposed Model Evaluation Criteria

In this stage, five established and reliable evaluation metrics were used for evaluation. The brief explanations of the proposed evaluation metrics are discussed below:

Mean Squared Error (MSE). It is utilized to evaluate quality by computing the average of squared errors between actual values and predictions [26]. MSE is non-negative; therefore, a value of zero demonstrates a high-quality estimator [36]. MSE is calculated for each individual observation 'a' across 'm' samples as the sum of squared differences between actual and predicted values, divided by the total no of samples [26, 36].

$$MSE = \frac{1}{m} \sum_{a=0}^{m-1} (Actual\ value_a - Predicted\ value_a)^2 \tag{4}$$

Root Mean Squared Error (RMSE). It provides the sample's standard deviation for the variations between actual values and predicted values [10, 36]. This evaluation is used to address a limitation in which MAE's sensitivity to moderate errors understates the impact of large errors. Evaluating larger errors is important as they signify critical deviations from predicted model performance. It is computed by finding the square root of the mean of the squared differences between actual and predicted values [15]. The equation is mentioned as follows:

$$RMSE = \sqrt{\frac{1}{m} \sum_{a=0}^{m-1} (Actual\ value_a - Predicted\ value_a)^2} \tag{5}$$

Mean Absolute Error (MAE). It serves as a risk evaluation metric that evaluates the predicted absolute error rate between actual values and predictions [6]. It is calculated for each individual data point 'a' among 'm' no of samples using the following formula [26]:

$$MAE = \frac{1}{m} \sum_{a=0}^{m-1} |Actual\ value_a - Predicted\ value_a| \tag{6}$$

Mean Magnitude of Relative Error (MMRE). It calculates the mean of the magnitude of the relative errors between actual and predicted values in a set of data points [1, 10]. The MMRE for every individual observation 'a' can be calculated using the following formula [6, 26, 29]:

$$MMRE = \frac{1}{m} \sum_{a=0}^{m-1} \left| \frac{Actual\ value_a - Predicted\ value_a}{Actual\ value_a} \right| \tag{7}$$

Coefficient of Determination (R-Square/R^2). It represents the proportion of the dependent variable's variance explained by the independent variable(s) in a regression model [6, 36]. This proportion is used to determine how accurately the actual values are predicted. A R^2 value close to 1 is regarded as the finest achievable score.

The R^2 for each individual data point 'a' can be computed over the total amount of samples 'm' as follows [26].

$$R_a^2 = 1 - \frac{\sum_{a=1}^{m} (\text{Actual value}_a - \text{Predicted value}_a)^2}{\sum_{a=1}^{m} (\text{Actual value}_a - \overline{y})^2} \tag{8}$$

where, $\overline{y} = \sum_{a=1}^{m} \text{Actual value}_a$

Figure 1 depicts the architecture of the DBEEST. The initial section of the figure depicts the processes of smart data preparation and hyperparameter optimization whereas the second section depicts the construction and training of six separate homogeneous ensembles through bagging (or Bootstrap Aggregation). The third section of the figure depicts the average method for integrating all six homogeneous ensemble predictions, and the figure's fourth and final section depicts the evaluation of the proposed model.

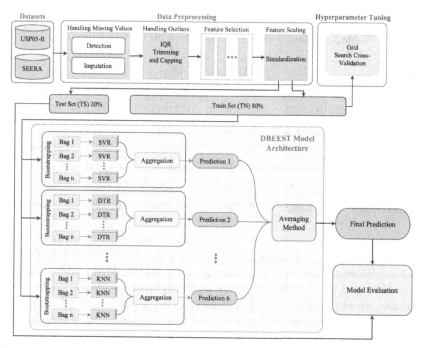

Fig. 1. Process of constructing the proposed model (DBEEST) to estimate software effort.

4   Results and Discussion

In this section, the experimental results of the proposed model (DBEEST) along with the results of six separate homogeneous ensembles based on bagging on both proposed datasets are presented individually. It was discovered that the smaller values of the MSE, RMSE, MAE, and MMRE values, along with an R^2 value nearer to 1, indicated a better-performing model. All experiments were performed using Jupyter Notebook (version 6.5.2) with the most recent version of Python 3.10.12.

4.1   Performance of Models

Tables 2 and 3 present the performance of the models on both proposed datasets. In Table 2, the DBEEST model exhibits the lowest values for MSE, RMSE, MAE, and MMRE, which are 0.02903, 0.17039, 0.13239, and 0.39513, respectively. Additionally, it achieves a higher R^2 value of 0.94554 compared to individual bagging ensembles on the USP05-FT dataset. Table 3 presents the performance of the models on the SEERA dataset, and the results demonstrate that the proposed model again performed well on this dataset, yielding a higher R^2 value of 0.93685 and lower values of 0.07322, 0.27059, 0.20363, and 0.29162 for MSE, RMSE, MAE, and MMRE, respectively.

Table 2. Evaluation results of models using the USP05-FT dataset.

Models	MSE	RMSE	MAE	MMRE	R^2
Bagging SVR	0.10648	0.32632	0.22532	0.66101	0.80027
Bagging DTR	0.05017	0.24042	0.23565	0.59417	0.90465
Bagging LR	0.15432	0.39284	0.31307	0.75264	0.71053
Bagging MLP	0.07768	0.27872	0.21129	0.59373	0.85429
Bagging RFR	0.04094	0.20235	0.24374	0.53931	0.91320
Bagging KNN	0.08173	0.28589	0.18244	0.69922	0.84669
DBEEST Model	**0.02903**	**0.17039**	**0.13239**	**0.39513**	**0.94554**

After a comparative evaluation of the models, it was determined that the DBEEST model outperformed, achieving low values for MSE, RMSE, MAE, MMRE, and high R^2 values on both datasets. In ML, every algorithm functions uniquely, with distinct methodologies and mechanisms for each dataset [10], a fact evident when observing the performance of bagging SVR and bagging KNN in Table 2 and 3. Bagging SVR exhibits good performance on the USP05-FT dataset by providing low error measures of MSE = 0.10648, RMSE = 0.32632, MAE = 0.22532, MMRE = 0.66101, and a high R^2 value of 0.80027, while on SEERA datasets, it appears slightly less accurate by providing marginally higher error measures of MSE = 0.55993, RMSE = 0.74828, MAE = 0.52431, MMRE = 0.74175, and a low R^2 value of 0.51716. Bagging KNN, on the other hand, performs poorly on the SEERA dataset by providing high error measures

Table 3. Evaluation results of models using the SEERA dataset.

Models	MSE	RMSE	MAE	MMRE	R^2
Bagging SVR	0.55993	0.74828	0.52431	0.74175	0.51716
Bagging DTR	0.09561	0.30596	0.24005	0.90759	0.90927
Bagging LR	0.49503	0.70358	0.60785	1.52982	0.57312
Bagging MLP	0.19033	0.43627	0.34446	1.23672	0.83587
Bagging RFR	0.09957	0.31555	0.23740	0.84309	0.91413
Bagging KNN	0.65338	0.80832	0.62331	1.28796	0.43658
DBEEST Model	**0.07322**	**0.27059**	**0.20363**	**0.29162**	**0.93685**

of MSE = 0.65338, RMSE = 0.80832, MAE = 0.62331, MMRE = 1.28796, and a low R^2 value of 0.43658, but performs well on the USP05-FT dataset by providing low error measures of MSE = 0.08173, RMSE = 0.28589, MAE = 0.18244, MMRE = 0.69922, and a high R^2 value of 0.84669. The diversity of estimators in the proposed DBEEST model can effectively mitigate this issue by leveraging the strengths of multiple algorithms. This can be proved by examining the evaluation metric results for the proposed model in Tables 2 and 3 across diverse datasets. The performance of the proposed model was thoroughly evaluated across these two diverse datasets, each representing a wide variety of projects with different characteristics and requirements. The SEERA dataset encompasses projects with varying software sizes, development methodologies, complexities, programming languages, application domains, and extensive feature sets, while the USP05-FT dataset focuses on smaller-scale projects from different domains with distinct characteristics and requirements. These projects represented scenarios with distinct challenges, such as the complexity of internal calculations, resource constraints, and intricate software architectures. The DBEEST model has demonstrated consistent and robust performance across these diverse datasets, showcasing its ability to predict software effort effectively in various project scenarios. Furthermore, the DBEEST model structure, which includes training base estimators on diverse subsets (bags) and integrating different bagging ensembles, enhances robustness and generalization while reducing individual model variability. Table 4 provides the DBEEST models' average overall prediction performance across both datasets for assessing their generalization ability, determined by taking the average of the evaluating metrics results. Additionally, Figs. 2 and 3 depict the graphical representation of actual effort values and the predicted effort values of a DBEEST model on the USP05-FT and SEERA datasets, respectively. The green grid lines with green square datapoints represent the actual effort values, whereas the blue grid lines with red circle datapoints represent the predicted effort values. The closer the actual and predicted effort values are, the lower the error and the better the model. The graphs demonstrate that the actual effort and predicted effort values are close to each other.

Table 4. Average overall performance of the DBEEST model on both proposed datasets.

Datasets	MSE	RMSE	MAE	MMRE	R^2
USP05-FT	0.02903	0.17039	0.13239	0.39513	0.94554
SEERA	0.07322	0.27059	0.20363	0.29162	0.93685
Overall Performance	**0.05112**	**0.22099**	**0.16801**	**0.39337**	**0.94120**

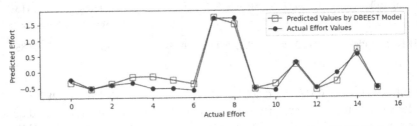

Fig. 2. Actual vs predicted effort using the DBEEST Model for the USP05-FT dataset.

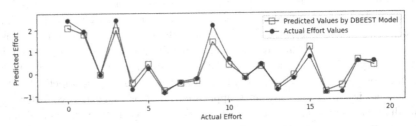

Fig. 3. Actual vs predicted effort using the DBEEST Model for the SEERA dataset.

5 Conclusion and Future Work

This study proposed a **D**iverse **B**agging **E**ffort **EST**imation (DBEEST) model to enhance software project effort estimation. Six separate homogenous bagging ensembles are constructed by using multiple diverse base estimators such as SVR, DTR, LR, MLP, RFR, and KNN. They are then combined through an averaging method to produce the final prediction. To further enhance the model's performance, data pre-processing techniques and hyperparameter tuning are employed on the USP05-FT and SEERA datasets. According to the evaluation results, the proposed DBEEST model provides consistent and good results with an overall average of low MSE, RMSE, MAE, and MMRE values (0.05112, 0.22099, 0.16801, and 0.39337, respectively) and an overall average of high R^2 values (0.94120) across both proposed datasets and outperformed all individual bagging ensembles. This research will significantly help software development companies enhance their software project management capabilities, resulting in heightened success and effectiveness in their software projects. The future prospects are to integrate the expert estimation technique with this proposed model (DBEEST). By integrating expert estimations, the machine learning model is able to capture the intuition and human experience for highly innovative projects.

References

1. Bakmeedeniya, T.: Estimation of software development effort based on decision tree approach (2021)
2. Ritu, Garg, Y.: Comparative analysis of machine learning techniques in effort estimation. In: 2022 International Conference on Machine Learning, Big Data, Cloud and Parallel Computing (COM-IT-CON). IEEE, pp. 401–405 (2022)
3. Issa, A., Odeh, M., Coward, D.: Software cost estimation using use-case models: a critical evaluation. In: Proceedings - 2006 International Conference on Information and Communication Technologies: From Theory to Applications, ICTTA 2006 (2006)
4. Shrivastava, A.K.: Comparative study of different project size estimation technique for the development of software. Int. J. Sci. Res. Sci. Technol., 231–236 (2018). https://doi.org/10.32628/IJSRST18401142
5. Assefa, Y., Berhanu, F., Tilahun, A., Alemneh, E.: Software effort estimation using machine learning algorithm. In: 2022 International Conference on Information and Communication Technology for Development for Africa, ICT4DA 2022 (2022)
6. Shivhare, J., Rath, S.K.: Software effort estimation using machine learning techniques. In: ACM International Conference Proceeding Series (2014)
7. Zakaria, N.A., Ismail, A.R., Ali, A.Y., et al.: Software project estimation with machine learning. Int. J. Adv. Comput. Sci. Appl., **12** (2021). https://doi.org/10.14569/IJACSA.2021.0120685
8. Marapelli, B.: Software development effort duration and cost estimation using linear regression and K-nearest neighbors machine learning algorithms. Int. J. Innov. Technol. Exploring Eng. (2019)
9. Satapathy, S.M., Acharya, B.P., Rath, S.K.: Early stage software effort estimation using random forest technique based on use case points. IET Softw. **10** (2016). https://doi.org/10.1049/iet-sen.2014.0122
10. Pospieszny, P., Czarnacka-Chrobot, B., Kobylinski, A.: An effective approach for software project effort and duration estimation with machine learning algorithms. J. Syst. Softw. **137** (2018). https://doi.org/10.1016/j.jss.2017.11.066
11. Kapoor, D., Gupta, R.K.: Software cost estimation techniques– a review of literature. Int. J. Res. Dev. Appl. Sci. Eng. (IJRDASE), 9359 (2014)
12. Sarro, F., Moussa, R., Petrozziello, A., Harman, M.: Learning from mistakes: machine learning enhanced human expert effort estimates. IEEE Trans. Softw. Eng. **48** (2022). https://doi.org/10.1109/TSE.2020.3040793
13. Moharreri, K., Sapre, A.V., Ramanathan, J., Ramnath, R.: Cost-effective supervised learning models for software effort estimation in agile environments. In: Proceedings - International Computer Software and Applications Conference (2016)
14. Fernández-Diego, M., Méndez, E.R., González-Ladrón-De-Guevara, F., et al.: An update on effort estimation in agile software development: a systematic literature review. IEEE Access **8** (2020)
15. Priya Varshini, A.G., Anitha Kumari, K., Varadarajan, V.: Estimating software development efforts using a random forest-based stacked ensemble approach. Electronics (Switzerland) **10** (2021). https://doi.org/10.3390/electronics10101195
16. Makris, C., Vikatos, P., Visser, J.: Classification model for predicting cost slippage in governmental ICT projects. In: Proceedings of the ACM Symposium on Applied Computing (2015)

17. Al Asheeri, M.M., Hammad, M.: Machine learning models for software cost estimation. In: 2019 International Conference on Innovation and Intelligence for Informatics, Computing, and Technologies, 3ICT 2019 (2019)
18. Amazal, F.A., Idri, A., Abran, A.: Analysis of cluster center initialization of 2FA-kprototypes analogy-based software effort estimation. J. Softw. Evol. Process **31** (2019). https://doi.org/10.1002/smr.2180
19. Hammad, M.: Software cost estimation using stacked ensemble classifier and feature selection. Int. J. Adv. Comput. Sci. Appl. **14** (2023). https://doi.org/10.14569/IJACSA.2023.0140621
20. Mustafa, E.I., Osman, R.: SEERA: a software cost estimation dataset for constrained environments. In: PROMISE 2020 - Proceedings of the 16th ACM International Conference on Predictive Models and Data Analytics in Software Engineering, Co-located with ESEC/FSE 2020 (2020)
21. Bilal, K., Wahab, K., Muhammad, A., Nazir, J.: Software cost estimation: algorithmic and non-algorithmic approaches. Int. J. Data Sci. Adv. Anal. **2** (2020)
22. Alhazmi, O.H., Khan, M.Z.: Software effort prediction using ensemble learning methods. J. Softw. Eng. Appl. **13** (2020). https://doi.org/10.4236/jsea.2020.137010
23. Scott, E., Pfahl, D.: Using developers' features to estimate story points. In: ACM International Conference Proceeding Series (2018)
24. Rahman, M., Roy, P.P., Ali, M., et al.: Software effort estimation using machine learning technique. Int. J. Adv. Comput. Sci. Appl. **14** (2023). https://doi.org/10.14569/IJACSA.2023.0140491
25. Han, W.M.: Discriminating risky software project using neural networks. Comput. Stand. Interfaces **40** (2015)
26. Kanneganti, A.: Using ensemble machine learning methods in estimating software development effort (2020)
27. Priya Varshini, A.G., Anitha Kumari, K., Janani, D., Soundariya, S.: Comparative analysis of machine learning and deep learning algorithms for software effort estimation. J. Phys. Conf. Ser. (2021)
28. Hu, Y., Feng, B., Mo, X., et al.: Cost-sensitive and ensemble-based prediction model for outsourced software project risk prediction. Decis. Support Syst. **72** (2015). https://doi.org/10.1016/j.dss.2015.02.003
29. Malhotra, R., Jain, A.: Software effort prediction using statistical and machine learning methods. Int. J. Adv. Comput. Sci. Appl. **2** (2011). https://doi.org/10.14569/ijacsa.2011.020122
30. Mahmood, Y., Kama, N., Azmi, A., et al.: Software effort estimation accuracy prediction of machine learning techniques: a systematic performance evaluation. Softw. Pract. Exp. **52** (2022). https://doi.org/10.1002/spe.3009
31. Hidmi, E.: Software development effort estimation using ensemble machine learning. Int. J. Comput. Commun. Instrum. Eng. **4** (2017). https://doi.org/10.15242/IJCCIE.E0317026
32. Desai, V.S., Mohanty, R.: ANN-cuckoo optimization technique to predict software cost estimation. In: 2018 Conference on Information and Communication Technology, CICT 2018. Institute of Electrical and Electronics Engineers Inc. (2018)
33. Ramaswamy, V., Suma, V., Pushphavathi, T.P.: An approach to predict software project success by cascading clustering and classification. IET Semin. Dig. (2012)
34. Ghotra, B., McIntosh, S., Hassan, A.E.: Revisiting the impact of classification techniques on the performance of defect prediction models. In: Proceedings - International Conference on Software Engineering (2015)
35. Rekha, T., Rai, P.K.: Machine learning methods of effort estimation and it's performance evaluation criteria. Int. J. Comput. Sci. Mob. Comput. **6** (2017)

36. Dada, E.G., Oyewola, D.O., Joseph, S.B., Duada, A.B.: Ensemble machine learning model for software defect prediction. Adv. Mach. Learn. Artif. Intell. **2** (2021). https://doi.org/10.33140/amlai.02.01.03

37. Mahdi, M.N., Mohamed, M.Z., Yusof, A., et al.: Design and development of machine learning technique for software project risk assessment - a review. In: 2020 8th International Conference on Information Technology and Multimedia, ICIMU 2020 (2020)

38. Sehra, S.K., Brar, Y.S., Kaur, N., Sehra, S.S.: Research patterns and trends in software effort estimation. Inf. Softw. Technol. **91** (2017)

39. Singh, R.: Machine learning algorithms and ensemble technique to improve prediction of students performance. Int. J. Adv. Trends Comput. Sci. Eng. **9** (2020). https://doi.org/10.30534/ijatcse/2020/221932020

40. Sagi, O., Rokach, L.: Ensemble learning: a survey. Wiley Interdiscip. Rev. Data Min. Knowl. Discov. **8** (2018)

41. Luong, A.V., et al.: A homogeneous-heterogeneous ensemble of classifiers. In: Yang, H., Pasupa, K., Leung, A.C.-S., Kwok, J.T., Chan, J.H., King, I. (eds.) Neural Information Processing. CCIS, vol. 1333, pp. 251–259. Springer, Cham (2020). https://doi.org/10.1007/978-3-030-63823-8_30

42. Wang, H., Zhuang, W., Zhang, X.: Software defect prediction based on gated hierarchical LSTMs. IEEE Trans. Reliab. **70** (2021). https://doi.org/10.1109/TR.2020.3047396

43. Idri, A., Amazal, F.A., Abran, A.: Accuracy comparison of analogy-based software development effort estimation techniques. Int. J. Intell. Syst. **31** (2016). https://doi.org/10.1002/int.21748

44. Sathesh, A., Hamdan, Y.B.: Analysis of software sizing and project estimation prediction by machine learning classification. J. Ubiquit. Comput. Commun. Technol. **3** (2022). https://doi.org/10.36548/jucct.2021.4.006

45. Nakai, M., Chen, D.-G., Nishimura, K., Miyamoto, Y.: Comparative study of four methods in missing value imputations under missing completely at random mechanism. Open J. Stat. **04** (2014). https://doi.org/10.4236/ojs.2014.41004

46. Pereira Barata, A., Takes, F.W., Van Den Herik, H.J., Veenman, C.J.: Imputation methods outperform missing-indicator for data missing completely at random. In: IEEE International Conference on Data Mining Workshops, ICDMW (2019)

47. Abdelhadi, S., Elbahnasy, K., Abdelsalam, M.: A proposed model to predict auto insurance claims using machine learning techniques. J. Theor. Appl. Inf. Technol. **98** (2020)

48. Jadhav, A., Pramod, D., Ramanathan, K.: Comparison of performance of data imputation methods for numeric dataset. Appl. Artif. Intell. **33** (2019). https://doi.org/10.1080/08839514.2019.1637138

49. Iwata, K., Nakashima, T., Anan, Y., Ishii, N.: Applying machine learning classification to determining outliers in effort for embedded software development projects. In: Proceedings - 2019 6th International Conference on Computational Science/Intelligence and Applied Informatics, CSII 2019 (2019)

50. Dovoedo, Y.H., Chakraborti, S.: Boxplot-based outlier detection for the location-scale family. Commun. Stat. Simul. Comput. **44**, 1492–1513 (2015). https://doi.org/10.1080/03610918.2013.813037

51. Elssied, N.O.F., Ibrahim, O., Osman, A.H.: A novel feature selection based on one-way ANOVA F-test for e-mail spam classification. Res. J. Appl. Sci. Eng. Technol. **7** (2014). https://doi.org/10.19026/rjaset.7.299

52. Gao, K., Khoshgoftaar, T.M., Wang, H., Seliya, N.: Choosing software metrics for defect prediction: an investigation on feature selection techniques. Softw. Pract. Exp. **41** (2011). https://doi.org/10.1002/spe.1043

53. Pedregosa, F., Varoquaux, G., Gramfort, A., et al.: Scikit-learn: machine learning in Python. J. Mach. Learn. Res. **12** (2011).

54. Tsamardinos, I., Rakhshani, A., Lagani, V.: Performance-estimation properties of cross-validation-based protocols with simultaneous hyper-parameter optimization. Int. J. Artif. Intell. Tools (2015)

55. Adnan, M., Alarood, A.A.S., Uddin, M.I., ur Rehman, I.: Utilizing grid search cross-validation with adaptive boosting for augmenting performance of machine learning models. PeerJ Comput. Sci. **8** (2022). https://doi.org/10.7717/PEERJ-CS.803

56. Popescu, M., Balas, V.E., Mastorakis, N.: Multilayer perceptron and neural networks LILIANA PERESCU-POPESCU. WSEAS Trans. Circuits Syst. **8**, 579–588 (2009)

Integrating Dual Strengths: A Hybrid Architecture Merging Decentralized Trust with Server-Side Efficiency for Enhanced Secure Transactions

Priya Mali, Parth Shirole$^{(\boxtimes)}$, and Sandip Shingade

Veermata Jijabai Technological Institute (VJTI), Mumbai, India
{ppmali_b20,pashirole_b20}@ce.vjti.ac.in, stshingade@it.vjti.ac.in

Abstract. The use of payment gateways (PGs) in conventional online stores' methods of accepting credit card and cheque payments drives up transaction fees. The fundamental difficulty is in guaranteeing the authenticity of digital payment QR codes and the safety of financial transactions. There are concerns over the security of these transactions and the possibility of phishing attempts in an environment where QR code adoption is trending for digital payments. In this study, we introduce a new "Secure Payment Model" that aims to solve all of these problems. The fundamental goals of this model are to guarantee non-repudiation and transaction integrity from the production of QR codes to the execution of the transaction. The suggested methodology assures the security of electronic payments and avoids the need for intermediary services like PGs by implementing a secure digital signature mechanism. Both the general safety of online purchases and the operational expenses of maintaining such services are greatly alleviated by this. To optimize the financial parts of e-commerce operations and promote trust and security in digital transactions, the secure payment model provides a comprehensive solution.

Keywords: Payment Gateway · Digital Signature · Integrity · QR Code

1 Introduction

In the digital world of today, where things change quickly, QR codes are becoming more popular. This is a sign of a move toward faster and easier ways to do things. The widespread use of these codes brings up a basic question: why QR codes? Before you can get into the details of this, you need to know how cryptographic methods protect transactions. But before getting into the details of safe transactions, it's important to look at the authentication steps that come before transactions.

O. Gervasi et al. (Eds.): ICCSA 2024, LNCS 14814, pp. 311–326, 2024.
https://doi.org/10.1007/978-3-031-64608-9_20

Because they are so flexible and easy to use, QR codes have become essential for making digital transfers possible. Building on this, cryptographic methods become very important for making sure that digital transactions are safe and honest. [1] is a source that talks about how important security methods are in many different areas.

Authentication of parties involved in transactions stands as a cornerstone in establishing trust within digital interactions. Two papers, [2,3], explore the multifaceted applications of Public Key Infrastructure (PKI) in authenticating parties before transactions occur.

The necessity of a blockchain-based electronic payment system is underscored by its reliance on fundamental elements such as public keys, private keys, and digital signatures. To fully interact with cryptographic technologies, it is necessary to understand the fundamentals of Public Key Infrastructure (PKI), as well as the roles of public and private key. In these systems, a public key is used to encrypt data, assuring secure transmission, and the corresponding private key, which is only in the recipient's hands, is used for decryption. This guarantees that access to the information is restricted solely to the intended recipients. The implementation of asymmetric encryption is vital in ensuring the security of communications. In addition, digital signatures serve as distinct electronic identifiers, which are indispensable for validating the genuineness and soundness of digital correspondence. The recipient is able to validate these signatures, which were generated with the sender's private key and appended to the transmitted data, using the sender's public key. It is crucial to validate this process in order to establish the message's provenance and ensure that it has not undergone any alterations throughout transmission.

Non-repudiation and trustworthiness are very important for users who use any system, so we need a safe way to authenticate the users. Authentication, which checks that people are who they say they are before a deal, is very important. Non-repudiation is important because it makes sure that a party can't say they weren't involved in a deal. Reliability is mostly achieved by digital signatures. The data transmitted by the special signature associated with a private key is closely related to the source. In digital transactions, integrity is maintaining data consistency and accuracy during transmission. Hashing algorithms are one of the cryptographic methods that help to guarantee that data is not altered while being sent. Digital signatures' tamper-evident character helps to preserve data integrity during transmission in a big way.

In this research, our contribution lies in addressing the integration of blockchain, QR codes, and cryptographic methods in secure electronic payment systems:

- We aim to elucidate how these technological elements can be synergistically combined to enhance the security and efficiency of digital transactions.
- Our approach involves the development of a system that not only incorporates these technologies but also adapts to the challenges of evolving digital landscapes, ensuring resilience and adaptability in payment platforms.

- We propose a novel framework for integrating these technologies in a way that transforms traditional payment platforms, making them more secure and versatile.
- The experimental implementation of our system is compared with existing models, using standard and novel algorithms. This comparison is crucial to demonstrate the effectiveness and innovation of our approach in the context of rapidly advancing digital transaction technologies.

The subsequent portions of the paper are structured as follows: This Sect. 2 provides an elaborate account of the incorporation of blockchain, QR codes, and cryptographic techniques in electronic payment systems. It discusses the existing difficulties and potential advantages in this field. Section 3 presents the first background knowledge that is relevant to our suggested methodology. It introduces the fundamental ideas of blockchain technology, QR codes, and cryptographic techniques. Section 4 explores the technological elements of our strategy, explaining how these technologies are used to improve the security and functionality of electronic payment systems. Section 5 presents our recommended methodologies, providing a comprehensive explanation of the precise techniques and algorithms utilized to seamlessly include blockchain, QR codes, and cryptographic procedures. The experimental results are extensively expounded upon in Sect. 6. This section showcases the results of our technique, contrasting it with existing ways to illustrate its effectiveness and originality. Section 7 ends with a concise overview of our discoveries, contributions, and a conversation on possible directions for future investigation in the field of secure electronic payment systems.

2   Literature Survey

The proposed blockchain e-commerce payment system by [4] involves a merchant, customer's smartphone application, and a blockchain system, ensuring secure and efficient transactions. The process includes payment requests through QR codes, confirmation from the blockchain, and transaction verification using digital signatures for integrity and non-repudiation. The subsystems, including Merchant, Customer Application, and Blockchain, collaborate to authenticate and process payments in real-time, addressing concerns related to security and efficiency in e-commerce transactions.

The research conducted by [5] introduces a novel QR-based visual cryptography approach. In this method, the merchant initiates a payment request, and a QR code is subsequently generated. The customer, in turn, scans the QR code to complete the payment process. The security aspect is anchored in the (2,2) Visual Cryptography Scheme (VCS), where two shares are generated, and these shares must be superimposed to reconstruct the original image, ensuring robust security measures.

The research conducted by [6] presents an innovative approach to enhance the security of QR code usage in a general context. The method involves converting the information intended for storage into a QR code, encrypting this QR code, and ultimately transforming the encrypted data into a final QR code.

[7] introduced a system to mitigate the risk of attackers embedding malicious content in QR codes, aiming to safeguard unsuspecting customers from potential device infections resulting from scanning such codes.

The research by [8] employs a qualitative method involving data collection, analysis, interpretation, and validation to develop a system for students' final project approval. It explores QR code methods, hash functions, and cryptographic algorithms, with a focus on the Elliptic Curve Digital Signature Algorithm (ECDSA) for data integrity and authentication.

[9] explores the integration of blockchain technology in payment gateways to enhance security and efficiency. It addresses concerns related to money laundering and terrorism financing by considering proposals to restrict blockchain access to government-identified individuals.

[10] introduces a robust system for secure digital transactions. Employing a two-layer security approach, the model utilizes dynamic QR codes to encapsulate unique order-specific information, enhancing security against cyber-attacks. The first layer involves generating dynamic QR codes with encrypted payment details, while the second layer employs digital signatures for verification. This innovative approach ensures the integrity and non-repudiation of transactions, providing a secure and efficient solution for digital payments in the e-commerce landscape.

The paper [11] proposes an innovative secure mobile payment model in their work. The authors introduce a two-layered approach emphasizing dynamic QR codes for unique order-specific information, reducing vulnerability to cyber-attacks. Notably, their model streamlines the registration process, avoiding the need for a general CA certificate, and ensures secure transactions with a robust two-factor authentication mechanism. The proposed work stands out for its user-friendly payment approval process, employing encrypted QR codes and a double-checking mechanism for enhanced security and integrity.

In the study by [12], the authors investigate the influence of technology anxiety, vulnerabilities, and privacy concerns on user resistance to facial recognition payment (FRP). Utilizing the Antecedent-Privacy Concern-Outcome (APCO) model, the research explores the relationships among these variables through an online survey involving 1058 Chinese users. The results reveal significant associations between technology anxiety and vulnerabilities, while privacy concerns positively correlate with user resistance to FRP. The study fills a research gap by addressing the psychological antecedents, such as technological anxiety and perceived vulnerability, within the context of FRP adoption in China.

The payment system proposed in [13] incorporates a multi-step authentication process. It begins with a registered mobile user logging into the system using a customer account and PIN. The system employs a secure session ID, a server certificate ID, and a public key for connections. The mobile user captures a QR code, decodes it to retrieve product information, and initiates a purchasing request with a digital signature. The merchant server authenticates the mobile client, processes the payment transaction, and sends a confirmed message with a QR code receipt. This integrated use of QR codes and digital signatures ensures secure authentication and transaction processes in the proposed payment system.

Specific gaps are present in all research: Research may not fully integrate blockchain technology into electronic payment systems, QR codes in transactions: Secure payment systems may have QR code integration issues, Cryptographic methods are well-studied, yet electronic payment systems may need new uses, Existing solutions may not handle digital transaction non-repudiation and integrity, Electronic payment systems struggle to adapt to rapidly changing technology. A secure, flexible, and scalable system to adapt to future technology is proposed in this research. All we brought to the gathering was consideration of the knowledge gaps that must be filled in our designed strategy. In this methodology:

- In our research project, we propose and contribute a novel approach to secure electronic payment systems, addressing gaps in prior literature. Our system uniquely integrates blockchain, QR codes, and advanced cryptographic methods, setting a new standard in digital transaction security. By emphasizing the critical roles of public and private keys, along with digital signatures, our approach not only enhances data encryption and decryption processes but also strengthens user authentication, non-repudiation, and data integrity. This comprehensive model addresses previous shortcomings in ensuring secure and authenticated transactions.
- The proposed system has implications that extend beyond the current technological landscape. It anticipates future challenges and evolves to meet them, offering a robust and adaptable framework for electronic payment systems. This foresight is crucial in an era of rapid digital transformation. Our research not only redefines the security paradigms of digital transactions but also provides a scalable model capable of adapting to emerging technologies and evolving cyber threats, thereby ensuring long-term resilience and reliability of electronic payment platforms.

3 Preliminary Background

The careful and strategic selection of critical components and technologies has been undertaken during the establishment phase of the Secure Payment Model project, with the aim of guaranteeing a payment experience that is both secure and efficient, while also being intuitive to users.

The Merchant Component utilizes Angular (version 16.2.0) and Angular CLI (version 16.2.9) as its front-end framework. Angular is well-known for its strong architecture and modular design, which makes it easier to create dynamic user interfaces that are important for merchant interactions in the payment system. By incorporating Angular CLI, the development process is made more efficient, improving the capacity to maintain and scale the code.

The Customer Component in the user interface is built using React (version 18.2.0). React's efficacy as a JavaScript library for constructing user interfaces is utilized to deliver customers with a prompt, engaging, and user-friendly payment interface. React's modular design enables the development of reusable components, enhancing the overall user experience.

The Server Component, which manages server-side operations, utilizes Node (version 20.10.0) and Express (version 4.18.2). Node is well-known for its asynchronous and event-driven architecture, which guarantees fast and efficient execution of server-side JavaScript. Express achieves this by offering a simple yet robust web application framework that enables smooth communication between client-side components and the server.

Tailwind CSS (version 3.3.5) is used in the project to create a uniform and visually appealing design across all components. This utility-first CSS framework simplifies the styling process, enabling efficient customization and scalability while keeping a consistent design language.

4   Proposed System

4.1   System Overview

The proposed e-commerce payment paradigm introduces three essential entities: Merchant, Customer, and Server. In order to begin a payment, the Merchant requests the Customer's participation, creating a payment request that is encoded as a detailed message. The Merchant's private key is used to authenticate this message, which contains customer and payment information. This authentication process generates the Merchant's Digital Signature. The combination of the message and the Merchant's Digital Signature creates QR data, which is then sent to the Customer for scanning.

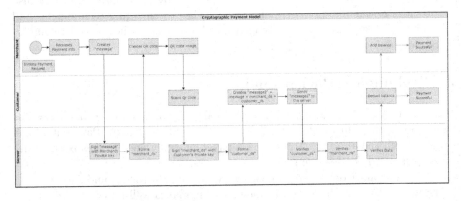

Fig. 1. Flowchart depicting cryptographic payment model

Upon scanning the QR code, the Customer's private key signs the digital signature, leading to the formation of the Customer's Digital Signature. Before the payment is executed, a second message, inclusive of payment details, the

Merchant's Digital Signature, and the Customer's Digital Signature is dispatched to the Server for authentication.

The Server meticulously verifies the information in Message2, ensuring the authenticity of both parties involved in the transaction. Following successful verification, the payment is duly processed, with the customer's account debited accordingly. This streamlined process not only establishes a secure authentication mechanism but also ensures the integrity of the e-commerce payment system.

Figure 1 depicts a payment model relying on cryptographic primitives to ensure secure and transparent transactions. The process initiates with a payment request, triggering the generation of a tamper-proof QR code containing an encrypted payload. Upon scanning, the device decrypts the information and signs it with the customer's private key, forming a digitally authenticated message. This signed message is transmitted to the merchant, who employs cryptographic verification techniques to validate the data and customer identity. Upon successful verification, the merchant deducts the amount from the customer's account via off-chain channels, potentially involving smart contracts or peer-to-peer interactions within the underlying blockchain network. Finally, a confirmation message relays the successful transaction completion.

This model eliminates the need for intermediary financial institutions, potentially reducing transaction fees and processing times. The cryptographic infrastructure safeguards against data breaches and fraudulent transactions, promoting user trust and financial security. Further research should investigate the scalability and privacy implications of this model, especially in large-scale deployments.

4.2   Comparison with Existing Blockchain Enhcanced QR Desgins

QR systems that are blockchain-enhanced have revolutionized cryptocurrency transactions by providing increased scalability, security, and transparency. Bitcoin Lightning Network, one of the extant systems, utilizes Bitcoin's blockchain in an efficient manner to facilitate swift and economical transactions. Integrating QR codes into its payment initiation process, Lightning Network ensures seamless and instant cryptocurrency transfers, improving user experience and accessibility. In contrast to our suggested payment model, Lightning Network places greater emphasis on scalability and speed, potentially neglecting specific facets pertaining to transparency and non-repudiation.

Ethereum Payment Channels is a significant system that enables the creation of programmable and secure payment channels using Ethereum's blockchain. By employing QR codes to initiate off-chain transactions, Ethereum Payment Channels guarantee the integrity of cryptocurrency transfers while reducing latency and transaction costs. Nevertheless, our payment model distinguishes itself by emphasizing non-repudiation and transparency through comprehensive verification processes. By incorporating digital signatures and meticulous data comparison, our system provides robust security measures against fraud and tampering, ensuring trust and accountability in transactions.

On the other hand, platforms such as Hyperledger Fabric, Ripple Interledger Protocol (ILP), and Stellar Anchor Systems prioritize high-quality blockchain solutions for businesses and payment networks that can function together seamlessly. Although these systems possess distinct attributes like secrecy and cross-ledger transactions, they might not possess the necessary speed and accessibility for consumer-oriented bitcoin transactions. Our payment approach resolves these concerns by integrating the security and transparency of blockchain technology with the rapidity and scalability required for streamlined customer transactions. Our method establishes a new benchmark for secure and smooth cryptocurrency payments over QR codes by giving utmost importance to security, non-repudiation, and transparency.

4.3   Choice of Architecture

Optimizing Security and Efficiency: A New Paradigm for Payment Systems: Even though decentralization is still an important idea in modern financial systems, our payment model is a big step forward because it uses a carefully planned design with server-side signing at its core. This method was created to not only provide security and user control, but also to unlock performance and scalability that have never been seen before. In the end, it will change the future of secure transactions.

Our commitment to user empowerment is unwavering. Unlike conventional models where sensitive keys reside on central servers, vulnerable to potential breaches, we prioritize user control. Private keys, the foundation of digital signatures, are never stored on the server. Instead, the keys are produced and securely stored on separate devices, guaranteeing that even in the event of a server breach, it would be extremely difficult to gain access to the keys. Adopting this strategy that prioritizes the needs and preferences of users helps to establish confidence and provide a strong basis for a secure financial system.

The strategic optimization of server-side signature goes beyond security. Offloading computationally difficult cryptographic tasks to dedicated servers speeds up transaction processing. Even as transaction traffic grows, this speeds confirmations, improves user experiences, and scales seamlessly. Client-side signature can be difficult on resource-constrained devices, but our approach works smoothly regardless.

The client-server architecture in Fig. 2 enables a sophisticated and proactive fraud detection strategy. Real-time sophisticated algorithm analysis is possible using server-side signed message and transaction data. These algorithms analyze patterns and discover abnormalities to forecast and prevent fraud before it affects users. Centralized fraud detection outperforms decentralized alternatives, protecting user assets and making financial markets safer.

Our method doesn't shy away from using the best parts of both fixed and decentralized systems. In line with decentralized ideas, we put user control and data privacy first by managing keys on the device. We also use the power of computer infrastructure to get the best processing speed, scalability, and fraud detection, which goes beyond what purely decentralized models can do. This

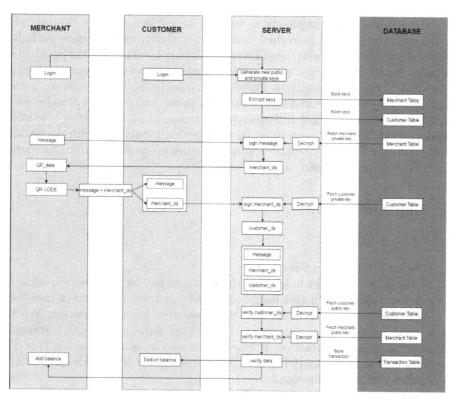

Fig. 2. Beyond client-side signing: Optimizing transaction performance and fraud prevention through server-side cryptographic processing

hybrid design is a big step forward. It shows how safe and effective payment systems can be, and how they can provide unmatched trust and performance in the future.

Furthermore, unlike the traditional method of SSL/TLS certificate issuing managed by Certificate Authorities (CAs), our approach to transaction security differs by emphasizing a decentralized and user-centric architecture. SSL/TLS certificates authenticate and secure websites by depending on a centralized Certificate Authority (CA) to issue digital certificates. However, our concept focuses on empowering users and boosting security through server-side signature.

Digital certificate applicants produce a private-public key pair during SSL/TLS certificate issuing. Data is encrypted and decrypted with these keys. After that, a Certificate Signing Request (CSR) with domain names and organizational details is created. The Certificate Authority (CA) authenticates the given data and applicant identity using the Certificate Signing Request (CSR). After verification, the CA digitally signs the certificate with its private key. Then, using the certification authority (CA) public key, the digital certificate can be checked, confirming the business's validity and protecting the sent data.

Nevertheless, in our architecture, we promote a shift away from this centralized method by granting individual users direct authority over private keys. Individual devices securely generate and store private keys, minimizing the possibility of server breach and increasing user authority over valuable cryptographic assets. Our design enhances security and efficiency by implementing server-side signature, resulting in accelerated transaction processing and proactive fraud detection. Our methodology revolutionizes secure transactions by utilizing a hybrid strategy that integrates centralized fraud detection capabilities with decentralized user control. This innovative approach ensures exceptional performance and confidence within the financial ecosystem

5   Implementation

5.1   Client-Side

1. *Merchant Application Subsystem*
   The implementation includes a user-friendly interface for merchants to initiate payment requests. Whether integrated into e-commerce platforms or financial apps, the core approach and default parameters remain consistent. When a merchant starts a request, a crucial payload named "message" transmits essential details like their email, transaction amount, and unique ID. This ID plays a vital role in verifying the QR code generated server-side, protecting against potential tampering.
   The message travels securely before getting to the consumer. It first goes to the server where it is digitally signed with the merchant's private key, producing a distinct "merchant_ds." Step two sees the server merge the signed "message" and "merchant_ds" into "qr_data," which it then sends back to the merchant. Lastly, the merchant creates a safe QR code that is shown to the customer to start payment using this "qr_data". The integrity and legitimacy of payment requests are ensured by this multi-layered procedure, which also strengthens transaction security generally and greatly lowers the possibility of QR code manipulation.

2. *Customer Application Subsystem*
   After scanning the QR code, the payment information is transferred from the merchant application to the client application. The communicated data consists of a collection of parameters, referred to as the "message," which contains important information such as the "merchant_email," "amount," "transaction_time," and "transaction_id." These parameters remain unchanged in our customer subsystem. At the same time, the "merchant_ds" is retrieved and sent to the server for additional processing.
   Following this, the server signs the received data, and a detailed explanation of this process can be found in the next section of our paper. This procedure generates the customer's digital signature, henceforth referred to as "customer_ds." Notably, the entire process is completed quickly after scanning the QR code.

Consumers must cross-check their device and merchant information. After verification, the customer can click pay. This action sends "message2," which includes "message," "customer_ds," and "merchant_ds" parameters for further verification.

Table 1. Software configuration for the experiment

Sr.no	Component	Software
1	Merchant	Angular 16.2.0, Angular CLI 16.2.9
2	Customer	React 18.2.0
3	Server	Node 20.10.0, Express 4.18.2
4	Styling	Tailwind CSS 3.3.5

5.2 Server-Side

1. *Account Creation*

   The account creation process for both businesses and customers is almost indistinguishable, necessitating the submission of crucial information such as name, email, and a password that is safe. After the user submits the data, it is transmitted to the server. At the server, the password is hashed using the bcrypt library. Next, a new record is generated in either the merchant or customer table, ensuring that the received data is safely kept. Significantly, at the initial account creation, both the private and public keys are initially set to the value of "null."

   When patrons or vendors re-authenticate, an additional set of private and public keys is generated utilizing the RSA algorithm, featuring a 2048-bit modulus. The private key is encoded in accordance with the Public-Key Cryptography Standards (PKCS) #8 format, while the public key is encoded in the Subject Public Key Info (SPKI) format. The format of both keys is Privacy Enhanced Mail (PEM). In order to validate the sensitivity of these keys, a precautionary encryption operation is executed prior to their storage in the database.

   The encryption technique described herein employs the "SERVER_KEY" in combination with an initialization vector ("IV") that implements the AES-256 CBC algorithm. Hexadecimal values are represented as the encrypted keys. Following this, the values from the database are substituted with the newly generated encrypted key values. By implementing this stringent procedure subsequent to every logon, security measures are fortified against the potential compromise or exposure of confidential data, underscoring a commitment to advanced data protection protocols.

2. *Digital Signature Creation*

All operations pertaining to digital signatures are executed server-side within the established system. When a merchant initiates a payment request, the creation of a digital signature becomes imperative for the formulation of the QR code. The server receives the payload, denoted as "message," encompassing crucial merchant data, including email, amount, transaction ID, among others. To facilitate the signing of this message, the server searches for the merchant's private key within the database. Given that the keys have been encrypted, a preliminary decryption process is undertaken utilizing the "SERVER_KEY" and "IV." Subsequently, the message undergoes signing through the crypto.sign function, employing the RSA-SHA256 algorithm. The resultant signature is then converted to base64 encoding. The resulting digital signature, termed "merchant_ds," is transmitted back to the merchant to facilitate QR code generation.

A similar procedure is activated when a customer scans the merchant's QR code, triggering the transmission of a payload containing the previously generated "merchant_ds." In a manner akin to the merchant's process, the customer's private key is retrieved from the database, decrypted using the "SERVER_KEY" and "IV," and then employed in the signing process. The crypto.sign function is again utilized, incorporating identical parameters and encoding. The resulting signature, denoted as "customer_ds," is communicated back to the customer application.

This systematic approach ensures the secure exchange of digital signatures, thereby contributing to the robustness of the payment verification process in our system.

3. *Verification*

The initiation of the verification process is triggered upon the activation of the pay button within the customer application, prompting the transmission of a payload comprising "message," "merchant_ds," and "customer_ds" to the server.

The verification process commences with customer authentication. To achieve this, the digital signature undergoes scrutiny utilizing the customer's public key, retrieved from the server. Following a decryption process akin to the one outlined in the previous section, a verification function is deployed. This function decrypts the "customer_ds" and subsequently compares it with the "merchant_ds." Verification that goes well opens the door for the next steps. As we transition to the process of verifying the merchant, a simultaneous procedure takes place where the merchant's public key is decrypted. Using a similar verification method, this step examines the decrypted "merchant_ds" in comparison to the original "message." If congruence is established, the algorithm advances to the next phase.

The last stage of the verification process involves a thorough examination and comparison of data from both the merchant and customer perspectives. More specifically, the fields "merchant_email" and "transaction_id" are carefully examined. Once all three verification processes are successfully completed, the payment is considered successful. Afterwards, notifications are sent to both subsystems, and the financial consequences of the transaction become apparent as the customer's balance is reduced and the merchant's balance is increased accordingly. In addition, a thorough log of the transaction is carefully maintained in a specialized table in the database, guaranteeing a comprehensive and orderly approach for storing records.

6 Experimental Results

Three critical workflows have been identified in our implementation as being indispensable to our payment system: the generation of digital signatures for the merchant and the consumer, and the verification of payment. In order to evaluate the efficacy of these procedures, we documented the duration of each process through its execution five times. The average time necessary to achieve optimal accuracy was then computed.

The process of creating a digital signature for a merchant commences when the user clicks the "Generate QR Code" icon. To ensure consistency, a fixed quantity was entered, accompanied by the automatic generation of a timestamp and transaction ID. Furthermore, the affiliated email was pre-populated with information from the verified vendor. To generate the digital signature, the QR code was generated in five separate instances. The exhaustive outcomes of these iterations are thoroughly recorded in Table 2, where the mean time is computed as 1.639 ms.

Table 2. Experimental Times (in milliseconds)

Experiment no.	Merchant DS Generation	Customer DS Generation	Verification
1	2.500	363.100	529.607
2	1.399	242.900	420.775
3	1.500	245.299	496.569
4	1.399	274.500	436.920
5	1.400	247.100	456.588

Similarly, the customer's digital signature is generated when the customer scans the QR code provided by the merchant. The process was replicated five times, and the corresponding times were accurately recorded in Table 2 as well. The resultant average time for customer digital signature generation is observed as 274.98 ms.

In a similar vein, the generation of the customer's digital signature occurs upon scanning the QR code that the merchant has supplied. The procedure was duplicated on five separate occasions, and the corresponding timings were recorded precisely in Table 2. The average time required to generate digital signatures for customers is determined to be 274.98 ms.

The final workflow consists of a multistage verification mechanism, which includes Retrieval and Decryption, Customer Verification, and Merchant Verification. At the outset, data pertaining to the merchant and the consumer is retrieved from the database by utilizing their respective email addresses. Concurrently, the relevant public keys undergo decryption, which establishes the foundation for subsequent phases of verification. Five repetitions of this meticulous procedure produced consistent results. The mean cumulative verification time was determined to be 468.09 ms

In addition, we assessed the frontend efficiency by monitoring CPU utilization and JavaScript (JS) heap size. Figures 3 and 4 present the facts pertaining to the customer application. Figure. 1 shows that the first peak corresponds to the moment when customers successfully log in, followed by a second rise during QR code scanning. After a successful scanning process, there is a subsequent decrease in CPU consumption, as depicted in Fig. 4. Significantly, the scale of the JS heap size in Fig. 4 is distinct from that of other photos.

Figure 5 presents data for the merchant app. Similar to the customer app, the first peak signifies merchant login, while the second peak indicates QR code generation by the merchant.

In summary, the merchant app exhibits comparatively better performance than the customer app. CPU usage for both applications remains below 30–35%, with JS heap size peaking around 15 MB.

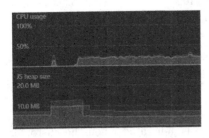

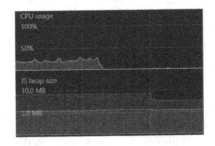

Fig. 3. Customer - Login and Start Scan performance

Fig. 4. Customer - Scan completed

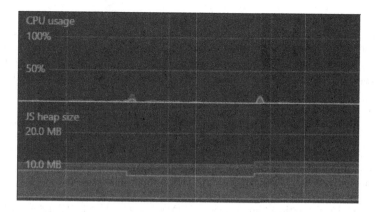

Fig. 5. Merchant - Login and QR code generation performance

7   Limitations

The design demonstrates deficiencies in error management, with a lack of intricate procedures that could potentially result in user perplexity, difficulties in debugging, and weaknesses in security. Duplications in the procedures of verifying signatures may hinder the efficiency of processing transactions and cause delays. Moreover, the lack of adequate inclusion of crucial security protocols, such as data encryption, supplementary authentication layers, and time synchronization, presents a threat to the security and reliability of transactions.

8   Conclusion and Future Work

The efficacy and security of our online payment processing system optimizes and simplifies the purchasing process. The hybrid architecture, which integrates decentralized elements with centralized processing, enhances the overall performance of the system. We showcase our commitment to enhancing the e-commerce payment experience by our rigorous criteria for maintaining data integrity and authenticity. Our model shines as an example of honesty and dependability since it follows industry norms. Essentially, our meticulous design establishes this payment model as a robust and efficient solution, ready to effortlessly handle the demands of modern e-commerce transactions.

This research serves as a solid foundation for future work that will delve into enhancing scalability and security, refining user experience, ensuring regulatory compliance, and integrating emerging technologies like AI and blockchain.

References

1. Qadir, A.M., Varol, N.: A review paper on cryptography. In: 2019 7th International Symposium on Digital Forensics and Security (ISDFS), Barcelos, Portugal, 2019, pp. 1–6 (2019). https://doi.org/10.1109/ISDFS.2019.8757514

2. Kfoury, E., Khoury, D.: Distributed public key infrastructure and PSK exchange based on blockchain technology. In: 2018 IEEE International Conference on Internet of Things (iThings) and IEEE Green Computing and Communications (GreenCom) and IEEE Cyber, Physical and Social Computing (CPSCom) and IEEE Smart Data (SmartData), Halifax, NS, Canada, 2018, pp. 1116–1120 (2018). https://doi.org/10.1109/Cybermatics_2018.2018.00203.

3. Dulia, O., Minochkin, D.: An exploration of public key infrastructure applications across diverse domains: a comparative analysis. Collect. Inf. Technol. secur. 11(1), 137–148 (2023). https://doi.org/10.20535/2411-1031.2023.11.2.293496

4. Kim, S.I., Kim, S.H.: E-commerce payment model using blockchain. J. Ambient Intell. Human. Comput. 13, 1673–1685 (2022)

5. Ahmad, L., Al-Sabha, R., Al-Haj, A.: Design and implementation of a secure QR payment system based on visual cryptography. In: 2021 7th International Conference on Information Management (ICIM), London, United Kingdom, 2021, pp. 40–44 (2021). https://doi.org/10.1109/ICIM52229.2021.9417129.

6. Gomathy, C.K.: Design and implementation of a secure QR payment system (2023)

7. Xu, R.: Optimized secure payment solution using QR code scanning based on operation-payment dual devices. BCP Bus. Manag. 17, 118–123 (2022). https://doi.org/10.54691/bcpbm.v17i.383

8. Wellem, T., Nataliani, Y., Iriani, A.: academic document authentication using elliptic curve digital signature algorithm and QR code. JOIV: Int. J. Inf. Visual. 6(3), 667–675 (2022). https://doi.org/10.30630/joiv.6.2.872

9. Duela, S., Raja, K., Umapathy, P., Rangnani, R., Patel, A.: Decentralized payment architecture for E-Commerce and utility transactions with government verified identities. Soft Comput. Signal Process. 313, 9 (2023).https://doi.org/10.1007/978-981-19-8669-7_2

10. Patil, N., Kondabala, R.: Two-layer secure mechanism for electronic transactions. In: 2022 International Conference on Recent Trends in Microelectronics, Automation, Computing and Communications Systems (ICMACC), Hyderabad, India, 2022, pp. 174–181 (2022). https://doi.org/10.1109/ICMACC54824.2022.10093478.

11. Suryotrisongko, H., Sugiharsono., Setiawan, B.: A novel mobile payment scheme based on secure quick response payment with minimal infrastructure for cooperative enterprise in developing countries. Procedia - Soc. Behav. Sci. 65, 906–912 (2012). https://doi.org/10.1016/j.sbspro.2012.11.218

12. Liu, Y., Yan, W., Hu, B.: Resistance to facial recognition payment in China: the influence of privacy-related factors. Telecommun. Policy. 45, 102155 (2021). https://doi.org/10.1016/j.telpol.2021.102155

13. Ashvini B., Vaishali B., Dhanashri B., Patil, Y.S.: Android mobile based payment system using QR (2016)

Optimizing On-Body Sensor Placements for Deep Learning-Driven Human Activity Recognition

Sakorn Mekruksavanich[1]([⊠])[iD] and Anuchit Jitpattanakul[2][iD]

[1] Department of Computer Engineering School of Information and Communication Technology, University of Phayao, Phayao, Thailand
sakorn.me@up.ac.th
[2] Intelligent and Nonlinear Dynamic Innovations Research Center Department of Mathematics, Faculty of Applied Science, King Mongkut's University of Technology North Bangkok, Bangkok, Thailand
anuchit.j@sci.kmutnb.ac.th

Abstract. The effective positioning of sensors and the appropriate data merging play a crucial role in advancing systems for recognizing human activities (HAR) using deep neural networks. This study thoroughly evaluates five well-known deep learning structures designed for HAR based on smartphone multi-position sensors. During various activities, the research analyzed data from accelerometers and gyroscopes placed in five different locations on the body. Convolutional neural network (CNN), Long short-term memory (LSTM), Bidirectional LSTM (BiLSTM), Gated recurrent units (GRU), and Bidirectional GRU models were assessed for the classification of activities, considering different sensor combinations across various positions. The study's main findings confirm that achieving accuracy and F1-scores exceeding 99% for the leading BiLSTM, GRU, and BiGRU models is possible by utilizing multi-modal data from well-suited sensor configurations across wrists, arms, pockets, and belts. These recurrent networks consistently outperform CNN and standard LSTM models, which depend on bimodal inputs. Notably, the wrist offers additional motion-sensing capabilities from both the accelerometer and gyroscope, thereby enhancing the fidelity of recognition across multiple positions. The insights derived contribute guidelines for designing robust sensor placements and strategies for fusing data to optimize HAR driven by deep learning, especially on common smartphones. Applications in various domains, such as automated fitness tracking, patient monitoring, and context-aware computing, can benefit from these on-body sensor-based deep models tailored to specific device locations.

Keywords: Human activity recognition · Sensor fusion · Sensor placement · Deep learning · Wearable sensors

O. Gervasi et al. (Eds.): ICCSA 2024, LNCS 14814, pp. 327–338, 2024.
https://doi.org/10.1007/978-3-031-64608-9_21

1   Introduction

Wearable devices show great potential in health and fitness monitoring applications, assisted living technologies, and context-aware computing [10,22]. The primary objective of human activity recognition (HAR) is to automatically identify individuals' physical activities through the analysis of data from on-body sensors, including inertial measurement units and accelerometers [4,8,11]. The continuous monitoring of activities has become feasible due to the widespread use of consumer-grade activity trackers and smartwatches. Nevertheless, the accuracy of inferred activities is heavily influenced by the placement of sensors on wearable devices [13].

Earlier research has conducted experimental examinations into the impact of placing wearable sensors on activity recognition effectiveness using traditional machine learning methods [15,19]. Repeatedly, the torso and wrist positions have been identified as offering the highest accuracy for classifiers, including decision tree, k-nearest neighbor, and support vector machine models. However, recent advancements in deep learning, particularly the progress of convolutional neural networks (CNN) and recurrent networks, have elevated results on benchmark datasets for HAR [17]. Deep models can acquire robust feature representations from multimodal sensor data in an end-to-end fashion. This shift in approach necessitates a fresh examination of suitable strategies for positioning wearable sensors.

The strategic arrangement of sensors and integration of data from various on-body locations play a crucial role in developing HAR systems using deep learning. Despite this importance, there needs to be a thorough examination that assesses strategies for placing sensors specifically designed for deep neural networks. This study aims to establish guidelines for the optimal configuration of wearable sensors, specifically tailored to the analysis of human activities driven by deep learning.

This study explores data from accelerometers and gyroscopes at five locations on the body: wrists, arms, belts, right pockets, and left pockets. During the investigation, participants engage in routine activities like walking, sitting, standing, and jogging. We evaluate five notable deep-learning structures to classify these activities across multiple positions through sensor fusion. The architectures under assessment include CNNs, long short-term memory (LSTMs), bidirectional LSTMs (BiLSTMs), gated recurrent units (GRUs), and bidirectional GRUs (BiGRUs).

The primary results confirm that integrating data from accelerometers and gyroscopes at specific wrist, arms, belt, and pocket locations improves accuracy and F1-score, surpassing 99% for the top-performing BiLSTM, GRU, and BiGRU recurrent networks. These recurrent networks consistently outshine CNN and regular LSTM models. Notably, the wrist plays a crucial role in providing essential signals for motion sensing from both modalities, enhancing recognition capabilities across various positions.

The remaining sections of this document are structured as outlined below. Section 2 reviews existing research on the analysis of sensor positions in HAR and the progress made in deep learning. Section 3 details our framework based on deep CNNs, along with the experimental setup and evaluation metrics used for analysis. The presentation of quantitative results, diagnostic inferences, and critical observations is covered in Sect. 4. Lastly, Sect. 5 provides concluding remarks and outlines directions for future works.

2   Related Works

2.1   Deep Learning for S-HAR

Recent significant investigations into HAR [25] have brought to light issues linked with traditional machine learning methods that impact the capability to identify human activities. The constraint is around opting for manually crafted features, a decision-making process heavily reliant on the expertise of the individual making the choices [27]. Deep learning has emerged as a viable alternative to tackle these limitations effectively in only a few years.

In recent years, there has been extensive exploration of advanced learning models to address challenges in classifying time-series data related to recognizing human activities. Researchers have scrutinized different complex structures on standard datasets to assess their effectiveness in accurately recognizing activities. Among the popular methodologies, CNNs [16] and LSTM networks [14] have demonstrated promising outcomes in HAR tasks involving data from smartphone sensors. These sophisticated models offer suitable assessment metrics for measuring performance in identifying periodic time-series signals. Encouraged by their proven capabilities, our study delves into applying CNN and LSTM models to classify hand gestures using motion data from smartwatches. We gauge the efficiency of both models in solving the hand movement recognition challenge based on pertinent evaluation criteria, providing insights into their suitability for HAR applications driven by wearable sensors.

In 1997, Schuster and Paliwal introduced the BiLSTM [23] to expand the knowledge capacity within the LSTM network. The BiLSTM is connected to two hidden layers operating in opposite directions, enabling it to gather information from preceding and succeeding sequences simultaneously. Unlike unidirectional models, the BiLSTM does not require any reconfiguration of input data and can incorporate future inputs while maintaining its current state. In their work on sensor-based HAR (S-HAR), Alawneh et al. [1] conducted a comparative analysis of unidirectional and bidirectional LSTM models. The findings revealed that the BiLSTM surpasses the unidirectional technique regarding recognition efficiency.

While LSTM has effectively mitigated the vanishing gradient problem associated with RNNs, the memory cells within its architecture result in increased memory consumption; in 2014, Cho et al. [5] introduced the GRU network as a new model based on RNNs. The GRU is a simplified version of LSTM, lacking a distinct memory cell in its structure [6]. Within the GRU network, update and reset gates are responsible for adjusting the modification degree of each hidden state. These gates determine the knowledge that should be transferred to the next state and what should not be transferred [20,21]. Addressing the S-HAR problem through data augmentation, Okai et al. [18] established a robust deep learning model based on the GRU network. In comparisons within this study, the GRU model outperformed and demonstrated greater resilience than the LSTM models.

An inherent drawback of this network lies in its unidirectional nature, meaning the output at a given time step relies solely on past information from the input sequence, excluding the current input. In specific scenarios, it could prove advantageous to consider the past and future when making predictions [12]. To address this, Alsarhan et al. [2] introduced a BiGRU model for HAR. The outcomes demonstrated that employing the BiGRU model for recognizing human actions through sensor data is also highly effective.

2.2   Position-Aware HAR

The recognition of on-body device positions has been a relatively neglected aspect of research. Initially, scholars delved into recognizing activities without considering the device's location [9]. However, they discovered that the recognition rate varies significantly based on the location. Subsequent experiments focused on the device's position and its impact on the recognition rate, indicating that this information enhances activity recognition accuracy. However, opinions on its impact remain divided [7]. A critical examination of their findings highlights that differing viewpoints may arise from the specific positions and activities considered. Notably, studies have yet to comprehensively explore all relevant on-body positions in everyday physical activities, leaving uncertainty about the accuracy of detecting each pertinent position for different activities.

In the broader context of recognizing activities, the positioning of sensors holds significant importance, prompting numerous researchers to explore the impact of various locations on activity performance [26]. These investigations reveal that seven distinct body locations — forearm, head, shin, thigh, upper arm, waist, and chest - exhibit varying behaviors in activity recognition. Subdividing these body parts into smaller regions does not yield improved accuracy. Moreover, additional research indicates that the optimal placement of sensors depends on the specific activity under consideration [3]. Consequently, the value of position information and the feasibility of deducing device positions from an accelerometer has been firmly established.

3   The Sensor-Based HAR Framework

This study employs a HAR system that is conscious of the positioning, encompassing four primary stages: 1) the collection of raw data from sensors, 2) the pre-processing of the gathered data, 3) the creation of processed features and samples, and 4) the training of machine learning models on the processed data and the assessment of their performance in classifying activities. Figure 1 depicts the comprehensive workflow involving these four phases.

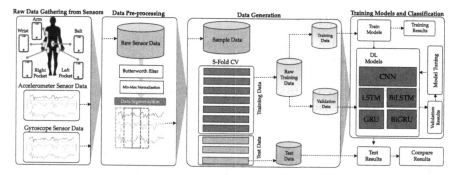

Fig. 1. The position-aware HAR framework based on smartphone sensors used in this work.

3.1   Pervasive Dataset

The dataset utilized for evaluating HAR, known as the Pervasive benchmark dataset [24], utilizes smartphone sensors to collect data on seven physical activities: walking, running, sitting, standing, jogging, biking, walking upstairs, and walking downstairs. These fundamental daily movements are commonly employed in similar research investigations. The data gathering process involved ten male participants aged between 25 and 30, each engaging in every activity for 3–4 minutes, with biking conducted outdoors. Indoor walking and running occurred in a university building corridor, while stair walking tasks were performed in a 5-floor building with stairs.

Five smartphones were strategically placed on each participant to capture motion data simultaneously from various on-body positions — right and left jeans pocket, belt area near right leg, upper right arm, and right wrist. Accelerometer samples were recorded at a rate of 50 samples per second across all devices and positions for the entire duration of each activity. Previous studies have affirmed the adequacy of this sampling frequency for recognizing fundamental human activities [28].

3.2   Data Pre-processing

Before extracting features, the initial sensor data underwent a pre-processing stage that involved denoising and normalization. Denoising was performed to filter out any noise artifacts, preventing contamination of the signals. Normalization was applied to standardize all sensor readings to a standard scale, ensuring consistency. The pre-processed data streams were then segmented into fixed-length portions using a sliding window approach. The segmentation utilized overlapping windows of 5-second durations, with a 50% overlap between consecutive windows. This process allowed for extracting distinctive time-series features from each window, facilitating subsequent activity classification. The inclusion of overlap ensures seamless transitions between the segmented data chunks.

3.3   The Deep Learning Model

This study assesses five well-known deep learning structures – CNNs, LSTMs, BiLSTMs, GRUs, and BiGRUs – for the task of recognizing human activities across various positions.

CNNs utilize a layered structure comprising convolutional layers for extracting features, pooling layers for achieving scale-invariant representations, flattened and fully connected layers for reducing dimensionality, and an output layer for classification. They excel at capturing local dependencies in data.

LSTMs tackle the vanishing gradient challenge in standard recurrent neural network models by explicitly modeling long-range context using specialized memory cells and gated operations. This allows for effective temporal modeling of extended time-series data.

GRUs offer a streamlined alternative to LSTMs, delivering competitive performance across various applications. Bidirectional versions of both LSTMs and GRUs enhance context modeling by considering information from both past and future time steps.

This comparative evaluation provides valuable insights into practical deep-learning approaches for addressing the multi-position activity recognition challenge.

3.4   Hyperparameter Tuning by Bayesian Optimization

In this research, Bayesian optimization served as an automated method for adjusting the hyperparameters of neural network architectures. This approach offers an effective way to optimize complex functions that lack explicit mathematical representations. By creating a probabilistic surrogate model of the target function, Bayesian optimization steers the search process toward global optima through iterative sampling.

Given the computational intensity and challenging gradient derivation in assessing neural networks, Bayesian treatment facilitates the efficient tuning of non-linear performance objectives. Unlike grid or random search methods, it reduces the necessary trial iterations, thereby reducing training expenses. Bayesian optimization proves particularly useful for optimizing intricate structures of deep neural networks, such as CNN, LSTM, and GRU, where multiple interconnected hyperparameters are involved.

The primary optimization objective is identifying the highest value at the sampling point for an unknown function f.

$$x^+ = \arg\max_{x \in A} f(x) \tag{1}$$

where A denotes the search space of x.

4   Experiments and Research Findings

Within this segment, we elucidate the experimental setup and present the results of our experiments conducted to assess the performance of five deep learning models in HAR, considering smartphone sensor data.

4.1   Experimental Environment

For this study, the experimental setup utilizes Google Colab Pro+ as a cloud-based notebook environment featuring Tesla V100 GPUs to expedite computations. All code is written in Python 3.6.9, employing widely used machine learning libraries. TensorFlow 2.2.0 is used for constructing models, Keras 2.3.1 for high-level neural network APIs, Scikit-Learn for training pipelines, Numpy 1.18.5 for numerical processing, and Pandas 1.0.5 for manipulating data structures.

This optimized configuration in Colab, coupled with established Python data science tools, streamlines the process of quickly prototyping and evaluating deep learning architectures for recognizing human activities across various sensor positions.

4.2   Experimental Results

In assessing the effectiveness of deep learning models in recognizing activities across positions, we applied a 5-fold cross-validation technique on the Pervasive dataset. This method ensures a balanced distribution of activity classes in each validation fold, mitigating sampling bias. The dataset was segmented into five stratified bins or folds, with four folds (80% data) allocated for training and one bin (20% data) for testing the model in each iteration. This process was iterated five times, each fold acting as the test set once. Consequently, every data point was included in both the training and evaluation stages throughout the cross-validation procedure.

The experiments involved testing five deep neural networks – CNN, LSTM, BiLSTM, GRU, and BiGRU – that underwent optimization using Bayesian hyperparameter tuning for recognizing activities based on smartphone sensor data from multiple positions. Performance in recognizing activities was compared among the models based on accuracy and F1-score. The results of the experiments are detailed in Tables 1 – 2, showcasing benchmark scores on important evaluation metrics for each network architecture. This enables a thorough examination of differences in the models' capabilities in classifying human activities across various positions.

The outcomes in Table 1, illustrating the accuracy of deep learning models on sensor data from various on-body positions, lead to the following key insights:

1. Accelerometer data analysis:
   - The BiLSTM and GRU models consistently achieve the highest accuracy across all sensor positions – left pocket, right pocket, belt, arm, and wrist.

Table 1. Accuracies of the deep learning models using sensor data from different positions.

Sensor	Model	Accuracy				
		Left Pocket	Right Pocket	Belt	Arm	Wrist
Accelerometer	CNN	99.53%	99.42%	99.04%	98.11%	96.70%
	LSTM	99.66%	99.66%	99.52%	98.27%	99.08%
	BiLSTM	99.86%	99.78%	99.70%	98.59%	98.88%
	GRU	99.80%	99.84%	99.60%	98.96%	99.20%
	BiGRU	99.78%	99.88%	99.82%	98.80%	99.08%
Gyroscope	CNN	94.72%	94.36%	95.20%	92.81%	98.27%
	LSTM	84.07%	78.33%	80.22%	82.51%	99.04%
	BiLSTM	84.88%	83.63%	80.98%	88.73%	99.32%
	GRU	86.27%	86.59%	86.61%	88.17%	99.24%
	BiGRU	88.29%	87.39%	88.31%	96.41%	99.38%
Accelerometer + Gyroscope	CNN	99.62%	99.50%	98.98%	98.21%	98.27%
	LSTM	99.58%	99.80%	99.56%	97.95%	99.04%
	BiLSTM	99.94%	99.90%	99.72%	98.47%	99.32%
	GRU	99.94%	99.92%	99.64%	99.16%	99.24%
	BiGRU	99.88%	99.88%	99.82%	99.46%	99.38%

- The BiLSTM attains the top accuracy of 99.86% on the left pocket, while the GRU reaches the peak score of 99.88% on the right pocket data.
- The CNN model, although slightly less accurate than BiLSTM and GRU on accelerometer data, still demonstrates competitive accuracy ranging from 96.7% to 99.53% across positions.

2. Gyroscope data analysis:
   - The BiGRU model attains maximum accuracy, peaking at 99.38%, specifically on wrist data. The wrist position consistently yields the highest gyroscope accuracy for all models, indicating its suitability for rotational motion sensing.
   - The LSTM and BiLSTM architectures exhibit noticeably lower gyroscope accuracy, ranging between 78–88%, and they are outperformed by other models, notably on non-wrist positions.

3. Combined accelerometer and gyroscope data analysis:
   - Utilizing accelerometer and gyroscope data further enhances accuracy across the models, reaching 99.94% for GRU and BiGRU networks.
   - Sensor fusion proves beneficial in augmenting overall recognition capability.

Here are the notable findings derived from the F1-score of deep learning models on sensor data from diverse positions, as illustrated in Table 2:

1. Accelerometer data F1-score analysis:

Table 2. F1-score of the deep learning models using sensor data from different positions.

Sensor	Model	F1-score				
		Left Pocket	Right Pocket	Belt	Arm	Wrist
Accelerometer	CNN	99.52%	99.42%	99.04%	98.10%	96.66%
	LSTM	99.66%	99.66%	99.52%	98.26%	99.08%
	BiLSTM	99.86%	99.78%	99.70%	98.58%	98.88%
	GRU	99.80%	99.84%	99.60%	98.96%	99.20%
	BiGRU	99.78%	99.88%	99.82%	98.80%	99.08%
Gyroscope	CNN	94.69%	94.31%	95.19%	92.77%	98.25%
	LSTM	80.28%	73.13%	76.44%	79.10%	99.04%
	BiLSTM	81.25%	80.10%	78.36%	88.01%	99.32%
	GRU	83.33%	83.66%	83.91%	87.33%	99.24%
	BiGRU	86.78%	85.42%	86.70%	96.39%	99.38%
Accelerometer + Gyroscope	CNN	99.62%	99.50%	98.98%	98.20%	98.25%
	LSTM	99.58%	99.80%	99.56%	97.94%	99.04%
	BiLSTM	99.94%	99.90%	99.72%	98.46%	99.32%
	GRU	99.94%	99.92%	99.64%	99.16%	99.24%
	BiGRU	99.88%	99.88%	99.82%	99.46%	99.38%

- The F1-scores exhibit patterns closely mirroring the accuracy results detailed in Table 1.
- The BiLSTM, GRU, and BiGRU designs achieve the highest F1-score, surpassing 99%, on accelerometer data from multiple positions.
- The CNN model achieves highly competitive F1-score, comparable to GRU's performance, reaching up to 99.52% on left pocket data. However, BiLSTM and BiGRU outperform CNN by slight margins.
2. Gyroscope data F1-score analysis:
    - Parallel to accuracy trends, gyroscope sensor F1-score are notably lower than accelerometer scores, except for the wrist position, where all models attain over 98% F1-score. This underscores the wrist's efficacy in sensing rotational motions.
    - LSTM and BiLSTM models demonstrate considerably lower F1-score, ranging between 73–86%, for classifying activities using gyroscope data from positions other than the wrist. Their ability to capture rotational motion needs to be improved.
3. Combined accelerometer and gyroscope data F1-score analysis:
    - The fusion of accelerometer and gyroscope data further amplifies the F1-score, reaching up to 99.94% for the BiLSTM architecture, leveraging the benefits from both motion modalities.

5   Conclusion and Future Works

This study thoroughly assessed deep learning methods for recognizing human activities across multiple positions, employing smartphone sensors. Five models, namely CNN, LSTM, BiLSTM, GRU, and BiGRU, underwent evaluation with data from accelerometers and gyroscopes at five on-body locations. The results confirm that combining sensor data and utilizing multiple positions improves accuracy and F1-score across all models.

Notably, the BiLSTM, GRU, and BiGRU models attain scores exceeding 99% with combined data from appropriate wrist, arm, belt, and pocket positions. These models consistently surpass the CNN and standard LSTM networks. Additionally, the wrist accelerometer and gyroscope offer complementary motion-capturing capabilities, enhancing the overall fidelity of activity recognition. These results guide effective deep learning design and strategic sensor placement strategies in position-aware HAR applications using smartphones. Practical applications in domains such as fitness tracking, health monitoring, and context-aware computing can benefit from these neural approaches customized for on-body device locations.

For future considerations, additional experiments with more extensive datasets can enhance the general applicability of the findings and identify an appropriate level of complexity for multimodal HAR using deep neural networks. Furthermore, assessing the models on data from alternative wearable gadgets such as smart glasses, rings, shoes, etc., positioned on different body parts, presents an avenue for further exploration.

Acknowledgments. This research project was supported by Thailand Science Research and Innovation Fund; University of Phayao under Grant No. FF67-UoE-214; National Science, Research and Innovation Fund (NSRF); and King Mongkut's University of Technology North Bangkok with Contract no. KMUTNB-FF-67-B-10.

Disclosure of Interests. The authors have no competing interests to declare that are relevant to the content of this article.

References

1. Alawneh, L., Mohsen, B., Al-Zinati, M., Shatnawi, A., Al-Ayyoub, M.: A comparison of unidirectional and bidirectional LSTM networks for human activity recognition. In: 2020 IEEE International Conference on Pervasive Computing and Communications Workshops (PerCom Workshops), pp. 1–6 (2020). https://doi.org/10.1109/PerComWorkshops48775.2020.9156264

2. Alsarhan, T., Alawneh, L., Al-Zinati, M., Al-Ayyoub, M.: Bidirectional gated recurrent units for human activity recognition using accelerometer data. In: 2019 IEEE SENSORS, pp. 1–4 (2019). https://doi.org/10.1109/SENSORS43011.2019.8956560

3. Atallah, L., Lo, B., King, R., Yang, G.Z.: Sensor positioning for activity recognition using wearable accelerometers. IEEE Trans. Biomed. Circ. Syst. 5(4), 320–329 (2011). https://doi.org/10.1109/TBCAS.2011.2160540

4. Attal, F., Mohammed, S., Dedabrishvili, M., Chamroukhi, F., Oukhellou, L., Amirat, Y.: Physical human activity recognition using wearable sensors. Sensors **15**(12), 31314–31338 (2015). https://doi.org/10.3390/s151229858

5. Cho, K., van Merriënboer, B., Bahdanau, D., Bengio, Y.: On the properties of neural machine translation: encoder–decoder approaches. In: Proceedings of SSST-8, Eighth Workshop on Syntax, Semantics and Structure in Statistical Translation, pp. 103–111. Association for Computational Linguistics, Doha, Qatar (Oct 2014). https://doi.org/10.3115/v1/W14-4012

6. Chung, J., Gulcehre, C., Cho, K., Bengio, Y.: Empirical evaluation of gated recurrent neural networks on sequence modeling. In: NIPS 2014 Workshop on Deep Learning, December 2014 (2014)

7. Coskun, D., Incel, O.D., Ozgovde, A.: Phone position/placement detection using accelerometer: impact on activity recognition. In: 2015 IEEE Tenth International Conference on Intelligent Sensors, Sensor Networks and Information Processing (ISSNIP), pp. 1–6 (2015). https://doi.org/10.1109/ISSNIP.2015.7106915

8. Fu, B., Damer, N., Kirchbuchner, F., Kuijper, A.: Sensing technology for human activity recognition: a comprehensive survey. IEEE Access **8**, 83791–83820 (2020). https://doi.org/10.1109/ACCESS.2020.2991891

9. Henpraserttae, A., Thiemjarus, S., Marukatat, S.: Accurate activity recognition using a mobile phone regardless of device orientation and location. In: 2011 International Conference on Body Sensor Networks, pp. 41–46 (2011). https://doi.org/10.1109/BSN.2011.8

10. Hnoohom, N., Mekruksavanich, S., Jitpattanakul, A.: Pre-impact and impact fall detection based on a multimodal sensor using a deep residual network. Intell. Autom. Soft Comput. **36**(3), 3371–3385 (2023). https://doi.org/10.32604/iasc.2023.036551

11. Jiao, W., Zhang, C.: An efficient human activity recognition system using WiFi channel state information. IEEE Syst. J. **17**(4), 6687–6690 (2023). https://doi.org/10.1109/JSYST.2023.3293482

12. Lynn, H.M., Pan, S.B., Kim, P.: A deep bidirectional GRU network model for biometric electrocardiogram classification based on recurrent neural networks. IEEE Access **7**, 145395–145405 (2019). https://doi.org/10.1109/ACCESS.2019.2939947

13. Mannini, A., Sabatini, A.M., Intille, S.S.: Accelerometry-based recognition of the placement sites of a wearable sensor. Pervasive Mob. Comput. **21**, 62–74 (2015). https://doi.org/10.1016/j.pmcj.2015.06.003

14. Mekruksavanich, S., Jitpattanakul, A.: LSTM networks using smartphone data for sensor-based human activity recognition in smart homes. Sensors **21**(5), 1636 (2021). https://doi.org/10.3390/s21051636

15. Mekruksavanich, S., Jitpattanakul, A.: Position-aware human activity recognition with smartphone sensors based on deep learning approaches. In: 2023 46th International Conference on Telecommunications and Signal Processing (TSP), pp. 43–46 (2023). https://doi.org/10.1109/TSP59544.2023.10197773

16. Mekruksavanich, S., Jitpattanakul, A., Youplao, P., Yupapin, P.: Enhanced hand-oriented activity recognition based on smartwatch sensor data using LSTMs. Symmetry **12**(9), 1570 (2020). https://doi.org/10.3390/sym12091570

17. Nouriani, A., McGovern, R., Rajamani, R.: Deep-learning-based human activity recognition using wearable sensors. IFAC-PapersOnLine **55**(37), 1–6 (2022). https://doi.org/10.1016/j.ifacol.2022.11.152, 2nd Modeling, Estimation and Control Conference MECC 2022

18. Okai, J., Paraschiakos, S., Beekman, M., Knobbe, A., de Sá, C.R.: Building robust models for human activity recognition from raw accelerometers data using gated recurrent units and long short term memory neural networks. In: 2019 41st Annual International Conference of the IEEE Engineering in Medicine and Biology Society (EMBC), pp. 2486–2491 (2019). https://doi.org/10.1109/EMBC.2019.8857288

19. Qamar, N., Siddiqui, N., ul Haq, M.E., Awais Azam, M., Naeem, U.: An approach towards position-independent human activity recognition model based on wearable accelerometer sensor. Procedia Comput. Sci. **177**, 196–203 (2020). https://doi.org/10.1016/j.procs.2020.10.028

20. Quadrana, M., Cremonesi, P., Jannach, D.: Sequence-aware recommender systems. ACM Comput. Surv. **51**(4), 1–36 (2018). https://doi.org/10.1145/3190616

21. Rendle, S., Freudenthaler, C., Schmidt-Thieme, L.: Factorizing personalized Markov chains for next-basket recommendation. In: Proceedings of the 19th International Conference on World Wide Web, pp. 811-820. WWW '10, Association for Computing Machinery, New York, NY, USA (2010). https://doi.org/10.1145/1772690.1772773

22. Rezaei, A., Stevens, M.C., Argha, A., Mascheroni, A., Puiatti, A., Lovell, N.H.: An unobtrusive human activity recognition system using low resolution thermal sensors, machine and deep learning. IEEE Trans. Biomed. Eng. **70**(1), 115–124 (2023). https://doi.org/10.1109/TBME.2022.3186313

23. Schuster, M., Paliwal, K.: Bidirectional recurrent neural networks. IEEE Trans. Signal Process. **45**(11), 2673–2681 (1997). https://doi.org/10.1109/78.650093

24. Shoaib, M., Bosch, S., Incel, O.D., Scholten, H., Havinga, P.J.M.: Fusion of smartphone motion sensors for physical activity recognition. Sensors **14**(6), 10146–10176 (2014). https://doi.org/10.3390/s140610146

25. Tüfek, N., Özkaya, O.: A comparative research on human activity recognition using deep learning. In: 2019 27th Signal Processing and Communications Applications Conference (SIU), pp. 1–4 (2019). https://doi.org/10.1109/SIU.2019.8806395

26. Vahdatpour, A., Amini, N., Sarrafzadeh, M.: On-body device localization for health and medical monitoring applications. In: 2011 IEEE International Conference on Pervasive Computing and Communications (PerCom), pp. 37–44 (2011). https://doi.org/10.1109/PERCOM.2011.5767593

27. Wang, J., Chen, Y., Hao, S., Peng, X., Hu, L.: Deep learning for sensor-based activity recognition: a survey. Pattern Recogn. Lett. **119**, 3–11 (2019). https://doi.org/10.1016/j.patrec.2018.02.010

28. Wu, W., Dasgupta, S., Ramirez, E.E., Peterson, C., Norman, G.J.: Classification accuracies of physical activities using smartphone motion sensors. J. Med. Internet Res. **14**(5), e130 (2012). https://doi.org/10.2196/jmir.2208

An Innovative Approach for Long ECG Synthesis with Wasserstein GAN Model

Thi Diem Tran[1]([✉]), Thi Thu Khiet Dang[2], and Ngoc Quoc Tran[3]

[1] University of Information Technology, VNU-HCM, Ho Chi Minh City 70000, Vietnam
diemtt@uit.edu.vn

[2] University of International, VNU-HCM, Ho Chi Minh City 70000, Vietnam
BEBEIU17015@student.hcmiu.edu.vn

[3] John Von Neumann Institute, University of Science, VNU-HCM, Ho Chi Minh City 70000, Vietnam
quoc.tran2020@ict.jvn.edu.vn

Abstract. Deep neural networks (DNNs) have set new standards in identifying and classifying irregular patterns in ECG (electrocardiogram) signals, surpassing previous methods. Despite the easy access and affordability of ECG sensors, a critical bottleneck remains the limited availability of reliable data for complex heart rhythms like second and third-degree atrioventricular block, ventricular tachycardia, and supraventricular tachycardia. This shortage has been a significant obstacle to improving DNN algorithms. Recent studies have turned to Generative Adversarial Networks (GANs) to create synthetic ECG data, enhancing the diversity of training datasets. However, much of this research has only managed to produce basic ECG components, missing the intricate details found in real patient data that includes multiple heartbeats. Our research has taken a groundbreaking approach by converting ECG signals into a two-dimensional format, allowing us to utilize advanced GAN models originally developed for image processing. This method has enabled us to generate extended, realistic ECG sequences closely mimicking those from actual patients. We have tested and refined our model using two databases, Physionet and Chapman, and have successfully produced 10-second ECG sequences showcasing a variety of heart rhythms previously unachieved in other studies. Our innovative technique not only surpasses existing methods in generating high-quality, realistic ECG data but also sets a new benchmark in ECG synthesis.

Keywords: ECG generating · Long ECG · Signal to Image · GAN

1 Introduction

An electrocardiogram (ECG) is a time-lapse recording of a re-polarization sequence in the human heart using a piece of standard non-invasive equipment. It is utilized for clinically diagnosing cardiac diseases by understanding abnormalities, for example, second and third-degree atrioventricular block, ventricular

© The Author(s), under exclusive license to Springer Nature Switzerland AG 2024
O. Gervasi et al. (Eds.): ICCSA 2024, LNCS 14814, pp. 339–351, 2024.
https://doi.org/10.1007/978-3-031-64608-9_22

tachycardia, or ventricular run supraventricular tachycardia, in the signal space [1]. Many applications have embedded DNNs to examine rhythms abnormal in patients, such as Medtronic Linq monitor, Zio monitor, or Apple Watch. Series 4 [2]. However, the performance of DNNs, particularly classification tasks, still needs to improve due to imbalanced data throughout the training model. Augmented data with artificial data generation by creating natural-looking samples that are not available in the original data set is a new approach to increasing the accuracy of DNNs. Furthermore, the ability to create realistic samples with specific attributes might be beneficial in comprehending the original data distribution.

Generative adversarial network, initially described in 2014 [3], is a recently suggested framework for producing generated data that shows remarkable results for producing artificial images. They successfully created and altered data in computer vision and NLP areas, such as high-quality picture production, style transfer, text-to-image synthesis [4,5], etc. GANs have mainly been created and used for picture creation, with just a few research addressing time series. Nonetheless, they have recently shown promising results for the generation of artificial audio [6]. Many current studies have used GANs for ECG signal creation to address the issue of data scarcity. Previous efforts for creating a time-series GAN have mainly relied on Recurrent Neural Network (RNN)-based architectures [7]. To synthesize ECG data, Brophy et al. [8] suggested a GAN architecture that included a Bidirectional LSTM-as Generator and an LSTM-CNN as Discriminator. However, the authors only employed the generator to synthesize ECG data and offered no evaluation of the discriminator network for the arrhythmia classification task. Besides, this GAN-RNN cannot handle lengthy sequential data that suffers from a vanishing gradient issue. Wasserstein GAN [9] claimed the ECG synthesis result was superior to the Denoising Diffusion Probabilistic Models (DDPM), but it was also stopped at one beat ECG generation. Some works have successfully inspired transformer architecture in GAN, intending to improve the quality of synthetic data or create a more efficient training procedure. One of the famous examples of trends using a transformer in 1D signal processing is the TTS-GAN [4]. This research had realistic synthetic time-series data sequences of any length for sinusoidal waves, jumping, and running from the UniMiB dataset. However, it also comes to a halt as it generates an artificial ECG with only one QRS complex (or one beat).

Several previous studies have investigated the synthesis of long ECG signals, but their purposes and methodologies differ from our research. For example, the study of Vo et al. (2021) [10] utilized P2E-WGAN for the reconstruction from the realistic Photoplethysmogram (PPG) to ECG signals. They suggested that while collecting high-quality ECG data remains challenging, deriving it from a wearable PPG device would be much more convenient for the patients. In other words, they did not try to generate a fake ECG signal but established a framework to predict ECG data based on the available PPG. As a result, their research still needs to address the lacking-data problem as one of our proposals. The study of Zhang et al. (2021) [7] considered the implementation of a 2D long short-term memory generative adversarial network (GAN) to produce ECG signals. Their approach generated representative beats and then attached 13 of the same representative beats to each other to form a 10-second ECG signal. The limitation of this approach is that such a framework is only suitable for generating normal rhythms with the defined morphology, not abnormal ones. Heart rate would be the same in all of the generated data because there are always 13 QRS complexes available in a 10-second signal. The research [11,12] had succeeded in long ECG generation with the DDPM model; however, the signal generation velocity in the inference stage of this strategy is a burden. As a result, an architecture that can automatically generate long ECG signals with various morphology and patterns in a short period is required.

Because of the vanishing gradient, instability, and quality of ECG generation, while training GAN directly for 1D long ECG signals, in this paper, we propose a new approach for a generative network that inspired GAN architecture for the image. We convert a 1D signal to a 2D image and optimize the network to achieve high performance on the GAN for images. Instead of a complex network, we toward our approach by using a simple architecture GAN named the DCGAN [13] as our baseline model. This research focuses on generating storage rhythms in ECGs such as second and third-degree atrioventricular block, ventricular tachycardia, or ventricular run supraventricular tachycardia. The Physionet (MIT-BIH Arrhythmia, European ST-T) [14] and Chapman [15] databases are utilized for the training model. We benchmark our proposal with other state-of-the-art architecture for the 1D ECG-GANs model. The result shows outperformance not only for one beat ECG but also for a 10-second ECG signal with various rhythms like acquiring from patients, which has yet to be reported.

2   Methodology

2.1   Premilinaries: Generative Adversarial Networks

Generative Adversarial Networks (GANs) and variants are powerful models for data synthesis. The strategy of GAN is to define a min-max game between two competing networks: a *generator* and a *discriminator*. The *generator* takes the role of generating a sample from random noise, while the *discriminator* is trained to classify a true sample or a generated sample as real or fake. Formally, given a random noise vector z sampled from a prior distribution $p(z)$ (e.g., uniform distribution) and real data sample x drawn from $p(x)$. The *generator* G aims to generate realistic-looking sample $G(z)$ and fool the *discriminator*, and the *discriminator* D tries to distinguish $G(z)$ from x. This game between the *generator* G and the *discriminator* D can be formulated as the following min-max objective function:

$$\min_G \max_D V(G, D) = \mathbb{E}_{x \sim p(x)}[\log(D(x))] + \mathbb{E}_{z \sim p(z)}[\log(1 - D(G(z)))] \quad (1)$$

Despite the interesting mechanism and good results in generating data, stabilizing GAN training is a challenge. Many approaches have been proposed to handle this problem, prominent among them are WGAN [16] and WGAN-GP [17].

WGAN stands for Wasserstein GAN, a variant of GAN whose loss function relies on the Wasserstein distance. In WGAN, the *discriminator* is no longer used as a binary classifier but as an evaluation component (called *critic*) used to fit the Wasserstein distance. The objective function of WGAN is formulated:

$$\min_{G} \max_{D \in \mathcal{D}} V(G, D) = \mathbb{E}_{x \sim p(x)}[D(x)] - \mathbb{E}_{z \sim p(z)}[D(G(z))] \qquad (2)$$

where $\mathcal{D}$ is the set of 1-Lipschitz functions. WGAN makes the loss function avoid the vanishing gradient problem and stabilizes the GAN training.

WGAN-GP has the same manner as WGAN except the term of *gradient penalty*. Specifically, WGAN-GP uses gradient penalty instead of weight clipping to enforce the 1-Lipschitz constraint for the *critic*, and the right term in the formula (2) becomes:

$$\mathbb{E}_{x \sim p(x)}[D(x)] - \mathbb{E}_{z \sim p(z)}[D(G(z))] + \lambda \mathbb{E}_{\hat{x} \sim p(\hat{x})}[(\|\nabla_{\hat{x}} D(\hat{x})\|_2 - 1)^2] \qquad (3)$$

where λ is the penalty coefficient and $p(\hat{x})$ is the uniform distribution sampled between points in $p(x)$ and $p(z)$. WGAN-GP has been proven to improve GAN training stability, produce high-quality samples, and become much faster convergence power than WGAN.

2.2 Generating Long ECGs Using GAN

Previous studies tackled the ECG synthesis challenge by constructing a direct GAN model or converting the best GAN model for an image to process the signal in the time domain. However, these results cannot provide long ECGs like those obtained from patients. As a result, the output cannot be employed in real-world applications such as rhythm categorization or detecting aberrant heart disorders.

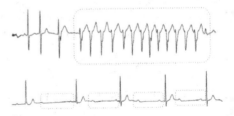

Fig. 1. Top: VT beat with signature V beat group. Bottom: AVB2 rhythm with regular repeats of two P waves.

In this paper, we choose the opposite approach that reuses the GAN model's power on the image and converts the ECG signal to the 2D domain. The intuition of converting the ECG signal into an image and working with it stems very much from the "morphology" character of the ECG signal. Unlike other biological signals (e.g., EEG), an ECG signal contains many morphological features like QRS complexes, P waves, T waves, etc., that professionals need to "see" to diagnose. These characters are more valuable when working with long ECG signals. Figure 1 shows an example of two types of ECG rhythms with different morphological features. To implement our intuition, we propose a new approach consisting of sequential steps: Split (for long ECGs) and draw an image of the ECG signal, train the GAN model with image data, and extract and convert to ECG signal from the generated image. Our proposal is illustrated in Fig. 2.

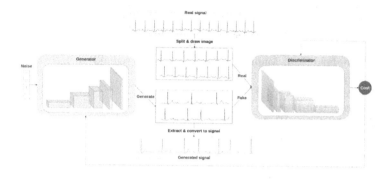

Fig. 2. Flowchart of our approach

In the first step, we plot an ECG signal without the information of magnitude or axes. We believe it is enough to represent the ECG signal on the image without adding extra details (like color). We aim to make our data as simple as possible but still contain the necessary information (like MNIST). The binary image met our expectations. We draw and convert the image to binary mode and then use image processing techniques to make the image look "smoother and softer". Besides, binary images bring convenience for the next steps. A binary image is formatted as a 2-dimensional array (matrix) instead of a 3-dimensional array (tensor) like a color image, making learning easier and reducing storage and computation costs. The extract signal step is done better with binary images, which will be shown in more detail in the following sections.

The next stage is to address the issue of the fit between the available data and the model. Such a problem is simpler to be addressed in one-beat synthesis when it can be fully represented in a symmetric image. Difficulties appear when working with longer ECG signals. Keeping the sample intact for a 10-second ECG signal will result in an extremely asymmetric image when one dimension is much larger than the other. On the other hand, using a symmetric image to represent the ECG signal in the image is shrinking and unnatural, especially when viewed from the perspective of signal amplitude. So we aim for an image of sufficiently large size and "acceptable" asymmetry. To solve this problem, we split the 10 s ECG into two 5 s ECG segments and put them in the same image. We searched through a dozen times and selected the image size that gives the best results as 128×128 for an ECG beat and 240×480 for a 10 s ECG signal. For the GAN model, we choose DCGAN [13] as our baseline model. DCGAN is a lightweight GAN model (compared to current GAN models) that is used a lot and achieves good results when working with image data. The architecture of DCGAN is built on top of convolution and convolution-transpose layers. We made a few adjustments to our problem.

We define $C(f, k, s)$ and $C_{ts}(f, k, s)$ to stand for convolution and convolution-transpose layers, f, k, and s are the number of filters, kernel size, and stride value, respectively. Not like the original DCGAN, we use the asymmetric kernel and stride in some convolution and convolution-

---

Algorithm 1. Convert image to 10-second ECG signal

Input: Input image: **I**, Binary image: **BI**, Width binary image: **W**: 120
Heigth binary image **H**: 480, Resize value **RS**: 2.5, Binary image threshold **BIT**: 250
Key **K**: 1, Threshold **T**: 5, Amplitude **Amp**: 1, Output signal **S**

1: **for** k *from* 0 *to* 1 **do**
2:     $BI = Resize(I, W \leftarrow W * RS, H \leftarrow H * RS)$
3:     **for** i *from* 0 *to* H **do**
4:         **for** j *from* 0 *to* W **do**
5:             $BI[i][j] = 1$ if $BI[i][j] < BIT$ else 0
6:         **end for**
7:     **end for**
8:     $BI = MedianFilter(\boldsymbol{BI})$
9:     *Remove pixel columns without information*
10:    *Placeholder target array: A*
11:    **for** i *from* 0 *to* H **do**
12:        *Placeholder index : O*
13:        **for** j *from* 0 *to* W **do**
14:            $A = LinearSearchAlgorithm(key \in BI[i][j])$
15:        **end for**
16:        $O = SearchMaxLengthRunAlgorithm(A)$
17:        $O = (Max(O) - Min(O)) * T\% + Min(O)$
18:        $S[k][i] = (\frac{W-1-O-\frac{W-1}{2}}{\frac{(W-1)}{2}}) * Amp$
19:    **end for**
20: **end for**
21: $S = Concatenate(S[0], S[1])$

---

transpose layers as our model works with asymmetric images. More specifically, for the *generator*, we build 8 convolution-transpose layers with the configuration $C_{ts}(512, 4, 1) - C_{ts}(256, 4, 2) - C_{ts}(256, 3, 2) - C_{ts}(128, 4, 2) - C_{ts}(128, (3, 4), (1, 2)) - C_{ts}(64, 4, 2) - C_{ts}(64, 4, 2) - C_{ts}(1, 4, 2)$. The input of the *generator* is a vector noise of length 100, and the output is an image of size $240 \times 480 \times 1$. For the *discriminator*, we also create 8 convolution layers with the configuration $C(64, 4, 2) - C(64, 4, 2) - -C(128, 4, 2) - C(128, (3, 4), (1, 2)) - C(256, 4, 2) - C(256, 3, 2) - C(512, 4, 2) - C(1, 4, 1)$. The input of the *discriminator* is an image of size $240 \times 480 \times 1$, and the output is a scalar. Following each convolution or convolution layer in both *generator* and *discriminator* are batch normalization layers, LeakyRelu as activation function and dropout layer with a ratio of 0.3 to prevent overfitting. To stabilize GAN training and give high-quality results, we also utilize WGAN-GP in our proposal. When using WGAN-GP, we replace the last convolution layer in the *discriminator* with a fully connected layer, the sigmoid activation function after the last layer in vanilla GAN is also removed.

The produced images are then translated into ECG signals in the final stage. We define a workflow, described in Algorithm 1, to enhance this stage. Specifically, the image would be separated into two halves with the shape of 120×480, one for each of the two five-second signal segments. Image dimensions are amplified 2.5 times to form the new image of 300×1200. This process is conducted to guarantee that the number of pixel columns in the picture is roughly equal to the length of the signals and that the ECG morphological features are not deformed if the two dimensions are not enlarged equally. The image would then be converted to binary using a threshold of 250 and filtered with a median filter to eliminate salt and pepper noise. The image is then evaluated in each pixel column to create the target array A consisting of the positions of pixel value equal to 1 using the Linear Search Algorithm. After that, the Search Max Length Run Algorithm is applied to determine the longest run in array A. After several attempts, the best ECG signals are obtained by setting the threshold T to 5 (choose the position in the longest run at the percentile T). These places would then be translated to the relevant value in the range (-Amplitude, Amplitude) and concatenated to produce an ECG signal. This algorithm shows the flexibility of our proposal when we can control the amplitude of the generated signal.

3   Experiments

3.1   Dataset

This study uses Physionet (MIT-BIH Arrhythmia, European ST-T) [14] and Chapman [15] datasets to evaluate performance. First, the MIT-BIH contains ECG signals from 48 participants captured at a sampling rate of 360 Hz. The second Physionet database used in this study is the European ST-T dataset, consisting of 90 annotated ECG recordings sampling at 250 Hz. Besides, the Chapman dataset consists of ECG signals collected from 10,646 patients at a 500 Hz sampling rate. All records were resampled into 250 Hz for convenience during the generation process. We investigate two types of ECG synthesizes, including one beat (one QRS complex) and 10-second signals. First, with case one beat synthesis, we use only the MIT-BIH database (lead II) and divide the dataset into four categories: **N** (Normal beat), **V** (Ventricular beat), **S** (Supraventricular beat), **F** (Fusion of the ventricular and normal beats). The dataset is split into two subsets, including DS1 and DS2 like Hossain et al. research [1]. If DS1 is used for training, DS2 is utilized for inference. In the case using DS1 and DS2 for training, we take N, S, V, and F samples and divide this into 80% and 20% for training and testing, respectively. Second, in the case of the long ECG synthesis, we utilize both Physionet and Chapman datasets to synthesize ECG signals. Due to the lack of rhythms on the atrioventricular block, our study focuses on three rhythms (sinus rhythm, ventricular tachycardia, and supraventricular tachycardia). Based on the notes from the annotation, N, VT, and SVT symbols denote sinus rhythm, ventricular tachycardia, and supraventricular tachycardia, respectively; we spit these rhythms into 10-second ECG signals to make up the data training of our GAN model. Total samples collected from two datasets for N, VT, and SVT include 2782 N, 252 VT, and 635 SVT. As a result, we have a Synthetic Minority Over-sampling Technique (SMOTE) to augment data.

3.2   Evaluation Metrics

To evaluate morphology similarity between the original ECG and ECG synthesis in case one beat, we use four various metrics: Mean Squared Error (MSE), Normalized Mean Squared Error (NRMSE), Structural Similarity Index (SSIM), and Cross-correlation coefficient. It is important to note that the best performance means lower MSE and RMSE and higher SSIM and Cross-correlation coefficient. Besides, we also use the CNN classification model for beat classification tasks with adversarial data made up as the training dataset, and MIT-BIH data is utilized for testing. Accuracy (ACC), Sensitivity(SEN), and Specificity(SPEC) metrics are considered for analysis and comparison with previous studies.

3.3   Setup Hyper-parameters

As described, our GAN model relied on WGAN-GP. We set the penalty coefficient $\lambda = 10$ in Eq. 3. The input vector noise of length 100 is sampled from a standard normal distribution. In this study, the Adam optimizer is used to train the model, employing a learning rate of 0.0002 with $\beta_1 = 0.5$ and $\beta_2 = 0.999$. We used Pytorch 1.11 to train the model in mini-batches with a batch size of 32 in 400 epochs on a GeForce RTX 2070 SUPER GPU.

4   Results and Discussion

4.1   Results on One Beat ECG Synthesis

Table 1. Comparing performance of ECG generator on one beat synthesis with previous research for MIT-BIH.

Dataset	MSE	RMSE	SSI	CCC
DS1 [1]	0.00038	0.0136	0.9982	0.9986
DS1 (ours)	**0.00032**	**0.00107**	**0.9981**	**0.9985**
MIT [1]	0.00241	0.0292	0.9977	0.9425
MIT (ours)	**0.00179**	**0.0237**	**0.9978**	**0.9546**

MIT: DS1+DS2

After training using the DS1 data part from the MIT-BIH dataset with our GAN model, the extracted signal from the image is compared with the types of beats from the DS2 part. Table 1 indicates the results when evaluating with MSE, NRMSE, SSIM, and Cross-correlation coefficient. Table 1 demonstrates that our adversarial examples generated from DS1 and DS1 + DS2 training datasets outperform previous work [1]. Significantly lower MSE and NRMSE scores, as well as greater SSIM and Cross-correlation coefficients, were found in both test scenarios. In Fig. 3, we provide real and generated ECG signals for each class for comparison and visualization. The graphic expositions that the synthesized signals are highly vibrant and lifelike visually. Comparison with GAN models that work on time domain LSTM-GAN [8], WGAN-GP 1D [9] TTS-GAN [4], Fig. 4 shows that our one-beat ECG synthesis has the same performance as these three studies. Specifically, the amplitudes of all QRS complexes have been normalized in the range [0, 1] for convenience in the comparison. The generated QRS durations in these four models are reasonable, with values of approximately 0.8 s. However, there are still some minor limitations. While the one of LSTM-GAN reveals significant fluctuations, the one of WGAN-GP 1D illustrates more fluctuation during the post-QRS-complex duration. The TTS-GAN approach seems trivial in the one-beat synthesis, whereas this method needs more verification while working with the longer ECG signal generation.

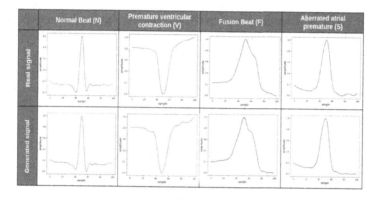

Fig. 3. Visualize a one-beat ECG synthesis on N, S, V, F types.

We also establish a classifier based on the Discriminator architecture of [1] to assess the efficient model and robustness on out-of-distribution and real-world data, which the adversarial scenario mimics for one-beat ECG synthesis. The network takes ECG signals as input and classifies the four categories (N, S, V, F) as output. Specifically, convolution is used four times for downsampling. Except for downsampling convolution, which uses a stride of two, we use a kernel size of three, a stride of one, and padding of one. Follow-

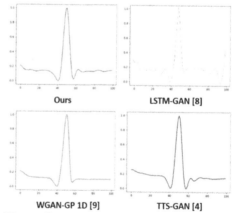

Fig. 4. Compare our generated ECG one beat with other GAN-based models.

ing the convolution layer are the Batch-normalization and Leaky-ReLU layers. Following that, we employ three dense layers. Eight convolution layers and two dense layers make up the encoder as described in [1]. Finally, we utilize the Softmax activation function as output for the prediction.

We would train and test this model on different datasets to evaluate the influence of generated signals on neural network architecture. Table 2 reveals that our adversarial samples have promoted the overall performance of the architecture. Specifically, while testing the fake dataset with models trained by 80% MIT or

DS1, the evaluated performance illustrates the approximate values, or in other words, slightly higher compared with the one tested with 20% MIT or DS2. This result reveals that our produced signals are similar and can replace the real ones in the training and testing processes. Besides, since all of these adversarial data mimics manually chosen one-beat ECG signals, nearly no noise would be generated, which would be helpful during the classification process. While combining the available training datasets with the fake ones, we noticed that the evaluation metrics of models improved significantly by approximately 0.3% in all of the values. This fact means the generated data has been successful in the augmentation procedure and model performance promotion.

Table 2. Classification results with different training and testing datasets

Training Data	Testing Data	ACC	N		S		V		F	
			SEN	SPEC	SEN	SPEC	SEN	SPEC	SEN	SPEC
80%MIT	20%MIT	99.31	99.28	94.36	94.56	99.64	94.93	99.94	95.54	99.54
	FAKE	**99.45**	**99.37**	**95.02**	94.91	99.6	**95.47**	**99.95**	**95.68**	**99.73**
DS1	DS2	97.72	95.87	96	88.19	99.6	93.75	99.64	90.9	96.53
	FAKE	**98.04**	**95.97**	**96.32**	**88.24**	**99.63**	**94.05**	**99.73**	**91.07**	**96.85**
TF1	20%MIT	**99.78**	**99.43**	**96.48**	**95.95**	**99.89**	**95.75**	**99.98**	**96.67**	**99.71**
TF2	DS2	**98.32**	**96.01**	**96.43**	**89.21**	**99.64**	**94.14**	**99.73**	**91.06**	**96.73**

MIT: DS1+DS2, **TF1**: 80%(DS1+DS2)+FAKE, **TF2**: DS1+FAKE

4.2   Results on Long ECG Synthesis

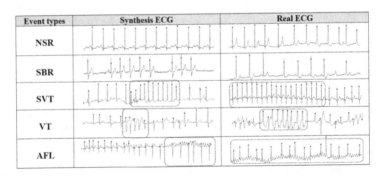

Event types	Synthesis ECG	Real ECG
NSR		
SBR		
SVT		
VT		
AFL		

Fig. 5. 10 s ECG synthesis examples for normal sinus (NSR), sinus bradycardia rhythm (SBR) supraventricular tachycardia (SVT), ventricular tachycardia (VT) and atrial flutter (AFL) rhythms

Figure 5 portrays the likenesses and dissimilarities between real and synthesized signals by detecting the R peak position of each with the PanTompkins algorithm. In summary, Fig. 5 illustrates some comparison of various rhythms, including normal sinus (NSR), sinus bradycardia rhythm (SBR), supraventricular tachycardia (SVT), ventricular tachycardia (VT), and atrial flutter (AFL) rhythms. The morphology shown in Fig. 5, the QRS complexes in the generated data, may be smoothly noticed, just like valid data. Furthermore, each data set accurately emphasized the different properties of event types. For instance, the AFL rhythm characters have a sawtooth appearance. A succession of V beats at higher heart rates causes the VT event. The created SVT data, with shorter RR intervals during the event, is also comparable to the genuine data, with shorter RR intervals.

A well-evaluated long ECG signal should include the acceptable P and T waves. However, after rebuilding and verification on models for 10-second ECG synthesis, a large amount of noise appears when testing with the work [8,9]. Figure 6 also compares the difference in the performance of our proposals with other architectures, including S12-ECG-GAN [7], TTS-GAN [4] and DDPM [11]. In terms of S12-ECG-GAN, the main problem is that the

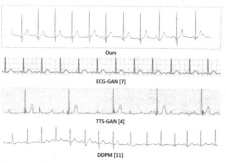

Fig. 6. Comparison 10 s ECG synthesis between our proposal with previous works

generated 10-second signals are formed from the same 13 representative beats attached. As a result, the generated signals in this framework have no diversity in RR intervals and morphological features. TTS-GAN seems to address such a problem, but the shapes of P and T waves are still unacceptable, with sharp peaks and illogical inclinations. The DDPM result with clear P and T morphology is acceptable like the real one. However, when we conducted this experiment again, the performance to synthesize one sample took approximately 2 min, which required nearly 30 s for our approach with the same heart rate and shape on one long ECG sample. In short, to compare the synthesis rate and output morphology on ECG generation, our suggestion has demonstrated the results outperformance of previous research.

5 Conclusion

This paper proposes a new approach that works on the image domain rather than the time domain for the long ECG synthesis. To generate 10-second ECG signals, we only utilize a baseline simple GAN (DCGAN). This novel idea has been handled in synthesizing particular features inside ECG, such as P and T waves. Our models cannot validate performance for atrioventricular block rhythms since none exist in the dataset. However, we have succeeded in 10-second ECG synthesis for sinus, ventricular tachycardia, or supraventricular tachycardia rhythms. In terms of creating realistic ECGs, our technique consistently outperforms state-of-the-art benchmarks. In the future, we may look at merging the differential privacy framework into our method to develop adaptable ECGs that can govern multiple frequencies and amplitudes.

Acknowledgments. This research is funded by Vietnam National University Ho Chi Minh City (VNU-HCM) under grant number DS2024-26-05.

References

1. Hossain, K.F., et al.: ECG-Adv-GAN: Detecting ECG adversarial examples with conditional generative adversarial networks. In: 2021 20th IEEE International Conference on Machine Learning and Applications (ICMLA), pp. 50–56, IEEE (2021)
2. Rajpurkar, P., Hannun, A.Y., Haghpanahi, M., Bourn, C., Ng, A.Y.: Cardiologist-level arrhythmia detection with convolutional neural networks. arXiv preprint arXiv:1707.01836 (2017)
3. Creswell, A., White, T., Dumoulin, V., Arulkumaran, K., Sengupta, B., Bharath, A.A.: Generative adversarial networks: an overview. IEEE Signal Process. Mag. **35**(1), 53–65 (2018)
4. Li, X., Metsis, V., Wang, H., Ngu, A.H.H.: TTS-GAN: a transformer-based time-series generative adversarial network. arXiv preprint arXiv:2202.02691 (2022)
5. Karras, T., Laine, S., Aittala, M., Hellsten, J., Lehtinen, J., Aila, T.: Analyzing and improving the image quality of StyleGAN. In: Proceedings of the IEEE/CVF Conference on Computer Vision and Pattern Recognition, pp. 8110–8119 (2020)
6. Su, J., Jin, Z., Finkelstein, A.: HIFI-GAN-2: studio-quality speech enhancement via generative adversarial networks conditioned on acoustic features. In: 2021 IEEE Workshop on Applications of Signal Processing to Audio and Acoustics (WASPAA), pp. 166–170, IEEE (2021)
7. Zhang, Y.-H., Babaeizadeh, S.: Synthesis of standard 12-lead electrocardiograms using two-dimensional generative adversarial networks. J. Electrocardiol. **69**, 6–14 (2021)
8. Brophy, E.: Synthesis of dependent multichannel ECG using generative adversarial networks. In: Proceedings of the 29th ACM International Conference on Information & Knowledge Management, pp. 3229–3232 (2020)
9. Adib, E., Fernandez, A.S., Afghah, F., Prevost, J.J.: Synthetic ECG signal generation using probabilistic diffusion models. IEEE Access **11**, 75818–75828 (2023)
10. Vo, K., et al.: P2E-WGAN: ECG waveform synthesis from PPG with conditional wasserstein generative adversarial networks. In: Proceedings of the 36th Annual ACM Symposium on Applied Computing, pp. 1030–1036 (2021)
11. Tran, D.T., Tran, Q.N., Dang, T.T.K., Tran, D.H.: A novel approach for long ECG synthesis utilize diffusion probabilistic model. In: Proceedings of the 2023 8th International Conference on Intelligent Information Technology, pp. 251–258 (2023)
12. Alcaraz, J.M.L., Strodthoff, N.: Diffusion-based conditional ECG generation with structured state space models. Comput. Biol. Med. **163**, 107115 (2023)
13. Radford, A., Metz, L., Chintala, S.: Unsupervised representation learning with deep convolutional generative adversarial networks. arXiv preprint arXiv:1511.06434 (2015)
14. Moody, G.B., Mark, R.G.: The impact of the MIT-BIH arrhythmia database. IEEE Eng. Med. Biol. Mag. **20**(3), 45–50 (2001)

15. Zheng, J., Zhang, J., Danioko, S., Yao, H., Guo, H., Rakovski, C.: A 12-lead electro-cardiogram database for arrhythmia research covering more than 10,000 patients. Sci. Data **7**(1), 1–8 (2020)
16. Arjovsky, M., Chintala, S., Bottou, L.: Wasserstein GAN, vol. 30, no. 4,arXiv preprint arXiv:1701.07875 (2017)
17. Gulrajani, I., Ahmed, F., Arjovsky, M., Dumoulin, V., Courville, A.C.: Improved training of wasserstein GANs. In: Advances in Neural Information Processing Systems, vol. 30 (2017)

PHD Showcase Papers

CFD Analysis of Turbine Cascade Unsteady Aerodynamics Using a Hybrid POD Technique

Vladyslav Skilskyy⬥, Viola Rossano⬥, and Giuliano De Stefano$^{(\boxtimes)}$⬥

Engineering Department, University of Campania Luigi Vanvitelli, 81031 Aversa, Italy
giuliano.destefano@unicampania.it

Abstract. This study presents a computational investigation into the unsteady aerodynamics of a low-pressure turbine cascade, utilizing computational fluid dynamics (CFD) with a primary focus on enhancing efficiency. The proposed approach combines a classical proper orthogonal decomposition with a modern machine learning technique. This hybrid methodology demonstrates its effectiveness by accurately predicting the unsteady flow over the turbine blade. Crucially, the solution retains the essential features of the original physics-based computational model. This study represents a potential significant advancement in improving the efficiency of CFD solutions, enabling future resource-conscious scale-resolving simulations of complex aerodynamic flows without sacrificing solution accuracy.

Keywords: Computational Fluid Dynamics · Compressible Turbulent Flow · Turbine Blade Aerodynamics · Proper Orthogonal Decomposition

1 Introduction

Low-pressure turbine (LPT) blades are intricately designed to enhance aerodynamic efficiency at low-pressure ratios, prioritizing the recovery of exhaust energy, while minimizing back pressure [1]. The airflow around one blade naturally becomes turbulent due to the wake produced by upstream blades, resulting in unsteady airflow that interacts with blade movements, creating a complex non-linear scenario. Accurately predicting this fluid-structure interaction (FSI) phenomenon is crucial, particularly concerning potential flutter instabilities, especially with extended blades. Despite advancements in understanding LPT flow dynamics under both laminar and turbulent conditions, addressing the transitional region in the flow remains challenging, especially considering the effects induced by the passage of wake flow from upstream blade rows [1]. Over the past decade, considerable efforts have been devoted to developing effective numerical approaches for aero-mechanical analysis, primarily tailored for industrial design considerations [2]. However, these approaches might prove insufficient when simulating flow patterns around the LPT blades, particularly for separated flow conditions. Therefore, there is a need to develop more accurate and detailed numerical models, especially to fully comprehend the complex airflow dynamics in modern LPT experiencing vibrations. For instance, a nonlinear frequency-domain technique was employed in [3] to predict pressure coefficients and aero-damping for multistage turbine blades, achieving good agreement compared to time-domain methods.

In the industrial context, low-fidelity methods remain desirable due to their particular emphasis on aero-damping analysis. However, this emphasis often comes at the cost of neglecting the intricate physics underlying FSI. This pragmatic approach introduces what is commonly referred to as a "black-box effect," wherein a deep understanding of fundamental physical processes is sacrificed. This becomes particularly critical in the design of modern aeronautical LPT blades featuring slender airfoils, where flutter may emerge as a significant constraint. In the current era of extensive data utilization, the pivotal role of data-driven models in industrial research cannot be overstated. In contrast to complex numerical approaches to turbulent flow modeling like large-eddy simulation (LES), which requires highly detailed grids to capture shocks and boundary layers, data-driven models emerge as a highly efficient alternative. Surrogate models have clearly proven their effectiveness in dealing with challenges related to optimizing shapes [4], positioning data-driven models as a very promising approach, surpassing the limitations of hybrid approaches based on Reynolds-averaged Navier-Stokes (RANS) and LES methodologies [5], and conventional wind tunnel experiments [6].

While commonly employed, there is a lack of comprehensive research explaining the reasons for preferring neural network (NN) or other artificial intelligence tools over alternative methods like proper orthogonal decomposition (POD) for the reconstruction of transonic flows. This becomes particularly crucial when considering sample efficiency, a factor frequently overlooked in such evaluations. Conventionally, the belief is that deep learning demands an extensive dataset compared to more traditional tools, but this viewpoint is questioned in our current research. This study aims at improving the accuracy of the POD approach by using a deep learning algorithm to estimate the unsteady compressible aerodynamics behaviour in a low-pressure turbine cascade.

This represents a significant advancement over previous works [7,8], which primarily focused on only one of these methods. The integration of POD and machine learning techniques brings about several benefits. Firstly, it significantly reduces computational complexity, making it more efficient than using a single method. Secondly, it allows for the extraction of essential flow features, which may not be possible with a single method, leading to a better understanding of the dynamic behavior of the turbine cascade. Finally, it preserves the essential features of the original physics-based computational model, ensuring that the solution's accuracy is not compromised.

The manuscript is organized as follows: Section 2 provides a comprehensive overview of the CFD model. The proposed methodology is introduced in Sect. 3, where the POD technique is briefly reviewed, and the hybrid POD-DNN method is presented. The preliminary results are presented in Sect. 4, accompanied by a thorough analysis of the main sources of error. Finally, Sect. 5 offers some concluding remarks.

2   CFD Model

In this study, the T106A LPT blade profile acts as a suitable benchmark for the proposed data-driven model, representing the mid-section of the PW2037 LPT rotor passage blade. Widely examined in previous studies, this profile offers valuable insights into complex phenomena like flow separation and transition in engine regions characterized by high-pressure gradients, along with moderate Mach and Reynolds numbers [9].

The computational domain, which is depicted in Fig. 1, outlines the geometric characteristics of the turbine blade, featuring a chord length of 1.0 m, an axial chord of 0.8663 m, a pitch of 0.9557 m, and a domain breadth of 2.287 m in the homogeneous spanwise direction. The domain's origin is situated at mid-span along the leading edge of the turbine blade, with the inflow plane positioned 0.92 m upstream from the leading edge, and the outflow plane situated 1.86 m downstream. In this configuration, the Reynolds number based on the chord of the turbine blade is set to 2×10^5, while the Mach number is 0.601. The air is assumed to behave as an ideal gas with constant viscosity and its dynamics is governed by the compressible Navier-Stokes equations. To highlight a nuanced aspect that has received limited attention in the existing literature, a cylindrical wake generator was intentionally positioned ahead of the blade, following the methodology proposed in [9].

The mesh generation process utilized the Pointwise software V18.6R2. Initially, a two-dimensional triangle-based unstructured mesh was created on the blade surface. To take into account the boundary layers near the various solid surfaces (of both blade and cylinder),the T-Rex method was employed to generate a boundary layer mesh consisting of 30 layers of quadrilaterals beneath the triangles. The minimum wall spacing was set at 3×10^{-5} m, with a growth rate of 1.2 from one layer to another.

Numerical simulations were conducted using the CFD code Ansys Fluent v23.R1 [10], employing a pressure-based solver, due to the relatively low Mach number. The freestream turbulence intensity was imposed to be 2%, and the blade surface was subjected to isothermal no-slip boundary condition. Using the finite volume (FV) method, the governing equations were discretized applying the conservation principles directly to each computational cell [11]. The SIM-PLEC procedure managed the coupling between pressure and velocity. A second-order upwind scheme was utilized for pressure discretization, energy, and turbulence variables, while a central differencing scheme was employed for momentum.

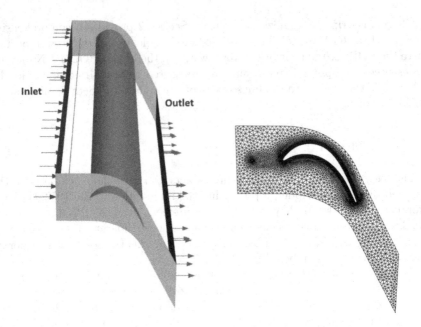

Fig. 1. Computational domain and spatial mesh.

Table 1. Flow specification

Parameter	Value
Total temperature at inlet (T_{in})	350 K
Static pressure at inlet (P_{in})	7,340 Pa
Total pressure at inlet $(P_{total,in})$	7,770 Pa
Static pressure at exit (P_{exit})	6,950 Pa

In the context of applied scientific research, our recent findings, e.g. [12, 13], suggest that employing unsteady RANS models offers a feasible and cost-effective alternative for predicting complex aerodynamic flows with engineering accuracy, even for rough walls [14], which is particularly important for turbine blades. Therefore, a hybrid RANS-LES model utilizing the Stress-Blended Eddy Simulation (SBES) technique was employed for turbulence modeling [15]. This approach dynamically switches between RANS and LES turbulence models using a shielding function dependent on the local mesh resolution [16].

Concerning boundary conditions, velocity inlet and pressure outlet conditions were specified in the streamwise direction. Periodic boundary conditions were applied to the upper, lower, and lateral walls. The inlet and outlet thermo-fluid dynamic conditions were set according to the specifications detailed in Table 1.

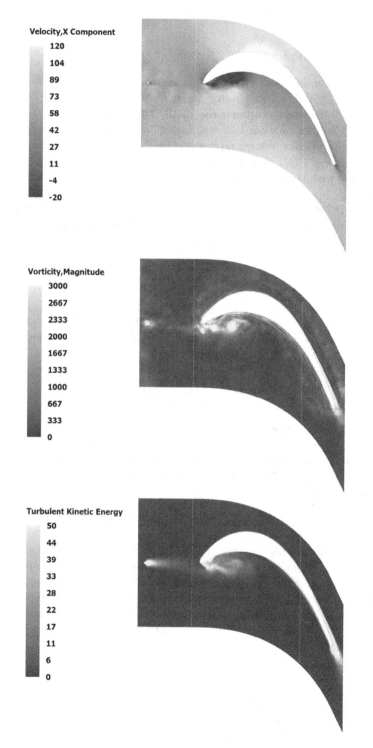

Fig. 2. Flow field variables from CFD analysis at $t = 0.01$ s.

3 Methodology

3.1 POD Technique

By now, POD can be considered a strong and widely used technique in the field of applied CFD. Originating from Lumley's work [17], POD has been refined by Sirovich, particularly through the method of snapshots [18]. The method is similar to Fourier analysis but stands out by often needing fewer modes to create a highly efficient system representation. This distinct feature emphasizes the importance of POD as a valuable option compared to Fourier-type analysis when dealing with the original partial differential equations describing fluid flow [19] (Fig. 2).

The POD expansion allows the representation of Fourier coefficients for a scalar variable $u(x,t)$ (representing a generic fluid dynamic variable), defined in the time interval $0 < t < T$ [20]. Mathematically, this variable is expressed as:

$$u(x,t) = \sum_{n=1}^{\infty} c_n(x)\phi_n(t),$$ (1)

where $\phi_n(t)$ denotes a set of orthonormal basis functions. The functions $c_n(x)$ are random variables, particularly relevant when dealing with random processes like fluid turbulence, and are given by:

$$c_n(x) = \int_0^T x(t)\phi_n^*(t)dt .$$ (2)

where $\phi_n^*(t)$ denotes the complex conjugate of the orthonormal basis function $\phi_n(t)$. The above integral captures the interaction between data and basis functions, yielding coefficients c_n that encapsulate the contribution of each mode to the overall system. The POD method minimizes the mean square error of projections, expressed as:

$$error = \langle \|u(x,t) - \hat{u}(x,t)\|^2 \rangle.$$ (3)

In this expression, where u represents the original data, $\hat{u}(x,t)$ signifies the reconstructed data using a reduced set of modes. The aim is to optimize this projection, ensuring that the reconstructed data closely approximates the original dataset. This minimization process allows for a more compact representation of the system's dynamics, emphasizing the most significant features while reducing computational complexity. To obtain POD modes, the following eigenvalue problem needs to be solved:

$$\int_0^T R(t_1, t_2)\phi_n(t_2)\, dt_2 = \lambda\phi_n(t_1).$$ (4)

Here, $R(t_1, t_2)$ is the auto-covariance of the fluid variable $u(x,t)$ evaluated in different time instants (t_1, t_2). The eigenvalues of each POD mode represent the energy contained in that mode, with magnitudes arranged in decreasing order $(\lambda_n > \lambda_{n+1})$.

In this approach, CFD data at a specific time interval are treated as a snapshot. The method of snapshots aims at reducing the computational cost of solving the eigenvalue problem in Eq. (4), which involves an $n \times n$ matrix. The auto-covariance matrix R is approximated as a sum of snapshots:

$$R_{ij} = \frac{1}{M} \sum_{n=1}^{M} x_i^n x_j^n. \tag{5}$$

Here, the snapshots are assumed to be sufficiently separated in time or space, beyond the correlation time or distance. While commonly employed, doubts arise about the applicability of this method in some kind of flows, due to its assumption of uncorrelated snapshots, as mentioned in [20].

3.2 Hybrid POD-DNN Method

In this study, we investigate the application of the back-propagation neural network (BPNN) to predict flow fields based on POD principles, following the method of Xie et al. [21]. Renowned for its well-established theory, exceptional performance, and broad applicability, BPNN proves to be a robust tool for flow field predictions.The BPNN minimizes the mean square error between predicted $(\hat{y}_i)$ and actual values (y_i). The neuron, which represents the fundamental unit of a neural network, combines weighted inputs and generates an output using an activation function. The network structure, enhanced by multiple hidden layers in a Deep Neural Network (DNN), influences the overall functionality.

The common activation function ReLU is preferred, owing to its near-linear response, simplifying the application of gradient-based optimization algorithms [22]. The network is trained to minimize output errors using a quadratic function. The training process aims at enhancing predictions by minimizing the disparity between actual and predicted values across all sample points, measured by the mean squared error (MSE) loss function:

$$J_{\mathrm{MSE}} = \frac{1}{N} \sum_{i=1}^{N} (y_i - \hat{y}_i)^2, \tag{6}$$

where N represents the total number of training examples. The optimization process, driven by the gradient descent algorithm, enhances the network's performance:

$$g_t(\theta) = \frac{\partial J}{\partial \theta} \tag{7}$$

In summary, the POD methodology allows the identification of primary modes and their associated modal coefficients, providing insights into the main characteristics of the resolved flow field. Essentially, POD discerns fundamental patterns and their respective strengths within the CFD dataset. Subsequently, the obtained modal coefficients are utilized to train a particular DNN, referred to as AI_Airfoil_CFD, which is available at https://github.com/Jameshin/AI_Airfoil_CFD. This DNN is specifically designed to predict the modal coefficients under unknown conditions, such as situations not previously observed.

In conclusion, once trained, the DNN can efficiently reconstruct the local flow field with a low computational cost based on the POD orthogonal basis. This implies that deep learning framework can predict the flow distribution without the need to solve higher-order non-linear partial differential equations. In practical terms, this methodology facilitates an efficient prediction of the flow field, proving applicable in scenarios where the direct numerical solution of flow equations would be computationally highly demanding.

4   Preliminary Results

In this showcase study, the ability of the POD-DNN method to reconstruct the velocity field is assessed by comparing velocity data to ground-truth values obtained through CFD, at four different time instants. The preliminary results, which are shown in Fig. 3 in terms of velocity contours, demonstrate the accurate modeling of separation zones by using the POD-DNN technique. In fact, the method provides results that are fully consistent with the expected physical scenario. Despite turbulent flow in the turbines, the hybrid POD-DNN algorithm accurately estimated fluid separation near the trailing edge, proving its effectiveness in resolving complex turbulence with high accuracy. The deviation between the values predicted by POD-DNN and CFD results was assessed through the computation of relative mean squared errors, as outlined in Table 2.

The POD-DNN approach offers a significant advantage not only in terms of accuracy but also in its ability to rapidly generate results compared to conventional numerical methods. To assess the difference in computational efficiency between CFD and POD-DNN, we conducted a comparative analysis, focusing on the computational time required. This involved running identical simulations using both approaches and recording the time taken to reach the solution. The speedup is eveluted as the ratio of computational time between CFD and POD-DNN methods, providing a quantitative measure of the efficiency of POD-DNN compared to traditional CFD simulations. The individual computational times for a single simulation, utilizing a dedicated GPU node are detailed in Table 3.

Table 2. Error estimation

Time (s)	RMSE
7.6×10^{-5}	1.835415×10^{-13}
0.0014	2.320662×10^{-13}
0.007	8.444527×10^{-13}
0.013	7.502180×10^{-13}

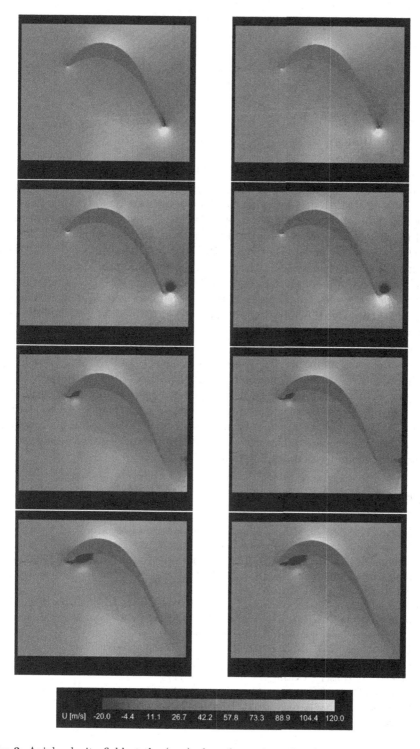

Fig. 3. Axial velocity field at the (x, y) plane for various time instants corresponding to $t = 7.6e - 05$ s, 0.0014 s, 0.007 s, 0.013 s, organized from top to bottom rows for CFD and POD-DNN, displayed from left to right columns.

Table 3. Computational time

Method	Time (s)	Speedup
CFD	864000	–
POD-DNN	11520	75

5   Conclusion

This study explores the feasibility of rapidly obtaining solutions for flow fields in turbomachinery applications. The objective is to test a novel approach that integrates POD with deep learning to estimate unsteady aerodynamic flows. To generate data for unsteady flows, hybrid RANS-LES simulations are performed, and the acquired dataset is employed to train the method, while validating the effectiveness of the model. The present POD-DNN framework demonstrated the ability of accurately capturing the features of the flow field. In addition, it is demonstrated the potential for conducting simulations with low computational cost, while addressing complexities in the resolved flow field. Finally, it is important to acknowledge the limitations of the POD-DNN method, particularly when extrapolating fields in strongly nonlinear conditions outside the parameter space for which the data are available, where the relationship between inputs and outputs can become unpredictable. Additionally, there exist several potential ways for improving the proposed method. The exploration of integrating alternative machine learning techniques, such as reinforcement learning or genetic algorithms, could prove beneficial in augmenting the performance of the methodology. Furthermore, the incorporation of experimental data holds the potential to enhance the model's accuracy by providing real-world insights that are not captured by computational simulations.

References

1. Besem, F.M., Kielb, R.E.: Influence of the tip clearance on a compressor blade aerodynamic damping. J. Propuls. Power **33**, 227–233 (2017)
2. Rahmati, M.T., He, L., Wells, R.G.: Interface treatment for harmonic solution in multi-row aeromechanic analysis. In: Turbo Expo: Power for Land, Sea, and Air, vol. 4, pp. 1253–1261 (2010)
3. Rahmati, M.T., He, L., Wang, D.X., Li, Y.S., Wells, R.G., Krishnababu, S.K.: Nonlinear time and frequency domain methods for multirow aeromechanical analysis. J. Turbomach. Trans. ASME **136**, 041010 (2014)
4. Liu, J., Song, W.-P., Han, Z.-H., Zhang, Y.: Efficient aerodynamic shape optimization of transonic wings using a parallel infilling strategy and surrogate models. Struct. Multidiscip. Optim. **55**, 925–943 (2017)
5. Rossano, V., De Stefano, G.: Testing a generalized two-equation turbulence model for computational aerodynamics of a mid-range aircraft. Appl. Sci. **13**, 11243 (2023)

6. Zhu, J., Liu, L., Liu, T., Shi, Y., Su, W., Wu, J.: Lift and drag in two-dimensional steady viscous and compressible flow: I. far-field formulae analysis and numerical confirmation. In: 45th AIAA Fluid Dynamics Conference, vol. 2305 (2015)

7. Pan, Y., An, X., Lei, Y., Ji, C.: An improved neural network for modeling airfoil's unsteady aerodynamics in transonic flow. Phys. Fluids **36**(1), (2024)

8. Fonzi, N., Brunton, S.L., Fasel, U.: Data-driven modeling for transonic aeroelastic analysis. J. Aircraft **61**(2), 625–637 (2024)

9. Iyer, A.S., et al.: High-order accurate direct numerical simulation of flow over a MTU-T161 low pressure turbine blade. Comput. Fluids **226**, 104989 (2021)

10. ANSYS Inc., ANSYS Fluent (Version 23R1)

11. De Stefano, G., Denaro. F.M., Riccardi, G.: High-order filtering for control volume flow simulation. Int. J. Numer. Meth. Fluids **37**, 797–835 (2001)

12. Rossano, V., Cittadini, A., De Stefano, G.: Computational evaluation of shock wave interaction with a liquid droplet. Appl. Sci. **12**, 1349 (2022)

13. Rossano, V., De Stefano, G.: Hybrid VOF-Lagrangian CFD modeling of droplet aerobreakup. Appl. Sci. **12**, 8302 (2022)

14. Salomone, T., Piomelli, U., De Stefano, G.: Wall-modeled and hybrid large-eddy simulations of the flow over roughness strips fluids **8**, 10 (2023)

15. Mendez, M.A., Ianiro, A., Noack, B.R., Brunton, S.L.: Data-Driven Fluid Mechanics: Combining First Principles and Machine Learning. Cambridge University Press (2023)

16. Rossano, V., De Stefano, G.: Scale-resolving simulation of shock-induced aerobreakup of water droplet. Computation **12**, 71 (2024)

17. Berkooz, G., Holmes, P., Lumley, J.L.: The proper orthogonal decomposition in the analysis of turbulent flows. Annu. Rev. Fluid Mech. **25**, 539–575 (1993)

18. Sirovich, L.: Turbulence and the dynamics of coherent structure. Part I, II, III. Quat. Appl. Math. **3**, 583 (1987)

19. Duggleby, A., Paul, M.R.: Computing the Karhunen-Loève dimension of an extensively chaotic flow field given a finite amount of data. Comput. Fluids **39**(9), 1704–1710 (2010)

20. Gorder, R.: Use of proper orthogonal decomposition in the analysis of turbulent flows. Report, Fluid Turbulence Course, University of Washington (2010)

21. Xie, C., Yuan, Z., Wang, J.: Artificial neural network-based nonlinear algebraic models for large eddy simulation of turbulence. Phys. Fluids **32**, 116610 (2020)

22. Jarrett, K., Kavukcuoglu, K., Ranzato, M., LeCun, Y.: What is the best multi-stage architecture for object recognition? In: 2009 IEEE 12th International Conference on Computer Vision, pp. 2146 (2009)

CFD Prediction of Supersonic Jet Impingement on Inclined Flat Plate

Antonio Mezzacapo$^{(\boxtimes)}$ (ID) and Giuliano De Stefano (ID)

Engineering Department, University of Campania Luigi Vanvitelli,
81031 Aversa, Italy
antonio.mezzacapo@unicampania.it

Abstract. This study aims at simulating the effects of turbulent supersonic jet impingement on an inclined flat plate, by examining the pressure distribution on the plate surface. Simulations are performed at the Mach number of 2.2, fixed the jet-to-plate distance, for different plate inclinations. Unlike previous studies, a modern turbulence modelling approach such as detached eddy simulation is followed, while comparing the current results to traditional unsteady Reynolds-averaged Navier-Stokes solution. It is determined that the DES solution is able to predict the correct pressure distribution on the plate, showing a quite good agreement against existing experimental and numerical data.

Keywords: Computational fluid dynamics · Turbulent supersonic jet · Unsteady Reynolds-averaged Navier-Stokes · Detached-eddy simulation

1 Introduction

Despite decades of research and progress, accurate and efficient computational fluid dynamics (CFD) simulation of wall-bounded supersonic turbulent flows still represents a challenging task, e.g. [1]. In particular, the research on free and impinging jets continues to receive a lot of attention by the applied CFD community, due to its high complexity. Indeed, the study of turbulent supersonic jets impinging on an inclined flat plate shows a strong interest in both theoretical research and engineering applications. The matter appears in various aerospace applications, including design of jet deflectors, and multistage rocket separation, among others [2].

The main advantage of CFD techniques is that they generally make less expensive to investigate a wider range of experimental parameters and configurations, compared to experimental methods. However, in spite of its geometric simplicity, the jet impingement on an inclined flat plate is very difficult to simulate, since the turbulent flow field involves a variety of complex fluid dynamics phenomena, including shock/shock and shock/boundary layer interactions. Due to the high computational cost, practically, the research resources have been mostly spent to investigate the impingement of perpendicular jets [3]. More recently, thanks to the surprising growth in computational power and the development of advanced numerical techniques, many research studies, as well as

O. Gervasi et al. (Eds.): ICCSA 2024, LNCS 14814, pp. 366–377, 2024.
https://doi.org/10.1007/978-3-031-64608-9_24

comprehensive reviews [4], have focused on the flow field and the shock structures generated after the impact of impinging circular supersonic jet flows on various geometries and configurations. Specifically, varying nozzle to wall distance, nozzle diameter, and impingement angle have been considered [5].

As to experiments, the study carried out by Lamont and Hunt [6] represents one of the more significant works on supersonic jet impingement on inclined plates. Such study highlights how inclined jet impingement exhibits more complex features against the perpendicular case, due to strong shock-shock interactions. The latter can cause the maximum pressure on the inclined plate to be several times larger than that one attained for the perpendicular case, leading to more severe damage of the plate surface. The nozzle-plate distance, the jet pressure ratios, and the inclined angle of the plate all significantly impact on the jet flow characteristics. Other studies [7] highlighted how the flow structures generated at the impingement location are influenced by compressibility effects and fluid turbulence. In the research by Nakai et al. [8], the supersonic jet impinging on an inclined flat plate at various plate angles, pressure ratios, and nozzle-plate distances, was experimentally studied by using the pressure-sensitive paint (PSP) surface pressure measurement and the Schlieren method. From these experiments, Nakai and co-workers observed that there are three different types of flow patterns, and that, if the flat plate angle, nozzle-plate distance, and shock cell length are known ahead of time, it is possible to anticipate the different forms of flow. Furthermore, Ito et al. [9] carried out experiments of the jet impingement at higher flat plate angles, where the location and angle of the plate were changed from 1 to 4.5, and from 60 to 90°, respectively.

Most of the works available in the literature are mainly focused on the study of the acoustic field nearby the impingement zone. Although complex numerical techniques have been involved, such as large-eddy simulation, and hybrid Reynolds-averaged Navier-Stokes (RANS)/LES methods, little attention seems to have been given to the aerodynamic flow field. The objective of this ongoing research is to underline how the study of the acoustic field is not sufficient when examining a complex flow system such as jet impingement, where analyzing the aerodynamics field becomes a crucial point. The reason why many researchers in the past have focused their attention on the noise produced by the jet is associated to the so-called acoustic fatigue [10]. The intense acoustic pressures waves produced at the nozzle exit can actually cause failure of light weight structures, such as skin panels, fuselage rings and tail plane structures. While these failures may not be catastrophic, the associated maintenance and repair costs may be considerable. On the other hand, what the authors seem to have not been investigated enough is also the implication of the aerodynamic field on the impingement surfaces. For example, during the take off of an aircraft (or missile), the local increase of velocity produces a decrease of the local pressure near the impingement area, leading to a lose of lift. The latter may cause either takeoff failure or an excessive fuel consumption. Such phenomenon is known as lift loss, and was studied for the first time by Wyatt [11], using a baffle plate to simply represent the under surface of an aircraft. Conducting a series of experiments to study the lift loss, due to a single air jet impinging on the ground at different heights, it found that closer was the ground surface from the jet, higher was the lift loss.

In this challenging context, the aim of this study is to determine and analyze the jet flow characteristics, and the pressure distribution on the flat plate, using modern CFD approaches. Unlike the similar previous study by Dharavath et al. [12], in which traditional unsteady RANS models were employed, a modern turbulence modeling approach that is detached-eddy simulation (DES) is investigated. The new results are compared with previous numerical and experimental data to demonstrate the capability of both approaches to predict and capture the correct pressure distribution over the plate and the complex flow structures created by the jet impingement, at several plate angles in the range between 30 to 50 °C.

2   CFD Model

2.1   Computational Domain

The flow geometry consists of an inclined flat plate and a convergent-divergent nozzle generating the supersonic jet. A schematic view of the computational domain is depicted in Fig. 1, with the flow region between the nozzle exit and the plate surface being represented in the zoomed-in picture. The domain extends up to $21D_j$, $75D_j$, $21D_j$, and $28D_j$, where D_j is the nozzle exit diameter, in the longitudinal direction, upper, lower, and lateral sections, respectively, in order to capture most of the complex flow field features. The rectangular flat plate has the dimensions of 50 m (length), 28 m (width), and 0.25 m (thickness). Note that the size of the present computational domain is reduced compared to reference simulations in [12]. Also, only the divergent section of the nozzle is simulated. Moreover, taking advantage of the expected symmetry of the resolved mean flow, only one half of the computational domain is actually considered in the practical simulations.

2.2   Computational Grid

Figure 2 shows an overview of the finite volume (FV) computational mesh, along with zoomed-in pictures corresponding to the flow region between the nozzle exit and the inclined plate. The method allows the complex compressible flow to be numerically approximated, with the conservation principles being applied over each control volume [13]. The FV mesh is made of a total of about 3 million cells, with structured elements in the close proximity of the plate (whose linear size is of the order of 0.05 m), and tetrahedral elements away from the plate. The meshing strategy allows on a smooth shift from structured to unstructured mesh elements, while reducing the computational complexity of the overall CFD model. In order to save computational time, the semi-empirical RNG $k - \epsilon$ turbulence model is employed, supplied with wall functions. The spatial discretization is performed

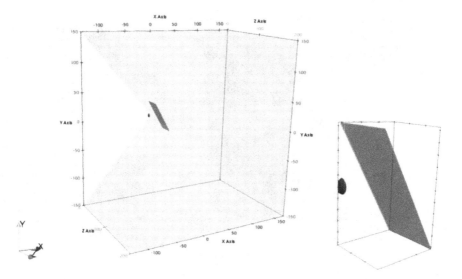

Fig. 1. Sketch of the computational domain, with zoomed-in picture of the flow region of primary interest.

by taking particular care to the height of the first computational cell, which is maintained at the order of 10^{-3} m, ensuring that $y^+ \approx 35$. The present wall modelled approach avoids to directly solve the entire boundary layer region, which would require a much more refined grid, resulting in saving approximately 4 million cells compared to the above mentioned reference work.

2.3   Boundary Conditions

Several numerical simulations are carried out using the commercial CFD software ANSYS Fluent [14], by considering different plate angles θ, fixed pressure ratio $PR = P_j/P_\infty$ (where P_j and P_∞ are nozzle exit and freestream pressures, respectively), and fixed distance between the nozzle exit and the plate surface L/D_j. The boundary conditions, which are based on the previous work by Dharavath et al. [12], are listed in Table 1. At the inlet, since the exact shape of the nozzle is given and known, a pressure-inlet boundary condition is imposed, where static pressure and temperature have been calculated under the assumption of isentropic flow. The pressure outlet condition is imposed at the outlet boundary. This allows to use the non-reflecting option, thus avoiding false reflections, but letting waves to pass through the boundaries.

Since the turbulent mean flow is expected to be symmetric, a symmetry boundary condition is imposed at $x = 0$, assuming a zero flux of all balanced quantities across the boundary. Finally, the no-slip boundary condition is used for the plate surface, where the fluid velocity is zero.

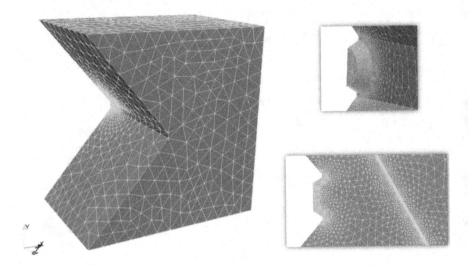

Fig. 2. Sketch of the computational grid, with zoomed-in pictures of the flow region of primary interest.

Table 1. Summary of boundary conditions

Boundary	Type
Inlet	Pressure inlet
Outlet	Pressure outlet
Plate	Wall
Symmetry	Symmetry plane

2.4 Numerical Parameters

For the different simulations that are conducted, the pressure ratio (P_j/P_∞) and the flat plate location (L/D_j) are kept constant, while varying the angle of inclination of the plate (θ). The characteristic compressible flow parameters are summarized in Table 2.

The double precision transient density-based solver is chosen for the following analysis due to its ability to handle highly compressible flows. Unlike the pressure-based solver, the pressure field is obtained from the equation of state while the density field is obtained using the continuity equation. Flow, energy and turbulence equations are accurately solved to obtain reasonable velocity and pressure gradients on the plate surface. The first order implicit Euler scheme is adopted for the time discretization, with the time step of $\Delta t = 10^{-4}$ s, making sure that the Courant number is kept approximately equal to 0.75 during all the time of the calculations. The threshold for the residual criterion for both momentum and energy is set equal to 10^{-6}, and the maximum iterative loop is made of 6 iterations for each time step. Finally, under-relaxation factors for turbulence kinetic energy (k) and turbulence dissipation rate (ϵ) are set to 0.75, in order to increase the stability of the iterative process.

Table 2. Characteristic flow parameters

Boundary	Values
Stagnation pressure, Pc	100 kPa
Stagnation temperature, Tc	298 K
Nozzle exit Mach number, M_j	2.2
Pressure ratio, $PR = P_j/P_\infty$	7
Specific heat ratio, γ	1.4
Plate angle, θ	30°, 40°, 50°
Nozzle exit diameter, D_j	7 m
Plate location, L/D_j	2

3   Results

Two different turbulence modeling approaches are employed in order to assess the predictive capabilities of the present CFD model to simulate the plume impingement flow field on the inclined flat plate. As preliminary step of the ongoing research, a variant of the standard semi-empirical $k-\epsilon$ turbulence model is investigated, namely, the RNG $k-\epsilon$ model [15]. This model is well known for its robustness, economy, and reasonable accuracy, for a wide range of industrial fluids engineering applications. It represents an improved version of the original $k-\epsilon$ model, resulting more accurate to simulate the spreading rate of both planar and round jets [16]. Although the original version of the model and its variations are known to be more suitable for free shear flow regions away from the wall, Dharavath et al. [12] demonstrated that different turbulence URANS methods (including the RNG $k-\epsilon$ model) provide similar surface pressure distributions for the present flow configuration with $\theta = 30°$. Here, the RNG $k-\epsilon$ turbulence model is confirmed to provide accurate mean flow results, in agreement with the reference study, where a different commercial code was employed [12].

The main point of the present CFD analysis involves the usage of a more innovative and sophisticated turbulence modeling procedure that is DES. In particular the realizable $k-\epsilon$ based DES model is employed. Figure 3 shows the pressure distribution on the plate for the two different solutions, namely URANS and DES, for varying plate incidence, compared to the experimental findings in [8]. In these plots, the distance Y is nondimensionalized by the nozzle exit radius R_n, whereas the pressure is nondimensionalized by the nozzle chamber pressure P_c. By inspection of this figure, both solutions appear to correctly reproduce the pressure peak and its location on the plate, when compared against experimental results, regardless of the plate incidence. In fact, a pretty good match of pressure distribution for the three different plate inclinations, which are $\theta = 30°$, 40°, and 50°, against the experimental data, is attained. It is interesting to note that the location and pattern of impingement seems to change with the plate inclination, and it becomes more noticeable at high incidences, confirming previous findings. The same trend is observed for both URANS and DES approaches.

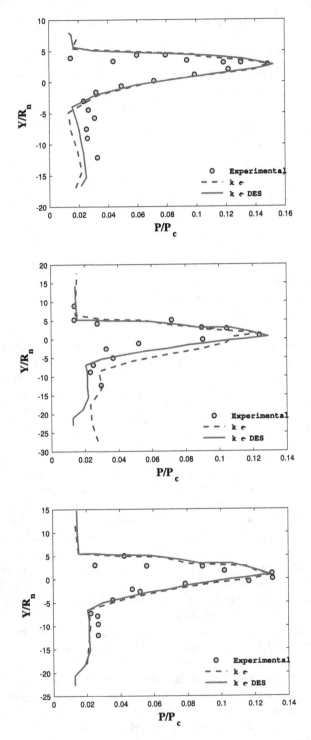

Fig. 3. Surface pressure distribution for $P_j/P_\infty = 7$ and $L/D_j = 2$, with different plate angles that are: (top) $\theta = 30°$, (middle) $\theta = 40°$, and (bottom) $\theta = 50°$, compared to experimental data [8].

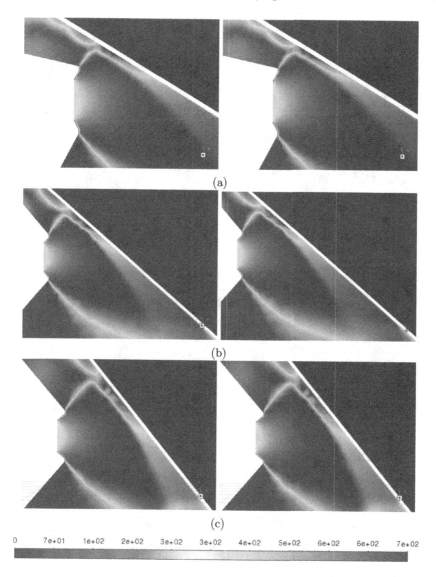

Fig. 4. Velocity contour map for URANS (left) and DES (right) calculations for P_j/P_∞ = 7 and $L/D_j = 2$ with different plate angles (a) $\theta = 30°$, (b) $\theta = 40°$, (c) $\theta = 50°$.

Figure 4 shows the velocity distribution in the symmetry plane corresponding to the flow region between the nozzle exit and the inclined plate. The complex structure of the three-dimensional mean flow field is apparent. The different characteristic features of the jet impingement, such as the jet boundary, jet shock, upper tail shock, front and behind plate shocks, are roughly captured. It is worth noticing how the expansion waves generated from the nozzle exit get reflected

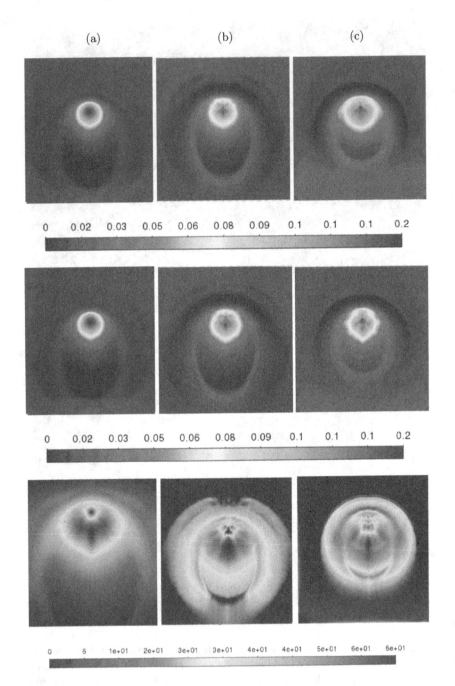

Fig. 5. Pressure (top), density (middle) and wall shear stress (bottom) contour maps for DES calculation at $P_j/P_\infty = 7$ and $L/D_j = 2$ with different plate angles (a) $\theta = 30°$, (b) $\theta = 40°$, (c) $\theta = 50°$.

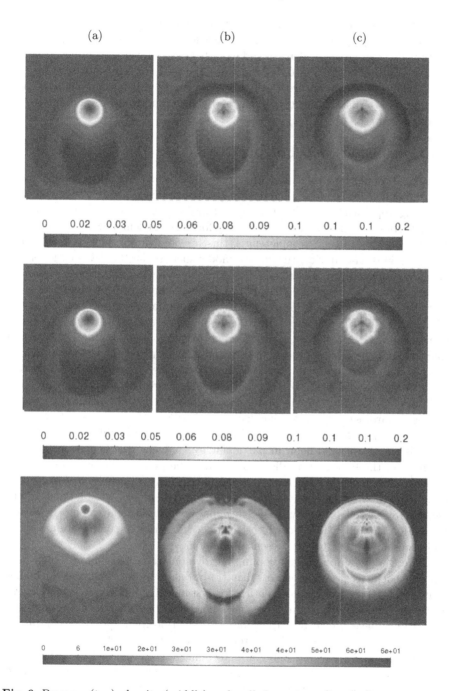

Fig. 6. Pressure (top), density (middle) and wall shear stress (bottom) contour maps for URANS calculation at $P_j/P_\infty = 7$ and $L/D_j = 2$ with different plate angles (a) $\theta = 30°$, (b) $\theta = 40°$, (c) $\theta = 50°$.

from the jet boundary and transform into compression waves which coalesce to form barrel shape jet shock. The Mach disc is formed very close to the plate. The contour maps of pressure, density and wall shear stress over the plate surface are presented in Fig. 5 and Fig. 6, for the URANS and DES solutions, respectively. These contour maps capture the features of the flow fields, for instance, the jet boundary. Again, the two different turbulence modeling procedures provide similar results.

4 Conclusions and Perspectives

Numerical simulations are carried out to simulate the supersonic jet impingement on an inclined flat plate at different angles of incidence, using two turbulence modeling approaches for predicting the mean flow field. Although more complicated turbulence models are widely used for this particular fluids engineering application, due to their completeness, this research shows that even a simpler (and faster) semi-empirical turbulence model such as the RNG $k - \epsilon$ model can be successfully adopted to the aim, resulting in saving computational resources.

Preliminarily, the overall CFD approach was validated using the RNG $k - \epsilon$ turbulence closure model supplied with wall functions, while reproducing the URANS data in the reference study, while making a comparison against experimental findings. Afterwards, a modern hybrid method, combining URANS and LES, namely, the DES approach was originally investigated. The results provided by the qualitative and quantitative analyses performed for the two different turbulence models demonstrate that both models correctly predict the pressure peak and its location on the plate, showing a good match with experimental results, regardless of the plate incidence.

As to future work, the next step of this ongoing research will be to extend our analysis to the thermal field, in particular by analysing the heat transfer coefficient, and the temperature distribution over the plate, in order to investigate the best pressure ratio ensuring the most efficient heat transmission. This will be done using innovative URANS approaches based on adaptive numerical methods [17,18], as well as improved DES formulations like the delayed detached-eddy simulation (DDES) [19], that will be examined in terms of computational effort and accuracy respect to the present methodologies.

Note that jet impingement cooling has demonstrated to achieve a high heat transfer coefficient compared to other traditional systems, resulting in higher heat transfer rates, which is essential, for instance, for modern hybrid vehicles. Since the main power source for such vehicles is provided by batteries, several studies have shown how these devices reach optimal operating conditions only when working in a particular temperature range, which is between 25 °C and 40 °C [20]. As a result, being able to manage their thermal performance is becoming crucial to their performance and safety. Jet air cooling systems also show several promising priorities when compared to other traditional methods such as: low cost, light weight and high reliability. Therefore, our future work for this particular fluids engineering application will also contribute to the development of jet cooling systems for hybrid and electric vehicles.

Acknowledgement. The authors acknowledge funding from the Italian Ministry of University and Research: PRIN research project 2022B2X937, "NextGenSProDesT Next Generation Space Propulsion Design Techniques."

References

1. De Stefano, G., Brown-Dymkoski, E., Vasilyev, O.V.: Wavelet-based adaptive large-eddy simulation of supersonic channel flow. J. Fluid Mech. **901**, A13 (2020)
2. Lubert, C.P., Kent, L.G., Seiji, T.: Supersonic jet noise from launch vehicles: 50 years since NASA SP-8072. J. Acoust. Soc. Am. **151**, 752–791 (2022)
3. Pamadi, B.N.: On the impingement of supersonic jet on a normal flat surface. Aeronaut. Quart. **13**, 199–218 (1982)
4. Chin, C., et al.: Investigation of the flow structures in supersonic free and impinging jet flows. J. Fluids Eng. **135**, 031202 (2013)
5. Nguyen, T., Maher, B., Hassan, Y.: Flow field characteristics of a supersonic jet impinging on an inclined surface. AIAA J. **58**, 1240–1254 (2020)
6. Lamont, P.J., Hunt, B.L.: The impingement of underexpanded, axisymmetric jets on perpendicular and inclined flat plates. J. Fluid Mech. **100**, 471–511 (1980)
7. Hadžiabdić, M., Hanjalić, K.: Vortical structures and heat transfer in a round impinging jet. J. Fluid Mech. **596**, 221–260 (2008)
8. Nakai, Y., Fujimatsu, N., Fujii, K.: Experimental study of underexpanded supersonic jet impingement on an inclined flat plate. AIAA J. **44**, 2691–2699 (2006)
9. Ito, M., Oyama, A., Fujii, K., Hayashi, K.: Flow field analysis of jet impinging on an inclined flat plate at high plate angles. In: Proceedings of the 44th AIAA Aerospace Sciences Meeting and Exhibit, Reno, Nevada, 9-12 January 2006 (2006)
10. Mixson J.S, Roussos L.A: Acoustic fatigue: overview of activities at NASA Langley. NASA Technical Memorandum 89143 (1987)
11. Wyatt L. A.: Static tests of ground effect on planforms fitted with a centrally-located round lifting jet. ARC/C **749** (1964)
12. Dharavath, M., Chakraborty, D.: Numerical simulation of supersonic jet impingement on inclined plate. Def. Sci. J. **4**, 355–362 (2013)
13. De Stefano, G., Denaro. F.M., Riccardi, G.: High-order filtering for control volume flow simulation. Int. J. Numer. Meth. Fluids **37**, 797–835 (2001)
14. https://www.ansys.com/products/fluids/ansys-fluent
15. Yakhot, V., Orszag, S.A., Thangam, S., Gatski, T.B., Speziale, C.G.: Development of turbulence models for shear flows by a double expansion technique. Phys. Fluids A **4**, 1510–1520 (1992)
16. Shih, T.-H., Liou, W.W., Shabbir, A., Yang, Z., Zhu, J.: A new $k-\epsilon$ eddy viscosity model for high Reynolds number turbulent flows. Comput. Fluids **25**, 227–238 (1995)
17. Ge, X., Vasilyev, O.V., De Stefano, G., Hussaini, M.Y.: Wavelet-based adaptive unsteady Reynolds-averaged Navier-Stokes computations of wall-bounded internal and external compressible turbulent flows. In: Proceedings of the 2018 AIAA Aerospace Sciences Meeting, Kissimmee, Florida, 8-12 January 2018 (2018)
18. Ge, X., Vasilyev, O.V., De Stefano, G., Hussaini, M.Y.: Wavelet-based adaptive unsteady Reynolds-averaged Navier-Stokes simulations of wall-bounded compressible turbulent flows. AIAA J. **58**, 1529–1549 (2020)
19. Salomone, T., Piomelli, U., De Stefano, G.: Wall-modeled and hybrid large-eddy simulations of the flow over roughness strips. Fluids **8**, 10 (2023)
20. Suh, I.S., Cho, H., Lee, M.: Feasibility study on thermoelectric device to energy storage system of an electric vehicle. Energy **76**, 436–444 (2014)

Development of a Value-Based Method for Identifying Priorities of City Development Programs

Boris A. Nizomutdinov[✉] [iD] and Alina S. Meteleva[iD]

Institute of Design and Urban Studies, ITMO University, Saint Petersburg, Russia
boris@itmo.ru

Abstract. The proposed study describes an innovative method for ranking budget allocations and the effectiveness of urban development programs based on the analysis of residents' value orientations. The central premise of the method is the idea that taking into account the value priorities of the population contributes to increasing social responsibility and expediency of public spending. The methodology includes several key stages: collecting primary data on the values of residents through sociological surveys, analyzing the information obtained using quantitative and qualitative analysis tools, including factor and cluster analyses, creating a scalable model for allocating budget funds, as well as forming a feedback mechanism for course correction and adaptation of the development program in order to an adequate reflection of the changing values of the citizens.

The results of preliminary testing of the method on the example of several municipalities showed a significant increase in residents' satisfaction with the dynamics of urban development and transparency of budget spending. The study provides tools for strategic planning, which can be integrated into the management practice of city administrations to optimize costs and implement the most significant initiatives for citizens. The results obtained are planned to be used in the role model of the ecosystem of urban digital services.

Keywords: Values · value-based approach · social networks · modeling · parsing · sustainable development · urbanism · smart city

1 Introduction

In modern conditions, sustainable urban development is becoming an increasingly urgent task. However, in order to achieve this goal, it is necessary that urban development programs of the city be based on the real needs of its residents. Unfortunately, nowadays it is often possible to observe that such programs do not take into account the actual interests and values of residents, but are based only on statistical calculations.

This approach hinders the achievement of sustainable development of the city, as it creates a gap between what is considered important for the city as a whole and what is really a priority for its residents. This gap can lead to discontent and distrust on the

O. Gervasi et al. (Eds.): ICCSA 2024, LNCS 14814, pp. 378–394, 2024.
https://doi.org/10.1007/978-3-031-64608-9_25

part of residents, as well as to the inefficient use of resources and funds allocated for the development of the city.

This article proposes a new approach to the development of urban development programs based on taking into account the values of residents. It is proposed to include the opinions and preferences of residents in the process of developing city development programs, which will allow creating more relevant and effective programs.

To implement this approach, it is proposed to use a method based on the definition and analysis of the values of residents. By conducting surveys and interviewing city residents, it is possible to identify their preferences, values and priorities in relation to various aspects of the city's development. This data can then be used to form urban development programs that will meet the real needs and interests of residents. However, this is a very expensive and slow method. In this paper, it is proposed to use social networks as a source of information about values and interpret them as needs.

The concept proposed in this article has the potential to lead to more sustainable urban development, since it allows you to take into account the opinions and preferences of the most important participants in the urban environment - its residents, practically online, using social networks. The proposed approach can be used by city authorities, planners and other stakeholders to develop more effective and relevant urban development programs. The results obtained are planned to be used in the role model of the ecosystem of urban digital services.

1.1 Subject of Study

Currently, more than 50% of the world's population lives in cities, and this number is expected to increase to ~70% by 2050. Urban sustainability is an urgent issue caused by the growing challenges of urbanization. Factors such as population growth, urban sprawl, land-use changes, unemployment and environmental degradation have a negative impact on the quality of life of urban residents. Therefore, drawing the attention of administrators, urban planners and academia to urban sustainability and its measurement is becoming increasingly important in terms of improving urban development and the well-being of the population.

In general, urban sustainability and its measurement are important aspects for achieving improved urban development and ensuring the well-being of urban residents. The balanced development of the urban economy, society and the environment is key to achieving this sustainability. Further research and development in this area is essential to ensure a sustainable and prosperous future for cities around the world.

The analysis of the regulatory framework has shown that in the current urban management, a list of administrative-territorial units and residential buildings located on their territory with estimates of the availability of all types of urban services is used to allocate the budget and rank the priority of development programs [1, 2]. This is the main metric that is used to determine development priorities, without taking into account the real needs of residents in this area, since surveys are not conducted, demand is not studied by other methods. And efficiency is assessed using outdated formulas that calculate the achievement of budgeting indicators and a planned approach, and again, without taking into account the real needs of the population and their satisfaction. This work is aimed at assessing the well-being of the population in terms of their real needs. The assessment and prioritization of the city's development is based on a needs model.

New approaches in urban development management focus on the formation of a high level of urban environment, which contributes to a better quality of life for residents and visitors of the city, as well as supports the long-term sustainability of the development of urbanized territories.

The article suggests adapting the principles of digital humanism for the management of modern urban agglomerations. In this concept, the main focus is on the value principles of managing changes in the structure of cities.

The main goal of such urban governance is to achieve sustainable development, improve the living conditions of citizens and their social well-being. The values that are the long-term stable guidelines for the life of individuals become fundamental in this management. These values serve as a kind of universal plan for the organization of human life, they take into account the cost of innovation and risks, and contribute to the harmonization of individual activity and social conditions for its implementation. They also guide both individual and group behavior, giving rise to the desire to act in certain circumstances, point the course towards selected goals and help make decisions in conditions of uncertainty. In addition, values can serve as the basis for a responsible decision between several alternatives.

It follows from this that it is possible to create a value-based management model for cities, which will be based on combining individual values into a single life structure of the city. We will rely on the basic concept of Schwartz's values. Values are not independent concepts, but interrelated, context-determined, culturally diverse and related to how we see ourselves and how we perceive the environment [3].

Sustainable urban development requires the integration of different values in order to achieve multifunctional goals. Blue-green infrastructure (BGI) projects can be considered as pioneers in the integration of values [4, 5].

An outstanding figure in the field of public administration, Mark H. Moore presents the results of his fifteen years of research, observations and teaching on what public sector managers should do to improve the efficiency of state-owned enterprises [6, 7]. Moore's answers reflect the well-understood difficulties of managing state-owned enterprises in modern society, recommending specific changes in the practice of individual state managers, namely, using the ideas of a value-based approach.

The role of values in urban governance is highly relevant, as such an idea is reflected in the world literature and requires further research and development. Value-oriented management systems for a large city are being formed [8], modern classifications of large cities and theoretical issues of strategic management are being revealed. The article highlights in detail the stages of the implementation of the balanced scorecard system in the municipalities of large cities, analyzes the concept of social values for strategic management in cities.

Value orientations are used in strategic city management in the provision of local public goods and services [9] the evolution of urban management theories and the possibility of adapting the ideas of value-oriented management in city management in the provision of local public goods and services are considered.

Special attention is paid to values and the smart city, so in the work [10, 11] the value-oriented management in a smart city is considered, the role of values in city management in the context of the development of smart technologies is explored. The authors consider the influence of values on decision-making in a smart city and propose approaches to taking values into account in the management process.

Value-oriented modeling of economic decision-making in the conditions of non-stationary environment is carried out [12] where the possibility of taking into account values in modeling decision-making in the conditions of environmental change is considered. The internal processes of an agent before making a decision are studied and the factors limiting rationality and risk assessment in the context of behavioral economics are analyzed.

Scientists define and classify the concept of city value in terms of subject utility, including three factors of high homogeneity and six factors of low homogeneity [13]. In ideal conditions, the increase in the value of the city occurs spontaneously. However, in reality, the process of increasing requires the active intervention of various marketing actors and the adjustment of the dynamic model. Adjustments such as defining customer requirements, developing an urban marketing strategy, linking value with integration, and improving the goal are described. The analysis of the situation in Paris confirms the dynamic model of increasing value in the course of urban marketing.

The paper [14] analyzes 12 sustainable Development Goals related to ensuring sustainable patterns of consumption and production. The authors identify two main points of view: one focuses on improving the efficiency of production and consumption, and the other emphasizes the need to take into account consumption volumes, distributional issues and related social and institutional changes. The role of social networks [15], in particular Twitter, in obtaining information about the values of the city is being investigated. The authors analyze tweets related to the city of Amsterdam and identify the basic values and preferences of residents expressed on social networks. As a result of the study, the authors come to the conclusion about the possibility of using social networks as a new source of information about the values of the city [16–18].

Our early papers [19] present the results of a pilot study of the possibility of using a value-based approach to managing urban development programs using social media data. It is proposed to determine the values of residents through social media profiles and user comments, which can be used to manage urban development programs.

However, the area remains insufficiently studied, which raises the question of what will happen if the city's development programs do not correspond to the interests and values of residents for a long time. In this paper, the hypothesis is put forward that in this case there may be a process called "social contradiction". In [20], group conflict is considered as a social contradiction. If the processes of social contradiction are not controlled, such negative processes for the city as an outflow of population, a decrease in the level of education, an increase in crime and other negative consequences can occur.

The article focuses on a common problem of modern urban development programs: they often ignore the true values and needs of residents, which jeopardizes their practicality and limits the sustainable development of urban areas. The authors insist on the importance of ranking urban programs based on the values and priorities of citizens to ensure that they respond to the most important demands of society and do not prove useless against the background of changing social needs. The initial approach, when the same program tries to cover many incompatible needs, should give way to a more finely tuned consideration of the values of citizens to ensure long-term well-being and development of the urban environment.

Ignoring the real values of residents in the urban development program can negatively affect the sustainability of development. Firstly, it can lead to the creation of projects and services that do not meet the needs and expectations of the population. Such programs often face insufficient levels of engagement and support from the public, which can reduce their effectiveness and longevity. When citizens' interests and preferences are ignored, there may be a mismatch between the resources invested in urban planning and the actual impact of these efforts. Development programs that are not based on the values of residents can end up being unsuccessful, wasting budgets and resources and failing to achieve development goals.

Also, ignoring values leads to a decrease in the loyalty of citizens, since they may feel that their needs and opinions are not taken into account in decision-making processes. This weakens social capital and trust in city authorities. In addition, programs that do not correspond to the values of residents can lead to social alienation and an increase in inequality, which is incompatible with the principles of sustainable development, including social justice and inclusivity.

Ultimately, ignoring the values of residents in the process of city development complicates the achievement of harmonious and sustainable development, which should be based on a balance of economic, social and environmental interests of the urban community.

In this paper, it is proposed to rank city development programs by taking into account values and needs so that they can primarily address the most important needs of citizens, in order of priority and thus meet the interests of citizens, taking into account the fact that one program can solve several needs.

2   Research Methodology

City development programs are strategic documents that define the directions and priorities for the development of the urban environment. They are developed by authorities at various levels with the participation of experts, local residents and stakeholders. City development programs include goals, objectives and specific actions to improve infrastructure, social development, environmental protection, economic development and other aspects of urban life.

As part of the city's development programs, projects can be implemented for the construction and reconstruction of roads, parks, residential complexes, social facilities, the development of education, healthcare, culture, sports and other areas. The goal of city development programs is to create a comfortable and sustainable urban environment that meets the needs and interests of residents, attracts investment, promotes economic growth and improves the quality of life.

This research work, aimed at introducing a value-based approach to the management of urban development programs, was implemented on the basis of one of the districts of St. Petersburg in 2021 and covered 18 different programs. List of programs:

- Health care development
- Development of education
- Social support for citizens
- Development of physical culture and sports
- Development of the transport system
- Ensuring the rule of law, law and order and security
- Integrated development of municipal infrastructure, energy and energy supply systems
- Development of the cultural sphere
- Providing affordable housing and housing and communal services to residents
- Landscaping and environmental protection
- The knowledge Economy
- Development of industry, innovation and agro-industrial complex
- Promotion of employment
- Development of entrepreneurship and the consumer market
- Improving the efficiency of public administration
- Economic and social development of territories
- Creating conditions for ensuring public consent
- Development of the tourism sector

The main task was to develop such a system for assessing the priorities of these programs so that it could meet the numerous needs of citizens as effectively as possible, while it is noticeable that one project can be aimed at solving not one, but several tasks.

The difficulty in implementing this approach is the fact that the regulations in force in the city evaluate programs mainly in terms of their infrastructural contribution, without delving into the study of the real needs of the population. The created method aims to eliminate this imbalance by offering a new way of analysis - using data from social networks. This makes it possible to abandon traditional, time-consuming and resource-intensive surveys, replacing them with innovative methods of analyzing large amounts of information reflecting real values and the needs of residents.

Within the framework of the presented work, a fundamentally new approach is proposed in the management of urban development programs, which consists in taking into account the values of residents and their transformation into specific needs. For this purpose, a unique model has been developed that allows, based on the analysis of data from social networks, to identify the values of citizens.

Using this model, it is possible to determine which aspects of life in the city are valued by residents the most, and then transform these value preferences into practical needs. This becomes the basis for the creation of adapted and effective development programs that will more accurately respond to the needs of the urban population and contribute to improving the quality of life.

This approach provides a more accurate and in-depth understanding of what is really important for citizens, and allows the city administration to implement measures that can actually improve the urban environment. This represents a departure from standard methodologies, when the development and evaluation of the effectiveness of programs is often carried out without taking into account the opinions of citizens themselves.

Within the framework of the presented work, a fundamentally new approach is proposed in the management of urban development programs, which consists in taking into account the values of residents and their transformation into specific needs. For this purpose, a unique model has been developed that allows, based on the analysis of data from social networks, to identify the values of citizens.

Using this model, it is possible to determine which aspects of life in the city are valued by residents the most, and then transform these value preferences into practical needs. This becomes the basis for the creation of adapted and effective development programs that will more accurately respond to the needs of the urban population and contribute to improving the quality of life.

This approach provides a more accurate and in-depth understanding of what is really important for citizens, and allows the city administration to implement measures that can actually improve the urban environment. This represents a departure from standard methodologies, when the development and evaluation of the effectiveness of programs is often carried out without taking into account the opinions of citizens themselves.

2.1   The Value Model

In previous work [6], reliably significant relationships were established between the components of a social network profile and the real values of users. In the work, regression analysis was applied to find relationships and, based on the results of the work, a model was developed to identify the values and needs of users based on data from social networks. The central idea of the model is to predict the user's value orientations based on the analysis of his social profile data. For this purpose, regression analysis is used, which allows us to identify the relationship between various characteristics of a user's profile on social networks and his value orientations, identified using the Schwartz technique.

The following steps are used to create a predictive model:

- Data loading: First, the model loads a preprocessed dataset with value orientations and user profile information.
- Data preprocessing: Includes data purification, normalization of numerical features, and conversion of categorical data into a format suitable for machine learning, for example, through coding.
- Feature identification: Identification and selection of relevant features to be used for model training.
- Dataset separation: The data is divided into training and test samples to ensure that the model can be evaluated.
- Model Training: At this stage, the selected regression model is trained based on the training sample.
- Model evaluation: Analysis of the accuracy of the model using a test sample and appropriate metrics such as standard error (MSE) or coefficient of determination (R2).
- Value prediction: Finally, a trained model is used to predict the values of new users based on their data from social networks.

Figure 1 shows the general scheme of data collection and processing to determine the values of citizens.

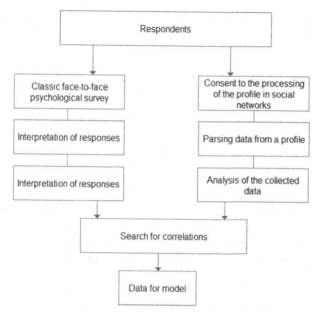

Fig. 1. General scheme of data collection and processing to identify values and needs

Such a model can be extremely useful in determining the needs and preferences of users in marketing and social research. It is this model that is used in this work to calculate values.

In this paper, the process of modeling urban processes over time is considered, in which 2 scenarios for managing city development programs will be considered - taking into account values and without taking into account.

2.2 A Model of Urban Infrastructure Development Needs

As noted earlier, a toolkit has been developed for conducting research, which allows determining the user's needs based on information in a social network profile. With the help of this model, having received an array of user profiles of an individual city, it is possible to calculate the needs of residents of the entire city. To conduct such a study, 980 urban and neighborhood communities were collected using the example of St. Petersburg, each community had an open list of subscribers and an accurate link to the city. The name and descriptions of the communities accurately linked them to the city and a specific area, which allowed us to conclude that the audience of these communities consists precisely of residents. By uploading subscribers of such communities, you can get a digital profile of residents of a particular city. Next, using the value model, identify the needs of each profile and summarize them for the entire audience.

To calculate the total assessment of each need for all residents of the district, we can use the following formula (Fig. 2):

$$C_i = \frac{\sum_{k=1}^{X} S_{ik}}{X} \times A_j$$

Fig. 2. The formula for calculating a separate need for all residents.

Where:

- (C_i) is the total indicator of the i-th need for the entire district, normalized from 0 to 10,
- (X)—the number of users in the area whose i-th need has been measured,
- (S_{ik})—assessment of the ith need of the kth user,
- (A_j)—coefficient of adaptation of the ith need to the total number of residents of the area (Y), $(A_j = frac\{Y\}\{X\})$ (if (X) is equal to (Y), then $(A_j = 1)$).

Explanation:

- The average value of each need is calculated for all users.
- The resulting average is multiplied by the adaptation coefficient to take into account the difference in the total number of residents of the area compared to the number of users.

2.3 Risks of Social Contradiction

As noted earlier, in a situation where city development programs do not take into account the real needs of residents, a process of social contradiction may develop. To analyze and identify such a risk, modeling was carried out on retrospective data reflecting the needs of citizens for 3 years in order to identify what would happen if the distribution of funding between programs was not adjusted and the old ranking methodology was used.

Using the ARIMA method to forecast needs for the next 3 years, we have identified the need that is expected to grow the most. ARIMA is an AutoRegressive Integrated Moving Average (AutoRegressive Integrated Moving Average), a statistical model used to analyze and predict time series. This model is capable of covering various types of time series data and is one of the most widely used forecasting methods.

Based on this analysis, a graph of historical data was constructed along with forecast values for this very need. It is determined that if the budget allocation is not adjusted, individual needs may increase, causing a social contradiction. Description of the model's work:

1. For input, the model receives a time series of each of the nine needs over the past five years.
2. For each need, an ARIMA model is built, which tries to describe time series using a combination of conditional autoregression and a moving average, taking into account the previous values of the series (to determine the trend), and integration to stabilize the series if it is non-stationary.

3. The model is trained on historical data and makes forecasts for the next three years.
4. A table is created containing the projected values of each requirement for the next three years.
5. An analysis of the projected data is being conducted to determine the three needs that are expected to increase the most.
6. A graph is being drawn to visually display the growth rates of these three needs.

In order to prevent an uncontrolled increase in infrastructure development needs, it is necessary to develop a model that will take into account the values and rank city development programs in such a way as to reduce critical needs and align the overall demand for city development, thereby achieving the goal of sustainable development (Fig. 3).

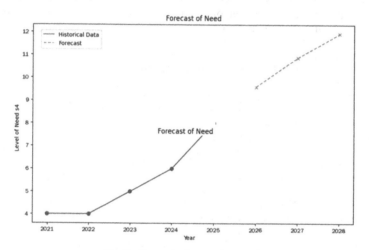

Fig. 3. Example forecasting needs

Now it is necessary to solve the problem of ranking urban programs so that funding is allocated to the highest priority programs in the first place and then in descending order. It is important to note that one program can solve several needs, which is why calculation is required.

To rank city development programs by importance, depending on the needs of residents, we can use the following formula (Fig. 4):

$$\text{Rank}(prog_i) = \sum_{s_j \in prog_i} w(s_j)$$

Fig. 4. A formula for ranking programs, taking into account that one program can solve several needs

Where:

– $(prog\_i)$—i-th city development program,

– (sj)—the jth need that the program (progi) solves,
– (w(sj))—the weight of the need (sj), equal to its value on a scale from 1 to 10. The higher the value, the higher the weight.

This formula allows you to get a list of programs in the order of their importance, based on the total importance of the needs they solve. Greater importance means that the program addresses the more urgent needs of residents. Calculation algorithm:

1. Definition of weights: We assign a weight to each need based on its value.
2. Summation of weights: For each program, we calculate the total weight of all the needs that it solves.
3. Ranking: Programs are ranked in descending order of their total weight.

Table 1 shows an example of calculating the rating of programs for ranking the budget and optimal budget planning of city development programs for the coming year, based on the developed methodology.

Table 1. Distribution of city development programs

№	The name of the program	Rating
1	Healthcare	8,41
2	Transport accessibility	7,52
3	Environmental sustainability	7,23
4	Educational resources	6,32
5	Security	6,03
6	Work and employment	5,55
7	Housing conditions	4,32
8	Social inclusion	4,30
9	Access to digital services	3,71
10	Tourism	3,62

2.4   A General Model for Ranking Programs

As a conclusion of this study, an algorithm for prioritizing urban development projects is proposed, integrating data from social networks to assess the needs and value indicators of residents, which will then form the basis for the distribution of priority directions for the development of the urban environment. The structural visualization of this algorithm is shown in Fig. 5.

Thus, with the help of a scientific approach integrating both quantitative and qualitative data obtained from open sources, it is possible to increase the efficiency of decision-making in the field of urban planning and development of urban agglomerations.

The results of preliminary testing of the methodology on the example of several municipalities showed a significant increase in residents' satisfaction with the dynamics of urban development and transparency of budget expenditures. The study provides strategic planning tools that can be integrated into the practice of city administration management to optimize costs and implement the most significant initiatives for citizens.

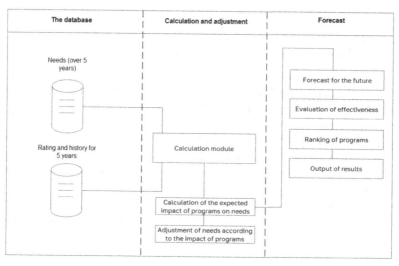

Fig. 5. General data processing scheme

2.5 Evaluating the Effectiveness of a Value-Based Approach

In the context of the proposed value-based approach to the management of urban development programs, the key change is the method of evaluating effectiveness. Instead of standardized performance indicators, such as compliance with planned budget expenditures or an increase in the number of infrastructure facilities, the emphasis is on a more practical and significant criterion: the degree of reduction of unmet needs of the population over time.

This means that the main measure of the success of development programs will not be the amount of money spent or facilities built, but a real improvement in the living conditions of citizens. This approach assumes that if, after the implementation of a particular urban development program, the needs of residents in some area decrease or are fully satisfied within a specified period, the program can be recognized as effective.

Thus, the value-based approach shifts the focus of evaluating the effectiveness of programs from formal, often abstract figures, to concrete changes in the life of the city and its residents. This helps to ensure that the development results are not just impressive figures in the reports, but have a real and tangible impact on the daily life of society.

In order to quantify the effectiveness of urban programs within the framework of a value-based approach, it is possible to introduce a formula that will measure the change in satisfaction of citizens' needs. Let's take the following metric as a basis (Fig. 6):
where:

$$E = \frac{P_b - P_a}{P_b} \times 100\%$$

Fig. 6. The formula for calculating efficiency

- E - the effectiveness of the program,
- Pb - general needs assessment before the implementation of the program,
- Pa - general needs assessment after the implementation of the program.

In this metric, Pb corresponds to the sum of the needs indices for all relevant categories before the start of the programs. Pa also represents a similar sum of needs indices after. These indexes can be calculated based on the analysis of data from social networks, surveys, statistics and other sources.

The percentage of reduced needs reflects the effectiveness of the program. If the E value is positive and high, this indicates a significant decrease in needs. If the value of E is zero or negative, this may indicate stagnation or deterioration of the situation, which, in turn, is an indicator of the inefficiency of the program.

For a more comprehensive approach, it is possible to introduce weight coefficients for each category of needs, depending on their priority, based on the values of citizens. So, the formula will take the following form (Fig. 7):

$$E = \frac{\sum(P_{b_i} \times W_i) - \sum(P_{a_i} \times W_i)}{\sum(P_{b_i} \times W_i)} \times 100\%$$

Fig. 7. The formula for calculating efficiency

where:

- Σ denotes the summation of all categories i,
- Wi is the weight coefficient of category i.

Thus, it is possible not only to quantify the effectiveness, but also to take into account the importance of various aspects of city life for its residents.

2.6 Personal Data

Within the framework of this study, special attention is paid to issues of confidentiality and ethical standards regarding the use of personal data. It should be emphasized that in the process of data collection and analysis, all necessary steps have been taken to ensure their anonymity and security.

First of all, we used methods of depersonalization of information, during which all personal data capable of identifying an individual user was deleted or changed to a stage at which any communication with specific persons became impossible. In particular, the accounts used in the study have been replaced with unique identification numbers (IDs), which eliminates the possibility of restoring the identity of the participants.

To collect and analyze data, we used statistical methods based on the aggregation of information and the derivation of general patterns. This approach allows us to extract meaningful information about people's behavioral patterns and preferences, while at the same time completely preserving their anonymity.

In addition to the aforementioned privacy measures, the language model involved has the functionality to automatically delete any data that identifies the user before such data is further analyzed. This level of processing provides additional protection for personal information and is an integral part of our project's data protection system.

To summarize, we would like to emphasize that the confidentiality of personal data is a priority for us. Our approach to data research and analysis strictly complies with all modern information security requirements and standards of research ethics.

3 Conclusion

In the course of this work, a model of values has been developed, which is of significant importance for the sustainable development of the city. With this model, we can not only identify the needs of residents, but also rank development programs based on their importance in order to solve primary tasks first. The originality of this study lies in the fact that the work combines classical methods of sociology and psychology with modern methods of machine learning and automated methods of information collection, opening up new prospects for the use of open data for urban management.

This decision is important in the context of the sustainable development of the city for the following reasons:

1. Meeting the needs of residents: The value model allows you to identify and understand the needs and preferences of city residents. This provides an opportunity for administrators and urban planners to prioritize various development programs and pay special attention to the most important aspects for residents. This approach provides a more accurate reflection of real needs and allows you to create a more satisfactory and favorable environment for living and working.
2. Efficient use of resources: Ranking city development programs allows you to determine which tasks should be solved first in order to achieve the greatest positive impact on sustainable development. This allows you to effectively allocate resources, both financial and human, and focus them on solving the most significant problems and challenges. This approach ensures optimal use of resources and increases the effectiveness of city development programs.
3. Strengthening sustainability: The development and implementation of value-based development programs contribute to strengthening the sustainability of the city. Programs that take into account the needs of residents and focus on solving problems of paramount importance can create a harmonious combination of economic development, social justice and environmental protection. This contributes to the creation of a city that is able to adapt to changing conditions, overcome challenges and ensure a sustainable and prosperous future for its residents.

The identification of the value system of the urban population is a fundamental element for the development of role models in the context of the Ecosystem of Urban Services "Digital Petersburg" (EUS). Empirical data on the value orientations of residents can serve as determinants for ranking the priority of urban services. Thus, such data obtained through sociological surveys, comments on social media or appeals to municipal services make a significant contribution to qualitative research and understanding of the motivations and preferences of the city's population.

The development of a role model of the EUS based on the identified values makes it possible to form a typology of users taking into account their individual, group and cultural characteristics. This contributes to the creation of a flexible and adaptive infrastructure that can best meet the needs of various segments of the urban population. For example, if the priority value is education, educational institutions, then the development of these services and infrastructure will be a priority.

The role model based on value analysis will provide urban planners and analysts with the opportunity to predict the needs of the population and influence their formation through targeted social policy and marketing communications. This will become the basis for the formation of a sustainable and functionally saturated urban space, where each service is aimed at maximum compliance with the expectations and requests of its users.

Thus, our value model plays an important role in ensuring the sustainable development of the city. It allows you to identify the needs of residents, rank development programs and focus resources on solving priority tasks. This approach contributes to the creation of a harmonious and sustainable urban space that meets the needs and values of its inhabitants and is able to adapt to changing conditions.

The importance of this solution for the sustainable development of the city is that it helps to establish a strong link between urban development programs and the real needs of residents. With this connection, urban programs become more effective and adaptive, and the development of the city is focused on the satisfaction of residents.

Further development of this research may include the following areas:

1. Expanding the Value model: Researchers can continue to develop and refine the value model to cover different contexts and aspects of urban development. This may include a detailed study of specific categories of values, such as sustainable mobility, accessibility of services, and even socio-cultural aspects.

2. Integration of collaborative research: Further development can be advanced by integrating collective research involving scientists, urban planners, administrators and residents of the city. This will help to link academic research with practical application, ensuring the practical relevance and effectiveness of the developed models.

3. Accounting for dynamism and variability: Cities are constantly changing and developing, and therefore the study should take into account the dynamism and variability of the values of residents. Researchers can conduct periodic updates and analyses to track changes in values and adapt urban development programs accordingly.

4. Extension of the methodology: Researchers can explore additional methods such as the use of modern data analysis and modeling technologies, as well as the integration of geographic information systems. This can help to analyze data more accurately and predict the needs of residents, taking into account spatial and temporal aspects.

5. Collaboration with city authorities and stakeholders: To better implement the developed models and recommendations, researchers can collaborate with city authorities and stakeholders. This will allow us to take into account practical limitations and

implementation factors, as well as make the research more practically oriented and applicable in the real world.

Overall, the development of this research is critically important for promoting sustainable urban development. This can help administrators, urban planners, and academia more accurately address the needs and values of residents in developing urban programs, which contributes to creating a sustainable and prosperous future for cities.

However, despite the promise of a value-based approach to evaluating the effectiveness of urban development programs, it has a number of limitations that do not allow it to completely replace traditional management methods. This approach serves as an additional tool supporting the decision-making process rather than a substitute for it.

One of the main drawbacks is the problem of data relevance, since information extracted from social networks can quickly become outdated. In a dynamically changing world, user preferences and values can easily change, making data less relevant to the current moment. The method needs to be improved in terms of online analysis and the ability to respond quickly to changes.

Acknowledgments. The study was carried out at the expense of a grant from the Russian Science Foundation and the St. Petersburg Science Foundation № 23-18-20079 "Research on the social effectiveness of electronic interaction between citizens and authorities in St. Petersburg on the example of urban digital services" (https://rscf.ru/project/23-18-20079/).

References

1. Turova, A.M.: The problem of managing the development of urban areas. Symbol of Science, No. 1 (2017). https://cyberleninka.ru/article/n/problema-upravleniya-razvitiem-gorods kih-territoriy. Date of Application 14 Apr 2024
2. Sutyagin, B.C.: On the correlation of scientific forecasts and state programs of socio-economic development. Prob. Forecast. **1**, 3–12 (1998)
3. Horlings, L.: Values in place; a value-oriented approach toward sustainable place-shaping. Reg. Stud. Reg. Sci. **2**, 256–273 (2015). https://doi.org/10.1080/21681376.2015.1014062
4. Kuitert, L., Willems, J., Volker, L.: Value integration in multi-functional urban projects: a value driven perspective on sustainability transitions. Constr. Manag. Econ. **42**(2), 182–198 (2023)
5. Kuitert, L., Van Buuren, A.: Delivering blue-green infrastructure: innovation pathways for integrating multiple values. Front. Sustain. Cities **4** (2022)
6. Moore, M.H.: Creating Public Value: Strategic Management in Government. Harvard University Press, Cambridge MA (1998)
7. Moore, M.H.: Managing for value: organizational strategy in for-profit, nonprofit, and governmental organizations. Nonprofit Volunt. Sect. Q. **29**, 183–204 (2000)
8. Kaisarova, V.: Formation of a value-based management system for a large city. Bull. St. Petersburg Univ. Econ. (4) (2009)
9. Kaisarova, V., Maleeva, T.: Value orientations in strategic city management in the provision of local public goods and services. Bull. Eng. Ser. Econ. **1**(28), 60–69 (2022)
10. Mityagin, S., Gornova, G., Drozhzhin, A.A., Sokol, A.: Value-oriented management in a smart city. Int. J. Open Inf. Technol. **12** (2021)

11. Mityagin, S.A., Drojjin, S.I., Tikhonova, O.B.: A value-oriented approach in smart city projects selection and ranking. In: Alexandrov, D.A., Boukhanovsky, A.V., Chugunov, A.V., Kabanov, Y., Koltsova, O. (eds.) Digital Transformation and Global Society. CCIS, vol. 745, pp. 307–318. Springer, Cham (2017). https://doi.org/10.1007/978-3-319-69784-0_26

12. Guleva, V., Kovantsev, A.N., Surikov, A., Chunaev, P., Gornova, G., Bukhanovsky, A.: Value-oriented modeling of economic decision-making in a non-stationary environment. Sci. Tech. Bull. Inf. Technol. Mech. Opt. 1 (2023)

13. Shen, L., Kyllo, J., Guo, X.: An integrated model based on a hierarchical indices system for monitoring and evaluating urban sustainability. Sustainability 5, 524–559 (2013). https://doi.org/10.3390/su5020524

14. Bengtsson, M., Alfredsson, E., Cohen, M.: Transforming systems of consumption and production for achieving the sustainable development goals: moving beyond efficiency. Sustain. Sci. 13, 1533–1547 (2018). https://doi.org/10.1007/s11625-018-0582-1

15. Leavesley, A., Trundle, A., Oke, C.: Cities and the SDGs: realities and possibilities of local engagement in global frameworks. Ambio 51, 1416–1432 (2022). https://doi.org/10.1007/s13280-022-01714-2

16. Karami, S., Ghafary, M., Fakhrayee, A.: Analyzing the correlation between urban spaces and place attachment. Evidence from: Narmak neighborhood in Tehran. Eur. Online J. Nat. Soc. Sci. 3(4) (2014)

17. Reynald, D., Elffers, H.: The future of Newman's defensible space theory. Eur. J. Criminol. 6(1), 25–46 (2009)

18. Negami, H.R., Mazumder, R., Reardon, M., Ellard, C.G.: Field analysis of psychological effects of urban design: a case study in Vancouver, pp. 106–115 (2018)

19. Nizomutdinov, B., Uglova, A., Antonov, A.: Value-oriented management of city development programs based on data from social networks. In: Gervasi, O., et al. (eds.) ICCSA 2023. LNCS, vol. 13957, pp. 369–382. Springer, Cham (2023). https://doi.org/10.1007/978-3-031-36808-0_24

20. Porello, D., Bottazzi, E., Ferrario, R.: Group conflict as social contradiction. In: D'Errico, F., Poggi, I., Vinciarelli, A., Vincze, L. (eds.) Conflict and Multimodal Communication. CSS, pp. 33–52. Springer, Cham (2015). https://doi.org/10.1007/978-3-319-14081-0_2

21. Marans, R.W., Stimson, R.J.: Investigating Quality of Urban Life: Theory, Methods and Empirical Research. Springer, Dordrecht (2011). https://doi.org/10.1007/978-94-007-1742-8

Short Papers

Identification of Malicious URLs:
A Purely Lexical Approach

Julio Rodrigues[1], Charles de Barros[1], Diego Dias[2]([⊠]) [iD],
Marcelo de Paiva Guimarães[3] [iD], Elisa Tuler[1] [iD], and Leonardo Rocha[1] [iD]

[1] Universidade Federal de São João Del Rei (UFSJ), São João Del Rei, Brazil
{charlesbarros,etuler,lcrocha}@ufsj.edu.br
[2] Universidade Federal do Espírito Santo (UFES), Vitória, Brazil
diego.dias@ufes.br
[3] Universidade Federal de São Paulo (UNIFESP), São Paulo, Brazil
marcelode.paiva@unifesp.br

Abstract. Internet users are increasingly exposed to security vulnerabilities stemming from malicious Uniform Resource Locators (URLs), which act as conduits for cyber threats. These threats, often orchestrated by sophisticated cybercriminals, underscore the importance of comprehending the intricate dynamics involved to devise robust defense mechanisms. This scholarly exposition delineates an efficacious approach for discerning diverse categories of malicious URLs leveraging machine learning algorithms. Notably, our methodology obviates the necessity of directly accessing such URLs for extracting pertinent information, relying solely on attributes inherent within the lexical composition of the URLs. The empirical analyses are predicated on meticulously curated datasets from reputable repositories such as Kaggle and PhishTank, culminating in competitive performance vis-à-vis existing literature that predominantly focuses on network-centric or content-based features.

Keywords: Machine Learning · Malware detection · Feature Extraction

1 Introduction

Users' vulnerability to internet security is one of the weakest points in the digital ecosystem. The URLs in our daily lives act as direct gateways to malicious online activities, requiring just a few clicks to carry out a cyber attack. This easy access facilitates the spread of digital threats, significantly increasing the potential for infection. However, the effectiveness of these attacks often depends on additional characteristics of the URL itself and the sophisticated camouflage techniques employed by cybercriminals. Understanding the dynamics behind these tactics is fundamental to developing more effective online protection strategies.

In 2019, the cybersecurity landscape in Brazil confronted formidable challenges with the proliferation of cyber attacks leveraging malicious URLs, as underscored by the findings of the Abranet report, which positioned Brazil among the fifteen nations with the highest incidence of victims. However, it is reasonable to posit that these alarming statistics have substantially exacerbated in subsequent years, particularly in light of the protracted duration of the COVID-19 pandemic. This unprecedented global crisis has accelerated the adoption of information technologies across diverse sectors, consequently enlarging the attack surface susceptible to potential cyber threats. The dynamic nature of cybersecurity perpetually undergoes evolution, with both defenders and adversaries engaged in an incessant pursuit of enhancing their respective strategies. While security teams diligently endeavor to devise more robust detection mechanisms, the perpetrators of cyber attacks persistently refine their tactics, particularly in the realm of obfuscating malicious URLs. Such perpetual flux necessitates implementing proactive and adaptive measures to mitigate the ever-looming specter of online security risks effectively.

Currently, two popular and practical strategies facilitate the detection of malicious URLs, the first of which is blacklisting services. These services keep a record of URLs that have been reported and identified as malicious, thereby checking whether a suspicious URL is present in their database. Although blacklisting services are helpful in the medium and long term, they often face limitations in detecting newly created or as yet uncatalogued malicious URLs. This gap in coverage of recent URLs highlights the need to complement this approach with other more dynamic and adaptable detection strategies.

The second approach involves building machine learning models to classify URLs. Although this strategy is more complex compared to blacklisting services, it offers a significant advantage in terms of effectiveness in the short, medium, and long term. A well-built machine learning model can accurately classify many URLs when successfully implemented. This approach takes advantage of sophisticated algorithms to analyze various attributes of URLs, identifying subtle patterns that can indicate whether a URL is malicious or legitimate. Using machine learning models represents a promising evolution in malicious URL detection, providing a more adaptable and efficient solution to the ever-changing challenges of the cybersecurity landscape.

The subsequent sections of this paper are delineated as follows: Sect. 2 expounds upon the employed methodology for development; Sect. 3 furnishes an analysis of the acquired results; Sect. 4 deliberates upon the principal conclusions derived from this study and posits a set of considerations for prospective future endeavors.

2   Methodology

In this section, we outline the development process and the crucial decisions in designing an effective method for classifying URLs based on machine learning. It is essential to highlight that the entire development of this work utilized the

Python[1] programming language in conjunction with the open-source scikit-learn[2] machine learning library.

2.1   Feature Extraction

In our endeavor to extract highly predictive information from URLs, we opted for a purely lexical approach, focusing solely on the URL's structure. This decision stemmed from the recognition that extracting features about content or network attributes, as elaborated upon in diverse related studies, typically necessitates direct URL access for data collection. However, our primary objective is to discern the essence of a URL without necessitating direct access, thereby mitigating potential exposure to cybersecurity threats.

The features can be divided into two groups: those related to the structure of the URL, such as the length and specific characters, and those linked to the content of the page, such as the use of pop-ups and cookies. Thus, the characteristics of malicious domains can include the presence of an IP address in the URL, the use of at, double slashes "//", hyphens, HTTPS, the domain's favicon, the use of pop-ups, the length of the URL, the number of links and the number of open ports.

In this investigation, we extracted a set of 21 characteristics from the URLs (Table 1), employing a methodology grounded in simple statistical analysis and examining pertinent literature. Among these features, seven emerged from statistical analysis of the databases, while the remaining 14 were identified through scrutiny of the existing literature. We meticulously extracted all these characteristics, focusing on the lexical attributes encapsulated within the URLs. However, after applying feature selection techniques, we reduced this number to 11 features, as shown.

One of the elementary features extracted encompassed the enumeration of distinct symbols (tokens) manifested within the URLs. Intriguing disparities emerged concerning these quantities, notably observed in the prevalence of the "=" symbol within URLs. Remarkably, URLs categorized under defacement exhibited an average occurrence of approximately 11 times more instances of this symbol than other URL types in the collected database.

In addition to the symbol count, we extracted characteristics related to the measurement of URL segments. In this context, metrics such as the length and number of characters of the URLs and the size of the directory were considered. These characteristics are potential indicators for distinguishing malicious instances from safe ones.

2.2   Feature Selection

Once the feature extraction process was complete, we began analyzing the relevance of each feature. To conduct this analysis, we adopted a strategy of recursive elimination of features with cross-validation. In other words, we utilized a

---

[1] More information at: https://www.python.org/.
[2] More information at: https://scikit-learn.org/stable/.

Table 1. Features Extraction

Features	Description
protocol	Communication protocol used
exclamation	Number of occurrences of the '!' character in the URL
slash	Number of occurrences of the '/' character in the URL (ignoring the protocol - https://)
dirs_qtd	Number of directories in the URL path
digits_qtd	Number of digits in the URL
equals	Number of occurrences of the '=' character in the URL
question	Number of occurrences of the '?' character in the URL
dots	Number of occurrences of the character '.' in URL
fstdir_length	Length in characters of the first directory in the URL path
url_length	Total length in characters of the URL
question	Number of occurrences of the '-' character in the URL
underscore	Number of occurrences of the character '_' in the URL
ats	Number of occurrences of the '@' character in the URL
commercial	Number of occurrences of the character '&' in the URL
plus	Number of occurrences of the '+' character in the URL
star	Number of occurrences of the '*' character in the URL
hashtag	Number of occurrences of the character '#' in the URL
cipher	Number of occurrences of the character '$' in the URL
percent	Number of occurrences of the character '%' in the URL
url_punc	Number of occurrences of non-alphanumeric characters in the URL
susp_words	Boolean indicating the presence of "suspicious" words in the URL (e.g., free, bonus, payment, extra, lucky, ...)

bottom-up approach, dividing the database into five parts and eliminating features with less relevance in the classification at each step. By the end of this process, we obtained a set of 11 features with greater predictive power.

We continue this process until we find the optimum number of features, meaning the total number of features eliminated has little or no impact on the model's performance. In Fig. 1, we observe the result of feature selection using the XGBoost algorithm [2] as a base. An apparent discrepancy exists between the predictive power of the communication protocol used by the URLs and the rest of the attributes. This behavior stems from the well-defined patterns found in the database, where all defacement URLs use the HTTP protocol, while phishing and malware URLs predominantly utilize the HTTPS protocol. The 11 features selected by the XGBoost algorithm can be described as follows:

- **protocol**: The protocol, also known as the scheme, is the first part of a URL and determines how different files on a web server are displayed and transferred to the user. The protocol can be HTTP or HTTPS.

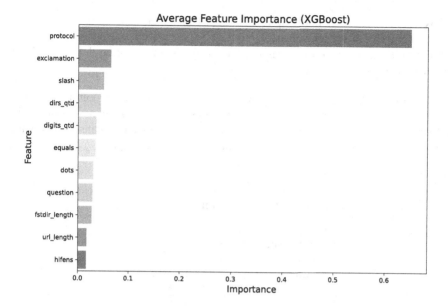

Fig. 1. The predictive power of the 11 features

- **exclamation**: The exclamation mark (!) is not commonly used in standard URLs. However, in some web applications, it can be used as part of a technique known as "hashbang" (#!) to enable client-side navigation.
- **slash**: The slash (/) separates different parts of a URL, such as the domain, path, and parameters1.
- **dirs_qtd**: This characteristic probably refers to the number of directories in a URL, which are the parts of the URL separated by slashes (/).
- **digits_qtd**: This characteristic probably refers to the number of digits in a URL.
- **equals**: The equals sign (=) is used in URLs to separate names and parameter values in query strings1.
- **dots**: These (.) are used in URLs to separate different parts of the domain1.
- **questions**: The question character (?) is used in URLs to start the query string, which contains additional parameters for the request1.
- **fstdir_lenght**: This characteristic probably refers to the length of the first directory in a URL.
- **url_lenght**: This characteristic refers to the total length of the URL.
- **hyphens**: These (-) are often used in URLs to separate words, especially in SEO-friendly URLs.

2.3 Database and Balancing

To build the supervised machine learning model, we used URLs from two databases:

- **Kaggle**[3]: Database made up of 651,191 URLs collected from various sources, distributed among four classes;
- **PhishTank**[4]: Database composed exclusively of phishing URLs. 105,905 instances were collected.

We observed a significant class imbalance after applying the join process and removing duplicate instances from the databases (Fig. 2). That necessitated the adoption of class balancing techniques before training the classifiers. The class distribution was Benign (57%), Defacement (27%), Phising (13%) and Malware (3%).

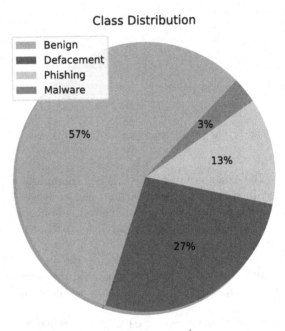

Fig. 2. Proportion of classes in the database

We used the F1-Score metric in our study. The F1 Score is a metric that combines precision (how many of the model's positive predictions are correct) and recall (how many of the actual positive instances were correctly identified by the model) into a single value. It is beneficial when we have an unbalanced data set, i.e., when one class is much more frequent than the others. In the context of classification metrics such as the F1 Score, the terms malware, benign, phishing, and defacement are usually referred to as classes or labels in a data set. Malware, a term derived from malicious software, is an umbrella term for

---

[3] Available at: https://www.kaggle.com/datasets/sid321axn/malicious-urls-dataset.
[4] Available at: https://phishtank.org/phish_archive.php.

any software designed to infiltrate a device without the user's consent and cause damage, system interruptions, or data theft.

There are several distinct categories of malware, each with its characteristics and infection methods. The most common examples of malware are adware, spyware, ransomware, and viruses. Benign usually refers to instances that are considered normal or safe. For example, in a malware detection dataset, samples free of malware would be labeled benign. Phishing refers to instances identified as phishing attempts (an online fraud technique where attackers try to trick users into revealing personal information, such as passwords or credit card details). Defacement refers to instances employing attacks where the visual content of a website is altered by the attackers, usually for vandalism or advertising purposes. They can be defined as follows:

– Adware is an abbreviation for "advertising-supported software", a form of malware that displays unwanted, sometimes malicious, advertising on a computer or mobile device's screen;
– Spyware is a category of malware that operates covertly on a device, monitoring user activity and stealing sensitive information such as financial data, account details, and login credentials;
– Ransomware, a particularly pernicious form of malware, is a serious threat that encrypts the user's data and demands a ransom for its recovery; and
– Virus is malicious code that spreads between computers and networks, often causing significant damage.

At this stage, we opted for a hybrid approach to applying balancing techniques to the database. While the most straightforward path would involve the indiscriminate application of random oversampling, duplicating instances of the minority classes, this approach might not add helpful information to the training and classification processes. It would also significantly increase the data volume, which would considerably increase the computational cost of training the models.

However, after conducting initial tests with the hold-out method, we observed that the F1 Score metric values were similar for the benign, phishing, and defacement URL classes. This preliminary result suggested the potential application of random undersampling to majority class instances (benign). Subsequently, we implemented this technique, reducing the number of safe URLs in the database from 428,081 to 200,000 instances. This approach provided a safety margin to prevent the loss of information if large numbers of non-redundant URLs were removed.

At this stage, we equalized the number of safe and phishing URL instances through random undersampling and data scraping from PhishTank's database. However, addressing the imbalance between defacement and malware URLs posed a challenge. Despite efforts in data scraping, similar to the approach taken for phishing URLs, we encountered difficulty locating databases of sufficient size to compensate for the shortage of such instances.

However, we chose to apply a balancing technique based on synthetic minority oversampling, known as SMOTE [1]. In other words, several synthetic instances of the defacement and malware classes were generated based on the existing URLs of these types in the database.

At the end of this process, we had a fully balanced database of 800,000 URLs, 200,000 instances of each class, and 11 characteristics. With this database prepared, we could select the machine learning algorithms, formulate the models, and then evaluate them.

2.4   Classifier Selection

We chose a set of three classifiers to build the supervised machine learning models. The first is XGBoost, classified as an ensemble method, which uses a set of several classifiers with the boosting technique, calibrating and reinforcing the classifiers at each iteration. The remaining two algorithms correspond to methods considered classic in the literature: logistic regression and KNN [3].

The main reason for selecting these algorithms is to observe and compare the performance of a more recent and sophisticated classifier, such as XGBoost, with older and more classic algorithms, such as KNN. At this point, important questions arise, such as the relationship between classifier performance and the computational cost associated with training. Another hypothesis to explore is the influence of the Knowledge Discovery in Databases (KDD) process on the final performance of the classifiers, i.e., whether there is a significant difference between the classifiers when applied to a well-prepared and refined database.

2.5   Model Evaluation

To evaluate the results, we employed the 10-fold cross-validation technique. Following the completion of the entire battery of tests, we derived the mean and standard deviation of the Macro F1 metric to assess the performance of each algorithm.

Finally, we fine-tuned the hyperparameters for each algorithm through a tripartite experiment using 5-fold. Subsequently, we conducted a two-tailed t-test for each pair of algorithms to determine whether the models exhibited statistically significant differences or similarities at a specified confidence level.

3   Results

After fine-tuning the hyperparameters, the results obtained with each 10-fold cross-validation algorithm are summarized in Table 2. Initially, we observe good and similar performance between the XGBoost and KNN algorithms, which will be discussed later with the statistical test. The low standard deviation is also a good indication of the model's performance. This characteristic could signify good uniformity in the base and a low presence of *outliers*.

Table 2. Macro F1 Scores achieved by the algorithms

Algorithm	Mean	Standard Deviation
Logistic Regression	73.39%	0.39%
XGBoost	94,76%	0,06%
KNN	92,29%	0,08%

To ascertain the superior performing algorithm, a two-tailed t-test was conducted with a significance level set at $\alpha = 0,05$, indicating a 5% probability of erroneously inferring a difference between the algorithms when such disparity does not exist. Following the execution of this statistical test across the algorithm pairs, it was discerned that all algorithms exhibited statistically significant differences. Consequently, XGBoost emerged as the optimal classifier, demonstrating the highest score in the Macro F1 metric.

4   Conclusion and Future Work

In this study, the initial objectives were successfully achieved, with the extraction of characteristics capable of defining the nature of each URL and obtaining satisfactory results. In addition, the metrics evaluated, analyzing only the lexical scope of the URL, are promising, showing comparable or slightly lower performance than related works that use characteristics related to the network and the content of URLs, which require direct access to them.

In conclusion, the methodology employed throughout the development of this work surpasses many of the cited related studies in terms of robustness and reliability. This superiority stems from the consistent application of cross-validation techniques for model evaluation, feature selection, and hyperparameter refinement, alongside the confident utilization of statistical tests to ascertain the optimal performing models for URL classification.

Future research endeavors could entail a more thorough investigation into the distinguishing characteristics of URLs, aiming to elucidate more precise demarcations between various malicious URLs. As depicted in Fig. 3, it becomes evident that additional pertinent features are requisite to effectively differentiate instances belonging to the malware class from other URL categories. The disparity in false negatives and positives surpasses any other URL classification, underscoring the critical need for refinement. Notably, false negatives in this classification possess significant potential for detrimental consequences, as they erroneously portray malware-infected URLs as safe, posing substantial security risks.

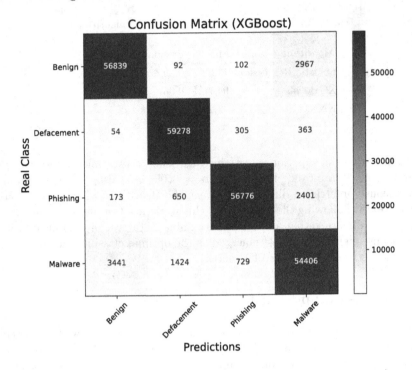

Fig. 3. False negative analysis

Another avenue for exploration could involve investigating the levels of correlation among different characteristics. Figure 4 illustrates a notable correlation between features. For instance, we can observe a conspicuous example between attributes corresponding to the count of directories and the count of "/" symbols within URLs. Given their direct proportional relationship, researchers could consider strategies for feature consolidation or similar approaches.

Lastly, contemplating the reduction of database volume could prove beneficial. That entails scrutinizing and eliminating redundant URLs from the database, specifically those that contribute minimal informative value to the classification task. Implementing the instance selection technique holds promise for substantially diminishing data volume while preserving model efficacy and curtailing the computational overhead associated with training.

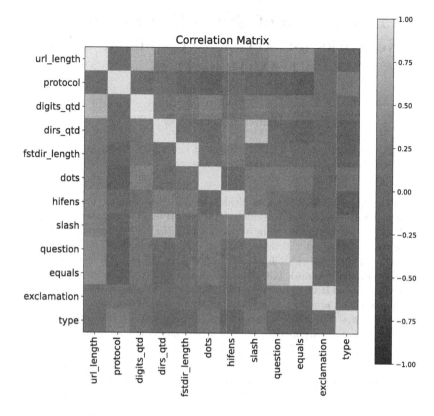

Fig. 4. Levels of correlation between characteristics

Acknowledgements. This study received partial financial support from AWS, CNPq, CAPES, FINEP, and Fapemig.

References

1. Bowyer, K.W., Chawla, N.V., Hall, L.O., Kegelmeyer, W.P.: SMOTE: synthetic minority over-sampling technique. CoRR **abs/1106.1813** (2011). http://arxiv.org/abs/1106.1813
2. Chen, T., Guestrin, C.: Xgboost: A scalable tree boosting system. In: Proceedings of the 22nd ACM SIGKDD International Conference on Knowledge Discovery and Data Mining, pp. 785–794. KDD '16, Association for Computing Machinery, New York, NY, USA (2016). https://doi.org/10.1145/2939672.2939785, https://doi.org/10.1145/2939672.2939785
3. Fix, E., Hodges, J.: Discriminatory Analysis: Nonparametric Discrimination: Consistency Properties. USAF School of Aviation Medicine (1951). https://books.google.com.br/books?id=4XwytAEACAAJ

Late Fusion of Graph Convolutional Networks for Action Recognition Using UAV Bone Data

Dinh-Tan Pham[✉][ID]

International School, Vietnam National University, Hanoi, Vietnam
tanpd@vnu.edu.vn

Abstract. Unmanned Aerial Vehicle (UAV) is becoming popular for surveillance, search, and rescue operations. Human action recognition (HAR) using UAV data is an important task that allows human behavior to be detected instantly from the visual data. UAVs' attitudes and motions make HAR for UAVs challenging. In recent years, Graph Convolutional Network (GCN) architectures have been mainstream for skeleton-based HAR. This paper proposes a Late Fusion GCN (LF-GCN) framework by applying late fusion to three graph-based deep learning architectures. The framework combines the advantages of different graph-based deep-learning models. The proposed model outperforms existing GCN schemes on the large-scale UAV-Human dataset.

Keywords: action recognition · bone data · deep learning

1 Introduction

Nowadays, Unmanned Aerial Vehicle (UAV) equipped with cameras is used to examine significant areas for surveillance, search, and rescue. Understanding human behavior using UAV-captured data has emerged recently. While there has been immense work on ground-camera data, study on UAV data is limited. For ground-camera scenes, human body size takes up a high portion of the scenes. However, compared to ground-camera data, human action recognition (HAR) from UAV data is more complicated. The difficulty arises from various UAV conditions, including altitude, motion, weather, and geography. A large-scale benchmark dataset, namely UAV-Human, is introduced in [6] to facilitate the development and evaluation of deep learning models. Various modalities, including RGB, optical flows, and skeleton data, are collected for HAR. Skeleton-based HAR has drawn much interest lately because of its compactness and robustness [3]. A variety of skeleton-based methods for HAR have been proposed [8].

While many methods for HAR on datasets captured by ground cameras have been proposed, the performance of these methods on UAV-Human has yet to be thoroughly studied. Because of their quick movements and constant changes in height and attitude while in flight, UAVs tend to capture video sequences with more diverse and unique viewpoints, noticeable motion blurs, and a more comprehensive range of target resolutions than ground cameras. Changes in UAV

O. Gervasi et al. (Eds.): ICCSA 2024, LNCS 14814, pp. 408–417, 2024.
https://doi.org/10.1007/978-3-031-64608-9_27

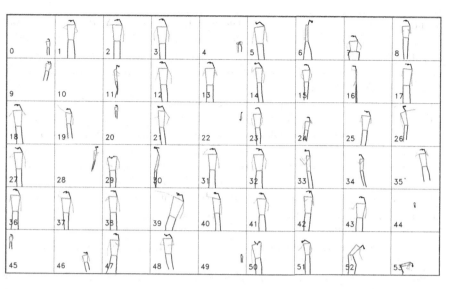

Fig. 1. UAV-Human action samples.

motion can easily cause image blurring. Moreover, UAV data are typically collected from a high altitude, so images have varying resolutions and are of low quality, as shown in Fig. 1. Pose estimation from UAV images is prone to errors, which makes skeleton-based HAR a challenging issue.

This paper makes two contributions.

- First, the performance of graph-based learning models for HAR is evaluated on the large-scale UAV-Human dataset.
- Second, a late-fusion framework is proposed to benefit from the advantages of these three graph-based learning models to improve the performance of HAR on UAV-Human.

The remaining sections of the document are arranged as follows: While Sect. 2 reviews deep learning models for HAR, Sect. 3 describes the proposed method. The dataset and experimental findings are thoroughly explained in Sect. 4. Section 5 concludes the paper.

2   Related Work

Deep learning methods for skeleton-based HAR can be categorized into three types: Convolutional Neural Network (CNN), Recurrent Neural Network (RNN), and Graph Convolutional Network (GCN). GCN has emerged as the mainstream for skeleton-based HAR recently. This paper will mainly focus on GCN models, as these are the building blocks of the proposed method.

Graph-based deep learning for HAR is first introduced in ST-GCN [18]. The network models skeletal dynamics using a graph. Every node in the graph represents a joint. Temporal edges link the same joints over successive frames, whereas spatial edges reflect the skeleton's structure. In [10], a Directed Graph Neural Network (DGNN) is presented by modeling the joint relationship using networks with directed connections. Double-Feature Double-Motion network (DD-Net) is proposed in [20]. The DD-Net's feature shape and graph structure are both reduced. A straightforward but efficient semantics-guided neural network (SGN) is proposed in [22]. The authors explicitly include the high-level semantics to improve the graph's capacity to represent features. There is a hierarchical link between joints using two modules: one at the joint level, which models the correlations between joints within the same frame, and another at the frame level, which models the dependencies between frames by considering all the joints. HARD-Net is proposed in [5] to target early HAR to forecast the action label before the action is completed. Shift-GCN, a lightweight GCN model, is presented in [1] using the shift convolution operator for the 2D convolution procedure. In [13], a multi-stream spatial-temporal relative transformer (MSST-RT) is proposed. The transformer breaks the inherent graph topology in spatial and temporal dimensions.

In [16], TE-GCN is proposed. A unique temporal-enhanced graph convolution network is described to consider temporal aspects. To prevent future information leakage and maintain the ordering information of the inputs, a Causal Convolution layer is added at each time step. In [17], Interacted Object SGN (IO-SGN) is proposed to support the accurate localization of interacted objects, aiding in action identification. The authors investigate the initial action cues and the characteristics of interacted objects. In [15], a lightweight channel-topology-based AGCN (LC-AGCN) is suggested as a solution. A multi-scale spatial-temporal CNN (MSSTNet) is proposed in [2] to capture high-level features for HAR. Rather than employing sophisticated graph convolution, the authors fully utilize multi-scale convolutions to capture the relationships of joints. In [21], combinatorial attention-enhanced adjacency matrix-based GCN (CA-EAMGCN) is proposed. First, an upgraded adjacency matrix is built to increase the model's perceptual field of features. Second, a feature fusion module is added to offer the best fusion ratio possible for the model's various input characteristics.

Since the skeleton model is a graph, representing skeleton data using nodes and edges is efficient and natural. The literature has proposed a variety of graph-based architectures. Among many GCN models for HAR, three models are selected for UAV-Human: AGCN, AAGCN, and MS-G3D. These are state-of-the-art methods for HAR on ground-camera datasets like Kinetics-Skeleton [4] and NTU RGB+D [9].

Three skeleton-based deep learning models, AGCN, AAGCN, and MS-G3D, for HAR on ground-camera data are presented in this section. Using data from ground cameras, these models represent HAR's state-of-the-art deep learning models. While these models perform well on ground-camera data, their accuracy on UAV data can be low. Human shapes only occupy a small portion of scenes. As skeleton data collected by UAVs suffers from extreme noise and varying resolution owing to UAV motion, HAR on UAV data is a complex issue.

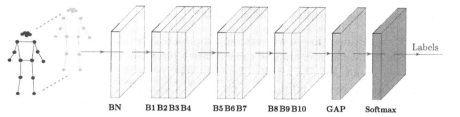

Fig. 2. Block diagram of AGCN and AAGCN. AAGCN differs from AGCN by the attention mechanism in the basic blocks.

2.1 Adaptive GCN (AGCN)

The framework involves cascading layers of graph convolution to analyze data in two dimensions: space and time. Adaptive GCN (AGCN) is introduced in [11]. Unlike ST-GCN, which uses a fixed adjacency matrix, AGCN adaptively learns the graph's topology. The model's generality is increased by this data-driven approach, which makes it more flexible and outperforms ST-GCN on large-scale datasets. AGCN is introduced in [11]. It is mentioned that only some samples of every action class will benefit equally from a single fixed graph topology. The model parameterizes two different graph types, whose structures are trained and updated with the model's convolutional parameters. A global graph is one kind that shows the overall pattern in all the data. An individual graph is another kind that shows a distinct pattern for every data sample. Because each of the two graph types is specifically tuned for a distinct layer, the hierarchical structure of the model can be better fitted. This data-driven approach gives the model more generality to adapt to different data samples and boosts its flexibility for graph creation. As seen in Fig. 2, the stack of fundamental blocks represents the AGCN system diagram. At the input, a Batch Normalization (BN) layer is applied. Ten fundamental blocks with varying numbers of output channels are present. There are 64 channels in the first four blocks. There are 128 channels in the next three blocks and 256 in the final three. The basic blocks are numbered from B1 to B10. A residual link is employed for every basic block to prevent gradient vanishing. The block stack's output is sent to a layer known as Global Average Pooling (GAP). A softmax classifier is utilized to forecast the action label.

2.2 Attention-Enhanced Adaptive GCN (AAGCN)

AAGCN is proposed in [12] to allow the model to pay attention to important data. The block diagram of AAGCN is the same as that of AGCN in Fig. 2. AAGCN differs from AGCN in that each basic block contains a Spatial-Temporal-Channel (STC) attention module, which can aid in teaching the model to focus on discriminative joints, frames, and channels selectively.

2.3 Multi-scale Graph 3D (MS-G3D)

MS-G3D is introduced in [7]. The system diagram of MS-G3D is shown in Fig. 3. The system is the concatenation of three Spatial-Temporal Graph Convolutional (STGC) blocks, a GAP, and a Fully Connected (FC)/Softmax layer. The original MS-G3D paper provides information on STGC blocks. To mitigate the biased weighting, a proposed multi-scale aggregation strategy involves cutting down on extra connections between neighborhood disentangling features. Consequently, more potent multi-scale operators may represent cooperative interactions at any distance.

Fig. 3. Block diagram of MS-G3D.

3 Proposed Method

Each graph-based deep learning model has advantages in inference for certain action categories. Every graph-based model makes use of a distinct skeleton data feature. Bone data are defined as the spatial offsets between adjacent joint pairs. Bone data are used in this work since they contain offset values between adjacent joint pairs. Figure 4 shows a schematic diagram of our proposed method. The framework comprises three streams that use bone data as the input to AGCN, AAGCN, and MS-G3D. Softmax scores of three streams are summed up for late fusion to calculate the final score.

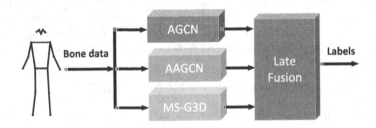

Fig. 4. System diagram of the proposed method.

- C: the number of channels, $C = 2$ for UAV-Human.
- T: the maximum frame length, $T = 263$ for UAV-Human.

- N: the number of joint in the skeleton model, $N = 17$ for UAV-Human.
- M: the maximum number of subjects in each frame, $M = 2$ for UAV-Human

Let $S^i_{...}(v)$ be the score that each stream returned for sample v, and let v be the action sample. The following is the expected class of v:

$$i^* = \arg\max_i((S^i_{AGCNbone}(v) + S^i_{AAGCNbone}(v) \\ + S^i_{MSG3Dbone}(v)) \tag{1}$$

where $\mathrm{argmax}(\cdot)$ returns the index of the class with the largest value.

4   Experimental Results

4.1   Dataset

The UAV-Human, a large-scale benchmark dataset, is introduced in [6]. The dataset includes skeletal, color, infrared, and depth data, among other data modalities. The dataset poses significant challenges for action detection for the following reasons: It was collected from 45 distinct locations, encompassing a wide range of indoor and outdoor environments, including forests, squares, streets, gyms, university campuses, farms, and many scenarios within buildings. It was gathered over three months by a drone flying in both rural and urban areas, days and nights. As a result, it includes a wide range of subjects, lighting, weather, and camera motion.

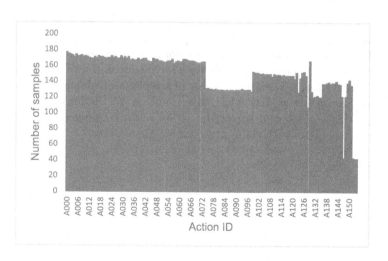

Fig. 5. Number of samples per action category.

Figure 6 depicts the UAV-Human skeletal structure. The construction of the skeleton has 17 joints, also known as joints. UAV-Human is a challenging dataset since it has 155 classes with action IDs ranging from A000 to A154. The list of 155 action classes can be found at [14]. Figure 5 shows the number of samples per action category.

Fig. 6. The skeleton model of the UAV-Human dataset.

4.2 Results and Discussions

All of the GCN schemes are considered to benefit from late fusion regarding HAR performance. With late fusion applied to all three streams, our proposed method achieves up to 43.90% accuracy on UAV-Human. Table 1 shows performance comparison with state-of-the-art methods. The proposed method outperforms the state-of-the-art methods MSSTNet and CA-EAMGCN with accuracies of 43.00% and 43.11%, respectively.

The top 10 action classes with the best accuracy are shown in Table 2. The list of 10 challenging action classes for the proposed method is shown in Table 3. This is an ordinary situation since having a model that outperforms other models in all action classes is difficult, especially for a large-scale dataset like UAV-Human with 155 action classes. The small number of samples for training partially causes low accuracies on action IDs A152, A153, and A154. Action *mow* is mainly confused with *dig a hole* and *set on fire*; action *cough* is confused with *blow nose* as these actions are of high similarity even for human eyes.

Table 1. Comparison with state-of-the-art methods by accuracy (%).

No.	Method	Year	Accuracy [%]
1	ST-GCN [18]	2018	30.25
2	DGNN [10]	2019	29.90
3	DD-Net [20]	2019	31.47
4	2s-AGCN [11]	2019	34.84
5	SGN [22]	2020	36.37
6	HARD-Net [5]	2020	36.97
7	Shift-GCN [1]	2020	37.98
8	AAGCN [12]	2020	34.45
9	MS-G3D [7]	2020	40.51
10	MSST-RT [13]	2021	41.22
11	TE-GCN [16]	2022	42.50
12	IO-SGN [17]	2022	39.99
13	LC-AGCN [15]	2023	40.49
14	MSSTNet [2]	2023	43.00
15	CA-EAMGCN [21]	2023	43.11
16	ViA [19]	2024	42.60
17	**Proposed**	2024	**43.90**

Table 2. Top 10 action classes with the best accuracies using the proposed method.

Action ID	Action	# Training	# Testing	Accuracy [%]
A092	move something with someone	93	35	82.86
A007	stand up	126	45	75.56
A134	comfort someone	85	34	73.53
A011	put on a coat	125	45	64.44
A023	jump on two legs	125	44	63.64
A112	rear right turn	106	41	63.41
A090	high five	93	35	62.86
A097	lend an arm to support someone	93	35	62.86
A132	wave a goodbye	86	34	61.76
A101	land at designated locations	109	41	60.98

Table 3. Top 10 action classes with the lowest accuracies using the proposed method.

Action ID	Action	# Training	# Testing	Accuracy [%]
A123	mow	87	38	21.05
A062	cough	122	45	20.00
A017	throw away a hat	127	44	18.18
A152	walk	20	22	18.18
A041	make a victory sign	123	45	17.78
A086	hit someone with something	92	35	17.14
A040	make an OK sign	122	45	15.56
A125	smoke	109	41	14.63
A154	close an umbrella	20	21	14.29
A153	open an umbrella	20	21	9.52

5   Conclusions

UAVs' automatic HAR is crucial for surveillance and rescue operations. This paper assessed the performance of various graph-based deep learning models on the large-scale UAV-Human dataset. Bone data are used in this work since they contain offset values between adjacent joint pairs. A late fusion framework is proposed to benefit the advantages of AGCN, AAGCN, and MS-G3D using UAV bone data. According to evaluation results, the proposed method outperforms existing methods on UAV-Human. Future studies should focus on improving pose estimation from UAV data, which will help improve HAR results.

Acknowledgments. Supported by International School, Vietnam National University, Hanoi, Vietnam.

References

1. Cheng, K., Zhang, Y., He, X., Chen, W., Cheng, J., Lu, H.: Skeleton-based action recognition with shift graph convolutional network. In: Proceedings of the IEEE/CVF Conference on Computer Vision and Pattern Recognition (2020)
2. Cheng, Q., Cheng, J., Ren, Z., Zhang, Q., Liu, J.: Multi-scale spatial-temporal convolutional neural network for skeleton-based action recognition. Pattern Analysis and Applications, pp. 1–13 (2023)
3. Degardin, B., Proença, H.: Human behavior analysis: a survey on action recognition. Appl. Sci. **11**(18), 8324 (2021)
4. Kay, W., et al.: The Kinetics human action video dataset. arXiv preprint arXiv:1705.06950 (2017)
5. Li, T., Liu, J., Zhang, W., Duan, L.: HARD-Net: hardness-aware discrimination network for 3D early activity prediction. In: Vedaldi, A., Bischof, H., Brox, T., Frahm, J.M. (eds.) Computer Vision - ECCV 2020, pp. 420–436. Springer International Publishing, Cham (2020)

6. Li, T., Liu, J., Zhang, W., Ni, Y., Wang, W., Li, Z.: UAV-Human: a large benchmark for human behavior understanding with unmanned aerial vehicles. In: Proceedings of the IEEE Conference on Computer Vision and Pattern Recognition (2021)
7. Liu, Z., Zhang, H., Chen, Z., Wang, Z., Ouyang, W.: Disentangling and unifying graph convolutions for skeleton-based action recognition. In: Proceedings of the IEEE/CVF Conference on Computer Vision and Pattern Recognition, pp. 143–152 (2020)
8. Pham, D.T., et al.: Deep learning models for skeleton-based action recognition for uavs. In: 2022 IEEE Ninth International Conference on Communications and Electronics (ICCE), pp. 343–348. IEEE (2022)
9. Shahroudy, A., Liu, J., Ng, T.T., Wang, G.: NTU RGB+D: a large scale dataset for 3D human activity analysis. In: Proceedings of the IEEE Conference on Computer Vision and Pattern Recognition, pp. 1010–1019 (2016)
10. Shi, L., Zhang, Y., Cheng, J., Lu, H.: Skeleton-based action recognition with directed graph neural networks. In: Proceedings of the IEEE/CVF Conference on Computer Vision and Pattern Recognition. pp. 7912–7921 (2019)
11. Shi, L., Zhang, Y., Cheng, J., Lu, H.: Two-stream adaptive graph convolutional networks for skeleton-based action recognition. In: Proceedings of the IEEE/CVF Conference on Computer Vision and Pattern Recognition, pp. 12026–12035 (2019)
12. Shi, L., Zhang, Y., Cheng, J., Lu, H.: Skeleton-based action recognition with multi-stream adaptive graph convolutional networks. IEEE Transactions on Image Processing, pp. 9532–9545 (2020)
13. Sun, Y., Shen, Y., Ma, L.: Msst-rt: multi-stream spatial-temporal relative transformer for skeleton-based action recognition. Sensors **21**(16), 5339 (2021)
14. SUTDCV: UAV-Human. https://github.com/SUTDCV/UAV-Human (2021). Accessed 02 May 2024
15. Wang, K., Deng, H., Zhu, Q.: Lightweight channel-topology based adaptive graph convolutional network for skeleton-based action recognition. Neurocomputing **560**, 126830 (2023)
16. Xie, Y., Zhang, Y., Ren, F.: Temporal-enhanced graph convolution network for skeleton-based action recognition. IET Comput. Vision **16**(3), 266–279 (2022)
17. Xu, L., Lan, C., Zeng, W., Lu, C.: Skeleton-based mutually assisted interacted object localization and human action recognition. IEEE Transactions on Multimedia (2022)
18. Yan, S., Xiong, Y., Lin, D.: Spatial temporal graph convolutional networks for skeleton-based action recognition. In: Thirty-second AAAI Conference on Artificial Intelligence (2018)
19. Yang, D., Wang, Y., Dantcheva, A., Garattoni, L., Francesca, G., Brémond, F.: View-invariant skeleton action representation learning via motion retargeting. Int. J. Comput. Vision pp. 1–16 (2024)
20. Yang, F., Wu, Y., Sakti, S., Nakamura, S.: Make skeleton-based action recognition model smaller, faster and better. In: Proceedings of the ACM multimedia Asia, pp. 1–6. ACM (2019)
21. Zhang, D., Deng, H., Zhi, Y.: Enhanced adjacency matrix-based lightweight graph convolution network for action recognition. Sensors **23**(14), 6397 (2023)
22. Zhang, P., Lan, C., Zeng, W., Xing, J., Xue, J., Zheng, N.: Semantics-guided neural networks for efficient skeleton-based human action recognition. In: proceedings of the IEEE/CVF Conference on Computer Vision and Pattern Recognition, pp. 1112–1121 (2020)

Detecting Outlier Segments in Uncertain Personal Trajectory Data

Sungsoon Hwang[1]([✉]), Kushal Navghare[2], Umer Huzaifa[2], Ilyas Ustun[2], Alex Dzewaltowski[3], and Christopher Connaboy[3]

[1] Department of Geography, DePaul University, Chicago, IL 60614, USA
shwang9@depaul.edu
[2] School of Computing, DePaul University, Chicago, IL 60604, USA
{knavghar,mhuzaifa,iustun}@depaul.edu
[3] Scholl College of Podiatric Medicine, Rosalind Franklin University of Medicine and Science, North Chicago, IL 600064, USA
{alex.dzewaltowski,christopher.connaboy}@rosalindfranklin.edu

Abstract. Uncertainties such as missing data, noise, and outliers, are common in personal trajectory data due to extended indoor time. To improve the usability of such data, it is necessary to detect and repair errors. While smoothing-based methods can be used to deflate noise, such methods are not well suited to cleaning trajectory data in the presence of spatial outliers represented by abrupt change in location. We propose detecting spatial outliers at the level of segments using supervised machine learning algorithms. We partitioned a trajectory into segments based on time gaps (greater than recording interval) and used smoothed values of relevant features including movement state at the level of segments for detecting spatial outliers. Experimentation results indicate that Extreme Gradient Boosting outperforms Random Forest and Light Gradient Boosting Machine methods. The study indicates that gaps and movement state can be considered to partition a trajectory and improve outlier detection.

Keywords: Trajectory Data Preprocessing · Outlier Detection · Machine Learning · Trajectory Segmentation · GPS Errors

1 Introduction

A large volume of personal trajectory data has become readily available as Global Navigation Satellite Systems (GNSS) and location-aware devices (e.g., smartphones) have become more pervasive. Personal trajectory data track a person' whereabouts and movement at fine spatiotemporal resolution (e.g., every second to minutes). The data refers to a set of consecutive track points with a tuple of location and time (x, y, t) given sampling rate for any duration (e.g., hours to years) [1]. There are many use cases of personal trajectory data. Spatially explicit activity patterns that are inferred from personal trajectory data can be used to develop location-based recommendation systems. A large collection of historical trajectory data on road networks can inform real-time car navigation,

O. Gervasi et al. (Eds.): ICCSA 2024, LNCS 14814, pp. 418–426, 2024.
https://doi.org/10.1007/978-3-031-64608-9_28

traffic congestion mitigation, and transportation/land use planning. The environmental etiology of diseases has been largely unaccounted for due to challenges with measuring environmental exposure at a full scale in space and time. Now those challenges are being overcome by advances in the technologies mentioned above [2].

Uncertainties in personal trajectory data, however, have been the barrier to realizing the potential of the data. There are three major sources of uncertainty in personal trajectory data: a gap, noise and outliers. A gap refers to incomplete track points (records) caused by signal loss, and the latter two refer to inaccurate records caused by measurement error. GNSS signals do not typically penetrate thick structures like buildings, tunnels, and tree canopies, resulting in incomplete/irregular sampling in the trajectory data. Multiple sources like ionospheric delay (signal reception deterred by particles in ionosphere), multipath interference (signal reception deflected off by structures nearby), clock errors in GNSS receivers, and geometry among satellites, contribute to measurement errors in the trajectory data.

Noises are expressed as back-and-forth movement typically around an indoor location or slight misalignment with road networks outdoors. Figure 1 depicts track points that were logged for an hour when a person was staying inside a single building in downtown Chicago with many high rises [3]. Individual deviational points (or outliers) can occur and are typically represented by a sudden jump in location as observed in different geographic scales in Fig. 2.

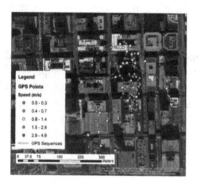

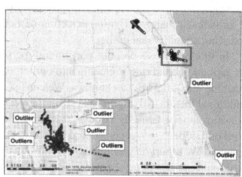

Fig. 1. Noise in personal trajectory data.

Fig. 2. Outliers in personal trajectory data.

Incomplete and inaccurate track points account for a large proportion in 'personal' trajectory data in contrast to 'vehicle' trajectory data due to extensive time spent indoors in an increasingly urban setting. These uncertainties deter the development of accurate and reliable activity/place recognition algorithms. Further, most of these algorithms are developed based on relatively clean 'vehicle' trajectory data and thus those algorithms do not work well at uncertain personal trajectory data. Untreated uncertainties lower the usability of personal trajectory data in many real-world applications discussed above. Observations on uncertain personal trajectory data reveal that a gap, noise, and outliers are not independent of each other. That is, a gap, noise and outliers are interspersed with each other as they relate to structural interference.

Review of related work on cleaning trajectory data suggests several findings. First, smoothing feature values over sliding windows is most widely used to clean trajectory data. It is, however, not highly effective at cleaning the 'personal' trajectory data due to high level of uncertainties. Smoothing-based methods are more geared toward filtering out slight noise in outdoor trajectory data. Furthermore, despite the dependence of uncertain events (a gap, noise, and outliers) in trajectory data, existing methods rarely consider those events altogether. Relatedly, a recent study combines constraint-based methods for detecting outliers and smoothing-based methods for repairing noise [4]. This method, however, may not be effective at detecting outliers that are spatiotemporally clustered, as depicted at the lower right of the inset map of Fig. 2.

In this paper we will focus on detecting outlier segments from personal trajectory data. An *outlier segment* is defined as a set of one or more consecutive track points that are regarded as an outlier whose location deviates from the actual location beyond the acceptable level of error. The acceptable level of error will be formulated depending on intended use. There are several reasons why we believe detecting outlier segments is significant or takes precedence over other uncertain events discussed above. First, imputing unknown location during signal loss (gap) in trajectory data is sensitive to the presence of outliers [5] as much as smoothing noise is. In other words, detecting outlier segments should precede handling a gap and noise to improve the overall performance of trajectory cleaning. Second, outliers and slight noise should be treated differently due to different variations in errors. Smoothing can reliably clean trajectory data if outliers are singled out and repaired first. Third, outliers typically exist in segments rather than in an isolated manner. That is, detecting outlier segments is a more general case than detecting an individual outlier.

In this paper, we propose partitioning personal trajectory data to segments based on gaps and classifying segments into outlier vs. non-outlier category using supervised machine learning (ML) techniques. We consider the movement state of segments as an additional feature. ML algorithms are employed to account for dynamic, non-linear relationships among features associated with the likelihood of outlier segments. Segment-level outlier detection is considered less computationally intensive than individual-level analysis. We report on preliminary findings on using the proposed approach to detecting positional outliers in personal trajectory data.

The paper is organized as follows. Section 2 reviews existing methods for detecting errors in trajectory data. Section 3 describes the process of collecting, processing, and labeling personal trajectory data as well as the proposed method. Section 4 describes experimentation results related to the choice of parameters and machine learning algorithms. Section 5 concludes the study.

2 Related Work

This section focuses on existing methods related to detecting 'spatial' errors in 'offline' personal trajectory data. A spatial error can be quantified as the degree to which a measured location deviates from a true location. It is known that standard GNSS receivers available in the market today have a spatial (positional) error between 2 and 10 m in ideal outdoor conditions. However, horizontal accuracy varies greatly due to reasons as discussed earlier. Due to difficulties with obtaining labeled data (i.e., track points with the actual location), error detection algorithms typically mark errors if a track point's measured location deviates from its 'expected' location. In general, data points with location deviation beyond acceptable level given intended use can be considered errors as a categorical variable.

Several methods have been proposed to deal with spatial errors in trajectory data. Those methods can be classified into smoothing-based, constraint-based, and modeling-based approach. Smoothing techniques can be used to detect errors by comparing a track point's measured coordinate to its smoothed coordinate within temporal sliding windows. Constraint-based approach attempts to detect errors based on conditions imposed on data (e.g., errors if signal quality is poor, errors if the distance from the previous track point is beyond possible). A modeling-based approach builds a model that estimates the probability of track points' being errors as a function of related features, and mark errors if the probability is high. Below we review existing methods that fall into these categories.

Smoothing-Based Methods: this approach smooths geographic coordinates of a track point using filtering techniques of different kinds (e.g., mean, median, Kalman, particle) over sliding windows. A sliding window is typically made of consecutive track points before and after a track point to be processed for any error. This works to replace original coordinates with expected coordinates within sliding windows. The intent is to deflate noise that exists in raw trajectory data.

This approach is well suited to correcting (repairing) the location of slight noise, but the effectiveness of error correction is put into question in the presence of outliers. Smoothing in the segment of trajectory data containing outliers (Fig. 2) can result in more distorted coordinates than original coordinates [6]. Research also shows that the performance of filtering is sensitive to the size and partitioning of sliding windows [7]. Sliding windows of fixed size are typically used for convenience. Using sliding windows with disregard to uncertain events (such as gap) is expected to lower the performance of filtering. Little is known about effective partitioning strategies of sliding windows for smoothing and cleaning personal trajectory data.

Constraint-Based Methods: this approach constructs conditional rules that detect spatial errors based on threshold values. Threshold values can be determined globally (i.e., relative to the entire dataset) or locally (i.e., relative to temporal neighbors). Examples of global threshold values include extreme speed, acceleration, and altitude, where extreme values can be statistically determined. Spatial errors can be detected based on poor quality of GNSS signal indicated by a combination of high Dilution of Precision (DOP) (e.g., > 4), low number of satellites used (NSAT) (e.g., <4), and low signal-to-noise ratio (SNR) (e.g., <150). Examples of local threshold values include abrupt changes in speed or altitude. A track point beyond the maximum possible distance from the previous track point can be marked as an outlier (called range constraint), where the maximum possible distance is estimated based on the maximum possible vehicle speed [4].

While this approach is easy to implement, it is challenging to identify threshold values that are universally applicable. Moreover, in the case of rules based on locally unexpected values, the assumption should be made about the state (e.g., constantly moving) and velocity of the previous track point or track points as a whole. If the previous data point is stationary, then the maximum possible distance from the previous data point is zero in theory, making it infeasible to detect outliers. Further, while a spatial outlier can occur individually in an isolated manner, the rule of 'range constraints' described above will fail to detect outliers if the previous track point is also an outlier. For this reason, we consider detecting *outlier segments* as a general case of an individual outlier. Lastly, it is difficult to construct rules that satisfactorily account for the dynamic, non-linear relations among different features; hence a modeling-based method is suggested as an alternative.

Modeling-Based Methods: this builds a model that classifies data points into a binary dependent variable y (error or not) based on a matrix of multiple features X. The relationship will be captured as coefficients (weights) of X in terms of mathematical models. Supervised machine learning (ML) algorithms for classification such as random forest and support vector machine (SVM) have been suggested as a method for detecting errors in trajectory data. A deep learning algorithm based on the Long Short-Term Memory (LSTM) was applied to detect outliers from outdoor data with about 86% accuracy [8].

3   Methods

We collected personal trajectory data around Chicago and its vicinity in the fall of 2023. A participant was asked to carry a GPS logger (QStarz BT-Q1000XT) all the time except for water activities for a total of 8 days. A GPS logger is configured to log a track point every second (i.e. with a 1-s recording interval) and stop logging it if a person is stationary for over 10 min. Total 170,488 track points were collected. A participant was asked to log the time and location at every start and end of trip made in a travel diary template provided to them during the tracking period. We ensure the accuracy of a travel diary that serves as ground truth before, during, and after data collection. That is, we directly supervise participants' completing a travel survey at the beginning of data collection, confirm the validity of a travel diary during data collection, and verify the accuracy of a travel diary against orthoimage of higher accuracy and independent sources (ESRI Imagery Hybrid) in ArcGIS Pro 3.0. We divided the collected trajectory data into training data (80%) and testing data (20%).

Trajectory data was partitioned into temporally consecutive segments, where a new segment starts whenever the difference in time from the previous track point exceeds a recording interval (1 s). This yielded a total of 143 segments. To label outlier segments in the collected trajectory data, research staff link the trajectory data to a travel diary based on timestamp and plot geographic coordinates of the trajectory data in ArcGIS Pro. The actual location of a track point is manually checked against a travel diary (for stop location) and ESRI Imagery Hybrid (for the location of a trip route and stop). Location deviation for each track point is calculated. For each of segments, research staff labels whether the segment can be marked as an outlier. An outlier segment is a set of temporally consecutive track points whose location unexpectedly deviates from the actual location. In Fig. 3, an outlier segment is depicted in pink line that is comprised of 11 track points in temporal sequence (labeled 1 to 11). These 11 track points (or traces) are not aligned with a road network, not constituting a trip.

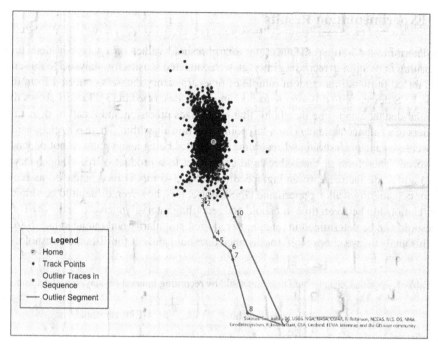

Fig. 3. An Outlier Segment in Personal Trajectory Data

The proposed method partitions the trajectory data into temporally consecutive segments as defined above and then flags outliers based on smoothed values of relevant features at the level of segments. For training machine learning (ML) algorithms, we consider descriptive statistics of the following features for each segment: speed, height, heading, PDOP, HDOP, VDOP, signal to noise ratio (snr_info), number of satellites used (sat_used), previous speed, previous heading, previous snr_info, previous sat_used, change in speed, change in heading, change in sat_used, distance from the previous track point (distance), the number of track points (num_points), and the number of track points falling into staypoints (total_staypoints).

To calculate total_staypoints, the individual track point is marked as staypoint or not using the staypoint-detection algorithm. The algorithm marks a staypoint if the distance among two or more consecutive track points exceeds a distance threshold and time span among those track points exceeds a time threshold [9]. In general, these threshold values should be chosen in relation to sampling rate, intended use, and data quality. These threshold values are chosen based on sensitivity analysis, to be discussed in the next section. For ML algorithms, we used random forest (RF), Light gradient boosting machine (LightGBM), and Extreme Gradient Boosting (XGBoost) for evaluation. Preliminary analysis indicates that these ML algorithms outperform k-nearest neighbor, support vector machine, and logistic regression.

4   Experimentation Results

To determine the optimal distance and time threshold values of a staypoint detection algorithm in relation to recording interval, we conducted sensitivity analysis. To this end we labeled outliers in a random sample of other trajectory datasets collected from the same GPS device with different recording intervals, described in [3]. Table 1 shows the optimal distance and time threshold (that maximizes precision and recall of detecting outliers in a balanced manner) for a staypoint detection algorithm. There is a relationship between distance threshold and recording interval as being a staypoint or not depends on speed. Therefore, distance threshold can be set to a product of recording interval (sec) and scale factor representing speed (in m/s). 3–6 m/s is recommended as scale factor considering walking speed and GNSS noise. It is, however, difficult to generalize the relationship between time threshold and recording interval given this analysis. Time threshold can be determined in relation to required granularity and intended use. Based on this analysis, we choose 3 m for distance threshold and 6 s for distance threshold.

Table 1. Optimal distance and time threshold by recording interval for staypoint detection

	Distance threshold	Time threshold
10-s interval	30 m	6 s
5-s interval	28 m	46 s
1-s interval	4 m	6 s

We evaluated classification accuracy of three ML algorithms (RF, LightGBM, XGBoost) on test data. Classification results with the best parameter values are shown in Table 2. Parameters are tuned to maximize F1-score. According to experimentation, XGBoost with precision 1 and recall 0.75 (F1-score 0.86) outperforms the other two ML algorithms (RF with F1-score 0.8 and LightGBM with F1-score 0.82).

Table 2. Precision, Recall, and F1-score for Detecting Outliers

	Precision	Recall	F1-score
Random Forest	1	0.67	0.8
Light GBM	0.9	0.75	0.82
XGBoost	1	0.75	0.86

Figure 4 plots relative importance of features used in classifying trajectory segments into outliers using XGBoost with 0.5 probability threshold. X axis in Fig. 4 shows the average gain of splits which use the feature. As expected, features indicating quality of GNSS signals (such as the number of satellites used and signal-to-noise ratio) contribute most significantly to this binary classifier. Other features like speed, distance, dilution of precision (DOP), height, the number of staypoints, and change in heading are shown to be important.

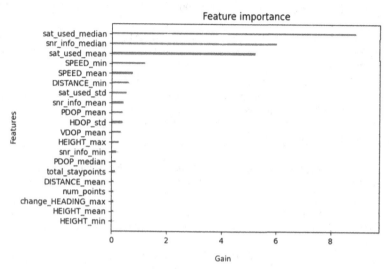

Fig. 4. Relative importance of features

5 Conclusions

In this paper, we consider methods for detecting positional outliers at the level of segments using supervised machine learning (ML) algorithms. We partition personal trajectory into segments based on time gaps and incorporate features pertaining to movement state using a staypoint detection algorithm, as well as other commonly available features. The study shows that segment-level classification with ML technique reaches an acceptable level of accuracy. The study also confirms that it is worthwhile considering movement states and uncertainties like gaps in detecting outliers.

The next step for the study is to devise and evaluate segmentation strategies that reflect movement state and detect spatial outliers at those segments. Such segmentation strategies are designed to incorporate movement state (whether a person was stationary or not) into feature space and aggregate track points into the spatiotemporally related unit of analysis that facilitates efficient error correction in the later step. Once outlier segments are identified, the location of outlier segments can be repaired in a different method than smoothing to make smoothing less sensitive to outliers. In the future research, other ML classifiers utilizing neural network will be considered. In general, the study indicates that it is necessary to consider interaction among uncertain events like gap, noise, and outliers in cleaning trajectory data.

Acknowledgments. This study was funded by the 2023 DePaul-RFUMS joint grant (project number 501763).

References

1. Liu, G., Gu, R., Wang, J., Yan, W.: Personal trajectory with ring structure network: algorithms and experiments. Secur. Commun. Netw. **2021**, e9974191 (2021). https://doi.org/10.1155/2021/9974191

2. Richardson, D.B., Volkow, N.D., Kwan, M.-P., Kaplan, R.M., Goodchild, M.F., Croyle, R.T.: Spatial turn in health research. Science **339**(6126), 1390–1392 (2013). https://doi.org/10.1126/science.1232257

3. Hwang, S., VanDeMark, C., Dhatt, N., Yalla, S.V., Crews, R.T.: Segmenting human trajectory data by movement states while addressing signal loss and signal noise. Int. J. Geogr. Inf. Sci. **32**(7), 1391–1412 (2018). https://doi.org/10.1080/13658816.2018.1423685

4. Fang, C., Wang, F., Yao, B., Xu, J.: GPSClean: a framework for cleaning and repairing GPS data. ACM Trans. Intell. Syst. Technol. **13**(3), 40:1–40:22 (2022). https://doi.org/10.1145/3469088

5. Hwang, S., Webber-Ritchey, K., Moxley, E.: Comparison of GPS imputation methods in environmental health research. Geospatial Health **17**(2) (2022). https://doi.org/10.4081/gh.2022.1081

6. Lee, W.-C., Krumm, J.: Trajectory preprocessing. In: Zheng, Y., Zhou, X. (eds.) Computing with Spatial Trajectories, pp. 3–33. Springer, New York (2011). https://doi.org/10.1007/978-1-4614-1629-6_1

7. Thalmann, T., Abdalla, A.: Assessing the influence of preprocessing methods on raw GPS-data for automated change point detection. In: Huerta, J., Schade, S., Granell, C. (eds.) Connecting a Digital Europe Through Location and Place. LNGC, pp. 123–139. Springer, Cham (2014). http://link.springer.com/chapter/10.1007/978-3-319-03611-3_8. Accessed 31 July 2015

8. Sbetti, D., Tessaris, S.: Cleaning outdoor activity logs using deep learning. Presented at the SIGNAL 2022, The Seventh International Conference on Advances in Signal, Image and Video Processing, May 2022, pp. 1–6. https://personales.upv.es/thinkmind/SIGNAL/SIGNAL_2022/signal_2022_1_10_60003.html. Accessed 7 Feb 2024

9. Li, Q., Zheng, Y., Xie, X., Chen, Y., Liu, W., Ma, W.-Y.: Mining user similarity based on location history. In: Proceedings of the 16th ACM SIGSPATIAL International Conference on Advances in Geographic Information Systems, GIS 2008, pp. 34:1–34:10. ACM, New York, NY, USA (2008). https://doi.org/10.1145/1463434.1463477

Deep Learning Techniques for Skeleton-Based Action Recognition: A Survey

Dinh-Tan Pham[(✉)] [iD]

International School, Vietnam National University, Hanoi, Vietnam
`tanpd@vnu.edu.vn`

Abstract. Interpreting human behavior from entirely performed actions is called human action recognition (HAR). HAR applications rapidly expand into robotics, CCTV surveillance, self-driving vehicles, gaming, and video retrieval. Among different data modalities, skeleton data offers compact representation and computational efficiency. In recent years, much work has gone into developing a robust and accurate deep-learning framework for skeleton-based HAR. The paper reviews state-of-the-art methods for skeleton-based HAR. The survey also summarizes evaluation results on a large-scale benchmark dataset. Trends in action recognition research are discussed.

Keywords: action recognition · skeleton data · deep learning

1 Introduction

In computer vision, human action refers to movements, from single-limb movements to complicated joint movements involving several limbs and the whole body. Human action recognition (HAR) is a fundamental job that identifies human activities by observing the entire execution of the action. The issue has been extensively researched for many years and remains challenging because of its numerous practical uses, such as visual surveillance and video retrieval. Much work has gone into developing an intelligent system that can recognize complicated human activities in congested situations, like humans. But an action is merely presented to a computer by a collection of pixels. The computer cannot interpret these pixels into a useful representation or deduce human behavior from that representation [7].

Psychological research shows that skeleton data are discriminative to present human actions [3]. A skeleton model with 25 joints is shown in Fig. 1. Furthermore, skeletons are invariant to changes in appearance and backdrop, facilitating the description of actions. The skeletal data for action representation contains interdependence between joints. Pixels in depth/color images do not directly provide these dependencies. Consequently, there has been a lot of research in skeleton-based HAR in recent years [19]. Noise and changes in illumination significantly impact action recognition in RGB video sets. Action recognition based

O. Gervasi et al. (Eds.): ICCSA 2024, LNCS 14814, pp. 427–435, 2024.
https://doi.org/10.1007/978-3-031-64608-9_29

on skeletons is resistant to these issues. Skeletal data can also enable privacy protection in the real world [32].

Motion capture (Mocap) system can be used to collect skeleton data. Since mocap devices are not affected by illumination or vision, they can provide high-quality skeleton data. Mocap systems are pricey and cumbersome, though. Therefore, skeletal data from color photographs or depth maps is used in various scenarios. Skeletal data are now readily available due to the widespread use of inexpensive depth sensors and advancements in pose estimation. Pose estimation can be used to color/depth data to provide skeleton information or obtained directly via depth sensors. Joint trajectories can be used to represent human action. Skeletal data HAR methods can prevent color data weaknesses such as background changes and lighting conditions. Additionally, skeleton data offers computation and storage efficiency.

Nevertheless, skeleton-based HAR is not the main focus of the surveys mentioned above. They draw attention to various taxonomies, uses, and theoretical stances of HAR. This serves as the driving force of this paper, providing a more thorough analysis of skeleton-based HAR. The remaining of the paper is organized as follows: Sect. 2 is the survey of skeleton-based HAR techniques. Section 3 is a comparative study on the performance of deep learning models using the benchmark dataset NTU RGB+D. The paper is concluded in Sect. 4 with a discussion of some future approaches.

2   Skeleton-Based HAR Techniques

Skeleton-based HAR techniques can be categorized as in Fig. 2. In recent years, deep learning-based HAR become dominant with remarkable performance. popular deep learning techniques are Convolutional Neural Network (CNN), Recurrent Neural Network (RNN), and Graph Convolution Networks (GCN).

2.1   Convolutional Neural Network (CNN)

The CNN-based approach retrieves the features from the texture color images created by first encoding the skeleton data. These approaches still consider skeleton data as picture characteristics. The skeleton-based action recognition of CNN-based techniques can also benefit from the experience obtained from the earlier CNN application. The ability of CNN to recognize patterns in images has been demonstrated. Nevertheless, it must still model temporal dependency for video action recognition. The skeleton sequence is represented as an image rather than processing individual frames. Both geographical and temporal information are considered in the resulting image. Deep CNNs can successfully learn the skeleton sequence's spatial and long-term temporal structure from the generated image. A normalization procedure produces three gray images for every skeleton sequence, corresponding to the sequence's 3D coordinates. CNN-based methods are shown in Table 2.

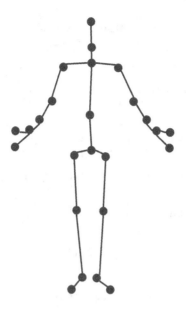

Fig. 1. Skeleton model with 25 joints.

2.2   Recurrent Neural Network (RNN)

RNN was first widely employed in the Natural Language Processing discipline. When processing sequential data, the RNN offers a significant benefit. Later, it was progressively used in many sequential data-related applications, including machine translation, sentiment analysis, picture captioning, time-series prediction, etc. RNNs may accommodate sequences of any length in theory. An excessively lengthy sequence during training can cause issues with gradient explosion and vanishing gradient during optimization. However, a maximum length is typically provided in practice because the extended feedforward neural network will consume too much memory. The series is terminated when it gets longer than the allowed length. RNN's shortcoming is addressed by Long Short-Term Memory (LSTM) networks. LSTM can handle the trajectories of skeleton joints as a time series and investigate the temporal structure of the skeleton sequences for action recognition. LSTMs help RNNs overcome recurrent issues like disappearing gradients by enabling training on lengthy sequences. Even though LSTM networks are meant to investigate long-term dependencies, they need help to learn the contents of a sequence with numerous timestamps. Furthermore, LSTM networks have trouble extracting high-level characteristics. Typical RNN-based methods are summarized in Table 2.

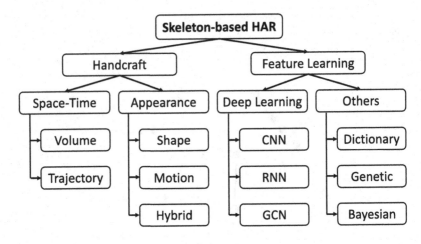

Fig. 2. Skeleton-based HAR techniques.

2.3   Graph Convolution Networks (GCN)

In contrast to the conventional CNN and RNN network model, GCN may handle data with a generalized topology structure and thoroughly mine its properties. This has much in common with the convolution kernel's weighted average and parameter-sharing mechanisms. Skeleton architecture data are transformed into standard grid structure data before applying CNN structure to the data. This significantly reduces CNN's effectiveness in skeleton-based HAR.

GCN extends the use of the convolution operator for images to the graph domain. Yan *et al.* first proposed GCN for HAR in Spatial-Temporal GCN (ST-GCN) [31]. The skeletal data are represented as graphs, with joints as graph nodes. The spatial graph is constructed using the innate joint connections seen in the human body. The temporal graph is made up of connections between joints in consecutive frames. Tang *et al.* provide a system in [28] that consists of two networks: the Graph-based CNN (GCNN) and the frame distillation network (FDNet). The FDNet aims to extract critical frames from input sequences. GCNN considers the human body a graph structure and uses this information for action recognition. The framework can identify the most illuminating frames in every sequence. A progressive approach is used to model how frame selection works. Action detection is performed using the chosen frames. In [11], the Actional-Structural GCN (AS-GCN) concept is presented, utilizing an inference block. The model creates a graph by combining structural and actional links. The structural linkages represent higher-order dependencies, and the actional links embed action-specific dependencies. In [1], Channel-wise Topology Refinement GCN (CRT-GCN) is proposed. A parameterized adjacency matrix known as the shared topology provides generic correlations between vertices and topological priors for all channels. The channel-specific correlations capture the nuanced interactions between vertices inside each channel, which are dynamically inferred for every sample. The multi-stream EfficientGCN-B4 model is proposed by Song *et al.* [26]. This model uses early fusion to merge the inputs, including joint locations and motion velocities. In [30], the Language Knowledge-Assisted GCN (LA-GCN) is proposed. The model directs the creation of new representations to highlight important node information at the data level and to replicate category prior knowledge in human brain.

3   Performance Evaluation

Table 1. Benchmark datasets with data modalities: Skeleton (S), Depth (D).

No.	Dataset	Modality	#Class	#Subject	#Sample
1	MSR-Action3D [15]	D,S	20	10	557
2	HMDB51 [8]	RGB	51	–	6,766
3	UCF101 [27]	RGB	101	–	13,320
4	UTKinect [29]	RGB,D,S	10	10	200
5	MSRAction-Pair [18]	RGB,D,S	12	10	360
6	NTU RGB+D [20]	RGB,D,S	60	40	56,880
7	Kinetics-400 [4]	RGB	400	–	306,245
8	UAV-Human [14]	RGB,D,S	155	119	67,428

There are many skeleton datasets in literature built for developing and evaluating HAR techniques as in Table 1. In this paper, the most popular large-scale dataset, NTU RGB+D, is selected as the benchmark dataset for evaluating deep learning methods. The NTU RGB+D dataset is introduced in [20], utilizing data modalities gathered from Kinect v2 sensors. The skeleton model has twenty-five joints as in Fig. 1. The dataset contains 56,880 sequences that are divided into 60 activity classes. There are forty people involved in the actions. The three Kinect sensors are positioned at different angles but at the same height. Seventeen camera sets with varying heights and distances are used to gather the dataset. The authors of the dataset suggest two benchmark protocols: (1) Cross-subject: half of the participants are trained, while the other half are tested. The training set consists of 40,320 sequences, whereas the testing set contains 16,560 sequences. (2) Cross-view: 18,960 sequences (from camera one) make up the testing set, while 37,920 sequences (from cameras two and three) make up the training set. A comparative study on the performance of deep learning techniques on NTU RGB+D is shown in Table 2. It can be seen that state-of-the-art methods for HAR are graph-based deep learning models. This comes from the graph nature of skeleton data in human action presentation. Action recognition in this case is a graph classification task.

Table 2. Performance evaluation by accuracy (%) on NTU RGB+D.

No.	Method	Year	Cross-subject	Cross-view
1	Bi-directional RNN [2]	2015	59.1	64.0
2	Part-based LSTM [20]	2016	60.7	67.3
3	ST-LSTM [16]	2016	69.2	77.7
4	STA-LSTM [24]	2017	73.4	81.2
5	VA-LSTM [33]	2017	79.2	87.7
6	Res-TCN [6]	2017	74.3	83.1
7	Clip CNN [5]	2017	79.6	84.8
8	Synthesized CNN [17]	2017	80.0	87.2
9	Motion CNN [10]	2017	83.2	89.3
10	Multi-scale CNN [9]	2017	85.0	92.3
11	ST-GCN [31]	2018	81.5	88.3
12	GCNN [28]	2018	83.5	89.8
13	IndRNN [13]	2018	81.8	88.0
14	SRN+TSL [23]	2018	84.8	92.4
15	ARRN-LSTM [34]	2019	80.7	88.8
16	Dense IndRNN [12]	2019	86.7	94.0
17	AS-GCN [11]	2019	86.8	94.2
18	AGCN [21]	2019	87.3	93.7
19	3 s RA-GCN [25]	2020	87.3	93.6
20	AAGCN [22]	2020	88.0	95.1
21	CTR-GCN [1]	2021	92.4	96.8
22	EfficientGCN-B4 [26]	2022	92.1	96.1
23	LA-GCN [30]	2023	93.5	97.2

4   Conclusion

Understanding human actions is essential in computer vision, robotics, security surveillance, and home monitoring applications. This paper provides a summary of the most recent research in this area. It suggests a classification based on deep learning techniques for skeleton-based action recognition. The analysis of the state-of-the-art methodologies and the methods employed for their validation are presented. Action recognition technology applied to real-world scenes may encounter several practical issues, including occlusion, non-unique characters and activities in the video, low picture resolution, and challenging access to vast numbers of labeled data sets. Due to these issues, many action recognition systems are still in the lab. The performance of HAR can be improved using multi-modal HAR or combining it with action-related object information.

Acknowledgments. This research is funded by International School, Vietnam National University, Hanoi, Vietnam.

References

1. Chen, Y., Zhang, Z., Yuan, C., Li, B., Deng, Y., Hu, W.: Channel-wise topology refinement graph convolution for skeleton-based action recognition. In: Proceedings of the IEEE/CVF International Conference on Computer Vision, pp. 13359–13368 (2021)
2. Du, Y., Wang, W., Wang, L.: Hierarchical recurrent neural network for skeleton based action recognition. In: Proceedings of the IEEE Conference on Computer Vision and Pattern Recognition, pp. 1110–1118 (2015)
3. Johansson, G.: Visual perception of biological motion and a model for its analysis. Percept. Psychophys. **14**(2), 201–211 (1973)
4. Kay, W., Carreira, J., Simonyan, K., Zhang, B., Hillier, C., Vijayanarasimhan, S., Viola, F., Green, T., Back, T., Natsev, P., et al.: The Kinetics human action video dataset, pp. 1–22. arXiv preprint arXiv:1705.06950 (2017)
5. Ke, Q., Bennamoun, M., An, S., Sohel, F., Boussaid, F.: A new representation of skeleton sequences for 3D action recognition. In: Proceedings of the IEEE Conference on Computer Vision and Pattern Recognition, pp. 3288–3297 (2017)
6. Kim, T.S., Reiter, A.: Interpretable 3D human action analysis with temporal convolutional networks. In: 2017 IEEE Conference on Computer Vision and Pattern Recognition Workshops (CVPRW), pp. 1623–1631. IEEE (2017)
7. Kong, Y., Fu, Y.: Human action recognition and prediction: a survey. Int. J. Comput. Vision **130**(5), 1366–1401 (2022)
8. Kuehne, H., Jhuang, H., Garrote, E., Poggio, T., Serre, T.: HMDB: a large video database for human motion recognition. In: 2011 International Conference on Computer Vision, pp. 2556–2563. IEEE (2011)
9. Li, B., Dai, Y., Cheng, X., Chen, H., Lin, Y., He, M.: Skeleton based action recognition using translation-scale invariant image mapping and multi-scale deep CNN. In: 2017 IEEE International Conference on Multimedia and Expo Workshops (ICMEW), pp. 601–604. IEEE (2017)
10. Li, C., Zhong, Q., Xie, D., Pu, S.: Skeleton-based action recognition with convolutional neural networks. In: 2017 IEEE International Conference on Multimedia and Expo Workshops (ICMEW), pp. 597–600. IEEE (2017)
11. Li, M., Chen, S., Chen, X., Zhang, Y., Wang, Y., Tian, Q.: Actional-structural graph convolutional networks for skeleton-based action recognition. In: Proceedings of the IEEE/CVF Conference on Computer Vision and Pattern Recognition, pp. 3595–3603 (2019)
12. Li, S., Li, W., Cook, C., Gao, Y.: Deep independently recurrent neural network (IndRNN), pp. 1–18. arXiv preprint arXiv:1910.06251 (2019)
13. Li, S., Li, W., Cook, C., Zhu, C., Gao, Y.: Independently recurrent neural network (IndRNN): Building a longer and deeper RNN. In: Proceedings of the IEEE Conference on Computer Vision and Pattern Recognition, pp. 5457–5466 (2018)
14. Li, T., Liu, J., Zhang, W., Ni, Y., Wang, W., Li, Z.: UAV-Human: a large benchmark for human behavior understanding with unmanned aerial vehicles. In: Proceedings of the IEEE/CVF Conference on Computer Vision and Pattern Recognition, pp. 16266–16275 (2021)

15. Li, W., Zhang, Z., Liu, Z.: Action recognition based on a bag of 3D points. In: 2010 IEEE Computer Society Conference on Computer Vision and Pattern Recognition-Workshops, pp. 9–14. IEEE (2010)

16. Liu, J., Shahroudy, A., Xu, D., Wang, G.: Spatio-temporal LSTM with trust gates for 3D human action recognition. In: Leibe, B., Matas, J., Sebe, N., Welling, M. (eds.) ECCV 2016. LNCS, vol. 9907, pp. 816–833. Springer, Cham (2016). https://doi.org/10.1007/978-3-319-46487-9_50

17. Liu, M., Liu, H., Chen, C.: Enhanced skeleton visualization for view invariant human action recognition. Pattern Recogn. **68**, 346–362 (2017)

18. Oreifej, O., Liu, Z.: HON4D: Histogram of oriented 4D normals for activity recognition from depth sequences. In: Proceedings of the IEEE Conference on Computer Vision and Pattern Recognition, pp. 716–723 (2013)

19. Ren, B., Liu, M., Ding, R., Liu, H.: A survey on 3D skeleton-based action recognition using learning method, pp. 1–8. arXiv preprint arXiv:2002.05907 (2020)

20. Shahroudy, A., Liu, J., Ng, T.T., Wang, G.: NTU RGB+D: a large scale dataset for 3D human activity analysis. In: Proceedings of the IEEE Conference on Computer Vision and Pattern Recognition, pp. 1010–1019 (2016)

21. Shi, L., Zhang, Y., Cheng, J., Lu, H.: Two-stream adaptive graph convolutional networks for skeleton-based action recognition. In: Proceedings of the IEEE Conference on Computer Vision and Pattern Recognition, pp. 12026–12035 (2019)

22. Shi, L., Zhang, Y., Cheng, J., Lu, H.: Skeleton-based action recognition with multi-stream adaptive graph convolutional networks. IEEE Trans. Image Process. **32** 9532–9545 (2020)

23. Si, C., Jing, Y., Wang, W., Wang, L., Tan, T.: Skeleton-based action recognition with spatial reasoning and temporal stack learning. In: Ferrari, V., Hebert, M., Sminchisescu, C., Weiss, Y. (eds.) ECCV 2018. LNCS, vol. 11205, pp. 106–121. Springer, Cham (2018). https://doi.org/10.1007/978-3-030-01246-5_7

24. Song, S., Lan, C., Xing, J., Zeng, W., Liu, J.: An end-to-end Spatio-temporal attention model for human action recognition from skeleton data. In: Proceedings of the AAAI Conference on Artificial Intelligence, vol. 31, pp. 1–7 (2017)

25. Song, Y.F., Zhang, Z., Shan, C., Wang, L.: Richly activated graph convolutional network for robust skeleton-based action recognition. IEEE Trans. Circuits Syst. Video Technol. **31**(5), 1915–1925 (2020)

26. Song, Y.F., Zhang, Z., Shan, C., Wang, L.: Constructing stronger and faster baselines for skeleton-based action recognition. IEEE Trans. Pattern Anal. Mach. Intell. **45**, 1474–1488 (2022)

27. Soomro, K., Zamir, A.R., Shah, M.: UCF101: a dataset of 101 human actions classes from videos in the wild, pp. 1–6. arXiv preprint arXiv:1212.0402 (2012)

28. Tang, Y., Tian, Y., Lu, J., Li, P., Zhou, J.: Deep progressive reinforcement learning for skeleton-based action recognition. In: Proceedings of the IEEE Conference on Computer Vision and Pattern Recognition, pp. 5323–5332 (2018)

29. Xia, L., Chen, C.C., Aggarwal, J.K.: View invariant human action recognition using histograms of 3D joints. In: 2012 IEEE Computer Society Conference on Computer Vision and Pattern Recognition Workshops, pp. 20–27. IEEE (2012)

30. Xu, H., Gao, Y., Hui, Z., Li, J., Gao, X.: Language knowledge-assisted representation learning for skeleton-based action recognition. arXiv preprint arXiv:2305.12398 (2023)

31. Yan, S., Xiong, Y., Lin, D.: Spatial temporal graph convolutional networks for skeleton-based action recognition. In: Thirty-second AAAI Conference on Artificial Intelligence, pp. 1–20 (2018)

32. Yue, R., Tian, Z., Du, S.: Action recognition based on RGB and skeleton data sets: a survey. Neurocomputing **512**, 287–306 (2022)
33. Zhang, P., Lan, C., Xing, J., Zeng, W., Xue, J., Zheng, N.: View adaptive recurrent neural networks for high performance human action recognition from skeleton data. In: Proceedings of the IEEE International Conference on Computer Vision, pp. 2117–2126 (2017)
34. Zheng, W., Li, L., Zhang, Z., Huang, Y., Wang, L.: Relational network for skeleton-based action recognition. In: 2019 IEEE International Conference on Multimedia and Expo (ICME), pp. 826–831. IEEE (2019)

Transformation of Local Communities from Neighborhoods to Urban Commons in the Production of Social Representations of Space

Aleksandr Antonov$^{(\boxtimes)}$ ⓘ, Galina Gornova ⓘ, Georgii Kontsevik ⓘ,
Leonid Turkov ⓘ, Vladimir Vorona ⓘ, and Sergey Mityagin ⓘ

ITMO University, Birzhevaya Line, 14, Saint Petersburg, Russia
asantonov@itmo.ru

Abstract. The paper explores new types of social interaction between urban communities. These include translocal and hyperlocal identities that reflect the uniqueness of urban areas at different levels. These two types of identities have become more widespread due to the increasing communication of city residents in digital ways, especially through social media. The method proposed in this paper is based on the application of thematic modelling, toponym and keyword extraction, and spatial knowledge graphs. It allows the identification of links between different territories and hotspots of activity resulting from such communication. It also provides the ability to identify the semantic properties of such phenomena, which could be useful in further urban identity research.

Keywords: Local communities · Translocal identity · Urban foundation models · Spatial semantic analysis

1 Introduction

Contemporary studies of sustainable communities are conducted within discourses of locality, translocality, and hyperlocality [1,2]. Within these discourses, the objects of study vary in scale and show different criteria of sustainability [3,4].

A local community is defined as a social group that is united by its place of residence, such as a district or city, and shares similar needs and values. When functioning effectively, a local community produces social capital that supports its sustainability. Social ties within local communities are strong and geographically bound.

Traditional notions of local communities are often linked to neighbourhoods. However, in metropolitan areas, neighbourhoods no longer provide the social support associated with the characteristics of urban lifestyles, changes in the nature of public practices, social ties and ways of accumulating social capital [3]. As a result, communities are transforming from locality to hyperlocality and translocality.

O. Gervasi et al. (Eds.): ICCSA 2024, LNCS 14814, pp. 436–447, 2024.
https://doi.org/10.1007/978-3-031-64608-9_30

Social media platforms support the development of hyperlocal communities by tailoring their messages to specific geographic contexts. Hyperlocality can encompass a street, a neighborhood, or a district. Public groups on social media serve as a digital medium for communication and public engagement. Social media platforms play a crucial role in supporting weak social ties, which are essential in urban settings for maximizing social support and facilitating the effective transmission of essential information relevant to daily life and professional advancement.

Translocal communities are formed by the interaction of people, ideas, and symbolic resources, located in different spaces but maintaining a local self-identity. They are 'imagined neighbourhoods' supported by digital and networked tools that convey local meanings across territorial boundaries. Translocal connections shape and sustain social representations of the specificity of urban places.

Digital technologies and the evolution of social media have contributed to "reassembling the social" within local communities. Central to this phenomenon are transformations in the dynamics of social connections at multiple levels: the micro level, characterized by hyperlocality; the meso level, associated with locality; and the macro level, encompassing translocality.

Modern cities have retained those features that were reflected in Georg Simmel's classic essay 'Big Cities and Spiritual Life', in the works of Chicago School theorists and a number of other authors. These include individualism and anonymity. The former has a destructive effect on traditional neighbourhoods, while the latter frees the individual from group pressure and excessive social control [5]. Research on social media enables the comprehension of effects engendered by the multiscalar nature of urban space, one of which is the transformation of urban interactions towards commons-based neighboring in the production of social space. Urban commons is the outcome of a series of multiscale processes [1].

The paper consists of the following sections. The Related Works section presents the theoretical developments underlying our study and an overview of digital methods that can be used to extract and analyse social media data. The Method section describes the algorithm of the developed method and its data structure. Experimental Results section presents the practical application of the method to test subjects and presents the results of its use.

2   Related Works

The transformation of society in the modern world, associated with the shift from modernity to postmodernity and caused by changes in network communications, is reflected in B. Latour's actor-network theory [6]. The classical concept of M. Granovetter presents the prevalence and effectiveness of weak ties over strong ties, including in the formation of communities of different types. Granovetter argues that weak ties serve as channels through which community members receive socially distant messages and information that are useful for their activities and life [7]. Weak ties form the foundation of hyperlocal and translocal communities. The term 'hyperlocal' refers to the online content of a small, geographically defined community such as a town, village, or neighbourhood, as defined in a 2012 study by the British Charitable Foundation Nesta when analysing the UK media [4]. A. Appadurai, who coined the term 'translocality', studied the differences between local communities, similar to traditional neighbourhoods, and translocal diasporas [2]. The transformation of communities due to globalisation processes that prevent the reproduction of traditional locality was also examined. The study 'Urban Commons: Moving Beyond State and Market' presents the conceptualisation of urban cohesion in conjunction with multiscale [1].

Researchers from various fields are actively working with the combination of spatial and semantic data. Urban data is analyzed at different scales, including several cities, the city as a whole, districts, neighborhoods, and streets [8,9]. These studies utilize a variety of data, such as social network data, open data, and spatial data [10,11]. Urban studies that utilise spatial semantic data typically concentrate on information agendas and people's activities related to events, as well as thematic modelling of the territory [9]. Additional attention is paid to the spatialisation of objects through textual data [12].

Kim [12] presents a technique for identifying and connecting space objects using their textual features obtained from online sources, including web documents and social. The authors suggest creating graphs with vertices representing particular locations and edges indicating their connections. Semantic and spatial similarities can be discovered by comparing textual descriptions, names, and nearby places. These graphs are compared to determine the most appropriate candidate for location in space. This approach allows the identification of location of objects based solely on text. However, this approach is not suitable for urban identity research. The authors do not conduct a semantic study of topics near identified physical objects.

Capela F. presents a method for identifying unique identities for different cities based on news texts [13]. The process begins with keyword extraction using TF-IDF, followed by the Latent Dirichlet Allocation (LDA) method to generate topic models [14]. The distribution of news texts across cities is then determined in the context of the generated topics. The approach focuses on the inter-city level. Our method uses a similar approach but applies it intra-city.

In the review of topic modelling and analysis methods by Kousis A., two main methods of topic identification are described: LDA and BERTopic [15]. BERTopic is noted as being more advanced. The input data used to create a topic map on smart cities includes news sources, academic articles, and social media comments. It is important to note that post-processing with expert judgement is necessary for BERTopic to generate a list of labels. The inter-city focus is a notable feature of this method.

Bok K. describes an approach for analysing Twitter data to identify event keywords and their relationships [16]. The study generates a graph of keywords associated with certain events by analysing social media data. Keywords are extracted from datasets with Twitter posts, and clusters are built. However, the study does not consider geographical labels in the context of keyword linking. The sampling is spontaneous, as no specific spatial framework is given for the study. Instead, toponyms are associated as normal words in text without geocoding.

B. Hawelka presents a method for studying interregional migration behaviour of people [17]. The study uses 944 million geo-tagged messages on Twitter to determine The study compared each user's geo-tagged posts over time to determine their place of residence based on the highest number of geo-tagged posts. It also identified places of current residence, such as tourist destinations. The authors then identify the main migration drivers of people's movements in each country.

The study conducted by Tan M.J. and Guan C. utilises Twitter message analysis to evaluate the sentiments of residents towards property prices [9]. The researchers analyse the tone of messages for a specific geographical label (address) to determine the tonal level of the label and create a tonal distribution of the area. Based on the tone level, hotspots are identified, reflecting attitudes towards property transactions on a scale of 0 to 100. The paper analyses property prices and assesses their tone, which is then grouped into a heat map. The study focuses on neighbourhood-level properties. Our research method does not include a sentiment score in the form of a scale that reflects the sentiment of an area. Instead, it conducts semantic analysis of words linked to geocoded address labels.

All of these methods aim to gather information about the city and its processes and patterns. However, these works focus solely on analyzing a specific topic and do not consider other aspects of the territories. The present study employs a distinct approach that considers the major themes in the information agenda.

The proposed methodology is focused on identifying multiple thematic areas that influence and shape individuals' perceptions of a particular urban area.

3 Method

3.1 Method Overview

The general scheme of the method is shown in Fig. 1. Blocks marked in blue characterize the information supplied to the input; blocks marked in green characterize the tools used.

Data is collected using the open API of the VKontakte social network, then toponyms (street names) and house numbers are extracted from each text and geocoded. Next, a keyword that describes each message is selected [18]. All keywords are collected into a text corpus and clustered. Thus, each message possesses an address and a semantic class. Next, each cluster is visualized on a map and grouped in a hexagonal grid. The hexagons are clustered by the number of messages that fall into them. Hexagons characterize the spatial proximity of messages of the same class. Thus, the parts of the space that fall into one cluster will show similarity with respect to the activity of residents in the selected category (semantic cluster) and space. The code implementation example and sample data are available in github repository [19].

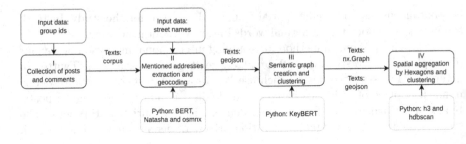

Fig. 1. Scheme of the method

3.2 Data Structure

Each post has comments that refer to it. Accordingly, a post and comments can contain an address (house and street), which is discussed within one post. Comments can have replies to them (discussions) within one post. Such links between comments and between comments and post allows to fill in geo-referencing information for comments within one post without the location mentioned in them.

3.3 Toponym Extraction

Geocoding was implemented according to a method and model similar to the article [20] in order to extract toponyms presented in the text.

3.4 Keyword Extraction

After extracting the toponyms, the text data is prepared for processing. This involves removing numbers, references, extracted toponyms, and words indicating toponyms such as 'street', 'avenue', and 'boulevard'. Additionally, stop words obtained from the nltk library [21] are filtered from the text to increase the relevance of keywords. The KeyBERT algorithm [22], based on the DeepPavlov/rubert-base-cased model [23], is used to extract them one per text. Only keywords with a semantic closeness higher than 0.6 to the source texts are used.

In the next step, the extracted toponyms are linked to the keywords according to the following rules:

1. If the toponym was extracted from a post, the words extracted from all comments that refer to it and the word extracted from the text where the toponym was, are linked to its node.
2. If the toponym was extracted from a commentary, the words extracted from all other commentaries that refer to the toponym, as well as the word extracted from the text where the toponym was, are linked to its node.
3. If the toponym was extracted from a comment that is not referenced by other comments, only the word extracted from the text of that comment is linked to its node.

This set of rules is demonstrated in Fig. 2.

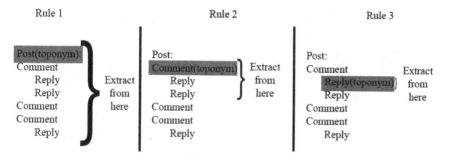

Fig. 2. Rules for toponym extraction from social media posts and comments

3.5   Graph Generation

Thus, the necessary set of nodes for the knowledge graph is obtained. The nodes consist of toponyms and keywords from related texts, connected by edges. As different texts may contain the same keywords, several edges may lead to one node with a keyword. This is how links between toponym nodes are formed. To enhance the number of links, we assess the semantic similarity of all keywords by encoding them into embeddings and calculating the cosine distance between them using the DeepPavlov/rubert-base-cased model. If the similarity of words exceeds a certain threshold (in this case, 0.75), we include the relationship between words in the graph as the edge. To map the graph in space, we add the coordinates of the centroids of the corresponding streets to the attributes of the toponym nodes.

3.6   Spatial Aggregation

Spatial aggregation as such was chosen because we need to consider parts of the city and not just the points themselves. The hexagonal grid is interpretable, in this paper we use level 7 of h3 hexagonal grid, which corresponds to a scale of 1 km for each edge of the hexagon. The use of the hexagonal grid rather than the boundaries of administrative units allows us to consider vernacular areas of the city. The process of spatial clustering is shown in Figs. 3a-3d.

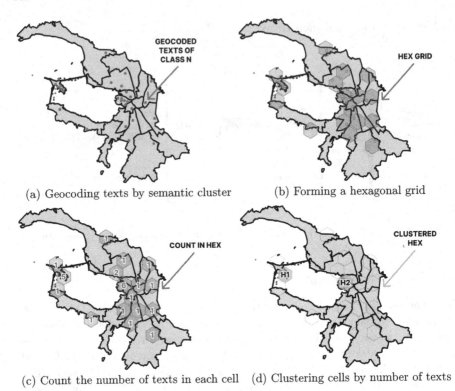

(a) Geocoding texts by semantic cluster   (b) Forming a hexagonal grid

(c) Count the number of texts in each cell   (d) Clustering cells by number of texts

Fig. 3. Spatial analysis steps

4   Experimental Results

4.1   Study Area

In order to identify similarities between community identities in different parts of the city, two experiments were conducted in St. Petersburg and Vyborg. Both cities are nuclei for their nearest agglomerations and are located in the north within drive accessibility from the border with Finland.

St. Petersburg is located in north-western Russia on the coast of the Gulf of Finland and at the mouth of the Neva River. It is bordered by the Leningrad Oblast to the south and has maritime borders with Finland and Estonia to the west. St. Petersburg has a population of over 5 million people and spans across 10 administrative districts, covering a total area of 1,439 square kilometers.

According to Federal State Statistics Service the most densely populated districts of Saint Petersburg by number of inhabitants are [24]:

1. Primorsky district (699,243 people)
2. Nevsky District (547,896 people)
3. Vyborgsky District (541,590 people)
4. Kalininsky District (536,794 people)
5. Krasnoselsky District (431,546 people)

Vyborg is located in the Leningrad Oblast on the coast of Vyborg Bay, which is located in the north-eastern part of the Gulf of Finland. Vyborg is smaller in size and population, and is considered part of the St. Petersburg agglomeration due to its good connectivity via public transportation (high speed trains connection). Vyborg is the second most populous city in the Leningrad Oblast, with a population of approximately 71,772 residents.

4.2   Data

The text data were obtained using open API of VKontakte social network [18]. Geospatial data for geocoding was obtained from OpenStreetMap.

For the experiment, we collected two sets of posts and comments. The first set covers the entire city of St. Petersburg, and includes posts and comments from 38 groups in 14 administrative districts for the period from 29.06.2022 to 12.02.2024. The second set pertains to the city of Vyborg, and includes texts from 5 groups for the period from 01.03.2023 to 01.03.2024.

4.3   Hypothesis

This paper examines the hypothesis that different parts of the city may be similar in terms of the projection of their identity through social media activity.

4.4   Results

The method was tested on a small scale in the city of Vyborg near St. Petersburg, using the dataset described in the previous section. The results are presented in Fig. 4.

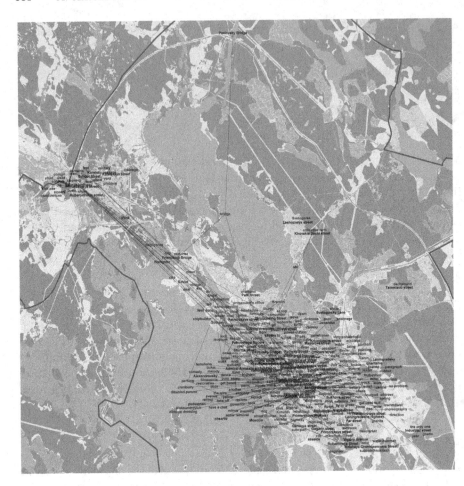

Fig. 4. Spatial-semantic graph of Vyborg

Based on visual and expert assessments, the city is divided into two enclaves of the most frequently mentioned areas, separated by a strait. The bottom right enclave refers to the older historic city, while the top left enclave refers to the newer Kalininsky district. Both areas are distinguished from other less active areas, such as the private residential areas near Kirovsky Dachas, Tammisuo and the industrial areas around Vyborg, by the presence of multi-storey apartment buildings. Additionally, they are connected by common semantic links that may indicate markers of translocal identity. These connections include 'fireman', 'hotel', 'city', 'soviet', 'prosecutor's office', and 'clean', which have some common meaning, typical for a small tourist town.

The application of proposed method on larger scale was performed for the area of St. Petersburg. The method was applied including additional aggregation

of social network texts on a hexagonal grid and clustering of hexes. The results
are presented in Fig. 5a and Fig. 5b.

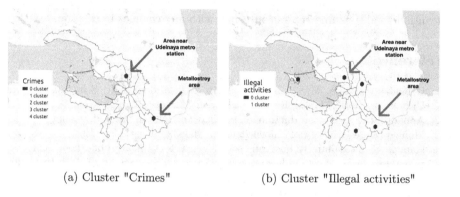

(a) Cluster "Crimes"   (b) Cluster "Illegal activities"

Fig. 5. Spatial clusters of messages by semantic clusters

Of particular interest are the topic clusters with the highest emotional load,
among a number of others. In this instance, clusters related to security threats
of varying degrees, such as 'murder', 'theft', and 'vandalism' were selected. The
analysis identified two territories belonging to the most active cluster in this
context. These territories are located in the settlement of Metallostroy (bottom
right of the figure) and near the Udelnaya metro and railway station (top of the
figure). These two areas are morphologically similar as they both contain green
spaces and industrial areas. They are often characterised by few regular visitors
and may be perceived as unsafe by residents.

5   Conclusion

The article outlined theoretical approaches to the study of identity, as well as
digital tools that facilitate the study of identity in the information space. It
also demonstrated experiments relying on the data from the VKontakte social
network with the method based on text analyses approach and presented the
interpretation of the received results of the work [18]. This research presents a
method for identifying spots of high intensity of individual thematic clusters in
a limited territory as manifestations of hyperlocal identity. As the semantic connection between some clusters concentrated in remote areas can be estimated by
the semantic similarity of text topic representations, it is reasonable to conclude
that some else of these areas' identities can be called translocal. As an example
of such a process, the case of districts of Vyborg and two locations in St. Petersburg in Russia is shown. It means that citizens of two or more remote areas can
be concerned about the same problems and processes depending on the found
topic.

By implementing this method in the decision-making process authorities and other actors can acquire a better understanding of the current urban processes in the agglomerations and give a basement for more precise prediction of different project results in urban development and management. It is essential to pay attention to all possible actors concerned with any changes in city life.

References

1. Dellenbaugh-Losse, M., Bieniok, M., Kip, M., Müller, A.K., Schwegmann, M.: Urban Commons: Moving Beyond State and Market (2015)
2. Appadurai, A.: The production of locality. In: Fardon, R. (ed.) Counterworks. Managing the Diversity of Knowledge, pp. 204–225. Routledge (1995)
3. Ganugi, G., Prandini, R.: Fostering social cohesion at the neighbourhood scale: the role of two social streets in Ferrara and Verona. SN Soc. Sci. 3 (2023). https://doi.org/10.1007/s43545-023-00688-6
4. Radcliffe, D.: Here and now: UK hyperlocal media today (2012)
5. Gornova, G.V.: Philosophy of the City. FORUM Publ., INFRA-M Publ., Moscow (2014)
6. Latour, B.: Reassembling the Social: An Introduction to Actor-Network-Theory. Oup Oxford (2007)
7. Granovetter, M.S.: The strength of weak ties. Am. J. Sociol. 78(6), 1360–1380 (1973)
8. Yu, Z., Zhu, X., Liu, X.: Characterizing metro stations via urban function: thematic evidence from transit-oriented development (TOD) in hong kong. J. Transp. Geogr. 99, 103299 (2022)
9. Tan, M.J., Guan, C.: Are people happier in locations of high property value? Spatial temporal analytics of activity frequency, public sentiment and housing price using twitter data. Appl. Geogr. 132, 102474 (2021)
10. Chen, Y., Niu, H., Silva, E.A.: The road to recovery: sensing public opinion towards reopening measures with social media data in post-lockdown cities. Cities 132, 104054 (2023)
11. Gao, Y., Chen, Y., Mu, L., Gong, S., Zhang, P., Liu, Y.: Measuring urban sentiments from social media data: a dual-polarity metric approach. J. Geogr. Syst. 24(2), 199–221 (2022)
12. Kim, J., Vasardani, M., Winter, S.: Similarity matching for integrating spatial information extracted from place descriptions. Int. J. Geogr. Inf. Sci. 31(1), 56–80 (2017)
13. de Oliveira Capela, F., Ramirez-Marquez, J.E.: Detecting urban identity perception via newspaper topic modeling. Cities 93, 72–83 (2019)
14. Blei, D.M., Ng, A.Y., Jordan, M.I.: Latent Dirichlet allocation. J. Mach. Learn. Res. 3, 993–1022 (2003). submitted 2/02; Published 1/03
15. Kousis, A., Tjortjis, C.: Investigating the key aspects of a smart city through topic modeling and thematic analysis. Future Internet 16(1), 3 (2023)
16. Bok, K., Kim, I., Lim, J., Yoo, J.: Efficient graph-based event detection scheme on social media. Inf. Sci. 646, 119415 (2023)
17. Hawelka, B., Sitko, I., Beinat, E., Sobolevsky, S., Kazakopoulos, P., Ratti, C.: Geo-located twitter as proxy for global mobility patterns. Cartogr. Geogr. Inf. Sci. 41(3), 260–271 (2014)
18. VKontakte: about VKontakte. https://vk.com/about (Year not provided)

19. Sloyka: a sample repository. https://github.com/GeorgeKontsevik/sloyka (2024)
20. Antonov, A., Kontsevik, G., Natykin, M., Mityagin, S.A.: Feedback2event: public attention event extraction from spontaneous data for urban management. Procedia Comput. Sci. **229**, 138–148 (2023). https://www.sciencedirect.com/science/article/pii/S1877050923020057, 12th International Young Scientists Conference in Computational Science, YSC2023
21. Project, N.: NLTK library. https://www.nltk.org/. Accessed 27 March 2024
22. Issa, B., Jasser, M.B., Chua, H.N., Hamzah, M.: A comparative study on embedding models for keyword extraction using keybert method. In: 2023 IEEE 13th International Conference on System Engineering and Technology (ICSET), pp. 40–45 (2023)
23. Kuratov, Y., Arkhipov, M.: Adaptation of deep bidirectional multilingual transformers for Russian language (2019)
24. Rosstat: Number of permanent population of the Russian federation by municipalities as of 1 January 2023. https://rosstat.gov.ru/storage/mediabank/Bul_MO_2023.xlsx (2023)

City Interactions in Urban Planning: The Square Example from an Ontological Analysis Point of View

Maria Rosaria Stufano Melone[1,2]([✉]), Stefano Borgo[2], and Domenico Camarda[1,2]

[1] Polytechnic University of Bari, Bari, Italy
mariarosaria.stufanomelone@poliba.it
[2] LOA, CNR-ISTC, Trento, Italy

Abstract. The evolution of cities and technologies for the city has generated the need and possibility of integrating data coming both from socio-technical and environmental systems, and individual and collective participation in the making of places - of the city in particular. The growth of the possibilities for managing and integrating knowledge has also led to managing, integrating and constantly monitoring the evolution of data and their respective impacts on the territory as in the vision push forward by Urban Digital Twins (UDT). In this paper, we delve into the possibility of managing knowledge and supporting decision making through ontological approaches, and consider the issue of which aspects an ontology should cover for effective disambiguation and interpretation sharing in urban scenarios where different agents and systems must interact. More specifically, we explore the square as an urban type with the goal of reassessing earlier formalization steps in view of the construction of a UDT. The study is a further step along an original research carried out by our group at the crossroads between formalization of complex knowledge and planning of urban complexity.

Keywords: City · Digital Twin · Ontological Analysis · Urban planning

1 Introduction

Planning the city and the territory turns out to be an increasingly complex and subtle activity. The amount of information we can collect, the variety of sources, and the different research methodologies have highly enriched the possibility of knowledge acquisition. Furthermore, today there is increased awareness of the limits of the rational-comprehensive planning approach which is now seen as rigid and divisive. It too often leads to choices that are blind of the existing connections in the present and future urban system. This awareness has pushed attention on how to intervene on territories and cities in a more appropriate, intuitive and empathic way, maintaining at the same

This research was financially supported by Italian National Operational Programme for "Research and Innovation" 2014–2020; Area: Smart Secure and Inclusive Communities, Project: "Resilient City- Everyday Revolution (ARS01_00592)".

O. Gervasi et al. (Eds.): ICCSA 2024, LNCS 14814, pp. 448–455, 2024.
https://doi.org/10.1007/978-3-031-64608-9_31

time a technically sound and pragmatically oriented use of the resources. In research, the need for an approach broader than the pure handling of surfaces, destinations and values, has also gained ground. From these changes, other perspectives also emerged like the necessity of reading, interpreting, extending, and integrating the dynamism and plurality of needs and viewpoints (not only human), or the need for sustainability and for a more equal resource sharing. Awareness has made the planners' lens multifaceted and rich in visions, offering them the possibility of working with a new humility in the complex and haunted world of 'vast' choices - that is, those affecting large territories or portions of space, affecting large quantities and qualities of relationships, which have an impact on the present and the future. Recently, this awareness has allowed for broadening the scope of knowledge and data in width and in-depth making possible the reading and analysis of sedimented layers.

The new tools developed over the last twenty years, supported by scientific and technological advancement, have given rise to a season of fertile research from the Multi-Agent System to Space Syntax, CAD, and GIS, from E-Governance tools to those crowd-sourced (a.k.a. volunteered) based on individual contributions, etc. alongside more traditional 'walks', meetings in parishes, and street movements.

Among the new tools, artificial intelligence, which has exploded in its disruptive speed and all-pervasive potential, has given rise to tools that have integrated modelling approaches with data coming from sensors distributed over certain portions of the territory, leading to the conception of the Digital Twin for the city [1].

Although it remains difficult to give a definitive definition of city [2, 3], cities can be understood as the result of a specific political, economic and social organisation. Nonetheless, the semantics of the social roles of an urban artefact remains difficult to understand and challenging to represent [4].

As a conceptual artefact which provides a common disambiguated vocabulary for the experts and the practitioners, an ontology is particularly suitable for disambiguation and knowledge sharing between different agents (including humans, non-human animals, and artificial agents) and useful to overcome the subtleties of natural and technical languages and their specificities [5]. In this research line, we have based our analysis on the foundational ontology DOLCE (Descriptive Ontology for Linguistic and Cognitive Engineering), developed at the Laboratory of Applied Ontology in Trento, within the broader European project WonderWeb [6–11].

In this paper, we propose a twofold analysis that moves in the direction explored and suggested by Stufano Melone et al. [5] towards an ontology-based Urban Digital Twin. The indeed goal is the exploitation of a fourth component of smart cities (along which the material, the agentive and the knowledge components), which we call the relation component (see Sect. 2), linked to the identification of roles in the use of urban places [2, 4]. In this case, we analyse a urban square (see Sect. 3). In it, we look at the urban square as an urban type and a role-dependent element as discussed in the work of Calafiore et al. [4]. In doing this, we begin an ontological modelling of collective uses of an urban place. Concluding reflections and follow-up perspectives are drawn out in Sect. 4.

2 The Fourth Component in the Ontological Analysis of the City

Ontological analysis helps to model the social content of the built environment besides its planned characterization [12, 13]. It offers support to decision-making and to defining the patterns of use and living of an urban place, as an example the urban square: local knowledge expressed by emerging social patterns is crucial [4].

Previously we conducted ontological analyses, in order to elicit the structuring components of the city within this perspective [2]. A city is a complex and rich system, composed of heterogeneous parts that interact in different ways and for different reasons. We therefore identified and discussed three core components of the city. The three elicited components are: (i) city-place; (ii) city agent; and (iii) city-knowledge.

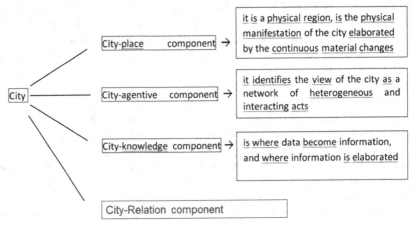

Fig. 1. City-components schema with a fourth layer component [3]

Certainly a city is not the mere juxtaposition of these disjoint components, due to its intrinsic systemic complexity. Rather, the city as a whole emerges from these interacting and intertwined components. The general vision is a city resulting from interactions between ontologically distinct components, where the nature of the interactions is as necessary as the qualification of the components themselves. In this framework, the level of development of the components of a city and the quality of mutual interactions can identify the type of that city. The main characteristic of these components is that they exist in the city as a whole, thus characterizing the ontological and conceptual structure of the city itself [2].

Interactions determine the relationships within and across the components in the complex system that the city is [14]. Therefore, the next step in the analysis is to make this interaction network of the city explicit. We suggest identifying it as the fourth component of city as a place (Fig. 1). The relationship component structurally shows up in both the natural and artificial spaces. In a Leibnizian sense, the relationship in the city is itself substance [15].

3   The Example of Square: The Market Square in Naples

The square is a representative element of the Western city, in its being an urban architectural type, and in its being a focal point of the life practices and habits of the inhabitants as well as a geometric space central to the historical layout of the towns themselves [16]. In villages with up to a few thousand inhabitants, the reference square is usually just one. It is identified by use, is central and barycentric in practices and space - despite the possible presence of a number of 'square-like' spaces in the residential/architectural fabric [17]. In fact, we often see oldest urban architectural fabrics with a constellation of small squares that innervate the distribution of urban 'voids'.

In larger cities the system of squares intrinsic to the urban fabric is multiplied and complexified. We will not go into detail here in the description of the various possible declinations, nor in the list of possible configurations and examples [e.g., 18]. We just want to highlight the constant and significant presence of the square element and many squares in the same urban fabric. Each of such squares in a larger city takes on its dimensions of use, semantic and role interpretations which depend on their location in the fabric itself and on the community that inhabits that part of the city [19].

In earlier studies we looked at the square to address the difficult integration and at the same time the importance of integrating literary sources for knowledge of the places on which planners and administrators are called to decide and act [5, 20, 21]. We also explored the square as an urban architectural type, concerning the elements of the city [22].

Fig. 2. An image of the Market Square in Naples [4]

Calafiore et al. (2017) aimed to formalize the dimension of the use of space, managing the reflection according to the identification of the concept of role to 'tell' and 'diversify' the uses of a space. That analysis aimed to be inclusive, consistent and coherent in managing the knowledge deriving from the different uses and roles that the square in question assumes and encounters cyclically, for example over a week, or is determined by management decisions - such as parking regulations in the square. In particular, the mentioned work analysed the Market Square of Naples (Fig. 2), a case of coexistence of formal and informal social practices manifested by different 'groups' during a certain time frame. The ontological analysis carried out in Calafiore et al. [4], which includes a formal proposal, shows the square as a point of convergence and tension between the "designed" city and the "lived" one, which has always had a primary interest in urban planning. Those formal clarifications form a basis for the construction of an ontology of the urban square as an element in an Urban Digital Twin [1]. Local knowledge of urban places is central and is often shared in specific communities but is generally the most difficult knowledge to be collected [23].

Figure 3 reports an ongoing formalized representation of the used language and conceptual framework, based on DOLCE ontology model [24].

$$UrbAct(x) \rightarrow PD(x) \land \exists y (PC(y,x) \land UrbArt(y)); \tag{1}$$

$$Rec(spr,y,t) \rightarrow SPr(spr) \land SoC(y) \land Time(t); \tag{2}$$

$$SoC(y) \rightarrow ASO(y); \tag{3}$$

$$SPr(spr) \rightarrow \exists x,t,y \, (CF(x,spr,t) \land Act(x) \land SoC(y) \land Rec(sty,y,t)); \tag{4}$$

$$Act(x) \land Spr(y) \land CF(x,y,t) \land PC(z,x) \land DF(y,w) \land SoP(w) \rightarrow CF(z,w,t) \tag{5}$$

Fig. 3. An excerpt of logic formalizations identifying urban actions and social practises (from [4])

It lists an initial formalization of the conceptual framework of the square and its roles, formal and informal, intended and unintended. We put down it here as a canvas to be integrated in a wider research path about the managing of knowledge for planning activities.

4   Conclusions and Follow-Up

In conclusion, the city can be seen as a complex reality of multiple dimensions: open, dynamic and varied. The city system is characterized by emerging properties [25] that integrate into the city entity giving rise to streams of differentiated and multiple behaviors offered by the peculiarity of the agents who live there, by the consolidated customs, by the knowledge expressed, by the relationships activated and interactions acted out.

Ontological analysis allows us to clarify and manage part of the complexity of references, constraints, and functional objectives and identify relationships and interactions [26]. The present study has presented possible paths of representation of the complex knowledge of a city system. This modeling attempt arises from the recent line of research developed around the so-called Urban Digital Twins. With the aim of identifying ways of representing knowledge within a digital urban model, we tried to explore partial modeling, in particular through the example of the urban square. The modeling perspective of the urban square cited here is rather original and based on our previous ontologically based research paths, concerning the organization of the components of a city [2, 27]. This study was therefore developed with a deliberately exploratory orientation.

In this contribution, we concentrated on two points, namely:

i) the identification of a fourth component to integrate the ontological model of the city and

ii) the need to construct an ontological model of the square following the formalization conducted by Calafiore et al. [4]. This has been carried out from the point of view of our previous reflections about the square as a crucial node from the architectural and social practices, and put under the vision of a Urban Digital Twin for the city.

In doing this, we try to lay the foundations for an ontologically based modelling of the square and, subsequently, of the city in an extensive and generalized form. The final goal is to manage and represent knowledge for decision support in planning.

From a general point of view it can be said that the research presents positive and promising perspectives. In fact, within the components of a city, the square appears as a representative element with intrinsic complexity, able to justify the approach used. The resulting suggestions were quite interesting despite the limited scope, just by virtue of these generalizable complexity perspectives. Of course, the limits of this study arise from the same partialisation, with respect to a context with such multiple and multidimensional complexities – i.e., the city itself. Modeling any element of the city, even a complex one, is not comparable to modeling a city as such, and the limits are clearly numerous – physical, spatial, temporal, perceptual, cognitive, emotional and so on. Towards a perspective of formalization of knowledge data, for the purposes of digital representation and management, these limits are evidently stringent and of unavoidable importance.

Just from the perspective of formalizing the collected databases, however, the ontological approach can provide integrability and interoperability features useful for achieving the objectives of interest [28]. Therefore, the next work within this line of research will be developed just in the ontological formalization perspective, starting by dealing with such challenges.

References

1. Ferré-Bigorra, J., Casals, M., Gangolells, M.: The adoption of urban digital twins. Cities **131**, 103905 (2022)
2. Borgo, S., Borri, D., Camarda, D., Stufano Melone, M.R.: An ontological analysis of cities, smart cities and their components. In: Nagenborg, M., Stone, T., González Woge, M., Vermaas, P.E. (eds.) Technology and the City: Towards a Philosophy of Urban Technologies, pp. 365–387. Springer, Cham (2021). https://doi.org/10.1007/978-3-030-52313-8_18
3. Stufano Melone, M.R., Borgo, S., Camarda, D.: Digital twins of cities vs. digital twins for cities. In: Marucci, A., Zullo, F., Fiorini, L., Saganeiti, L. (eds.) INPUT 2023. LNCE, vol. 467, pp. 192–203. Springer, Cham (2024). https://doi.org/10.1007/978-3-031-54118-6_18

4. Calafiore, A., Boella, G., Borgo, S., Guarino, N. (eds.): Urban Artefacts and Their Social roles: Towards an Ontology of Social Practices, vol. 86. Dagstuhl Publishing, Leipzig (2017)
5. Stufano Melone, M.R., Camarda, D.: Spatial-cognition ontology models in policymaking: dealing with urban landmarks in literary narratives. TeMA – J. Land Use Mob. Environ. SI(1), 29–44 (2024)
6. Guarino, N. (ed.): Formal Ontology in Information Systems (FOIS 1998), vol. 46. IOS Press, Trento (1998)
7. Masolo, C., Borgo, S., Gangemi, A., Guarino, N., Oltramari, A., Schneider, L.: WonderWeb deliverable D17. In: The WonderWeb Library of Foundational Ontologies and the DOLCE Ontology. ISTC-CNR (2002)
8. Borgo, S., Masolo, C.: Foundational choices in DOLCE. In: Staab, S., Studer, R. (eds.) Handbook on Ontologies, pp. 361–381. Springer, Cham (2009). https://doi.org/10.1007/978-3-540-92673-3_16
9. Gaio, S., Borgo, S., Masolo, C., Otramari, A., Guarino, N.: Un'Introduzione all'Ontologia DOLCE. AIDA Informazioni, pp. 107–127 (2010)
10. Borgo, S., et al.: DOLCE: a descriptive ontology for linguistic and cognitive engineering. Appl. Ontol. **17**, 45–69 (2022)
11. Stufano Melone, M.R., Camarda, D.: Non-knowledge and the unexpected in planning: an experimentation account. In: Gervasi, O., et al. (eds.) ICCSA 2023, pp. 331–340. Springer, Cham (2023). https://doi.org/10.1007/978-3-031-37129-5_27
12. Searle, J.R.: Social ontology: some basic principles. Anthropol. Theory **6**, 12–29 (2006)
13. Lai, S., Zoppi, C.: An ontology of the strategic environmental assessment of city masterplans. Future Internet **3**, 362–378 (2011)
14. Billen, R., Zaki, C., Servières, M., Moreau, G., Hallot, P.: Developing an ontology of space: application to 3D city modeling. In: Usage, Usability, and Utility of 3D City Models, 02007 (2012)
15. Messina, J., Rutherford, D.: Leibniz on compossibility. Philos Compass **4**, 962–977 (2009)
16. Lamberti, C.: Der Städtebau nach seinen künstlerischen Grundsätzen: La piazza come fondamento dell'urbanistica. Turris Babel **66**, 64–65 (2005)
17. Lynch, K.: The Image of the City. The MIT Press, Cambridge (1960)
18. Lévy, B.: The European town square as an ideal place, or Camillo Sitte revisited. Environ. Land Soc. Architectonics **1**, 24–37 (2008)
19. Hillier, B.: Studying cities to learn about minds: some possible implications of space syntax for spatial cognition. Environ. Plann. B. Plann. Des. **39**, 12–32 (2012)
20. Camarda, D., Stufano Melone, M.R., Borgo, S., Borri, D.: Toward clarification of meanings via ontological analysis method in environmental planning processes and actions. In: Leone, A., Gargiulo, C. (eds.) Environmental and Territorial Modelling for Planning and Design, pp. 427–435. FedOAPress, Napoli (2018)
21. Stufano Melone, M.R., Camarda, D.: Reflections about non-knowledge in planning processes. In: La Rosa, D., Privitera, R. (eds.) Innovation in Urban and Regional Planning. LNCE, vol. 146, pp. 205–212. Springer, Cham (2021). https://doi.org/10.1007/978-3-030-68824-0_22
22. Stufano, R., Borgo, S.: Towards an understanding of shapes and types in architecture. SHAPES, pp. 47–54 (2015)
23. Holsapple, C.W., Joshi, K.D.: A formal knowledge management ontology: conduct, activities, resources, and influences. J. Am. Soc. Inform. Sci. Technol. **55**, 593–612 (2004)
24. Gangemi, A., Guarino, N., Masolo, C., Oltramari, A., Schneider, L.: Sweetening ontologies with DOLCE. In: Gómez-Pérez, A., Benjamins, V.R. (eds.) Knowledge Engineering and Knowledge Management: Ontologies and the Semantic Web. LNCS (LNAI), vol. 2473, pp. 166–181. Springer, Heidelberg (2002). https://doi.org/10.1007/3-540-45810-7_18
25. McPhearson, T., Haase, D., Kabisch, N., Gren, Å.: Advancing understanding of the complex nature of urban systems. Ecol. Ind. **70**, 566–573 (2016)

26. Guarino, N., Bottazzi, E., Ferrario, R., Sartor, G.: Open ontology-driven sociotechnical systems: transparency as a key for business resiliency. In: De Marco, M., Te'eni, D., Albano, V., Za, S. (eds.) Information Systems: Crossroads for Organization, Management, Accounting and Engineering, pp. 535–542. Springer, Heidelberg (2012). https://doi.org/10.1007/978-3-7908-2789-7_58

27. Stufano Melone, M.R., Borri, D., Camarda, D., Borgo, S.: Knowledge of places: an ontological analysis of the social level in the city. In: Papa, R., Fistola, R., Gargiulo, L. (eds.) Smart Planning: Sustainability and Mobility in the Age of Change, pp. 3–14. Springer, Cham (2018). https://doi.org/10.1007/978-3-319-77682-8_1

28. Michal, K., Michal, Š., Zdeněk, B.: Interoperability through ontologies. IFAC Proc. Vol. **45**, 196–200 (2012)

Author Index

A

Abreu, Alexandre Augusto Alberto Moreira de   I-125
Ahuja, Rohit   I-180
Aktaş, Mehmet S.   II-83
Alam, Md. Golam Rabiul   II-31
Alves, Juan Mangueira   II-49
Amarante, Gabriel   II-151
Amorim, Glauco   I-3
Andrade, Yan   II-151
Ann, Victoria Grace   I-221
Anna, Solovyeva   I-450
Antonov, Aleksandr   II-436
Araújo, Anna Luíza Damaceno   I-151
Argyrakis, Panagiotis   I-422
Arora, Paluck   I-180

B

Barros, Charles de   II-397
Bashirov, Roman   I-364
Basly, Hend   I-165
Batista, Fabrício Martins   I-96
Binh, Nguyen Thanh   II-31
Borgo, Stefano   II-448
Brandão, Diego   I-3
Brega, José Remo F.   I-96
Brito, Bruna Alice Oliveira de   II-243
Bui, Thiloan   II-101

C

Camarda, Domenico   II-448
Cardoso, Luis Eduardo Pelin   II-198
Caspar, Marvin   I-346
Cavuldak, Cansu   II-83
Chua, Fang-Fang   II-293
Chunga-Palomino, Sara L.   I-209
Churiakova, Tatiana   I-285
Clementino, Tiago Lucas Pereira   II-213
Connaboy, Christopher   II-418
Cruz, Juliano E. C.   II-133

D

d'Orazio, Laurent   I-298
d'Ovidio, Francesco Domenico   I-29, I-239
da Silva, Arnaldo V. Barros   I-151
da Silva, Jamicel   II-151
da Silva, João Paulo   II-151
Dang, Thi Thu Khiet   II-339
Daverona, Anna Christina   I-422
de Carvalho, André C. P. de Leon F.   II-198
de Carvalho, André C. P. L. F.   I-151
de Freitas, Sergio Antônio Andrade   II-49
de Jesus, Enéas Mendes   I-112
de Souza, Eduardo Santos Carlos   I-151
De Stefano, Giuliano   II-355, II-366
Dias, Diego   II-397
dos Santos, Isaac Pinheiro   I-112
Dzewaltowski, Alex   II-418

F

Faria, Antônio Hot   II-151
Farias, Mylena Angélica Silva   II-49
Fauzi, Akhmad   I-379
Fava, Felipe Bedinotto   II-17
Ferreira, Renato   II-151
Filho, Itamir de Morais Barroca   II-243
Firza, Najada   I-29, I-239

G

Ghosh, Rajib Chandra   I-46
Ginige, Athula   II-273
Giraldi, Gilson Antônio   I-65
Gonzaga de Oliveira, Sanderson L.   I-3, I-125
González, Pedro Henrique   I-3
Goonetillake, Jeevani   II-273
Gornova, Galina   II-436
Guimarães, Marcelo de Paiva   II-397
Gurgel, André Morais   II-243

H

Hakvar, Hakan   II-83
Haris, Mohammad   II-293

O. Gervasi et al. (Eds.): ICCSA 2024, LNCS 14814, pp. 457–459, 2024.
https://doi.org/10.1007/978-3-031-64608-9

Printed in the United States
by Baker & Taylor Publisher Services